C0-ASZ-765

What They Said
In 1991

The Yearbook Of World Opinion

Compiled and Edited by

ALAN F. PATER

and

JASON R. PATER

MONITOR BOOK COMPANY

R.F.
D
410
.W46
1991

To

The Newsmakers of the World . . .

May they never be at a loss for words

COPYRIGHT © 1992 BY MONITOR BOOK COMPANY

All rights reserved. Copyright under International Copyright Union.
All rights reserved under International American Convention (1910).

TWENTY-THIRD ANNUAL EDITION

Printed in the United States of America

Library of Congress catalogue card number: 74-111080

ISBN number: 0-917734-24-6

WHAT THEY SAID is published annually by Monitor Book Company,
Palm Springs, California 92263. The title, "WHAT THEY SAID," is a
trademark owned exclusively by Monitor Book Company and has been
duly registered with the United States Patent Office. Any unauthorized
use is prohibited.

LONGWOOD COLLEGE LIBRARY
FARMVILLE, VIRGINIA 23901

Preface to the First Edition (1969)

Words can be powerful or subtle, humorous or maddening. They can be vigorous or feeble, lucid or obscure, inspiring or despairing, wise or foolish, hopeful or pessimistic . . . they can be fearful or confident, timid or articulate, persuasive or perverse, honest or deceitful. As tools at a speaker's command, words can be used to reason, argue, discuss, cajole, plead, debate, declaim, threaten, infuriate, or appease; they can harangue, flourish, recite, preach, discourse, stab to the quick, or gently sermonize.

When casually spoken by a stage or film star, words can go beyond the press-agentry and make-up facade and reveal the inner man or woman. When purposefully uttered in the considered phrasing of a head of state, words can determine the destiny of millions of people, resolve peace or war, or chart the course of a nation on whose direction the fate of the entire world may depend.

Until now, the *copia verborum* of well-known and renowned public figures—the doctors and diplomats, the governors and generals, the potentates and presidents, the entertainers and educators, the bishops and baseball players, the jurists and journalists, the authors and attorneys, the congressmen and chairmen-of-the-board—whether enunciated in speeches, lectures, interviews, radio and television addresses, news conferences, forums, symposiums, town meetings, committee hearings, random remarks to the press, or delivered on the floors of the United States Senate and House of Representatives or in the parliaments and palaces of the world—have been dutifully reported in the media, then filed away and, for the most part, forgotten.

The editors of *WHAT THEY SAID* believe that consigning such a wealth of thoughts, ideas, doctrines, opinions and philosophies to interment in the morgues and archives of the Fourth Estate is lamentable and unnecessary. Yet the media, in all their forms, are constantly engulfing us in a profusion of endless and increasingly voluminous news reports. One is easily disposed to disregard or forget the stimulating discussion of critical issues embodied in so many of the utterances of those who make the news and, in their respective fields, shape the events throughout the world. The conclusion is therefore a natural and compelling one: the educator, the public official, the business executive, the statesman, the philosopher—everyone who has a stake in the complex, often confusing trends of our times—should have material of this kind readily available.

These, then, are the circumstances under which *WHAT THEY SAID* was conceived. It is the culmination of a year of listening to the people in the public eye; a year of scrutinizing, monitoring, reviewing, judging, deciding—a year during which the editors resurrected from almost certain oblivion those quintessential elements of the year's *spoken* opinion which, in their judgment, demanded preservation in book form.

WHAT THEY SAID is a pioneer in its field. Its *raison d'etre* is the firm conviction that presenting, each year, the highlights of vital and interesting views from the lips of prominent people on virtually every aspect of contemporary civilization fulfills the need to give the *spoken* word the permanence and lasting value of the *written* word. For, if it is true that a picture is worth 10,000 words, it is equally true that a verbal conclusion, an apt quote or a candid comment by a person of fame or influence can have more significance and can provide more understanding than an entire page of summary in a standard work of reference.

The editors of *WHAT THEY SAID* did not, however, design their book for researchers and scholars alone. One of the failings of the conventional reference work is that it is blandly written and referred to primarily for facts and figures, lacking inherent "interest value." *WHAT THEY SAID*, on the other hand, was planned for sheer enjoyment and pleasure, for searching glimpses into the lives and thoughts of the world's celebrities, as well as for serious study, intellectual reflection and the philosophical contemplation of our multifaceted life and mores. Furthermore, those pressed for time, yet anxious to know what the newsmakers have been saying, will welcome the short excerpts which will make for quick, intermittent reading—and rereading. And, of course, the topical classifications, the speakers' index, the subject index, the place and date information—documented and authenticated and easily located—will supply a rich fund of hitherto not readily obtainable reference and statistical material.

Finally, the reader will find that the editors have eschewed trite comments and cliches, tedious and boring. The selected quotations, each standing on its own, are pertinent, significant, stimulating—above all, relevant to today's world, expressed in the speakers' own words. And they will, the editors feel, be even more relevant tomorrow. They will be re-examined and reflected upon in the future by men and women eager to learn from the past. The prophecies, the promises, the "golden dreams," the boastings and rantings, the bluster, the bravado, the pleadings and representations of those whose voices echo in these pages (and in those to come) should provide a rare and unique history lesson. The positions held by these luminaries, in their respective callings, are such that what they say today may profoundly affect the future as well as the present, and so will be of lasting importance and meaning.

ALAN F. PATER
JASON R. PATER

Beverly Hills, California

Table of Contents

PART THREE: GENERAL

Editorial Treatment

ORGANIZATION OF MATERIAL

Special attention has been given to the arrangement of the book—from the major divisions down to the individual categories and speakers—the objective being a logical progression of related material, as follows:

(A) The categories are arranged alphabetically within each of three major sections:

Part One:	"National Affairs"
Part Two:	"International"
Part Three:	"General"

In this manner, the reader can quickly locate quotations pertaining to particular fields of interest (see also *Indexing*). It should be noted that some quotations contain a number of thoughts or ideas—sometimes on different subjects—while some are vague as to exact subject matter and thus do not fit clearly into a specific topic classification. In such cases, the judgment of the Editors has determined the most appropriate category.

(B) Within each category the speakers are in alphabetical order by surname, following alphabetization practices used in the speaker's country of origin.

(C) Where there are two or more quotations by one speaker within the same category, they appear chronologically by date spoken or date of source.

SPEAKER IDENTIFICATION

(A) The occupation, profession, rank, position or title of the speaker is given as it was *at the time the statement was made* (except when the speaker's relevant identification is in the past, in which case he is shown as "former"). Thus, due to possible changes in status during the year, a speaker may be shown with different identifications in various parts of the book, or even within the same category.

(B) In the case of a speaker who holds more than one position simultaneously, the judgment of the Editors has determined the most appropriate identification to use with a specific quotation.

(C) The nationality of a speaker is given when it will help in identifying the speaker or when it is relevant to the quotation.

THE QUOTATIONS

The quoted material selected for inclusion in this book is shown as it appeared in the source, except as follows:

(A) *Ellipses* have been inserted wherever the Editors have deleted extraneous words or overly long passages within the quoted material used. In no way has the meaning or intention of the quotations been altered. *Ellipses* are also used where they appeared in the source.

(B) *Punctuation and spelling* have been altered by the Editors where they were obviously incorrect in the source, or to make the quotations more intelligible, or to conform to the general style used throughout this book. Again, meaning and intention of the quotations have not been changed.

(C) *Brackets* ([ ]) indicate material inserted by the Editors or by the source to either correct obvious errors or to explain or clarify what the speaker is saying. In some instances, bracketed material may replace quoted material for sake of clarity.

(D) *Italics* either appeared in the original source or were added by the Editors where emphasis is clearly desirable.

Except for the above instances, the quoted material used has been printed verbatim, as reported by the source (even if the speaker made factual errors or was awkward in his choice of words).

Special care has been exercised to make certain that each quotation stands on its own and is not taken "out of context." The Editors, however, cannot be responsible for errors made by the original source, i.e., incorrect reporting, mis-quotations, or errors in interpretation.

DOCUMENTATION AND SOURCES

Documentation (circumstance, place, date) of each quotation is provided as fully as could be obtained, and the sources are furnished for all quotations. In some instances, no documentation details were available; in those cases, only the source is given. Following are the sequence and style used for this information:

Circumstance of quotation, place, date/Name of source, date:section (if applicable), page number.

Example: *Before the Senate, Washington, Dec. 4/The Washington Post, 12-5:(A)13.*

The above example indicates that the quotation was delivered before the Senate in Washington on December 4. It was taken for *WHAT THEY SAID* from *The Washington Post*, issue of December 5, section A, page 13. (When a newspaper publishes more than one edition on the same date, it should be noted that page numbers may vary from edition to edition.)

(A) When the source is a television or radio broadcast, the name of the network or local station is indicated, along with the date of the broadcast (obviously, page and section information does not apply).

(B) An asterisk (*) before the (/) in the documentation indicates that the quoted material was written rather than spoken. Although the basic policy of *WHAT THEY SAID* is to use only *spoken* statements, there are occasions when written statements are considered by the Editors to be important enough to be included. These occasions are rare and usually involve Presidential messages and statements released to the press and other such documents attributed to persons in high government office.

INDEXING

(A) The *Index to Speakers* is keyed to the page number. (For alphabetization practices, see *Organization of Material*, paragraph B.)

(B) The *Index to Subjects* is keyed to both the page number and the quotation number on the page (thus, 210:3 indicates quotation number 3 on page 210); the quotation number appears at the right corner of each quotation.

(C) To locate quotations on a particular subject, regardless of the speaker, turn to the appropriate category (see *Table of Contents*) or use the detailed *Index to Subjects*.

(D) To locate all quotations by a particular speaker, regardless of subject, use the *Index to Speakers*.

(E) To locate quotations by a particular speaker on a particular subject, turn to the appropriate category and then to that person's quotations within the category.

(F) The reader will find that the basic categorization format of *WHAT THEY SAID* is itself a useful subject index, inasmuch as related quotations are grouped together by their respective categories. All aspects of journalism, for example, are relevant to each other; thus, the section *Journalism* embraces all phases of the news media. Similarly, quotations pertaining to the U.S. President, Congress, etc., are in the section *Government*.

MISCELLANEOUS

(A) Except where otherwise indicated or obviously to the contrary, all universities, organizations and business firms mentioned in this book are in the United States; similarly, references made to "national," "Federal," "this country," "the nation," etc., refer to the United States.

(B) In most cases, organizations whose names end with "of the United States" are Federal government agencies.

SELECTION OF CATEGORIES

The selected categories reflect, in the Editors' opinion, the most widely discussed public-interest subjects, those which readily fall into the over-all sphere of "current events." They represent topics continuously covered by the mass media because of their inherent importance to the changing world scene. Most of the categories are permanent; they appear in each annual edition of *WHAT THEY SAID*. However, because of the transient character of some subjects, there may be categories which appear one year and may not be repeated the next.

SELECTION OF SPEAKERS

The following persons are always considered eligible for inclusion in *WHAT THEY SAID*: top-level officials of all branches of national, state and local governments (both U.S. and foreign), including all United States Senators and Representatives; top-echelon military officers; college and university presidents, chancellors and professors; chairmen and presidents of major corporations; heads of national public-oriented organizations and associations; national and internationally known diplomats; recognized celebrities from the entertainment and literary spheres and the arts generally; sports figures of national stature; commentators on the world scene who are recognized as such and who command the attention of the mass media.

The determination of what and who are "major" and "recognized" must, necessarily, be made by the Editors of *WHAT THEY SAID* based on objective personal judgment.

Also, some persons, while not generally recognized as prominent or newsworthy, may have nevertheless attracted an unusual amount of attention in connection with an important issue or event. These people, too, are considered for inclusion, depending upon the specific circumstance.

SELECTION OF QUOTATIONS

The quotations selected for inclusion in *WHAT THEY SAID* obviously represent a decided minority of the seemingly endless volume of quoted material appearing in the media each year. The process of selecting is scrupulously objective insofar as the partisan views of the Editors are concerned (see *About Fairness*, below). However, it is clear that the Editors must decide which quotations *per se* are suitable for inclusion, and in doing so look for comments that are aptly stated, offer insight into the subject being discussed, or into the speaker, and provide—for today as well as for future reference—a thought which readers will find useful for understanding the issues and the personalities that make up a year on this planet.

ABOUT FAIRNESS

The Editors of *WHAT THEY SAID* understand the necessity of being impartial when compiling a book of this kind. As a result, there has been no bias in the selection of the quotations, the choice of speakers or the manner of editing. Relevance of the statements and the status of the speakers are the exclusive criteria for inclusion, without any regard whatsoever to the personal beliefs and views of the Editors. Furthermore, every effort has been made to include a multiplicity of opinions and ideas from a wide cross-section of speakers on each topic. Nevertheless, should there appear to be, on some controversial issues, a majority of material favoring one point of view over another, it is simply the result of there having been more of those views expressed during the year, reported by the media and objectively considered suitable by the Editors of *WHAT THEY SAID* (see *Selection of Quotations*, above). Also, since persons in politics and government account for a large percentage of the speakers in *WHAT THEY SAID*, there may exist a heavier weight of opinion favoring the philosophy of those in office at the time, whether in the United States Congress, the Administration, or in foreign capitals. This is natural and to be expected and should not be construed as a reflection of agreement or disagreement with that philosophy on the part of the Editors of *WHAT THEY SAID*.

Abbreviations

The following are abbreviations used by the speakers in this volume. Rather than defining them each time they appear in the quotations, this list will facilitate reading and avoid unnecessary repetition.

ABC:	American Broadcasting Companies
ACLU:	American Civil Liberties Union
A&E:	Arts & Entertainment Network
AIDS:	acquired immune deficiency syndrome
AMA:	American Medical Association
ANC:	African National Congress
BBC:	British Broadcasting Corporation
BCCI:	Bank of Credit and Commerce International
CBS:	Columbia Broadcasting System (CBS, Inc.)
CEO:	chief executive officer
CIA:	Central Intelligence Agency
CNN:	Cable News Network
CPSU:	Communist Party of the Soviet Union
D.C.:	District of Columbia
DLC:	Democratic Leadership Council
DOE:	Department of Energy
DOT:	Department of Transportation
EC:	European Community
EEOC:	Equal Employment Opportunity Commission
EPA:	Environmental Protection Agency
FBI:	Federal Bureau of Investigation
FDA:	Food and Drug Administration
FDIC:	Federal Deposit Insurance Corporation
F.D.R.:	Franklin Delano Roosevelt
FMLN:	Farabundo Marti National Liberation Front (El Salvador)
GCC:	(Persian) Gulf Cooperation Council
GEC:	graduate equivalency diploma
GNP:	gross national product
GOP:	Grand Old Party (Republican Party)
HBO:	Home Box Office
HHS:	Department of Health and Human Services

HIV:	human immunodeficiency virus (AIDS virus)
HUD:	Department of Housing and Urban Development
IBM:	International Business Machines Corporation
IOC:	International Olympic Committee
IRA:	individual retirement arrangement; or, Irish Republican Army
IV:	intravenous
KGB:	Soviet State Security Committee
KJV:	King James Version
L.A.:	Los Angeles
LAPD:	Los Angeles Police Department
MFN:	most favored nation trade status
MPAA:	Motion Picture Association of America
m.p.g.:	miles per gallon
MTV:	Music Television
NAACP:	National Association for the Advancement of Colored People
NASA:	National Aeronautics and Space Administration
NATO:	North Atlantic Treaty Organization
NBA:	National Basketball Association
NBC:	National Broadcasting Company
NCAA:	National Collegiate Athletic Association
NEA:	National Endowment for the Arts
NFL:	National Football League
NHL:	National Hockey League
NIH:	National Institutes of Health
NSC:	National Security Council
OMB:	Office of Management and Budget
OPEC:	Organization of Petroleum Exporting Countries
PAC:	political action committee
PBS:	Public Broadcasting Service
PGA:	Professional Golfer's Association
PLO:	Palestine Liberation Organization
POW:	prisoner of war
PRC:	People's Republic of China
ROTC:	Reserve Officers' Training Corps
R&R:	rest & relaxation
SACP:	South African Communist Party
SAT:	Scholastic Aptitude Test
SDI:	Strategic Defense Initiative

SEC:	Securities and Exchange Commission
S&L:	savings-and-loan association
SSA:	Social Security Administration
START:	strategic arms reduction talks
TV:	television
U.K.:	United Kingdom
UN:	United Nations
U.S.:	United States
USIA:	United States Information Agency
USOC:	United States Olympic Committee
U.S.S.R.:	Union of Soviet Socialist Republics
VCR:	video cassette recorder

Party affiliation of United States Senators, Congressmen, Governors and state legislators:

D: Democratic
I: Independent
R: Republican

The Quote of the Year

What you believe matters less than your capacity for belief—and your willingness to translate belief into constructive action . . . It is your moral compass that counts far more than any bank balance, any resume and, yes, any diploma. Whether on the floor of Congress or in the boardrooms of corporate America or in the corridors of a big city hospital, there is no body of case studies which can supplant the force of character which provides both a sense of direction and a means of fulfillment. It asks not what you want to be, but who you want to be.

—**ELIZABETH HANFORD DOLE**
President, American Red Cross;
former Secretary of Labor
of the United States.
At Dartmouth College commencement,
Hanover, N.H., June 9.

PART ONE

National Affairs

The State of the Union Address

Delivered by George Bush, President of the United States, at the Capitol, Washington, January 29, 1991.

Mr. President and Mr. Speaker and members of the United States Congress, I come to this house of the people to speak to you and all Americans, certain that we stand at a defining hour.

Halfway around the world we are engaged in a great struggle in the skies and on the seas and sands. We know why we're there. We are Americans, part of something larger than ourselves.

For two centuries, we've done the hard work of freedom. And tonight we lead the world in facing down a threat to decency and humanity.

What is at stake is more than one small country, it is a big idea—a new world order where diverse nations are drawn together in common cause to achieve the universal aspirations of mankind: peace and security, freedom and the rule of law. Such is a world worthy of our struggle, and worthy of our children's future.

The community of nations has resolutely gathered to condemn and repel lawless aggression. Saddam Hussein's unprovoked invasion, his ruthless, systematic rape of a peaceful neighbor, violated everything the community of nations holds dear. The world has said this aggression would not stand, and it will not stand.

Together, we have resisted the trap of appeasement, cynicism and isolation that gives temptation to tyrants. The world has answered Saddam's invasion with 12 United Nations resolutions, starting with a demand for Iraq's immediate and unconditional withdrawal, and backed up by forces from 28 countries of six continents. With few exceptions, the world now stands as one.

The end of the cold war has been a victory for all humanity. A year and a half ago, in Germany, I said that our goal was a Europe whole and free. Tonight, Germany is united. Europe has become whole and free, and America's leadership was instrumental in making it possible.

U.S.-Soviet Relations

Our relationship to the Soviet Union is important, not only to us but to the world. That relationship has helped to shape these and other historic changes. But, like many other nations, we have been deeply concerned by the violence in the Baltics, and we have communicated that concern to the Soviet leadership.

The principle that has guided us is simple: our objective is to help the Baltic peoples achieve their aspirations, not to punish the Soviet Union. In our recent discussions with the Soviet leadership we have been given representations, which, if fulfilled, would result in the withdrawal of some Soviet forces, a re-opening of dialogue with the republics, and a move away from violence.

We will watch carefully as the situation develops. And we will maintain our contact with the Soviet leadership to encourage continued commitment to democratization and reform.

If it is possible, I want to continue to build a lasting basis for U.S.-Soviet cooperation, for a more peaceful future for all mankind.

America and World Freedom

The triumph of democratic ideas in Eastern Europe and Latin America, and the continuing struggle for freedom elsewhere all around the world all confirm the wisdom of our nation's founders.

Tonight, we work to achieve another victory, a victory over tyranny and savage aggression.

We in this Union enter the last decade of the 20th century thankful for our blessings, steadfast in our purpose, aware of our difficulties, and responsive to our duties at home and around the world.

For two centuries, America has served the

world as an inspiring example of freedom and democracy. For generations, America has led the struggle to preserve and extend the blessings of liberty. And today, in a rapidly changing world, American leadership is indispensable. Americans know that leadership brings burdens and sacrifices.

But we also know why the hopes of humanity turn to us. We are Americans; we have a unique responsibility to do the hard work of freedom. And when we do, freedom works.

The conviction and courage we see in the Persian Gulf today is simply the American character in action. The indomitable spirit that is contributing to this victory for world peace and justice is the same spirit that gives us the power and the potential to meet our toughest challenges at home.

We are resolute and resourceful. If we can self-lessly confront evil for the sake of good in a land so far away, then surely we can make this land all that it should be.

If anyone tells you that America's best days are behind her, they're looking the wrong way.

Tonight, I come before this house, and the American people, with an appeal for renewal. This is not merely a call for new government initiatives, it is a call for new initiative in government, in our communities, and from every American—to prepare for the next American century.

America has always led by example. So who among us will set the example? Which of our citizens will lead us in this next American century? Everyone who steps forward today, to get one addict off drugs; to convince one troubled teen-ager not to give up on life; to comfort one AIDS patient; to help one hungry child.

We have within our reach the promise of a renewed America. We can find meaning and reward by serving some higher purpose than ourselves—a shining purpose, the illumination of a thousand points of light. And it is expressed by all who know the irresistible force of a child's hand, of a friend who stands by you and stays there, a volunteer's generous gesture, an idea that is simply right.

The problems before us may be different, but the key to solving them remains the same: it is the individual, the individual who steps forward.

And the state of our Union is the union of each of us, one to the other, the sum of our friendships, marriages, families and communities.

We all have something to give. So if you know how to read, find someone who can't. If you've got a hammer, find a nail. If you're not hungry, not lonely, not in trouble, seek out someone who is. Join the community of conscience. Do the hard work of freedom. And that will define the state of our Union.

Since the birth of our nation, "we the people" has been the source of our strength. What government can do alone is limited, but the potential of the American people knows no limits.

We are a nation of rock-solid realism and clear-eyed idealism. We are Americans. We are the nation that believes in the future. We are the nation that can shape the future.

And we've begun to do just that, by strengthening the power and choice of individuals and families.

Together, these last two years, we've put dollars for child care directly in the hands of parents instead of bureaucracies, unshackled the potential of Americans with disabilities, applied the creativity of the marketplace in the service of the environment, for clean air, and made home-ownership possible for more Americans.

The strength of a democracy is not in bureaucracy, it is in the people and their communities. In everything we do, let us unleash the potential of our most precious resource: our citizens, our citizens themselves. We must return to families, communities, counties, cities, states and institutions of every kind the power to chart their own destiny and the freedom and opportunity provided by strong economic growth. And that's what America is all about.

The Economy

I know, tonight, in some regions of our country, people are in genuine economic distress. And I hear them.

Earlier this month Kathy Blackwell of Massachusetts wrote me about what can happen when the economy slows down, saying, "My heart is aching, and I think that you should know—your people out here are hurting badly."

I understand. And I'm not unrealistic about the future. But there are reasons to be optimistic about our economy.

First, we don't have to fight double-digit inflation. Second, most industries won't have to make big cuts in production because they don't have big inventories piled up. And third, our exports are running solid and strong. In fact, American businesses are exporting at a record rate.

So let's put these times in perspective. Together, since 1981, we've created almost 20 million jobs, cut inflation in half and cut interest rates in half.

And, yes, the largest peacetime economic expansion in history has been temporarily interrupted. But our economy is still over twice as large as our closest competitor.

We will get this recession behind us and return to growth soon. We will get on our way to a new record of expansion and achieve the competitive strength that will carry us into the next American century.

We should focus our efforts today on encouraging economic growth, investing in the future and giving power and opportunity to the individual.

The Budget

We must begin with control of Federal spending. And that's why I'm submitting a budget that holds the growth in spending to less than the rate of inflation. And that's why, amid all the sound and fury of last year's budget debate, we put into law new, enforceable spending caps so that future spending debates will mean a battle of ideas, not a bidding war.

And though controversial, the budget agreement finally put the Federal Government on a pay-as-you-go plan, and cut the growth of debt by nearly $500 billion. And that frees funds for saving and job-creating investment.

Now, let's do more. My budget again includes tax-free family savings accounts, penalty-free withdrawals from I.R.A.'s for first-time homebuyers and, to increase jobs and growth, a reduced tax for long-term capital gains.

I know there are differences among us about the impact and the effects of a capital gains incentive. So tonight I am asking the Congressional leaders and the Federal Reserve to cooperate with us in a study, led by Chairman Alan Greenspan, to sort out our technical differences so that we can avoid a return to unproductive partisan bickering.

But just as our efforts will bring economic growth now and in the future, they must also be matched by long-term investments for the next American century.

Economic Plan of Action

And that requires a forward-looking plan of action, and that's exactly what we will be sending to the Congress. We've prepared a detailed series of proposals, that include:

• A budget that promotes investment in America's future—in children, education, infrastructure, space and high technology.

• Legislation to achieve excellence in education, building on the partnership forged with the 50 governors at the education summit, enabling parents to choose their children's schools and helping to make America No. 1 in math and science.

• A blueprint for a new national highway system, a critical investment in our transportation infrastructure.

• A research and development agenda that includes record levels of Federal investment and a permanent tax credit to strengthen private R. and D., and create jobs.

• A comprehensive national energy strategy that calls for energy conservation and efficiency, increased development and greater use of alternative fuels.

• A banking reform plan to bring America's financial system into the 21st century, so that our banks remain safe and secure and continue—can continue to make job-creating loans for our factories, our businesses and home buyers. You know, I do think that there's been too much pessimism. Sound banks should be making more sound loans, now. And interest rates should be lower, now.

In addition to these proposals, we must recognize that our economic strength depends on being competitive in world markets. We must continue to expand American exports. A successful Uruguay Round of world trade negotiations will create more real jobs, and more real growth, for all nations. And you and I know that if the playing field is level, America's workers and farmers can outwork, outproduce anyone, anytime, anywhere.

And with a Mexican Free Trade Agreement and our Enterprise for the America's Initiative we can help our partners strengthen their economies and move toward a free trade zone throughout this entire hemisphere.

The budget also includes a plan of action right here at home to put more power and opportunity in the hands of the individual. And that means new incentives to create jobs in our inner cities by encouraging investment through enterprise zones. It also means tenant control and ownership of public housing. Freedom and the power to choose should not be the privilege of wealth. They are the birthright of every American.

Civil Rights

Civil rights are also crucial to protecting equal opportunity. Every one of us has a responsibility to speak out against racism, bigotry and hate. We will continue our vigorous enforcement of existing statutes, and I will once again press the Congress to strengthen the laws against employment discrimination without resorting to the use of unfair preferences.

We're determined to protect another fundamental civil right: freedom from crime and the fear that stalks our cities. The Attorney General will soon convene a crime summit of our nation's law-enforcement officials. And to help us support them we need tough crime control legislation, and we need it now.

And as we fight crime, we will fully implement our national strategy for combating drug abuse. Recent data show we are making progress, but much remains to be done. We will not rest until the day of the dealer is over, forever.

Good health care is every American's right, and every American's responsibility. And so we are proposing an aggressive program of new prevention initiatives—for infants, for children, for adults and for the elderly—to promote a healthier America and to help keep costs from spiraling.

Elections

It's time to give people more choice in government by reviving the ideal of the citizen politician who comes not to stay, but to serve. And one of the reasons that there is so much support across this country for term limitations is that the American people are increasingly concerned about big-money influence in politics. So we must look beyond the next election, to the next generation. And the time has come to put the national interest above the special interest—and to totally eliminate political action committees.

And that would truly put more competition in elections and more power in the hands of individuals. And where power cannot be put directly in the hands of the individual, it should be moved closer to the people—away from Washington.

The Federal Government too often treats government programs as if they are of Washington, by Washington and for Washington. Once established, Federal programs seem to become immortal.

Federal and State Programs

It's time for a more dynamic program life cycle. Some programs should increase. Some should decrease. Some should be terminated. And some should be consolidated and turned over to the states.

My budget includes a list of programs for potential turnover totalling more than $20 billion. Working with Congress and the governors, I propose we select at least $15 billion in such programs and turn them over to the states in a single consolidated grant, fully funded, for flexible management by the states.

The value of this turnover approach is straightforward. It allows the Federal Government to reduce overhead. It allows states to manage more flexibly and more efficiently. It moves power and decision-making closer to the people. And it reenforces a theme of this Administration: appreciation and encouragement of the innovative power of "states as laboratories."

This nation was found by leaders who understood that power belongs in the hands of people. And they planned for the future. And so must we—here and all around the world.

America's Fighting Forces

As Americans, we know that there are times when we must step forward and accept our responsibility to lead the world away from the dark chaos of dictators, toward the brighter promise of a better day.

Almost 50 years ago, we began a long struggle against aggressive totalitarianism. Now we face another defining hour for America and for the world.

There is no one more devoted, more committed to the hard work of freedom, than every soldier and sailor, every marine, airman and coastguardsman—every man and woman now serving in the Persian Gulf.

Oh, how they deserve—what a fitting tribute to them. You see—what a wonderful, fitting tribute to them. Each of them has volunteered—volunteered to provide for this nation's defense. And now they bravely struggle to earn for America, for the world and for future generations, a just and lasting peace.

Our commitment to them must be the equal to their commitment to their country. They are truly American's finest.

Persian Gulf Crisis

And the war in the gulf is not a war we wanted. We worked hard to avoid war. For more than five months we, along with the Arab League, the European Community, the United Nations, tried every diplomatic avenue. U.N. Secretary General Perez de Cuellar; Presidents Gorbachev, Mitterand, Ozal, Mubarak and Bendjedid; Kings Fahd and Hassan; Prime Ministers Major and Andreotti—just to name a few—all worked for a solution. But time and again Saddam Hussein flatly rejected the path of diplomacy and peace.

The world well knows how this conflict began, and when: it began on August 2d, when Saddam invaded and sacked a small, defenseless neighbor. And I am certain of how it will end. So that peace can prevail, we will prevail.

Tonight I am pleased to report that we are on course. Iraq's capacity to sustain war is being destroyed. Our investment, our training, our planning—all are paying off. Time will not be Saddam's salvation.

Our purpose in the Persian Gulf remains constant: to drive Iraq out of Kuwait, to restore Kuwait's legitimate government, and to insure the stability and security of this critical region.

Let me make clear what I mean by the region's stability and security. We do not seek the destruction of Iraq, its culture or its people. Rather, we seek an Iraq that uses its great resources not to destroy, not to serve the ambitions of a tyrant, but to build a better life for itself and its neighbors. We seek a Persian Gulf where conflict is no longer the rule, where the strong are neither tempted nor able to intimidate the weak.

Most Amerians know instinctively why we are in the gulf. They know we had to stop Saddam now, not later. They know that this brutal dictator will do anything, will use any weapon, will commit any outrage, no matter how many innocents suffer.

They know we must make sure that control of the world's oil resources does not fall into his hands only to finance further aggression. They know that we need to build a new, enduring peace, based not on arms races and confrontation, but on shared principles and the rule of law.

And we all realize that our responsibility to be the catalyst for peace in the region does not end with the successful conclusion of this war.

Democracy brings the undeniable value of thoughtful dissent, and we've heard some dissenting voices here at home, some—a handful—reckless, most responsible. But the fact that all voices have the right to speak out is one of the reasons we've been united in purpose and principle for 200 years.

Commitment to Defense

Our programs in this great struggle is the result of years of vigilance and a steadfast commitment to a strong defense. And now, with remarkable technological advances like the Patriot missile, we can defend against ballistic missile attacks aimed at innocent civilians.

Looking forward, I have directed that the S[trategic] D[efense] I[nitiative] program be refocused on providing protection from limited ballistic missile strikes, whatever their source. Let us pursue an S.D.I. program that can deal with any future threat to the United States, to our forces overseas and to our friends and allies.

The quality of American technology, thanks to the American worker, has enabled us to successfully deal with difficult military conditions, and help minimize precious loss of life. We have given our men and women the very best. And they deserve it.

We all have a special place in our hearts for the families of our men and women serving in the gulf. They are represented here tonight by Mrs. Norman Schwarzkopf. We are all very grateful to General Schwarzkopf, and to all those serving with him. And I might also recognize one who came with Mrs. Schwarzkopf, Alma Powell, the wife of the distinguished Chairman of the Joint Chiefs. And to the families let me say, our forces in the gulf will not stay there one day longer than is necessary to complete their mission.

International Support in Gulf

The courage and the success of the R.A.F. pilots—of the Kuwaiti, Saudi, French, the Canadians, the Italians, the pilots of Qatar and Bahrain—all are proof that for the first time since World War II, the international community is united. The leadership of the United Nations, once only a hoped-for ideal, is now confirming its founders' vision.

And I am heartened that we are not being asked to bear alone the financial burdens of this struggle. Last year our friends and allies provided the bulk of the economic costs of Desert Shield, and now, having received commitments of over $40 billion for the first three months of 1991, I am confident they will do no less as we move through Desert Storm.

But the world has to wonder what the dictator of Iraq is thinking. If he thinks that by targeting innocent civilians in Israel and Saudi Arabia, that he will gain advantage, he is dead wrong. And if he thinks that he will advance his cause through tragic and despicable environmental terrorism, he is dead wrong. And if he thinks that by abusing the coalition prisoners of war he will benefit, he is dead wrong.

We will succeed in the gulf. And when we do,

the world community will have sent an enduring warning to any dictator or despot, present or future, who contemplates outlaw aggression.

The world can therefore seize this opportunity to fulfill the long-held promise of a new world order—where brutality will go unrewarded, and aggression will meet collective resistance.

Yes, the United States bears a major share of leadership in this effort. Among the nations of the world, only the United States of America has both the moral standing, and the means to back it up. We are the only nation on this earth that could assemble the forces of peace.

U.S. Leadership

This is the burden of leadership, and the strength that has made America the beacon of freedom in a searching world.

This nation has never found glory in war. Our people have never wanted to abandon the blessings of home and work for distant lands and deadly conflict. If we fight in anger it is only because we have to fight at all. And all of us yearn for a world where we will never have to fight again.

Each of us will measure, within ourselves, the value of this great struggle. Any cost in lives—any cost—is beyond our power to measure. But the cost of closing our eyes to aggression is beyond mankind's power to imagine.

This we do know: Our cause is just. Our cause is moral. Our cause is right.

Let future generations understand the burden and blessings of freedom. Let them say, "We stood where duty required us to stand."

Let them know that, together, we affirmed America and the world as a community of conscience.

The winds of change are with us now. The forces of freedom are together, united. And we move toward the next century, more confident than ever, that we have the will at home and abroad to do what must be done—the hard work of freedom.

May God bless the United States of America. Thank you very, very much. Thank you all. Thank you.

The American Scene

Robert Borosage
Senior fellow,
Institute for Policy Studies

1

The President [Bush] has a contradiction he has to resolve—that the American government has the capacity to impose order and our values on an unruly world [through U.S. military strength], but has no ability to address our own real disorders here at home. You can't say you can have stability in the [Persian] Gulf, but that a child can't walk down the streets without being under fire in our [American] cities.

The Washington Post, 2-4:(A)4.

Bill Bradley
United States Senator,
D-New Jersey

2

I would say America's always been about the future—whether it's the frontier, people moving on to a new day; or whether it's immigrants coming to the United States for a better life; or whether it's what you teach your kids about hard work and the belief that you can get ahead if you get an education in advance.

Interview,
Washington/
Los Angeles Times, 9-29:(M)3.

William F. Buckley, Jr.
Editor-at-large,
"National Review"

3

[Saying the U.S. performance during the recent Persian Gulf war shows it should be able to handle its other problems]: Who can mount [Operation] Desert Storm should be able to police Central Park, and who created the Patriots [anti-missile missile] should be able to handle [foreign competition from] Sony and Mercedes.

The New York Times, 3-4:(A)9.

George Bush
President of the United States

4

Now [that Operation Desert Storm, the U.S.-led war in the Persian Gulf, has ended victoriously], let's use our strength and our credibility to take on challenges here at home. We can make our schools the best in the entire world, and we will. We can restore order to our streets, and we will. We can build a society in which people who want to work will have opportunities, in which people who seek to build a just society will conquer the diverse forces of prejudice. We will build that society. If we didn't know it before Desert Storm, we know now: Nothing can stop us. So let's all of us, you and me, your family and our family, make this America the best it can possibly be.

At Independence Day celebration,
July 4/
Los Angeles Times, 7-5:(A)20.

Robert C. Byrd
United States Senator,
D-West Virginia

5

Most rock musicians and actors in music videos emerge as sneering, anti-social, unkempt, undisciplined and arrogant punks, male and female alike. Schools, jobs, home life, nuclear families, patriotism, self-discipline, religion, fathers and mothers, policemen, soldiers and other conventional figures—most of the people and institutions with which we live today—are portrayed day after day as oppressive, square, boring, fascist, un-cool, hypocritical and outdated. Contrarily, those who reject these institutions of responsibility in our society are lionized, romanticized and glorified. The central message of most of these music videos is clear: Human happiness and fulfillment are experienced by becoming a sociopath and rejecting all responsibility . . . We do indeed reap as we have sown. If we in this nation continue to sow the images of murder, violence, drug abuse, sadism, arrogance,

(ROBERT C. BYRD)

irreverence, blasphemy, perversion, pornography and aberration before the eyes of millions of children, year after year and day after day, we should not be surprised if the foundations of our society rot away as if from leprosy.

Before the Senate, Washington/
The Washington Post, 10-16:(C)7.

Randy "Duke" Cunningham
United States Representative,
R-California

1

If only the President [Bush] could have the kind of domestic support he had for the [U.S.-led war against Iraq in the] Persian Gulf, think what we could do in education. If we had the national resolve of the American people and a united Congress, think what we could do on the war on drugs. We could lick it. We could do it if we could get Congress together and forget the politics of it.

Interview/
The Washington Post, 3-11:(A)15.

David Duke
Louisiana State
Representative (R);
Candidate for the 1992
Republican Presidential
nomination

2

[Saying there is too much immigration to the U.S.]: I think the time has come . . . to begin to limit and stop the illegal immigration. Our traditions are being torn away. Our values are being torn away. Our environment is being threatened by massive immigration and a massive increase in demographic problems in America.

News conference,
Washington, Dec. 4/
Los Angeles Times, 12-5:(A)34.

Thomas S. Foley
United States Representative,
D-Washington;
Speaker of the House

3

We have problems here at home [in the U.S.] that are dramatic in a long-term sense, are conclusive and defining in a long-term sense, though not with the intensity or the focus of this recent war [in the Persian Gulf]. But if we ignore our problems at home, if we ignore the failings of our own system in this country—economic, political, educational and health—we will be inviting a time in the next century when the United States will simply not have the capacity, will not have the power, to lead the world to an undertaking such as the Desert Storm or Desert Shield operation [in the Persian Gulf].

At legislative conference
of American Federation of State,
County and Municipal Employees,
Washington, March 4/
The New York Times, 3-5:(A)9.

Mary Ann Glendon
Professor of law,
Harvard University
Law School

4

While rights have been proliferating, we have paid little attention to the seedbeds of civic virtue from which rights derive their surest protection. Now we are beginning to sense this erosion, and it scares us. People for the American Way recently completed a survey of the political attitudes of young Americans. The students were asked, "What makes America special?" Overwhelmingly, the young people answered, "Our rights and freedoms," which they characterized in a way that classical philosophers would recognize not as liberty but as license. People for the American Way, a group not noted for worrying about excessive liberty, said it's time to sound the alarm that America's youth has learned only half of the democratic equation: They have almost no sense of civic participation and responsibility.

Panel discussion, Philadelphia/
Harper's Magazine, February:44.

Henry Grunwald
Former editor-in-chief,
Time, Inc.

5

What we have in common as Americans is a political and social tradition that has created a

(HENRY GRUNWALD)

unique degree of freedom in action and conscience, a society more open to newcomers than
any so far known. American law and custom
have blended diverse groups more successfully
than any other community. Further, we have in
common a system that—for all its serious flaws
and injustices—has shown an unprecedented
ability to correct itself. Certainly we must
become more aware of other cultures and their
contributions. But the top priority should be to
equip children for life in the modern world, to
preserve and expand the unity America needs to
function better, for the sake of all, and to avoid
the destructive effects of intellectual tribalism.

Interview/Time, 7-8:20.

Thomas W. Kelly
Lieutenant General,
United States Army;
Director of Operations,
Joint Chiefs of Staff

1

[On U.S. home support for the recent U.S.-led
war against Iraq's occupation of Kuwait]: The
support of the American people can't be underestimated. In Saudi Arabia, the military felt the
American people were squarely behind them,
and this didn't happen during Vietnam. From
that, I derive that it's time for Americans to take
off the hair shirt. We are a very self-critical
people, and it's about time we started a little
bragging about America being able to do things
well.

Interview/USA Today, 3-20:(A)13.

Clara Sue Kidwell
Historian, University of California,
Berkeley

2

History should not teach a kind of uniform
identity or a commonality of American culture.
So much of American history really does involve
struggle and conflict and different groups trying
to come to terms with one another. I think it tells
us that the melting pot has not served the function of melting people into a kind of common

identity so much as the fact that people still retain
their own senses of identity. It's easy for teachers
to look for easily teachable generalizations for
students. But what history tells us more than anything else is how complex our experiences have
been.

Interview/Time, 7-8:20.

Kiichi Miyazawa
Former Minister of Finance
and former Deputy Prime Minister
of Japan

3

I firmly believe America is still a great country. Really wonderful people—not just the
famous, but ordinary Americans. So many of
them are honest, hard-working, decent. Of
course, there are problems like the homeless,
drugs and education. But the American people
have the freedom to discuss them . . . and the
willingness to fix them. The real problem in the
U.S. has been one of confidence. But after the
[recent Persian] Gulf war, Americans seem to
have regained their confidence.

To foreign reporters,
Tokyo, Oct. 18/
The Washington Post, 10-19:(A)16.

Shoichi Osada
Chairman, Tokyo Sowa Bank
(Japan)

4

Before the war, America was a good country. It
made good cars, developed good science . . .
That was a white country then. Now there are
blacks, Puerto Ricans, Mexicans, Japanese,
Koreans, Jews, Arabs, and that one-race, white-
only state has come to disappear. We used to
think of the United States as an emperor. Now we
think you're weak. You've become a multi-racial
nation. You won't get any better.

Los Angeles Times, 12-6:(A)1.

Turgut Ozal
President of Turkey

5

There is one interesting fact [about the U.S.]:
You contribute constantly to self-renewal. This

(TURGUT OZAL)

probably comes from the free expression of ideas, free thinking. There is also free enterprise, the ability of people to take risks. A man can even jump from Niagara Falls. I mean, there is no difference between a man jumping, or making money, or the astronauts going to the moon.

Interview, New York/
Time, 5-13:14.

Douglas "Pete" Peterson
United States Representative,
D-Florida

1

[On the recent U.S.-led victory over Iraq in the Persian Gulf war]: The Gulf war may not have had this original goal, but it unified this nation in a way it has not been since 1941. It made people feel good about the nation and the armed forces and about themselves. If we take this unity and the bipartisanship and apply it now to domestic needs of our society, we can do great things.

Interview/
The Washington Post, 3-11:(A)15.

Rinaldo Petrignani
Italian Ambassador
to the United States

2

[On the U.S.]: This is the universal nation, the nation that contains the world within herself, whose nationalism therefore excludes nobody.

Interview, Washington/
The New York Times, 5-27:7.

David E. Skaggs
United States Representative,
D-Colorado

3

[On the recent victory of U.S.-led forces in the Persian Gulf war against Iraq's occupation of Kuwait]: What I most want to see come out of this is a public identification that this is what the country can do when it puts its mind to making a difference. That is a lesson that can be applied at home as well as in international affairs. Let's get

serious about being first in math and science by the end of this century, as the President [Bush] has touted, and get serious about taking care of the 35 million people who can't get health insurance. I hope we can bolster our can-do spirit out of this.

Interview/
The Washington Post, 3-11:(A)13.

Michael I. Sovern
President,
Columbia University

4

[Saying the U.S. should show the same resolve in tackling other problems that it displayed fighting Iraq in the recent Persian Gulf war]: Let us give the lie to the proposition that our adversary must be an evil tyrant to bring out the best in us. Must we fight and die to feel proud of our country?

At Columbia University commencement,
May 15/
The New York Times, 5-16:(A)11.

Al Strachan
Sports columnist,
"Toronto Globe and Mail"

5

There's nothing wrong with being born American or opting to live there. The problem is that Americans *think* like Americans. It has been said that a Canadian who makes $5-million will retire and enjoy his money. An American who makes $5-million will work harder than ever to turn it into $10-million.

Los Angeles Times, 3-7:(A)12.

Marty Strange
Director,
Center for Rural Affairs

6

[On the decrease in young people staying on the family farm]: What it all adds up to is [more] shriveling of the rural community. It means an atrophying of Main Street. What rural communities live on is not commodities. Rural communities live on rural people. If you don't have people

(MARTY STRANGE)

out there populating the land, you're not going to have small towns.

Los Angeles Times, 7-23:(A)10.

Laurence H. Tribe
Professor of constitutional law,
Harvard University

1

It's terribly important for the United States to hold on to what it is that makes our country and our society so unique and distinctive. While we export our greatest commodity—our Bill of Rights and our dedication to principles of privacy and freedom—we shouldn't neglect the domestic dangers to those principles and freedoms.

USA Today, 9-17:(A)11.

Ben Wattenberg
Senior fellow,
American Enterprise Institute

2

If this [current Persian Gulf war] doesn't do away with the idea that, quote, America is in decline, unquote, nothing will. When the dust settles, you will have had several billion people watching [the war] in real time and noting the fact that America is the preeminent political, diplomatic and military force in the world, coming at a time when our popular culture and our political system is the most widely copied, and when English is the international language.

The Washington Post, 1-31:(A)21.

L. Douglas Wilder
Governor of Virginia (D)

3

Although the U.S. Constitution provides us a working blueprint for protecting the liberties and freedoms of the American people, unfortunately not everyone in this land has been committed to following that blueprint . . . The watering and nurturing of those seeds [of democracy] remains an evolutionary process . . . Americans should hope, pray and work to ensure that our leaders will provide the moral leadership and unconditional commitment needed to make America a land where all Americans participate in the American dream.

At University of North Carolina
commencement, May 12/
USA Today, 5-20:(A)11.

Civil Rights • Women's Rights

Clifford L. Alexander
*Former Chairman,
Equal Employment
Opportunity Commission
of the United States;
Former Secretary
of the Army of the United States*

1

During my lifetime, no black person will join your exclusive Senate club, run a Fortune 500 company, be president of NBC, CBS, CNN or ABC. You are determined to reserve those powerful positions for your own kind. Yes, we [blacks] nibble at the edges while you [whites] enjoy hearty meals . . . You see us as less than you are. You think we are not as smart, not as energetic, not as well suited to supervise you as you are to supervise us, that we are looking for something extra—a government program that gives us something we do not deserve . . . If you see a black man, you think you had better cross the street before something bad happens to you. These are the ways you perceive us, and your perceptions are negative. They are fed by motion pictures, ad agencies, newspapers and television. If you want to show [something] clean, brave and reverent, color it white. If it is shiftless, crime-ridden and over-crowded, color that black.

*Before Senate Banking, Housing
and Urban Affairs Committee,
Washington, May 21/
Los Angeles Times, 5-22:(A)4.*

Merle Black
*Professor of politics
and government,
Emory University*

2

[Comparing current Presidential candidate David Duke, who has a racist background, with former Alabama Governor George Wallace, who ran for President in 1968]: The issues George Wallace raised in 1968 are the issues Duke is addressing now. When you talk about affirmative action, preferential treatment [for minorities], busing for school desegregation— these are issues which came up in the 1960s in which whites were in direct opposition to blacks, and these are issues that have never been reconciled.

The New York Times, 11-25:(A)8.

Lawrence Bobo
*Professor of sociology,
University of California,
Los Angeles*

3

Once you have well ensconced some system of unequal relations between majority and minority groups, a set of ideas that sort of justifies that societal order are likely to take shape, and that will include a set of ideas about the traits of minority-group members that putatively explain why it is they should occupy a lesser, subordinated status.

The Washington Post, 1-9:(A)1.

Clint Bolick
*Director, Landmark Center
for Civil Rights*

4

The insistence on quota-type remedies by the civil-rights lobby is what keeps that issue alive. [NAACP leader] Ben Hooks created [former Ku Klux Klan member and now Louisiana state legislator] David Duke, and we're going to see a lot more David Dukes until we finally move away from that issue.

The New York Times, 4-3:(A)12.

5

What we have thought of in recent years as affirmative action is really all too often a form of racial preference. A quota is any form of racial preference in which a person's race is a determining factor in eligibility for opportunities.

The Washington Post, 6-5:(A)9.

David A. Bositis
*Senior research associate for
politics, Joint Center for
Political and Economic Studies*

1

The reason people have stereotypical perceptions [about minorities] is because they don't spend very much time in any genuine actions with other types of people. Usually what happens when people spend quality time with other people, they start thinking that people are more like themselves than different.

*Jan. 8/
Los Angeles Times, 1-9:(A)13.*

2

There are a lot of people who long for the days of "We Shall Overcome," when [blacks] all stood together. But part of the consequence of the civil-rights movement is that it allowed for a much greater measure of differentiation in the black community. They're not used to it right now, but they will get used to it.

The New York Times, 7-19:(A)10.

Barbara Boxer
*United States Representative,
D-California*

3

[Criticizing a Bush Administration order prohibiting doctors in Federally funded family-planning clinics from counseling women about abortion]: This isn't about abortion. This is about freedom of speech. It's about telling a physician, who takes the Hippocratic oath, that he or she cannot tell the truth to a patient. Now, there is something in my mind very un-American about this . . . That frightens me because I don't want the government teaching its values, its ideas to my children.

*Before Rotary Club,
Alturas, Calif./
Los Angeles Times, 10-7:(A)3.*

Bill Bradley
*United States Senator,
D-New Jersey*

4

Why don't you [President Bush] spend some of the political capital represented by your 70 per cent [public] approval ratings and try to move our glacial collective humanity one inch forward? . . . I'm asking you to take the issue of race out of politics and put it on a moral plane where healing can take place. Racial tension is too dangerous to exploit and too important to ignore. America yearns for straight talk about race, but, instead, we get code words and a grasping after an early advantage in the 1992 election.

*Before the Senate,
Washington, July 10/
Los Angeles Times,
7-11:(A)15.*

5

[Criticizing President Bush's record on civil rights]: The record is there. When he was running for the Senate in Texas in 1964, he opposed the Civil Rights Act of 1964, which desegregated public accommodations. That's restaurants, restrooms, buses. He has said he wants a full funding for the Head Start program, but only 25 per cent of the funds are there. He did run the Willie Horton ad in [the 1988 Presidential election campaign]. So do I think President Bush is racist? No. But I don't think he's been above using race to get votes. That is what is reprehensible. A person running for President or a President should not divide America, he should unite America.

*Interview,
Washington/
Los Angeles Times, 9-29:(M)3.*

Lee P. Brown
*Commissioner of Police
of New York City*

6

Considering history, considering cultural acceptance of segregation, considering that most police departments were predominantly or exclusively white, it should come as little surprise that the police in the American South were willing, if not eager, to deny basic rights to blacks. The police enforce the status quo, which is admirable only when the status quo protects the rights of individuals. When the status quo is corrupt by virtue of its repression of others, then

(LEE P. BROWN)

the police become instruments of repression and are corrupted in the process.

At "Policing the New South Africa"
conference, Pietermaritzburg,
South Africa, June 5/
The New York Times, 6-10:(A)4.

Gro Harlem Brundtland
Prime Minister of Norway

1

If you look at the '70s, in the U.S. and in other European countries, feminism was a kind of high-level intellectual and cultural debate, focused through novels, through speeches. It never came deep into reality.

The New York Times, 5-22:(A)4.

George Bush
President of the United States

2

The prevalance of abortion on demand in America calls into question our respect for the fundamental right to life . . . While sincere persons may disagree, my position is that the lives of both [mother and child] must be cherished and protected. We must recognize the dignity and worth of every human being in our laws, as well as in our hearts . . . All levels of government and all sectors of society should promote policies that encourage alternatives such as adoption and make adopting easier for families who want children and will give them loving homes, particularly children with special needs.

Proclamation of "National
Sanctity of Human Life Day,"
Washington, Jan. 14/
The Washington Post, 1-15:(A)19.

3

We must free people who have been held back by barricades of discrimination. This Administration will fight discrimination vigorously, because a kinder, gentler nation must not be gentle or kind to those who practice prejudice.

At Hampton (Va.) University
commencement, May 12/
The Washington Post, 5-13:(A)4.

4

I'm going to take my case every chance I get to black Americans and say, "Hey, listen, we got a good record on civil rights, and we're going to continue it" . . . We got a good civil-rights bill. Don't listen to all these people out there that say it's bad . . . In terms of a civil-rights bill, if they want to pass one, pass mine, pass mine now. And it moves against discrimination in the workplace. And you don't hear anything about it because others want to do something [quotas] that we can't accept.

News conference,
Washington, July 10/
The New York Times, 7-11:(C)18.

5

[On criticism that he is siding with anti-abortion protestors who have been blocking an abortion clinic in Wichita, Kansas]: I've been perfectly prepared to say all along . . . that I disapprove of breaking the law [by blocking the clinic entrance]. I don't think it helps the cause, whether the cause is anti-abortion or pro-abortion, or whether it's AIDS, whatever it is. And so what I'm saying is the American people get turned off by the excesses, the denial of the rights of others, for example. I disapprove of throwing blood. I don't like interrupting people's speeches. I think that's probably protected under the First Amendment, but I think it hurts the cause, whatever the cause is. I don't think people like just plain rudeness.

Aug. 17/
Los Angeles Times, 8-19:(A)14.

Anthony James Catanese
President,
Florida Atlantic University

6

[Criticizing the U.S. Education Department's stand against the granting of race-based scholarships to minority students]: This may represent the neo-racism of the 1990s. This says that neo-racists are not illiterate Southerners in hoods and sheets trying to burn crosses, but people who are well-educated, wearing three-piece suits, who are raising questions obscured in issues of

(ANTHONY JAMES CATANESE)

legality and Constitutionality, when in fact they are trying to say the same thing as old-time-racism—that the economic and social problems of this country are due to giving minorities an even chance.

The New York Times, 12-7:9.

William S. Cohen
United States Senator,
R-Maine

1

Civil rights is whispered to be a politically-defining issue, a so-called wedge issue that can be used to drive middle-class white voters into the arms of the Republican Party. But I believe the short-term political success is going to prove to be a long-term public-policy disaster . . . Success, for a party and for our country, ought to mean something more than he who dies holding the most votes.

Before the Senate,
Washington, Oct. 23/
Los Angeles Times, 11-5:(A)19.

James H. Cone
Professor of systemic theology,
Union Theological Seminary,
New York

2

When you look at the successes of the women's movement, or the gay-rights movement, or the anti-abortion movement, you can see the impact that the civil-rights movement—which was, to a degree, a black church movement—has had on their activism. So many people, with so many agendas, have turned to the black church and civil-rights movement as a model for protest.

Ebony, August:70.

Edith Cresson
Former Minister of European
Affairs of France

3

There are three places where women have always been excluded: the military, religion and politics. I would say that today it is still in politics where they have the least access.

Interview/
The New York Times,
5-16:(A)3.

John J. Curtin, Jr.
President,
American Bar Association

4

There are some polls which indicate that Americans would be willing to modify or abrogate the Bill of Rights in order to accomplish some good ends—fighting crime, the drug war, the flag issue or whatever. But you can't have the Bill of Rights protect only what the majority wants to protect . . . The whole purpose of the Bill of Rights is to protect the minority, and you can't turn it on and off like some sort of electric switch. Once you allow encroachments on the Bill of Rights even for very good ends, then the Bill of Rights no longer is there to protect you when you need it the most.

Interview/
USA Today, 8-8:(A)9.

John C. Danforth
United States Senator,
R-Missouri

5

There's been a heated debate going on among blacks as to how to accomplish the objective of equality in America. The view of a significant part of the civil-rights leadership is that the key to equality is a variety of preference systems. There is another, emerging group of black intellectuals, including [Supreme Court nominee] Clarence Thomas, who have seriously questioned that. They take the position that the job of improving equality is better served by different tactics than the traditional race-based preference. Clarence Thomas would argue that the best strategy for equality would include improved education, job training, an effective war on drugs and on crime, and very tough enforcement in cases of specific discrimination.

USA Today,
9-10:(A)11.

Benjamin O. Davis, Jr.
*General, United States
Air Force (Ret.);
First black General
in the Air Force*

1

Black [volunteers] are in the military for two reasons. Number 1, they're patriotic. Number 2, they are in an equal opportunity and treatment environment. A reflection, really, on society in the United States which is not an equal opportunity and treatment environment . . . Blacks in the military are treated in a way that Americans ought to be treated, in a non-racist atmosphere that exists in the military as opposed to the racist attitude that exists in work-places here in the United States.

Interview/USA Today, 2-18:(A)9.

David N. Dinkins
Mayor of New York

2

[Referring to a recent incident of violence by blacks against Jews in New York City]: I cannot help but think how sad [the late black civil-rights leader Martin Luther] King would be to know that in New York in 1991, the mob that had to be restrained was not wearing [Ku Klux Klan] hoods but came from the [black neighbor-] 'hood and that the man of God they lynched was not a black preacher who gave a fiery talk but a Jewish divinity student out for a quiet walk.

*At forum on race relations,
New York, Sept. 25/
The New York Times, 9-26:(A)17.*

Sharon Pratt Dixon
Mayor of Washington

3

It is abdundantly clear that America's reluctance to accept the African-American in all of our diversity continues to this very day in 1991 . . . Yet, claim this America, we must. For America cannot reach her full majesty until such time as all African-Americans have full and equal ownership of the rock [Plymouth Rock] . . . Our task is clear. We must educate not just the "talented tenth" but each and every African-American so that we become producers and manufacturers—distributors of products and services in the expanding global marketplace. It is not enough that a Michael Jordan or a Janet Jackson or an M. C. Hammer [black sports and entertainment personalities] achieve economic success. We, as a community of people, must achieve a corner on a critical American industry.

*At Howard University commencement,
May 11/
USA Today, 5-20:(A)11.*

4

While some may argue . . . that we [women] are the weaker sex, I suggest that all the facts and evidence would point to the reality. If it is so, we have a mighty strong way of showing it. We out-survive men from conception to the casket. We out-register them and we out-vote them . . . When we gather 20 years from today, let it be said that we are in every position and every corridor of power in matters that reflect our strength in this country. Let it be that we exist not only in the state houses but in the White House as well.

*At National Women's Political
Caucus convention,
Washington, July/
Los Angeles Times, 7-16:(E)8.*

Howard Dodson
*Chief, Schomburg Center for
Research in Black Culture*

5

Experts have been predicting the demise of black men for more than three centuries. The first slave masters assumed they would work them to death in seven or eight years. Later, they predicted that a decade or two of freedom would sound their death knell. But as Sterling Brown stated so eloquently, black men have been strong men! And they have kept on coming! Despite incredible odds, despite suffering numerous casualties, black men have found ways of overcoming the obstacles and making remarkable contributions to black people and all of humankind. They will survive today's crisis. They will be around to make 21st-century America.

Ebony, August:113.

Robert K. Dornan
United States Representative,
D-California

1

[Supporting the Supreme Court ruling that Federally financed family-planning clinics cannot give abortion advice to women]: I do like seeing Planned Parenthood take a heavy hit because they are as political a group as there is in the United States and they are the main perpetrators of the lie that *Roe vs. Wade* only legalized abortion in the first three months. The legal fact is that *Roe* legalized abortion for the entire nine months period for any reason whatsoever.

May 23/
Los Angeles Times, 5-24:(A)30.

Peter F. Drucker
Professor of social sciences
and management,
Claremont (Calif.)
Graduate School

2

All through history, men and women have had equal labor-force participation. The idea that women weren't in the labor force was a 19th-century notion. Women worked more hours than men. What is new is that they are [now] doing the same work . . . That's a new experiment in human history.

Interview/Los Angeles Times,
9-17:(D)7.

Marlin Fitzwater
Press Secretary to President
of the United States George Bush

3

[Criticizing the NAACP for threatening to expel members of its Compton, Calif., branch who endorsed Clarence Thomas for the Supreme Court over the objections of the national NAACP]: It's very troubling that the NAACP, which has a long and distinguished record of civil rights, would choose to threaten one of its chapters for endorsing Judge Thomas. They're ignoring individual rights and personal freedom at the expense of their own liberal political agenda . . . It serves to strengthen our conten-

tion that many of these organizations don't reflect the mainstream of America or even the mainstream of their own membership.

To reporters, Kennebunkport, Maine/
The Washington Post, 8-10:(A)11.

Arthur A. Fletcher
Chairman, United States
Civil Rights Commission

4

In the next decade, 75 to 80 per cent of America's work-force will be blacks, women and other minorities. The question, then [is], is America going to have a work-force that can compete? If that work-force is denied access to education and training, the answer is obviously no. And if they don't have the education, training and skills to compete with the rest of the world, how can they keep America secure, stable and prosperous? So a secure and stable America, not justice and fair play, is the *real* reason blacks and whites must learn to live in harmony. The national security depends on it.

Interview/Ebony, July:22.

Nancy Fulco
Human-resources attorney,
United States Chamber
of Commerce

5

[Opposing the 1991 Civil Rights Act because she says it would lead to hiring quotas]: Employees would be able to go into court based strictly on the numbers. They would not have to allege that the employer is doing anything that's causing a disparity of numbers [in the balance of minority and women employees]. A basic tenet of our legal system has always been that, in a lawsuit, a plaintiff not only has to show that harm occurred but also must show what caused the harm. This bill would reverse a legal tenet that's been around since the founding of the republic . . . How is [the employer] going to [try to avoid such lawsuits]? He's going to make certain that his work-force is statistically balanced to match the relevant labor pool from which he draws—which is, basically, quotas.

Interview/USA Today, 4-9:(A)9.

Geoffrey Garin
Democratic Party consultant

1

I think we're at a crucial juncture in terms of how we think about civil rights as a country. If civil rights is defined as quotas, it's a losing hand. If it's defined as protection against discrimination and efforts to promote opportunity, then it will remain a mainstream value in American life.
The New York Times, 4-3:(A)12.

Katharine Graham
Chairman,
The Washington Post Company

2

[On women in the corporate world]: They've made enormous progress. A lot of women say there's a "glass ceiling" at the mid-level range. That's true to some extent. Men who aren't used to dealing with women are still in charge, so there's probably some prejudice. But women started coming into the work-place in great numbers only 15 to 20 years ago, so time will eventually solve a lot of the problem.
Interview/USA Today, 4-4:(A)9.

Augustus F. Hawkins
United States Representative,
D-California

3

[On whether President Bush will sign a civil-rights bill this year]: I doubt seriously if he will sign one. I doubt if one will be passed that differs much from the one we passed last year. Assuming that is true, I would think he would not sign it. If Bush's position is that a civil-rights bill will create an atmosphere in which some employers think it necessary to use quotas in order to guard themselves against a lawsuit—I don't think you can ever guarantee against that. Consequently, if standing on that particular principle, if you can call it that, I would think that it would be practically impossible to pass a bill that is completely immune against lawsuits. It's the nature of business that a lawsuit may arise.
Interview/
Los Angeles Times,
7-7:(M)6.

Wade J. Henderson
National legislative director,
National Association for the
Advancement of Colored People

4

[On the large proportion of blacks in the U.S. military]: African-Americans are patriotic people and their commitment to the full freedoms of this country and to the protection of American interests has been strong. We are disturbed, however, that many African-Americans see opportunities in the general society so severely constricted that, for some, the military option is the only viable one.
Feb. 25/
The New York Times, 2-26:(A)11.

5

[On the 1991 Civil Rights Act]: [It is causing] tremendous anxiety [in the business community]. It's understandable but not justifiable. The stories of people who have been victimized in the work-place will chill you—the kinds of things that women have been subjected to under the guise of humor or fair play or joking. It's clear that juries will respond with great sympathy to those stories. Employers will begin to take control of these kinds of unjustifiable practices only if they feel real monetary pressure.
Interview/USA Today, 4-9:(A)9.

Benjamin L. Hooks
Executive director,
National Association for the
Advancement of Colored People

6

I don't think America was [ever] ready to end segregation. I don't think it has ever been ready to extend full equality. I can't think of anything we've gained as black people that has not come without a struggle.
The New York Times, 4-3:(A)12.

7

[On the NAACP]: There are so many things we try to do with meager resources because the problems are so deep. But one thing we won't do

(BENJAMIN L. HOOKS)

is abandon the fight against racism. If we do, who's left? I don't know if our critics understand; our charter is to fight discrimination. If they're telling me there's no longer a problem with police brutality, no more job and housing discrimination and most people are not worried about it, they're wrong. We're not struggling to find a mandate; we've got one.

Interview/The New York Times,
6-10:(C)10.

Henry J. Hyde
United States Representative,
R-Illinois

1

[Criticizing a current Democratic-sponsored civil-rights bill which he says will result in racial quotas[: This bill will accomplish precisely what the 1964 civil-rights bill stood four-square against—a color-conscious society. This bill codifies racial preference.

Before the House,
Washington/
Los Angeles Times, 6-5:(A)9.

Patricia Ireland
National vice president,
National Organization
for Women

2

[On the Senate's confirmation of Clarence Thomas for the Supreme Court despite allegations that he sexually harassed a female assistant of his 10 years ago]: It is obvious that Clarence Thomas is hostile to women's rights and indifferent to the realities of women's lives. Despite the Judiciary Committee's attempted cover-up and lopsided hearings, Thomas faces serious, credible, corroborated charges of sexual harassment. We will build a new political force to challenge incumbents who have abandoned the dream of equality and to challenge the unresponsive and outdated political parties.

Oct. 15/
Los Angeles Times,
10-16:(A)6.

Jesse L. Jackson
Civil-rights leader

3

[Criticizing President Bush's rejection of the Democratic Party's civil-rights bill]: Bush in the White House is more dangerous than [former Alabama Governor George] Wallace was in the schoolhouse door . . . It is a sad day when an American President consciously promotes racial fear and division in our country as his means of governing and of being re-elected.

At National Rainbow Coalition
convention, Washington, June 6/
The Washington Post, 6-7:(A)5.

4

[Saying the Republican Party is using the racial-quota issue for political gain]: Race is a decoy that sets America against America. It is a way for a politician to win, and the people to lose. It is morally wrong to polarize the country this way. Moreover, it is economically destructive. Race-baiting is a smokescreen that hides how vulnerable Americans really are.

Speech/
The New York Times,
6-27:(A)1,10.

5

President Bush has raised the specter of race to divide the nation, while neglecting our real economic needs. It seems to me that President Bush is a bully and he has us in a buzz saw. He continues his race signals and sinister plots, from Willie Horton [election-campaign commercials about crime] to [racial] quotas to the Supreme Court nominee [Clarence Thomas]. If we do nothing, we are humiliated. If we spend all our energy on it, we martyr him.

At NAACP convention,
Houston, July 10/
Los Angeles Times, 7-11:(A)15.

John Paul II
Pope

6

[Calling on Poland to stop practicing abortion]: Understand, all you who are careless in

(JOHN PAUL II)

these matters, understand that they cannot fail to concern me and cannot fail to hurt me. And it should hurt you as well. You should not carelessly destroy any more. Each and every child is a gift from God. That gift is always priceless, even if it is sometimes difficult to accept.

Mass, Kielce, Poland, June 3/
Los Angeles Times, 6-4:(A)6.

Bob Jones
Executive director, National
Conference of Christians and
Jews of Southern California

1

I do feel that racism is more acted out in the last dozen years than ever before . . . I think government has to accept responsibility for the trend. They've moved civil rights down the list of priorities, allowing education and business to follow suit. We have turned back the clock in affirmative action and equal-opportunity employment, which has been exacerbated by the current economic downturn. When the civil-rights groups lost several key leaders—Martin Luther King, Jr., Malcolm X, Robert Kennedy—the momentum was lost.

Interview, Los Angeles/
The Christian Science Monitor,
10-10:7.

Barbara Jordan
Professor of government,
Lyndon Johnson School
of Public Affairs,
University of Texas, Austin;
Former United States Representative,
D-Texas

2

I see reverse discrimination as imposing an unfairness on the majority. You cannot achieve an appropriate solution or correct a wrong by creating a further wrong. Now, when I speak of redress, I believe you must act affirmatively to try to place the complaining party, the victim, in the position he or she *would* be in were it not for discrimination.

Interview, Austin, Texas/
Los Angeles Times, 9-8:(M)3.

John R. Lewis
United States Representative,
D-Georgia

3

[Supporting affirmative action]: We must continue to move toward a truly interracial society. We must use every available instrument in government and in the private sector in order to do what we must to make up for some of the wrongs of the past . . . Sometimes we have to all pay a little price, we have to be part of the solution, and in some instances it can be a little painful—in the work-place or in a college, or wherever.

The Washington Post,
1-15:(A)4.

Jill Long
United States Representative,
D-Indiana

4

It was not too long ago that a colleague of mine complimented me on my appearance and then said he was going to chase me around the House floor. Because he was not my boss, I was not intimidated. But I was offended and embarrassed. Sexual harassment is serious; it's not funny and it's not cute and it certainly is not complimentary.

Before the House,
Washington, Oct. 9/
The Christian Science Monitor,
10-11:2.

Glenn C. Loury
Professor of political economy,
Kennedy School of Government,
Harvard University

5

It will sound paradoxical to many that affirmative action is not in the interest of blacks . . . But in the longer term, preferential treatment is inconsistent with blacks' attainment of equal status in society as independent contributors respected for their contribution.

Los Angeles Times,
7-15:(A)16.

Joseph E. Lowery
President, Southern Christian
Leadership Conference

1

The [civil-rights] issues in the 1950s were very simple—whether you [can] sit in a restaurant or whether you can vote. And the opposition was defending the indefensible and doing it by very offensive means. Now we have to find a way to simplify very complicated issues, and we haven't been able to do it yet.

The New York Times, 4-3:(A)12.

Thurgood Marshall
Associate Justice,
Supreme Court
of the United States

2

. . . when I was a youngster, a Pullman porter told me that he had been in every city in this country . . . and he had never been in any city in the United States where he had to put his hand up in front of his face to find out if he was Negro. I agree with him.

News conference,
Washington, June 28/
The Washington Post, 6-29:(A)10.

Thurgood Marshall
Former Associate Justice,
Supreme Court
of the United States

3

[Referring to new black Supreme Court Justice Clarence Thomas, who rose from poverty to success]: None of us [blacks] has gotten where we are solely by pulling ourselves up from our own bootstraps. We got here because somebody—a parent, a teacher, an Ivy League crony or a few nuns—bent down and helped us pick up our boots.

Newsweek, 10-28:23.

George J. Mitchell
United States Senator,
D-Maine

4

[On recent Senate Judiciary Committee hearings into charges by Anita Hill that Supreme Court nominee Clarence Thomas sexually harassed her 10 years ago]: Under the circumstances it was fair and it was appropriate to subject Professor Hill to careful, rigorous, even skeptical questioning. But what took place went beyond that. For some it became not a search for truth, but a search-and-destroy mission [against Hill]. No doubt Judge Thomas and his supporters would make the same argument in reverse. But what happened to Professor Hill, unfortunately, if unchallenged, sends a clear and chilling message to women everywhere: If you complain about sexual harassment, you may be doubly victimized. We must not let that message stand unchallenged. Victims of illegal sexual harassment must know that they have the force of law and the support of society behind them, just as much as the victims of rape or any other violation of human dignity. What happened to Professor Hill showed that our society has a long way to go before an attack on a woman's integrity and reputation are treated as seriously as one on a man's.

Before the Senate,
Washington, Oct. 15/
The New York Times, 10-16:(A)12.

Ralph Neas
Executive director,
Leadership Conference
on Civil Rights

5

The right wing has not been able to defeat civil-rights bills on their merits, so they have always attempted to convert the debate to a debate over quotas when all these issues have nothing to do with quotas.

The New York Times, 4-3:(A)12.

Sandra Day O'Connor
Associate Justice,
Supreme Court
of the United States

6

As [female] students today, your challenge will come not so much in breaking new paths—as your mothers, grandmothers and I have done—but in deciding which to choose among the many

23

(SANDRA DAY O'CONNOR)

paths now open to you, and in knowing how you should travel along them . . . As even larger numbers of women enter the work-force and our population grows ever more diverse racially and ethnically, we need to make structural and innovative changes in how our families are managed, how jobs are designed . . . and in our cultural and institutional attitudes toward women and minorities.

At Widener University commencement/
USA Today, 5-20:(A)11.

Nancy Pelosi
United States Representative,
D-California

1

[Criticizing the Senate Judiciary Committee for not taking seriously an allegation of past sexual harassment made against Supreme Court nominee Clarence Thomas by a woman who used to work with him]: They are men; they can't possibly know what it's like to receive verbal harassment, harassment that is fleeting to the man and lasting and demeaning to the woman. These allegations may not be true. But women in America have to speak up for themselves and say we want to remove all doubt that the person who goes to the Supreme Court has unquestioned respect for women. What's the rush [toward confirmation of Thomas]? We need a little more time to follow up on allegations so that we can send a signal to women in America that we take sexual harassment seriously.

Oct. 7/
The New York Times, 10-8:(A)1.

Derryl L. Reed
President,
National Association of Black MBAs

2

This is a good and bad time for blacks in the corporate world. On the one hand, you probably have the largest corps of well-educated, highly skilled black executives ever coming out of business schools and working their way into management right now. At the same time, we're seeing a

lessening of opportunity for those same men and women. Because of the current environment of corporate downsizing, mergers and acquisitions, their jobs are being eliminated. And with the lack of support from the Federal government with regard to discrimination suits, companies are no longer as inclined to seek out or promote minority managers.

Ebony, October:108.

John D. (Jay) Rockefeller IV
United States Senator,
D-West Virginia

3

The sad reality is that, for the Republicans, civil rights isn't a cause—it's a political issue. This issue isn't about racial quotas. It's about racial politics.

Raleigh, N.C., April/
Los Angeles Times, 4-23:(A)24.

Eleanor Smeal
President, Fund for the
Feminist Majority

4

A group of men have classified abortion and family planning as controversial, although women have long ago decided they want abortion. Forty-six per cent will have one in their lifetime. Three-quarters of all couples use some form of birth control. Yet it's deemed as controversial. We are made to feel less than moral, and then the men determine which class of women can get full access. And of course, their women, they'll arrange for it. They are the gatekeepers. The ones they keep regulating are the poor, the young, the sick and the helpless.

The Washington Post, 7-19:(D)3.

Margaret Chase Smith
Former United States Senator,
R-Maine

5

My feeling is that women have come a long, long way in a relatively short time. I think that they have made some great gains. I think it's time for them now to be looked upon as people and not

(MARGARET CHASE SMITH)

women and men. I realize there's a difference between men and women—no one would realize it more than I do. But it is not reasonable for women to stand out and want equal rights and, at the same time, all the special privileges that come with it . . . I never was a woman candidate. I never was a woman Senator or woman representative—I was [just] one of them.

Interview, Skowhegan, Maine/
Los Angeles Times, 12-8:(M)3.

Shelby Steele
Professor of English, San Jose
(Calif.) State University

1

[On his criticism of affirmative-action programs]: My position on affirmative action comes right out of the civil-rights movement. What the civil-rights movement wanted was a fair and equal society, where everyone had an equal opportunity to advance in the society. That's what I'm still very much for. Affirmative action, it seems to me, does the opposite of that—grants me a special entitlement based on my pigmentation . . . This business of cosmetically arranging the work-place . . . or universities by color, and presuming then that you have equality, is ridiculous.

Interview, San Jose, Calif./
Los Angeles Times, 1-13:(M)3.

2

Under affirmative action, the quality that earns us [blacks] preferential treatment is an implied inferiority. However this inferiority is explained—and it is easily enough explained by the myriad deprivations that grew out of our oppression—it is still inferiority.

Los Angeles Times, 7-15:(A)16.

Nadine Strossen
President,
American Civil Liberties Union

3

[On the ACLU]: I think this is the most important organization in the country, if not the world.

To say what we're doing is controversial is to say the Bill of Rights is controversial.

The New York Times, 1-28:(A)11.

4

In a time of perceived national crisis there's the greatest pressure on civil liberties. The government will always invoke the need to combat drugs, Communism, attacks on the sanctity of the family, [Iraqi President] Saddam Hussein—whatever the particular bogeyman of the time is.

Interview, New York/
The Washington Post,
2-13:(B)1.

5

[On advertisers who pull out of sponsorship of controversial material because of pressure groups]: Those of us who believe in free speech have an obligation [to advertisers] to help instill in them a notion they're just not in business to make money, but to face a responsibility to make the First Amendment a living reality. [But] the basic problem we face is that the urge to censor is the most fundamental in human nature.

At symposium sponsored by
Playboy Foundation and Nation
Institute, New York, Oct. 16/
The New York Times,
10-18:(C)15.

Louis W. Sullivan
Secretary of Health
and Human Services
of the United States

6

I firmly believe that enduring solutions to the problems of the black community will be found within the black community. We must transform a culture of violence which defeats and destroys into a culture of character which uplifts and empowers.

Before Senate Banking, Housing
and Urban Affairs Committee,
Washington/
The Christian Science Monitor,
8-6:12.

Robert M. Teeter
Republican Party
public-opinion analyst

1

I have often argued that one central characteristic of the baby-boom voters is that they are anti-special privilege, no matter whether that is [racial] quotas [as a means of addressing civil-rights problems] or tax breaks for big companies or wealthy people. In that sense, being opposed to [racial] quotas is a good idea and good politics.

The Washington Post, 1-15:(A)4.

Clarence Thomas
Judge,
United States Court of Appeals
for the District of Columbia;
Nominee for Associate Justice,
Supreme Court of the United States

2

I think it is important to state this unequivocally, and I have said this unequivocally in speech after speech: There is discrimination, there is sex discrimination in our society . . . You know, I used to when I can remember in my own classrooms looking around and realizing that 7 or 8 of the top 10 students in my classroom in grammar school were the smartest students and wondering at that age, if 8 of the 10 of them are the brightest, then why aren't there women doctors and why aren't there women lawyers.

At Senate Judiciary Committee
hearing on his nomination,
Washington, Sept. 10/
The New York Times, 9-11:(A)13.

3

I guess as a kid we heard the hushed whispers about illegal abortions and individuals performing them in less than safe environments, but they were whispers. It would, of course, if a woman is subjected to the agony of an environment like that, on a personal level, certainly, I am very, very pained by that. I think any of us would be. I would not want to see people subjected to torture of that nature . . . As difficult as it is for me to anticipate or to want to see that kind of illegal activity, I think [expressing my position on abor-

tion rights at these hearings] would undermine my ability to sit in an impartial way on an important case like that.

At Senate Judiciary Committee
hearing on his nomination,
Washington, Sept. 10/
The New York Times, 9-12:(A)12.

George C. Wallace
Former Governor
of Alabama (D)

4

When I first ran for Governor [in the 1960s] . . . I had to stand up for segregation or be defeated, but I never insulted black people by calling them inferior. That statement in 1963 about "segregation forever" and my stand in the classroom door [blocking blacks] reflected my vehemence, my belligerence, against the Federal court system that seemed to be taking over everything in the South. I didn't write those words about segregation now, tomorrow and forever. I saw them in the speech written for me and planned to skip over them. But the wind-chill factor was 5 below zero when I gave the speech. I started reading just to get it over and read those words without thinking. I have regretted it all my life.

Interview/
The Washington Post, 9-5:(A)21.

Catharine Wells
Professor,
University of Southern
California Law Center

5

The meaning of equality [for women] has changed radically in the past 10 years. The original idea of treating women as having the same rights as men has given way to a view that recognizes the differences between them.

U.S. News & World Report, 6-17:48.

Cornel West
Professor of religion
and director of Afro-American
studies program,
Princeton University

6

[On the alienation of many whites from the black civil-rights movement because of per-

(CORNEL WEST)

3

ceived preferential treatment embodied in current proposed civil-rights legislation]: The power of the civil-rights movement under [the late black leader] Martin Luther King was its universalism. Now, instead of the civil-rights movement being viewed as a moral crusade for freedom, it's become an expression of a particular interest group. Once you lose that moral high ground, all you have is a power struggle, and that has never been a persuasive means for the weaker to deal with the stronger.

The New York Times, 4-3:(A)1.

L. Douglas Wilder
Governor of Virginia (D)

1

[President] Bush, are you going to make this a gentler, kinder nation? Then quit this nonsense about the civil-rights act being a quota bill. Quit it. You know darn well that it's not a quota bill. If they want to know what real quotas are, I could tell them—sitting in the back of the bus, herded into neighborhood theatres, not being able to get a book out of the neighborhood library. Denied the opportunity to vote—by law. Denied the opportunity to hold elective office—by law. Talk about quotas—come on, let's get real now.

Interview/
The New York Times,
9-4:(A)14.

Roger Wilkins
Professor of history
and American culture,
George Mason University

2

Racial fairness in this country is essentially counter-cultural. Because of the weight of our history, for institutions and individuals to be racist is kind of like water flowing downhill. And in order to make water not flow downhill you have to make a dam. You have to do something counter-cultural to stop people from doing something that is not the normal, easy thing to do.

The New York Times,
4-3:(A)12.

I think [the race issue] will continue to heat up. When we're in uncertain economic times, white people become insecure and frightened, and they look around for scapegoats. The racial advances we've had usually have come in times of economic expansion, when people feel good about themselves. I don't think the American people are going to feel very optimistic for some time to come.

The New York Times, 10-19:7.

Joel Williamson
Professor of humanities,
University of North Carolina

4

The role that blacks play today is the role they have always played in the South. If you look at the black and white bodies and their mutual proximity to one another, there's been a revolution. But if you look at ideas, opinions and notions, if you push it out toward the subconscious, very little has changed.

The New York Times, 10-19:7.

Charles Willie
Professor of education
and urban studies,
Harvard University

5

[On the busing of schoolchildren to achieve racial integration]: It's just transportation. We use transportation to go to and from churches, jobs, etc. Health centers, jobs and churches don't operate on a neighborhood basis; why should schools? Busing has no relationship to the quality of education. It's sad to see an entire nation fall for the propaganda of busing, as if that was important to learning.

The Christian Science Monitor,
3-1:7.

Raul Yzaguirre
President, National Council
of La Raza

6

[On Spanish-speaking people in the U.S.]: Once they get here, they begin to be viewed as

(RAUL YZAGUIRRE)

aliens, regardless of where they came from. Even if they came here legally or under political asylum, they're viewed as illegal aliens. They're viewed as subhuman people because they are racially different. Their accents are taken as evidence of lower intelligence, even though these folks may speak two or three languages. Monolingual-English-speaking people will interpret that accent as evidence that they are mentally incapacitated.

Interview/USA Today, 5-9:(A)11.

The '80s were a horrible decade in terms of progress for the Hispanic community. But the '90s seem to offer a lot more promise. We're becoming more sophisticated, and we've gone way past the time when we were simply interested in getting Hispanics elected. We now want to make sure that they vote for civil-rights legislation, that they become aggressive in looking out after the interests of the Hispanic community and that they speak out and become visible on our issues.

Interview/USA Today, 9-30:(A)11.

Commerce • Industry • Finance

John F. Akers
Chairman, International
Business Machines
Corporation

1

[To IBM managers]: The tension level [among IBM employees] is not high enough; everyone is too damn comfortable when the business is in crisis . . . I'm sick and tired of visiting plants to hear nothing but great things about quality and cycle times, and then to visit customers who tell me of problems . . . I used to think my job as a [sales] rep was at risk if I lost a sale. Tell [IBM workers] theirs is at risk if they lose one.

U.S. News & World Report,
6-10:16.

James Autry
President, magazine group,
Meredith Corporation

2

Emotionally, so many times, managers think that in the office they've got to be this stoic, aloof, tough, emotionless person. Then when they go home, they can be this nice, soft, nurturing, supportive human being. It creates a kind of emotional dualism: that there is life and there is work. In fact, work is part of life. It's not only healthy but it's good management to be the same person wherever you are—home, church or work.

Interview/USA Today, 2-13:(A)11.

Geoffrey Beene
Fashion designer

3

I think that retail executives and buyers talk too much to themselves. They are constantly having meetings in their stores rather than keeping in daily touch with the markets that supply their goods. There used to be a one-on-one relationship between the retailer and the designer or producer. Now it's all internal meetings with a consequent lack of outside contact. It seems to me that in U.S. stores the immediacy that made

them so exciting has shifted to what's going on in the board room.

Interview, New York/
The New York Times, 5-27:19.

Nicholas F. Brady
Secretary of the Treasury
of the United States

4

We must modernize our banking laws to deal with the reality of the marketplace. We now have one United States bank in the top 30 internationally. Twenty years ago, we had nine banks in the top 30.

News conference,
Washington, Feb. 5/
The New York Times, 2-6:(A)1.

5

The difference between the banking industry and the S&Ls is the difference between chalk and cheese.

USA Today, 2-8:(A)12.

6

There is simply no bank insurance fund large enough to protect the taxpayer unless and until we address the underlying problems. If we leave the job half done—if we tinker with the problem—then we'll probably be back again, sooner or later, recapitalizing the bank insurance fund, perhaps the next time with taxpayer money.

Before Senate Banking Committee,
Washington, Feb. 26/
The New York Times, 2-27:(C)6.

Richard C. Breeden
Chairman, Securities and
Exchange Commission
of the United States

7

[On supervision of the government-securities market]: Questions about the regulatory structure are not just questions of turf; they go to

(RICHARD C. BREEDEN)

whether we can design a system that is likely to achieve our objectives. And our objectives here must be to finance government at the lowest cost, but also to maintain a respect for law and integrity in the market.

Interview, August/
The New York Times, 9-3:(C)5.

Leon Brittan
Vice president for
competition policy,
European Commission

1

A company's interests are to maximize profits, and there is nothing wrong with that. But sometimes a company is tempted to take the easy way out by swallowing up competitors, carving up the market with them or driving them out of business. The consumer's interest, of course, is to have a wide choice of goods and services . . . When you look around the world for examples of genuinely competitive industries, lack of competition at home is not a common feature. In fact, companies taking on world markets are more likely to be fit and able to do so successfully if they have been training competitively at home.

At Yale University, Jan. 14/
Los Angeles Times, 2-12:(H)3.

George E. Brown, Jr.
United States Representative,
D-California

2

I've honestly come to believe that the Federal government is too damned inept to determine what is in the best interest of major private-sector players. The Federal government doesn't even know what private industry is *trying* to do. The biggest thing the Federal government can do is to balance the budget. That would make it much easier to provide larger pools of reasonably priced capital. At the same time, we need to provide supportive environments that allow more cooperation among various parts of American industry without risking, say, antitrust violations. The thing most lacking is leadership.

Interview/
The Washington Post, 10-15:(A)21.

Nicolas Browne-Wilkinson
Vice Chancellor,
High Court of Justice
of the United Kingdom

3

[On the financial scandal involving the BCCI]: It is a matter of profound regret to me that there is no . . . convention regulating international insolvency. This case, I hope, if it does nothing else, may concentrate people's minds on the necessity for such a convention.

The Washington Post, 8-9:(B)3.

Richard H. Bryan
United States Senator,
D-Nevada

4

I find it difficult to believe that allowing banks to enter securities and insurance will make them more profitable. Expanded powers and diversification for S&Ls in the 1980s were justified on the theory that they were needed to make them more competitive. [After the recent S&L scandals,] you can surely understand why many of us feel uncomfortable when some of these same arguments are used now with respect to banks.

Addressing Treasury Secretary
Nicholas Brady at Senate Banking
Committee hearing,
Washington, Feb. 26/
The New York Times,
2-27:(C)6.

Daniel Burstein
Global business and
financial analyst

5

When we look back, we'll see that the 1990s were the years when the industrial-policy orientation of Germany proved superior to America's *laissez-faire* capitalism. The Germans are dedicated to government-determined policies that allow for state intervention and force the marketplace to operate in a much more narrow band than we favor in the United States.

Interview/
U.S. News & World Report,
4-1:50.

George Bush
President of the United States

1

[On his Administration's proposals to ease banking rules to allow more loans to be made]: Good banks should make good loans, but they've got to determine what that is. And what we want to do is be sure the Federal government is not in the way but fulfills its responsibilities, and that's the way it's going to be working here.

To reporters, Washington, Oct. 8/
The Washington Post, 10-9:(A)9.

Clark M. Clifford
Former chairman,
First American Bankshares,
Washington

2

[Saying he was not aware of his bank's involvement with the BCCI financial scandal]: Were we deceived? Apparently we were deceived. I don't know that it's any comfort, but the Bank of England was deceived . . . My judgment is questionable. I guess I should have learned it some way. I've been in this business a long time; it's been a very active life; you learn a good deal from government. I guess I should have some way sensed it. I did not. Others perhaps should have sensed it. I don't know what happened within our government. I read about all that government agencies knew. I know that you gentlemen will want to give a lot of attention to that . . . Still, however, I face it. And I face it in a manner that would indicate that I shall continue to do everything that I can to be helpful to the government. I want to know how this could happen. I want to know how it can be prevented in the future, and that is a main aim of mine.

Before House Banking, Finance
and Urban Affairs Committee,
Washington, Sept. 11/
The New York Times, 9-12:(C)5.

Bill Clinton
Governor of Arkansas (D)

3

Let's not forget that the most irresponsible people of all in the 1980s were not the people on the bottom. They were those who sold out our savings and loans with bogus deals and nearly bankrupted the country with [corporate] mergers and acquisitions when they should have invested that money to create jobs and produce new products.

Announcing his candidacy
for the 1992 Democratic
Presidential nomination,
Little Rock, Ark., Oct. 3/
Los Angeles Times, 10-4:(A)24.

E. Gerald Corrigan
President,
Federal Reserve Bank
of New York

4

What the marketplace tells us with almost unfailing regularity is that in times of stress, some parts of a financial entity cannot safely be insulated from the problems of affiliated entities.

Before Senate Banking Committee,
Washington/
The New York Times, 2-21:(C)18.

Graef S. Crystal
Adjunct professor,
School of Business,
University of California,
Berkeley

5

[Saying high executive pay seems to have little to do with company performance]: I'm looking at my data, and I'm saying, this isn't working. If pay for performance really worked, then all the people in this country who have the highest pay will give the highest performance, and all those people who have the lowest pay will have the lowest performance. And that just isn't true.

The Washington Post,
7-15:(Washington Business)20.

6

[Saying executive compensation should be linked to company performance]: Executives are only in the same boat as shareholders when the stock price rises. When the stock price tanks,

(GRAEF S. CRYSTAL)

shareholders are in a tiny little rowboat going down the drain, while the executives are sitting on the deck of the QE2 waving goodbye.

Los Angeles Times, 7-15:(D)1.

Richard Dale
Professor of international banking,
Southampton University (Britain)

1

[On the financial scandal involving the Bank of Credit and Commerce International]: What is needed now is new guidelines and better supervisory arrangements. There must be [international] consolidated regulation, with free exchange of information. That will not be easy to achieve . . . Unfortunately, the British inquiry into BCCI's collapse will not address this question. International bank regulation is a complicated area, and responsibility has to be distributed among national authorities. There has to be a full-scale review of present arrangements.

The Christian Science Monitor,
7-31:8.

W. Edwards Deming
Management consultant

2

What does a school of business teach? They teach the present system, how to get jobs in it, how to perpetuate what we have. That's exactly what we don't want. The school of business ought to educate people for the future, the transformation—but how could they? That would require knowledge.

To Congressmen and their staffs/
The Washington Post, 7-25:(A)17.

Kenneth T. Derr
Chairman,
Chevron Corporation

3

[On public resentment of oil companies' profits]: There is a lot of confusion on the part of the American public . . . I know it's complicated . . . I sympathize a little bit with the general public, which has trouble understanding . . . I think the American consumer doesn't like oil companies. We sort of epitomize bigness.

To journalists,
San Francisco, Jan. 14/
Los Angeles Times, 1-15:(D)5.

Michael Dertouzous
Professor, Massachusetts
Institute of Technology

4

This weakening in [U.S.] industrial performance is not because we're losing inventions. It's because we are not able . . . to make products that are simultaneously high-quality, low-cost and fast to market. It doesn't matter where they're invented; we have trouble making them. That's why we're losing our shirt.

The Christian Science Monitor,
3-14:9.

Daniel Diamond
Dean of the undergraduate school,
Stern School of Business,
New York University

5

Historically, corruption, unethical behavior, is unfortunately an integral part of the financial world . . . There is no canon of ethics in the U.S. securities industry.

The Christian Science Monitor,
8-21:8.

David Duke
Louisiana State
Representative (R);
Candidate for the
1992 Republican
Presidential nomination

6

[On Japanese trade barriers]: I come from Louisiana. We produce rice. We must go to the Japanese and say, "You no buy our rice, we no buy your cars."

News conference,
Washington, Dec. 4/
Los Angeles Times, 12-5:(A)34.

Barry Eichengreen
Professor of economic history,
University of California,
Berkeley

1

The Great Depression was caused by a collapse of the whole banking system. [But because of Federal deposit insurance,] depositors today know that they'll get back 100 cents on the dollar no matter what. So banks fail; depositors don't.

Newsweek, 1-21:44.

Steve Gardner
Assistant Attorney General
of Texas

2

[On downsizing, the practice by some companies of secretly decreasing the size or contents of their products while keeping them at the same price]: Any time the economy drops, we see across the spectrum of marketers an increased willingness to engage in deceptive activity. In this case, they aren't playing fair. The consumer is going to be tricked into buying something that doesn't exist.

The Washington Post, 2-4:(A)8.

Richard A. Gephardt
United States Representative,
D-Missouri

3

For years, we have been trying to get Japan and other countries to be more like us [in foreign trade matters], to play by our rules. We've got to continue this fight. But at the same time, if a country wants to exclude our products, they will face similar restrictions on access to the U.S. market. That's reciprocity and fair play.

Before Institute for International
Economics, Washington, Sept. 10/
Los Angeles Times, 9-11:(D)2.

Henry B. Gonzalez
United States Representative,
D-Texas

4

We must figure how to conceptualize the kind of banking system the country must have. One

thing seems certain: We can't go on with the crazy patchwork of giant banks and small ones . . . There's no way the tiny banker can compete with an institution that has no bad loans and that has grown with the help of government underwriting of its take-overs. The small guy is going to go under. We have in a sense nationalized the system. And the diminished bank competition is aggravating the credit crunch.

Interview/Time, 1-21:57.

Allan Goodman
Associate dean,
School of Foreign Service,
Georgetown University

5

We [the U.S.] are not competitive economically. Our industries are cumbersome, don't deliver value, and are not as quality-control conscious as the Japanese. If the Japanese market opened tomorrow to U.S. goods, we still make poor cars or electronics. Somehow, American industry has got to get galvanized.

Interview/
USA Today, 12-2:(A)13.

Joseph Gorman
Chairman, TRW, Inc.

6

The principal reason we're [the U.S.] not competitive is attributable to management. Too much short-term thinking. Not enough focus on the customer, on quality for the customer. Not enough focus on lean production techniques, on doing it right the first time. Not enough focus on advanced manufacturing processes, not enough focus on research and development and product development.

Interview, Cleveland/
The Christian Science Monitor,
8-8:8.

Alan Greenspan
Chairman,
Federal Reserve Board

7

I would think that there are a number of [banking] institutions which probably would be better

33

(ALAN GREENSPAN)

off if they merged, and there's no question in my mind that some significant, real cost in savings would occur under those conditions. That is talking about individual institutions. But as far as the system as a whole, the basic issue is that we've got a large number of community banks out there who do very well, and they serve their communities in an exceptionally effective manner. When we know that is when big banks try to come in and take their business away, they [the big banks] fail. So, unless you're going to argue that a lot of those community banking institutions are somehow not serving your community or are unprofitable or unsafe and unsound, none of which one can argue, you can't just merely make a generic statement that we should collapse the number of banks. It is true that we should in certain areas and certain individual institutions.

Interview, Washington/
The New York Times, 1-31:(C)5.

Kenneth Guenther
Executive vice president,
Independent Bankers Association

1

[Criticizing the "too-big-to-fail" doctrine under which the Federal government would bail out very large banks that are in trouble but limit coverage of smaller banks]: You are setting up a system where the financial giants of the world, whose failure would cause the greatest systemic risk, would have 100 per cent coverage, while tens of thousands of community banks would find their insurance capped. This is a prescription for slowly encouraging the migration of deposits from small banks to the too-big-to-fail institutions.

The New York Times, 2-21:(C)18.

Steve Hayden
Chairman, BBDO/Los Angeles,
advertising

2

When times are grim in corporate America, risky advertising is defined as anything that is interesting, human or entertaining. Therefore,

you end up with advertising that is uninteresting, inhuman and dull.

Los Angeles Times, 4-2:(D)6.

Ernest F. Hollings
United States Senator,
D-South Carolina

3

Congress is fed up playing Uncle Sucker. Japan and Europe, after reaping the benefits of one-sided, give-away trade agreements with the United States for decades, are about to meet the America that can say no.

U.S. News & World Report,
4-15:46.

Claude Hutchison
Chairman,
CivicBank of Commerce,
Oakland, Calif.

4

We're [banking] an industry that has to attract additional capital. The interests of the economy and the people and the banking industry are served by creating an environment where banks can legitimately compete. The industry is holding its own, but if we're going to have globally competitive banks, we have to look to ways to enhance earnings by offering a broader base of service. If we don't, we're going to lose out internationally. And by losing out internationally, our own domestic economy is going to continue to erode *vis a vis* the other economies that we are competing with in a global sense. The United States does not have a bank in the top 10 in the world any more.

Interview/
Los Angeles Times, 3-3:(D)7.

Lee A. Iacocca
Chairman,
Chrysler Corporation

5

[Accusing Japan of unfair trade practices, such as "dumping" in the U.S.]: I send Jeeps to Japan, and when they cross the international date line, magic happens—they go from $22,000 to

(LEE A. IACOCCA)

$34,000. The Toyota minivan, which we just had a dumping case against—like magic it's $22,000, [but] it drops to $15,000 when it gets to San Francisco. Now, why can't sane Americans figure out that there's something wrong with that? It's unfair. So long as it's unfair, I'll keep shouting.

Broadcast interview/
"Nightline," ABC-TV, 6-11.

Alan M. Johnson
Managing director of
executive pay practices,
Handy Associates, consultants

1

Corporate America operates by the John Wayne school of management. There are one or two powerful guys at the top who have the power to bet the company on a new project or a huge investment, and that requires John Wayne-type pay. The Germans and Japanese, by contrast, run companies collegially, spreading the responsibility around among top managers.

The New York Times, 3-18:(C)4.

Herbert D. Kelleher
Chairman and president,
Southwest Airlines

2

I talk to people about leadership, rather than managing or administering, and I think there are key, substantive differences. What we try to breed at Southwest Airlines are leaders, not managers or administrators. We want everyone to be a leader in their job; you're a leader not just in what you say, but in the way you listen and respond to others, in what you do, and, most importantly, how you do it. A baggage handler who does his job promptly is as much a leader as I am, setting an example and showing the others how to do it properly. That's why we value individuality: It gives us leaders. And, yes, it makes for a whole lot of fun.

Interview/
Nation's Business,
October:59.

John Kerry
United States Senator,
D-Massachusetts

3

[On the financial scandal involving the BCCI]: The target of our investigation [is] this enormous under-government that's out there—a mixture of various kinds of nefarious types of people within countries, who share no standards, who know no laws.

Interview, Washington, Aug. 2/
The Christian Science Monitor,
8-5:9.

Paul R. Krugman
Economist, Massachusetts Institute
of Technology

4

Free-trade areas are not necessarily a good thing economically, because they lead to trade diversion rather than trade creation. In the highly imperfect politics of international trade, regional free-trade zones could upset the balance of forces that has allowed the creation of a fairly liberal world trade system . . . [But] the prospects of trade diversion from free-trade areas are limited because the prospective trading blocs mostly fall along the lines of "natural" trading areas, countries that in any case do a disproportionate amount of their trade with one another.

At economic conference,
Jackson Hole, Wyo., August/
The Washington Post, 9-4:(C)3.

Jim Leach
United States Representative,
R-Iowa

5

[Criticizing Bush Administration proposals to ease banking rules to allow more loans to be made]: It's my judgment the Treasury got took by the weak banks. We're in a cyclone in the economy, banks are running scared and have pulled in their horns. You don't improve that by allowing banks to weaken their standards.

Oct. 8/
The Washington Post,
10-9:(A)9.

35

WHAT THEY SAID IN 1991

Carl Levin
United States Senator,
D-Michigan

1

[Saying shareholders should be allowed to have some say on company executives' pay]: In the 1980s, pay increases for American CEOs shot far above the pay increases for other workers. Often, executive pay rose while corporate profits stalled and in some cases plummeted. The government ought to get out of the way of stockholders who are angry about runaway pay. It's their money.

USA Today, 5-23:(A)10.

Alice Tepper Marlin
Executive director,
Council on Economic Priorities

2

When the Council began two decades ago, the vast majority of companies thought that information on their social programs [which the Council disseminates] was nobody's business. Today, hardly any companies will argue with the concept that consumers and investors care about good social performance and that it is integral to good financial performance . . . Good social performance often goes with good financial performance because they both are evidence of good management. Management that understands social changes, as well as the impact of company operations on society and public opinion on the company, realizes that it's wiser to stay two steps ahead of the sheriff rather than one step behind.

Interview/
USA Today, 4-8:(A)11.

John B. McCoy
Chief executive, Banc One,
Columbus, Ohio

3

Banks are a little like lemmings. If someone comes up with a good idea, the next guy does it, the next guy does it and the next guy does it. When the 127th guy does it, it's not a good idea any more.

Los Angeles Times,
4-17:(A)15.

Lenny Mendonca
Banking consultant,
McKinsey & Company

4

The banking industry needs mergers. We have far too many banks and bank branches. The United States has over 12,000 banks, which is 50 banks per million people. The United Kingdom and West Germany have six banks per million people. The banking industry spends over $113-billion a year on things like people and branches and systems. And it's been growing at 10 per cent for the past decade. If the industry consolidated, competition would be increased. Even a small-scale consolidation could take $10-billion to $15-billion out of the industry's expenses, and you would still have two to three major banks and hundreds of small ones in an area, and they would still be competing as aggressively for deposits, with lower costs.

Interview/
Los Angeles Times, 3-3:(D)7.

Nel Minow
President,
Institutional Shareholders
Services

5

If [actor] Jack Nicholson, [entertainer] Janet Jackson or [baseball player] Darryl Strawberry don't perform, their salaries can drop to zero. When a [corporate] CEO does badly, his pay almost never goes down.

Newsweek, 6-17:44.

James C. Morgan
Chief executive,
Applied Materials, Inc.

6

No question. We learn more from our Japanese customers than we do from our American ones . . . That's beginning to change, but much of our success in the rest of the world comes from what we learn from our best Japanese customers.

The Washington Post,
6-21:(F)3.

Robert M. Morgenthau
District Attorney of Manhattan
(New York City)

1

[On the financial scandal involving the BCCI]: I think what it illustrates is that the United States cannot afford to have a foreign bank doing business in this country that is not regulated by any strong central bank, and is protected by the secrecy laws of its headquarters operation . . . If they do business here, they've got to be regulated by the Federal Reserve, in conjunction with the states. But they should not be able to evade regulation by our central bank.
Interview, New York/
Los Angeles Times, 8-4:(M)3.

Robert A. Mosbacher
Secretary of Commerce
of the United States

2

[On product liability suits against companies]: . . . we find case after case where businesses have to stop making products, not because they've already been sued or that they're faulty products but because the insurance for them is so high they can't afford to make them . . . [We in the Administration] have proposed for the last two years that the Congress pass a law in the product-liability area that gave alternatives to going to court. It did not allow these out-of-size damages to be put through, have some relation to the hurt, to the damage actually made, and that would diminish the number of cases, find alternative ways to settle these things, because we saw that it's costing American business hundreds of billions of dollars, and that's costing the consumer and it's costing our competitive position around the world.
Broadcast interview, Aug. 15/
The Washington Post, 8-20:(A)14.

3

A major cause of the credit crunch is over-regulation [of the banks], and there is no doubt about it. The regulators are intimidating bankers, so that in many cases the bankers have not been able to use their experience to work with lenders.
Interview/
The New York Times, 10-5:16.

Frank H. Murkowski
United States Senator,
R-Alaska

4

Retaliation [by the U.S. against unfair trade practices by other countries] is the only possible recourse. We welcome foreign investment in the United States. It's good for the economy and U.S. consumers. But we simply cannot tolerate trading partners that don't believe in reciprocity.
Los Angeles Times, 4-27:(A)19.

George C. Parker
Professor,
Graduate School of Business,
Stanford University

5

It's a little difficult to identify areas where American banks have a competitive edge in the global market. My first reaction is to ask, "My goodness, why should they bother?" American banks will never in our lifetimes dominate global banking the way they did 15 or 20 years ago. But this only reflects the fact that our dominance of the global economy has declined considerably, and will never be the same.
Los Angeles Times, 8-16:(D)4.

Lee A. Pickard
Former Director,
Division of Market Regulation,
Securities and Exchange Commission
of the United States

6

Financial intermediaries regulated by the SEC—broker-dealers, investment advisers and mutual funds, for example—have experienced very few insolvencies over the past several years, unlike the savings-and-loan and banking industries, where literally hundreds of billions of dollars of public monies have been lost due to insolvencies. The SEC wants more funding to oversee the financial integrity of the stock market and its professionals. It also wants to engage in more intensive "risk assessment" of the markets and their participants with an objective of avoiding the type of debacle we have experienced with depository institutions. Moreover, the SEC is

37

(LEE A. PICKARD)

being confronted with an array of new financial products and trading techniques . . . This is going to require that they have the personnel and resources to both understand these products and trends and fashion a proper regulatory response.

Feb. 4/The Washington Post,
2-5:(A)17.

Dan Quayle
Vice President
of the United States

1

[Excessive regulations on business] threaten the loss of American jobs, place billions of hours of needless government paperwork on America's small-businessmen and women, impose millions of dollars of unnecessary Federal mandates on our cities and towns, and last—but certainly not least—raise the cost of products to America's consumers. Obviously, some regulations are necessary to protect public health and safety. But the reality is that many regulations are unnecessary and don't really protect anyone.

Speech to business group,
Washington, Oct. 22/
Los Angeles Times, 10-23:(A)10.

Donald W. Riegle, Jr.
United States Senator, D-Michigan

2

[On government regulation of the securities industry in the wake of the recent Salomon Brothers scandal]: There remain outstanding questions as to who should be the primary enforcer over this marketplace. Authority over the market seems to be divided between the Treasury, the Federal Reserve and the SEC, possibly resulting in enforcement actions falling between the cracks.

Washington, Sept. 10/
The New York Times, 9-11:(C)2.

John D. (Jay) Rockefeller IV
United States Senator,
D-West Virginia

3

There is no *free* trade in the world except as practiced by the U.S. and to some extent

Canada. There is no real choice. The only choice is *fair* trade, reciprocity.

Los Angeles Times, 7-4:(A)22.

Felix G. Rohatyn
Senior partner,
Lazard Freres & Company,
investment bankers;
Chairman, Municipal
Assistance Corporation
of New York

4

The cost structure of Wall Street has been so dramatically increased over the past decade that even though you may see a minor increase in profitability, it is not enough to recapitalize the industry. There still has to be a real re-examination, probably by each [Wall Street] firm, about what is its business, and maybe a redefinition of what the business is all about.

The New York Times, 3-7:(C)7.

Richard M. Rosenberg
Chairman,
BankAmerica Corporation

5

By the end of this decade, the U.S. banking system will look entirely different. There are likely to be only 3,000 to 5,000 banks in the year 2000, instead of the 12,000 to 14,000 existing today. But those that remain will be better, stronger banks.

Before American Chamber of Commerce,
South Korea, May/
The New York Times,
8-14:(C)1.

Louis Rukeyser
Host, "Wall Street Week,"
PBS-TV

6

Karl Marx was wrong about many things, and one of the things he was wrong about was that Wall Street was a bunch of warmongers. In fact, they yearn for stability in the investment world. They're scared by war and rumors of war, and no placard-carrying peacenik of the '60s yearned for a peaceful settlement [of the current Persian Gulf war] more than the investors now do.

Interview,
New York/
Lear's, March:22.

John Rutledge
Chairman,
Claremont Economics Institute

1

The argument that a low dollar will reduce the trade deficit is a very standard and very narrow-minded view. To me, trade balance is something that should only happen by accident. If you went through a 10-year period where it made sense to move capital goods from the United States to Germany, as I think the next will be, that would be recorded as a U.S. trade surplus and a German deficit. If those tools are more needed in Germany than they are in the United States during that period, then that's a great thing to do. For 75 years during the 19th century, the United States was in a trade deficit because we were importing tools to take advantage of our investment opportunities. And that's when we did our tremendous growth.

Interview/
Los Angeles Times,
2-10:(D)9.

Walter Scott
Professor of management,
Kellogg Graduate School
of Management,
Northwestern University

2

[In the recent Persian Gulf war, the U.S.] built and fought well with some of the most sophisticated instruments ever designed. The biggest dividend at home may be instilling that same kind of aggressiveness into our own business competitiveness. People may be willing to roll up their sleeves and think Japan isn't such an indomitable rival after all.

Time, 3-11:68.

L. William Seidman
Chairman, Federal
Deposit Insurance Corporation

3

[Criticizing Bush Administration proposals that would put savings-and-loans and national banks under Treasury Department supervision and state-chartered banks under the Federal Reserve, taking away supervisory control from the FDIC]: It looks to me like an invitation to civil war, regulatory civil war. The Treasury would be under the Administration and the Fed would be free—it would be half-free and half-slave. It never worked before and I don't think it will work well this time. With respect to the FDIC, it would take away essentially all of our powers to protect the [deposit-] insurance fund. One thing you need to protect the taxpayer is an agency who can protect the insurance fund and has the power to do so.

Before House Budget Committee,
Washington, Feb. 7/
The Washington Post, 2-8:(F)2.

4

There is no free market—only markets that operate freely with proper government control. That's why so much of international competition is more like a barroom brawl than a prize fight. And why government has become more important in our lives.

Los Angeles Times Magazine,
5-5:54.

5

We have some problems in the banking system. They are primarily involved in geographic areas that are having a very stiff recession, particularly a real-estate recession. We are in a period that tests management of banks. As has been said, "When the tide goes out, we find out who's swimming without a suit."

Interview/USA Today, 10-16:(A)13.

Karen Shaw
Consultant,
Institute for Strategic Development

6

The old saying is that trade follows finance. American companies will never be strong in

(KAREN SHAW)

international markets unless [U.S.] banks are, too. No foreign bank really wants to finance imports into its own market.

Los Angeles Times, 8-16:(D)4.

C. J. "Pete" Silas
Chairman,
Phillips Petroleum Company;
Chairman, United States
Chamber of Commerce

1

Top performance is at the heart of our corporate mission. This doesn't always mean being the biggest or the most profitable. But it does mean getting the most mileage from our assets and delivering the highest returns to shareholders. Top performance also means making decisions today that set the stage for even bigger achievements later on.

Nation's Business, June:45.

Bruce F. Vento
United States Representative,
D-Minnesota

2

[On government proposals to allow commercial companies to own banks]: We marry the titans of industry to the biggest banks and hope they don't find the bedroom.

USA Today, 2-8:(A)12.

Ralph Whitworth
President, United
Shareholders Association

3

[Criticizing high executive pay which seems to have little to do with company performance]: The system is bankrupt. There really is no restraint on these people, and the only thing that limits them is their own gall . . . It's like a bear loose in a honey factory.

The Washington Post,
7-15:(Washington Business)20.

Crime • Law Enforcement

Charles T. Banner-Haley
Assistant professor of history,
Colgate University

1

[On the excessive beating of a suspect by Los Angeles police officers, which was recorded by an amateur videotape camera]: People are re-awakening to the same realities that shocked them when civil-rights footage showed blacks being hosed and cattle-prodded in the '60s . . . What is most disturbing is, this episode is not an aberration; it is the tip of the iceberg in cities big and small.

The Christian Science Monitor,
3-11:1.

Henry G. Barr
Deputy Attorney General
of the United States

2

Republicans have sought to reverse two decades of liberal activism and bring the law more into the mainstream. While this effort is largely succeeding, perhaps the main unfinished business is the criminal law, where society's ability to protect itself from crimes still suffers from the excesses of the Warren [Supreme] Court.

The New York Times, 3-26:(A)12.

Joseph R. Biden, Jr.
United States Senator,
D-Delaware

3

[President Bush's new drug program] makes some improvements, but it commits most of the same old mistakes of the last three strategies. It does not put nearly enough emphasis on dealing with the hard-core cocaine addict population, which is rising. It does little or nothing to deal with tens of thousands of addicted prisoners [who] . . . after they have served their term, go out and commit these crimes again. It continues to emphasize, in the area of interdiction, mili-tary assistance to countries abroad rather than economic aid and debt relief, which is the best way to get at the root of the problem . . . It falls short on education . . . When I introduce my drug strategy and the President his, we always emphasize those portions which are different. Eighty-five percent of what we are both proposing is the same thing. The question comes down to where the emphasis should be to have the biggest impact on the problem, and some of the things don't cost any money, like dealing with assault weapons. It doesn't cost any money, it just requires a commitment.

Jan. 31/
The Washington Post, 2-6:(A)16.

Sherman Block
Sheriff of Los Angeles County,
Calif.

4

We've had people in this department who have been brutal. In the future, I'm sure we'll have people who will be brutal. We've had people in this department who have just been plain stupid, who have done some dumb things which have gotten them in trouble and have brought great discredit to the department, and I'm sure that will happen in the future. But I think the larger question is not that these incidents occur but what is the organizational response? How do we deal with these people who are, in fact, engaged in misconduct?

At media open house,
Los Angeles, Aug. 28/
Los Angeles Times, 8-29:(A)1.

Bill Bradley
United States Senator,
D-New Jersey

5

. . . you've got to be tough [against violent crime], which means death penalty for drug kingpins who murder, which means long sentences for drug dealers who use a gun in the commission of a drug crime. Gun control in terms of a waiting period and in terms of registration . . . In addition to that, you need community policing, where you engage the community to help secure safety for them. Right now, a lot of police departments basically patrol areas of our cities like an occupying army. That's not the way it should be. Local residents should be a part of the process.

Interview, Washington/
Los Angeles Times, 9-29:(M)3.

Robert Burgreen
Chief of Police of San Diego

1

In today's police work, the chief of police has to be in touch with the community . . . A chief who believes in and exercises community outreach on a personal level—that would be the Number 1 job requirement. A chief who also maintains regular contact with the officers on the street, so that the chief knows what the officers are thinking and doing and the problems they are having—that is equally important.

Interview/
Los Angeles Times, 7-28:(M)1.

George Bush
President of the United States

2

[Comparing the high crime rate in the U.S. with the danger of being in the Persian Gulf during the recent war there]: Think of it—one of our brave National Guardsmen may have actually been safer in the midst of the largest armored offensive in history than he would have been on the streets of his own hometown. It's outrageous, it's wrong and it's got to change . . . Now that the shooting has stopped overseas, we've got to redouble our efforts to silence our guns here at home. The kind of moral force and national will that freed Kuwait City from abuse can free America's cities from crime.

At Attorney General's Summit on
Law Enforcement Responses
to Violent Crime,
Washington, March 5/
The Washington Post, 3-6:(A)5.

3

We need a crime bill that will stop the endless, frivolous appeals that clog our *habeas corpus* system, one that guarantees that criminals who use serious weapons face serious time, and one that ensures that evidence gathered by good cops acting in good faith isn't barred by technicalities that let bad people go free. And for the most heinous of crimes, we need a workable death penalty, which is to say, a real death penalty.

At Attorney General's Summit
on Law Enforcement Responses
to Violent Crime,
Washington, March 5/
Los Angeles Times, 3-6(A)4.

4

[On the beating of a suspect by Los Angeles police officers which was captured on amateur videotape]: Law-enforcement officials cannot place themselves above the law that they are sworn to defend . . . It was sickening to see the beating that was rendered, and there's no way, there's no way, in my view, to explain that away. It was outrageous.

Washington, March 21/
The Washington Post, 3-22:(A)4.

5

The time has come to show less compassion for the architects of crime and more compassion for its victims. Our citizens want and deserve to feel safe . . . We must remember that the first obligation of a penal system is to punish those who break our laws . . . You can't turn bad people into saints.

Before Fraternal Order of Police,
Pittsburgh, Aug. 14/
The Washington Post, 8-15:(A)8.

William R. Celester
Director of Police
of Newark, N.J.

6

[President] Bush and his guys have to stop saying more police and jails are the answer [to the drug problem]. No local police department can

(WILLIAM R. CELESTER)

stop the flow of drugs. It has to come from the Federal government. They're the only ones who can go across country [borders] and go state to state. They have the money and the manpower to go after the big shots.

Interview, Newark, N.J./
The Christian Science Monitor,
11-22:9.

Warren Christopher
Chairman,
commission investigating
the Los Angeles Police Department

1

[Saying Los Angeles Police Chief Daryl Gates should step down in the wake of the commission's investigation showing brutality and racism among police officers]: We've said we think the time has come for a transition because we think [that] 10 years is an appropriate period of time [for a police chief to serve; Gates has been in office 13 years]. We think . . . term limits are desirable so we can have an infusion of new leadership . . . so there is not a time when the chief of police outlives his effectiveness, his creativity.

News conference,
Los Angeles, July 9/
Los Angeles Times, 7-10:(A)20.

Mark Clark
Former president,
Houston Police Officers Association

2

Police see the sorry side of it all. A policeman can start out bright-eyed and bushy-tailed, but it goes away quickly on the street. It takes a mature officer not to stereotype people.

Time, 4-1:21.

John Conyers, Jr.
United States Representative,
D-Michigan

3

We can build all the jails we think we need and slam the doors down on thousands of people, but it won't make a bit of difference until we address the fundamental causes of crime.

USA Today, 1-7:(A)2.

4

[On the current national investigation of alleged police brutality triggered by videotapes of Los Angeles police beating a suspect]: We are on our way to relieving the crisis of confidence [in the police] that now exists. I see this as a way to expunge a national problem from our law-enforcement system. It isn't often we get a case that leaves so little to question, so few defenses to be raised.

March 14/
Los Angeles Times, 3-15:(A)31.

Alfonse M. D'Amato
United States Senator,
R-New York

5

[On criticism that his proposals to increase the number of crimes that fall under Federal jurisdiction would create too big a burden for Federal courts]: I could care a hoot about the fact that it may create a burden for the [Federal] courts. Better a burden for the courts than the continued killing and violence on our streets . . . When a woman gets shot and killed and loses three babies, you're telling me I should be worried about whether the courts should take on additional cases? The Federal government cannot simply say this is a local responsibility. The domestic tranquility has been lost . . . The predators have taken over . . . The people of America are bleeding. They're living as prisoners in their own home.

Interview/
The Washington Post, 7-22:(A)8.

6

[Advocating putting many local crimes committed with guns under Federal jurisdiction]: We're in a crisis era; we're losing control of our urban centers. Let's get the Feds involved in this battle. The Feds shouldn't just walk away from these crimes saying, "It's not dignified."

Interview/
The New York Times, 7-24:(A)9.

43

Ron DeLord
Director,
Combined Law Enforcement
Associations of Texas

1

The bulk of police forces are white males of the middle class. Yet we send them into large urban centers that are black and Hispanic and poor, with no understanding of the cultural differences, to enforce white, middle-class moral laws. Doesn't that create a clash?

Time, 4-1:20.

Edward F. Feighan
United States Representative,
D-Ohio

2

. . . I think that there has been a dramatic change in public opinion over the past several years on the issue of gun control. The terrible tragedies that we've seen across this country from Stockton, California, to Washington, D.C., have made the public very much aware and very much sensitive to the need for some change in America's gun laws. In addition to that, I think that we have, ironically, one of our allies in the National Rifle Association itself, which has through its own irrationality and extremism now demonstrated to the American people that there is no room for compromise with this organization, that there is no willingness to even consider the most moderate, the most rational forms of gun legislation; demonstrated, obviously, through its most recent efforts, its legal maneuvering to make machine-gun ownership legal and easy once again.

News conference, Jan. 3/
The Washington Post, 1-9:(A)18.

Isaac Fulwood, Jr.
Chief of Police
of the District of Columbia

3

In my personal conversations with young people who have been involved in violence, there is no remorse, there is not the first tear, there is no sense that this is wrong.

The Washington Post, 1-2:(A)1.

Mary Hatwood Futrell
Associate director,
Center for the Study
of Education and National
Development;
Former president,
National Education Association

4

[On crime]: We have to focus more attention on families and on communities. I grew up in a poor community in the heart of the ghetto of Lynchburg, Virginia. But even though we were poor, we looked out for each other. One night a guy tried to break in our window, and my sister and I were beating him over the head with a hammer. The neighbors all came running. Today's kids need that kind of community support. What will the next generation be like? Are we creating a generation that doesn't care?

USA Today, 1-3:(A)9.

Daryl F. Gates
Chief of Police
of Los Angeles

5

[On calls for his resignation following an amateur videotape showing Los Angeles police excessively beating a suspect]: I'm Chief of Police. This was a shocking thing, a horrible situation and so I think they're aiming it right at me. And I understand that. I really do. I'm a little resentful, but I understand it. I'm Chief. And you said, "The buck stops here." And where in the hell do you think it stops? It never stopped with the [Police] Commission. It never stopped with the Mayor. Anybody else take any of the heat on any of these issues? No. Always been the Chief of Police. And that's the way it is . . . To my best knowledge, [when charges of police brutality have been made in the past] we've done complete investigations and, where we have determined they were at fault, we have taken very, very stringent action. I'm not an easy disciplinarian. They say you can't fire people in the civil-service system. You can. I fire them every year. I fire police officers every year.

Interview,
Los Angeles, March 14/
Los Angeles Times, 3-17:(M)3.

Ira Glasser
Executive director,
American Civil Liberties Union

1

[On review boards that investigate charges of police brutality]: Most review boards are creatures of the police department, and it's very difficult to get a fair and objective hearing. The police usually charge people whom they beat up with what are called "cover charges." And the more the beating the heavier the charges. If they shoot somebody, they usually charge him with attempted murder; if they beat him they charge him with resisting arrest and assaulting a police officer... If there are no witnesses and no proof, frequently a cross-complaint is filed against the police by the person who's beaten. It ends up in a bargain that they'll drop the charges against you if you drop the charges against them.

Interview/USA Today, 3-12:(A)9.

Herman Goldstein
Professor of criminal law,
University of Wisconsin

2

Community policing [citizens cooperating with police] is a deterrent to the improper use of [police] force because it strengthens officers' relationships with the community. The neighborhood support gives police a greater sense of confidence and authority, which reduces their need for using force. If police officers feel they don't have the authority, the power, to handle a situation, they're more likely to resort to brute force.

Time, 4-1:22.

Reuben Greenberg
Chief of Police
of Charleston, S.C.

3

Police are not going to be successful [against violent crime]. In case of homicide, police are effective—if you want to call it effective—after someone is killed or assaulted. The exception is domestic violence. The drive-by killings, the drug-related killings—we make excuses for this kind of activity. The solution is not going to be this "40 acres and a mule" position that's so

popular with liberals. We've got a very serious problem and a large proportion of it is black-on-black crime. The way you maintain order in a democracy is not through the police or the courts; it's through social order.

Interview/USA Today, 1-3:(A)9.

William Greenhalgh
Professor of law,
Georgetown University

4

[Criticizing a Supreme Court ruling that will prevent automatic overturning of guilty verdicts in trials where confessions coerced by police were used]: The message the police will take from this is that you can lean on them [suspected criminals] harder now and get away with it. That's the wrong message to send, and it couldn't come at a worse time [in light of recent revelations of police brutality].

March 26/
Los Angeles Times, 3-27:(A)10.

Frank Hartmann
Executive director,
criminal-justice program,
Harvard University

5

The four classical purposes of imprisonment are incapacitation, deterrence, punishment and rehabilitation. Right now, the balance has gone. You'd have to say rehabilitation is out and incapacitation and punishment are in.

The New York Times,
1-18:(B)11.

Orrin G. Hatch
United States Senator,
R-Utah

6

One does not need to know anything about *habeas corpus* to know that when it takes 10 years or more to carry out a death sentence, something is terribly wrong with the system.

Before the Senate,
Washington/
The New York Times, 6-27:(A)12.

Franklyn G. Jenifer
President, Howard University

1

The whole notion that one is going to cure the drug problem in America by stopping the supply is contradicted by history . . . Wherever there is a demand, there will always be somebody who is creating the supply. The demand has to be addressed. I think education is the long-term answer.

Interview, Washington/
Los Angeles Times, 2-10:(M)3.

Cassandra Johnson
Executive director,
National Organization
of Black Law Enforcement Executives

2

[On the Christopher Commision report showing brutality and racism in the Los Angeles Police Department]: From the chiefs I've been talking to [around the country], no one is surprised at what the report had to say. Everyone had been predicting that if patterns were found of derogatory remarks, and behavior not held in check, there would be nothing for [LAPD] Chief [Daryl] Gates to say. The only way things like this happen in a department is if officers feel they will not be held accountable for it. Every police chief is now sitting around hoping that they don't ever have to face a situation like this. They want to take every step possible to make sure it doesn't happen in their back yard.

Los Angeles Times, 7-15:(A)3.

Michael Keating
Chairman, Task Force on Justice
(sponsored by Boston Bar Association
and Boston's Crime and
Justice Foundation)

3

Every element of the [Massachusetts] criminal-justice system—from the courts, to probation, to the corrections system, to parole—is overwhelmed and imbalanced. What is out of balance today, we believe, will be out of control tomorrow unless systematic and comprehensive changes are made.

The Christian Science Monitor,
3-14:7.

Jack Kemp
Secretary of Housing and
Urban Development
of the United States

4

The vast majority of crime, I think, is caused by the poverty, the despair. So an all-out national assault on crime has to include as part of its strategy an all-out assault on despair. An all-out assault on lack of education. An all-out assault on impoverishment, poverty and lack of employment.

Interview/USA Today, 8-13:(A)11.

Edward Koren
Staff attorney,
National Prison Project,
American Civil Liberties Union

5

What we have right now is a terribly dangerous situation in terms of [prison] over-crowding. It's been going on for the last 15 years. We've been trying to solve all of our crime problems essentially by locking up as many people as we possibly can. And the system cannot handle the numbers that are coming into the system . . . We have generated many, many, many people due to our sentencing policies—getting rid of parole, going to mandatory minimum sentences, determinant sentences rather than indeterminant sentences—and that has meant there are more people coming in the front door and not enough people going out the back door.

Interview/USA Today, 5-30:(A)13.

Michael A. Kroll
Executive director,
Death Penalty Information Center

6

The interesting thing about capital punishment is that while politicians reaped a tremendous electoral reward for beating on the capital-punishment drum, and while the public apparently wants it, there seems to be an ambivalence about it. Theoretically, we like it but, in practice, we are very reluctant about it . . . We want to execute people who go this final step and commit the ultimate crime: taking life. But then, when

(MICHAEL A. KROLL)

you start looking at the fact that there are 23,000 murders in this country, you have to arrive at some system of selection unless you're willing to execute 23,000 people a year, and no country engages in that kind of slaughter. So once you agree that some system has to be enacted for picking out who among us is qualified or appropriate for this final solution, then you find all sorts of unacceptable and unfair considerations enter the process.

Interview/USA Today, 7-8:(A)11.

James Marquart
Sociologist,
Sam Houston State University

1

[On charges of police brutality against minorities]: White police officers don't understand a lot of things that go on in [non-white] areas. One way to deal with that is to use force. It goes across all cultural boundaries.

Time, 3-25:17.

LeRoy Martin
Superintendent of Police
of Chicago

2

If you recruit [as a police officer] a better-educated person, especially someone who has been college-educated, or at least has completed two years of college, you recruit a person with a different mentality. But most police departments around the country require only a high-school diploma or GED. As a result, you are recruiting some people who have dropped out of school at one time or another, and if you look into their backgrounds, you find some people who come from battered homes themselves, who may not have extensive police records, but who have been problem people themselves.

Ebony, July:60.

3

[Saying some Constitutional rights should be suspended in the fight against crime]: A lot of our communities are under siege, and police find themselves helpless because of civil rights. When we come in contact with evidence that hasn't been seized properly as part of the court, we can't use that evidence even though the evidence has been found on the person . . . and the person is guilty and walks away free to commit another crime . . . We need to take a look at it [the Constitution] and maybe from time to time curtail some of those rights because they have gotten us into a position where we're living in an armed camp.

Broadcast interview, Chicago/
The Washington Post, 7-13:(A)6.

Bob Martinez
Nominee for Director,
Federal Office of
National Drug Control Policy

4

[Saying he does not support a ban on private ownership of assault weapons]: An act of violence will be carried out, one gun or another. Some weapons, obviously, are more effective than others. Saying you ban, or outlaw, one weapon, or any other, does not, in my view, reduce drug traffic.

At Senate Judiciary Committee hearing
on his nomination,
Washington, Feb. 26/
The Washington Post, 2-27:(A)23.

Bob Martinez
Director,
Federal Office of
National Drug Control Policy

5

Certainly, the Persian Gulf conflict put everything else on the obit page. But I can tell you this: If you go out to the neighborhoods of this country, the intense feeling about drugs has not in any way waned. And our job is to make certain that feeling from the citizens of this country are not forgotten here . . . I intend to be a constant reminder that this is an issue that remains yet to be solved—that we've made improvements but we still have a long way to go.

Interview, March 25/
The Washington Post, 3-26:(A)15.

(BOB MARTINEZ)

1

You will often hear it said that the so-called real drug problem isn't on our college campuses— "college campuses" used, in this case, is a misleading shorthand for middle-class white kids. The real problem is addiction, this argument goes. And addiction is in the ghetto, nowhere else. Here's my view of that argument. It is arrogant nonsense . . . Schools receiving Federal funds— and almost all of them do—must implement drug-prevention programs for their students, must impose strict standards of conduct prohibiting unlawful activity, must make known to all students all applicable Federal, state, and local laws, must describe available counseling services and must distribute a clear statement that college disciplinary sanctions—quite apart from that provided by law—do exist and will be applied. This is the first and best stage in fighting drugs. It's not testing, it's not arrest, it's not treatment; it's information and clear messages and sanction that everyone understands.

Before Fraternity Executives Association,
Washington, April 5/
The Washington Post, 4-9(A)20.

2

There is now solid evidence that the percentage of violent crimes that are drug-related is declining, yet violent crime over-all is not. There are other social pathologies at work which will continue to foster violence, especially in our inner cities . . . When this crusade [against drugs] began, many of us assumed that crime would drop as drug use declined. Unfortunately, there are now some preliminary indications that success in the war on drugs does not necessarily translate into success in the war on crime.

At National Press Club,
Washington, Sept. 5/
Los Angeles Times, 9-6:(A)20.

Howard M. Metzenbaum
United States Senator,
D-Ohio

3

[Criticizing the crime bill before the Senate, which has a heavy emphasis on capital punish-

ment]: I cannot support a bill which does so little to deter violent crime and which, in the name of being tough on crime, puts at risk the lives of innocent people [who may be wrongly convicted]. There is too much death penalty with too few protections.

The Washington Post, 7-12:(A)12.

Patrick V. Murphy
Former Commissioner
of Police of New York City;
Former president,
Police Foundation

4

The strongest trend in police work today is community policing-prevention, or preventative policing. One way it's been described is "small-town policing in a big city." It's not the police alone, it's not the community alone, it's the teamwork that works.

USA Today, 1-3:(A)9.

5

The work of police officers, no matter how idealistic, energetic or motivated, can never transcend the caliber of their bosses. Leadership will either be a constant inspiration or instant depression. Cops at the lower rungs cannot escape the management of the chief. The L.A. officers [who have recently been charged with use of excessive force against a suspect] would not have done what they did if they knew they would be reported by other officers. The problem is the tone set at the top.

Time, 4-1:25.

6

I'm a firm believer in [police] accountability . . . In no uncertain terms I would say, "I will not tolerate [police] brutality. I'll hold you [officers] accountable." If you're smart, you'll hold the people under you accountable right down the line, because "I'll chop your head off as fast as I'll look at you" . . . [But] it is a sad commentary on this society that thousands of police officers have to put bulletproof vests on every day. Unlike the soldier in combat who's taken off the line for

(PATRICK V. MURPHY)

R&R, we have police officers putting bullet-proof vests on every day for 20 years . . . That affects the way you think. "Why am I having to put this uncomfortable thing on and perspire? Because there are guns out there. Because cops are getting shot. And because if I work in a certain precinct and it's Friday or Saturday night, I am going to respond to eight calls with a gun" . . . When they roll up on these calls and say, "Freeze! Throw your hands up!" and [the suspect] keeps walking, you're thinking, "I'm in the funeral parlor."

Interview, Washington/
Los Angeles Times, 4-7:(M)3.

1

There's not enough proper political oversight of police departments—simply because Mayors and elected officials don't know how complex the job is. The citizen walking down the street thinks he could do a police officer's job in a minute, and most people think they could do the chief's job better. It's not like that. It's very complex work because you're dealing with human behavior.

Interview, Washington/
Los Angeles Times, 4-7:(M)3.

Daniel P. O'Brien
Assistant to the Commissioner
of Corrections of Minnesota

2

There is no relationship between the incarceration rate and violent crime. We're in the business of tricking people into thinking that spending hundreds of millions for new prisons will make them safer.

The New York Times, 1-18:(B)11.

Ronald Reagan
Former President
of the United States

3

[Supporting proposed Federal legislation requiring a seven-day waiting period for the purchase of a handgun]: With the right to bear arms comes a great responsibility to use caution and common sense on handgun purchases. And it's just plain common sense that there be a waiting period to allow local law-enforcement officials to conduct background checks on those who wish to purchase handguns.

At George Washington University,
March 28/
The New York Times, 3-29:(A)1.

Edgardo Rotman
Specialist in criminology,
University of Miami

4

[On the parole system]: The United States imprisons people at a greater rate than any other nation. Parole is an absolutely essential tool to unload a dangerously overloaded system. That's one of its main functions. It allows making sentences more fair. Any uncompromising position in this field is dangerous. To reach fairness, you need a certain amount of flexibility. Over-crowding is one of the greatest generators of crime now.

Interview/
USA Today, 9-19:(A)13.

Robert Rufo
Sheriff of Suffolk County, Mass.

5

I understand the concept that we can't . . . build our way out of the crime problem [with bigger prisons], and I do not believe that every person, every first-time incarcerant, should be [put] behind bars . . . But I think that what we have to do as a society, and we are beginning to do this, is to carve out certain criteria . . . for the types of people that really should not be [at large].

The Christian Science Monitor,
3-7:13.

William S. Sessions
Director,
Federal Bureau of Investigation

6

White-collar crimes are difficult to detect . . . How do we prove that a judge accepted a bribe

(WILLIAM S. SESSIONS)

from a lawyer for deciding a case in a certain way? Generally, there is no crime scene to search . . . Bank-fraud and embezzlement investigations are extremely complex and extremely time-consuming. Many times the fraud is being committed by an owner, by members of the board or by other high-ranking bank officials, and cooperation from their employees is thus very difficult to obtain. This, in turn, necessitates more labor-intensive avenues of investigation. Thousands of documents must be examined . . . hundreds of witnesses must be interviewed and . . . a grand-jury investigation is almost always necessary in order to obtain essential documents and witness testimony.

At George Washington University
Law Center, Feb. 5/
The Washington Post,
2-8:(A)18.

Jerome H. Skolnick
Professor of law,
University of California,
Berkeley

1

. . . I believe that racist police are more likely to be brutal and brutal police are more likely to be racist.

Time, 3-25:17.

Eleanor Smeal
President, Fund for the
Feminist Majority

2

[Saying more women police officers will make for better police forces]: They're less authoritarian and use force less often than their male counterparts. They gain compliance without excessive force on the average more than men do. They're better at defusing potentially violent confrontations. They possess better communications skills. And they respond more effectively to incidents of violence against women.

Interview/
USA Today, 7-24:(A)11.

Dewey R. Stokes
President,
Fraternal Order of Police

3

I suffer frustrations. It appears we don't have any way to stop the recidivism that's going on among the 3 per cent or 4 per cent of the population that's committing crime after crime. You arrest, basically, the same people. They're the ones committing the crimes, the harassments, going through the penal system two or three times.

Interview/
USA Today,
3-12:(A)9.

4

A major thing [in the last 20 years] is a breakdown of respect for law enforcement, a more aggressive society toward law enforcement. That's a direct result of court cases over the years saying that this person has an excuse or excuses for his or her actions when they violate the law. They came from a broken home, they didn't have an educational opportunity to progress, they're downgraded because they've received some type of state or Federal subsidy. I don't believe that.

Interview/
USA Today,
8-6:(A)9.

Xavier Suarez
Mayor of Miami

5

Miami has experienced a substantial drop in its homicide and serious-crime rate in recent years. The most important factor in this decline has been citizen involvement. Ultimately, crime must be deterred by prompt and predictable punishment. Our system of bail bonds, illogical technicalities used by defense attorneys, and endless appeals makes prosecution of drug kingpins a costly, unworkable odyssey that frustrates law enforcement officials and drains society's resources.

USA Today,
1-3:(A)9.

Louis W. Sullivan
Secretary of Health and
Human Services
of the United States

1

Do you realize that the leading killer of young black males is young black males? As a black man and a father of three, this reality shakes me to the core of my being.

At Hampton (Va.) University,
March 13/
The Washington Post, 3-14:(A)1.

Morris Thigpen
Commissioner of Corrections
of Alabama

2

[The rate of prison incarceration in the U.S. reflects a] philosophy that all of us have allowed to become so [entrenched]: that the way we handle criminals is by totally removing them from society, by locking them up. I think that people are beginning to question whether that really solves anything. Some people realize now that just to routinely turn to incarceration [in cases of property and non-violent crime] is an unwise decision.

The Christian Science Monitor,
3-7:12.

Dick Thornburgh
Attorney General
of the United States

3

We are not here to search for the roots of crime or to discuss sociological theory. The American people demand action to stop criminal violence whatever its causes. The debate over the root causes of crime will go on for decades, but the carnage in our own mean streets must be halted now.

At Attorney General's Summit
on Law Enforcement Responses
to Violent Crime,
Washington, March 4/
The New York Times, 3-5:(A)13.

Anthony Travisono
Executive director,
American Corrections Association

4

. . . we have bond issues for new [prison] buildings. But buildings, new or old, have never cured anyone of anything. If they [the public] want corrections to lock people up just to vegetate and fester, then we [in corrections] don't want to take the rap when these folks come out the same as they went in, or worse. There has got to be much greater public discourse on the problems.

The New York Times,
1-18:(B)11.

Joseph Wambaugh
Author; Former police officer

5

Premature cynicism is the hallmark of a cop. They start mistrusting everyone, thinking that nobody's any good, except members of [their] group. They start palling around with police exclusively because they're the only ones who understand.

Los Angeles Times, 7-1:(A)18.

6

[On whether there should be more female police officers]: Oh God, yes—50 per cent women or more. I've always been a strong believer in that . . . I do not believe you need a strong back to be a cop. You need a strong back to be a firefighter. I think female cops can go a long way toward helping to mitigate the super-aggressive, paramilitary macho myth of the gung-ho cop and introducing the sobering element of maturity in police work . . . Police work is not about physical altercations; it's not about shooting people—it's not any of that. It's about talking to people. Women are awfully good at talking to people. They're awfully good at revealing their own emotions. They're awfully good at eliciting the other side to reveal their emotions. They're awfully good at problem-solving and that's all police work is. The very best cops are the ones who can get people to talk to them. That's what detective work is. It's not about all sorts

(JOSEPH WAMBAUGH)

of scientific breakthroughs—it's about getting people to talk. Women are eminently better qualified at that.

Interview,
Rancho Santa Fe, Calif./
Los Angeles Times, 7-14:(M)3.

Maxine Waters
United States Representative,
D-California

1

It's time for a revolution in management in police departments around this country. The old approach has long ago outlived its usefulness and the business of trying to rule the streets with the billy club and the gun is over. The police institution has not gone through a revitalization in my lifetime and in most people's lifetime. It's an antiquated operation. They [the police] are not prepared to deal with new attitudes, new diversity, and that's the main problem in the cities. They're now dealing with Asians and Mexican-Americans and African-Americans who come from a new generation of people, who look different, dress differently, whose ideas about freedom are different. Some of these young African-Americans are not going to kowtow to these officers and treat them as though they are something special.

Ebony, July:59.

Bob Watson
Commissioner of Corrections
of Delaware

2

[There's] a valuing of freedom . . . reflected in [high U.S. and state prison-] incarceration rates—that when someone breaks our laws we're quick to lock them up. We have in this culture a right/wrong, black/white, good/bad, true/false [mentality]. We don't have much tolerance for in-betweens.

The Christian Science Monitor,
3-7:12.

Hubert Williams
President, Police Foundation;
Former Director of Police
of Newark, N.J.

3

[On the effect on police departments around the country of the recent investigation into the Los Angeles Police Department which showed brutality and racism in the LAPD]: We'll see police leaders taking more responsibility for ensuring that their subordinate command officers are doing their jobs on enforcement of policy. We're going to see more scrutiny of police departments by government officials on whether or not their police department is racist and brutal. You're going to see more scrutiny of these incidents when they occur. You're going to see some effort made on the Federal level to create some kind of system where we know how much of this abuse is occurring. And when there are officers who are in violation, you'll see a greater willingness to take the officers to court and penalize them.

Interview/USA Today, 7-16:(A)13.

4

[Advocating a ban on private ownership of assault weapons]: These military weapons have no place in our cities. You still get people talking about their right to have an assault weapon for practice on the range or for hunting purposes . . . You might as well dynamite a river, drain it, take out all the fish, and say "I went fishing—look what I caught."

The Christian Science Monitor, 7-22:8.

Franklin Zimring
Director,
Earl Warren Legal Institute,
University of California, Berkeley

5

[On the high crime rate in the U.S.]: The conservative camp blames the evil that lurks in the hearts of men and wants to build more prisons. The liberal camp goes off in every other direction, essentially arguing that we can't cure social problems by locking people up. [Now] our crime rate is sufficiently large that we can bow generously to both camps.

Newsweek, 3-25:35.

Defense • The Military

Dwayne Aaron
Lieutenant Colonel,
United States Army;
Head of Civil Military Affairs
of XVIII Corps

1

[On the Army's dealings with civilians in wars such as the recent one in the Persian Gulf]: On the one hand, we will be viewed primarily as liberators, and on the other as invaders. This is an interesting part of the Army. To do it right you have to be part soldier and part humanitarian. You try to do as much as you can to reduce the suffering of the people who get caught in this mess.

USA Today, 3-6:(A)3.

James Abrahamson
Lieutenant General,
United States Air Force (Ret.);
Former Director,
Strategic Defense Initiative
(space defense system)

2

SDI was the right answer when the Soviets were a strong adversary, and a modified SDI is still important primarily when we're facing a larger and larger number of countries around the world that have some missile capability. We don't know when and where they will get a nuclear capability to go with the missile capability. But we have to deal with that.

Interview/USA Today, 1-9:(A)9.

Gordon Adams
Director,
Defense Budget Project

3

[On the strain on defense contractors caused by shrinking military budgets]: No one has proposed abolishing the armed forces, so we're going to have to keep a production base in place. If we're not careful how we manage the build-down, the risk is that we're going to lose the

research-and-development teams and our manufacturing capabilities. Then it's going to be difficult, and more expensive, and take longer to ever get it back.

The Washington Post, 1-5:(E)2.

Kenneth L. Adelman
Vice president, Institute
for Contemporary Studies;
Former Director,
Arms Control and
Disarmament Agency
of the United States

4

The problems of the '90s are the proliferation of nuclear weapons, the proliferation of ballistic missiles and the proliferation of very high-technology weaponry. First World weaponry in Third World hands is the worst of all combinations . . . The best thing for nuclear non-proliferation is the spread of freedom around the world. Free people do not choose to develop nuclear weapons. Free people have open societies where we can see, outsiders can see, the international inspectors can see, the UN family can see exactly what they're up to.

Interview/USA Today, 7-18:(A)11.

Sergei F. Akhromeyev
Military adviser
to Soviet President
Mikhail Gorbachev;
Former Chief,
Soviet Armed Forces General Staff

5

Everyone in the world is happy about [the end of the Cold War], including me. But U.S. policy is contradictory. I don't understand why under present conditions the Americans preserve a military organization like NATO and refuse to carry on reductions of naval forces—while the Soviet Union is reducing all other kinds of arms. Let's be frank. The initiative for preserving the North Atlantic Treaty Organization comes

(SERGEI F. AKHROMEYEV)

not from the European countries, but from the United States.

Interview/Newsweek, 1-21:40.

Les Aspin
United States Representative,
D-Wisconsin

1

Strength in defense is an issue that Democrats have had problems with in the past. We need a [Presidential] candidate who is looked on as strong in national security. People look at the candidates and they make a judgment: "Can I trust the national security of the country in their hands?" And if the answer is no, I think that kind of closes out the debate. I don't think they get a hearing on anything else.

April 17/USA Today, 4-18:(A)11.

2

[On the proposed strategic defense initiative]: The case for the theatre ballistic-missile defense of the kind the Patriot [anti-missile missile] was used for [against Iraqi Scud missiles in the recent Persian Gulf war] was strong before; political support is even stronger now. There is a greater agreement to take a look at some kind of defense against limited strikes [against the U.S.]. The Soviet threat was always a harder case to make for SDI, and I don't think it's been improved. But the case can be made for some kind of defense against three contingencies: 1) Third country attacks. 2) An accidental launch from the Soviet Union. 3) An unauthorized launch from the Soviet Union.

Interview/USA Today, 4-18:(A)11.

Robert H. Barrow
General (Ret.) and
former Commandant,
United States Marine Corps

3

[Opposing women in combat roles]: It's uncivilized and women can't do it. Women give life, sustain life, nurture life; they can't *take* it. If you want to make a combat unit ineffective, assign women to it.

Before Senate Armed Services
Committee, Washington, June 18/
Los Angeles Times, 6-19:(A)15.

Joseph R. Biden, Jr.
United States Senator,
D-Delaware

4

[On the Conventional Forces in Europe Treaty which has been submitted to the U.S. Senate for approval]: This treaty will eliminate a fundamental cause of tension in Europe since the end of World War II—that is, the huge numerical advantage of Soviet conventional forces. This superiority threatened the security and prosperity of the West for many years. This superiority also fueled the nuclear arms race. In every strategic doctrine adopted by NATO for 40 years, from massive retaliation to flexible response, nuclear weapons were intended to compensate for the Soviet edge in conventional arms.

Washington, July 11/
The New York Times, 7-12:(A)4.

5

Must we continue to accept a world in which the capability to detonate tens of thousands of Hiroshimas is deemed a necessary and normal fact of international life?

At arms-control hearing/
The New York Times, 7-30:(A)7.

Barbara Boxer
United States Representative
D-California

6

Under the NATO umbrella, we're [the U.S.] spending $190-million to defend Norway. Did you know Norway was in trouble? I didn't think so either. I think they're doing very well, thank you very much. But the fact is that's where the money is and we just need the guts to stand up and say it's a new time—bring it home now.

Before Democratic women,
Carson, Calif./
Los Angeles Times, 10-7:(A)3.

Bill Bradley
United States Senator,
D-New Jersey

1

I believe that at a minimum over the next five years we could cut the defense budget by $70- to $80- to $90-billion—or more than we have. And I believe that that money should be returned to American taxpayers first and primarily. And second, it could be used for a combination of deficit reduction and some pressing domestic needs. But primarily, it should be returned to taxpayers.

Interview,
Washington/
Los Angeles Times, 9-19:(M)3.

Alan Brinkley
Professor of history,
City University of New York

2

[On the victory by U.S.-led forces in the recent Persian Gulf war]: Our irrational fears that the military can't do the job may be replaced with the equally unrealistic belief that they're invincible and should be used for any and all problems. There's a healthy aspect to the end of this "Vietnam syndrome," and there's a dangerous one.

Los Angeles Times, 3-2:(A)14.

Harold Brown
Former Secretary of Defense
of the United States

3

[On the current war between U.S.-led coalition forces and Iraq, which invaded and took over Kuwait last year]: One effect of this crisis is that it will raise the appetite of all countries, developed and Third World, for high-technology weapons because they are seen to have worked in the hands of the coalition. Although few countries are going to be as aggressive as Iraq, those that think of themselves as threatened will want superior technology.

Los Angeles Times,
1-18:(A)11.

Richard Burt
Former chief U.S. negotiator,
strategic arms reduction talks
(START)

4

[I] believe that we will need to get on with a new agenda of arms control in the 1990s, an agenda some might call north-south arms control—that is, coping with the proliferation of ballistic missiles in the Third World, of chemical weapons, of nuclear [weapons]. This is an important arms-control agenda, and I think it will be easier for us to do that if we can in a sense finish the east-west . . . arms-control agenda for both conventional and nuclear arms.

Before Senate Foreign Relations
Committee, Washington, April 17/
The Washington Post, 4-19:(A)22.

George Bush
President of the United States

5

To those who question the [large] proportion of blacks in the armed services today, my answer is simple. The military of the United States is the greatest equal-opportunity employer around. Every soldier, sailor, airman, coast-guardsman and marine have enlisted because they want to be a part of the American armed services, because they know it is a place of openness and true meritocracy, and because they know that every serviceman and woman receives equal training and the finest training, and equal treatment every step of the way.

At ceremony marking black history
month, Washington, Feb. 25/
The New York Times, 2-26:(A)11.

6

[On the recent Persian Gulf-war victory by U.S.-led forces commanded by General H. Norman Schwarzkopf]: What he and his troops did . . . in terms of fulfilling our objectives is fantastic. What he and his troops did for the morale of the United States of America is unbelievable. We have a great team in [Defense Secretary Dick] Cheney and [Joint Chiefs Chairman General Colin] Powell and General Schwarzkopf,

(GEORGE BUSH)

and the country knows it. You can feel it. Any time you get out of this place, why, you sense it. It is fantastic.

Washington, April 23/
Los Angeles Times, 4-24:(A)12.

1

[On the signing of the U.S.-Soviet START treaty]: The treaty we sign today is the most complicated of contracts governing the most serious of concerns. Its 700 pages stand as a monument to several generations of U.S. and Soviet negotiators, to their tireless efforts to carve out common ground from a thicket of contentious issues, and it represents a major step forward for our mutual security and the cause of world peace . . . The START treaty vindicates an approach to arms control that guided us for almost a decade: the belief that we could do more than merely halt the growth of our nuclear arsenals. We could seek more than limits on the number of arms. In our talks we sought stabilizing reductions in our strategic arsenals. START makes that a reality. In an historic first for arms control, we will actually reduce U.S. and Soviet strategic nuclear arsenals. But reductions alone are not enough, so START requires even deeper cuts of the most dangerous and destabilizing weapons. The agreement itself is exceedingly complex but the central idea at the heart of this treaty can be put simply: Stabilizing reductions in our strategic nuclear forces reduce the risk of war.

At signing of START treaty
Moscow, July 31/
The Washington Post, 8-1:(A)25.

2

It's ironic that just a few, few days ago when [the failed coup in the Soviet Union aimed at ousting President Mikhail Gorbachev] was under way, there started a debate [in the U.S.] about are we spending enough on defense . . . Now [that the Soviet coup has failed], the debate comes: well, maybe we've got too much in defense. I'd say let's take a little time and sort this

thing out intelligently . . . Right now I simply cannot endorse that, and I notice so many people are jumping up and saying what we must do now is cut defense spending more. I think we've cut defense spending a lot and I want to be sure that our forces are properly structured to meet the needs that we were talking about just 12 months ago, standing in this very same place.

News conference,
Kennebunkport, Maine, Aug. 29/
The New York Times, 8-30:(A)10.

3

[On military spending in the wake of the end of the Cold War]: I wouldn't predict large cuts . . . I think we've got to guard against the sirens' call: "Now is the time to slash defense spending" . . . I'm not going to cut into this muscle of defense of this country in a kind of an instant sense of budgetary gratification . . . I'm not going to be stampeded into what I would think of as kind of mood of euphoria that misleads the American people about the national-security interests of this country.

News conference,
Kennebunkport, Maine, Sept. 2/
USA Today, 9-3:(A)11.

4

I am directing that the United States eliminate its entire world-wide inventory of ground-launched short-range, that is theatre, nuclear weapons. We will bring home and destroy all of our nuclear artillery shells and short-range ballistic-missile warheads. We will, of course, insure that we preserve an effective air-delivered nuclear capability in Europe. That is essential to NATO's security. In turn, I have asked the Soviets to go down this road with us—to destroy their entire inventory of ground-launched theatre nuclear weapons; not only their nuclear artillery, and nuclear warheads for short-range ballistic missiles, but also the theatre systems the U.S. no longer has—systems like nuclear warheads for air-defense missiles, and nuclear land mines. Recognizing further the major changes in the international military landscape, the United States will withdraw all tactical nuclear weapons

(GEORGE BUSH)

from its surface ships, attack submarines, as well as those nuclear weapons associated with our land-based naval aircraft. This means removing all nuclear Tomahawk cruise missiles from U.S. ships and submarines, as well as nuclear bombs aboard aircraft carriers. The bottom line is that under normal circumstances, our ships will not carry tactical nuclear weapons . . . As we implement these initiatives, we will closely watch how the new Soviet leadership responds. We expect our bold initiatives to be met with equally bold steps on the Soviet side. If this happens, further cooperation is inevitable. If it does not, then an historic opportunity will have been lost. Regardless, let no one doubt we will still retain the necessary strength to protect our security and that of our allies, and to respond as necessary.

Broadcast address to the nation,
Washington, Sept. 27/
The New York Times, 9-28:4.

Bill Busse
Director of Soviet relations,
Beyond War Institute

1

The time is right to restrict arms sales. Everyone always says, "If we don't sell them, someone else will." But the 34 nations that make up the Helsinki Accords sell 89 per cent of the world's weapons. These nations could certainly come down hard on total arms sales. It's time for this nation to be a moral influence, rather than playing power politics.

USA Today, 2-28:(A)4.

Dick Cheney
Secretary of Defense
of the United States

2

[The] assumption of U.S. military policy now for forty-some years has been the need to prepare for a global conflict with the Soviet Union that would begin with a Soviet-Warsaw Pact attack into Western Europe. We believe that that threat has very significantly diminished, that it's no longer necessary for us to size our forces based

on that . . . We believe that we can, in the future, reconstitute forces to deal with that kind of threat, should that become necessary, and that the long pole in the tent, if you will, the driving factor in the equation for the future with respect to U.S. military strategy, ought to be the need to deal with what we describe as regional contingencies—specifically, the kind of situation we're faced with in the Persian Gulf today.

Before American Enterprise
Institute Forum, Feb. 21/
The Washington Post, 2-22:(A)22.

3

[On the performance of U.S. forces in the Persian Gulf war]: There's no question that Operation Desert Shield and Desert Storm has transformed the public thinking about the United States military. I think the country's been tremendously impressed with the capability . . . of the people . . . When you have, day after day . . . and hour after hour, repetition of the television coverage of our people out there in the Gulf, it's just one tremendous piece of advertising for the United States military and the people who serve in it.

Interview, Washington, Feb. 22/
The Washington Post, 2-27:(A)25.

4

The military itself, as an institution in the United States, stands higher today than it has at any time since World War II. A lot of the criticism that was part and parcel of the '70s and '80s—stupid Generals, equipment that doesn't work, idiots running the Pentagon who don't know what they're doing—clearly wasn't valid.

Interview, Washington/
The Washington Post, 4-3:(C)2.

5

[On his proposal for closing 31 major U.S. military bases]: Smaller forces need fewer bases. It's as simple as that . . . The fact is that a shrinking budget clearly requires us to make some hard choices and to establish priorities. We have to concentrate on unglamorous things in the future,

(DICK CHENEY)

like operations and maintenance, if we're going to maintain a combat-ready force ... My first obligation as Secretary is to provide for the nation's defense. And the judgments and decisions the departments, the services, have made were driven first and foremost by military value, not by economic considerations [of the surrounding communities], although economic factors were taken into account.

News conference,
Washington, April 12/
Los Angeles Times, 4-13:(A)1;
The New York Times, 4-13:1,8.

1

[Saying his plans for cuts in military spending will meet resistance from many in Congress]: We want the absolute best possible force we can have, regardless of what size it is. Everybody will pay lip service to this philosophy. But it comes down to the vote. There is a big constituency out there to keep all the production lines open, keep all the bases open, keep all the units activated; don't mothball the [batttleships] *Missouri* and *Wisconsin*; don't close my fort.

Interview/
U.S. News & World Report,
4-15:42.

2

My biggest concern is that, as we go through these next few years, [Congress] will do what we have always done before when we've downsized the [military] force, and that is get it wrong. We'll end up protecting force structure that we can't support. We'll end up keeping open production lines instead of investing in new technology. We'll end up keeping bases open because that involves jobs back home in the district and we won't have the gumption and the courage to make the right cuts. That's my Number 1 concern these days.

Interview/USA Today, 6-27:(A)11.

3

We've got the most massive reduction in U.S. military force, the most fundamental change in our strategy since the beginning of the Cold War back in the 1940s. [But] I think that the prospects for peaceful evolution in the Soviet Union are still questionable. While they've had enormous positive elements politically in the last few weeks, they still are in deep, deep trouble in terms of their nationality problems, in terms of their economy. So I think a little caution is in order before we automatically assume, based on one week's news, that we can now dismantle our own defenses.

Broadcast interview/
"Today" show, NBC-TV, 9-9.

4

[Criticizing those who are calling for deeper cuts in U.S. defense spending in light of the ending of the Cold War]: Let me get something off my chest. One of the sources of frustration is having a lot of people operate on the assumption that we have not yet done anything to change our defense posture. [Many of those people speak as though] it's still 1985 ... and we're at our absolute peak in terms of military spending, "and you guys in the Pentagon haven't done anything to respond to the new world." And that's just garbage.

Interview, Washington, Sept. 10/
The Washington Post, 9-11:(A)4.

5

One factor in the [recent Persian] Gulf war was our superior technology, and it was phenomenal, no question about it . . . I remember . . . critics who said that we were wasting the taxpayers' money on weapons that were too complex, that would not work. And we were told last fall that our weapons would not work in the desert environment, systems like the M1A1 Abrams tank, the Tomahawk cruise missile, the F-117 Stealth fighter . . . If we'd listened to the critics, we never would have had those systems when we needed them.

At conference sponsored by
Committee for Economic Development
and the U.S. Army, Oct. 8/
The Washington Post,
8-10:(A)22.

Jim Courter
Chairman,
Defense Base Closure and
Realignment Commission
of the United States

1

[On his Commission's job to close military bases deemed unnecessary]: This is as much a conservative issue as it is a liberal issue. This thing cuts across party lines. It cuts across ideology. As a conservative, I don't want to spend money on bases we don't need. I want to spend that Department of Defense money on training people, on having modern equipment, on having enough exercises, making sure our men and women have that quality of life that makes them want to re-enlist.

Interview, Washington/
The New York Times, 6-4:(A)7.

2

[On his Commission's recommendations regarding which military bases in the U.S. should be closed]: The process, I think, is about as fair as you can possibly make it. The decisions were based on the merits. It wasn't based on Republican, Democrat, region. It wasn't based on some important chairman of an appropriations committee saying: "Don't close this, close that one over there." Our arguments were made in public and on the record. They may not be accepted by some people. They are accepted by the majority, and the majority rules.

July 1/
Los Angeles Times, 7-2:(A)18.

John C. Danforth
United States Senator,
R-Missouri

3

[Saying the Federal budget agreement should be broken so that funds earmarked for defense can be shifted to other areas in light of a diminished Soviet threat]: The budget agreement reached last year with such agony is obsolete. Clearly, the likelihood of our going to war with the Soviet Union today is zero and will be for as far as we can see.

Aug. 28/
Los Angeles Times, 8-29:(A)10.

Steven David
Director of international studies
Johns Hopkins University,
Homewood campus

4

There should be a list of countries not permitted to have nuclear weapons. If need be, hopefully in a coalition, [any renegade] facility would be bombed. I'd put Iraq, Syria, Libya and some radical Palestinian groups on the list. Israel [reportedly] has nuclear weapons, but they don't constitute a threat to American interests. You may call that hypocritical. But you have to discriminate. If Norway developed nuclear weapons, I wouldn't like it, but I wouldn't wake up at night screaming.

USA Today, 3-1:(A)6.

Alan J. Dixon
United States Senator,
D-Illinois

5

[Anticipating a new round of military-base closings in the U.S.]: Bases are going to be closed, depend on that. And in the end, someone is going to be unhappy, depend on that. And I might be one of them. Closing of bases is a crazy process.

April 10/
The New York Times, 4-11:(A)11.

Robert J. Dole
United States Senator,
R-Kansas

6

[On calls in the U.S. for cuts in defense spending in light of changes in the Soviet Union which have ended the Cold War]: We'll see no shortage of efforts to slash defense spending to pay for a laundry list of big domestic spending programs. But if the incredible turn of events in the Soviet Union taught us anything, it's that the only certainty is uncertainty. And, if you ask me, uncertainty in the nuclear world and unilateral disarmament just don't mix.

Washington, Sept. 10/
The Washington Post, 9-11:(A)4.

59

Mark Eitelberg
Professor, U.S. Naval
Postgraduate School

1

[On charges that the volunteer armed forces have a disproportionately large number of blacks]: I don't think it's anything to worry about in peacetime, but when people start dying [in war], the burden of service outweighs the benefits... When the war finally arrives, we have to think about distributing the burdens more carefully throughout all segments of society.

USA Today, 1-9:(A)5.

Andrew A. Feinstein
Specialist on military bases,
staff of the House Subcommittee
on Military
Installations and Facilities

2

[On the proposed closing of 31 military bases in the U.S. and the effects it will have on the surrounding communities]: The history of base-closings has been that many communities often prosper in the long run, although jobs and income are lost at first. Many bases have excellent buildings and roads and other infrastructure that can be turned around for community use. When the government surrenders the bases, the cost to the buyer is usually minimal, or maybe even nil if the buyer is a local government... No matter who gets the property in the end, the Federal government hardly ever recovers its original investment in land and buildings.

The New York Times, 4-13:8.

Marlin Fitzwater
Press Secretary to President
of the United States
George Bush

3

We never said that there would be no arms sales [to foreign countries in the future], only that we wanted to diminish [them]. Defense exports have become more important to our own defense industrial base as U.S. defense procurement declines. The survival of a number of important programs are already tied to foreign sales, in-cluding the M1-A2 Abrams main battle tank, the UH-60 Blackhawk helicopters, Hawk missiles and... aerial refueling tankers.

Los Angeles Times, 3-19:(A)1.

Raymond Garthoff
Former United States
arms-control negotiator

4

Arms control as a whole will continue to be important, but it won't be as important as it used to be—if only because a lot of other things have become more important. It is quite possible that START will end up being the last major strategic-arms agreement of this kind. There may be smaller efforts in one area or another, but the enthusiasm for big, comprehensive treaties like START has waned. There's a feeling that smaller, more limited efforts could mean more progress sooner.

Los Angeles Times, 7-30:(H)4.

Valery Giscard (d'Estaing)
Former President of France

5

I am for an army of volunteers and professionals [rather than compulsory universal military service] for two reasons: One is the end of the Cold War, and the second is the [recent Persian] Gulf war, which has shown that only the scientific arms used by men very well prepared are efficient.

Los Angeles Times, 8-13:(H)1.

Mikhail S. Gorbachev
President of the Soviet Union;
General Secretary,
Communist Party
of the Soviet Union

6

[On the signing of the U.S.-Soviet START treaty]: In both countries we face the complex process of the ratification of the new treaty. There will be critics. Here in Moscow, some will point to our unilateral concessions, while in Washington there will be talk about concessions made to the Soviet Union. Some will say the new

(MIKHAIL S. GORBACHEV)

treaty does not really fulfill the promise of a [monetary] peace dividend since considerable resources will be required to destroy the missiles. And if the missiles are not destroyed, critics will say they're obsolete and must be replaced with new ones. And that will be even more expensive. Sharp criticism is to be expected, also, from those who want to see faster and more ambitious steps toward abolishing nuclear weapons. In other words, the treaty will have to be defended. I'm sure we have achieved the best that is now possible and that is required to continue progress.

At signing of START treaty,
Moscow, July 31/
The Washington Post, 8-1:(A)25.

Mikhail S. Gorbachev
President of the Soviet Union

1

Demilitarization is directly related to human rights. [Amassing arms] not only drains the economy and ecology, it drains the human condition physically and spiritually.

At Conference on Security and
Cooperation in Europe,
Moscow, Sept. 10/
Los Angeles Times, 9-11:(A)6.

Alfred M. Gray, Jr.
General and Commandant,
United States Marine Corps

2

[Opposing women in combat roles]: We believe our women understand that you need women and you need men, and they're different.

Before Senate Armed Services
Committee, Washington, June 18/
Los Angeles Times, 6-19:(A)1.

Richard Grimmett
Authority on Third World
military affairs,
Congressional Research Service

3

[On the advanced U.S. arms used against Iraq in the recent Persian Gulf war]: Look at what our Apache helicopters did to their tanks with Hellfire missiles. It's the old argument that the Israelis have always used: a qualitative advantage compensates for a quantitative disadvantage.

The New York Times, 3-26:(A)6.

Gary Hart
Former United States Senator,
D-Colorado

4

At no time during my more than decade-long involvement with the military-reform movement has it ever been argued that technology per se, especially high technology, was an evil. [Rather, we reformers insisted] that technological sophistication was not an end in itself, and that the cost of super technology should not be permitted to drive down the over-all numbers of weapons available.

Before House Armed Services
Committee, Washington, April 30/
The Washington Post, 5-1:(A)17.

Siegfried S. Hecker
Director, Los Alamos
National Laboratory

5

The build-down of the nation's [nuclear] warhead stockpile means that the warheads we retain must be all the more reliable and effective, if we are to maintain a credible nuclear deterrence.

The New York Times, 8-3:8.

Duncan L. Hunter
United States Representative,
R-California

6

[On the Patriot missiles, which are being used successfully by the U.S. to shoot down Iraqi missiles in the current Persian Gulf war]: Patriots are demonstrating that you can stop missiles with missiles. We now live in an age of missiles, and we're going to have to be able to stop missiles with missiles. It's going to take an increasingly more sophisticated missile defense.

Los Angeles Times, 1-28:(A)5.

61

Bruce Jacobs
Major General,
United States Army (Ret.)

1

It is hard to convince me that [in a war] you own a piece of property until you can stand on it. You might fly over it, spit on it, napalm it or make it an uninhabitable moonscape, but there are people who would dispute whether you own it. To control the town, you have to be able to sit in city hall.

Los Angeles, 1-29:(H)1.

Christopher Jehn
Assistant Secretary for Force
Management and Personnel,
Department of Defense
of the United States

2

[On U.S. forces in the current Persian Gulf war]: I, for one, am convinced [that the success of the U.S. operation] is a direct product of . . . the fact that you have high quality [of personnel] coming into the [all-volunteer] service. They stay longer, they're more experienced and, above all, are more dedicated and motivated than conscripts.

Interview/
The Washington Post, 2-27:(A)22.

Jeane J. Kirkpatrick
Former United States Ambassador/
Permanent Representative
to the United Nations

3

[The current war in the Persian Gulf] shows the conservative vision of a strong America was correct: It's important to be strong, it's important to be prepared, and it's important to be able to defend ourselves from incoming missiles [as the U.S. Patriot anti-missile missiles are showing in the Gulf war].

At Conservative Political Action
Conference, Washington,
February/
The New York Times, 2-9:8.

John F. Lehman, Jr.
Former Secretary of the Navy
of the United States

4

[On the U.S. bringing in high-tech weapons in its buildup of forces in the Persian Gulf area aimed at getting Iraq out of Kuwait]: The desert is the perfect environment out there [for high-tech weapons]: You don't have the moisture degradation that affects electronics in Europe. Precision weapons using TV cameras can find their targets because of the visual contrast between a tank and the sand . . . Every weapon that's in the inventory—everything we've got that's good—is there. The Iraqis have no idea what they're getting into.

The Washington Post, 1-11:(F)3.

Hans Mark
Chancellor,
University of Texas;
Former Secretary
of the Air Force
of the United States

5

[Criticizing the idea that, because the Cold War is over, the U.S. can pay less attention to its military capability]: Peace isn't breaking out. We just fought a war [in the Persian Gulf]. If anything, the ability to retaliate quickly and accurately anywhere in the world is more important now than in the past as weapons of mass destruction proliferate . . . You can't let down your guard.

The New York Times, 8-20:(B)5.

George J. Mitchell
United States Senator,
D-Maine

6

It is and ultimately will be clear to all Americans that the basis of military strength in our society, as in all societies in history, is economic strength.

Interview/
The Washington Post, 2-4:(A)4.

John Myers
Colonel, United States Army;
Director of Advertising and
Public Affairs,
Army Recruiting Command

1

It's [been] a very historic period [for military recruitment]. You had the Army downsizing in the wake of probably the most important event of this half century—the fall of the Berlin Wall and everything that came along with it—then a major war [in the Persian Gulf], then the need to get the forces back and where they need to go while you continue downsizing.

The New York Times, 3-16:6.

Albert Narath
President,
Sandia National Laboratories

2

[On proposed cuts in U.S. nuclear-weapons programs]: We all know that we'll have to take our knocks, but if the cuts are so deep that we lose our pools of experts, the nation will lose nuclear competence—an indispensable asset in a world where nuclear proliferation has yet to be halted.

The New York Times, 8-3:8.

Delton Nichols
Major, United States Army;
Chaplain,
U.S. Army Armor School

3

It is difficult for one person to kill another if that person is looked at as being just like you or me, having a family back home. We encourage our soldiers to view the enemy in a very humane sense, somewhat like in the book *The Warriors,* where the first vision of the enemy should be as a human obstacle between the soldier and that soldier's objective, and not to consider the enemy as less than human. That's the high professional calling for the soldier. It will take a mature soldier and positive leadership for that image to be embraced, however.

Interview/
USA Today, 2-25:(A)11.

Paul Nisbet
Aerospace analyst,
Prudential Bache Securities

4

[On the competition among aerospace companies to land the Defense Department's $75-billion contract for a new fighter jet]: It is pure politics. Any time you have $75-billion at stake, you better believe that the Congress is not going to sit idly by and watch the program get awarded on the basis of merit. They get paid to bring home the bacon.

Los Angeles Times, 4-20:(A)26.

William Odom
Lieutenant General,
United States Army (Ret.);
Former Director,
National Security Council

5

[On the professionalism of the volunteer armed forces used by the U.S. in the recent Persian Gulf war]: What the Gulf war shows [the Soviets] is that the training competency required for soldiers and field-grade officers is not easy to obtain [with conscripts]—and when you have it, it's awesome. You are not going to deal with [an army of this caliber with] two-year draftees.

The Christian Science Monitor,
3-6:7.

Major R. Owens
United States Representative,
D-New York

6

When people can't get jobs, they find the Army and the Navy and the other military units as an opportunity to be utilized. There are many very bright young people who never looked for a job but who are recruited from high school and told that you can go to college after you go through the military and get those advantages. And there are many . . . [who] are African American men and women who went to military academies or they used the benefits of the ROTC as the only way they could make it. For this reason you have this disproportionate number [of blacks in uniform]. These are the same people who are penalized

(MAJOR R. OWENS)

when President Bush refuses to pass a civil-rights bill because he claims it has a quota. There is some kind of ugly reverse quota operating when 33 per cent of the troops on the front line [in the Persian Gulf] are poor and African American.

Before the House,
Washington, Jan. 11/
The New York Times, 1-12:6.

Colin L. Powell
General, United States Army;
Chairman, Joint Chiefs of Staff

1

[On the opportunities for minorities in the military]: I wish that there were other activities in our society and in our nation that were as open as the military is to upward mobility, to achievement, to allowing them in. I wish that corporate America, I wish that trade unions around the nation would show the same level of openness and opportunity to minorities that the military has.

Before House Armed Services
Committee, Washington, Feb. 7/
Los Angeles Times, 2-8:(A)19.

Dan Quayle
Vice President
of the United States

2

[On the prospects for proceeding with development of SDI in the wake of the positive performance of Patriot anti-missile missiles in the current Persian Gulf war]: [The war] not only vindicates the Strategic Defense Initiative but it makes SDI much more of a reality. People are amazed at the capability of the Patriot. But they will be amazed at the capability of SDI when it's deployed. The basic question is: Can a bullet hit a bullet? Well, we have certainly proved that with the Patriot. Every test that we have had in SDI has been successful. The fact of the matter is that you *can* have a bullet hit a bullet. As we get into more sophisticated ballistic missiles and Scuds, as other countries acquire ballistic-missile capability and chemical or nuclear capability, it is going to make eminent sense, to protect Ameri-

can lives, to be able to knock those missiles down over the country which launches them.

Interview, February/
U.S. News & World Report,
2-18:27.

Dana T. Rohrabacher
United States Representative,
R-California

3

Why did we win in the [recent] Persian Gulf [war against Iraq] with so few [U.S.] casualties? Yes, we would have won if we fought it out on an equal basis with [Iraqi President] Saddam Hussein, but would we have wanted to have had hundreds of thousands of casualties? The reason our boys and our young men and women were able to come home with very low casualties is that we invested in technology in the 1980s. It was that investment that saved the lives in the 1990s . . . I happen to believe . . . that if freedom has a chance anywhere in the world and if the world is going to have any stability, it will depend on a strong United States of America and a United States of America that is equipped with what it needs to get the job done.

Before the House,
Washington, May 20/
The Washington Post, 5-23:(A)22.

Alan Sabrosky
Senior fellow,
Center for Strategic
and International Studies

4

The decision to activate the National Guard early in the [current Persian Gulf] crisis reflects the [Bush] Administration's appreciation of the strategic and political consequences of not doing so during the Vietnam war . . . By reverting to pre-Vietnam tradition, the Administration is placing both the country and the Congress on notice that the American people should be prepared for major sacrifices in a major war.

The Christian Science Monitor,
1-25:3.

Carl Sagan

Professor of astronomy and
space science and director of
the Laboratory for Planetary Studies,
Cornell University

1

[Criticizing the proposed SDI space defense system]: It's just supposed to shoot out of the sky missiles that are coming in. It does nothing about airplanes or boats; it does nothing about nuclear weapons in suitcases or in the basements of embassies. And for any issue of the strategic confrontation between the superpowers, "star wars" [SDI] is worse than worthless because it gives a false sense of security.

Interview/USA Today, 1-9:(A)9.

Roald Sagdeyev

Director emeritus,
Space Research Institute
(Soviet Union);
Professor of physics,
University of Maryland

2

We have let ourselves be hypnotized into forgetting about this nuclear arsenal. I think START is necessary and I support it and it should be ratified as soon as possible, but it is so modest. It is only bringing us back to the early '80s when we already had enormous overkill. I think what happens in the Soviet Union [the recent failed coup] indicates that nuclear superpower could be hijacked just like any kind of airplane. We need to move boldly further beyond the START treaty. Keep people conscious about the nuclear arms and their danger.

Interview/
Los Angeles Times, 8-25:(M)3.

H. Norman Schwarzkopf

General, United States Army;
Commander, Operation
Desert Storm (U.S.-led forces
in the Persian Gulf war)

3

I really think of myself as a soldier who tries to do his duty with honor, serving his country. Contrary to what has been said about me, I have never had any illusions of grandeur, of leading huge armies into battle, and I will confess that sometimes the awesome responsibility that is placed on my shoulders flat scares me to death. But I do recognize that is what I have been trained for, and that's what the United States has a professional military for. And certainly a crisis is not the time for me to be weak of heart or timid about my responsibilities. All I can do is my best, and when this [war] is all over if I can still say to myself that I did my very best, then that is what is really important to me.

Interview, Saudi Arabia/
U.S. News & World Report,
2-11:37.

4

I think that there is one really fundamental military truth. And that's that you can add up the correlation of forces, you can look at the number of tanks, you can look at the number of airplanes, you can look at all these factors of military might and put them together. But unless the soldier on the ground, or the airman in the air, has the will to win, has the strength of character to go into battle, believes that his cause is just, and has the support of his country . . . all the rest of that stuff is irrelevant.

Broadcast interview/
"Talking With David Frost," PBS-TV, 3-27.

H. Norman Schwarzkopf

General, United States Army;
Former Commander,
Operation Desert Storm
(U.S.-led forces in the recent
Persian Gulf war)

5

[Addressing West Point cadets]: Out there among you are the cynics, the people who scoff at what you're learning here. The people that scoff at character, the people that scoff at hard work. But they don't know what they're talking about, let me tell you. I can assure you that when the going gets tough and your country needs them, they're not going to be there. They will not be there, but you will . . . After Vietnam, we had a whole cottage industry develop, basically in

(H. NORMAN SCHWARZKOPF)

Washington, D.C., that consisted of a bunch of military fairies that had never been shot at in anger who felt fully qualified to comment on the leadership ability of all the leaders of the United States Army. They were not Monday-morning quarterbacks, they were the worst of all possible kind; they were Friday-afternoon quarterbacks. They felt qualified to criticize us before the game was even played. And they are the same people who are saying, my goodness, we have a terrible problem in the armed forces because there are no more leaders out there, there are no more combat leaders. Where are the Pattons? Where are the Eisenhowers? Where are the Bradleys? Where are the MacArthurs? Where are the Audie Murphys? . . . Coming from a guy who's never been shot at in his entire life, that's a pretty bold statement.

At U.S. Military Academy,
West Point, N.Y., May 15/
The Washington Post, 5-17:(A)23.

Lawrence Skibbie
President, American Defense
Preparedness Association

1

Arms control is very hard to do. President [Jimmy] Carter felt it was inappropriate to sell arms overseas and put on tight restrictions. We found that constrained U.S. industry and allowed other countries to sell more of their arms. Those countries gained influence. That's detrimental to our interests and probably peace over-all. Even with global restrictions, some countries will get around them.

USA Today, 2-28:(A)4.

Richard Thomas
Director, Center for
Strategic Technology,
Texas A&M University

2

The strategic threat to the United States is increasing. [Despite recent changes in the Soviet Union,] the Soviets continue to deploy four SS-24s and -25s [missiles] aimed at you and me

every month. The Soviets recognize that their existence as a superpower—a status that they very much desire—rests on their ability to threaten the United States. And so the Soviet threat is not going to go away.

The Christian Science Monitor,
8-29:6.

Caspar W. Weinberger
Former Secretary of Defense
of the United States

3

[On whether the Vietnam-war experience is still haunting the U.S. military]: It isn't haunting them; it's a learned lesson. It's a lesson that may very well be governing a lot of the conduct of the leadership and the Administration. And I hope it is. It's not a lesson which paralyzes you or says you could never act. It's a lesson which says that that was the wrong way to do it and that a terrible set of losses were incurred for a cause that was not considered important enough to win. And we must never do that again.

Interview/USA Today, 2-4:(A)9.

4

It's important for us to realize we have the military strength to ensure the kind of foreign policy we want. But we have to keep that military strength. There are many people who keep talking about how the threat is over. The [recent war in the Persian] Gulf was a very good example of how quickly you have to use it. You can't acquire military strength quickly if you dismantle it.

Interview/USA Today, 8-20:(A)9.

Manfred Woerner
Secretary General, North Atlantic
Treaty Organization

5

We can't dis-invent nuclear weapons. We believe that nuclear weapons are an essential instrument to prevent any kind of war simply by keeping the risks high enough. I do not see a situation in which we would de-nuclearize Europe.

Taormina, Sicily, Oct. 18/
Los Angeles Times, 10-19:(A)12.

The Economy • Labor

Lloyd Bentsen
United States Senator,
D-Texas

1

Trade has assumed a new importance in our economic future. Here we are, in the middle of a recession. More than any time in the past, America will have to export its way back to prosperity.

Los Angeles Times, 5-15:(A)4.

Howard L. Berman
United States Representative,
D-California

2

So long as poor Mexican parents see little hope of supporting their families in Mexico . . . no laws, no fences or ditches are going to protect U.S. jobs from undocumented workers.

Los Angeles Times, 5-24:(A)16.

Joseph Blasi
Professor, Rutgers University

3

[On the strike against the *New York Daily News*]: I think this is one in a long series of very difficult confrontations that we're going to continue to see in unionized companies until the issue of permanent replacement workers is resolved. Labor-management law was originally set up to encourage both sides to come to a settlement. Using permanent replacement workers basically says that it's okay for one side [management] to eliminate the need for the other side [striking workers].

Los Angeles Times, 3-13:(D)2.

David E. Bonier
United States Representative,
D-Michigan

4

[Calling for an amended Federal budget reflecting the changes in the Soviet Union which

make that country less of a threat to the U.S.]: I don't know how you can keep that [budget] agreement together in light of the realities of the world situation and, even more importantly, the situation at home. There's been a prolonged recession [in the U.S.], and a lot of people are hurting, crying for help. We've got to meet their needs. As far as I'm concerned, Americans come first. I'm not for spending a penny for the Soviet Union beyond helping them avoid starvation in winter.

Los Angeles Times, 9-7:(A)2.

Michael J. Boskin
Chairman, Council of
Economic Advisers
to President
of the United States
George Bush

5

[On the current recession]: While no recession is ever a good thing . . . the decline in GNP . . . has been less than half of the average for post-World War II recessions. The unemployment rate, while far too high . . . is still below the rate in any . . . month in the first years of the economic expansion of the 1980s . . . A good way to think about . . . a large, diverse, complex economy like the United States . . . [is to make] a formal list of all the industries, regions and sectors of the economy. And you could put some in a positive column and some in a negative column . . . Even when the economy is booming— like in 1987 and 1988—there are still a few entries in the negative column. And . . . in a deep recession, there are still a few entries in the positive column . . . It's not like being at a traffic light—when you're in a recession, on red, with every part of the economy stopped; and . . . when a recovery begins, the light turns to green, and every industry, region and sector steps on the gas and is doing well and growing again.

At Export-Import Bank conference,
May 16/
The Washington Post, 5-17:(A)24.

67

(MICHAEL J. BOSKIN)

1

[Without an improved education system,] our labor force will not remain the world's leader. We can't be the world's leading economy without the world's leading labor force.

The Christian Science Monitor,
6-25:2.

Barry Bosworth
Economist,
Brookings Institution

2

America is not good at dealing with a shrinking pie. Our whole system is based on the idea of endless economic growth. But that ain't gonna happen in the 1990s.

Los Angeles Times, 11-25:(A)14.

3

[Arguing against a tax cut for the middle class]: It's the wrong message to send to American voters when they have a Federal deficit of over $300-billion . . . We have too much consumption, not too little. Temporary tax cuts—and we have four recent examples to look at—have shown that they reduce household debt; they don't stimulate financing. A very large percentage of the money is saved, and there's a very small impact on spending.

The Christian Science Monitor,
12-30:9.

Bill Bradley
United States Senator,
D-New Jersey

4

By the year 2000, only 57 per cent of people entering the work-force will be native-born whites. White Americans have to understand that their children's standard of living is inextricably bound to the future of millions of non-white children who will pour into the work-force in the next decades. To guide them toward achievement will make America a richer, more successful society. To allow them to self-destruct because of penny-pinching or timidity about

straight talk will make America a second-rate power.

Before the Senate,
Washington, July 10/
The Washington Post, 7-12:(A)18.

Nicholas F. Brady
Secretary of the Treasury
of the United States

5

[Criticizing proposed legislation that would put a cap on interest rates charged by credit-card companies]: Let me tell you what's wrong with it. It was tried in 1980 by [then-President] Jimmy Carter. They put credit controls in in February of 1980. It was so bad for the economy—it caused the recession in 1980—that by May of that year, they took it off the books. That's what's wrong with it. It doesn't work . . . If you lower the interest rates on [credit cards] . . . you wipe out the profit for the banks [that issue the cards]. The whole system will change. There will only be credit cards for the very, very rich. This is elitist legislation.

Broadcast interview/
"Meet the Press," NBC-TV, 11-17.

Fred Breimyer
President,
Northeast Economic Project

6

The consensus view is that the [U.S. economic] recovery began in the late spring or early summer. But it has been modest by historical standards . . . If the test of recovery is [people] feeling better, then this is not a recovery. We have an end of decline, but not the beginning of rapid growth.

Los Angeles Times, 9-23:(D)1.

William E. Brock
Chairman,
Federal Commission on
Achieving Necessary Skills;
Former Secretary of Labor
of the United States

7

Unless we're willing to settle for declining living standards and the end of the American

(WILLIAM E. BROCK)

dream, we have to make some very fundamental changes in our classrooms and our workplaces. For one, we have to start acting like we really believe people are America's most important competitive resource.

July 2/
Los Angeles Times, 7-3:(D)5.

Ron Brown
Chairman,
Democratic National Committee

1

We've been in a deep recession for a long time. The President [Bush] hasn't been engaged in these issues of the economy or domestic issues. He's been enthralled by, engaged in, entranced by, excited by foreign-policy matters. But, clearly, he has been bored with the kinds of problems facing average, middle-income, working men and women and working families . . . The President's policy has been to do nothing in the hope that [the economy] will turn around. It was kind of "don't-worry-be-happy" talk. It was a blame game. First, you blame the Congress, then you blame banks for not lending, then you blame consumers for not spending, then you blame the Fed, then you blame credit-card companies. It's their fault we're in a recession. [But] the blame game is over. It's time for some action.

Interview/
USA Today, 12-18:(A)13.

2

There's been a tremendous redistribution of wealth over the last 10 or 12 years. That's got to be reversed. While [former President] Ronald Reagan and [President] George Bush were telling Americans: "Your taxes aren't going up," the taxes of 9 out of 10 families went up during the 1980s and most heavily on middle-income people. The people at the top end who can afford it most have to pay their fair share of taxes. They're not paying their fair share now.

Interview/
USA Today, 12-18:(A)13.

George Bush
President of the United States

3

If I can borrow a term from Wall Street, I am bullish on the economy—not overly optimistic, not Pollyannic about it, but while some sectors are still sluggish, on the whole a turnaround in the economy appears to be in the making . . . I think there's a reason to be optimistic. This recession has lasted perhaps longer than we would have thought. It hasn't been as deep as many had predicted. But let's see where we go. I think things are looking much more promising as I speak to you here.

To American Advertising Federation,
Nashville, Tenn.,
via closed-circuit TV, June 11/
Los Angeles Times, 6-12:(D)5.

4

A free economy is nothing more than a system of communication. It simply cannot function without individual rights or a profit motive, which give people an incentive to go to work, an incentive to produce. And it certainly cannot function without the rule of law, without fair and enforceable contracts, without laws that protect property rights and punish fraud. Free economies depend upon the freedom of expression, the ability of people to exchange ideas and test out new theories.

Before Ukrainian Parliament,
Kiev, U.S.S.R., Aug. 1/
The New York Times, 8-2:(A)5.

5

A free economy demands engagement in the economic mainstream. Isolation and protectionism doom its practitioners to degradation and want.

Before Ukrainian Parliament,
Kiev, U.S.S.R., Aug. 1/
The Washington Post, 8-2:(A)21.

6

[On his refusal to implement an extension of unemployment benefits passed by Congress]: I

69

(GEORGE BUSH)

won't bust the budget, bust the caps on the budget that were agreed to by Democrats and Republicans alike . . . It looks like the national economy is recovering. It's pretty hard to say to someone that's out of work, hey, things are getting better . . . [But] one way to guarantee a less bright future is to have the Federal government keep doing what often in the past is done—recklessly spend money.

News conference,
Kennebunkport, Maine, Aug. 16/
The Washington Post, 8-17:(A)1,8.

1

. . . the world has learned that free markets provide levels of prosperity, growth and happiness that centrally planned economies can never offer. Even the most charitable estimates indicate that, in recent years, the free world's economies have grown at twice the rate of the former Communist world. Growth does more than fill shelves. It permits every person to gain, not at the expense of others, but to the benefit of others. Prosperity encourages people to live as neighbors, not as predators. Economic growth can aid international relations in exactly the same way.

At United Nations,
New York, Sept. 23/
The New York Times, 9-24:(A)6.

2

While Americans demand action [on economic recovery], it remains business as usual up on Capitol Hill. And business as usual can only hurt people who want to work or want to move on into better jobs . . . There are a number of steps we can take to get our economy booming again, and steps that, in my judgment, Congress should have taken long ago when I proposed them. These include—and I know I sound like a broken record to some—capital-gains tax cuts, research-and-development tax credits, expanded IRAs, comprehensive banking reform legislation, international trade liberalization and a job-intensive, sound transportation bill. And this is just part of

the litany . . . I'm concerned about the people that are hurting, and, although we technically have pulled out of recession on a national basis and although we enjoyed a very modest economic growth in the third quarter, in recent months many people still feel the pinch of an economy that isn't growing as it should. No honest observer can tell you that things are great. They're not. And when people are hurting, I worry about it.

Speech delivered by satellite
to Southern Newspaper Publishers
Association, Nov. 19/
Los Angeles Times, 11-20:(A)14.

Ronald Carey
President-elect,
International Brotherhood
of Teamsters

3

[On his victory in the just-held Teamsters election]: It's goodbye to the mafia. This union will now work in the interests of its members. It's the members that will come first.

News conference,
Washington, Dec. 12/
The New York Times, 12-13:(A)16.

Robert L. Crandall
Chairman, AMR Corporation
(American Airlines)

4

This country needs a growth economy. We have to recognize that unless we create wealth, we cannot spend it. That's the problem today. We are a great country whose economy is simply not strong enough to do all that it needs to do, and we are worsening the situation by trying to do more than we can afford.

Interview/
USA Today, 10-14:(B)7.

Mario M. Cuomo
Governor of New York (D)

5

[The Bush Administration] appears content to believe that it doesn't have to act, that however hard life is now, the hardships felt by millions of

(MARIO M. CUOMO)

Americans will dissipate as soon as the cyclical economic gods choose once again to smile upon us. I don't think you can wait. Not when nearly 10 million Americans are out of work. Not when the nation has had virtually zero economic growth since 1989.

At American Stock Exchange,
New York, July 25/
The New York Times, 7-26:(C)2.

1

[On New York State's large budget deficit]: The story of our fiscal situation has become better understood as it has become clear that it is not a New York story but a tale of national economic and fiscal failure. New York has made mistakes, as have the governments of other states and local areas, but the dominant force of the deficit has been a powerful unrelenting collapse of national confidence that has produced an intractable recession affecting most Americans and most of America.

Nov. 25/
Los Angeles Times, 11-26:(A)18.

Alfonse M. D'Amato
United States Senator,
R-New York

2

[On his proposed legislation to put a cap on interest rates charged by credit-card companies]: We see seven out of 10 of the largest banks charging the identical interest rate. There's no free market. They're charging 19.80 [per cent]— right to the decimal, 19.80—seven of the largest 10. So what I'm saying is . . . there's no competition. If there was competition, this legislation wouldn't be necessary.

Broadcast interview/
"Meet the Press," NBC-TV, 11-17.

Robert J. Dole
United States Senator,
R-Kansas

3

[Criticizing a bill to require employers to give unpaid leave to workers to deal with family

medical needs]: It's a tax increase . . . It's the long arm of Washington, D.C., reaching out across America.

The Washington Post, 10-3:(A)11.

Thomas J. Downey
United States Representative,
D-New York

4

Now that most economists recognize that the economy is in recession, our attention has been turned to unemployment insurance as our first line of defense. What we find, however, is a system in need of repair. Only about two out of five unemployed workers receive unemployment benefits.

Los Angeles Times, 3-10:(D)2.

Peter F. Drucker
Professor of social sciences
and management,
Claremont (Calif.)
Graduate School

5

If you ever run into an industry that says it needs better people, sell its shares. There *are* no better people. You have to use ordinary, every-day people and make them capable of doing the work.

Interview/
Los Angeles Times, 9-17:(D)7.

Raymond L. Flynn
Mayor of Boston

6

When you're not working, the most simple issue is the need for a job. The best social program I know of is a job.

At U.S. Conference of Mayors,
Cape Cod, Mass./
The Christian Science Monitor,
8-12:8.

Thomas S. Foley
United States Representative,
D-Washington;
Speaker of the House

7

[On the House vote to extend unemployment benefits for up to 20 additional weeks to the long-

(THOMAS S. FOLEY)

term unemployed]: A veto [by President Bush, who is against the extension] is never easy to override, but I believe, in this case, the votes will be there. Nearly 9 million Americans are looking for work, 2 million more than a year ago, and only 37 per cent [of them] are getting unemployment benefits. These workers have no doubt that an emergency exists.

News conference,
Washington, Sept. 17/
Los Angeles Times, 9-18:(A)15.

1

Providing [tax] relief to middle-income tax-payers can help stimulate the economy. Many of the problems today are that people who are in this income area who want to buy houses don't have the down payment, who want to buy auto-mobiles can't see themselves making the monthly payments . . . That's what's drying up demand around the country.

To reporters, Washington, Oct. 22/
Los Angeles Times, 10-23:(A)12.

2

It's very clear that the signal has gone out from the White House to resist and oppose any reductions in taxes as a part of dealing with the recovery, or as a part of providing tax fairness. I regret that, but it's very clear that's the case, and under those circumstances the enactment of such a tax bill will be extraordinarily difficult if not impossible.

To reporters, Washington, Oct. 30/
The Washington Post, 10-31:(A)16.

Wendell H. Ford
United States Senator,
D-Kentucky

3

[Supporting a bill to require employers to give unpaid leave to workers to deal with family medical needs]: The bottom line is, for as little as $6 per employee per year, this bill will bring both stability and increased productivity to our work-force by assuring workers that they will not lose their jobs if they put their family first.

The Washington Post, 10-3:(A)11.

Audrey Freedman
Labor economist,
The Conference Board

4

[On today's job situation]: You have a kind of sea-change in the way people's working relation-ships are carried on. They are no longer fixed relationships with one employer. Now it's really people working to cobble together a piece of income . . . They're hustling, in other words.

Los Angeles Times, 11-28:(A)24.

John Kenneth Galbraith
Professor-emeritus of economics,
Harvard University

5

[On economists' forecasts about the current recession]: I do urge that all prediction, however great the authority, be received with something varying between amusement and contempt.

Before Senate Labor Committee,
Washington/
The Christian Science Monitor,
1-16:9.

Louis Gerstner
Chairman, RJR Nabisco, Inc.

6

We are preoccupied in this country with our daily dose of [economic] statistics. We focus on bank credit, we focus on unemployment, on M2. These are interesting statistics. They aren't irrelevant. But what do we mean by the economy? What are we trying to accomplish? We are trying to raise the living standards of Americans. That requires increases in productivity in the economy—both in the public and private sector . . . There isn't a quick fix. That's the problem. We tend to look at quick fixes in terms of "Gee, what happened this week?"

Interview/
USA Today, 10-14:(B)7.

Jackie Goldberg
President, Los Angeles Board
of Education

1

[In the past,] if you didn't do too well [in school], you could go to a factory and you could get a union job where you would assemble something or you would be a part of an assembly line. And, frankly, you could make a good living and you'd get good benefits and retirement and nobody really cared one bit whether your English-language or your history skills were particularly good or not. Now those jobs are gone. Now you've got to go to an office where you have got to make decisions about what to do with the information that is in your computer's data bank . . . It takes much more to be an employee now.

Interview/
Los Angeles Times, 3-10:(M)3.

Alan Greenspan
Chairman,
Federal Reserve Board

2

Concern about the appropriateness of [the U.S.] maintaining a policy of fiscal restraint during a period of weak economic performance are understandable. However, they must be balanced against the benefits that will flow from adhering to a budget strategy that is geared to the longer-run needs of the economy. Those needs can best be met by keeping the underlying or structural deficit firmly on a downward path, even as the actual deficit is being swollen temporarily by the effects of a weak economy. That path promises to improve prospects for increased capital accumulation and higher productivity. It will complement monetary policy in the attainment of the nation's over-all economic objective in the long run.

Before Congressional Joint
Economic Committee,
Washington, March 13/
The Washington Post, 3-15:(A)22.

3

Inadequate domestic savings is impairing our economic prospects for the long run. By choosing to consume more now and to save less, we are limiting our ability to expand and upgrade our stock of capital.

At Senate Hearing,
Washington, May/
The New York Times, 5-22:(C)2.

4

[On the current recession]: Consumers appear to be more apprehensive than one might expect given the broad macroeconomic circumstances. For example, the level of employment, and particularly the layoff rate, are well below those experienced in periods of economic weakness. This would not seem to square with the deep concerns expressed in surveys about perceived labor-market conditions . . . I suspect that what concerns consumers, and indeed everyone, is that the current pause may be underscoring a retardation in long-term growth and living standards. So long as the recovery proceeded, this latent concern did not surface. But, as balance-sheet constraints held the recovery in check, earlier worries about whether the current generation will live, as well as previous ones, resurfaced . . . The essential shortcomings of this economy is the lack of saving and investment. It's here that our major policy focus should rest. Investment is the key to enhanced productivity and higher living standards.

Before House Ways and Means
Committee, Washington, Dec. 18/
The New York Times, 12-19:(C)2.

Gene Guerrero
Washington legislative representative,
American
Civil Liberties Union

5

[On employer monitoring of employees]: The whole trend toward Big Brother monitoring is something that ought to be of great concern to us because if we're not careful, we're going to find ourselves in the kind of 1984 society that George Orwell predicted. It will be a few years late, but it's coming in bits and pieces . . . Constant surveillance is an infringement of an employee's basic right and in the long run costs companies

73

(GENE GUERRERO)

because it's very stressful to be working a job where you know that somebody is looking over your shoulder all the time.

Interview/
USA Today, 8-5:(A)11.

Tom Harkin
United States Senator,
D-Iowa

1

The issue, [President] George Herbert Walker Bush, is not jobs. Hell, slaves had jobs. What we want in this country are decent, well-paying, secure jobs.

The New York Times, 8-5:(A)8.

Tom Harkin
United States Senator,
D-Iowa;
Candidate for the 1992
Democratic Presidential nomination

2

When I'm President of the United States, every double-breasting, scab-hiring, union-hurting employer in America will know the working people of America have a friend in the White House.

At AFL-CIO convention,
Detroit, Nov. 12/
Los Angeles Times, 11-13:(A)4.

Sylvia Ann Hewlett
Economist

3

We are facing a growing labor shortage in this country. Yet because of the rising skill demands of the work-place, many of our [high-school] dropouts are simply unemployable. A technology-based economy cannot absorb workers who are not literate and who lack rudimentary mathematical skills . . . Even high-school graduates are coming up short in meeting the demands of the work-place. Chemical Bank has reported that it must interview 40 high-school graduates to find one person who can be trained

to become a teller. All they are seeking is eighth-grade-level skills, and they cannot find them in most high-school graduates.

Interview, New York/
Time, 8-26:12.

Leon Hirsch
Chairman, U.S. Surgical
Corporation

4

. . . a capital-gains-tax reduction would actually help the average worker. It means there is more capital invested. And that means more jobs and more economic production. Democrats are very mistaken when they say capital-gains-tax reduction only benefits the rich. That's absolutely not true. Everybody benefits—particulary the middle class and the working man.

Interview/
USA Today, 10-14:(B)7.

Jack Kemp
Secretary of Housing
and Urban Development
of the United States

5

. . . I've argued to lower the top tax rate to 25 per cent ever since I started running [for public office]—on the theory that the way to get more revenue is not to tax people the way [former President] Jimmy Carter did. I'd rather get 25 per cent of the revenue of a lot of wealthy people than 70 per cent of the wealth of almost no one. When the tax rates were at 70 per cent, people were only investing offshore or in nothing but tax-free municipal bonds.

Panel discussion, Washington/
Harper's Magazine, July:44.

6

Recessions scare me. And this [current one] is a man-made recession. It was caused by policies that were passed by real, live human beings, and it can be corrected with policy. I mean, the one thing we learned in the '80s is that you can change policy for good or bad . . . Recessions cause big government. Recessions cause people to lose hope. Recessions are absolutely inimical

(JACK KEMP)

to the interest of the [Federal] budget and to the interest of the poor . . . I don't think we're out of the recession yet. And that's one reason why I so strongly support President Bush's call for a cut in the capital-gains [tax] rate, why I want to eliminate it in the inner city, why I think there should be a labor-based incentive by rolling back the payroll tax. And why the family, the most over-taxed institution in the United States of America, needs a higher exemption for our children.

Interview/USA Today, 8-13:(A)11.

1

I think the time is right, personally—I haven't yet convinced everybody in Congress or the White House—to have a joint [President] Bush and Congressional tax-rate reduction, not to bust the budget, but to get America growing again. I think it could be done this year . . . This is the real debate, both in the Congress as well as the Administration. And it's a friendly debate, it really is, but it's a vigorous one. And I think this is a defining moment for our country in terms of getting the type of growth that can meet both economic as well as social goals . . . The economy, while technically, perhaps, out of recession, is limping, it's anemic and it needs some oxygen in the body economic to create more jobs, to create more growth.

Broadcast interview/
"Face the Nation," CBS-TV, 11-10.

Edward M. Kennedy
United States Senator,
D-Massachussetts

2

The Bush Administration has no anti-recession program, no strategy to preserve jobs or relieve the suffering of those who have lost work, home, savings, or businesses. It is time for the Administration to get as serious about fighting this recession as they are about fighting in the Persian Gulf.

At Senate Labor and Human
Resources Committee hearing,
Washington, Jan. 7/
The New York Times, 1-8:(A)10.

Bruce Llewellyn
Chairman, Philadelphia
Coca-Cola Bottling Company

3

[The U.S. needs] to reorder priorities overseas. Charity begins at home. You can't be a world power if your basement is falling apart. That's what's happening. We're able to find millions upon millions for Poland, Czechoslovakia and Russia. Yet [President Bush] doesn't have any money for programs at home. These countries are asking for money that the American taxpayer has put in the pot. But the American taxpayer has first call on that pot.

Interview/
USA Today, 10-14:(B)7.

Edward P. Madigan
Secretary of Agriculture
of the United States

4

[On the U.S. decision to provide loan guarantees to help the Soviet Union get through its food shortages this winter]: This is not a foreign program. This is a [U.S.] domestic program that has as its intent moving U.S. grain [which the Soviets would buy with the loaned money] out of the U.S. market for the benefit of American farmers who will make these sales and then will spend that money in the American economy—buying pickup trucks and buying other things that are manufactured in urban areas.

News conference,
Washington, Nov. 20/
Los Angeles Times, 11-21:(A)10.

Lynn Martin
Secretary of Labor
of the United States

5

[On the "glass ceiling," an invisible block to advancement of women and minorities in the business world]: The glass ceiling . . . deprives our economy of new leaders, new sources of creativity—the would-be pioneers of the business world. If our end game is to compete successfully in today's global market, then we

(LYNN MARTIN)

have to unleash the full potential of the American work-force.

News conference,
Washington, Aug. 8/
Los Angeles Times, 8-9:(A)1.

1

The economic world has changed over. Products get modernized faster than ever. Industries disappear overnight. The demographics of the work-place are defined by the striking rise in the participation of women, minorities. These developments drive us, therefore, to a fundamental choice: Do we try to manage the change or do we try to prevent it, because change always brings uncertainty and fear? . . . Post World War II America gave us an unprecedented capacity to deliver on the commitments of economic security. But with the changes that have taken place, they're not working today. Employers' needs change every single day. They change from week to week, and that means the jobs change, too. Workers are called upon to become more adaptable, to display greater levels of skills . . . Unions can't stop companies from changing. Companies can't stop changing, and individual relationships are undergoing often difficult times.

Speech, Washington,
Nov. 7/
The Washington Post,
11-15:(A)22.

William C. Melton
Chief economist,
IDS Financial Services

2

[On the Federal Reserve's handling of economic problems]: What really counts is the Fed's ability to change policy in the early stages of an emerging problem, rather than waiting until momentum has built up . . . Twice during the last three years, the Fed nipped incipient inflation boomlets in the bud, before they could do serious damage.

The Washington Post,
4-19:(F)2.

Howard M. Metzenbaum
United States Senator,
D-Ohio

3

My goal is simple and straightforward: save consumers money by protecting them from price-fixing and price gouging . . . The damage caused by price-fixing may not be immediately obvious because consumers cannot know how low the price might have been in an open, competitive market. A consumer also may be unaware that a particular product is not for sale at discount stores or is no longer offered at a discount price because the manufacturer has refused to continue to supply a discounter.

Before the Senate, Washington/
The Washington Post, 4-7:(D)2.

George J. Mitchell
United States Senator,
D-Maine

4

The capital-gains tax cut as proposed by the President [Bush] would primarily benefit those whose incomes exceed $200,000 a year. We [Democrats] want to primarily benefit those in the middle. Instead of cutting taxes for one family whose income is $300,000 a year, we think we ought to cut taxes for 10 families whose income is $30,000 a year.

Oct. 20/
Los Angeles Times, 10-21:(A)19.

5

[On President Bush]: Not since President [Herbert] Hoover told Americans the country had turned the corner has an American President been so consistently wrong in his judgment of the economy . . . President Bush's record for economic growth and job creation is worse than for any other President since Herbert Hoover. During Bush's Presidency, our country has grown at a slower rate, with fewer jobs created than during any other Presidency in the last 60 years.

Before Center for National Policy,
Oct. 31/
The Washington Post, 11-1:(A)16.

H. Ross Perot
Entrepreneur

1

We always tend to juice the economy [before an election]. But that's like taking a racehorse with bad legs and shooting it with dope. That's going to tranquilize, homogenize everything until the election is over . . . My biggest fear is that nothing will be done. It will require sacrifice. But if we don't fix [the economy] pretty soon, it's going to create a tremendous scar, thousands will be out of work and it will take a decade to clean it up. Watching the economy is like looking at the instrument panel of a jet going Mach 2 headed straight down and 100 feet off the ground.

Interview/
USA Today, 10-14:(B)7.

Robert B. Reich
Professor of political economy
and management,
Kennedy School of Government,
Harvard University

2

Around the world, the global economy is rewarding those individuals who have "symbolic analytic" skills with ever greater incomes. Yet 12,000 people are coming into that economy every hour, the vast majority of them unskilled and unemployed. The overarching goal for America should be to enlarge the number of people that can be understood to do symbolic-analytic work, who are problem-solvers, problem-identifiers and brokers of the two. In decades to come, people will not be talking about the "competitiveness" of the U.S. economy but rather the competitiveness of Americans. The only difference between, say, the Japanese and American economies will be in the percentage of the population equipped with symbolic-analytic capacities. If the present trends continue, something like 40 to 50 per cent of the Japanese population will be engaged in symbolic-analytic tasks while not more than 20 per cent of the American work-force will be.

Interview/
U.S. News & World Report,
4-22:46.

3

[Criticizing companies for laying off large numbers of employees in the current recession]: For every person who's laid off, there are 20 more who fear that their jobs may be next. Nothing inhibits consumer purchases like that fear. It has a very depressive effect on the economy . . . It makes sense for companies to hold on to their workers. Companies can't be flexible and innovative without the full commitment of workers. [The labor pool is] the one unique aspect of a firm. With their skills, insights and commitment, workers become more valuable because they are ready to solve the next, more-complex problem. Layoffs deplete know-how and drive, leaving only the machinery.

The Christian Science Monitor,
12-4:1,2.

Robert Reischauer
Director,
Congressional Budget Office

4

[On the likelihood that the U.S. faces its biggest Federal budget deficit in history]: It is going to face Congress with a very difficult situation with the American people, who will be shaken in their faith in Congress. Congress just enacted the largest deficit-reduction package in the nation's history, and now we will be treated to the largest deficit in the nation's history.

The Washington Post, 1-8:(A)1.

Donald W. Riegle, Jr.
United States Senator,
D-Michigan

5

[Criticizing a proposed free-trade agreement between the U.S. and Mexico]: We know there will be tens of thousands, hundreds of thousands— I think millions—[in the U.S.] who will lose their jobs [as a result of such an agreement]. We need a jobs strategy for America—that should be our first goal. And instead, here we are with a jobs program for Mexico. This is an appalling policy.

Washington, May 24/
The Washington Post,
5-25:(A)4.

John D. (Jay) Rockefeller IV
United States Senator,
D-West Virginia

1

I have always believed in an America of industrial might and agricultural bounty where a steelworker's strong arms could earn enough to own a modest home and send a child to college. Despite the talk of values and responsibility, our leaders abandoned them. Instead of raising standards and expectations, they lowered them . . . They built a Berlin Wall through our economy, lavishing tax breaks and corporate perks on the lucky few, taxing and ignoring those on the other side.

Announcing he would not run
for the 1992 Democratic
Presidential nomination,
Charleston, W.V., Aug. 7/
The Washington Post, 8-8:(A)9.

Felix G. Rohatyn
Senior partner,
Lazard Freres & Co.,
investment bankers;
Chairman, Municipal Assistance
Corporation of New York

2

If I were 30 years old, I would move to Europe. [The American economy] is going no place. The assumption is that all the problems are too hard to tackle. We say we can't do anything about the real issues, like education, health, so no one even talks about them. Washington is pushing everything back to the state and local level. But Europe is forward-looking, driven by a confident government-business partnership. They want to widen out the frontiers. People are thinking about and accepting a United Europe. Sure, they have problems, but they assume they can be dealt with.

Interview/
The Washington Post, 7-18:(A)17.

William A. Schreyer
Chairman, Merrill Lynch
and Company

3

[Telling graduating students not to be overly discouraged if they find it difficult getting a job]:

Things weren't much different when I graduated from Penn State in 1948. Inflation was heating up and most people suspected we were heading back toward depression. How could we know, just over the horizon, the biggest economic boom in history was about to start?

At Pennsylvania State University
College of Earth and Mineral
Sciences commencement/
The New York Times, 5-20:(A)13.

John Sharp
Texas State Comptroller

4

[On his plan for cutting government spending in Texas to fight the state's budget problem]: What's different about this plan is that it's not coming from a bunch of people who hate government. We're people who think government is a good thing, a beneficial thing, and that there are ways to make it more efficient . . . As long as the public views national Democrats as those folks who believe spending is the answer to every single problem, we're [Democrats] in trouble. That's what comes across to old Bubba out there [the average citizen]. The lesson we're trying to send the national Democrats is you can save money and provide important services at the same time.

The Washington Post, 7-15:(A)5.

George P. Shultz
Former Secretary of State
of the United States;
Former president, Bechtel Group, Inc.

5

As a management person, if I'm running my shop and I don't have a [labor] union, I don't want them. But I'm trying to look at this more broadly and ask a question about where we're heading, and I think the monkey is really on the unions' back as much as anything to show a function in a world that is changing rapidly—the whole work-place is changing, the patterns of competition are changing. [Yet,] as a society, we have a great stake in freedom and a lot of that is anchored, somehow, historically [in the labor movement].

Before National Planning Association/
The New York Times, 12-13:(C)2.

Jim Slattery
United States Representative,
D-Kansas

1

I consider myself to be a representative of the blue-collar workers of America. But there are two basic factors to keep in mind. One is that the number of workers who are members of labor unions has dramatically declined. In many Congressional districts there are more small-businessmen and women than there are members of labor unions. Second, in the last 10 years with the emergence of political action committees, the Democratic Party is less dependent on the contributions of organized labor than it was 15 years ago.

The New York Times, 4-19:(A)12.

Richard A. Snelling
Governor of Vermont (R)

2

[Criticizing previous Governors for not putting aside enough funds in the state treasury during the prosperous 1980s, so that now, during a recession, the state must increase taxes]: It is disingenuous to say that states have been popped by an economic cycle. Taxpayers have a legitimate gripe when they ask, "Why did you spend everything you could take from us in the good times and then raise taxes in the bad times?"

The New York Times, 7-27:8.

Bo Sodesten
Professor of economics,
Lund University (Sweden)

3

The capitalist market economy is an unavoidable condition. You can't skip this stage. Social democracy is clearly a superstructure that became possible at a rather late stage in the development of capitalism. Anyone who believes the contrary and puts the cart before the horse will see that it won't work.

Interview/
World Press Review,
March: 40.

Sung Won Sohn
Chief economist,
Norwest Corporation

4

The euphoria immediately after the [Persian Gulf] war probably will pick up the economy temporarily. But the reason we're in a recession right now is not because of [Iraqi President] Saddam Hussein. It's because of too much debt by consumers, corporations and the U.S. government.

Los Angeles Times, 2-23:(D)2.

David A. Stockman
Former Dirctor,
Federal Office of
Management and Budget

5

[On the current high levels of consumer debt]: I think they are going to have an impact on consumer savings, which have been at historically minimal levels over the last four or five years. They are also going to affect consumer spending, which has actually exceeded available cash flow since the early 1980s. After consumers pay their taxes, which are rising, and pay the interest on the huge debt balance that accumulated in the '80s, and after you account for sources of income that we never really see, such as mandatory employer contributions for pensions and other fringe benefits, the available share of current income that ends up being spent is going to fall significantly. This represents a key weakness in the [economic] recovery that lies ahead.

Interview/
U.S. News & World Report,
5-6:62.

Margo Thorning
Chief economist,
American Council
for Capital Formation

6

We shouldn't push the panic button yet; the economy is not in such bad shape. Unemployment is holding steady at 6.8 per cent, inflation is low and inventories aren't high. [President] Bush

(MARGO THORNING)

is doing the right thing now by sitting tight, riding this [recession] out and not putting out a big, costly tax cut for the middle class.

The Christian Science Monitor,
11-22:2.

Robert G. Torricelli
United States Representative,
D-New Jersey

1

Just as the world had confidence in American products because they were amazed at our ability to execute the Apollo [space] program, when this [current Persian Gulf] war is over, people are going to to be reminded that a nation that can place a bomb from 10,000 feet through a doorway can also manufacture a good machine tool.

The Washington Post,
1-31:(A)24.

Paul E. Tsongas
Candidate for the
1992 Democratic
Presidential nomination;
Former United States Senator,
D-Massachussetts

2

Democrats have been famous for dividing the pie fairly. Now there's no pie left. So Democrats must learn how to produce wealth.

Time, 6-24:19.

3

Our [Democratic Party's] mandate is not to elect a Democrat [as President in 1992]. It is not to do polls and focus-groups and figure out what sells. Our mandate is to rescue the country from economic decline. If you're going to be pro-jobs, you better be pro-business, because that's where the jobs are.

Before Association of
State Democratic Chairs,
Chicago, Nov. 22/
Los Angeles Times, 11-23:(A)22.

Stansfield Turner
Former Director
of Central Intelligence
of the United States

4

The security of our country is more dependent today than ever before on our economic competitiveness. It rivals our military preparedness as the key to national security.

Interview/
USA Today, 9-16:(A)13.

Robert Vanasek
Speaker of the
Minnesota House (D)

5

One of the mistakes we [in the states] made in the '80s is that as the Feds cut back on domestic spending, we picked up a lot of the difference. So the public never felt the effect of Reaganomics. We cushioned them, and it sort of worked until we had a downturn like we have now.

The Washington Post, 1-14:(A)5.

Murray Weidenbaum
Director, Center for the Study
of American Business,
Washington University;
Former Chairman, Council
of Economic Advisers to the
President of the United States
(Ronald Reagan)

6

[On why there is still a Federal budget deficit]: When you really assess blame, there's enough blame to go along both ends of Pennsylvania Avenue, the Capitol on one side and the White House on the other. Neither one really has a stomach for saying no to powerful spending groups. What you have to do is follow [the late President] Harry Truman's attitude, at least when he was Chairman of the Senate Appropriations Committee: He never saw a budget that couldn't be cut.

Interview/
USA Today, 7-17:(A)13.

Alan Westin
*Professor of public law
and government,
Columbia University*

1

[On employer monitoring of employees]:
Supervisory monitoring goes back as far as the
pyramids where employers watched how many
bricks workers made. What you have today is a
new capacity to use that supervisory monitoring
made possible by computers . . . An overwhelming majority of over a thousand workers who
were interviewed felt it was legitimate for
employers to monitor, as long as certain standards were met: that they were aware of the
monitoring, and could see any records and results
and could challenge their accuracy.

*Interview/
USA Today, 8-5:(A)11.*

Michael R. White
Mayor of Cleveland

2

Jobs provide the balance, the stability, the
foundation not only for the individual, but for
families. This is not only a local problem but it is
a national one . . . The best social program in this
country is a job for every single American, especially young people who have not seen their
parents or their grandparents work.

*Interview, Cleveland/
The Christian Science Monitor,
8-12:9.*

L. Douglas Wilder
Governor of Virginia (D)

3

Gramm-Rudman [the Federal budget-balanc-
ing guidelines] falsely led the public to believe
that it would reduce spending automatically,
because otherwise the government would shut
down. Have you ever heard such nonsense!
How does the government shut down? Gramm-
Rudman turned out to be a recipe for "spending
as usual." We haven't seen any commitment in
Washington to limit spending . . . Why not put
the case before the American people by sending
down a balanced budget, which has not been

done in the last several years, and promising to
veto any Congressional budget legislation that
differs substantially?

*Interview/
The Washington Post, 1-17:(A)20.*

John Q. Wilson
*Chief economist,
Bank of America*

4

[On just-released numbers indicating a new
loss of a large number of jobs in the current reces-
sion]: This reinforces a pretty pessimistic view of
the economy. These numbers feed into lower
confidence. People out there are getting paranoid
about unemployment, and they are not going to
spend more. Consumers are on the sidelines
waiting for the economy to improve, and the
government is on the sidelines waiting for the
consumer to start spending, and we're going
nowhere.

*Dec. 6/
Los Angeles Times, 12-7:(A)24.*

Clayton K. Yeutter
*Chairman,
Republican National Committee*

5

You can yell all you wish about [economic]
leadership from this Executive Branch, but there
are two branches of government in Washington.
There is a whole lot of responsibility on the
shoulders of the U.S. Congress in all of these
issues, and the Congress has not had high marks
from anybody.

*Interview/
USA Today, 12-18:(A)13.*

6

We ought not raise taxes on anyone. Tax
increases that start out limited to the very upper-
income spectrum will not generate very much
additional revenue. Then our friends on Capitol
Hill will gradually widen the coverage of such
proposals further into the middle-income categories. Instead of having middle-income tax
relief, we'll have middle-income tax increases.

*Interview/
USA Today, 12-18:(A)13.*

81

Education

John T. Agresto
President, St. John's College,
Santa Fe, N.M.;
Former Acting Chairman,
National Endowment for the
Humanities of the United States

1

[Supporting a strong tilt toward the teaching of Western culture and civilization in American education and humanities]: I cannot imagine people functioning intelligently in this civilization without knowing about the Greeks, the Romans, the Bible, the heritage of English liberty, the American Revolution and the Civil War, no matter what race or ethnic heritage they are. A kid who has read Indian fairy tales in Sanskrit, but who has never read the Bible, is a person who is, for this culture, not appropriately educated.

Interview, Santa Fe, N.M./
Los Angeles Times, 7-5:(A)23.

Lamar Alexander
Secretary of Education
of the United States

2

I think that telling parents where they must send their children to school is an alien idea in America. So far as we're concerned, if it's okay with the local school district and okay with the Supreme Court, then [Federal] dollars will follow the child.

Interview, Washington, April 19/
The New York Times, 4-20:8.

3

We're going to have to radically change what it is we teach. The first target for this is the teachers in the classroom who will need to change what they are doing. If it is true that only 15 to 20 per cent of our students know what it is we want them to graduate knowing in math, we must change the teachers in place . . . Most Americans instinctively know that caring for and loving and raising

and educating children and educating themselves is principally their own responsibility or the responsibility of their community and their state. The remedies we are prescribing are not for everyone else, but for a child right now, right in a class.

Interview, Washington/
The Christian Science Monitor,
8-27:12.

4

A Phi Delta Kappa survey shows that when asked what's the most important thing for this country for the next 25 years, Americans far and away choose having the best education system in the world. The second thing is that while only 21 per cent would give the U.S. system an A or B, 73 per cent say their own school deserves an A or B. In other words, most people say the nations' at risk, but their school is okay. Somehow, we have to ring an alarm bell, stir people up, get people not just to realize that the nation is at risk but that they are, too.

Interview/USA Today, 8-28:(A)11.

James B. Appleberry
President, American Association
of State Colleges
and Universities

5

We're [the U.S.] treating [higher] education in many cases as if it is a consumer product. We're expecting the individual who gets the education to pay for that education. It's seen less as an investment in the future of our country. We happen to be an association that says for a whole lot of reasons that we think that tuition ought to remain low.

Interview/USA Today, 8-7:(A)9.

Robert Atwell
President, American Council
on Education

6

If you're a private-sector [college] president, you get judged on the basis of how well you raise

(ROBERT ATWELL)

money. All presidents seem to be judged on increases in the SAT scores of their entering students, which tells you precisely nothing about what's going on in the institution. Sometimes you even get judged by how well the basketball team is doing.

The Christian Science Monitor,
3-18:13.

Marguerite Barnett
President,
University of Houston

1

We are in the midst of a transfer in our economy from an industrial economy to sophisticated service industry. With most of our people living in cities, a diverse new population, it is the urban university that is on the cutting edge of change . . . Very few public urban research institutions will simply be located in their cities in the 21st century. They will have to be a partner in their cities if they're going to continue to thrive.

The New York Times, 8-13:(A)8.

George Batsche
President,
National Association
of School Psychologists

2

It's a different child who comes to the schoolhouse door today . . . We're talking about students who may have short attention spans. Students who have not experienced persistence at a reading task, a coloring task or a writing task. We're also talking about children who solve problems by being aggressive because, in the world that they come from, aggression is both a self-defense and a method of getting what you want. We have children coming to school who have problems with authority figures. They do not respond to directions; they are defiant . . . We have kids who are anxious. They're worried about their ability to succeed or are depressed because they're not succeeding. Instead of acting out, as some kids do when they're frustrated, these kids withdraw. We also are beginning to see in the schools the effects of drugs.

Interview/USA Today, 9-4:(A)11.

Terrel H. Bell
Professor of educational
administration,
University of Utah;
Former Secretary of Education
of the United States

3

[Calling for ranking of schools based on test scores and other qualitative measurements]: We propose that the schools let it all hang out, that we rank schools each year because we think it will motivate parents and others to rally around the schools. We know who is last in the football league. Let's not be shy about doing it academically.

Interview/
The Washington Post, 8-9:(A)19.

William J. Bennett
Former Secretary of Education
of the United States

4

When it comes to equal opportunity [in education for all], we [the U.S.] have the best hearts. The problem is our education system doesn't produce the best minds.

Newsweek, 12-2:52.

Douglas Besharov
Researcher,
American Enterprise Institute

5

Young people, especially those who've dropped out of school, have been having a progressively tougher time in our economy. They have the lowest seniority and the lowest educational attainment, and many of them are competing with low-wage workers around the world for jobs . . . If we look at the nature of the underlying trend, which is fewer opportunities for those with lower educational levels, then we would realize we ought to be spending money and improving their schools so that they can compete in what has become a post-industrial Western economy.

Los Angeles Times,
11-26:(A)12.

Ernest L. Boyer
President,
Carnegie Foundation for the
Advancement of Teaching

1

Moral and civic education have almost disappeared. We've become increasingly preoccupied with the economic impact of education.

The Washington Post, 9-28:(A)8.

Bill Bradley
United States Senator,
D-New Jersey

2

[On financing of scholarships]: I've always tried to do a self-reliant scholarship that says you can get up to $33,000 in exchange for paying back a per cent of your income into a trust fund, an education trust fund, and that that should be available to any American up to the age of 50. You then are beginning to give people some hope that they will be able to get the education they need to equip them to earn money that they will need in order to have a more prosperous life than their parents had.

Interview, Washington/
Los Angeles Times, 9-29:(M)3.

Frank Burtnett
Executive director,
National Association of
College Admission Counselors

3

[On the current recession's effect on students paying college tuition]: Any way you look at it, it's going to be a tough year. There's no longer a prescribed formula on how to pay for college. I can see more kids taking five and six years to get through four years, dropping out to work to meet the costs.

The New York Times, 2-9:8.

George Bush
President of the United States

4

If we want America to remain a leader, a force for good in the world, we must lead the way in educational innovation. Think about every problem, every challenge we face. The solution to each starts with education . . . People who want Washington to solve their educational problems are missing the point. What happens here in Washington won't matter half as much as what happens in each school, each local community and, yes, in each home.

To Congressional, business and
education leaders,
Washington, April 18/
The Washington Post, 4-19:(A)1.

5

[Saying he supports the idea of young urban black males being able to attend all-boy public schools]: I'm for as much innovation as possible. We've got to abide by the law of the land, and if our experience shows us that we need to get modifications to accommodate academies of that nature, we ought to do it because I do believe that something of that nature has some merit . . . I think the Boy Scouts—it's perfectly okay to have only boys in it . . . Maybe I'm old-fashioned.

Interview, Washington, Sept. 9/
The Washington Post, 9-10:(A)2.

Jose A. Cabranes
Judge, United States District Court
for Connecticut

6

[On the "Western Civilization" course requirement at Columbia College in the 1950s]: Columbia College can take pride in having demanded the most of *all* of us, regardless of background [he is Puerto Rican-born]. It can be proud of having made *all* of us quite uncomfortable—uncomfortable as we encountered new and unfamiliar ideas and as we pursued together an understanding of the Western heritage. Columbia College did not define its academic program on the basis of the ethnicity or the race of any of us. It invited us all, regardless of our origins, to join in the common study of our heritage, and to do so with an appreciation that criticism and reform of our institutions is an integral part of the tradition we describe as "Western Civilization."

Upon receiving Columbia's
John Jay Award, March/
The Wall Street Journal, 5-3:(A)12.

Steven Carbo
Legislative counsel,
Mexican-American Legal
Defense and Educational Fund

1

[Multiple-choice tests] are an inaccurate indicator of future education and employment performance. They just give a snapshot of what a test-taker might know in certain areas, at a particular time and place, and within a particular time frame. What they don't show is how well a student is able to think creatively. They don't show how well the student is able to work with other people. They don't reflect the student's experience. They don't reflect a variety of contributions a student can make which also indicate how well he or she will perform in the future.

Interview/USA Today, 6-10:(A)11.

Linda Chavez
Chairman,
National Commission
on Migrant Education

2

America is simply more mobile today than it was in the 19th century and most of the 20th century. It is very rare for most students to stay in the same school district throughout their school lives. We're going to see some movement in the direction of more standardized curriculum, more emphasis on certain basic courses being required to graduate from high school. Whether this is done voluntarily or by the encouragement of the Federal government is yet to be seen.

Interview/USA Today, 4-29:(A)11.

John Chubb
Senior fellow,
Brookings Institution

3

No matter what [President Bush] stands for [in education], there are going to be voices that say, "If he doesn't stand for billions and billions of new money for education, then he doesn't deserve to be called the education President." But I'd argue that if he's willing to speak out loudly and clearly for the evaluation of schools by performance, if he's willing to speak out

strongly that academic excellence is the most important goal of the schools, if he's willing to take to task the existing system as the source of failure, then he deserves to be regarded as a serious player.

Newsweek, 4-22:28.

4

[On the idea of giving parents a choice as to which school their children will attend]: The unions are opposed [to the idea], not because they are not concerned about the poor, but obviously because they are in business to protect the livelihood of all union members. A choice system is a potential threat to the incompetent or the marginal teacher. People who are doing a poor job, obviously, will not be chosen. And unions cannot support a program that will jeopardize the jobs of some of their teachers.

The Saturday Evening Post,
May-June: 32.

5

There's nothing inherently "private" about private schools' success—they have strong relationships with families, they're sharply focused on academics, they provide a professional environment for teachers and they're concerned with producing tangible results. Public schools ought to be able to do the same things. But public education is intensely bureaucratized and politicized. That drives a wedge between schools and families, creates a non-professional teaching environment, confuses the schools' objectives and cuts incentives and accountability for tangible results. As a result, it's practically impossible, at least in our big cities, for public schools to apply the lessons of private schools.

Interview/
U.S. News & World Report,
12-9:78.

John L. Clendenin
Chairman,
BellSouth Corporation

6

The problems of how to get a trainable workforce are really looming larger for all of us. Our

(JOHN L. CLENDENIN)

initial conclusion was that we really needed to fix the school curriculum . . . But when we started to look at it we suddenly realized that we had loaded onto the schools a whole host of society's problems, everything from teen-age pregnancy to drug problems to the breakup of families. And the school can't handle the overload.

Before House Budget Committee,
Washington, March 6/
The Washington Post, 3-7:(A)21.

Susan M. Collins
Associate professor of economics,
Harvard University

1

[President Bush's] declaration, "I am the education President," excites people and makes education a national issue. That increased awareness will be an election issue, and then "the education President" will have to do something.

The Christian Science Monitor,
6-25:2.

Dolores Cross
President,
Chicago State University

2

It takes considerable energy to run a university. You not only formulate the plan for the institution, you have to get people motivated and involved in that plan so it can be carried out. It's a big job.

Ebony, November:27.

Linda Darling-Hammond
Professor of education,
Teachers College,
Columbia University

3

We've always been able to produce wonderful demonstration schools. You can always get terrific teachers in one school, but we're not doing enough to address the fact that we're not producing enough terrific teachers for all schools.

Newsweek, 4-22:28.

Sharon Pratt Dixon
Mayor of Washington

4

[Educators] need to have the authority to instill standards and values and discipline in young people, especially in a society where so many women are working and trying to rear children alone. There's got to be some kind of authoritative figure in their lives . . . Young people respond to discipline. [Schools need] the authority to discipline, including, if need be, spanking young people.

Broadcast interview, April 9/
The Washington Post, 4-10:(A)1.

Elizabeth Hanford Dole
President, American Red Cross;
Former Secretary of Labor
of the United States

5

A university is a paradoxical place, where ancient tradition thrives alongside the most revolutionary hypothesis.

At Dartmouth College commencement,
June 9/
The New York Times, 6-10:(A)12.

Peter F. Drucker
Professor of social sciences
and management,
Claremont (Calif.)
Graduate School

6

Since the public schools aren't going to reform, we need a voucher system [to allow students to go to the school of their choice] . . . There are six schools within biking distance in Claremont. There's no reason for all of them to have the same pedagogical philosophy. [Without vouchers,] you'll never get any competition going.

Interview/
Los Angeles Times, 9-17:(D)7.

Richard Elmore
Professor of eduction,
Graduate School of Education,
Harvard University

7

We need to have a fundamental debate about the role that private education plays and what

(RICHARD ELMORE)

responsibilities come with accepting public money. People are basically deceiving themselves if they think that opening up choice is going to pull government out of people's lives. If it's fair and equitable, it's going to involve government.

The Christian Science Monitor,
3-11:12.

Chester E. Finn, Jr.
Professor of education
and public policy,
Vanderbilt University;
Director, Educational
Excellence Network

1

The politics of education have been dominated for most of this century by what I call now producer politics, where the people who make the major decisions about what goes on in the education system are those who are employed by the education system. It has not been a consumer-oriented system.

Interview, Washington/
The New York Times, 8-2:(A)9.

2

Have you talked to any teen-ager lately? Every fourth word is "like" and only about a third of the sentences parse, i.e., are grammatically correct. Their vocabularies are stunted and the gap between idea and explication is wide, such that you often don't quite get the point, except at the crudest and most simplistic level.

USA Today, 8-27:(D)2.

3

I don't think there's any industrialized country right now that's complacent about their educational system. The Eastern-bloc countries are thinking about reform because of their recent escape from the Soviet system. England's problems are closer to [those of the U.S.]—a faltering economy and anxiety about that . . . Japan wants to win Nobel Prizes, not just produce others' inventions more efficiently.

Newsweek, 12-2:52.

Edward B. Fiske
Former education editor,
"The New York Times"

4

[President] George Bush is trying to do the two most important things that a President can do. One is to define the stake that the country has in a very decentralized system of 16,000 local school districts; and to say it's an urgent national priority. Secondly, he has said we will not solve it with "business as usual." We need some fundamental changes . . . [But] he has not addressed the problems of restructuring the system.

Interview/
The Christian Science Monitor,
9-16:13.

John E. Frohnmayer
Chairman,
National Endowment for the Arts
of the United States

5

I would like to persuade those who really care about education that the arts ought to be central to the curriculum. Arts education is not recreational; it's not secondary; it's not "nice" if you have a lot of money and a lot of time. It's critical to the process of learning to think, of learning to be a productive citizen, of learning to make connections of disconnected items, which is the real substance of genius . . . If we can show that arts education is really critical not just to a better-educated citizenry and more able citizenry, a citizenry that includes the skills that the Department of Labor says are necessary for people in the job market, then we will have accomplished two things: One, we will have improved the education *en toto* of the United States; and secondly, we will have improved the appreciation for the arts in the United States.

Interview, Washington/
Los Angeles Times, 12-22:(Calendar)88.

David P. Gardner
President,
University of California

6

It is increasingly difficult to find people who are interested in the [college] institution as a

(DAVID P. GARDNER)

whole. People see the schools as a means of giving expressions to their own particular interests irrespective of the impact that might have on the rest of what the school does. So these schools get thrown in several directions at once, making it very hard for those trying to take an overview of their work to get support for it in general.

Interview/
The Christian Science Monitor,
11-20:9.

Howard Gardner
Professor of education,
Harvard University

1

A classroom teaches you a certain kind of knowledge, but it doesn't teach you how to activate that knowledge—how to activate the principles you've learned in your everyday life . . . Essentially, what goes on in school is a giant deception where I ask you certain kinds of questions, you give certain kinds of answers. If you perform well, I say "You're educated." So school creates a superstructure on the mind, but in 99 percent of cases, the superstructure doesn't survive beyond the day you leave school. Pretty frightening . . . Students, like novices, need to witness experts exhibiting their knowledge. And there aren't many experts. Experts are people who not only have knowledge, but understand how it relates to their everyday lives. They don't need to be Nobel Prize winners, but they have to be people who understand the relationship between what's in the textbook and what's outside it. I think it's important that we see kids in schools as novices, and teachers as mentors or masters of their discipline.

Interview/USA Today, 12-10:(D)4.

Richard A. Gephardt
United States Representative,
D-Missouri

2

It is natural that war [such as the recent Persian Gulf war] begets metaphors. If we can build "smart" bombs, surely we can graduate smart kids. If 90 per cent of our soldiers have graduated from high school, how can we be satisfied when only 60 per cent of our civilian workers have?

Speech, February/
The Washington Post, 3-27:(A)21.

Jackie Goldberg
President, Los Angeles
Board of Education

3

If you really want to do something for the low-income minority students, you would provide funding for the kinds of services that it would take to make those students able learners . . . And I think every student can be an able learner if [he or she] has everything they *need* to be an able learner. They need to have the right set of conditions, and we must be willing to spend what it takes.

Interview/
Los Angeles Times, 3-10:(M)3.

Edmund Gordon
Professor of psychology,
Yale University;
Member, New York State
Curriculum Committee

4

The primary reason youngsters need to study multiple cultures is to learn how to develop multiple perspectives. This capacity is essential to developing intelligence. We have, I hope, elevated the question from a political debate concerning whose history to teach to the question of how to enable youngsters to use broad, often conflicting bodies of information to arrive at sound judgments.

Interview/Time, 7-8:19.

Duncan Graham
Chief executive,
National Curriculum Council
(Britain)

5

[On his organization's role of prodding along a national curriculum in Britain]: The educational

(DUNCAN GRAHAM)

establishment, left to its own, will take a hundred years to buy a new stick of chalk. In the end, to say, "It's time you guys got on with it; here's an act and a crisp timetable," was probably necessary . . . When I was first appointed, I used to need a bodyguard when I was going round the country. Now I don't find much opposition at all, though there are great worries about assessment. Not many people, if you ask them if we should abandon the national curriculum, would say yes. It's like sliced bread: Once you've got it, you begin to see some of the benefits. You might change the way you cut the slices, but you keep the principle of the sliced loaf.

Interview/
The Atlantic, May:28,36.

Fred Grandy
United States Representative,
R-Iowa

1

There is an educational bias in this country toward people who follow an education system from kindergarten through college. Sixty per cent of Federal education funds are spent on higher education—but only 30 per cent of high-school students go to college. The lack of attention given to the other 70 per cent has surfaced in the decline of individual income, lagging productivity and an under-educated and non-competitive work-force. My bill [encouraging private-sector investment in high schools and community colleges] corrects these problems by empowering that 70 per cent who chose a different, but no less legitimate, track to the workplace.

Los Angeles Times, 7-14:(D)2.

William Hawkins
Director of financial aid,
Western Connecticut
State University

2

[Saying that, because of economic conditions, many students will be attending lower-tuition state universities rather than costlier insti-

tutions]: Kids that in the past might have gone to Trinity or Wesleyan or the University of Vermont are coming here. Or they're transferring here from private colleges because their parents have lost a job or are afraid of losing it. The middle class is getting hammered, and they are telling their kids, "Hey, we don't have the money for those schools."

The New York Times, 2-9:8.

Pat Henry
President, National
Parent-Teacher Association

3

For a long time, I have watched our nation address priorities, and it seems like kids are never Number 1. There's no way you can talk about education without talking about other social issues that impact a child's life. I'd like to see us put children first. No matter how much money we think we need for defense or the savings-and-loan crisis, we don't knock children down eight rungs and not fund their needs.

Interview/USA Today, 6-24:(A)13.

Paul Hill
Senior researcher,
Rand Corporation

4

The first lesson private schools teach is that schools need a clear mission and they need to be simple. That creates a greater sense of common purpose among students, teachers and administrators alike. It's a false assumption that because public schools are publicly funded they have to be all things to all people. Public-school authorities should create portfolios of schools, each with a different focus, in math and science, say, or vocational education.

Interview/
U.S. News & World Report,
12-9:78.

Bill Honig
California State Superintendent
of Public Instruction

5

[Arguing against too much change too soon in reforming the education system]: Is this the

(BILL HONIG)

French Revolution where everyone tries to outpace the last person in moving further to the left? Well, that ended with everybody killing each other. The real issue we face is how to teach more demanding curricula to a greater number of kids.

Newsweek, 4-22:29.

Judith Richards Hope
Member, selection committee
for the presidency
of Harvard University

1

[For a university president,] you need someone with enormous energy, a brilliant scholar, who has done undergraduate teaching, who gives wonderful testimony before Congress, who is a fabulous fund-raiser . . . God is not good enough to be a university president.

Newsweek, 4-8:49.

Jesse L. Jackson
Civil-rights leader

2

[On school-choice proposals]: Choice by the [President] Bush definition is spraying the leaves and not watering the roots. It's choosing a few children, like one school in 435 districts, but leaving the masses unchosen. It's kind of trickle-down education. Only dogs and fire hydrants seem to get some benefit from trickle down. A sound educational plan must begin with pre-natal care, Headstart, day care, compensatory education, vocational education, scholarships, adequate funding. Not choice for the selected few.

Interview, May 7/
USA Today, 5-8:(A)11.

Franklyn G. Jenifer
President,
Howard University

3

[On using affirmative-action programs when selecting students for admission to universities]: When we talk about affirmative action, it should not be—and has not been in my interpretation—a circumstance of giving special breaks to a population or people. What it should mean, and hopefully does mean, is that you're looking for a diverse population of individuals and you give weight to an individual's differences. That should be no more the case for black students than it should be for students from the Midwest or from the East. You try to choose a student population of different socio-economic circumstances, so that the classroom is not a monotonous environment. That, I believe, is appropriate affirmative action . . . Unfortunately, that's not the way it has worked in America. And many people believe that people are allowed to get in when standards would not normally admit them. Where that is the case, I think those people have bastardized it. That was never its intent.

Interview, Washington/
Los Angeles Times, 2-10:(M)3.

4

[On being a college president]: Today, universities are so much more complex. You are not only expected to be the academic leader of the institution, you must cultivate a series of managerial skills that are not normally achieved in the traditional hierarchy of higher education.

Ebony, November:27.

Donald Kagan
Dean, Yale College

5

Discussion, argument and persuasion are the devices appropriate to the life of the mind—not suppression, obstruction and intimidation. Yet, for more than two decades, our colleges and universities have often permitted speakers to be shouted down [by dissenters] or prevented from speaking, buildings to be forcibly occupied and access to them denied, and various modes of intimidation to be employed, with much success. Most of the time, the perpetrators, in fact, have gone unpunished in any significant way. Colleges and universities that permit such attacks on freedom and take no firm and effective action to deter and punish those who carry them out sabotage the most basic educational freedom. To defend those freedoms is the first obligation

(DONALD KAGAN)

of anyone who claims to engage in liberal education.

At Wooster University, Sept. 30/
The Wall Street Journal,
10-15:(A)18.

Laurel M. Kanthak
Director of middle-level education,
National Association
of Secondary School Principals

1

Many schools are organized as if students are sponges that will absorb whatever comes their way. Instruction is very passive. Students sit at their desks while information is presented to them.

Washington, Jan. 10/
Los Angeles Times, 1-11:(A)25.

Thomas H. Kean
Head, Educate America;
Former Governor
of New Jersey (R)

2

The [high-school] diploma is more a proof of age than it is any kind of achievement.

To reporters/
USA Today, 2-5:(D)8.

David T. Kearns
Deputy Secretary
of Education
of the United States

3

[On education reform]: Business should support the educators and the politicians that are pushing for systematic and structural reform. I believe this is the Number 1 thing business can do—support those individuals who are for real change, not people playing around the edges. Secondly, it is very important for business to play an interactive role with the educators so that on an ongoing basis the educators understand what business requires in the work-place. Thirdly, reform is going to get done community by com-

munity, school by school . . . Lastly, business must agree to create a new learning environment and new American schools. A coalition has to be formed. I think the chambers of commerce can play a role in bringing together the business community, the educators and the politicians.

Interview/
Nation's Business, October:25.

Leroy Keith
President, Morehouse College

4

[On being a college president]: No, this certainly isn't an ivory-tower kind of position. As a college president, you are managing an enterprise that is unique to any enterprise one can imagine. So you not only have to be a good manager with good communication skills, you have to have the talent and foresight to deal with a diverse population with diverse needs.

Ebony, November:27.

Donald Kennedy
President, Stanford University

5

There's a lot of evidence that the public mistrusts all institutions more these days. So why should people like universities? After all, they don't like government, they don't like large corporations, they don't like media and they don't like church—right? . . . We may be part of a more general phenomenon.

Interview/
The Washington Post, 5-6:(A)13.

Jonathan Kozol
Educator

6

States now provide, at most, half of local funding [for schools]. They should pay 80 per cent of the bill. The Federal government, which now pays about 6 per cent, should add another 20. [School funding through the use of local] property tax is nothing more than a form of hereditary privilege for the children of the fortunate.

Interview/
People, 10-7:105.

Richard Lapchick
Director, Center for the Study
of Sport in Society,
Northeastern University

1

Somewhere along the line, the mission of the university has possibly been lost. Sometimes it becomes an athletic mission as opposed to an athletic and educational mission.

The Washington Post, 7-4:(B)8.

Edward A. Malloy
President,
University of Notre Dame

2

[On his school's new multi-million-dollar contract with NBC for televising Notre Dame football games, despite criticism of the contract by other colleges]: With limits to money available from the tax base of states and limits to what the Federal government is making, the great fear at Notre Dame is that we will outstrip our market, that we could not maintain the diversity of our student body. The only way we can remain affordable is by supplementing financial-aid packages from other sources. The primary reason I approved the NBC contract was that it would allow us to substantially increase the resources for financial aid, and a majority of it would be targeted to the students from the poorer socio-economic backgrounds, many of them minorities . . . Every other reason was secondary. It allows us to exercise a resource that is fairly unique to our history.

Interview, Notre Dame, Ind./
The Washington Post, 9-5:(B)4.

Peter McWalters
Superintendent,
Rochester (N.Y.) City
School District;
Commissioner-designate
of Education of Rhode Island

3

[In education,] there are roles to be played at the school level, at the state level, and at the Federal level. And of those right now . . . the state plays the biggest role in whether or not we're going to move toward an outcomes-driven system or a highly regulated system . . . we can talk about the school having more and more authority to make decisions it needs to make. But [state] issues of teacher certification, the minutes a subject is required, the test that's administered by the state, the number of days in a school year—these decisions lock the system in a way that makes some of this discussion about local decision-making really marginal.

Interview, Rochester, N.Y./
The Christian Science Monitor,
12-30:12.

Joe Nathan
Director,
Center for School Change,
University of Minnesota

4

[On proposals for a national student achievement test]: American children are among the most over-tested and under-achieving in the world. We don't need another test; we need to do better with the ones we've got.

USA Today, 2-5:(D)8.

5

More and more school districts are recognizing that traditional schools don't work for all kids and are developing new kinds of options . . . Choice can be used to promote equity. But it does not always do so. We need to be careful about what we do.

The Christian Science Monitor,
3-11:12.

Frank Newman
President, Education
Commission of the States

6

We haven't created a setting in our schools where verbal skills are developed. There is not enough reading because classes aren't reading-oriented. There is not enough debate and discussion because classes aren't debate-and-discussion oriented.

USA Today, 8-27:(D)2.

Gregory M. St. L. O'Brien
President,
University of New Orleans

1

[On the importance of universities located in cities]: Urban universities are doing for the cities in the 1990s what the land-grant colleges did for the rural areas in the 1800s.

The New York Times, 8-13:(A)8.

Donald E. Petersen
Former chairman,
Ford Motor Company

2

I carry with me a horrible worry about the inadequacies of our education system. When you start talking long term, my mind starts visualizing young people coming through K-12 without anything approaching an adequate preparation for higher education—hopelessly inadequate numbers of young people with any real understanding and capabilities in the sciences or math. We must redress that as a society, or Japan will just keep rolling right over us.

Interview/
USA Today, 10-21:(A)15.

James J. Renier
Chairman, Honeywell, Inc.

3

The initial response of the business community with regard to education was to look at it and say, "Gee, we need more math courses and we need more science courses and all of that." But in looking at it we began to understand, also, that we have a giant social agenda that . . . is diluting the ability of the educational system to deliver the academic agenda. One of the major factors is what has happened to little kids. And so, going down that logic tree, one of the best things you can do to help solve the educational crisis in the United States today is to work on the problems that affect little kids from minus nine months to the time they get to kindergarten.

Before House Budget Committee,
Washington, March 6/
The Washington Post,
3-7:(A)21.

F. C. Richardson
President, State University College
of New York at Buffalo

4

Clearly, being a college president is not a matter of making a lot of money. But what it offers is an opportunity to provide a learning environment for young people in which they can become more than they thought they could become. The anticipation that we have the power to make that kind of difference is the real reward.

Ebony, November:34.

David Riesman
Sociologist,
Harvard University

5

What we have now in universities is a kind of liberal closed-mindedness, a leveling impulse. Everyone is supposed to go along with the so-called virtuous positions.

The Atlantic Monthly, March:52.

Robert Rivinius
Member,
California Community College
Governing Board

6

[In the past,] community colleges had veered off course and were out of touch with the economic needs of the state and the training needs of the work-force. [But] today, they provide an ideal setting for companies to retrain their work-force and a place to find new people with real skills.

Los Angeles Times, 5-12:(D)2.

Roy Romer
Governor of Colorado (D)

7

There is a very large malaise in this country on the part of parents as to what it is a youngster needs to reach for to be an educated youngster. We need to have resources and we need to have a re-examination of our own role as parents, and as community leaders, and as educators as to what it is we expect of ourselves and of our children.

Interview/USA Today, 10-1:(A)11.

Robert M. Rosenzweig
President,
Association of American Universities

1

[Being president of a university is] a combination of being a CEO and an elected politician—without the powers of command of a CEO and without the steady constituency of the politician. It's about the hardest job in the United States.

Newsweek, 4-8:48.

2

Universities have lost their immunity from public criticism. There's no longer a presumption in favor of their virtue.

The Washington Post, 5-6:(A)13.

Neil L. Rudenstine
President-designate,
Harvard University

3

[Saying he will speak out nationally on education issues]: I don't see the presidency of Harvard as a bully pulpit. But I am good at listening and gentle persuasion. Instead of throwing rocks and bricks around, I prefer using one's voice in a civilized way.

Interview,
Cambridge, Mass., March 25/
The New York Times, 3-27:(B)9.

Steven B. Sample
President, University of
Southern California

4

[On the "publish or perish" syndrome for professors]: I don't think we will get rid of that. And I don't think we should get rid of it. What I think will happen though is that the balance between research and scholarship will change. One of the interesting things about people, human beings—all of us, for some reason, tend to think in absolutes, either-or terms. So we either emphasize research or we emphasize teaching. Now, let's imagine a research university where the emphasis is 80 per cent upon research and

scholarship for purposes of promotion and tenure, and 20 per cent on teaching. You can change that balance to 60 per cent on scholarship and research and 40 per cent on teaching, and still have primary emphasis on scholarship and research . . . What I think will happen here—and at a lot of other research universities—is that very good teaching will increasingly become an absolute necessity, not sufficient to advance the person, but an absolute necessity.

Interview, Los Angeles/
Los Angeles Times, 9-15:(M)3.

5

I think higher education is on the defensive. I think it has been a target of attack, a kind of preferred target, certainly for the last five and probably for the last 10 years, and I think some of that criticism is well-deserved, but . . . it's become a little mean-spirited and counter-productive. And we've lost sight of a larger truth, a larger reality, which is simply this: The United States has, far and away, the best system of higher education in the world . . . There aren't very many areas of human endeavor left where the United States is the unquestionable best in the world. So to the extent that this criticism is exposing some areas of weakness that need attention—can be fixed—I think it's good. But when it becomes just plain destructive, that's silly.

Interview, Los Angeles/
Los Angeles Times, 9-15:(M)3.

Thomas C. Sawyer
United States Representative,
D-Ohio

6

Urban universities form a very special function in education. That same engine that drove the economy of this nation during the shift from agriculture to urban industrial dominance has the same potential in an urban setting.

The New York Times, 8-13:(A)8.

Benno C. Schmidt, Jr.
President, Yale University

7

[On a new Yale course in Western civilization]: It is one of the aims of liberal education to

(BERNADETTE TOOMEY)

are difficult to refuse. Our experience in working in school systems as different as New York City and Salt Lake City is that when parents and students are offered alternatives, they'll not only choose them, they'll compete for them. And that competition generates new life and new energy in schools.

The Saturday Evening Post,
May-June:30.

Mike Tranghese
Commissioner, Big East
College Football Conference

1

[On statistics showing white college athletes graduating within five years at a rate close to double that of black athletes]: It's troubling to me. A two-to-one difference [between whites and blacks] better be troubling to all of us. If people tell me whites are smarter than blacks by two to one, that's the most absurd conclusion anyone could reach. If people tell me whites work harder than blacks by two to one, that's inconceivable to me. I think it involves the quality of education [received prior to college]. I think it involves socio-economic factors and factors that we don't even understand. It's a very complicated issue, and one that needs further study.

July 3/
The Washington Post, 7-4:(B)1.

Marc Tucker
President, National Center on
Education and the Economy

2

By the time [students in Germany] are 19, they have higher academic skills and higher voca-

tional skills [than students in the U.S.]. Our 19-year-olds are working at Wendy's.

Newsweek, 12-2:62.

Peter V. Ueberroth
Former Commissioner
of Baseball

3

Please teach sometime in your life . . . It's the most honored profession. Unless we care about education, both economically and with our efforts and with our passion, we're not going to be competitive in the next century.

At Rensselaer Polytechnic Institute
commencement, May 17/
USA Today, 5-20:(A)11.

George Will
Political columnist

4

Universities are entrusted with nothing less than a task. Theirs is the task of transmitting the best of the West [-ern civilization]. The real danger is not cultural hegemony but cultural amnesia. A society unaware of itself cannot endure.

At Duke University commencement,
May 12/
The New York Times, 5-13:(A)10.

Pete Wilson
Governor of California (R)

5

It is time for the great American university to return to the abandoned role of moral teacher—not by handing down prefabricated precepts, but by challenging and stretching minds, by compelling analysis to reach a judgment.

At Stanford University, Oct. 1/
Los Angeles Times, 10-2:(A)15.

The Environment • Energy

Nordine Ait-Laoussine
Minister of Energy of Algeria

1

The problem is that there is not now, and there never was, a free oil market. There has always been interference of one sort or another in the oil markets. What we advocate is stability. We can agree on at least that which is good for both consumers and producers so that we can do our economic planning on a sound basis.

> *At Ministerial Seminar for Oil-*
> *Producing and Consuming Countries,*
> *Paris, July 2/*
> *The New York Times, 7-3:(C)4.*

Richard H. Bryan
United States Senator,
D-Nevada

2

We have seen the cost of energy dependence [by the U.S. on foreign oil]—[the Persian Gulf] war. I supported the President's [Bush] policy at every step of the way [regarding the war], but we should not delude ourselves into thinking that wars are always concluded so fast or are so low in casualties [as the recent Persian Gulf war]. The Congress, the President and the auto industry can move forward and reduce our dependence on foreign oil.

> *Los Angeles Times, 4-7:(D)2.*

George Bush
President of the United States

3

Some will argue that reducing our energy vulnerability [dependency on foreign sources] is not enough and that we should embark upon more drastic measures designed to achieve total energy independence. The reality is that we are a long way from total energy independence. We must avoid unwise and unnecessary measures that would seriously hurt American consumers, American jobs and American industries.

> *Before Economic Club*
> *of New York, Feb. 6/*
> *The Washington Post, 2-7:(A)4.*

Ben Nighthorse Campbell
United States Representative,
D-Colorado

4

[Criticizing environmentalists who make it difficult for constituents in his district who make their living from timber, cattle, mining, etc.]: I've never met an environmentalist yet who is in favor of an oil well, a coal mine or a dam. You'd like to think that people out here [in Colorado], who make a living from the land, would have something more to say about it. But what are you going to do? They're Americans. Everybody owns the Federal lands.

> *Interview/*
> *The New York Times, 8-28:(A)12.*

Fernando Collor (de Mello)
President of Brazil

5

Just as the question of development has yielded to other issues on the international agenda, I am concerned that the issue of the environment may also yield to other aspects of the day-to-day life of the world . . . Lasting solutions to global problems require the commitment of the international community as a whole, each country according to its responsibility relating to the origin of these problems and to their management, as well as to its economic and technological capacity to overcome them.

> *At United Nations,*
> *New York, Sept. 23/*
> *The New York Times, 9-24:(A)8.*

Barber B. Conable
President, World Bank

6

Environmental success and failure have already yielded one invaluable truth: that development and environmental protection are mutually dependent. Population size and growth are an urgent manifestation of this relationship. At present rates of increase, 8 billion people will

(BARBER B. CONABLE)

be jostling for space on our planet by the year 2025. As many as 90 per cent of the young will be in developing countries. Sheer pressure of numbers threatens to overwhelm the environment and perpetuate poverty. More hungry mouths to feed means more pressure on fragile soils and rain-forest reserves . . . Good environmental policy is good economic-development policy in almost every sense. Preventing the erosion of millions of hectares of soil helps the environment and small farmers as well. Preventing the poisoning of rivers helps the environment and lengthens the lives of those who drink from those rivers. The reverse is also true—good economic policy is good environmental policy. When, as in too many countries, energy is heavily subsidized, patterns of production are distorted, fiscal balance is threatened and the environment is damaged.

London, March 19/
The Washington Post, 3-21:(A)20.

Bert M. Concklin
Former Assistant Secretary,
Occupational Safety and
Health Administration,
Department of Labor
of the United States

1

With the exception of water and air pollution, which the Environmental Protection Agency is charged with ameliorating, occupational safety and health, and especially health, remains one of the nation's most neglected areas of public policy . . . Reducing health-hazard enforcement to a "cost-benefit" equation . . . has always been highly controversial on conceptual, analytical and moral grounds. However, that system exists and must be dealt with. The often daunting reality of the cost-benefit numbers—for example, the equation says that it costs $2.8-million for each death avoided because of control of grain dust in the work-places—makes it easy to justify going slow or suspending enforcement related to deadly health hazards.

Feb. 4/
The Washington Post, 2-5:(A)17.

William E. Dannemeyer
United States Representative,
R-California

2

[Saying the various environmental groups really make up an "environmental party"]: I think the American public better wake up to the direction the environmental party seeks to take our society. When I say they're green on the outside and red on the inside—they're *red* in the sense that they favor the totalitarian system, you know. The socialist model is the only model that has relevancy [for them] . . . And some of them in the movement believe that all undeveloped land belongs only in public ownership.

Speech to Orange County, Calif.,
business leaders/
Los Angeles Times, 11-18:(A)18.

J. Michael Davis
Assistant Secretary
for Conservation
and Renewable Energy,
Department of Energy
of the United States

3

Renewable energy has enormous promise for clean and abundant supplies. Hydropower, biomass and waste-to-energy technologies are mainstream contributors, and wind, geothermal and solar thermal facilities are becoming increasingly viable . . . Collectively, it offers a diverse and virtually inexhaustible resource . . . It is substantially less harmful to the environment . . . It can contribute significantly to our economic and energy security. [In fact,] the size of the resource is orders of magnitude larger than our foreseeable demand.

The Christian Science Monitor,
8-27:6.

John D. Dingell
United States Representative,
D-Michigan

4

[On the current average price for a gallon of gasoline in the U.S. of $1.10]: What incentive is there to produce an alternative fuel when gasoline is cheaper than bottled water?

USA Today, 3-6:(A)4.

99

Jean Dure
Mayor of Montreal

1

National governments can't really tackle the [environmental] problem without involving cities. As centers of knowledge and creativity with the capacity to mobilize people . . . cities also have the potential to develop solutions.

New York/
The Christian Science Monitor,
7-12:4.

Richard Fineberg
Executive vice president,
Overseas Development Council

2

There is no question the World Bank is taking environmental problems with increasing intensity. There is growing awareness, world-wide, that no-holds-barred development defeats itself if environment spillovers are not addressed.

Los Angeles Times, 5-3:(A)8.

Christopher Flavin
Vice president for research,
Worldwatch Institute

3

The greenhouse [global warming] issue is serious. We need to begin reducing our use of fossil fuels, particularly coal, which is the leading contributor to the problem. But we can reduce our use of coal without turning to nuclear power. Using natural gas to generate electricity would be environmentally superior to nuclear power or coal. We can invest in more energy-efficient technologies: better light bulbs, refrigerators, air conditioners. Every appliance that uses electricity can be made more efficient. Within the next decade, we're going to turn toward solar power, wind power geothermal energy and other sources that have less environmental impact than coal or nuclear power.

Interview/USA Today, 4-25:(A)15.

4

The key problem in terms of oil dependence is clearly transportation, particularly the auto-mobile. The country is going to have to come up with some politically feasible way of getting new technology into the automotive industry and improving the level of fuel economy. Detroit has obviously tended to resist those kinds of policy measures. All of the emphasis seems to go into discussing mandatory standards rather than discussing financial incentives that might move us in the same direction.

Interview/USA Today, 10-17:(A)11.

Judy Knight Frank
Leader, Mountain Ute Indians
of Colorado

5

[Criticizing environmentalists who are fighting against a water-diversion project that they say would imperil the endangered squawfish, but which she says would benefit her tribe]: The environmentalists tell us: "Wait, this isn't the right project. There is something better for your people." But they have yet to tell us what that better thing is. For 100 years, we did not have running water on this reservation. Where were the environmentalists then? They weren't hollering about the terrible conditions for our children. But now, suddenly, the squawfish is so important. More important than the Indian people, apparently.

Interview, Mountain Ute Indian
Reservation, Colorado/
The New York Times, 12-28:8.

Marvin L. Goldberger
Director, Institute for
Advanced Study

6

A truly frightening force that carries the potential for war or general chaos is the population explosion—the unwillingness to come to grips with that, the consumption of resources by our throwaway society. If developing countries strive to achieve standards of living comparable to standards of the developed countries, if you think about that in terms of automobiles, gasoline, air quality, it's terrifying. Those countries say, "Look, you guys can talk all you like about conservation and pollution and the atmosphere, but

(MARVIN L. GOLDBERGER)

we want to eat and we want to live." So it's rather hard to be optimistic.

Interview, Princeton, N.J./
Lear's, June: 16.

Albert Gore, Jr.
United States Senator,
D-Tennessee

1

Global warming is the single most serious manifestation of the violent collision between industrial civilization as it's currently organized and the ecological system of this planet on which life as we know it depends. Other symptoms include the burning of a hole in the ozone layer, the loss of living species at an incredible rate, the loss of tropical rain forests, the polluting of the oceans and freshwater system and the air, and a variety of other related problems . . . We, right now, have an assumption that guides us in our perceptions of the global-warming problem that just ain't so. The assumption is that the Earth is so big, we can't possibly do any lasting damage to it. Nature is so powerful, we can't possibly do any irreparable harm. That used to be so. It is no longer so.

At symposium sponsored by
Environmental Defense Fund, May 17/
The Washington Post, 5-22:(A)20.

Dmitri M. Grodzinsky
Soviet biologist;
Member, Ukrainian
Academy of Sciences

2

[On the 1986 explosion at the Soviet Chernobyl nuclear-power plant]: The scope and the degree of the radioactivity [released] was seriously underestimated from the beginning. It was thought the main danger was from cesium 137, that the strontium 90 fallout had been contained within 30 kilometers of the reactor, the plutonium within 10. But now we are turning up plutonium and strontium right here in Kiev [80 miles south of Chernobyl]. This means that many more people than we believed were subjected to greater doses initially and to continued radiation. It means that they are at far greater health risk than we thought. It means that the cleanup will take more work and more time than we expected. It means, in short, that the long-term consequences of Chernobyl can only be assessed now.

Los Angeles Times, 4-23:(H)6.

Jack Hanna
Director,
Columbus (Ohio) Zoo

3

Someone once asked me whether a zoo is for people or animals. Maybe it's for people, but the animals in captivity are ambassadors for their cousins in the wild. What you're doing is teaching conservation in a fun way. People need to understand what's happening to the earth's wildlife. They need to understand that they have to protect the resources animals need to survive. Because if animals survive, people will survive.

Interview, Columbus, Ohio/
Cosmopolitan, February: 110.

Garrett Hardin
Professor emeritus
of human ecology,
University of California,
Santa Barbara

4

One . . . fundamental [concept about population] rests on the idea of carrying capacity—the limit to the number of animals a given territory can safely support for an indefinite period . . . without damage to the environment. Unless the limitedness of carrying capacity is admitted, there is little point in counting the number of living bodies. When we come to the human species, the concept of carrying capacity must be enlarged to that of the cultural carrying capacity. Human beings are not content to live at the lowest possible level of resource exploitation . . . We prefer to use resources with some extravagance . . . The greater the extravagance—the higher the material standard of living—the lower must be the cultural carrying capacity of the environment.

The Washington Post, 7-25:(A)16.

Walter Hickel
Governor of Alaska (R)

1

[Saying oil drilling should be allowed in Alaska's Arctic National Wildlife Refuge]: If the American people want a national energy policy, if they want to produce more than they buy or import, then [the Refuge] is the best potential . . . I know of no industry on Earth anyplace that spends as much for protection of the environment as [the Alaskan oil industry] . . . They know how to do it right . . . This makes good environmental and good economic sense, and good national security for the free world to have an [oil] field like that available.

USA Today, 3-13:(A)5.

H. Russel Holland
Judge, United States District Court for Alaska

2

[Rejecting a $100-million fine agreed to by Exxon Corporation and the Justice Department stemming from the 1989 Alaskan oil spill, saying the fine is too low]: The fines that were proposed to me were simply not adequate. They do not adequately achieve deterrence. I'm afraid these fines send the wrong message, suggesting that spills are a cost of business that can be absorbed. There is no question that the *Exxon Valdez* oil spill was off the chart.

April 24/
The New York Times, 4-25:(A)1.

Robert Horton
Chairman,
British Petroleum Company

3

[On conservationists and others who urge that the U.S. not open up more areas for oil-drilling]: It's your choice and yours alone not to make the most of your domestic resources. But I would remind you that the competitive costs of that strategy could be considerable.

The Christian Science Monitor,
3-12:8.

James R. Janis
Former Deputy Assistant
Secretary for Planning
and Evaluation,
Department of Energy
of the United States

4

[Then-President] Ronald Reagan came to town in 1981 saying that he wanted to shut down the Energy Department. The demoralizing effects of such rhetoric are still remembered at the DOE's headquarters on Independence Avenue. Casting aside Reagan's anti-bureaucratic themes, [President] George Bush has proposed a DOE budget for fiscal 1992 that increases not only the over-all level of spending, but the number of professional staff members as well—a most welcome departure from the norm.

Feb. 4/
The Washington Post,
2-5:(A)17.

J. Bennett Johnston
United States Senator,
D-Louisiana

5

We're now dependent on imports for 50 per cent of our crude oil. We will be two-thirds dependent in a few years. This is a very, very serious thing, both for the foreign policy of our country and particularly for the economy of the country. It now constitutes over a third of our trade imbalance. And the trends are getting much worse as domestic production goes down and domestic consumption goes up . . . One of the problems of democracy is its inability to think long term. We do that in politics, we certainly do that in energy. These are long-term trends. If we drill and are successful in the Arctic, it will be 10 years before that oil comes to the market. If we provide for a possibility of using nuclear energy, it will probably be eight or 10 years before those plants are on line. As a nation, we've got to think far in the future. And that is part of the challenge.

Interview/
USA Today,
10-17:(A)11.

Patrick J. Leahy
United States Senator,
D-Vermont

1

At a time when we are toughening [pesticide] standards at home, it makes no sense to allow American companies to use a loophole in current law to dump unsafe pesticides abroad—only to have these chemicals show up in imported foods in America's supermarkets.
The Christian Science Monitor,
6-20:10.

Norman Lear
Motion-picture and television
producer

2

You do what you can [to improve the environment], [but] it's very damned hard reorienting your life. I haven't bought a new car in three years. I asked how can I be an environmentalist and not buy a fuel-efficient car. I'm sorry, I wasn't ready to do it. I bought a Mercedes. It's the same human dichotomy everywhere.
Interview, Culver City, Calif.,
Sept. 30/
The New York Times, 10-2:(B)1.

Joseph I. Lieberman
United States Senator,
D-Connecticut

3

[On the oil-market pricing system, especially during the current conflict in the Persian Gulf]: You've got this crazy system of pricing without regard to supply and demand. Do we really want a system where a bunch of young guys screaming in a pit in New York set the price of oil? . . . It's just not good for the rest of us. People see an opportunity to make money, so they're coming in to make money at our expense.
The Washington Post, 1-12:(A)1.

4

[On Iraqi President Saddam Hussein, whose forces set ablaze Kuwaiti oil installations, which polluted the skies, as they were being pushed out

of Kuwait by U.S.-led forces]: I would put him to death. I would impose capital punishment without hesitation. [There is] substantial sentiment [in the U.S. Congress to create] some kind of treaty or convention that would make clear that vindictive assaults on the environment like this would be punished—and punished severely.
Dhahran, Saudi Arabia,
March 17/
Los Angeles Times, 3-18:(A)1.

Ray MacSharry
Commissioner of Agriculture
of the European Community

5

Rural areas are not just where many of our people live, but they are where the rest of us can breathe. The countryside is a source of reassurance and stability in an increasingly and in many respects artificial and synthetic society.
Los Angeles Times, 8-6:(H)3.

Rex Maughan
Chairman, Conference of
National Park Concessioners

6

[Criticizing the suggestion that private-sector concessions in the national parks result in excessive commercialism]: One of the reasons national parks are liked so much is that they have the greatest visitor facilities because the private sector has put money in. If we go to another system and the government gets involved, we will see the degradation of our national parks.
Time, 1-14:46.

J. Michael McCloskey
Chairman, Sierra Club

7

[Criticizing the proposed National Energy Strategy being worked on by the Bush Administration]: One would think the President's advisers would be encouraging him to seize international leadership by reversing the policies that have led the world into yet another energy crisis [Iraq's invasion and take-over of Kuwait in the oil-rich

103

(J. MICHAEL McCLOSKEY)

Persian Gulf]. Instead, the National Energy Strategy options . . . are simply a lump of coal in the stockings of all those who care about the health of the planet that we are leaving to our children. It seems clear that the whole process has been designed to ensure safe profit markets for Exxon and General Motors, not a safe energy future for the American people.

The Washington Post, 1-7:(A)6.

David McTaggart
Executive director,
Greenpeace International

1

You can talk about the "green wave" in the West, where corporations are putting nice pictures of pine trees on their product labels, but the green wave in the Soviet Union is a massive tidal force that is knocking politicians, nuclear-power plants and Western multinationals out of the way. We have had some successes already. The unilateral Soviet moratorium on nuclear testing was straight out of a briefing paper we submitted to [Soviet President Mikhail] Gorbachev . . . The Soviet decision to stop whaling, and to support the creation of a world park in Antarctica, are other areas where we've managed to get our foot in the door.

Interview/
Mother Jones, March-April:33.

Susan Merrow
President, Sierra Club

2

[Arguing against allowing oil drilling in Alaska's Arctic National Wildlife Refuge]: It is the last pristine arctic ecosystem on Earth. [Drilling] is too high a price to pay to sacrifice this national treasure . . . Even under the best of circumstances, by the government's own estimates, there's only a 1-in-5 chance of finding oil, and then only about 3 billion barrels [a 6-month U.S. supply].

USA Today, 3-13:(A)5.

George J. Mitchell
United States Senator,
D-Maine

3

[On the phenomenon of global warming caused by emissions of "greenhouse gases"]: We [the U.S.] are alone among industrialized nations in opposing even the concept of setting an emissions reduction target and deadline. Ignoring this problem will simply make it worse . . . Delay reduces our options and increases the final cost of action . . . The decade of the 1980s includes some of the warmest years on record. This week, temperature records are being broken across the country as we experience April in February. The potential of temperature shifts that previously occurred over thousands of years instead taking place in a matter of decades, confronts us with an unprecedented event . . . Even as we are forced to focus our attention on the deadly clash of military forces [in the current Persian Gulf war], the long-term survival of our planet demands that we keep a focus on natural forces as well. In the long term, those forces will determine how we live as certainly as the outcome of war.

Before the Senate,
Washington, Feb. 5/
Los Angeles Times, 2-6:(A)17.

W. Henson Moore
Deputy Secretary of Energy
of the United States

4

[Saying the U.S. should boost its oil output]: I'm not aware of any country that has the capacity [to produce oil] that is saying, "Let's save it" . . . That's a strategy that we don't understand, nor do we see any logic to it.

The Christian Science Monitor,
3-12:8.

Allen E. Murray
Chairman, Mobil Corporation

5

[Saying the U.S. has too many environmental restrictions against oil and gas drilling]: Does our government *really* think other governments don't care about the environment? The fact is, they *do*

(ALLEN E. MURRAY)

care. But they also include economic factors in their decision-making. They recognize the risks. They also recognize that this industry has proven its ability to develop the world's energy supplies while taking care of the environment. Drilling goes on in the North Sea where violent storms can be unrelenting . . . In Africa, emerging nations recognize the need to build their economies for their people . . . In the Soviet Union and other nations of Eastern Europe, the U.S. petroleum industry is being sought after for its technology, its investment capability, its know-how. And we will go. To Eastern Europe, to Africa, to Latin America. To wherever the search leads us. We will explore. We will develop the energy resources of other lands and, in the end, import some of those same resources into the United States. By importing energy instead of finding and producing economic supplies ourselves, the country is, in essence, exporting jobs and the paychecks that go with them. It is sending profits and royalty revenues overseas. It is losing government funds that would otherwise be gained by taxing the money that could be earned here. Most important, it is surrendering the opportunity for economic growth.

Before American Petroleum Institute,
Houston, Nov. 19/
USA Today, 11-21:(A)11.

Hisham Nazer
Minister of Petroleum
of Saudi Arabia

1

[On Iraqi forces setting Kuwaiti oil fields ablaze as they were being driven out of that country, which they invaded and occupied last year]: The purpose of the Iraqis was to put the Kuwaitis out of production for a long while. They probably feel that if everything goes back to normal [in Iraq], they will be able to export more oil if Kuwait production is shut in. [The destruction of Kuwait's oil facilities] is disastrous for Kuwait. But, on the world level, consuming nations have shown they can do without both Kuwait and Iraq for the time being . . . [Iraqi President] Saddam Hussein was practicing economic despotism on

prices, demanding they be raised to $25 to $30 a barrel whatever market conditions said. He is doing the same thing now in burning the Kuwait fields. He imposes political or military conditions on oil.

Interview, Riyadh, Saudi Arabia/
The Washington Post, 3-5:(D)4.

Dixy Lee Ray
Former Assistant Secretary,
Bureau of Oceans and
International Environmental
and Scientific Affairs,
Department of State
of the United States

2

In 1989, the Food and Drug Administration made a very extensive survey of foods on the market and found that 61 per cent of all the food that we eat had absolutely no pesticide residue at all. And of the remainder, only 1 per cent had enough pesticide that it actually exceeded the very, very conservative standards that are set . . . The Environmental Protection Agency bends over backward to be conservative. And that's right. But the risks are vastly exaggerated. A Stanford University study showed the risks of any pesticide residue on tomatoes is exaggerated 2,600 times. And so it goes with lots of other foods.

Interview/
USA Today, 4-22:(A)7.

William K. Reilly
Administrator,
Environmental Protection Agency
of the United States

3

In 1989, we made more referrals for civil action against corporations than ever in EPA history. We exceeded that record last year. More criminal actions, more fines, significantly more jail time. If you break the law, you're going to pay. Environmental crimes are every bit as serious as any other kind of crime.

Interview/
USA Today, 4-3:(A)13.

(WILLIAM K. REILLY)

1

The National Academy of Sciences has said that 10 per cent to 40 per cent of greenhouse gases could be reduced without serious economic disruption, possibly with net savings. I accept that estimate. I tell you why I believe that, and why economists sometimes miss it: I once served on the board of an electric-power company. When the company had great trouble winning permission to locate plants for new generating capacity, it turned to conservation, and found the opportunities were enormous. Through insulation, installing boilers, financing new conservation equipment, it was surprisingly easy to cut fuel use, and thus also greenhouse-gas emissions, in a way that enhanced the bottom line.

Interview, Washington/
Los Angeles Times, 6-2:(M)3.

2

Environmental protection requires a formidable array of analytic tools, but it is not purely a technocratic affair. Cost-benefit and risk analysis are vitally important, but there is something more fundamental, too: an ethical imperative to restore and conserve the natural order . . . We enter into the dimension of morality here, morality that instructs politics and stands above economics. One of the first concerns of a moral order must be to clarify and uphold principles of conduct that promote the survival and fulfillment of the species. That compels us to recognize and correct the disharmony in the relationship between nature and humankind . . .

At Conference on Environment for Europe,
Dobris Castle, Czechoslovakia, June 21/
The Washington Post, 7-10:(A)20.

Greg Rueger
General manager,
Pacific Gas & Electric Company

3

[Saying the Bush Administration should not be ignoring renewable energy sources]: They seem to have a belief . . . that renewables are not going to be cost-effective in this country for many years. [But] many renewable-generation options are technically feasible today, and with encouragement can prove to be fully cost competitive . . . within 10 years . . . Federal and state agencies and regulators have not generally endorsed renewables as a significant part of their energy-policy objectives. This has created a self-fulfilling prophecy in terms of the role of renewables. Because they are unrecognized, they are under-used. And because they are under-used, they remain unrecognized.

Interview/
The Christian Science Monitor,
3-14:6.

John Sawhill
President,
Nature Conservancy

4

Attitudes [about the environment] are changing. As I travel around the country, I really get the sense that everyday Americans are really becoming more and more concerned about their environment. They realize that one of the great things we have in this country is an abundance of land, and if we don't protect it, it's just going to get developed and we'll lose it forever.

Interview/
USA Today, 5-13:(A)7.

Janette Sherman
Physician;
Specialist in toxicology

5

The residues in pesticides can result in problems ranging from respiratory difficulties to diarrhea, from birth defects in a child born to a mother who consumed them, to cancer . . . If your broccoli is contaminated with pesticide A, and your oranges are contaminated with pesticide B, and your office is sprayed by a pest-control company, and your neighbors have their lawn sprayed, it accumulates. None of us is exposed to just a single source. The problem becomes cumulative.

Interview/
USA Today, 4-22:(A)7.

C. J. "Pete" Silas
Chairman,
Phillips Petroleum Company;
Chairman, United States
Chamber of Commerce

1

Right now, public policy in the U.S. actively discourages the development of domestic energy supplies... The energy strategy we've employed is to import more and more crude oil. We've shut down nuclear-power plants, taken away the investment tax credit, and taken away lease land [available for oil and gas exploration]. This policy of discouragement has to change. More domestic energy would diminish the importance of Middle Eastern oil, substantially improve our balance of payments—imported oil has accounted for 55 per cent of our foreign trade deficit the last two years—and encourage economic activity here in the U.S. As an oil man, I think it is a shame that we have locked away the areas of this country that have the greatest potential for oil and gas discoveries.

Before Carnegie Council on Ethics
and International Affairs,
New York/
Nation's Business, June:46.

Derek Spencer
Senior scientist, Woods Hole
Oceanographic Institute

2

[Saying deep-sea dumping of garbage may be an appropriate method of dealing with the growing waste problem]: I don't think anyone wants to advocate ocean dumping. But the waste problem is there and it's not going away. Indeed, it is going to get far worse. Perhaps the bottom of the sea is the best place for some wastes. Yet nobody wants to hear that.

Woods Hole, Mass., Jan. 10/
The Washington Post, 1-11:(A)3.

James D. Watkins
Secretary of Energy
of the United States

3

[Saying higher fuel taxes to cut gasoline use are unpopular with Americans]: Americans . . .

really do believe the Bill of Rights gave them $1.06-a-gallon unleaded regular [and they say] "that's what the government better give us, or we'll get the bums out of office" . . . [Taxes] simply won't get through [Congress] because people want to get elected again. It's easy to say, "We should change our life-style [to save energy], and we should be more conservative. We shouldn't be so self-interested." I agree with all that. After that's all over, what do you do about it? . . . I don't believe that we're going to go in and tell the American people how to live. They want to drive. They want to drive on the open plains, and we've got to somehow use our technological genius, which is the best in the world, and help them do that.

At meeting sponsored by
Center for Strategic and
International Studies/
The Christian Science Monitor,
3-4:8.

4

[Criticizing the shutdown of the Shoreham, Long Island, New York, nuclear-power plant for safety reasons]: The Federal government made a serious mistake in 1987 by not immediately attacking the flawed rationales for Shoreham shutdown. It's silly to shut down a plant that cost $6-billion, that had 1,000 megawatts of capacity in an electricity-starved area, where the risks were extremely small, if not negligible. To replace the lost power will require fossil sources producing carbon dioxide, at the time the same people who don't like Shoreham are talking about global warming. It's preposterous . . . For people to be hyped by politicians and warped science into irrational terror of nuclear power is sin. The rate-payers of Long Island don't understand that they are going to experience a significant growth in their rate base and get nothing in return . . . So many nuclear-power opponents and people in the media just don't know what they are talking about. That's why anyone in the science business, like DOE, must now be in the education business.

Interview,
Washington/
Los Angeles Times, 8-11:(M)3.

Brooks Yeager
*Vice president,
National Audubon Society*

1

[Criticizing President Bush's new energy plan]: The only balance I can find in the strategy is the balance between the oil industry and the nuclear industry. The oil industry gets the nation's premier wildlife refuge [the Alaska National Wildlife Refuge] and the nuclear industry gets quick one-stop licensing for reactors that no one can afford. There is nothing to do with automobile fuel economy, no gas-guzzler tax, no oil import fee, nothing to move us away from oil reliance in the long term.

Feb. 8/Los Angeles Times, 2-9:(A)19.

Government

Jack Anderson
Political columnist

1

[On leaks of secret government information to the press]: The American people cannot find out what their government is doing from official spokespersons. And because there is no press secretary who can churn out the other side of the story, we have to rely on confidential sources . . . If we [in the press] are to perform our function, which is to be the eyes and ears of the people who own the government and who are entitled to know what their government is doing, then we must have leaks. They're more valuable than official spokespersons.

USA Today, 10-28:(A)13.

Benjamin Barber
Professor of political science,
and director of the
Walt Whitman Center,
Rutgers University

2

There's no question that at the local level democracy works naturally and works well. But it is also the case that we live in a world of institutions and problems that are not only national but also international and interdependent. Solutions that re-emphasize the local level run up against the historical reality that we are a nation, as well as the facts that power is being deployed in international arenas and that reaction at the local level is ineffective. Besides, at this national level the rhetoric of duty *is* alive and well. Consider that the President [Bush] has dispatched almost a half million American troops abroad, without Congressional authorization and with considerable public discontent and a little of my own, but with an overwhelming majority agreeing that the young still have a duty to respond to the country's call.

Panel discussion/
Harper's Magazine,
February:50.

Robert S. Bennett
Special Counsel to the U.S. Senate
Ethics Committee

3

[On five Senators charged with ethical wrongdoing in a savings-and-loan scandal involving financier Charles Keating]: This Congress faces many very difficult choices. It faces a Federal deficit of disturbing dimensions. Our financial institutions and their viability are being called into question and, most importantly, there is an imminent possibility of military action of enormous consequence [in the Persian Gulf]. In comparison to these crises, some may say that ethics [in government] is unimportant; but I say to you that to accept this conclusion would be a terrible mistake. Because, with an economy in trouble and a war hanging over our heads, it is all the more important that the American people have confidence in their representatives, that they have confidence in the Senate, that they have confidence in you, in your ability to judge your peers and reach an honorable and ethical decision . . . The ultimate constituent disservice that you can perform is to tell the American people that you just don't have the standards to deal with this case. The ultimate constituent disservice that you can deliver in this case is to allow partisanship or friendship or relationships or the need for each other not to make the tough judgments in this case. And the ultimate disservice that you can perform to this institution is to allow the Keating Five to exist today, tomorrow and for all time. The ultimate constituent disservice is to tell the American people, "Well, we don't have any rules, but we'll take care of it in future legislation. We won't make the tough judgments in this case" . . . Once and for all, members of this Committee, so this travesty never happens again, you, with future legislation and with tough judgments in this case, must tell the people that this institution which you call a temple has no room for the money changers of the world like [financier] Charles Keating.

Closing presentation at the "Keating Five" hearings,
before Senate Ethics Committee, Washington, January/
The Wall Street Journal, 1-31:(A)14.

(ROBERT S. BENNETT)

1

Let me talk briefly about standards [of ethics in the Senate]. Senate Resolution 338 . . . encompasses conduct that is improper in and of itself and conduct that is improper because it creates the appearance of impropriety. These are two separate and distinct bases on which this Committee can conclude whether or not any particular Senator before you has violated the standards of conduct . . . It is no defense in an ethics case to say, "I didn't commit a political act in return for money." If that were a defense, the standard of ethics of this body would be "anything short of bribery is permissible." The world is not divided between felons and ethical people. The standards of this body must be the highest.

Closing presentation at the
"Keating Five" hearings,
before Senate Ethics Committee,
Washington, January/
The Wall Street Journal,
3-4:(A)10.

Joseph R. Biden, Jr.
United States Senator,
D-Delaware

2

[On the recent sensational Senate Judiciary Committee hearings into allegations that Supreme Court nominee Clarence Thomas sexually harassed a female assistant 10 years ago]: I know of no system of government where when you add the kerosene of sex, the heated flame of race and the incendiary nature of television lights, you're not going to have an explosion. I know of no institution that has been created by mankind that can contain that conflagration.

Washington, Oct. 15/
Los Angeles Times, 10-16:(A)6.

Barbara Boxer
United States Representative,
D-California

3

We're 40 years [after the first woman U.S. Senator, Margaret Chase Smith] and there are

[now only] two women [in the Senate]. The only way to put that in optimistic terms is to say it is a 100 per cent increase. [At that rate,] our children's children's children's children would be fossils [before women made up 50 per cent of the Senate as they do the population]. There's really something wrong with a democracy that doesn't represent more than half its population. Just remember when [President] George Bush calls his advisers into the back rooms of the White House, they all look like him.

Beverly Hills, Calif./
Los Angeles Times, 10-7:(A)3.

Edmund G. Brown, Jr.
Candidate for the 1992
Democratic Presidential nomination;
Former Governor of California (D)

4

[On his Presidential campaign]: I admit I have some problems to overcome. But I've got to try to turn this system around. Somebody's got to try. Our democracy has been the object of a hostile take-over. Government has become a Stop & Shop for every conceivable greedy and narrow interest. There are no new ideas and no real debate. We're down to a single political party: the incumbent party.

Interview,
Manchester, N.H./
The New York Times, 12-28:7.

Ron Brown
Chairman,
Democratic National Committee

5

People are very cynical now and very disillusioned with politicians and gridlock in government. We've had the unfortunate confluence of events where in 1980 [then-President] Ronald Reagan rode into Washington beating up on government. Government was the enemy and that attitude has permeated the American psyche. That's very dangerous for a democracy.

Interview/
USA Today,
12-18:(A)13.

Willie L. Brown, Jr.
*Speaker of the California
Assembly (D)*

1

The [ballot-] initiative process has no place in government. In a democracy, there really should not be the availability of the initiative . . . In a representative form of government, there ought to be an opportunity to intelligently debate issues, to suggest proposed solutions and then to build a consensus based upon a majority. That's best handled through the representative process where fair and objective evaluations are given, where the implications from a management standpoint as well as a cost standpoint are always properly assessed and properly produced.

Interview/USA Today, 4-16:(A)11.

George Bush
President of the United States

2

. . . government programs have tried to assume roles once reserved for families and schools and churches. This is understandable, but dangerous. When government tries to serve as a parent or a teacher or a moral guide, individuals may be tempted to discard their own sense of responsibility, to argue that only government must help people in need. If we've learned anything in the past quarter century, it is that we cannot Federalize virtue.

*At University of Michigan
commencement, May 4/
The Wall Street Journal,
5-10:(A)12.*

3

The most common challenge to Presidential powers comes from a predictable source . . . the United States Congress.

*At Princeton University, May 10/
Los Angeles Times, 5-11:(A)16.*

4

[In Presidential relations with Congress] there is a frustration level, and . . . it is harder, given the fact the other party controls both houses of the Congress, to get the things done that I want done—or to put it more broad-mindedly, get the things done that I think I was elected to do. Therein lies a frustration. But I have to accept the fact that the Executive Branch is ours [Republicans'], the Congressional Branch is controlled by the [Democratic] leaders

*Broadcast interview,
Los Angeles, June/
The Washington Post, 6-21:(A)15.*

5

America's problem-solving does not begin or end with the Congress nor with the White House. The Congress can refer our proposals to its hundreds of committees, tie itself up with debate and produce complicated, expensive, unworkable legislation. But, in the end, we must carry forward the magic of America.

*Speech to guests on White House lawn,
June 12/
The Washington Post, 6-13:(A)8.*

6

[On rumors of scandal that adversely affect the confirmation of high Presidential appointees, such as current allegations that CIA Director nominee Robert Gates was involved in the Iran-contra affair]: They [reporters and politicians] ought not to accept a rumor. They ought not to panic and run like a covey of quail because somebody has made an allegation against a man whose word I trust. What have we come to in this country where a man has to prove his innocence against some fluid, movable target? . . . I just don't think it's the American way to bring a good man down by rumor and insinuation.

*To reporters,
Kennebunkport, Maine/
Newsweek, 7-22:21.*

7

. . . all the world's woes cannot be solved by voluntary service. Our society can't survive without an efficient, compassionate government that can preserve people's liberties, that can establish a rule of law vital for civilized life and

111

(GEORGE BUSH)

that can do its part to help those in need in many, many ways.

At ceremony honoring Point of
Light award winners,
Orlando, Fla., Sept. 30/
Los Angeles Times, 10-1:(A)18.

1

Congress ought to follow the same laws that it imposes on everyone else. More than a dozen laws apply to the Executive Branch but not to Congress. Most of these laws apply to everyone in America except members of Congress. Congress does not have to comply with the Equal Pay Act of 1963. It does not have to follow Title VII of the Civil Rights Act of 1964, a title that prohibits sexual harassment and discrimination on the basis of race, color, sex, religion and national origin. It doesn't have to obey the provisions of the Americans with Disabilities Act of 1990, the Age Discrimination in Employment Act. I would wager that the American people do not know that Congress has exempted itself from the sexual-harassment laws private employers and the Executive Branch must obey . . . When Congress exempts itself from the very laws that it writes for others, it strikes at its own reputation and shatters public confidence in government. These exemptions encourage special-interest groups to press them for reckless regulations, knowing that Congress might adopt such laws if it won't feel the sting of these laws. This practice creates the appearance and reality of a privileged class of rulers who stand above the law.

October 24/
The Wall Street Journal,
10-28:(A)14.

2

The genius of the Bill of Rights is that it limits its attention to truly important things—and to things over which a just and limited government can exercise some actual control. Today, one often hears the concept of rights attached to specific social services or material standards of living. The framers, however, did not elevate

acquisition of even the most vital goods and services to the status of rights.

Speech commemorating 200th
anniversary of Bill of Rights,
Orange, Va., Dec. 16/
The New York Times, 12-17:(A)16.

Robert C. Byrd
United States Senator,
D-West Virginia

3

The Senate honoraria system is widely perceived as being one of the most serious ethics problems in Washington today. [There is a] widespread perception that elected officials are untrustworthy, corruptible and purchasable.

The Washington Post, 5-22:(A)4.

Bill Clinton
Governor of Arkansas (D)

4

I may be wrong about this, but I have a feeling . . . that one of the things [former] President Reagan tried hard to do was lower the expectations of the American people about the Presidency in terms of an instrument for solving domestic problems, and President Bush has continued that.

The Washington Post, 7-26:(A)17.

Bill Clinton
Governor of Arkansas (D);
Candidate for the 1992
Democratic Presidential nomination

5

[Criticizing President Bush's emphasis on volunteerism rather than Federal action]: Here in Arkansas, we worked very hard against very steep odds to create more jobs and educate our people, and every one of us in our own way tried to be one of the 1,000 points of light [mentioned by Bush in his Presidential campaign in 1988]. But I can tell you, my friends . . . where there is no national vision . . . a thousand points of light leaves a lot of darkness.

Announcing his candidacy for the
1992 Democratic Presidential nomination,
Little Rock, Ark., Oct. 3/
Los Angeles Times, 10-4:(A)24.

(BILL CLINTON)

1

Because they want to use government to help people, Democrats have to put Congress in order. Congress should live by the laws it applies to other work-places. No more midnight pay raises . . . No more bounced checks. No more bad restaurant debts. No more fixed [parking] tickets. Service in Congress is privilege enough.

Speech at Georgetown University,
Oct. 23/
The Washington Post, 10-24:(A)32.

John D. R. Cole
Director,
Public Management Institute,
George Mason University

2

There's an automatic tendency for government organizations to grow rather than to stay constant or shrink. You find changes of direction, growth or increases in program initiatives, [but] you see very few proposals to decrease or abolish [existing] government functions.

The Washington Post, 9-16:(A)8.

Alan Cranston
United States Senator,
D-California

3

[On his being reprimanded by the Senate for doing special favors for financier Charles Keating in exchange for political contributions]: I ask you this: How can you rationally refuse to give legal and proper help at any time to someone who seems to have a reasonable grievance, because he or she has contributed to your campaign? Can you only help people who haven't contributed? Or can you only help people who haven't contributed lately? How lately? And must you refrain from helping people who might contribute in the future? How far in the future? . . . I believe the only remedy is to get money out of politics. Therein lies salvation for you, for the Senate, and most of all for the American people who are the ultimate losers until we end the role money plays or seems to play in our decision-making, and end the business of Senators and would-be Senators having to spend more and

more of their time chasing the money needed to fund a successful [election] campaign.

Before the Senate,
Washington, Nov. 20/
Los Angeles Times, 11-21:(A)26.

Robert Dallek
Professor of history,
University of California,
Los Angeles;
Author of a biography of the
late President and Senator,
Lyndon B. Johnson

4

I think [Lyndon Johnson] was the greatest Senate majority leader in history. His personal power made the position important. The Johnson "treatment" is legendary. He'd back you into the corner, press his nose against yours, tower over you, put his arm around you. He also understood when to speed up or slow down debate, when to settle things in a back room. He knew what each Senator liked to eat and drink, needed politically, wanted personally. He changed the seniority rules and provided choice assignments to younger Senators. That was good for the Senate, and it obligated them to him.

Interview/Time, 7-29:6.

Christopher J. Dodd
United States Senator,
D-Connecticut

5

[Calling for a ban on honoraria to Senators from special interests]: Let's not delude ourselves. You are not being invited [to appear before special-interest groups] because you are a great orator, because you are Cicero. They are paying you $2,000 because they think you might listen to them . . . We must end the perception that the men and women who serve in this body have a price tag on them.

Before the Senate,
Washington/
Los Angeles Times,
5-22:(A)4.

John Eck
Associate director,
Police Executive Research Forum,
Washington

1

My feeling is the cultural differences between the United States and Canada are more than we tend to give them credit for. The public in the United States and Canada have very different notions of what is the role of government. In the United States, people seem to think the government is something to be worried about. Canadians seem to have very much more the idea that the government is on their side.

Los Angeles Times, 4-23:(H)4.

Marlin Fitzwater
Press Secretary
to President of the United States
George Bush

2

Chances are, when I can't be found I don't want to be found. In many ways, silence is the only weapon I have, and I use it very carefully.

People, 2-11:35.

3

[On criticism of Vice President Dan Quayle's use of military aircraft wherever he flies, even on vacations]: The Vice President of the United States flies on military aircraft wherever he goes. That is right and proper and in accordance with all of the concerns for that office, and for the security of a Vice President and his role in our Constitutional process. And that will not change. The American people do not ask their elected officials to give up their lives to take these positions. [Top Administration officials should not be expected] to live like hermits while they're in these offices.

Los Angeles Times, 5-3:(A)28.

Thomas S. Foley
United States Representative,
D-Washington;
Speaker of the House

4

[On President Bush's announced plan to turn over certain Federal programs to state govern-

ments]: It's very easy to say that they [state governments] are closer to the people, but I don't think as a general rule we would say that every local program in every city is the best administered in the country simply because it is at a local level. I mean, that's sort of a warm thought, but it isn't our practical experience.

The Washington Post, 1-31:(A)7.

Anthony M. Frank
Postmaster General
of the United States

5

The Postal Service is not a business. It's a business-like public service. I could cut out $5-billion in one day. But our charter is to provide universal, uniform service to the American people, which means everybody gets the same service at the same rate. Compared to almost any other country, we are certainly the cheapest postal service and probably the best and getting better. People don't seem to understand. Would companies compete [with the Postal Service to deliver mail in] Manhattan? Yes. Would they compete for the Bronx? I don't think so.

Interview/
U.S. News & World Report,
3-4:12.

Bill Frenzel
Former United States Representative,
R-Minnesota

6

[Supporting term limits for members of Congress]: Congress has become a professional legislature, where members come early, stay late, and die with their boots on.

Nation's Business, November:25.

Leonard Garment
Lawyer; Former Adviser to the
President of the United States
(Richard M. Nixon)

7

Political life in a democracy requires elbow room, play in the joints. If we try to codify the complexity of American life and culture—make

(LEONARD GARMENT)

it all square corners—we're going to stumble into rigidity, anger, hostility. It will be different species talking to each other rather than a conversation within a common culture where there are differences that are resolved, negotiated, reconciled.

Interview, Washington/
The Christian Science Monitor,
11-26:14.

William H. Gray III
United States Representative,
D-Pennsylvania

1

The power of the Speaker [of the House] is overestimated. The power of the Congress is overestimated. It's the Executive Branch [that has the power]. Congress reacts, alters slightly, deflects and, when lucky, stops.

USA Today, 9-10:(A)2.

Tom Harkin
United States Senator,
D-Iowa;
Candidate for the 1992
Democratic Presidential nomination

2

[On how he plans to finance the government programs he is espousing]: Implicit in that question is the assumption that we're poor, we're broke. Well, let me disabuse you of that notion. We may be 14th out of the 16 industrialized [nations] in what we spend on education. We may be 10th in infant mortality. But guess what? We're the richest country in the world. The money's there. We've just got to start spending it smarter.

The New York Times, 12-10:(A)14.

Vaclav Havel
President of Czechoslovakia

3

In a number of professions, you can immediately see the results of your work. If you're a bricklayer, you see the wall you've built; and if you're a writer, you can see the book you've written. In politics, your work is never visible enough. And that's what I don't like.

Interview, Prague/
Vanity Fair, August:159.

Stephen Hess
Senior fellow,
Brookings Institution

4

Leaks have been around as long as governments have had secrets. In the early days of Congress, from time to time a journalist was actually jailed in the Congress for leaking. As long as people have information that they think is useful for them to get out through informal channels, and as long as there are reporters anxious to publicize this information, there are going to be leaks.

Interview/
USA Today, 10-28:(A)13.

Jesse L. Jackson
Civil-rights leader

5

[Advocating statehood for the District of Columbia]: We [D.C.] had more youth in the Persian Gulf [war] than 20 states. Yet when our youth come home and the parade is over on June 8, they will not have the same rights at home for which they risked their lives in the Persian Gulf [D.C. has no Congressmen or Senators]. The people who live here have no rights that Congress is bound to respect. We can't even elect our own judges. Why does the cradle of democracy deny the citizens of its capital those basic rights that we affirm for people around the world? We were taught to be willing to die for a place we had never been and for people that we've never seen, Kuwaitis [in the recent Persian Gulf war], on that principle of self-determination. How can you love and be committed to the liberation of a land that you've never been to, people you've never seen, and not have that same regard for the neighbor next door? We [who live in D.C.] are the neighbor next door.

Interview, May 7/
USA Today, 5-8:(A)11.

J. Bennett Johnston
United States Senator,
D-Louisiana

1

[Approving the Senate's recent vote to increase their own salaries]: No one can fail to grasp the significance of the fact that there are staff members on the House side making more than U.S. Senators, that Federal judges make more, that Federal bureaucrats make more.

July 18/
The New York Times, 7-19:(A)10.

Barbara Jordan
Professor of government,
University of Texas, Austin;
Former United States Representative,
D-Texas

2

I am very disheartened by the public perception of politicians not having the public welfare at heart because I absolutely believe politics is an honorable profession. I wish more people would see politicians as public servants, because that's what they are . . . When ethical problems arise, the base is usually some act of greed or self-interest or money. I believe only a very small percentage of people who are in public office are guilty of wrongdoing, of abusing their public trust . . . [But] if ever you decide you want to get rich, then get out of government because, if you don't, I'll visit you in jail.

Interview/Time, 6-3:9,10.

Robert M. Kimmitt
Under Secretary for Political Affairs,
Department of State
of the United States

3

I've always felt that the best way that one can serve in public service is to maintain as low a profile as possible and keep your boss out front where the proper focus belongs. I respect the senior-subordinate relationship [with Secretary of State James Baker], just as Secretary Baker does in his relationship with President Bush.

Interview, Washington/
The New York Times, 1-3:(A)4.

Scott Klug
United States Representative,
D-Wisconsin

4

[On Congressional scandals, such as the recent revelation that some members bounced checks through the House bank and were not penalized by the bank]: This House continues to act as if its routine business affairs are classified information. That is wrong. If the Freedom of Information Act applied to Congress, these records would have been public for years, and this scandal would have ended a decade ago . . . Now we are going to see reporters mailing out surveys again to find out who has eaten thousands of dollars of free lunches [without paying for them] at the House dining room. Now Congress is trying to shush up those names, too. If that information was public, I know those outstanding bills, some dating back to 1985, would have been paid long, long ago. This has never been a fight to embarrass individual members. It has been about the institution's attempts to hide everything, and that is the big embarrassment for us all.

Before the House,
Washington, Oct. 3/
The Washington Post, 10-8:(A)18.

Peter H. Kostmayer
United States Representative,
D-Pennsylvania

5

[On revelations that some members of Congress have bounced checks at the House bank, which did not penalize them]: I don't think I or anyone else should get away with it. I made a mistake and it's wrong. We [members of Congress] have to live like everyone else, we have to eat like everyone else, we have to bank like everyone else and we have to park like everyone else.

The Washington Post, 10-4:(A)16.

Lloyd Leonard
Legislative director,
League of Women Voters

6

[Arguing against term limitations for members of Congress]: The Presidency is a very

(LLOYD LEONARD)

powerful office, and our system is based on a balance. It is our feeling that by cutting back too sharply on the ability of members of Congress to gain expertise and knowledge about government, the President would become much too powerful.

The Christian Science Monitor,
7-29:8.

Thomas E. Mann
Director of governmental studies,
Brookings Institution

1

[As a politician in government,] it's hard to be both responsible and provocative. To take on problems seriously is to anger as many people as to please them. And to take actions merely to please people is to weaken one's credibility as a governing party.

At Democratic National Committee's
spring meeting, March 22/
The Washington Post, 3-23:(A)6.

Romano L. Mazzoli
United States Representative,
D-Kentucky

2

[On public criticism that the House of Representatives' bank honored many overdrawn checks of House members and did not impose penalties on those checks]: I had had a meeting with some constituents the day the news broke. It was an issue raised by the constituents, and raised in a way that was very hurtful to me in that it reflected extremely unfavorably on the House as an institution. It's a minuscule amount of money, but it says that members of Congress are saying that the normal rules don't apply to them.

Interview, Sept. 30/
The New York Times, 10-1:(A)12.

John McCain
United States Senator,
R-Arizona

3

In public life you not only have to be careful

about what you do but you have to be careful about what you appear to do.

At Senate Ethics Committee hearing
investigating possible wrongdoing
by him and four other Senators,
Washington, Jan. 4/
The Washington Post, 1-5:(A)4.

Steven A. Merksamer
Former Chief of Staff
to the Governor of California
(George Deukmejian)

4

Nothing is more euphoric, heady or fun than doing a gubernatorial transition [from one administration to another] because you have the luxury of time . . . But after you take office, that's when the rubber meets the road. That's when the tough choices have to be made. It's very sobering. The fun has ended and the work begins. And each day generally gets harder in the first year—you're doing so many things for the first time: learning the players, which legislators can you trust, which legislators can't you trust.

Los Angeles Times, 1-11:(A)28.

Edmund Morris
Presidential biographer

5

[On the possibility of war in the Persian Gulf area between U.S.-led forces and Iraq]: At times of crisis, the Commander-in-Chief [the President] represents the best or the worst in us. If the war goes badly, so does the President. On the other hand, the Presidents we consider the greatest—Washington, Lincoln, F. D. R.—were all warrior Presidents.

The New York Times, 1-16:(A)6.

Frank H. Murkowski
United States Senator,
R-Alaska

6

[On the controversy over the Senate's recently voting itself a raise in salary]: I have no problem with my salary being [raised so that it is] equal to the House. It's kind of amusing from our point of

(FRANK H. MURKOWSKI)

view. We haven't seen the world fall in as a result of the House getting their raise.

July 18/
The New York Times,
7-19:(A)10.

Ralph Nader
Lawyer; Consumer advocate

1

[Criticizing the Senate's recent vote to increase their own salaries]: [The Senate leaders] led a narrow majority of avaricious Senators to a huge pay increase directly in the face of massive deficits, cutbacks in critical programs, S&L bailouts, scandals and unemployment.

July 18/
The New York Times,
7-19:(A)10.

Neil Newhouse
Republican Party
public-opinion analyst

2

As successful as [President] Bush was and the U.S. was in the [recent] Persian Gulf war, Americans seem to expect that same kind of success, or at least the same vigor and energy, on the domestic front. So they become frustrated... They see how quickly we can marshal our resources to attack a foreign enemy, but they are frustrated with how slowly we attack our domestic problems.

The Christian Science Monitor,
7-25:2.

William Proxmire
Former United States Senator,
D-Wisconsin

3

Being a U.S. Senator is the best job on the face of the earth. If the perks were reduced, you'd still have the same number of people running.

USA Today,
10-4:(A)8.

Diane Ravitch
Assistant Secretary
for Educational Research and
Improvement, Department of
Education of the United States

4

[On her leaving a professorship at Columbia University to work in the U.S. government]: I now work for an organization and I can't say all the outrageous things I might have said as a private person... I look at the way the money is spent, and I find it time and again very frustrating. I find studies about studies and research about research. I say to myself, who is this helping? It's like a job program for the research community. Now, I like the research community. I'm from it. I'm one of them. But I think research should help people.

Interview, Washington/
The Washington Post, 8-22:(A)21.

William K. Reilly
Administrator,
Environmental Protection Agency
of the United States

5

One thing you learn about Washington is how many power centers have to be consulted and mollified to get policy made. And that the system can become paralyzed when confronting issues that require sacrifice or changed habits.

Interview, Washington/
Los Angeles Times, 6-2:(M)3.

James Reston
Journalist

6

In my mind, the principle is fairly well established that a politician's personal behavior is not relevant until it clearly is interfering with his public responsibility. Franklin Roosevelt's fiddling around—I don't think that was important. Jack Kennedy's, I think, was important... As a general rule, I'm not at all sympathetic to those who say that we in the press are too nosy. I'm for being nosy. I don't even rule out the prospect that if a guy will cheat on his wife, he'll cheat on a lot of other things. I don't make an apology

(JAMES RESTON)

for feeling that there is a connection between character, keeping promises and telling the truth in private life and applying those principles to public life.

Interview/
U.S. News & World Report,
10-28:81.

Rozanne L. Ridgway
President, Atlantic Council;
Former Assistant Secretary
for European and Canadian
Affairs, Department of State
of the United States

1

There is still a sense in government that the traditional fields of national security, defense, nuclear policy and intricate diplomacy are just not things that women do. Women do social policy. Women do environment. Women do humanitarian things.

The New York Times, 5-20:(A)16.

David Roberti
President Pro Tem
of the California State Senate

2

The whole business of government is building majorities.

Los Angeles Times, 11-29:(A)30.

Barbara Roberts
Governor of Oregon (D)

3

The states are where the action is. There is not a lot of movement at the Federal level. The Governors are the innovators.

Interview/
The New York Times, 8-22:(A)16.

Sharon Rodine
President, National Women's
Political Caucus

4

Congress is 94 per cent male and the vast majority run for re-election, so you have a very

small window of opportunity for women—or any other new blood—to enter that . . . arena. They're all in pin-striped suits, striped shirts and red power ties.

USA Today, 7-12:(A)8.

Edward J. Rollins
Co-chairman, National
Republican Congressional
Committee

5

There are a lot of people in this town (Washington) who . . . think they are very important—special assistants think they are very important. But there really are really 537 people who have votes—the President, the Vice President, 100 Senators and 435 House members. Just about everybody else lives off their reflected power.

To reporters, Washington, July 23/
The Washington Post, 7-24:(A)17.

Warren Rudman
United States Senator,
R-New Hampshire

6

[Saying he is not interested in being U.S. Attorney General]: It's important to be independent. It's a problem in that kind of policy-making post, where anyone who has strongly felt views about the law and how it is administered could run afoul of some third-level, 29-year-old wimp in the White House. I think one of the major problems Cabinet officials have is not the President himself. It's a coterie of people about the President who don't like people who are independent-minded.

Interview/
The Washington Post, 6-7:(A)21.

Martin Olav Sabo
United States Representative,
D-Minnesota

7

It used to be that in order for groups to pass legislation, they had to speak to groups other than themselves. Since then, the arena shifted from politics to the courts. Some political skills were lost in the process. The rhetoric of speaking to your most loyal constituents is very different from trying to speak to persuadables. When your rhetoric is designed to mobilize the committed, you can alienate the persuadables.

The Washington Post,
6-6:(A)15.

Ron St. John
Executive director,
Citizens for Congressional Reform

1

[Calling for term limits for members of Congress]: It's in the American tradition. Thirty-one Governors have their terms limited; the President has. With more people involved in the process, it would have to become more responsive to the people and more good legislation would be passed because you wouldn't have people so obsessed with re-election.

Interview/
USA Today, 8-14:(A)9.

Bernard Sanders
United States Representative,
I-Vermont

2

[On his being the only socialist in the House]: Let me be frank. Do I think there are people who will dislike me in the Congress because of my style and because of my views? I do. I did not come here to be one of the nicest guys or be elected the most pleasant member of Congress. The people of Vermont did not send me down here to get patted on the back. If there are some people who don't like me, there's nothing I can do about it . . . But I hope people don't confuse bluntness with rudeness. Too many times around here people say, "My honorable good friend, colleague this and that." I say, "Okay, come on, let's get to the issues."

Interview,
Washington/
The Washington Post,
7-9:(D)2.

Terry Sanford
United States Senator,
D-North Carolina

3

[On Senators who are suspected of ethical misdeeds and are investigated by the Ethics Committee]: Anybody that in any way gives the appearance of wrongdoing is going to go through an ordeal. You know, just the ordeal of being heard, the ordeal of having all of this played in the papers is, I think, a pretty good signal. Certainly my experience [as a member of] the Ethics Committee has made me a lot more careful.

Washington, Aug. 2/
The New York Times, 8-3:11.

L. William Seidman
Chairman,
Federal Deposit Insurance
Corporation

4

This government of ours doesn't so much govern as decide among interests. A huge amount of bargaining and compromising is going on at all times. But more compromising went on at the Constitutional Convention. It's the only way to run a country like this.

Los Angeles Times Magazine,
5-5:42.

John Seymour
United States Senator,
R-California

5

[Criticizing the Senate's recent vote to increase their own salaries]: It's an issue of merit pay. If you're running a business, you don't give yourself a raise when you're in the red and your firm isn't producing.

July 18/
The New York Times, 7-19:(A)10.

Christopher D. Stone
Professor of law,
University of Southern California
Law Center

6

A citizen's character is not being nourished when a good civic act is made to be a duty. Take

(CHRISTOPHER D. STONE)

voting. In some countries, the government compels you to vote. But if liberty is to mean something, I think we should be free *not* to vote. The founders understood that liberty implied such a choice. By definition, duties are antithetical to liberty, because they oblige you to do something whether you want to or not.

Panel discussion/
Harper's Magazine,
February:46.

Roger Stough
Professor of Northern Virginia
local government,
George Mason University

1

[On the large growth of local government, such as in the area around Washington, D.C.]: You had 10 years of growth, and governments got quite used to anticipating that. They are not bottom-line organizations like the private sector. They are looking at whether they are satisfying 10,000 interest groups.

The Washington Post, 9-16:(A)1.

Nadine Strossen
President,
American Civil Liberties Union

2

There is a trend for government to become more and more involved in intimate aspects of individual life and of family life. Though much civil-rights legislation has been positive, it is inevitable that any government, of no matter what party, what ideology, has a tendency to aggrandize its own power.

U.S. News & World Report,
3-25:12.

Anita A. Summers
Professor of public policy
and management,
Wharton School of Business,
University of Pennsylvania

3

Since the beginning of the 1980s, the prevailing political philosophy has been that govern-

ments should shed what services they can [and turn them over to private business to do]. When you add to that prevailing philosophy the fiscal imperatives that are arising in a lot of cities . . . you add a lot more momentum to the privatization process.

The New York Times, 5-14:(A)8.

John H. Sununu
Chief of Staff to President
of the United States
George Bush

4

[Defending his use of a White House limousine and driver to make a trip to New York on private business]: The White House counsel said that that travel was both proper and appropriate . . . Let me make a couple of things clear . . . Number one, my job is a seven-day-a-week, 24-hour-a-day job. That's why I have a door-to-door car and driver assigned to me. I have to be able to communicate, to work on sensitive papers, to coordinate the White House activities, even while I'm traveling . . . While driving. Constantly on the phone, dealing with issues that needed an immediate involvement. That is a real part of my job . . . And it is not only a critical part of my being able to do that, but it is in the national interest . . . And even while involved in other activities, I constantly have to go and communicate back to the White House every 10 or 15 minutes to make sure what's going on . . . I'm going to continue to utilize the tools that are necessary for me to meet my responsibility to the President of the United States.

Broadcast interview/
"This Week with David Brinkley,"
ABC-TV, 6-16.

Dick Thornburgh
Attorney General
of the United States

5

We [at the Justice Department] are all here to serve the President. If the President wants advice on how best to combat an element of crime, say the savings-and-loan problem, he looks to us. We make recommendations, and I don't think we've

(DICK THORNBURGH)

ever been turned down. On civil rights, we work closely with the people who are calling the policy shots at the White House, but the legal work is done here. Supreme Court appointments are probably a little different. That's the President's appointment, and everybody circles the wagons to serve him.

Interview/
The New York Times, 3-26:(A)12.

Lawrence E. Walsh
Independent Counsel
investigating the Iran-contra scandal;
Former president,
American Bar Association

1

The greater the number of people [in government] responsible for wielding executive power, the greater the chances there are that power will be abused. [The American people] are not prepared to impeach a President who did not rein in one or two of his advisers who have acted improperly. It is thus not surprising that while Presidents since Truman routinely "accept responsibility" for the actions of their subordinates, the President's supporters usually portray misdeeds as isolated incidents. As a result, no one is truly held accountable.

Lecture sponsored by New York City
Bar Association, April 18/
The Washington Post, 4-19:(A)21.

Murray Weidenbaum
Director, Center for the Study
of American Business,
Washington University;
Former Chairman, Council of
Economic Advisers to the
President of the United States
(Ronald Reagan)

2

The day that members of the Congress can run for re-election saying, "Look at the pork-barrel legislation that I killed, including the pork in our own district," the day they can campaign on that and get re-elected, that's when we'll begin to see light.

Interview/USA Today, 7-17:(A)13.

William F. Weld
Governor of Massachusetts (R)

3

Our government should be driven not by standard operating procedures and incrementally drawn budgets but by clearly defined goals . . . Fewer rules and more results—that's my definition of entrepreneurial government. The result of such an approach will be a leaner, more flexible government and a healthier economy to support a generous social conscience.

Inaugural address, Boston, Jan. 3/
The Washington Post, 1-4:(A)3.

L. Douglas Wilder
Governor of Virginia (D)

4

Perhaps the single most important role of any public official is to be an independent voice speaking for the people, particularly when it becomes abundantly clear that so-called conventional wisdom is actually working against the best interests of the people.

New Hampshire, August/
Los Angeles Times, 9-3:(A)15.

Jim Wright
Former United States Representative,
D-Texas;
Former Speaker of the House

5

How would I describe life after Congress? It was like stepping off a treadmill onto stationary earth.

At unveiling of his portrait in the
Capitol's Statuary Hall,
Washington, July 10/
The Washington Post, 7-11:(A)13.

Walter Zelman
Executive officer-designate,
Los Angeles City
Ethics Commission

6

I am concerned with declining public participation in politics and declining public confidence in governmental institutions. When public

(WALTER ZELMAN)

confidence in government institutions erodes, people stop participating in government. And when people stop participating in government, then private interests and special interests tend to be strengthened because they will always participate. So the current crisis in public confidence and in public participation erodes the capacity of the general public to have its voice heard in political and governmental decision-making.

Interview/Los Angeles Times, 1-13:(D)9.

Law • The Judiciary

Jimmy Banks
Executive director,
Committee for Judicial Merit Selection
(Texas)

1

[Saying judges should not be required to go through the political-campaign election process as politicians do]: There's a big difference between a good judge and a good politician. [Judges] should be influenced by the law and the facts of the case, and not by . . . public sentiment.

The Christian Science Monitor,
6-27:7.

Joseph R. Biden, Jr.
United States Senator,
D-Delaware

2

[On his Judiciary Committee's questioning of Supreme Court nominees at their confirmation hearings, which now include queries as to the nominee's judicial philosophy]: This Committee used to dance around character and dance around judicial temperament rather than frontally saying we have a right to know . . . what direction the nominee would take this country in. The irony is, once we've crossed that threshold finally, now we find ourselves in a position where the process is viewed as a caricature of itself.

To abortion-rights advocates/
The Washington Post, 9-21(A)7.

3

[Saying he does not support confirmation of Clarence Thomas for the Supreme Court]: I do not share the certainty of some who are voting against Judge Thomas that he will be as extreme as some of his statements could lead one to believe he might be. As a matter of fact, my heart tells me he won't. My heart tells me he'll be a solid Justice. So some might ask, why not vote your heart, Biden? Why not vote your instincts? I might be prepared to vote my instincts and my heart were the state of the Court and the state of

the nation different than it is now. But I am not prepared to rest on an instinctual feeling and in my heart, at a time when the Court is on the verge—separate and apart from the issue of [abortion]—on the verge of making some truly profound decisions that will or could reverse the 40 years of progress . . . And so I'm casting this vote [against Thomas] with my head and not with my heart.

At Senate Judiciary Committee hearing
on the Thomas nomination,
Washington, Sept. 27/
The New York Times, 9-28:8.

4

[On being Chairman of the Senate Judiciary Committee, which is holding hearings into charges of sexual harassment made against Supreme Court nominee Clarence Thomas]: I must start off with a presumption of giving the person accused the benefit of the doubt. I must seek the truth and I must ask straightforward and tough questions, and in my heart I know that if that woman [Anita Hill, who is making the allegations of harassment] is telling the truth it will be almost unfair to her. On the other hand, if I don't ask legitimate questions, then I am doing a great injustice to someone [Thomas] who might be totally innocent. It's a horrible dilemma, because you have two lives at stake here.

Interview, Washington, Oct. 9/
The New York Times, 10-11:(A)12.

Harry A. Blackmun
Associate Justice,
Supreme Court
of the United States

5

Having been appointed by a Republican President and being accused now of being a flaming liberal on the Court, the Republicans think I'm a traitor, I guess, and the Democrats don't trust me, and so I twist in the wind, I hope, beholden to no one, and that's just exactly where I want to be.

Columbus, Ohio, Oct. 24/
USA Today, 10-25:(A)3.

124

Robert H. Bork
Former Judge,
United States Court of Appeals
for the District of Columbia;
Former nominee for
Associate Justice,
Supreme Court
of the United States

1

A lot of Americans are confused about the [Supreme] Court. They think the Court is a sort of big daddy legislature that does good things regardless of what the Constitution says. As a result, the courts have become the place to go if you can't get what you want from the legislature. [Former President] Ronald Reagan said he wanted judges who would interpret the Constitution. Most people agree with that. But most people also can't believe there isn't something in the Constitution protecting what they think ought to be done . . . If you say to the American Civil Liberties Union, "That's not in the Constitution," they always say, "Aha, the Ninth Amendment says there are things not in the Constitution that judges should do." But that's reading the Amendment incorrectly. The framers thought of the Federal judiciary as an insignificant branch of government. There would have been enormous debate if they had had any idea that the Ninth Amendment would be used to make up rights, because that would defeat the democratic process. It goes back to the fact that the people who resisted a Bill of Rights were fearful that we would get the impression that only what was stated as a freedom was important. But it's not a warrant for judges to make up rights. It's an admonition to the body politic.

Interview/Life, Fall:98.

Bill Bradley
United States Senator,
D-New Jersey

2

[On the proposed Senate judiciary Committee hearings into allegations by Anita Hill that Supreme Court nominee Clarence Thomas sexually harassed her 10 years ago]: The real issue here for the Senate is the truth. And that is what the American people expect us to find out when serious allegations are made about a nominee to a lifetime appointment to the highest court in the land. To settle for less than the truth, instead of a sincere attempt to discover the truth, is to tell the American people that the process is seriously flawed.

Before the Senate,
Washington, Oct. 8/
The Washington Post, 10-11:(A)2.

Steven Brill
Founder, "American Lawyer"
magazine

3

I'm frustrated that the average guy driving a taxi thinks the legal system works the way it does for Clint Eastwood in [the movie] *Dirty Harry,* with weak judges and stupid prosecutors and dumb juries, or as it does on [TV's] *L.A. Law,* where people who have a dispute at 10 past 10 can get it solved by 10:35.

The New York Times, 6-28:(B)10.

George Bush
President of the United States

4

Nowadays, many respond to misfortune by asking, "Whom can I sue?" Even worse, many would-be Samaritans wonder, "Will someone sue me?" Talented, concerned men and women avoid such noble professions as medicine for fear that unreasonable and undefined liability claims will force them to spend more time in court than in the office or in the hospital.

At University of Michigan
commencement, May 4/
The Wall Street Journal,
5-10:(A)12.

5

[On Clarence Thomas, Bush's nominee to fill the vacancy on the Supreme Court created by Justice Thurgood Marshall's announced resignation]: The fact that he is black and a minority has nothing to do with this sense that he is the best qualified at this time. I kept my word to the American people and to the Senate by picking

(GEORGE BUSH)

the best man for the job on the merits. And the fact that he's a minority, so much the better.

News conference,
Kennebunkport, Maine, July 1/
The Washington Post, 7-2:(A)6.

Robert C. Byrd
United States Senator,
D-West Virginia

1

[On Anita Hill's allegations that Supreme Court nominee Clarence Thomas sexually harassed her 10 years ago]: I believe Anita Hill. I believe what she said. I watched her on that [TV] screen intensely and I replayed . . . her appearance and her statement. I did not see on that face the knotted brow of satanic revenge. I did not see a face that was contorted with hate. I did not hear a voice that was tremulous with passion . . . This woman was not fantasizing. As one who has lived a long life and who has had the opportunity to see many people in this life and all walks of life, I think I have some ability to judge another person when I listen to that person, when I look into his eyes to determine in my own view what he is fantasizing, whether he is out of his mind, whether he is some kind of nut, whether he is a psychopath. It comes through. None of that came through in Anita Hill's statements.

Before the Senate,
Washington, Oct. 15/
The New York Times, 10-16:(A)12.

Guido Calabresi
Dean,
Yale University Law School

2

[On the nomination of Clarence Thomas for the Supreme Court]: None of the great [Supreme Court] Justices of the past—not Justice [Hugo] Black, nor Justices [John] Harlan or [Potter] Stewart, nor Justice [Oliver Wendell] Holmes nor Justices [Louis] Brandeis or [Benjamin] Cardozo, not even Justice [Felix] Frankfurter, for all his years of Constitutional law—came to the Court fully formed. The Court itself and the

individual cases that came before them shaped them, even as they shaped the Court . . . [Thomas'] history of struggle and his past openness to argument, together with his capacity to make up his own mind, make him a much more likely candidate for growth than others who have recently been appointed to the Supreme Court.

At Senate Judiciary Committee
hearing on the Thomas nomination,
Washington, Sept. 17/
The New York Times, 9-18:(A)10;
Los Angeles Times, 9-18:(A)15.

George Cochran
Professor of law,
University of Mississippi

3

[On Rule 11, which gives Federal judges the right to fine lawyers and their clients for bringing frivolous cases to court]: Everyone's concerned about the rule, but the civil-rights bar in particular feels aggrieved. There is a perception among civil-rights and public-interest lawyers in this country that they may be practicing law at their own peril before the wrong judges.

The Washington Post, 4-12:(A)17.

Mario M. Cuomo
Governor of New York (D)

4

[Criticizing Supreme Court nominee Clarence Thomas]: From everything I hear and the more I hear, the less I like about his instinct, which is apparently to diminish the importance of individual rights, of individual freedom, of the part of the Constitution that gives you privacy, that gives you personal freedom from undue intrusion. I think he's weak on that.

Broadcast interview/
"Face the Nation," CBS-TV, 7-14.

John J. Curtin, Jr.
President,
American Bar Association

5

[Criticizing Vice President Dan Quayle's statements that the U.S. has too many lawyers

(JOHN J. CURTIN, JR.)

and too much litigation]: Anyone who believes a better day dawns when lawyers are eliminated bears the burden of explaining who will take their place. Who will protect the poor, the injured, the victims of negligence, the victims of racial discrimination and the victims of racial violence?

At American Bar Association convention,
Atlanta, Aug. 13/Time, 8-26:54.

John C. Danforth
United States Senator,
R-Missouri

1

[On Senate Judiciary Committee confirmation hearings for Supreme Court nominees]: The forum is a very unnatural forum for anybody. To appear [as a nominee] in the Senate caucus room with batteries of cameras and 14 Senators peppering you with questions is not the typical evening around the fireplace.

USA Today, 9-10:(A)11.

2

[Criticizing allegations of sexual harassment made against Clarence Thomas, nominee for the Supreme Court]: This whole confirmation process has been turned into the worst kind of sleazy political campaign, with no effort spared to assassinate the character of Clarence Thomas. [Senate] staff members, interest-group representatives, fanning out over the country, trying to drum up whatever they can to attack [Thomas'] character . . . One hundred days ago today, Clarence Thomas was nominated for the Supreme Court of the United States. For 100 days the [anti-Thomas] interest groups and their lawyers and various staff members of the Senate have combed over the record of Clarence Thomas. For 100 days they have examined footnotes and law-review articles to question him about, sentences and articles taken out of context, speeches made in a political context, which are then analyzed and criticized before the Judiciary Committee. One hundred days this has gone on. And [now, because of these last-minute sexual harassment allegations,] people say, oh, no, wait,

we need more, we need more time. That's a tactic, Mr. President . . . I don't think there should be a delay [in Senate voting on the confirmation of Thomas]. This poor guy has been tortured enough . . . I have said in my opinion a delay would serve no purpose whatever. And that's how I feel about it . . . But Clarence Thomas has said to me on the phone, "I have to clear my name. I have to restore what they have taken from me. I have to appear before the appropriate forum and clear my name" . . . And [so] I ask for a delay [in the vote].

Before the Senate,
Washington, Oct. 8/
The New York Times, 10-9:(A)10.

3

[Criticizing the recent leak of a secret FBI report that has led to public allegations by Anita Hill that Supreme Court nominee Clarence Thomas sexually harassed her 10 years ago]: What's the reason for the secrecy of FBI reports? What is the reason for Senate rules providing that FBI reports are not supposed to be released to the public? What is the reason why a Senator who releases an FBI report can be expelled from the United States Senate? The reason is that it is manifestly unfair to an individual to release an FBI report, and that's what happened here. And you talk about unfairness. What is more unfair than to have a person's character called into question as the lead item on the network news? What is more unfair to an individual than to have Senator after Senator go on the [Senate] floor and say, oh, we don't know enough [about the nominee]?

Before the Senate,
Washington, Oct. 8/
The Washington Post, 10-9:(A)25.

Alan M. Dershowitz
Professor of law,
Harvard University

4

[Criticizing the rule in some states prohibiting trial lawyers from speaking with jurors after a trial]: We just are afraid of finding out how juries work. The American judicial system is like

(ALAN M. DERSHOWITZ)

making sausages. You eat them, but you don't want to know what's in them.

The New York Times, 10-18:(B)11.

Sara-Ann Determan
President,
District of Columbia
Bar Association

1

I am sympathetic to the idea that the community be aware of what the bar is doing to protect them from the very, very occasional bad actor within our ranks . . . But I am concerned about the potential for mischief and serious damage particularly when . . . the complaint grows out of heated litigation.

The Washington Post, 5-22:(A)17.

Alan J. Dixon
United States Senator,
D-Illinois

2

[On allegations by Anita Hill that Supreme Court nominee Clarence Thomas sexually harassed her 10 years ago]: Under our system, the burden falls on those making allegations. Under our system, the person being accused gets the benefit of the doubt. That is not a legal loophole; it is a basic, essential right of every American. If we are not to become a country where being charged is equivalent to being found guilty, we must preserve and protect that presumption. Since the Judiciary Committee hearings [into the allegations] did not overcome that presumption, that means Professor Hill's allegations cannot be used to justify a vote against [confirmation of] Judge Thomas.

Before the Senate,
Washington, Oct. 15/
The Washington Post, 10-16:(A)19.

Alan Ellis
President,
National Association of Criminal
Defense Attorneys

3

[Saying the Supreme Court, which is already cracking down on the ability of prosecutors to turn down potential jurors based on race and sex, may put the same restrictions on defense attorneys]: In a line of cases over the past five years, the Court has slowly but surely been moving toward a moment of truth on this issue. There's quite a bit of language in the decision this week to suggest that the Court will be just as hard on race-based jury exclusions by defenders as it already is on prosecutors.

The New York Times, 4-5:(B)12.

Marlin Fitzwater
Press Secretary
to President
of the United States
George Bush

4

[On the forthcoming Senate confirmation hearings for Supreme Court nominee Clarence Thomas]: We do not question judicial nominees about their positions on specific issues that may come before the courts and we expect the Senate would be no different. [The Supreme Court needs] open-minded individuals who have no prior commitments to us or the Congress on specific issues.

Sept. 9/Los Angeles Times, 9-10:(A)4.

Kenneth Geller
Partner, Mayer, Brown & Platt,
attorneys at law;
Supreme Court specialist

5

Footnotes [on Supreme Court opinions] are the repository of a great number of unnecessary and often ill-considered legal pronouncements, many of them drafted by one law clerk answering another. Yet, lower courts and litigants are bound to follow the Supreme Court's footnoted musings.

The New York Times, 1-4:(B)11.

William F. Gibson
Chairman,
National Association for
the Advancement of
Colored People

6

[Announcing the NAACP's opposition to Supreme Court nominee Clarence Thomas, a

(WILLIAM F. GIBSON)

black]: In the final analysis, Judge Thomas' judicial philosophy is simply inconsistent with the historical positions taken by the NAACP. We have concluded that Judge Thomas' confirmation would be inimical to the best interests of African Americans . . . [At the same time,] we were very troubled by having to confront [the idea of opposing Thomas]. We believe the importance of an African American as a replacement for [retiring black Justice] Thurgood Marshall should not be underestimated.

News conference, July 31/
The Washington Post, 8-1:(A)1,4.

Todd Gitlin
Professor of sociology,
University of California,
Berkeley

1

[On the Senate Judiciary Committee hearings into allegations by Anita Hill that Supreme Court nominee Clarence Thomas sexually harassed her 10 years ago]: There is something appalling in this process that couches it as a melodrama offering only two roles. There's this notion that either someone is telling the truth or lying, either someone is heinous or magnificent . . . I think it would be a great service to try to change the terms of it, so it's not either he's lying or she is, but something else.

The Washington Post, 10-15:(E)1.

Ira Glasser
Executive director,
American Civil Liberties Union

2

[On selection of a successor to Thurgood Marshall, who just announced his retirement as Associate Justice of the U.S. Supreme Court]: We're calling on the Senate to take an aggressive role as a barrier to any appointment of anybody who does not view the role of the Court as a bulwark of liberty and the role of the Court in curbing legislative and political excess.

June 27/
The Washington Post, 6-28:(A)19.

Charles E. Grassley
United States Senator,
R-Iowa

3

[Supporting confirmation of Clarence Thomas for the Supreme Court]: Of course, Judge Thomas did not [during his confirmation hearings] give us his legal or personal view of the most contentious of issues that have been raised, and of course the most contentious issue of our day, and that's abortion. And he was not obligated to do so. I'd like to remind my colleagues and also the American people that the confirmation process was never intended to be a campaign trail.

At Senate Judiciary Committee hearing
on the Thomas nomination,
Washington, Sept. 27/
The New York Times, 9-28:8.

Orrin G. Hatch
United States Senator,
R-Utah

4

[Supporting confirmation of Clarence Thomas for the Supreme Court]: I find the suggestion that Judge Thomas may have been following a "political strategy" in declining to answer certain questions [during his confirmation hearings] to be extremely ironic. I think some in the majority on this [Senate Judiciary] Committee have done more to politicize the confirmation process than anybody in history, and I believe Judge Thomas is trying to preserve the independence of the Judiciary . . . [As for his experience,] of the 105 Justices on the Supreme Court, 41 of them had no judicial experience whatsoever. And [I'm] talking about some of the greatest Justices who ever sat on the Court . . . There are 10 more who had less than two years experience. So [Thomas has] had as much experience on the court in judicial circles as better than half of the Supreme Court of the United States of America who have ever sat there.

At Senate Judiciary Committee hearing
on the Thomas nomination,
Washington, Sept. 27/
The New York Times, 9-28:8.

Drew Hays
Professor of law,
Yale University;
Former Assistant Attorney General
for Civil Rights,
Department of Justice
of the United States

1

[On President Bush's forthcoming decision on whether to appoint a black to the Supreme Court to fill the vacancy to be created by black Justice Thurgood Marshall's resignation]: George Bush has an opportunity to approach greatness. He can do something that is extraordinary—to demonstrate that he is not an ideologue. If he appoints someone who is not ideologically kindred [to Bush], if he feels the Court as an institution needs a certain amount of balance and variety of perspectives and different senses of how the law operates in this country—that would be greatness.

Los Angeles Times, 6-28:(A)24.

Wade J. Henderson
National legislative director,
National Association for the
Advancement of Colored People

2

[On the nomination of Clarence Thomas, a black, for the Supreme Court]: We really want that kind of [racial] diversity on the Court. At the same time, race alone is not the criterion for selecting an individual for the Court. We believe Judge Thomas is entitled to a fair evaluation of his record. We believe his views and his stated positions are far more important than his race. We think it's extremely harmful if a black person on the Court tends to provide legitimacy to efforts to roll back substantial protections and rights, which we believe Judge Thomas would do.

Interview/USA Today, 9-10:(A)11.

Anita F. Hill
Professor of law,
University of Oklahoma

3

[On her allegations that Supreme Court nominee Clarence Thomas sexually harassed

her 10 years ago]: [Some people say] that this is somehow a political ploy that I am involved in [to keep Thomas from being confirmed to the Court]. Nothing could be further from the truth. There is absolutely no basis for that allegation, that I am somehow involved in some political plan to undermine the nominee. And I cannot even understand how someone could attempt to support such a claim. But I would ask that what you do is to look at the fact that this has taken a great toll on me personally and professionally, and there is no way that I would do something like this for political purposes . . . I want an official resolution of this. My integrity has been called into question, by people who have never spoken to me, that have not considered the facts carefully as far as I know, and I want an official resolution of this because, at this point, the issue is being deflected. People are talking about this as a political ploy . . . I resent the idea that people would blame the messenger for the message rather than looking at the content of the message itself and taking a careful look at it, and fully investigating it. And I would hope that the official process will continue, and that careful investigation of this information be done.

News conference,
Norman, Okla., Oct. 7/
The Washington Post, 10-8:(A)10.

4

[On her allegation of past sexual harassment made against Supreme Court nominee Clarence Thomas]: I believe that [his] conduct reflects his sense of how to carry out his job. That, in effect, he did not feel himself compelled to comply with the guidelines that were established by the EEOC [where they had both worked and where she claims he engaged in sexual harassment], and therefore it undermines his ability to faithfully enforce those guidelines. And I think that what has to happen is really for the members of the Senate to consider that [when deciding on Thomas' confirmation]. And that's all that I want to bring forth. If the members of the Senate carefully consider this and investigate it and make a determination, then I have done what I'm obligated to do. But until that happens, I think that none of us have done our jobs . . . This

(ANITA F. HILL)

should not be judged on the basis of whether or not there was sexual harassment [in the legal sense] or not. It seems to me that a person shouldn't have to violate a law in order for his character to be called into question. So I'm not talking about an allegation of a violation of a Federal law.

News conference,
Norman, Okla., Oct 7/
The New York Times, 10-8:(A)12.

1

[On her allegations that Supreme Court nominee Clarence Thomas sexually harassed her 10 years ago]: It is only after a great deal of agonizing consideration that I am able to talk of these unpleasant matters to anyone except my closest friends. As I've said before, these last few days have been very trying and very hard for me and it hasn't just been the last few days of this week. It has actually been over a month now that I have been under the strain of this issue. Telling the world is the most difficult experience of my life ... I have no personal vendetta against Clarence Thomas. I seek only to provide the Committee with information which it may regard as relevant. It would have been more comfortable to remain silent. I took no initiative to inform anyone. But when I was asked by a representative of this Committee to report my experience, I felt that I had to tell the truth. I could not keep silent.

At Senate Judiciary Committee hearing
on the Thomas nomination,
Washington, Oct. 11/
The New York Times, 10-12:11.

2

[On the recent Senate hearings into allegations of sexual harassment she made against Supreme Court nominee Clarence Thomas]: It seemed that every 15 minutes I was being subjected to yet another new theory as to why I broke my [10-year] silence. It was suggested that I had fantasies, that I was a spurned woman and that I had a martyr complex. I will not dignify those theories except to assure everyone that I am not imagining the conduct to which I testified. I have been deeply hurt and offended by the nature of the attacks on my character. I had nothing to gain by subjecting myself to the process. In fact, I had more to gain by remaining silent.

News briefing,
Norman, Okla., Oct. 14/
Los Angeles Times, 10-15:(A)1.

John E. Jacob
President,
National Urban League

3

[On the nomination of Clarence Thomas for the Supreme Court]: Our position is not to oppose him—not to be his advocate, not to be his defender—but simply not to oppose him and let the Senate do its job [in the confirmation hearings] . . . The truth of the matter is that Clarence Thomas' addition to the Court is an academic one because if you lose 5 to 4, or if you lose 6 to 3, you still lose in that arena. I think, fundamentally, we're prepared to live with what we don't think is going to be a favorable position for us for a long time.

Atlanta, July 21/
The New York Times, 7-22:(A)8.

Yale Kamisar
Professor of law,
University of Michigan

4

[On the Supreme Court's ruling that the use of a coerced confession does not automatically void a conviction in a criminal trial]: The reason given most often for throwing out coerced confessions is that no confession can be harmless. But the real reason is that the Court used to feel so strongly about this that it wanted to condemn, in the strongest terms, police threats of violence. The Court also didn't want a prosecutor to say, "I've got a pretty good case without this confession, but I'm going to throw it in to clinch my case." The Supreme Court decision encourages the prosecutor to gamble.

March 27/
The New York Times, 3-28:(A)13.

Nancy Landon Kassebaum
United States Senator,
R-Kansas

1

[On Anita Hill's allegations that Supreme Court Nominee Clarence Thomas sexually harassed her 10 years ago] ... it appears that she never agreed to a full-scale investigation of these charges, which would mean that her name could be used in FBI interviews and committee inquiries with anyone who might know anything about this matter. If this is true, I find it difficult to comprehend what was intended in the raising of these charges. Is it possible that Professor Hill, an experienced attorney and law professor, believed that Judge Thomas' appointment [to the Supreme Court] could be killed in secret? Was she led to believe that mere raising of these charges could force the judge to withdraw, or lead the [Senate Judiciary] Committee to reject his nomination with no explanation to the full Senate or the public? ... On the question before us [the Thomas nomination], some women suggest that I should judge this nomination not as a Senator but as a woman, one of only two in the Senate. I reject that suggestion.

Before the Senate,
Washington, Oct. 15/
The New York Times, 10-16:(A)12.

Edward M. Kennedy
United States Senator,
D-Massachusetts

2

[Saying he does not support confirmation of Clarence Thomas for the Supreme Court]: If we play Russian roulette with the Supreme Court, if we confirm a nominee who has not demonstrated a commitment to core Constitutional values, we jeopardize our rights as individuals and our future as a nation. We cannot undo such a mistake at the next election or even in the next generation ... In effect, [former] President [Ronald] Reagan and President Bush have carried out a triple play against the role of Congress. First, in the guise of executing the laws, they used their Executive Branch power to rewrite and constrict statutes they dislike. Second, they persuade the Justices they have

named to the Supreme Court to disregard plain legislative history about Congressional intent and sustain narrow Executive Branch readings as minimally plausible in interpretations of the law. Third, they dare Congress to try and pass a new law to restore the correct interpretation in the face of a veto by the President. My concern is that Judge Thomas, based on his record, is likely to become a willing disciple of these search-and-destroy missions of the Court.

At Senate Judiciary Committee hearing
on the Thomas nomination,
Washington, Sept. 27/
The New York Times, 9-28:8.

3

[Saying the Senate should delay a confirmation vote on Supreme Court nominee Clarence Thomas so that hearings may be held into allegations against him of sexual harassment made by Anita Hill]: We have a Constitutional duty to the nation, to the Supreme Court and to the Senate to review Professor Hill's allegations before casting our votes. If confirmed by the Senate, Judge Thomas will receive a lifetime appointment to the Supreme Court. He may well serve on the Court for the next 30 or 40 years. And there is no justification for an unseemly rush to judgment in a few hours when a delay of a few days can make such an important difference ... Any vote on the merits of his nomination today would be painfully premature. It is not a question of having the Senate train run on time, but whether we can stop the Senate train from running off the track.

Before the Senate,
Washington, Oct. 8/
The New York Times, 10-10:(A)13.

4

[Criticizing negative comments about Anita Hill, who has made allegations of sexual harassment against Supreme Court nominee Clarence Thomas]: I hope we're not going to hear any more comments, unworthy, unsubstantiated comments, unjustified comments about Professor Hill and perjury, as we heard in this room [where hearings into the allegations are being held by the Senate Judiciary Committee] yester-

(EDWARD M. KENNEDY)

day. I hope we're not going to hear any more comments about Professor Hill being a tool of the various advocacy groups . . . I hope we're not going to hear more about politics. You can imagine what Professor Hill would have gone through if she had been a Democrat . . . I hope we're not going to hear a lot more comments about fantasy stories, picked out of books and law cases after we've heard from this distinguished panel [of pro-Hill witnesses], or how there have been attempts in the 11th hour to derail [the Thomas] nomination. I hope we can clear this room of the dirt and innuendo that's been suggested [about] Professor Hill as well, about over-the-transom information, about faxes, about proclivities. We heard a good deal about character assassination yesterday, and I hope we're going to be sensitive to the attempts of character assassination on Professor Hill. They're unworthy. They're unworthy.

At Senate Judiciary Committee hearing
on the Thomas nomination,
Washington, Oct. 13/
The New York Times, 10-14:(A)13.

Arthur J. Kropp
President,
People for the American Way

1

[Criticizing Supreme Court nominee Clarence Thomas]: We discover a man with a singular disrespect for the rule of law, an apparent indifference to fundamental civil liberties, contempt for Congress and the judiciary and a painfully cramped view of government's role in repairing the damage of [racial] discrimination.

News conference,
Washington, July 30/
Los Angeles Times, 7-31:(A)4.

Charles Lawrence
Professor,
Stanford University
School of Law

2

[On the nomination of Clarence Thomas for the Supreme Court]: This is a political nomina-

tion; let there be no mistake about that. The Framers [of the Constitution] anticipated this inevitability and gave to the Senate the job of checking the President's power to make a Supreme Court in his own image. This President [Bush] is determined to do just that, to push the Court even more solidly to the ideological right than it already is. When this is so, it is the especially important role of the Senate not to shirk its responsibilities in this process. It is your duty to insure that there remains on the Court some meaningful diversity of judicial philosophy and political orientation, that there remains some voice for those who too often go unheard. It is your duty to reject this nomination and reject each nomination that follows, until you are assured that this new Justice will stand against the current Court's assault on *Roe v. Wade, Brown v. Board of Education,* and *Griggs v. Duke Power.* It is not enough to guess, to hope, or even to pray, as I have, that, if confirmed, Judge Thomas will grow and change.

At Senate Judiciary Committee hearing
on the Thomas nomination,
Washington, Sept. 17/The New York Times, 9-18:(A)10.

Patrick J. Leahy
United States Senator,
D-Vermont

3

[Saying he does not support confirmation of Clarence Thomas for the Supreme Court]: Last year at the hearing on his nomination to the D.C. Circuit, Judge Thomas said that he was not someone who has had the opportunity or the time to formulate an individual, well-thought-out Constitutional philosophy. After five days of testimony in this room [on his Supreme Court nomination], Judge Thomas' judicial philosophy remains unformed and inconcise. Judge Thomas lacks the experience and qualifications that a Supreme Court Justice ought to have. He fled from his record and he refused to answer legitimate questions . . . His stated rationale for not answering questions was that such responses would compromise his impartiality. But if that is a standard, he was erratic in the application of it.

At Senate Judiciary Committee hearing
on the Thomas nomination,
Washington, Sept. 27/The New York Times, 9-28:8.

(PATRICK J. LEAHY)

1

[On the Senate Judiciary Committee hearings into allegations by Anita Hill that Supreme Court nominee Clarence Thomas sexually harassed her 10 years ago]: They are both credible, intelligent, well-educated, both lawyers, both testifying under oath, and one is lying. There's no conclusion I could reach. Which one it is, I don't know.

To reporters, Washington/
The Christian Science Monitor,
10-15:1.

Thurgood Marshall
Associate Justice,
Supreme Court
of the United States

2

[On whether President Bush should choose a black or other minority to replace him on the Supreme Court, from which he has announced his resignation]: I don't think [race] should be used as an excuse one way or the other . . . I mean for picking the wrong Negro, and saying, "I'm picking him because he is a Negro." I am opposed to that. There's no difference between a white snake and a black snake. They'll both bite.

News conference,
Washington, June 28/
Los Angeles Times, 6-29:(A)22.

3

For the past four or five years, one of the questions I asked prospective law clerks was, "How do you like writing dissenting opinions?" If they said no, they didn't get the job.

News conference,
Washington, June 28/
The Washington Post, 6-29:(A)10.

Howard M. Metzenbaum
United States Senator,
D-Ohio

4

[Addressing Supreme Court nominee Clarence Thomas]: Our only way to judge you is by

looking at your past statements and your record. And I will be frank: Your complete repudiation of your past record makes our job very difficult. We don't know if the Judge Thomas who has been speaking and writing throughout his adult life is the same man up for confirmation before us today. And I must tell you it gives me a great deal of concern. For example, yesterday, in response to a question from Senator [Joseph] Biden, you said that you support a right to privacy. Frankly, I was surprised to hear you say that. I have not been able to find anything in your many speeches or articles to suggest that you support a right to privacy.

At Senate Judiciary Committee hearing
on the Thomas nomination,
Washington, Sept. 10/
The New York Times, 9-12(A)12.

Barbara A. Mikulski
United States Senator,
D-Maryland

5

[Criticizing the treatment by Senate Judiciary Committee Republicans of Anita Hill, who has made allegations that Supreme Court nominee Clarence Thomas sexually harassed her 10 years ago]: What we saw was not a hearing but an inquisition, and there were Republican Senators who rushed into the role of the grand inquisitor. From the very first day of this nomination, the [Bush] Administration and their Senators made a decision to treat the nomination of Clarence Thomas as a political campaign and not a nomination process. We watched White House handlers and spin doctors mask the convictions and obscure the beliefs of Judge Thomas. He himself refused to answer questions or gave answers that were simply, plainly unbelievable. That's the wrong way to decide.

Before the Senate,
Washington, Oct. 15/
The New York Times, 10-16:(A)12.

George J. Mitchell
United States Senator,
D-Maine

6

In 1980, the Republican National Convention adopted a platform which called for the

(GEORGE J. MITCHELL)

appointment of judges committed to the pro-life position on abortion. Since 1980, in honoring that commitment, Presidents [Ronald] Reagan and Bush have established as a litmus test for a potential nominee to the Supreme Court: that person's position on abortion. The President [Bush] opposes a woman's right of choice. In order to have any hope of being nominated to the Supreme Court, so must any potential nominee. The President selects nominees because of their views, not despite them. That is his privilege. It is the reward of election to the Presidency. He is answerable for the quality of his choices to the voters and to history. But by the same token, the Senate is not required to be a rubber stamp, to approve any nomination simply because it's been made by a President. It is illogical and untenable to suggest that the President has the right to select someone because of that person's views and then to say that the Senate has no right to reject that person because of those very same views.

Before the Senate,
Washington, Oct. 15/
The New York Times, 10-16:(A)12.

Sandra Day O'Connor
Associate Justice,
Supreme Court
of the United States

1

Juries are permitted to target unpopular defendants, penalize controversial views and redistribute wealth. Multimillion-dollar losses are inflicted on a whim.

USA Today, 3-7:(A)12.

Dan Quayle
Vice President
of the United States

2

[Calling for reform of the U.S. legal system]: Does America really need 70 per cent of the world's lawyers? Is it healthy for our economy to have 18 million new lawsuits coursing through the system annually? . . . In 1989 alone, more than 18 million civil suits were filed in this

country—one for every 10 adults—making us the most litigious society in the world. Once in court, many litigants face excessive delays, some caused by overloaded court dockets, others by adversaries seeking tactical advantage. In addition, many of the costs confronting our citizens are enormous and often wholly unnecessary. And in resolving conflicts, Americans don't have enough access to avenues other than the formal process of litigation . . . We believe the system should provide a "multi-door courthouse," where parties have options other than formal litigation . . . Nobody is talking about eliminating lawyers. Nobody is talking about not allowing individuals to have their day in court. So let's not be extreme. Let's focus on the very fundamental problem and that is we should challenge the status quo. I am convinced we can have a better legal system in America if we sit down and work together.

Before American Bar Association,
Atlanta, Aug. 13/
Los Angeles Times, 8-14(A)1;
The Washington Post, 8-14:(A)1;
The Washington Post, 8-15:(A)20.

William H. Rehnquist
Chief Justice
of the United States

3

A constitution's impressive catalogue of individual rights or limitations on government power is not enough if the judges who are called upon to enforce these rights have no independence from the other branches of government.

Speech at National Archives,
Washington, Dec. 15/
The New York Times, 12-16:(A)15.

John Sexton
Dean, New York University
Law School

4

Lawyers must be broad-gauged people who have a historical perspective and understand terms of the debate [in whatever area they practice]. No discussion of communications law [for example] can ignore changes in communications technology.

U.S. News & World Report, 4-29:72.

Paul Simon
United States Senator,
D-Illinois

1

[On the forthcoming Senate hearings on the nomination of Clarence Thomas for the Supreme Court]: [Thomas] is a likeable person [and] in some ways the personality things are the toughest things that we deal with here. It's easier [for the Senate] to say no on an issue than to say no on a person.

The Washington Post, 8-3:(A)6.

2

[Saying he does not support confirmation of Clarence Thomas for the Supreme Court]: Would we elect a President or a Senator who told us that he or she never discussed the *Roe v. Wade* [abortion] decision and had no thoughts on it? Should we approve a Supreme Court nominee who gives us that same answer? His frequent attempts in testimony to escape past writings and statements would have been more understandable if he had simply said, "I changed my mind." He strained to please an audience of 14 on this Committee, and his lack of candor troubles me . . . If evasiveness before the Committee is rewarded, we warp the process. Thomas' evasiveness adds to my doubts.

At Senate Judiciary Committee hearing
on the Thomas nomination,
Washington, Sept. 27/
The New York Times, 9-28:8.

Alan K. Simpson
United States Senator,
R-Wyoming

3

[On criticism by some members of the Senate Judiciary Committee of the way Supreme Court nominee Clarence Thomas has been answering their questions at his current confirmation hearings]: [The solution is] stop smearing them [the nominees], stop ridiculing them, stop tearing their past lives to shreds . . . and they'll start talking. Until then, they won't, and who would?

To panel of Thomas opponents,
Sept. 19/
The Washington Post, 9-21:(A)7.

4

[On the forthcoming Senate Judiciary Committee hearings into allegations by Anita Hill that Supreme Court nominee Clarence Thomas sexually harassed her 10 years ago]: Anita Hill will be sucked right into the maw, the very thing she wanted to avoid most. She will be injured and destroyed and belittled and hounded and harassed—real harassment, different from the sexual kind, just plain old Washington-variety harassment, which is pretty demeaning in itself . . . Maybe we can ruin them [Hill and Thomas] both, leave them both wounded and their families wounded. Maybe, in cynical array, we can bring the curtain down on them both, and maybe we can get them both to cry. That will be something that people will be trying to do.

The Washington Post, 10-11:(A)2.

Nadine Strossen
President,
American Civil Liberties Union

5

[Saying liberals are looking to Congress to help their cause rather than to the now-conservative Supreme Court]: We are no longer seeking out the Supreme Court to take corrective action to restore the individual liberties that the Supreme Court has taken away.

Time, 7-8:22.

John H. Sununu
Chief of Staff
to President
of the United States
George Bush

6

[On the possibility that Supreme Court nominee Clarence Thomas will be rejected by the Senate]: There is always the possibility. Things can come out in a [confirmation] hearing, there may be difficulty in the hearing by the nominee and so on. But we are comfortable going into this hearing that the confirmation process will go forward smoothly and that Clarence Thomas will be confirmed . . . We think he is still in good shape and will be confirmed, but the fact is the climate in this country for nominations in general

(JOHN H. SUNUNU)

has become a little bit more of a partisan situation and the country would probably be better off if it were not in that mode.

Broadcast interview/
"Meet the Press," NBC-TV, 9-8.

Robert W. Sweet
Judge, United States District Court
for the Southern District
of New York

1

[Criticizing a proposal to put some local crimes under Federal jurisdiction]: Federal courts are unique in this country. We have a special role. We stand at the gate. We say what the Constitution means. Now, under the guise of an immediate problem, they have ignored our character and task and assigned us a different task.

The New York Times, 7-24:(A)9.

Clarence Thomas
Judge, United States Court
of Appeals for the
District of Columbia;
Nominee for Associate Justice,
Supreme Court
of the United States

2

. . . I don't see a role for the use of "natural law" in Constitutional adjudication. My interest in exploring natural law and natural rights was purely in the context of political theory. I was interested in that. There were debates that I had with individuals, and I pursued that on a part-time basis . . . The founders of our country, or at least some of the drafters of our Constitution and our Declaration [of Independence], believed in natural rights. And my point was simply that in understanding over-all Constitutional government, that it was important that we understood how they believed—or what they believed in natural law or natural rights.

At Senate Judiciary Committee hearing
on his nomination,
Washington, Sept. 10/
The New York Times, 9-11:(A)12.

3

A judge must be fair and impartial. A judge must not bring to his job, to the court, the baggage of preconceived notions, of ideology, and certainly not an agenda. And a judge must get the decision right because, when all is said and done, the little guy, the average person . . . the real people of America will be affected not only by what we as judges do, but by the way we do our jobs.

At Senate Judiciary Committee hearing
on his nomination,
Washington, Sept. 10/
Los Angeles Times, 9-11:(A)22.

4

[Asked about his opinion of *Roe vs. Wade*, the Supreme Court ruling legalizing abortion]: I do not think that at this time that I could maintain my impartiality as a member of the judiciary and comment on that specific case . . . No judge worth his or her salt will prejudge a case. You have to sit to listen, to hear the arguments and allow the adversarial process to go forward. I don't sit on any cases I have prejudged.

At Senate Judiciary Committee hearing
on his nomination,
Washington, Sept. 10/
The New York Times, 9-11:(A)13.

5

. . . the role of a judge is a limited one. It is to interpret the intent of Congress, the legislation of Congress, to apply that in specific cases, and to interpret the Constitution, where called upon, but at no point to impose his or her will or his or her opinion in that process, but, rather, to go to the traditional tools of Constitutional interpretation or adjudication, as well as to statutory construction, but not, again, to impose his or her own point of view or his or her predilections or preconceptions.

At Senate Judiciary Committee hearing
on his nomination,
Washington, Sept. 10/
The New York Times, 9-11:(A)13.

(CLARENCE THOMAS)

1

... it is important for any of us who are judges, in areas that are very deeply contested, in areas where I think we all understand and are sensitive to both sides of a very difficult debate, that ... for us who are judges, we have to look ourselves in the mirror and say, are we impartial? I think that to take a position [on a controversial issue] would undermine my ability to be impartial, and I have attempted to avoid that in all areas of my life after I became a judge. And I think it is important.

*At Senate Judiciary Committee hearing
on his nomination,
Washington, Sept. 10/
The New York Times, 9-12:(A)12.*

2

[On his switch from running a government agency to becoming a judge]: When one becomes a judge, the role changes, the roles change. That is why it is different. You are no longer involved in those battles. You are no longer running an agency. You are no longer making policy. You are a judge. It is hard to explain, perhaps, but you strive—rather than looking for policy positions, you strive for impartiality. You begin to strip down from those policy positions. You begin to walk away from that constant development of new policies. You have to rule on cases as an impartial judge. And I think that is the important message that I am trying to send to you; that, yes, my whole record is relevant [at these confirmation hearings], but remember that that was as a policy-maker, not as a judge.

*At Senate Judiciary Committee hearing
on his nomination,
Washington, Sept. 12/
The New York Times, 9-13:(A)10.*

3

With respect to judges and what happens when you become a judge, I, quite frankly, don't know any of us who, prior to becoming judges, understood exactly how it would change us. I could not have told you when I was here for the Court of Appeals [confirmation hearing] exactly how it would change me. I can tell you, and I think most judges would tell you, that it is not necessarily like an eraser, but it is a profound change.

*At Senate Judiciary Committee hearing
on his nomination,
Washington, Sept. 13/
The New York Times, 9-14:6.*

4

[On allegations by Anita Hill that he sexually harassed her 10 years ago]: I have endured this ordeal [the Senate confirmation process] for 103 days. Reporters sneaking into my garage to examine books that I read. Reporters and interest groups swarming over divorce papers, looking for dirt. Unnamed people starting preposterous and damaging rumors. Calls all over the country specifically requesting dirt. This is not American. This is Kafkaesque. It has got to stop. It must stop for the benefit of future [Supreme Court] nominees and our country. Enough is enough ... No job is worth what I've been through—no job. No horror in my life has been so debilitating. Confirm me if you want. Don't confirm me if you are so led. But let this process end. Let me and my family regain our lives. I never asked to be nominated. It was an honor. Little did I know the price, but it is too high ... I am a victim of this process. My name has been harmed. My integrity has been harmed. My character has been harmed. My family has been harmed. My friends have been harmed. There is nothing this Committee, this body or this country can do to give me my good name back. Nothing.

*At Senate Judiciary Committee hearing
on his nomination,
Washington, Oct. 11/
The New York Times,
10-12:(A)10.*

5

[Criticizing the current Senate Judiciary Committee hearings into allegations by Anita Hill that he sexually harassed her 10 years ago]: This is a circus, it's a national disgrace, and from my standpoint as a black American ... it's a high-tech lynching for uppity blacks. It's a message that ... you will be lynched, destroyed, carica-

(CLARENCE THOMAS)

tured by a committee of the U.S. Senate rather than hung from a tree.

At Senate Judiciary Committee hearing
on his nomination,
Washington, Oct. 11/
Newsweek, 10-21:26.

1

[On his being confirmed by the Senate for the Supreme Court following hearings on allegations by Anita Hill that he sexually harassed her 10 years ago]: I'd like to thank America for the things it stands for. And I'd like to think that at least in my life, in our lives, that we can uphold those ideals. I'd also like to make it unequivocally clear that throughout this process, and especially the last painful week, that I give God thanks for our being able to stand here today and I give God thanks for our ability to feel safe, to feel secure, to feel loved, and I give God thanks that the Senate approved me in this process. No matter how difficult or how painful the process has been . . . this is a time for healing in our country. We have to put these things behind us.

News briefing,
Springfield, Va., Oct. 15/
Los Angeles Times, 10-16:(A)11.

Laurence H. Tribe
Professor of constitutional law,
Harvard University

2

[On Supreme Court nominee Clarence Thomas' belief in the principle of "natural rights"]: No one sitting on the Court since the 1930s and no one nominated for the Supreme Court, including [1987's unsuccessful Supreme Court nominee] Robert Bork, seems to have held views of that sort. The philosophy that fundamental liberties are to be implied from one's personal reading of religious sources and the Declaration of Independence represents a departure from both liberal and conservative thought that has characterized the past half-century. If

taken seriously, if applied the way Judge Thomas seems to suggest, [his philosophy] would outlaw minimum-wage laws, child-labor laws and laws protecting the rights of reproductive choice . . . Invocation of the natural law in the history of the Court has much more often been used to subjugate and subordinate people than to liberate them.

The Washington Post,
7-8:(A)4.

3

The greatest danger of judges who tend to defer to the government, who say that the government is right unless the Constitution very clearly says otherwise, is that in their hands the Bill of Rights becomes just so much paper, a beautiful set of platitudes . . . I see the Ninth Amendment as perhaps the most basic principle in the whole Constitution. I would say it is a message from those who wrote the Constitution to those who read it about *how* to read it. And it says that the fact that the document lists certain rights must never be used as an excuse to say that there are no others. That's why the failure of the Constitution to enumerate rights of personal intimacy or marital privacy or reproductive freedom seems to me not at all decisive. The Ninth Amendment makes it clear that the failure to mention those words is immaterial . . . I think a judge's role is to identify the basic values that are expressed in the [Constitution] and to give those values life in the context of contemporary society.

Interview/
Life, Fall:98.

W. Scott Van Alstyne
Professor of law,
University of Florida

4

Law schools talk about providing a Renaissance education, but they really don't do it. There is such waste in upper-level courses that many graduates are not prepared to deliver legal services to anybody.

U.S. News & World Report,
4-29:71.

Lawrence E. Walsh
Independent Counsel
investigating the
Iran-Contra scandal;
Former president,
American Bar Association

1

The classified-information problem is frustrating because there is no review of the subjective judgment of the intelligence agencies in saying they will not release information that a court has held necessary to a fair trial. It's not just information that the government needs to prosecute the case. The problem also arises when the defendant asks for information he says is necessary for a fair trial and the judge agrees with him. And then the intelligence agency holds back that information on what sometimes seems to be an excessive claim of the need for the secrecy of information that is already publicly known. In an ordinary prosecution by the Department of Justice, the Attorney General can overrule that determination. But the Independent Counsel does not have the power to do so. That decision remains with the Attorney General. Whereas the Attorney General is fully familiar with prosecutions by his own department, he is not comparably familiar with a prosecution by the Independent Counsel—and indeed, I think he has less concern for it.

Interview/Time, 7-29:17.

Harriet Woods
President, National Women's
Political Caucus

2

[Criticizing the way Supreme Court nominee Clarence Thomas has been answering questions during his current confirmation hearings before the Senate Judiciary Committee]: The millions who are watching this process, what are they going to think about advice and consent if a nominee can appear before you [the Committee] and stonewall you and refuse to answer, be evasive, and yet be confirmed? I want to say to you that you may be dooming us to a similar game plan for all future nominees.

At Senate Judiciary Committee hearing
on the Thomas nomination,
Washington, Sept. 20/
The Washington Post, 9-21:(A)7.

Politics

William J. Bennett
Former Director,
Federal Office of National
Drug Control Policy;
Former Secretary of Education
of the United States

1

This [Republican] Party needs to attract more black voters. You don't achieve that end by saying, "Where there are black voters, we will assume they will vote Democratic and try to district them so their votes won't count against us." That's not a good outreach program.

Interview, May/
The New York Times, 5-9:(A)9.

Richard N. Bond
Former deputy chairman,
Republican National Committee

2

Every time the [Bush] Administration goes to [Capitol] Hill, it will lose, no matter how well conceived the policy is. I think you underestimate the problem any Republican domestic agenda will have with this Congress. With an imminent national election, with the Democrats on the run, with the Democrats lacking any credible [Presidential] candidate, with the Democrats fearing they might lose Congressional seats if they don't have a strong name on the ticket, they will stop at nothing to discredit Bush and any Republican domestic agenda.

Panel discussion, Washington/
Harper's Magazine, July:42.

Bill Bradley
United States Senator,
D-New Jersey

3

So much of political rhetoric today is so full of cliche and stereotype that you begin to say, "Where's the real behind the words?" The real is not always there to a public, because people don't confront what the real issues are out there . . . I think that for too long we've [Democrats] tried to be too many things to too many people. For too long we have not apparently said no to anyone. For too long we have not been the bearers of truth, and I frankly don't think we have been true to the best of our Democratic heritage. It begins by knowing where you are in that great American historical narrative. What you believe; where you stand. It also means thinking through how you address the real needs of real people.

Interview, Washington/
Los Angeles Times, 9-29:(M)3.

Joseph Brodsky
Poet Laureate
of the United States

4

[On the U.S. political system]: It has its ills and evils but they appear to be organic in nature, not ideological evils. And sometimes people chance upon something that works; and to my eye, to say the least, this system here works. It doesn't make everyone happy, but there is no blueprint for happiness.

Interview,
Washington/
The New York Times, 12-10:(B)3.

Edmund G. Brown, Jr.
Former Governor
of California (D)

5

[Saying he is considering running for the U.S. Senate from California]: I want to figure out a way to do this in a way that does not require spending 80 per cent of my time going to cocktail parties in affluent neighborhoods, doing my tap dance to get people to give me money to buy the consultants to buy video film to get myself elected.

To reporters,
Los Angeles, Jan. 11/
Los Angeles Times, 1-12:(A)30.

(EDMUND G. BROWN, JR.)

1

[Criticizing election campaigns in the U.S.]: What an irony that the spirit of democracy is bursting out all over the world, while in America democratic choice narrows and is rendered almost illusory. In place of debate and serious public discourse, we are bombarded with 30-second TV ads and short sound bites that obscure and distort the truth.

Speech/
The Christian Science Monitor,
10-21:8.

Edmund G. Brown, Jr.
Candidate for the
1992 Democratic
Presidential nomination;
Former Governor
of California (D)

2

[On his running for President]: You've probably heard a lot of things about me. Governor Moonbeam, the man who went to Africa with [singer] Linda Ronstadt, the man who drove a Plymouth, who didn't live in the [Governor's] mansion, slept on the floor. I don't know what images you have of me. But I'll tell you this—I have been around politics since the day I was born . . . And I can tell you this: We [in the U.S.] are in a crisis! The very idea of America is being killed!

Campaigning, Moline, Ill./
Los Angeles Times, 12-9:(A)22.

3

The aim of my [Presidential] campaign is to take back America from the manipulative big-money interests and the beholden, self-preservationist politicians who those interests elect and keep in office . . . This candidacy, this cause, will only work if it sparks a grass-roots revolution and the people rise up, one by one, then by the thousands, then by the millions. A revolution is not an easy thing to pull off.

Interview/
The New York Times, 12-28:7.

George Bruno
Democratic National Committeeman
from New Hampshire

4

[On the lack of more than one announced candidate for the 1992 Democratic Presidential nomination]: What is it about our times and our leadership on the 200th anniversary of the Bill of Rights that causes our Party to be so devoid of direction? It's five months before New Hampshire's [Presidential] primary and there's [only] one announced candidate. The situation is deplorable.

The New York Times, 8-26:(A)9.

Patrick Buchanan
Political commentator;
Candidate for the
1992 Republican
Presidential nomination

5

Why am I running [for President?] Because we Republicans can no longer say it is all the liberals' fault. It was not some liberal Democrat who declared, "Read my lips, no new taxes," and then broke his word to cut a seedy backroom deal with the big spenders on Capitol Hill . . . No, that was done by the man [President Bush] in whom we placed our confidence and our trust, and who then turned their backs on us and walked away from us.

The Christian Science Monitor,
12-12:6.

George Bush
President of the United States

6

[On suggestions that when he was running for Vice President in 1980, he was involved in secret negotiations with Iran to hold back the release of American hostages until after the election]: I can only say categorically that the allegations about me are grossly untrue, factually incorrect, bald-faced lies . . . I can categorically deny any contact with the Iranians or anything having to do with it . . . To assign a motive to a person that he'd want to keep an American in prison one day

(GEORGE BUSH)

longer I think is vicious, and I am really turned off by this . . .

News conference,
Washington, May 8/
The New York Times, 5-9:(A)12.

1

[On whether he might reconsider having Vice President Dan Quayle on the ticket next year when he runs for re-election, in light of Quayle's low poll ratings]: I've expressed my support for Dan Quayle. I think he's getting a bum rap in the press, pounding on him when he's doing a first-class job. And I don't know how many times I have to say it, but I'm not about to change my mind when I see his performance and know what he does.

News conference,
Washington, May 8/
The New York Times, 5-9:(A)12.

2

[On Democratic Party criticism that he has no domestic program]: We've got excellent programs, and the only way when the other party controls the Congress is to defeat some of their lousy ideas and then keep saying to the American people, "Have your Congressman try the President's ideas." We need more farsighted people like me in Congress. So please, American people . . . please do not listen to the charges by frantic Democrats who are trying to say we don't have a domestic policy when we have a good one. Give it a chance. Let the President's programs come up, and let's have some support for what he was elected to do.

News conference,
Washington, Aug. 2/
The Washington Post, 8-3:(A)4.

Mangosuthu Gatsha Buthelezi
President,
Inkatha Freedom Party
of South Africa;
Chief of the Zulu people

3

I have always regarded constituency politics as being vitally important . . . It is all too easy in protest politics to whip up emotions and to generate mass-action programs in which celebrity leaders could come and go and among whom the media could make kings. When leaders are elected by committees from nominations made by other committees, and when representatives are elected to represent representatives and not people, then political structures move out of grass-roots reach.

Before Carnegie Endowment,
Washington, June 18/
The Washington Post, 6-19:(A)16.

James Carville
Adviser to the recent
re-election campaign
of U.S. Senator Harris Wofford,
D-Pennsylvania

4

[Saying national Democrats are being too optimistic that Wofford's recent victory in Pennsylvania signifies trouble for President Bush in next year's Presidential election]: There's far too much attention being paid [by Democrats] to the message and not enough to the candidate . . . It's like we say where I come from: "Right string, wrong yo-yo." The right string is the middle-class message, but you may have a lot of wrong yo-yos [trying to deliver it].

The Washington Post, 11-11:(A)4.

Bill Clinton
Governor of Arkansas (D)

5

Too many of the people who used to vote for us [Democrats], the very burdened middle class we're talking about, have not trusted us in national elections to defend out national interest abroad, to put their values in our social policy at home or to take their tax money and spend it with discipline. We've got to turn these perceptions around or we can't continue as a national party.

At Democratic Party conference,
Cleveland, May 6/
The Washington Post, 5-7:(A)3.

6

A lot of people don't think we [Democrats] can be trusted with their tax dollars, or that we'll ever

(BILL CLINTON)

stand up to our own bureaucracies. And I'll tell you that, just as [former President] Richard Nixon was the only person who could go to China in 1972 because he spent all his time being an anti-Communist, it's only the Democratic Party that can reform government, because we believe in government. You think the Republicans want to fix it? If they fixed it, what would they run against?

New Hampshire/
The New York Times, 8-14:(A)9.

Mario M. Cuomo
Governor of New York (D)

1

[On President Bush's high opinion polls following the successful outcome of the Persian Gulf war]: The President was greeted as a hero. He should be. He earned that. But when he turned to the domestic program, he made it apparent that he was not going to deal with the problems . . . You cannot stay at 91 per cent in the polls by cheering yesterday's war.

Interview, March 7/
The Washington Post, 3-8:(A)7.

2

I believe with everything in me that the most glaring omission in today's politics, especially for the Democrats, is a clear articulation of values, something you believe in. The ideal for me would be to write down about what you believe in government and politics on a card and carry it that way, the way Catholics used to carry the Apostles' Creed, and take it out and cite what you believe.

Interview/
Los Angeles Times, 4-26:(A)27.

3

[On speculation that he may run for the Democratic Presidential nomination next year]: I'm not a candidate. I'm not a potential candidate. I'm not a make-believe candidate.

News conference,
Albany, N.Y., May 17/
The New York Times, 5-18:7.

4

[Criticizing the Democratic Leadership Council for saying the Party needs to change its position and move to the political center]: I don't like those people at the DLC [and the] implicit position that we have something we have to apologize for and now we have to move to the middle. I don't personally feel that I have to move two inches . . . What did [1984 Presidential nominee Walter] Mondale say that he should apologize for? What did [1988 Presidential nominee Michael] Dukakis say that he should apologize for? If it's not them, then who are they talking about? It's a straw man.

Interview, Albany, N.Y., June/
The Washington Post, 6-7:(A)8.

5

[Saying that, despite his outspoken views on national issues, it should not be assumed he will be running for President next year]: Why should it be that if you happen to have eight-and-a-half years as Governor, having all that background, having a platform to discuss national issues, if you do it in any plausible way then it follows you should be running for President? And if you're not, then there's something wrong with you. Either you've got a Mafia uncle hidden away in a closet or you've got some serious illness or you've got some psychic indisposition. Why should that be?

Before New York State
Broadcasters Association,
Saratoga Springs, N.Y., July 22/
The New York Times, 7-25:(A)14.

Dennis DeConcini
United States Senator,
D-Arizona

6

[Supporting Vice President Dan Quayle against criticism of him in the press]: I didn't vote for Dan Quayle. [But] whatever one thinks of Dan Quayle's politics, the argument that he is unqualified to be President is ridiculous. And the press knows it. In their hearts, they know it.

Before the Senate,
Washington, May 16/
The Washington Post, 5-17:(A)23.

Pierre S. (Pete) du Pont
Former Governor
of Delaware (R)

1

[Presidential] popularity is an opportunity. If you don't use it, it evaporates.

Los Angeles Times, 3-9:(A)15.

Lane Evans
United States Representative,
D-Illinois

2

[We Democrats must show that we] stand up for the average people who are the basis of our constituency, middle-income and poor people. Our leadership needs to understand there are people hurting in our country and they don't see a hell of a lot of difference between Democrats and Republicans . . . If you want to turn voters out, you have to turn them on before Election Day, and we are not turning them on.

The Washington Post, 6-24:(A)5.

Edwin J. Feulner, Jr.
President,
Heritage Foundation

3

The bad news for America, and for American conservatism, is that Washington's power elite—the [former Massachusetts Governor Michael] Dukakis-style technocrats who believe it is their duty to tell us how to spend whatever money they allow us to keep—are clearly in charge [in the Bush Administration] . . . The further Washington strays from the low-tax, anti-regulatory agenda of the [Ronald] Reagan era, the worse the economy will get, the better conservatism will look.

Jan. 7/
The Washington Post, 1-8:(A)4.

Geoffrey Garin
Democratic Party consultant

4

[On the effect on liberals if President Bush appoints another conservative to the Supreme Court to replace retiring liberal Justice Thurgood Marshall]: Liberals got used to relying on the [more liberal] Court, sometimes to the detriment of their political skills. I think civil rights is a good example of that. Liberals have become accustomed to winning the legalisms, but not winning the hearts and minds of the people. This will force a new kind of political discipline on the liberal side.

The Washington Post, 6-29:(A)10.

Valery Giscard (d'Estaing)
Former President of France

5

The performance of [U.S. President] George Bush [during the recent Persian Gulf war] has been remarkable. He has shown three qualities of a head of state in a media age: firmness, clarity of positions and moderation of tone.

Los Angeles Times, 3-2:(A)7.

Albert Gore, Jr.
United States Senator,
D-Tennessee

6

[Criticizing Republicans who are trying to make political hay out of the vote by many Democrats against the recent U.S.-led war in the Persian Gulf in which Iraq was ousted from Kuwait]: This seems to me to be an intentional effort to win votes by poisoning our national politics and dishonoring a debate in this chamber that was in our finest traditions. [President Bush] should stop those who are trying to earn a fast political buck off one of our nation's finest moments . . . Did Republicans consider their votes as political chips to be cashed in later? Did Republicans consider the arguments in this historic debate like cards in a poker game, playing the hand that offered the largest political payoff?

Before the Senate,
Washington, March 6/
The Washington Post, 3-7:(A)6.

7

[On his campaign strategy if he decides to run for President next year]: You make the decision. Then you go out and run with all your heart and

(ALBERT GORE, JR.)

soul—then you rip the lungs out of anyone else.

To reporters, July 17/
USA Today, 7-18:(A)2.

Phil Gramm
United States Senator,
R-Texas

1

[Criticizing Democrats in Congress who voted against the U.S. going to war in the Persian Gulf this year, a war in which U.S.-led forces were victorious in driving Iraq out of Kuwait]: [The vote in January] fits a pattern that is 20 years old. It is so damaging because it is exactly in the pattern of [former Democratic standard-bearers] Jimmy Carter, Walter Mondale and Michael Dukakis. It says to the nation once again that Democrats cannot be trusted to define the destiny of America.

Feb. 28/
The Washington Post, 3-1:(A)33.

Tom Harkin
United States Senator,
D-Iowa

2

If you believe strongly in something and you share fundamental values with the voters, they will give you a lot of running room. They don't want to know how you are going to dot every I and cross every T, as long as they feel you believe in something.

Los Angeles Times, 8-19:(A)23.

3

[On the possibility that he may run for President against President Bush in 1992]: [The Bush people have] never come up against anybody like me. I know how to run against Republicans. Never defend and always attack. And I fight on my territory, never theirs.

Interview/
Newsweek, 8-26:22.

Tom Harkin
United States Senator,
D-Iowa;
Candidate for the
1992 Democratic
Presidential nomination

4

[Conservatives have] tried to define liberalism like if you're a liberal, you're some kind of social degenerate. Somehow you're soft on crime or you're smoking dope or you're for pornographic movies or that kind of stuff. That is total nonsense.

Interview/USA Today, 9-20:(A)2.

5

[On his Presidential campaign]: A lot of people say you've got to be a little more like a Republican. You've got to walk a little more like a Republican, talk a little more like a Republican. But, as Harry Truman said, any time you run a Republican against a Republican, you're going to get a Republican as President.

At University of New Hampshire/
The New York Times, 12-10:(A)14.

Harrison Hickman
Democratic Party
political consultant

6

The Democratic [Presidential] candidate most likely to win a general election is one who can at once challenge the country to greatness while being skeptical toward the ability [of government] to stimulate the changes needed.

The Washington Post, 7-26:(A)17.

Jesse L. Jackson
Civil-rights leader

7

[On deciding whether or not to run for the 1992 Democratic Presidential nomination]: It is excruciating and agonizing. I realize the amount of trust that people invest in the candidate, and you want to honor their trust in the face of all kinds of pressures. In both instances when I ran [in the past], I received more physical threats than any

(JESSE L. JACKSON)

candidate in history. Virtually all day and all night, you have a fishbowl living style for a year. So that means you must reach an accommodation with your family, because the family has to make the economic adjustments, the family has to live at the risk of the danger, the family has to campaign. It completely disrupts the rhythm of one's household.

Aug. 8/
The Washington Post, 8-9:(D) 4.

1

The assumption [of the Democratic Party] must be [that] we can end slums, that we can have a national health-care plan, that we can reinvest in America, that we can build affordable housing. I hope that our Party can really embrace that assumption. If not, it will not survive the loyalty of people whose needs those are. My loyalty is to the needs of the people. I've worked hard for the Democratic Party. I registered more voters than anybody in the Party. I put more critical issues on the table. In effect, I stopped a third party, seeking to expand this one.

The Washington Post, 8-15:(A) 7.

Marvin Kalb
Director, Barone Center
on the Press,
Politics and Public Policy,
Harvard University

2

The 1988 Presidential campaign could have depressed anyone, even Republicans who won. Photo ops in flag factories or tanks, sound bites running all of 9.6 seconds . . . There seemed to be no end to the trivialization of American democracy.

The Washington Post, 9-5:(A) 6.

Edward M. Kennedy
United States Senator,
D-Massachusetts

3

Democrats have to identify with the kinds of needs the average family has. If we are able to

identify in those areas in a constructive and positive way, I think Democrats can be very successful. And if we don't, we don't deserve to win. It's as simple as that.

Broadcast interview/
Los Angeles Times, 3-28:(A) 20.

4

[On the controversies surrounding his personal life and behavior]: I am painfully aware that the criticism directed at me in recent months involves far more than honest disagreement with my positions, or the usual criticism from the far right. It also involves the disappointment of friends and many others who rely on me to fight the good fight . . . As I approach my 60th birthday, I am determined to give all that I have to advance the causes for which I have stood for almost a third of a century . . . In short, I will continue to fight the good fight . . . Our [liberals] day will come again, and we must keep the faith until it dawns. Individual faults and frailties are no excuse to give in—and no exemption from the common obligation to give of ourselves.

Speech, Harvard University, Oct. 25/
Los Angeles Times, 10-26:(A) 20.

Bob Kerrey
United States Senator,
D-Nebraska;
Candidate for the
1992 Democratic
Presidential nomination

5

[Announcing his candidacy for President]: I want to lead because I believe almost everyone but our present [Bush Administration] leadership knows what we must do. I believe Americans know deep in their bones that something is terribly wrong and that business as usual—the prescription of the '80s—will not work for the future . . . The year 1992 offers us a chance to break from a decade in which our leaders invited a season of cynicism. They invoked morality but winked at greed. They criticized the public sector but then robbed it blind. They spoke of balanced budgets but never submitted one. They railed against taxes but raised them on the middle class.

(BOB KERREY)

They called for civil rights but practiced racial politics. They wrapped their cause in mother-hood but tried to strip motherhood of choice [on abortion] or meaningful opportunities. [President Bush] reminds me of some managers I've known in business; great person to be around; all the employees love him. But the business is losing money, its future is impaired, and all he's offering is excuses as to why nothing can be done.

Speech, Lincoln, Neb., Sept. 30/
Los Angeles Times, 10-1:(A)1,15.

1

I don't assert that there is any special quality about me, in and of itself, that qualifies me to be President. What matters is the ideas, the values, the willingness to persevere toward the objective.

Interview/
The New York Times, 12-31:(A)12.

Kenneth L. Khachigian
Former speech writer
for Presidents
Richard M. Nixon
and Ronald Reagan

2

[On whether Vice President Dan Quayle will run again with President Bush in the 1992 election in light of Quayle's low ratings in public-opinion polls]: Quayle will be on the Republican ticket in 1992 because Bush is a man of his word. No one understands or sympathizes with the Vice Presidency more than someone who's held the job. The President has been in Quayle's shoes—and when he pledged that the Vice President would stay on the ticket, he knew whereof he spoke. As the President showed throughout [the recent Persian Gulf crisis], he won't be cowed by pack journalism or the mood swings of public opinion. The other reason Quayle will stay on the ticket is that the President could be hurt politically if he changes. Quayle has been tested and—his critics should admit—has not failed. His life has been examined fully. He has built up support for himself and the GOP across the country. And while a new candidate might be the delight of some faint-hearted Republicans and anxious Democrats, the fact is that few people have made the campaign grade at the Presidential and Vice-Presidential level. Bush knows that, and he knows that a new face could be far riskier than the current Vice President who is fulfilling his duties admirably.

Los Angeles Times, 5-12:(M)1.

Leonid M. Kravchuk
Candidate for President
of the Ukrainian Soviet
Socialist Republic

3

I find it is always the case that the direction a politician follows is determined by the posi-tioning of political forces in the society . . . A politician must take into account this force and that force, and listen to one and the other, and on that basis come to a conclusion. If he takes only one side, then he necessarily loses.

Uzhorod, Ukraine/
The Christian Science Monitor,
11-29:2.

Sander M. Levin
United States Representative,
D-Michigan

4

I don't want my entire political career [in Washington] to be under a Republican Presi-dency. Everything else is secondary. I want us [Democrats] to have a sense of direction again . . . Contrary to common opinion, we are not the majority party. We are out of power.

The Washington Post, 6-24:(A)5.

Ann F. Lewis
Former political director,
Democratic National Committee

5

[On whether Vice President Dan Quayle will run again with President Bush in the 1992 election in light of Quayle's low ratings in public-opinion polls]: Yes for '92, no for '96. Quayle still has the support of his only important consti-tuent, Bush. Even as the '92 race tightens,

(ANN F. LEWIS)

keeping Quayle is easier for Bush than replacing him. A change at this stage would raise questions of Presidential judgment and require choosing among potential successors. But Quayle's political base apparently can't grow; after two years of public appearances on apple-pie issues like space and competitiveness, Quayle's poll rating went down. People don't see him as President, and I don't think they ever will.

Los Angeles Times, 5-12:(M)6.

Jim Ross Lightfoot
United States Representative,
R-Iowa

1

[Criticizing proposals for public financing of Congressional election campaigns]: It's bad enough [that members of the House are] accused of writing rubber checks and running up [unpaid] restaurant tabs. Now some misguided members of the Democratic Party are suggesting we restore Congress' image with the taxpayers by having them pick up the tab for our elections. [This proposal sends a message] to the very people who are disenchanted with us: "Stick 'em up."

Before the House,
Washington, Nov. 25/
The New York Times, 11-26:(A)10.

Eugene J. McCarthy
Former United States Senator,
D-Minnesota

2

Being in politics is like being a football coach. You have to be smart enough to know the game and stupid enough to think it is important.

Los Angeles Times, 10-7:(C)2.

George S. McGovern
Former United States Senator,
D-South Dakota;
1972 Democratic
Presidential nominee

3

If we Democrats defeat [President] Bush in 1992, it will not be by surrendering our liberal principles. Indeed, if we surrender our principles, we don't deserve to win.

At National Press Club,
Washington, May 23/
The Washington Post, 5-24:(A)25.

4

[On the dearth of Democratic candidates who are willing to declare for the 1992 Presidential race]: Prophecies become self-fulfilling. If enough of the Party's spokesmen keep sending signals that it's hopeless, well, it becomes hopeless . . . Let me tell you: If I were 49 and not 69 and hadn't run before, there's no way anybody could keep me out of this race.

USA Today, 8-8:(A)4.

Robert H. Michel
United States Representative,
R-Illinois

5

[On a forthcoming Congressional investigation into allegations that representatives of the Ronald Reagan 1980 Presidential campaign secretly negotiated with Iran to delay release of American hostages until after the election]: [Congressional Democrats are] wasting an awful lot of money on a charade. It's going to end up with nothing being resolved except a lot of political shenanigans. There is nothing there, and the people back home don't give two hoots about it.

Aug. 5/
The Washington Post, 8-6:(A)1.

George J. Mitchell
United States Senator,
D-Maine

6

[President Bush's] strategy is very clearly a negative veto strategy. He has very little in the way of a domestic program of his own, and I think what you'll see is a political plan over the next year [leading up to the 1992 Presidential election], which will be for the President simply to veto whatever the Congress does and then to run against Congress.

Broadcast interview/
"Meet the Press," NBC-TV, 8-4.

Ralph Nader
Lawyer; Consumer advocate

1

[Saying election ballots should have a "none of the above" choice on them]: Elected officials are totally frightened of "none of the above." It's a powerful tool. Can you believe how insulting it is to be beaten by "none of the above"?

New Hampshire/
USA Today, 12-2:(A)4.

Kevin P. Phillips
President, American Political
Research Corporation

2

The Democrats' problem is that they address every issue piecemeal. One response comes from the education specialist, another from the guys associated with fiscal policy, then the leaders of the Party have something to say. The Democrats never present a coordinated reaction, so their beliefs will never cohere in the mind of the American public. These guys have no inkling how to achieve a common front that has depth on anything. Instead of having an instinct for the jugular, the Democrats have an instinct for the capillary.

Panel discussion, Washington/
Harper's Magazine, July:44.

3

The polls show [President Bush] has, besides the recession and the fate of the economy, three specifics that people don't like. The first is that he's seen as too close to the rich, a sort of messenger for the interests of the rich. The second is that he's seen as spending too much time overseas, of being interested in foreign affairs much more than he should be. The third point is the feeling people have that he doesn't have a domestic or economic policy to speak of, that there's no management coming on those fronts . . . If the economy slides, then the Democrats can get back on the right side of caring about the average American. But if it picks up, voters will put Bush back in. Maybe by a weak majority that gives him problems in Congress and in running the country. But back in.

Interview/USA Today, 11-4:(A)13.

Burton Yale Pines
Senior vice president,
Heritage Foundation

4

[Saying conservatives are unhappy with President Bush]: There's no joy in this. It is with profound sadness that we are criticizing George Bush in the terms that we are . . . We have learned some things about George Bush, and we don't like them. [But] we think he still has [conservative ideals] there someplace. We do not believe he was in the White House [as Vice President] with [former President Ronald] Reagan for eight years [and] didn't learn something . . . [It could be like then-President Harry Truman's tough midterm election setback in 1946 that] promoted in Truman's case a significant change of behavior which led to [his] 1948 victory. George Bush now has a choice. He can become Harry Truman. Or he can become Herbert Hoover.

The Christian Science Monitor,
1-10:1,2.

Dan Quayle
Vice President
of the United States

5

[Saying that despite the Republican Party's official platform against abortion, even pro-choice advocates are welcome in the Party]: It's necessary to restate the President's [Bush] viewpoint, very clearly, and that is that we are a party that is diversified, we are a party that though we have a position on abortion, that those who disagree with us should not feel excluded because of that issue. We do, in former [Republican National Committee] chairman Lee Atwater's words, offer the Party as a big tent, and therefore that message has to be clear.

To reporters, Washington, Oct. 8/
The Washington Post, 10-9:(A)2.

Ann Richards
Governor-elect of Texas (D)

6

[On whether politics continues to be a "men's club"]: There will still continue to be some

(ANN RICHARDS)

vestige of that, but as full participants in politics, women have been in the pipeline for a long time. Like anyone else, we had to prove ourselves. We had to do so at lower elected levels like school boards and city councils, and as we demonstrated our ability, the public was more willing to move us up . . . We've had to work harder to be successful—understandable when you're breaking new ground. So far, we have a better record of honesty than our predecessors, but perhaps that's because there have been relatively few of us.

Interview, Austin, Texas/
Cosmopolitan, April:124.

John D. (Jay) Rockefeller IV
United States Senator,
D-West Virginia

1

For 10 years, [President] Bush and [former President Ronald] Reagan pursued a policy of greed and malignant neglect pretending to be a pragmatic domestic policy. No wonder he [Bush] plays the politics of fear, division and greed. If George Bush had to run on his record, he'd be run out of town.

At AFL-CIO conference
on community service,
Washington, July 24/
The Washington Post, 7-25:(A)22.

Charles "Buddy" Roemer
Governor of Louisiana (R)

2

[On his switching from Democrat to Republican]: At my position in life, and with my vision for meeting the challenges of a new world, a choice must be made. Independence, though admirable, is not enough. My choice is Republican. And the reason is simple. After more than 10 years of public service, it has been my observation and increasing conviction that it is the Republican Party that is becoming the most open to new ideas, new thinking, new people—

most open to team-building, to opportunity-building.

To reporters,
Baton Rouge, La., March 11/
The Christian Science Monitor,
3-14:8.

Edward J. Rollins
Co-chairman,
National Republican
Congressional Committee

3

[On Presidential Chief of Staff John Sununu, who has been criticized for using government transportation for personal travel]: I think John Sununu is a very bright man—at nuclear engineering. And I am sure he knows a lot of things, but I think his view of the world is that Republicans are conservatives from New Hampshire and Democrats are liberals from Boston . . . John Sununu lives off the reflected power of [President] George Bush. When he reflects back on the President, reflects back negatively, then I think he does a great disservice.

To reporters, Washington, July 23/
The Washington Post, 7-24:(A)17.

4

In politics, you have controllables and uncontrollables. You better hit 100 per cent on the controllables because there's always some uncontrollable element out there that you misfire on.

At symposium on Presidential politics,
University of California at San Diego,
Dec. 6/Los Angeles Times, 12-7:(A)29.

Dan Rostenkowski
United States Representative,
D-Illinois

5

The problem with Democrats is we promise more than we can deliver, and then we don't deliver on the promises we make, and people view us as irresponsible.

The New York Times, 8-5:(A)9.

John Sears
Republican Party analyst

1

[On whether Vice President Dan Quayle will run again with President Bush in the 1992 election in light of Quayle's low ratings in public-opinion polls]: Quayle will be on the ticket. It's the President's call and he wants him. Both Dwight D. Eisenhower and Richard M. Nixon wanted to change running mates when each sought re-election—and they couldn't. So there is little reason to believe that Bush, who is pleased with Quayle's performance, would make a change. Besides, making a change would be an admission that you made a mistake in the first place, something that a popular President has no reason to admit and an unpopular President can ill-afford to do.

Los Angeles Times, 5-12:(M)1.

John Seymour
United States Senator,
R-California

2

[On whether the recent U.S.-led victory in the Persian Gulf war will be enough to ensure Republican victories in next year's national elections]: Let me tell you, no way am I going to ride on the laurels of a war vote and gamble that that's enough to get you home. If we're not out of this recession, I might as well pack my bags, because people are going to vote their pocketbooks.

Los Angeles Times, 3-16:(A)2.

Robert J. Shapiro
Vice president,
Progressive Policy Institute

3

[On President Bush's widespread popularity, in part a result of public support for U.S. policy in the current Persian Gulf crisis]: The conservatives have to be unhappy right now because Bush has finally found a circumstance which his predisposition is suited for: to be a President who elevates himself above ideological conflict. This has got to be a blow to conservatives whose agenda is change. [Bush] for the first time has the potential to be independent of the hard-core conservative base.

The Washington Post, 1-31:(A)9.

Robert Shrum
Democratic Party consultant

4

[On whether the Republican Party will try to politically capitalize on the recent U.S.-led victory in the Persian Gulf war, a war which many Democrats voted against]: They [would] run the risk of doing to the war what they did in the flag-burning issue: that is, cheapening and devaluating it. Any attempt to wrap the Republican Party in the war and say, "Elect us because we were for it and the other [Democratic party] side was for [Iraqi President] Saddam Hussein," isn't going to work. Patriotism is the last refuge of a party without any other ideas.

The New York Times, 3-8:(A)11.

Paul Simon
United States Senator,
D-Illinois

5

[Recalling his 1988 bid for the Democratic Presidential nomination]: I think you start with the assumption that "I could do better than the other people who are talking about [running]," and I don't think that's a big hurdle. I think the hurdle comes when you ask the question: If you win, it changes your life-style completely for the rest of your life—and is this something you want?

The Washington Post, 8-9:(D)1.

Robert S. Strauss
Former chairman,
Democratic National Committee

6

[On the chances for a Democratic President being elected this year in light of Republican President Bush's successful handling of the Persian Gulf war]: I will admit that today it looks somewhere between unlikely and impossible that a Democrat will win the Presidency. But six months from now I don't know what it will look like. They haven't called off the election, and as long as it stays set there, the Democrats should field someone who can responsibly make the case on the issues the country must face.

The New York Times, 3-11:(A)10.

(ROBERT S. STRAUSS)

1

We [Democrats] need a . . . tough-looking, middle-America-looking, progressive candidate [for President in 1992]. The truth of the matter is, [New York Governor] Mario Cuomo looks like a fellow ought to look. He looks . . . like he ought to be playing first base for somebody, or like he'd just gone six rounds. He looks tough, he sounds tough, and he acts tough.

The Christian Science Monitor,
4-24:8.

John H. Sununu
Chief of Staff to President
of the United States
George Bush

2

[On whether Republicans will try to politically capitalize on the recent U.S.-led victory in the Persian Gulf war, a war which many Democrats voted against]: Oh, I think the country's going to have to make a decision on people's records in the election process, and I can't believe that the Democrats who fought really on a party basis to resist the President are going to expect that individual [Republican] candidates may not bring that up. We're not going to bring it up out of the White House, but I can't believe that they're going to expect everyone to ignore the vote they cast on the most important issue this country has had to deal with in about 40 years.

Broadcast interview/
"Today" show, NBC-TV, 3-7.

Robert G. Torricelli
United States Representative,
D-New Jersey

3

[Calling for a formal inquiry into allegations that members of Ronald Reagan's 1980 Presidential campaign secretly negotiated a delay in the release of U.S. hostages held captive by Iran until after the election]: The charges are so serious that even partisan members don't want to believe them. Unfortunately, there's been too much testimony and too much evidence to ignore them. The charges just won't go away . . . There

is a perception that continuing with the investigation has obvious political benefit for Democrats and that this is a relatively easy decision to make. Nothing could be further from the truth. This has caused great apprehension for Democrats . . . We should begin, not because we're convinced of anyone's guilt, but because we want to find out.

The Christian Science Monitor,
7-8:1,2.

Paul E. Tsongas
Candidate for the
1992 Democratic
Presidential nomination;
Former United States Senator,
D-Massachusetts

4

[On his being the first Democrat to announce his candidacy for President in next year's election]: It's like Economics 101. There's an enormous demand for a candidate out there and at the moment I'm the only supply.

Time, 4-8:27.

5

The definition of liberalism, as I see it, is the expansion of the economic pie. If Democrats don't understand how to create jobs, and the pie shrinks . . . there is nothing liberal about that.

The Christian Science Monitor,
9-17:7.

Gore Vidal
Author

6

The American Republic disappeared nearly 40 years ago, and nobody noticed. There are not two political parties—there is only one. People notice it instinctively. Fifty per cent of them won't vote, and fifty per cent don't read newspapers. I hope it's the same fifty per cent.

Interview/Emmy, May-June:85.

Maxine Waters
United States Representative,
D-California

7

[On whether Vice President Dan Quayle will run again with President Bush in the 1992 elec-

(MAXINE WATERS)

tion in light of Quayle's low ratings in public-opinion polls]: Yes, I think Quayle will be on the ticket, but that doesn't mean he should be. Quayle is a lightweight who makes a mockery of the word "qualified." He is the epitome of the privileged white male who has bypassed the hurdles that the average citizen must overcome in order to achieve position, status or recognition.

Los Angeles Times, 5-12:(M)1.

L. Douglas Wilder
Governor of Virginia (D)

1

It bothers me, it really bothers me, when people say [President] Bush can't be beaten [in the 1992 Presidential election]: Why? Who says so? [People said former British Prime Minister] Margaret Thatcher couldn't be beaten; [the late British Prime Minister] Winston Churchill couldn't be beaten; [Soviet President Mikhail] Gorbachev couldn't be. All [of them] were considered experts on foreign policy, but hoist on the petard of domestic inactivity.

Interview/
The New York Times, 9-4:(A)14.

2

[On how to broaden the appeal of the Democratic Party]: My point is, rather than say my pitch to the black voter is this or my pitch to the labor voter is this, you concentrate on the problem. And in the process of doing that, you bring into the Party a large number of persons who believe the same way that we do on the issues.

Los Angeles Times, 9-17:(A)15.

3

[On his running for the Presidency]: I know it's difficult for people like you to understand that people like me could want to be the top. Maybe you never wanted to be the top. But I've always wanted to be at the top. When I say people like you, I don't mean it personally. It is difficult—very, very, difficult—for people to assume that an

African-American could actually believe that he could be the top. And it always has happened to me in reference to elections that people have said, oh come on, you got to be kidding. Governor? Of the state of Virginia?

Interview, Richmond, Va./
The New York Times, 12-30:(A)10.

Pete Wilson
Governor of California (R)

4

We must reject the flawed straw-man characterization of conservatives by liberals as uncaring. We need an honest characterization that fairly and accurately portrays our approach of compassionate, creative conservatism.

At 50th anniversary celebration
of Stanford University's Hoover Institution,
July 18/Los Angeles Times, 7-19:(A)3.

Clayton K. Yeutter
Chairman-designate,
Republican National Committee

5

[On those Democrats who voted against authorizing President Bush to begin military action against Iraq in the current Persian Gulf war]: They are certainly [politically] vulnerable on their votes on the Persian Gulf conflict. I would guess that about 90 per cent of those folks wish now that they [had] cast their votes the other way, because they picked the wrong side in the viewpoint of the American public. And if the conflict continues to go well, that will be a very significant factor in the near future.

Before Lincoln, Neb., Rotary Club,
Jan. 22/
Los Angeles Times, 1-25:(A)10.

Clayton K. Yeutter
Chairman,
Republican National Committee

6

[On a recent meeting between Democratic Party leaders and donors in Middleburg, Va.]: [The Democrats] can't see beyond the end of their political strategists' noses as they confer

(CLAYTON K. YEUTTER)

with their six-figure special-interest contributors in fox-and-hound country. No wonder they can't communicate with working men and women any more.

At Republican National
Committee meeting, Houston,
June 21/The New York Times, 6-22:7.

1

[On David Duke, who is running for the 1992 Republican Presidential nomination and who has a racist past]: With respect to David Duke, as far as I'm concerned he's not in the Republican Party. If he wishes to have his own party, that's obviously his privilege in a democratic society. But I am confident his racist and bigoted appeal will be rejected in Presidential campaigns, irrespective of his identification, as it was in [the recent gubernatorial election] in Louisiana. We do not view Mr. Duke as a legitimate candidate.

Interview/
USA Today, 12-18:(A)13.

Ed Zschau
Former United States Representative,
R-California

2

If we [moderate Republicans] are going to lead in the 1990s, we have to understand and communicate your values with the kind of intensity that's usually associated with the extremes. In other words, we must become "flaming moderates" in order to inspire [the people's] support.

Before California Republican League,
Walnut Creek, Calif.,
Nov. 17/
Los Angeles Times, 11-18:(A)3.

Social Welfare

Bruce Babbitt
*Former Governor
of Arizona (D)*

1

Sending the same size Social Security check to a millionaire and to a widow living in a cold-water flat doesn't make sense. If we're serious about getting the economy moving and balancing the budget, we can't automatically exclude [Social Security and Medicare from cuts].

USA Today, 1-4:(A)2.

Derek C. Bok
President, Harvard University

2

An eerie indifference hangs over the land. Instead of a popular outcry to end the urban violence, the poverty, the homelessness, the hunger of children, the loudest clamor we hear from the public today is "no new taxes."

*At Harvard University commencement,
June 6/The New York Times, 6-7:(A)10.*

Tom Bradley
Mayor of Los Angeles

3

[Criticizing those who do not want subsidized housing built near their neighborhoods]: One of the things that I know you recognize as an impediment to the development of affordable housing in this city is that those who are already in place, those who have their homes in neighborhoods very nicely built up, somehow seem to believe that they don't have a responsibility to those who follow them. And now the NIMBY [not in my back yard] attitude takes over. My friends, we've got to get over that attitude . . . There are too many people in this country who are without housing, and there is no place to turn except to say to every community that you've got to assume your share.

*Before Los Angeles Housing
Department, Aug. 14/
Los Angeles Times, 8-15:(A)1.*

James S. Brady
*Vice chairman, National
Organization on Disability;
Former Press Secretary
to the President
of the United States
(Ronald Reagan)*

4

Excluding mentally retarded individuals from a restaurant is not in the spirit of this nation. Requiring a blind person to present a driver's license as identification for cashing a check can be humiliating. Removing physical barriers in existing facilities, where it can be done easily and at no great expense, is only right and fair. Installing a ramp, lowering some shelves, raising some tables in restaurants so I can get my wheelchair under, creating designated accessible parking spaces—all this will be good for our economy. Opening up public accommodations means more demand for the goods and services produced by the private sector . . . We are at the beginning of the last great inclusion in American life—the inclusion of people with disabilities. The ADA [Americans with Disabilities Act] is just the beginning, because full participation in all aspects of life will require changing attitudes toward people with disabilities. The ADA will not automatically do that. The opportunity for enduring change lies in the communities of America, where disabled and non-disabled people go about their daily lives.

*Washington, March 14/
The Washington Post, 3-20:(A)18.*

Mario M. Cuomo
Governor of New York (D)

5

We had a victory parade [after the recent Persian Gulf war] in New York City, and it certainly was marvelous. But I'm looking forward to a different kind of victory parade, one which regrettably we could not hold at this moment. I would just love to march through inner-city and middle-class neighborhoods where all the chil-

(MARIO M. CUOMO)

dren and all the people had health care. I'd love to be in a parade where I could clap my hands and throw my fists in the air as we marched through neighborhoods where every school is a good one, where the streets were safe, where children could be children, where they would get a chance to go to college, one day even have the chance to own their own homes.

Before executive committee
of U.S. Conference of Mayors,
Hyannis, Mass., Aug. 9/
The Washington Post, 8-10:(A)7.

Marian Wright Edelman
President, Children's
Defense Fund

1

If we are serious about getting out of our [Washington, D.C.'s city] budget crisis, then we better start taking care of our kids before they get into trouble, before they are mowed down in the streets, before they end up in the neonatal intensive-care nursery. You cannot not invest in prevention if you are serious about your children . . . The budget crisis is not the children's fault.

News conference,
Washington, Sept. 16/
The Washington Post, 9-17:(A)8.

David T. Ellwood
Professor of public policy,
Kennedy School of Government,
Harvard University

2

The chief source of economic insecurity in America used to be growing old; now it's being born into or raised in a single-parent family. If Social Security were being designed today, I suspect it would have taken this new reality into account.

The Washington Post, 2-22:(A)21.

Mike Espy
United States Representative,
D-Mississippi

3

Empowerment [of the poor] is not a Republican philosophy or a Democratic philosophy; it is

an American policy goal. I am a practical Democrat, and I know that some of the programs that emanated from [the läte] President [Franklin] Roosevelt have not worked. Programs that help people subsist don't really help people out of poverty. To escape poverty, people need assets. That is why Project HOPE [Home Ownership for People Everywhere] is so important. On the cotton plantations of the Mississippi Delta, experience taught us that whoever controls your home controls your life. Project HOPE is about helping people who are stuck in public housing attain the assets that will give them self-sufficiency.

To employees of U.S. Department
of Housing and Urban Development/
The Washington Post, 9-11:(A)23.

Donald M. Fraser
Mayor of Minneapolis

4

We know that we have a welfare system, frankly, that discourages marriage. If you're the father of a child and you can't get a good job, that mother is crazy to marry you because she goes off welfare. She has no health care for her child. She can't live on a minimum-wage job. We have a public policy that is designed to destroy families, and nobody talks about it. We've got a crazy system. We've got to get out of this liberal-conservative polarization and start to focus on what we are doing to families and kids.

Panel discussion at National League
of Cities' annual legislative conference,
Washington, March 10/
The Washington Post, 3-11:(A)4.

John Guidubaldi
Professor of psychology,
Kent State University;
Former president,
National Association
of School Psychologists

5

For years experts said, "Once the trauma [of divorce] wears off, kids make adjustments." Well, so do people in prisons and mental institutions. The pertinent question is: Are those adjust-

(JOHN GUIDUBALDI)

ments healthy? The weight of the evidence has become overwhelming on the side that they aren't . . . People simply aren't putting enough effort into saving their marriages. I think the old argument of staying together for the sake of the kids is still the best argument.

The Washington Post, 1-29:(A)6.

Cheryl Hayes
Executive Director, National
Commission on Children

1

A whole series of realizations seem to have sunk in simultaneously. One is that millions of children are in deep poverty. Another is that the earthquake that shuddered through the American family over the past generation took its greatest toll on children, regardless of economic circumstance. The third is that children are a declining segment of the population and, if we're going to have a competitive work-force, we can't afford to lose any of them.

The Washington Post, 3-27:(A)1.

Sylvia Ann Hewlett
Economist

2

What we've done in this country in the past few decades is socialize the cost of growing old and privatize the cost of childhood. From an economic perspective, it makes no sense; children are an investment in our future. From the standpoint of compassion, we might have been able to get away with treating children this way in Norman Rockwell times, but not today, when so many families are fragile, brittle and dysfunctional.

The Washington Post, 2-22:(A)21.

Benjamin L. Hooks
Executive director,
National Association for the
Advancement of Colored People

3

[On the great disparity in wealth between white families and minority families]: It means

that [in black and Hispanic households] you have grinding poverty, the absence of amenities, books, newspapers, magazines, encyclopedias, health care, college funds, the kinds of things that build the environment that move people toward upward mobility.

Jan. 10/
The Washington Post, 1-11:(A)3.

Barbara Jordan
Professor of government,
Lyndon Johnson School
of Public Policy,
University of Texas, Austin;
Former United States Representative,
D-Texas

4

I have thought that perhaps we should redirect our efforts away from civil rights per se and toward addressing the problems of the inner cities and of poverty without regard to race. Nor do we need to reinvent the wheel or to come up with new solutions. Many anti-poverty programs have been tried and they worked. Model Cities and other programs from [the late President] Lyndon Johnson's Great Society did work, they did move people out of poverty. We need only put them into place and to persevere.

Interview, Austin, Texas/
Los Angeles Times, 9-8:(M)3.

Jack Kemp
Secretary of Housing
and Urban Development
of the United States

5

[Saying there is a diminishing supply of affordable housing in the U.S.]: One of the biggest problems is the level of regulations that has grown up over the years. I don't think anybody set out 10 or 20 years ago to reduce the stock of affordable housing. I don't think anybody sat down to look at what the impact would be of zoning or building fees or impact costs or wetlands and environmental legislation—all of these generic, regulatory laws that have built up topsy-turvy . . . [But] today close to 60 per cent of the American families cannot afford a median-priced home.

Interview/USA Today, 8-13:(A)11.

Lisa K. Mihaly
Senior program specialist,
Children's Defense Fund

1

Children, in the most horrible circumstances, maintain their sense of hope and their sense of humor and their desire to learn. I find that very inspiring. When I see them, I just feel so strongly that society has an obligation to try to help them hold on to that, and that the way to do that is to make sure that they have a safe place to live, a safe place to sleep and enough to eat, a good place to go to school and the health care they need. As adults, when we talk about public policy, those are the things that we really have to do.

Interview/USA Today, 7-30:(A)9.

John D. (Jay) Rockefeller IV
United States Senator,
D-West Virginia

2

Half a million children drop out of school every year. Too often, those who do graduate can't read or add well enough to get a job. Half of them have tried illegal drugs. More than half drink. For the last decade, the political air has been clouded with slogans and buzzwords about "family values" . . . that concealed a sad reality: Life has been getting worse for our children and their families. And we have done almost nothing.

Speech/
The Christian Science Monitor,
7-22:2.

3

America's parents and America's children are speaking directly to Washington through this [recent] survey [on families]. They are telling us that they are being tested and torn by too little time, by too little money, by too many absent parents and by their growing fears about crime . . . [But] despite the pressures, most families are making heroic efforts to hold themselves together. They're swimming upstream—but they're making it.

Nov. 21/
Los Angeles Times, 11-22:(A)4.

Stanford G. Ross
Former Commissioner,
Social Security
Administration
of the United States

4

The Social Security Administration accounts for about two-thirds of the expenditures—more than $400-billion—and one-half the personnel of HHS—65,000 employees . . . While SSA will do as good a job as it can with what it is given, its workload is backlogged and its efficiency is likely being hindered by the [Bush] Administration's proposed administrative budget. From a public management standpoint, SSA's administrative budget ought to be formulated to reflect the needs of the constituencies it serves, which would be consistent with its now being treated as an off-budget trust-fund account.

Feb. 4/
The Washington Post, 2-5:(A)17.

Dan Rostenkowski
United States Representative,
D-Illinois

5

If I were President, I'd focus on children. They've been in the dark cellar of policy debate for too long. Their problems are stark. They cannot plead their own case . . . And kids are a good investment. If we help them today, they'll strengthen our economy tomorrow . . . There's a depressingly logical momentum here. Kids who start off on the wrong foot spend a lifetime trying to catch up. And they often don't. Kids who don't have enough to eat tend to get sick. Kids who lack adequate medical care tend to miss a lot of school. Kids who aren't in class don't learn how to read. Teen-agers who are illiterate tend to drop out of high school. High-school dropouts can't get good jobs. Often they can't get jobs at all. Those who become dependent on the government for aid divert resources that could be used better in other areas.

Before National Association of
Children's Hospitals and Related
Institutions, March 18/
The Washington Post, 3-19:(A)6.

Patricia Schroeder
United States Representative,
D-Colorado

1

[The Bush Administration says] the right words [on child abuse], but words don't provide any real comfort to a child who is being abused. You don't need to convince people [that] child abuse is bad. It's not like cigarette smoking, which at one point was socially acceptable. There's no place in America where it's socially acceptable to be a child abuser. Talk doesn't cure it. You need a multidisciplinary approach, and that isn't cheap.

Los Angeles Times, 4-17:(A)12.

Louis W. Sullivan
Secretary of Health
and Human Services
of the United States

2

So many of our problems—drug and alcohol abuse, the spread of AIDS, teen pregnancy, infant mortality, youth homicide, among others—reflect the personal isolation, alienation and despair that follow from the widespread erosion of family and community in our society.

At National League of Cities'
annual legislative conference,
Washington, March 10/
The Washington Post, 3-11:(A)4.

3

The collapse of the American family in the past few decades is historically unprecedented in the U.S., and possibly in the world. Nowhere is this trend more apparent than in the black community, where 86 per cent of children spend part of their childhood living in a mother-only family. Some argue that the high rate of single parenthood has not adversely affected our children. But sadly, the research does not bear them out . . . Study after study has shown that children from single-parent families are five times more likely to be involved in criminal activity, to abuse drugs and alcohol, to suffer ill health, and to become trapped in welfare dependency.

At Hampton (Va.) University,
March 13/The Washington Post, 3-14:(A)14.

Michael Wald
Professor of law,
Stanford University

4

Child advocates like to use the generic term "children" as if here should be a big movement on behalf of all children. But most of the programs that advocates can agree upon really focus on the needs of poor children, primarily children of color. And the bulk of the electorate in this country is unwilling to support programs for other people's children if those people are perceived predominantly as people of color . . . The bulk of Federal money that is spent on children is spent on families earning $30,000 or more. The dependent allowance, the deductions for medical care, the fact that in education most of the money is going into suburban schools, plus the mortgage deductions, which allow middle-class kids to live in much better housing—we are in fact subsidizing children, but we're subsidizing richer children to a large degree. Now, those children do have problems, but it's not medical care. What they really want is for us to think of a way to keep their parents from getting divorced, because their biggest problem is the conflicts around divorce.

Panel discussion/
Mother Jones, May-June:35,38.

Fred Wertheimer
President, Common Cause

5

The cost of health care and housing are two of the most important issues facing American citizens today. The AMA PAC gives millions of dollars to influence House members; there is no patients' PAC. The realtors PAC gives millions of dollars to influence House members; there is no homebuyers' PAC.

USA Today, 7-15:(A)4.

Walter Williams
Professor of economics,
George Mason University

6

We don't have the decency to treat poor people the right way. We do to them what we would never do to someone that we loved. We want to give the poor money without demanding responsibility. Would you do that to your children? If we love our children, we teach them responsibility. My mother told me, "You gonna make your bed hard, you gonna lay in it."

The Christian Science Monitor,
9-23:9.

Pete Wilson
Governor of California (R)

1

Homelessness is a social tragedy that results from any number of personal tragedies: drug abuse, alcoholism, mental illness, battered wives, runaway kids . . . Providing shelter alone is not going to solve the problems, not those problems.

At conference of homeless-advocate
groups, Sacramento, Calif., March 12/
Los Angeles Times, 3-13:(A)19.

Nicholas Zill
Executive director,
Child Trends, Inc.

2

We want to be careful not to say that every child who has been through a divorce will be scarred for life . . . or that every child raised in a traditional two-parent family will turn out fine. But if you looked at the kind of long-term risk factors that divorce creates for kids and translated them to, say, heart disease, people would be startled.

The Washington Post,
1-29:(A)6.

Karl Zinsmeister
Adjunct scholar,
American Enterprise Institute

3

In this country today, family structure is the most important determinant of economic standing—more important than race, geography, anything else. We have study after study which shows that children in single-parent families are more likely to have problems in schools, to have psychological and behavioral problems . . . [Yet] the polite party line on family trends continues to be that families are not falling apart, they are just evolving, bless their hearts.

At forum sponsored by Progressive
Policy Institute, April 12/
The Washington Post,
4-13:(A)6.

Transportation

Robert L. Crandall
Chairman, AMR Corporation
(American Airlines)

1

Over the next decade, the [airline] industry is clearly going to have to do a better job of pricing its product to cover its costs and provide a reasonable margin of profitability. In the long term, an unprofitable industry isn't going to generate healthy competition. That's bad news for consumers.

U.S. News & World Report,
5-13:57.

2

[On the airline industry]: Much, indeed most, of our [financial] problems can be attributed to managements who seem to believe their mission in life is to put every living human being on an airplane at any price. This get-'em-on-the-plane mentality is exacerbated by the fact that more than 25 per cent of our industry's capacity is being operated by bankrupts and near-bankrupt carriers.

To group of analysts,
September/
The Washington Post,
10-15:(A)11.

3

Non-stop flights cost more, and a lot of people choose them. If you are in Dallas-Fort Worth and you want to go to La Guardia, you can fly non-stop and pay a premium for that convenience. Or you can save some money by flying a connecting flight, say through Chicago. The notion that we [airlines] are gouging people is crazy. It's sort of like asking, What's the average room rate at the Ritz-Carlton and Motel 6? Well, it's nicer at the Ritz-Carlton. It's nicer there. You get what you pay for. If you want a lower price, you can go to Motel 6.

Interview/
Time, 10-28:18.

John D. Dingell
United States Representative,
D-Michigan

4

The domestic auto industry is very, very important to America's well-being and the citizenry as a whole. Not only from an economic standpoint, but for the security of the entire country and our way of life.

At gathering sponsored by Chrysler,
Ford and General Motors,
Hamtramck, Mich., April 26/
Los Angeles Times, 4-27:(D)2.

Thomas Donohue
President,
American Trucking Association

5

The trucking industry does $250-billion worth of business. We employ 7.5 million people. We carry almost 80 per cent of the dollar value of everything that is manufactured, shipped, consumed, imported, exported and hauled around this country. We're somewhere between 5 per cent and 6.5 per cent of the economy. The railroads, on the other hand, do $30-billion worth of business. Obviously, it is absolutely essential that you use trucks. About 70 per cent of communities find the only type of service they can physically get is by trucks.

Interview/USA Today, 1-8:(A)11.

Jalal Haidar
Authority on aviation security

6

If you fly from Athens to Rome to Geneva to New York to Chicago, everything will be done according to international standards *except* security. Private security firms hire part-time help because it's cheap. So you've got high-school dropouts, senior citizens and people holding second jobs handling security. They aren't well-trained and don't take their job seriously.

USA Today, 2-11:(A)4.

162

Lee A. Iacocca
Chairman,
Chrysler Corporation

1

[Saying U.S. car-makers should consider supporting legislation to place quotas on imports of Japanese automobiles]: We've never favored a complete restriction, but we'll have to decide our collective position. We have to deal with our own self-interests. At some point, you have to decide what you stand for. [The U.S. is] out of the electronics business, the VCR business, and soon we could be out of the car business.

At dedication of Chrysler Corporation
technology center,
Auburn Hills, Mich., Oct. 15/
The New York Times, 10-16:(C)10.

Robert Lutz
President,
Chrysler Corporation

2

[On current poor automobile sales]: Nobody is selling anything. Times couldn't be worse. The only people buying are those with 90,000 miles on their cars or people who have had their cars stolen or burned.

Time, 1-28:73.

Carolina L. Mederos
Former Deputy Assistant Secretary
for Safety,
Department of Transportation
of the United States

3

There are several Departments of Transportation—the DOT that builds and maintains the nation's infrastructure, the DOT that operates a portion of it, primarily aviation, and the DOT that regulates its safety and security . . . The real challenge goes to those who must operate the system day in and day out. Once again, the Department has proposed incremental increases in operations. It proposes adding 450 air traffic controllers and 260 air maintenance personnel. Perhaps this is all the system can absorb, but one

wonders if it isn't a race to stay even. Every year the system suffers new expected setbacks, such as the costly and lagging modernization of the national airspace system, and unexpected setbacks such as the retirement of a significant number of key aviation personnel last year.

Feb. 4/
The Washington Post, 2-5:(A)17.

Norman Y. Mineta
United States Representative,
D-California

4

We have demonstrated our ability to build highways to move *vehicles*. Now we must tackle the more difficult challenge of moving *people* within the heavily congested urban and suburban communities connected by these highways.

The Washington Post, 6-22:(A)4.

Bud Shuster
United States Representative,
R-Pennsylvania

5

. . . we must realize that America's growing, and with that growth we not only have to maintain the Interstate [highway] system, but we have to recognize those highways of national significance which are not on the Interstate system . . . A modest increase in the gas tax is absolutely essential if we are going to provide the American people with a sound, efficient, productive, safe transportation system as we move into the 21st century.

TV broadcast/Nation's Business,
September:23.

Samuel K. Skinner
Secretary of Transportation
of the United States

6

[If the airline industry does not control its costs,] it cannot grow, it cannot remain productive and we will find ourselves 10 years from now

(SAMUEL K. SKINNER)

going to a situation that we all found uncomfortable last week, when Congress mandated settlements for management and labor in the rail industry. You cannot raise costs without increases in productivity at an annualized rate of 10 per cent a year for your flight crews when inflation is 4 per cent and claim you've got costs under control.

Before Society of American Business
Editors and Writers,
Washington, April 29/
The New York Times,
4-30:(C)15.

James D. Watkins
Secretary of Energy
of the United States

1

[On reducing the size of cars to conserve fuel]: The American people do not like midget cars on big highways. There are 51-m.p.g. cars on the market today. Few people buy them. Why? Americans want a high-performance machine they will be comfortable in out there on the L.A. freeways. To impose on the American people things they find distasteful is not this Administration's policy.

Interview, Washington/
Los Angeles Times, 8-11:(M)3.

Jerry Abramson
Mayor of Louisville, Ky.

1

[Criticizing Bush Administration plans to transfer the Federal Community Development Block Grants program to the states]: The Federal government pulled the rug out from under us [cities] before [with cuts in aid]. This would not only pull the rug out, it would remove the house, and we'd be standing in the middle of the field.

Feb. 4/
Los Angeles Times, 2-5:(A)20.

Sidney Barthelemy
Mayor of New Orleans

2

When people move outside the city, they still have an obligation to the city, because most of those people still come into the city to work. It is still the place where most of their children will get educated, where the museums, theatres and the arts are located. Cities are important, and I think Americans should look across the ocean to Europe. What is France without a Paris? What is England without a London? There is a commitment among the Europeans that their cities are important.

Interview/USA Today, 3-18:(A)11.

John A. Bohn
President,
Moody's Investors Service

3

[A] creditworthy [city] government has *credibility* with all its constituents, meaning its citizens as taxpayers present and future and as consumers of services, but also meaning its investors, present and prospective. Credibility is no longer achieved by paying a fat retainer to a public-relations firm. Credibility must be *earned* by facing the tough questions of urban government, and facing them *together with* those constituents. Credibility requires owning up to what those constituents suspect in any case: that we

can't afford everything we want, and therefore must make choices, however painful. Credibility must be achieved by honest accounting, by presenting a rigorously honest bill of the costs involved for all proposed objectives. Authorities too often take the position that citizens aren't interested in such details. What this usually means is that the authorities themselves feel threatened by an open accounting.

At U.S. Conference of Mayors,
San Diego, June 18/
The Wall Street Journal,
6-19:(A)14.

David N. Dinkins
Mayor of New York

4

[Criticizing Commerce Secretary Robert Mosbacher's decision not to adjust the 1990 census results to compensate for an apparent undercount of over 5 million people, which the Mayor says could result in some cities not receiving their fair share of Federal aid]: The Secretary's decision is a deplorable one, driven more by politics than by sound public-policy considerations. It is sure to have crushing consequences for our city, and our entire country.

July 15/
The Washington Post, 7-16:(A)1.

Sharon Pratt Dixon
Mayor of Washington

5

What we have on the streets of Washington, D.C., is almost a type of revolution—people who feel no interest, no stake in the world at hand. The malady ultimately impacts us all. We may shove it aside and kind of move it over there, but ultimately it comes back to hit us in another kind of way . . . One [side of the city] is blessed by great talent and wealth . . . including one of the most prosperous, successful black middle-class communities of anywhere in the world. Another Washington—alienated, angry and isolated . . .

(SHARON PRATT DIXON)

is too often reflected by an angry teen-ager with a gun, a crack-cocaine baby, a homeless panhandler.

*Speech, at Metropolitan Memorial
United Methodist Church,
Washington, Sept. 22/
The Washington Post, 9-23:(A)7.*

Raymond L. Flynn
Mayor of Boston

1

Over the past week, we have seen [in the Persian Gulf war] what extraordinary feats can be accomplished militarily when the Federal government focuses talent and resources on a particular challenge. Let us resolve now that America's urban agenda is next in line.

*Washington, Jan. 23/
The Washington Post, 1-24:(A)19.*

2

There has been a really callous indifference [at the Federal level] toward America's cities. And that's the reason why we're seeing some of the problems that are being played out each and every night in our communities—problems of crime and problems of violence and homelessness and problems with our young people. It would be a mistake to say that it's just the President [Bush] alone that has been ignoring American cities. It has been the whole Washington bureaucracy, and that includes the White House, the Congress, Democrats as well as Republicans. There has been no policy whatsoever dealing with building strong families, strong neighborhoods, strong American cities.

*Broadcast interview/
"Meet the Press," NBC-TV, 9-1.*

Joseph A. Giacalone
*Associate professor of economics,
St. John's University,
Jamaica, N.Y.*

3

There's a political demand [on cities] to do more and more—and most are "good" things like

providing health care, taking care of the homeless, concerts in the park. But it's difficult to do everything and do it well. People say [that with any cutbacks] everything will collapse. Well, it won't. We've got to do some long-term serious downsizing.

*The Christian Science Monitor,
6-28:2.*

Maynard Jackson
Mayor of Atlanta

4

We are a nation of failing cities. And therefore we are a failing nation, because 80 per cent of the people in America live on 2 per cent of the land. We are a nation of cities. And we have an infrastructure . . . that is being completely ignored.

*Broadcast interview/
"Meet the Press," NBC-TV, 9-1.*

Ruth Messinger
*President of the Borough
of Manhattan, New York City*

5

[On the recent victory of the U.S.-led Operation Desert Storm against Iraq's occupation of Kuwait]: Now that the liberation of Kuwait has been accomplished, my colleagues and I propose that the Federal government immediately undertake the liberation of millions of Americans in our cities trapped by the tyranny of poverty, illiteracy, hunger, unemployment, crime and hopelessness. We propose, in short, the launching of Operation Urban Storm.

*Before House Government Operations
Committee, Washington, March 12/
The Washington Post, 3-13:(A)3.*

Robert A. Mosbacher
*Secretary of Commerce
of the United States*

6

[Saying that, despite protests, he will not adjust the 1990 census results to compensate for an apparent undercount of over 5 million people]: After a thorough review, I find the evidence in

(ROBERT A. MOSBACHER)

support of an adjustment to be inconclusive and unconvincing. While we know that some [cities] will fare better and some will fare worse [in Federal aid] under an adjustment, we don't really know how much better or how much worse. If the scientists cannot agree on these issues, how can we expect the losing cities and states as well as the American public to accept this change?

News conference,
Washington, July 15/
The Washington Post, 7-16:(A)1.

Peter O. Muller
Professor of geography,
University of Miami

1

[On the rapid population growth of suburbs in the 1980s]: This is one of the most historic changes in the history of the American city. The suburbs are no longer sub to the urb . . . We always thought this would be the future—the Census tells us it is the present.

USA Today, 3-4:(A)9.

Joseph P. Riley, Jr.
Mayor of Charleston, S.C.

2

[Criticizing Bush Administration plans to transfer the Federal Community Development Block Grants program to state control]: We think that [such a transfer] would be a huge mistake. If ever there is a classic example of "if it isn't broke, don't fix it," it's certainly the Community Development Block Grants.

Feb. 4/
Los Angeles Times, 2-5:(A)20.

Albert Scardino
Press Secretary
to New York Mayor
David Dinkins

3

There are Governors around the country who distract attention from their own problems by pointing to the cities as cesspools of sin and degradation. It's a pattern that's as predictable as

sunrise. And the louder it gets, the more you can be sure that their own problems are growing in severity.

The New York Times, 1-7:(A)17.

Raymond Eugene Shipman
City Manager of Hartford, Conn.

4

[Criticizing a Bush Administration proposal to convert billions of dollars in state and local categorical grants for social services, education and housing into a single block grant to states]: The state has no idea what the problems of the urban communities are. We'll get more of the doughnut syndrome, with the cities being the hole and all of the resources going to the suburbs.

At National League of Cities'
annual legislative conference,
Washington, March 10/
The Washington Post, 3-11:(A)4.

Michael Stewart
Commissioner,
Salt Lake County, Utah;
President, National
Association of Counties

5

There's not a lot of competition between cities and counties [for Federal money] because, of the roughly 112 to 120 services that we deliver, 13 or 15 of those would be delivered by cities—fire, police, street lighting, planning and zoning, garbage, animal services, highways and so on. That's what cities do. We [counties] do that for the vast suburbia of America. We do compete for property tax because largely that's the only source that counties have. We're competing with school districts, which are funded by property taxes. But basically, we are competing at the Congressional level.

Interview/USA Today, 3-18:(A)11.

Michael R. White
Mayor of Cleveland

6

[On the amount of money the government is spending on the current Persian Gulf war compared with the amount of Federal aid to U.S. cities]: I'm not frustrated; I'm angry. I'm the Mayor of one of the largest cities in the country

(MICHAEL R. WHITE)

1

while we have an Administration [in Washington] that is completely oblivious to the problems of human beings in this country. I sit here like everyone else watching [war coverage on] CNN, watching a half-billion dollar a day investment in Iraq and Kuwait, and I can't get a half-million increase in investment in Cleveland or any other city.

Washington, Jan. 23/The Washington Post, 1-24:(A)19.

You can't have a great town with only a great downtown. I've said to corporate Cleveland over and over again that I'm going to work on the agenda of downtown Cleveland, but I also expect them to work on the agenda of neighborhood rebuilding.

Interview,
Cleveland/
The Christian Science Monitor,
8-12:9.

PART TWO

International

Foreign Affairs

Morton I. Abramowitz
President,
Carnegie Endowment for
International Peace

1

The fundamental problem of the CIA is not flying planes and listening in. It's analytical. There has to be a conscious effort to improve the quality of analysis and to maintain and nurture people who understand the countries and societies we are dealing with.

The New York Times,
9-2:7.

Madeleine Albright
President,
Center for National Policy
(United States)

2

[Saying the recent U.S.-led victory in the Persian Gulf War against Iraq's occupation of Kuwait should not lead to the use of force as a normal part of foreign policy]: All [international] problems can't be solved by bombing the bejesus out of some small country.

Panel discussion at meeting of
House Democrats,
Leesburg, Va., March 8/
Los Angeles Times, 3-9:(A)14.

Robert E. Allen
Chairman,
American Telephone
& Telegraph Company

3

Like the cobbler raising barefoot children, we [Americans] seem more intent on outfitting the world for freedom than fulfilling our obligations at home.

Before House Budget Committee,
Washington, March 6/
The Washington Post,
3-7:(A)21.

Kofi Nyidevu Awoonor
Ghanian Ambassador
to the United Nations

4

[On who will replace outgoing UN Secretary General Javier Perez de Cuellar]: There is no need for a superstar. The drama is within the UN already because of the collapse of the Cold War. A superstar may only muddy water. You don't need a *prima donna*. The opera is already written.

Los Angeles Times, 5-27:(E)2.

James A. Baker III
Secretary of State
of the United States

5

Two weeks ago we had some very contentious items—I call them old-agenda items—on our agenda with the Soviet Union. One of those was independence for the Baltic states. That is off the agenda. The Baltic states have their independence. Cuba—a very, very difficult issue, a thorny issue in U.S.-soviet relations for a long, long time. You heard what [Soviet] President [Mikhail] Gorbachev said on that issue [that his country is disengaging from its military and economic ties with Cuba]. That old-agenda item is disappearing from the agenda. Afghanistan—an issue where the Soviet Union and the United States have been directly in confrontation and at loggerheads for quite some time. This agreement this morning [the two countries agreeing to stop arms shipments to Afghanistan]—something we have sought to work out for the last two years—has now been worked out, at least in terms of a willingness on the part of both of us to say that no more military supplies are going to be shipped in there after the first of January. This removes three of the most contentious and "old-agenda" items that have impeded and obstructed progress in this relationship, and I just have to tell you we are delighted to see these old-agenda items being removed.

Verbal statement to the press, Moscow,
Sept. 13/The New York Times, 9-14:4.

Abolhassan Bani-Sadr
Exiled former President
of Iran

1

. . . the reality is that no country in the Third World likes the United States . . . What they see is the American power. The question is, what is wrong with America implementing policies so that these countries and these people like the United States instead of hating it? . . . Look at my case. I was elected by my people, very freely. I'm against fanaticism, against terrorism, I'm for freedom, I'm for democracy. But then, people from your government [the U.S.] go and make deals secretly with the group who's in power now [in Iran], and deprive my people of democracy . . . The question is, how long are these secret relations going to continue; how long is this type of policy going to continue?

Interview, Washington/
The Washington Post, 5-6:(B)4.

Gudrun Biffl
Labor economist, Austrian Institute
of Economic Research

2

[On the emigration from poorer countries to richer countries]: The traditional argument has always been that if you help them realize strong economic growth, foreigners will stay home. But if you take the case of Asia, you see there has been 8 to 10 per cent economic growth [in] "miracle" countries like Korea and Thailand, but still they have emigration.

The Christian Science Monitor,
8-7:13.

Daniel J. Boorstin
Historian; Former Librarian
of Congress of the United States

3

In America you become a democrat simply by crossing the ocean and becoming part of the American community. It's easy . . . We have developed a series of institutions and traditions that help us keep in balance our sense of community and quest for independence . . . But the Soviets or Yugoslavs cannot become democrats by simply dropping a few phrases. You need the right institutions.

Interview/
The Christian Science Monitor,
7-18:19.

David L. Boren
United States Senator,
D-Oklahoma

4

Two separate [intelligence] empires have been built up over the years—civilian intelligence and military intelligence. Two separate empires with a lot of duplication and overlap. We just can't afford it any more. We've got to force them together for budgetary reasons . . . We've really got to blend these two cultures in a much more effective way. Each side has some reason for distrusting the other, but we've got to bring them more closely together.

The Washington Post, 7-5:(A)9.

Bill Bradley
United States Senator,
D-New Jersey

5

I think there are some basic things that any intelligence agency would have to do, and that's continue to monitor the various military threats that might exist around the world. But then I think it will have to concentrate on terrorism, terrorist threats, and I then think it becomes a much broader-gauged agency than it has been in the past. I think broad trends in demography and ethnicity, broad changes in economic development in certain places of the world, environmental threats . . . The legitimate question is: What's the nature of our leadership in the world? I think increasingly it will come from our ability to essentially lead by example, through example of the pluralistic society that takes all its citizens to the higher economic ground, and does so in a way that remains open to the rest of the world—both in terms of economics and in terms of changes around the world.

Interview, Washington/
Los Angeles Times, 9-29:(M)3.

John Bryant
United States Representative,
D-Texas

1

Some 45 years after World War II, we Americans are still spending upwards of $200-billion a year paying the cost of defending other countries on the other sides of two oceans, countries which are doing better economically, have more resources than we do economically and yet do not come forward with their fair share of the policy of paying for their own defense. What do they do with the money that they save? They do a better job of educating their children, a better job of caring for their old people, a better job of protecting their environment and, much worse, a better job of competing with us in international trade. It is an expense we can no longer afford . . . Read the figures: Every year during the 1980s the American taxpayers paid $160-billion to $170-billion, and that is every year of the 1980s, to defend our allies in Europe and $30-billion to $40-billion to defend countries in Asia . . . The European members of NATO have a collective gross national product greater than that of the United States and at least two times greater than that of the Soviet Union. Yet America spends more on NATO defenses than all the other 15 alliance members combined.
Before the House,
Washington, May 21/
The Washington Post, 5-29:(A)18.

Zbigniew Brzezinski
Counsellor, Center for
Strategic and International
Studies (United States);
Former Assistant to the
President of the United States
(Jimmy Carter) for
National Security Affairs

2

The [current] war in the Persian Gulf is not the decisive issue for the future. The decision issue for the future still is what happens in the wake of the collapse of Communism. That's where most of the resources are. That's where the future of democracy will be determined. And I don't think we should ignore these problems. What happens in Eastern Europe, the Soviet Union and China ultimately is more important than what happens in Kuwait.
Broadcast interview/
Los Angeles Times, 2-8:(A)26.

Patrick Buchanan
Political commentator;
Candidate for the 1992
Republican Presidential
nomination

3

Today, we call for a new patriotism, where Americans begin to put the needs of Americans first, for a new nationalism where in every negotiation . . . the American side seeks advantage and victory for the United States. It is time to phase out foreign aid and to start looking out for the forgotten Americans right here in the United States.
The Christian Science Monitor,
12-12:6.

George Bush
President of the United States

4

Clearly, the U.S. has a disproportionate responsibility when it comes to helping secure the world. I would not call it the world's policeman, because there are certain areas where we wouldn't be in a position to act or want to act. But we have a disproportionate responsibility for the freedom and the security of various countries . . . We have got the credibility where others might not have as much. We are still respected, and we are still looked to for this kind of leadership.
Interview, Washington/
Time, 1-7:33.

5

I think because of [the U.S. involvement in the recent Persian Gulf war] we won't have to use U.S. forces around the world. I think when we say something that is objectively correct—like don't take over a neighbor or you're going to bear some responsibility—people are going to listen. Because I think out of all this will be a new-

(GEORGE BUSH)

found—let's put it this way: a re-established credibility for the United States of America. So I look at it the opposite. I say that what our troops have done [in the Persian Gulf] will not only enhance the peace but reduce the risk that their successors have to go into battle some place.

News conference,
Washington, March 1/
The New York Times, 3-2:5.

1

Until now, the world we've known has been a world divided—a world of barbed wire and concrete block, conflict and Cold War. Now [with the defeat of Iraq by U.S.-led coalition forces in the recent Persian Gulf war] we can see a new world coming into view. A world in which there is the very real prospect of a new world order. In the words of Winston Churchill, a "world order" in which "the principles of justice and fair play . . . protect the weak against the strong . . . " A world where the United Nations, freed from Cold War stalemate, is poised to fulfill the historic vision of its founders. A world in which freedom and respect for human rights find a home among all nations. The Gulf war put this new world to its first test. And, my fellow Americans, we passed that test.

Before joint session of U.S. Congress,
Washington, March 6/
The New York Times, 3-7:(A)4.

2

Some argue that a nation as moral and just as ours should not taint itself by dealing with nations less moral, less just. But this counsel offers up self-righteousness draped in a false morality. You do not reform a world by ignoring it.

At Yale University commencement,
May 27/
The New York Times, 5-28:(A)4.

3

[On his penchant for personal diplomacy, direct talks with world leaders, frequently by telephone, when problems arise]: I think a per-

sonal relationship can be extraordinarily helpful. I got kidded about that—maybe not kidded, needled about it, I guess—sometimes on telephone diplomacy . . . What they guard against is what I talk about, about ships passing in the night. Got an agricultural problem with Japan? Let's talk about it. Got a big reorganization or Baltic problem with the Soviets? Let's talk about that . . . And if you can't get agreement, so be it. But at least you've tried in an environment that has the best chance to succeed. And that's why I do spend a lot of time on this personal side.

To foreign journalists, July 8/
The Washington Post, 7-17:(A)18.

4

[On the rise of nationalistic movements and civil wars in the wake of the collapse of Communism]: Communism held history captive for years. It suspended ancient disputes and it suppressed ethnic rivalries, nationalist aspirations and old prejudices. As it has dissolved, [the] suspended hatreds have sprung to life . . . In Europe and Asia, nationalist passions have flared anew, challenging borders, straining the fabric of international society. Around the world, many age-old conflicts still fester . . . And, although we now seem mercifully liberated from the fear of nuclear holocaust, these smaller, virulent conflicts should trouble us all. No one here can promise that today's borders will remain fixed for all time. But we must strive to ensure the peaceful, negotiated settlement of border disputes.

At United Nations,
New York, Sept. 23/
Los Angeles Times, 9-24:(A)6.

5

You may wonder about America's role in the new world [the post-Cold War era]. Let me assure you, the United States has no intention of striving for a *Pax Americana*. However, we will remain engaged. We will not retreat and pull back into isolationism. We will offer friendship and leadership. And in short, we seek a *Pax Universalis*, built upon shared responsibilities and aspirations.

At United Nations, New York, Sept. 23/
The New York Times, 9-24:(A)6.

(GEORGE BUSH)

1

Anyone who says we should retreat into an isolationistic cocoon is living in the last century, when we should be focused on the next century and the lives our children will lead. And they should know America's destiny has always been to lead. And if I have anything to do with it, lead we will . . . I'm not going to let liberal Democratic carping keep me from leading. [During the recent Persian Gulf war,] thank God I didn't have to listen to these carpers telling me how to run that war.

At Republican fund-raising dinner,
Houston, Oct. 31/
The Washington Post, 11-1:(A)1.

Ted Galen Carpenter
Director of foreign-policy studies,
Cato Institute (United States)

2

The Persian Gulf intervention [by the U.S. during the Iraq-Kuwait crisis] is not a workable model for managing problems. We can't send 500,000 troops to fight a major war every time aggression occurs. Many colonial-era boundaries don't make sense from an ethnic, linguistic or economic standpoint. Without the restraining hand of rival superpowers, many nations will try to revise boundaries. The New World Order is more likely to be the New World Disorder . . . We ought to encourage regional balances of power or, when feasible, regional security arrangements. The U.S. doesn't have to be a major player.

USA Today, 2-28:(A)4.

Dick Cheney
Secretary of Defense
of the United States

3

[Lauding the performance of U.S. forces in the current Persian Gulf war]: We have to remember that we don't have a dog in every fight, that we don't want to get involved in every single conflict . . . By the same token, to the extent that we've been able to demonstrate our ability to do it successfully, I think we give an enormous boost to the credibility of the United States govern-

ment for a long time to come. When we say we are interested in guaranteeing the security of a friend or an ally, it will—by golly—mean something. There won't be any doubt in anybody's mind about the United States' willingness and ability to keep those commitments. But again, caution is the word.

Interview, Washington, Feb. 22/
The Washington Post, 2-27:(A)25.

Barber B. Conable
President, World Bank

4

Eight hundred fifty million poor people will be born into the developing world between now and 2000. That's nine out of every 10 people born. No issue poses such a crucial barrier to development . . . It's pretty obvious that population must be addressed if poverty is to be significantly reduced.

Interview, Washington/
The Christian Science Monitor,
8-28:9.

Marie M. Cuomo
Governor of New York (D)

5

There is no foreign policy nowadays that is not economic policy. This is a global economy. If you fall behind the Japanese and the Germans, you have lost the foreign-policy race. You cannot be dominant with military might and diplomacy. That's the way we did it for 40 years. But you can't be powerful with just that. Ask the Russians. You can't just do it with just military might in the new global economy . . . It is an economic struggle now.

Interview, Nov. 6/
Los Angeles Times, 11-7:(A)27.

Paula J. Dobriansky
Associate Director for Programs,
United States Information Agency

6

The universality of democracy . . . is demonstrated by the fact that democratic appeal transcends geographic, racial and cultural boundaries. In that respect, our Founding Fathers were right:

(PAULA J. DOBRIANSKY)

All men are created with certain inalienable rights. To be sure, democracy has ebbed and flowed in the past . . . I believe firmly, however, that the current round of democratic revolutions is unique—the advent of modern means of communications combined with an innate human aspiration for democracy means that all tyrants are living on borrowed time. These trends are reinforced by the fact that we and our allies have made the pursuit of democracy a key part of our foreign policy.

Speech, Washington/
The Washington Post,
10-16:(A)26.

Byron L. Dorgan
United States Representative,
D-North Dakota

1

This country this year will have an increase in its gross indebtedness of $405-billion. That's borrowing well over $1-billion a day every day, seven days a week, all year long. And strange as it seems, while we do that, we are borrowing money from our allies in order to pay for their defense. Well, the free ride [for our allies] is over. [The U.S.] can't any longer afford it, and our allies are not war-torn, war-tattered economies; they are tough, shrewd international competitors well able to contribute the amount of money they should contribute for the common defense of the world.

News conference,
Washington, May 16/
The Washington Post, 5-21:(A)20.

Roland Dumas
Foreign Minister of France

2

[On the collapse of the Soviet Union as a superpower]: American might reigns without balancing weight. I am telling our American friends: They must realize that being the world's top power creates not only possibilities and rights but also duties.

At French Socialist Party meeting,
Ramatuelle, France, Sept. 2/
The New York Times, 9-3:(A)8.

Lawrence S. Eagleburger
Deputy Secretary of State
of the United States

3

I believe very, very deeply that the world my kids have to live in in the 21st century is going to be quite different but not necessarily better. If the U.S. doesn't stay engaged in the process of formulating the new order, that world is going to be in great trouble.

Interview,
Washington/
The Washington, Post,
2-5:(C)2.

Elizabeth II
Queen of England

4

All our history in this and earlier centuries underlines the basic point that the best progress is made when Europeans and Americans act in concert. We must not allow ourselves to be enticed into a form of continental insularity.

Before joint session
of U.S. Congress,
Washington,
May 16/
Los Angeles Times, 5-17:(A)4.

Yves Fortier
Canadian Ambassador/
Permanent Representative
to the United Nations

5

[In the wake of the U.S.-led victory in the Persian Gulf war,] there is a perception out there that Big Brother—the United States—leads the [UN] Security Council and that the United States is going to marginalize the Third World here. The United States is going to have a major, major role here in showing itself to be supportive of the United Nations in other areas and in showing itself not to be the Big Bully and the Odd Man Out on many issues.

Los Angeles Times,
4-5:(A)5.

Robert M. Gates
*Assistant to President
of the United States George Bush
and Deputy for
National Security Affairs;
Nominee for Director
of Central Intelligence
of the United States*

1

Who would have thought that just five years ago we would stand where we are today? Certainly not the intelligence analyst sitting before you. Talk about humbling experiences. The old verities that have guided this country's national-security policy for 45 years and, thus, its intelligence service, have disappeared in an historical instant. Communism is dead or dying. A number of long-standing regional conflicts are coming to an end. The Cold War is over. The Communist Party lies mortally wounded in the Soviet Union, wounded by its own hand . . . The path to a new and brighter day is finally apparent but will require still American leadership, strength and vision; the willingness to act against those who would prey on the weak; and skillful navigation around the many obstacles that can thwart progress or send newly free but fragile democracies hurtling back into the darkness.

*At Senate Select Committee
on Intelligence hearing on his
nomination, Washington,
Sept. 16/The New York Times,
9-17:(A)14.*

2

[The challenge for the U.S. intelligence community] is to adapt to this changing world, not just in places like the Soviet Union and Europe, but to the very idea of change, the idea that for years to come, change and uncertainty will dominate international life, that the unthinkable and the not-even-thought-about will be commonplace.

*At Senate Select Committee
on Intelligence hearing on his
nomination, Washington,
Sept. 16/
The Christian Science Monitor,
9-23:8.*

3

[The late] President [John] Kennedy once said that CIA successes remain a secret while its failures are trumpeted. However, things have gotten out of hand when the most outrageous allegations against the Agency are taken seriously, when the honor and integrity of thousands of patriotic public servants are suspect merely by virtue of where they work . . . We know that many Americans are uneasy about CIA and U.S. intelligence activities. They understand the need for information, and even on occasion for covert action, but they are uncomfortable with secrecy. And therein lies the value of Congressional oversight. The reassurance to Americans that the laws are being obeyed and that there is accountability. This then puts a special responsibility on intelligence agencies to be truthful, straightforward, candid and forthcoming in dealings with Congress.

*At Senate Select Committee
on Intelligence hearing on his
nomination, Washington,
Sept. 16/The New York Times,
9-17:(A)14.*

4

[On a 1980s decision by the U.S. to swap arms for American hostages held by Iran]: The President of the United States made the decision to sell arms for hostages. He may have made that decision in the context of larger objectives and an opening to Iran and so on and so forth, but that was his decision. It was a policy decision . . . It seems to me that it is not the role of CIA to question the policy decision. We should have questioned how our part of that operation was carried out and the fact that it was in violation of all the procedures and approaches that we normally would take in one of these covert actions. In that area, I think we were negligent as an agency.

*At Senate Select Committee
on Intelligence hearing on his
nomination, Washington,
Sept. 17/The New York Times,
9-18:(A)12.*

5

[On how close the CIA should get to the policy-makers]: [One] view is that you remain at

(ROBERT M. GATES)

a distance and that a distance is the best place in which you can protect your objectivity and your integrity, and so forth . . . I have the other view. My view has been, all along from the beginning of my career—and perhaps it's due to the fact that I've served on the NSC—that the intelligence community has to be right next to the policy-maker, that he has to be at his elbow, that he has to understand what is on his mind, he has to understand what his future concerns are, he has to understand what his agenda is. He has to understand some of the initiatives that he's thinking about taking . . . I think that having a [CIA] Director who has a close personal relationship with the President offers a unique opportunity for the intelligence community to provide relevant intelligence and sharper intelligence to the policy process and, frankly, also to the Congress.

At Senate Select Committee
on Intelligence hearing on his
nomination, Washington,
Sept. 17/
The New York Times,
9-18:(A)12.

Richard A. Gephardt
United States Representative,
D-Missouri

1

[On the American public's support for U.S. involvement in international affairs]: Without economic growth [at home], the American people will reject these lofty, though self-interested, goals, and they will rationally demand that we simply turn inward. Public support will evaporate for international commitments at precisely the time President Bush is trying to expand them. His neglect of the domestic economy, then, may have the paradoxical consequence of undermining his foreign policy, the *raison d'etre* of his Presidency.

At Northwestern University,
Nov. 8/
The Washington Post,
11-15:(A)23.

Mikhail S. Gorbachev
President of the Soviet Union;
General Secretary,
Communist Party
of the Soviet Union

2

[Saying the U.S. should be more cooperative and warmer in its relations with his country]: If what has been gained at the end of the term of the previous [U.S.] Administration and under President George Bush is undermined, the world will again plunge into a "cold" or "semi-cold" war, into an atmosphere of political dampness that will negatively affect the health of international life as a whole.

At meeting with international media
executive Rupert Murdoch, Moscow,
May 5/The New York Times, 5-7:(A)3.

3

If we fail to reach an understanding regarding a new phase of [East-West] cooperation, we will have to look for other ways, for time is of the essence. But if we are to move to that new phase, those who participate in and even shape world politics must continue to change, to review their philosophic perception of the changing realities of the world and of its imperatives. Otherwise, there is no point in drawing up a joint program of practical action.

Lecture as winner of 1990 Nobel Peace Prize,
Oslo, Norway, June 5/
Los Angeles Times, 6-6:(A)9.

4

The beginning of a new era in history has been a tough test indeed for leaders of states, requiring enormous efforts, a sense of high responsibilities, strictest realism and vision. A great deal in world politics will continue to depend on how the Soviet Union and the United States interact with each other. For the first time ever, our two countries have a chance to build their relations on the natural basis of universal human values and national interests. We are beginning to realize that we need each other, that the security, internal stability and dynamic development of each of our two countries benefits both of them. Not only

(MIKHAIL S. GORBACHEV)

our two nations, but the entire world needs this kind of U.S.-Soviet relationship. The world has realized this and has given us support in our joint efforts.

At opening of summit conference
with U.S. President George Bush,
Moscow, July 30/
The New York Times, 7-31:(A)4.

Albert Gore, Jr.
United States Senator,
D-Tennessee

1

[Criticizing the U.S. Bush Administration's muted responses to Soviet and Chinese crackdowns on human rights]: Is a cool amoralism to be the foundation of the New World Order? We should speak out for democracy. We should be willing to stand for the principles upon which our nation is based and for which our nation stands throughout the world.

Speech/
Los Angeles Times, 7-4:(A)23.

Tom Harkin
United States Senator,
D-Iowa

2

[On the possibility of war between U.S.-led forces and Iraq, which invaded and took over Kuwait last year]: Certainly naked aggression must be responded to. But what about a few weeks ago, when there was naked aggression in Chad by Libya? We didn't rush over there with our troops. How about Syria? Not too long ago, Syria—now one of our allies—Syria went into Lebanon and massacred 750 civilians. Well, that's naked aggression. We didn't do anything about it . . . So what does this mean that we want to stop naked aggression? Does this mean that we are now going to say that the United States will indeed become the policeman of the world, and that we will respond to every instance of naked aggression? Or does it mean that we're just going to kind of pick and choose which ones we want to respond to or not? How about the Soviets put-

ting down the Lithuanians? Are we going to respond to that? I dare say we're not. So we're just going to kind of pick and choose which kind of naked aggression we want.

Before the Senate,
Washington, Jan. 11/
The New York Times, 1-12:6.

Kempton B. Jenkins
Former Deputy Assistant Secretary
for East-West Trade,
Department of Commerce
of the United States

3

The President's [Bush] budget proposal for national-security objectives is an accurate reflection of the President's priorities with which few would argue . . . [But] one may question the continued support for Radio Free Europe after the liberation of the East European satellites on the one hand and the minimal growth in the Voice of America and other U.S. Information Agency programs on the other hand. In a world where American credibility is now facing a mosaic of hostile forces rather than a singular overriding challenge from Moscow, USIA should be sharply expanding its traditional programs . . . The State Department will cost the U.S. less than $2.5-billion—as General H. Norman Schwarzkopf [head of U.S.-led forces in the Persian Gulf war] would say, a mosquito on the elephant of the massive U.S. budget.

Feb. 4/
The Washington Post, 2-5:(A)17.

Richard J. Kerr
Deputy Director
of Central Intelligence
of the United States

4

The problems of intelligence are more demanding of detailed information and more demanding of analysis involving that information. Terrorism is a good example. You work terrorism at a very fine grain of analysis that is nearly an investigative level, the way you might think of the FBI involved in an investigative problem. This puts different demands on our

(RICHARD J. KERR)

analysts. It requires a different kind of product because you are less interested in writing a research paper about it than you are in doing something about it. And that puts you then back into using information, whether it's with law-enforcement officials or foreign governments, and to try to do something about what you've uncovered.

Interview/
U.S. News & World Report, 6-3:30.

1

While we [in the intelligence community] may have to live with less because of the reality of our own [U.S.] economic situation and drawdowns in the military, the kinds of problems [the U.S. faces] require more information and more analysis, not less. Uncertainty about the Soviet Union and the [Soviet] republics is greater now than it was 15 years ago when you had a relatively stable, unchanging Soviet Union. From an intelligence point of view, that very instability demands a lot more work.

Interview, McLean, Va./
The New York Times, 9-2:(A)1.

Bob Kerrey
United States Senator,
D-Nebraska

2

[Criticizing the possible use of U.S. military force to get Iraq out of Kuwait, saying such use would be part of the old world order, not the new]: It seems to me that what we have to try to do is not just get a victory here but try to develop some lessons upon which we can build a sound foreign policy. And one of the things in the old world order, of course, was that it's got to be a quick military solution . . . What I'm suggesting is that the minute you narrow the options between choosing this military option or that military option, you begin to lose the opportunity to build a policy that is less dependent upon military [action].

Interview, Los Angeles/
Los Angeles Times, 1-6:(M)3.

3

The evidence is very clear that American policies can liberate human beings. We can create an environment where liberation is possible, even without the application of force. And, indeed, what I learn from the events in the [recent] Persian Gulf [war], from [the U.S.-led Operation] Desert Storm [against Iraq], is that unless you meddle in internal affairs [of other countries], you create the seeds of your own destruction; you create the possibility that you may have to resort to military force at some point.

Interview/
U.S. News & World Report,
7-15:28.

Robert M. Kimmitt
Under Secretary for Political Affairs,
Department of State
of the United States

4

The most difficult thing is policy formulation and implementation when you are trying to keep many different policy balls in the air. How do we get a cease-fire in Angola? How do we avoid tensions on the subcontinent? How do we continue to advance the prospects of democracy in this hemisphere, particularly in Panama and Nicaragua?

Interview, Washington/
The New York Times, 1-3:(A)4.

Mauno Koivisto
President of Finland

5

There is a new world order [following the U.S.-led military victory forcing Iraq out of Kuwait, which it invaded and occupied last year]. The only question is, how orderly? What kind of order? In [the] case of the Kuwaiti occupation, the permanent members of the United Nations Security Council were able to cooperate [in backing the U.S. effort]. There was something quite new that happened. Evidently, they will be able to work together. So that gives a new hope for many problems. There's some hope that many of the old problems have dissolved and that new ways of solving problems peacefully might

(MAUNO KOIVISTO)

be found. So the United Nations has to find a new importance.

Interview/USA Today, 5-8:(A)11.

Bernard Kouchner
State Secretary for
Humanitarian Action of France

1

We are starting to discover the right to intervene [in other countries for humanitarian reasons]. It will be a long, difficult process to construct, but this is new, this idea of a world consciousness where we will continue to respect states' sovereignty, but will no longer be indifferent to the suffering of people inside of countries . . . In the 21st century the right to intervene will exist. Those who do not agree are going to be left behind by history.

The Washington Post, 6-10:(C)1.

Michael Mandelbaum
Director of East-West studies,
Council on Foreign Relations
(United States)

2

For the first time, the [Group of Seven] economic summit may be more important than a U.S.-Soviet summit meeting . . . The U.S.-Soviet bilateral relationship has been significantly devalued . . . In the West, it's not just the United States that's important, it's the entire G-7 . . . The United States does not dominate international economic relations today in the way that it dominated international political and military relations during the Cold War.

Los Angeles Times, 7-18:(A)6.

Thomas E. Mann
Director of governmental studies,
Brookings Institution
(United States)

3

[The outcome of the U.S. involvement in the current Persian Gulf crisis] will have a lot to do with the future sentiment of Americans toward the U.S. role in the world. If this has an unhappy ending, I can see a resurgence of isolationism. The potential is there; certainly you already see it in some pockets in the country. But if the U.S. is successful in the Gulf, I can see us building a new world role for ourselves.

USA Today, 1-3:(A)2.

John McCain
United States Senator,
R-Arizona

4

We have made the mistake of considering some nations friends and others enemies, and we eventually find out that, in some cases, our friend is really our enemy.

USA Today, 2-28:(A)10.

Gene McNary
Commissioner, Immigration
and Naturalization Service
of the United States

5

[The Immigration Act of 1990 has] just extended the numbers [of legal immigrants annually accepted into the U.S.] from 500,000, roughly, to 700,000. One of the virtues, in my judgment, of the law is that it provides for a triennial review. So it's a means of opening the valve a little bit to see what will happen and how it works in this country. Whether [admitting more legal immigrants] has some adverse repercussions on our own labor market, how it fits in with productivity—[the new law] gives us a chance to see what the experience is. If the new law proves successful and increased numbers would be even more beneficial, then we would increase the numbers in three or four years.

Interview, Washington/
Los Angeles Times, 5-5:(M)3.

Carlos Saul Menem
President of Argentina

6

[Leftist ideology is] finished every place . . . Don't tell me that some European Presidents are leftists just because they wave that label. What

181

(CARLOS SAUL MENEM)

does socialism have to do with what is going on in Spain or France?

Interview/Newsweek, 7-15:28.

Robert H. Michel
United States Representative,
R-Illinois

1

When patience and delay become foreign-policy goals by themselves, they are no longer virtues . . . Patience at any price is not a policy, it's a cop-out.

Before the House,
Washington, Jan. 10/
The Washington Post, 1-11:(A)1.

Benjamin Netanyahu
Deputy Foreign Minister
of Israel

2

The source of terrorism is terrorist states and not the front organizations that use proxies . . . If you want to stop terrorism, you must defeat the terrorist. If terrorism is to be stopped, the terrorist states have to be stopped.

Interview, Israel/
USA Today, 1-29:(A)11.

Robert G. Neumann
Senior adviser and director
of Middle East studies,
Center for Strategic and
International Studies
(United States)

3

Terrorism is almost as old as history. It has lived for a long time and it is by no means dead [despite the recent release of U.S. hostages who had been held in Lebanon]. But, in my experience, terrorism seems to grow in certain cycles, 20 years at a time. I don't know why. It dies down for a while and then, for some other reason, it comes up again. So we have not seen the last of it yet, but I hope we've seen the last of it for a while.

Interview/USA Today, 12-4:(A)11.

Sam Nunn
United States Senator,
D-Georgia

4

[Saying the U.S. intelligence and foreign-affairs communities need more education in foreign languages and international studies]: We had to put 500,000 American men and women in our armed services in harm's way [in the recent Persian Gulf war] because our intelligence community failed to anticipate an impending military crisis and because our diplomatic and policy communities were unable to avert the need for American military action. The lesson is clear. We need policy-makers, diplomats and intelligence analysts expert in cultures and languages that encompass all regions of the world.

News conference,
Washington, July 18/
The Washington Post, 7-19:(A)19.

Joseph Nye
Professor of international affairs,
Kennedy School of Government,
Harvard University

5

[On the end of the Cold War and the fall of Communism in the Soviet Union]: We had a bipolar world, and we had a bipolar intellectual debate. The fact that there was a clear and present danger from an ideological enemy with enormous power had the effect of polarizing the domestic debate [in the U.S.] . . . Even though there's now no equivalent to American power and no real alternative to liberal democratic ideology, there's going to be a diffusion of power and ideas. In this sense, it's not the end of history but a return of history.

Interview/
The New York Times, 8-31:10.

Sadako Ogata
United Nations
High Commissioner
for Refugees

6

The number of refugees throughout the world is increasing, reflecting the enormously changing

(SADAKO OGATA)

world. Most come from developing countries, which means that economic development and political stability have a great bearing on the flow of refugees. At the same time, if you really look at the refugees, they are not the same people as before. I was overwhelmed by the number of Kurdish refugees [after the recent Persian Gulf war]. There were long lines of people carrying as much as they could. When you see that many people on the move, you feel there is little you can do to change the life of each person. I was daunted. At the same time, I feel that this is when organized efforts are really required, and I am terribly challenged in that sense. You have to believe in being able to make even a little difference by your efforts, by your appeals, by trying to do as much as you can.

Interview/
World Press Review, July:11.

Olara Otunnu
Ugandan Ambassador/
Permanent Representative
to the United Nations

1

The African countries hope very much that the swift reaction of the UN in the case of the [Iraqi] invasion of Kuwait will be repeated in other, similar situations in other parts of the world, because they recall—with a deep disquiet—situations in the past where invasions have taken place and the UN has not acted in the same way. So they hope that this will form a precedent for the future, and that the international community will be just as concerned, as vigorous in its reaction, in other incidents of invasion.

Interview, New York/
The Christian Science Monitor,
2-5:14.

Turgut Ozal
President of Turkey

2

If the superpower is managed by democracy's rules, there is no danger.

Los Angeles Times, 3-2:(A)14.

Boris D. Pankin
Foreign Minister
of the Soviet Union

3

The philosophy of new international solidarity, which is finding its way into practice, signifies a de-ideologization of the United Nations. In renewing our organization [the UN], we should once and for all leave behind the legacy of the Ice Age, like the obnoxious resolution equating Zionism to racism.

At United Nations,
New York, Sept. 24/
Los Angeles Times, 9-25:(A)6.

Anthony Parsons
Former British Ambassador
to the United Nations

4

In coming years we are likely to see a lot of civil wars, not only in Europe but in places such as Africa and the Americas. Regional organizations such as the European Community are going to have to overcome their inhibitions about involving themselves in the domestic affairs of states. It is possible for diplomatic action to be taken by the great powers toward the party that looks to be a potential aggressor in an ethnic conflict. It should be made clear to that party that if it advances against a weaker neighbor, it can expect stringent action to be taken—for example, immediate . . . economic sanctions.

The Christian Science Monitor,
11-19:3.

Javier Perez de Cuellar
Secretary General
of the United Nations

5

As Secretary General of the United Nations, my only strength is a moral strength.

Jan. 9/
Los Angeles Times, 1-10:(A)22.

Nikolai S. Petrushenko
Member, Supreme Soviet
of the Soviet Union

6

[On the U.S. leadership of coalition forces pushing Iraqi forces out of Kuwait]: [We] can see

(NIKOLAI S. PETRUSHENKO)

that the United States, feeling itself the victor of the Cold War and the policeman of the world, proceeds from a different philosophy [than the Soviet Union] in addressing international problems . . . We must ask ourselves: "Is this a partner for the Soviet Union in developing a new world order?"

Los Angeles Times, 2-26:(H)6.

Colin L. Powell
General, United States Army;
Chairman,
Joint Chiefs of Staff

1

One of the fondest expressions around is that we [the U.S.] can't be the world's policeman. But guess who gets called when suddenly someone needs a cop.

Life, March:53.

2

[On U.S.-Soviet relations]: We have seen our implacable enemy of 40 years vaporize before our eyes, a victim of its own contradictions, its imperial ambitions destroyed. The Soviet Union, or whatever we are calling it now, turns inward to try to make something of itself, and in this process there is enormous hope, in my view, as these two superpowers combine their efforts rather than confront each other as they have for four decades.

Before Senate Armed Services
Committee, Washington, Sept. 27/
The Washington Post, 9-28:(A)22.

Yevgeny M. Primakov
Director-designate,
First Chief Directorate
(Soviet intelligence service)

3

If you think that spies are people in gray coats, skulking around street corners, listening to people's conversations and wielding iron bars, then my appointment is unnatural. We must use analytical methods, synthesize information. This is scientific work.

News conference, Moscow, Oct. 2/
The Washington Post, 10-3:(A)1.

Muammar el-Qaddafi
Chief of State of Libya

4

[Criticizing Soviet President Mikhail Gorbachev's foreign policy]: Politically, what have we benefited from Gorbachev? Why should we congratulate him? Why this hypocrisy? Who sent the [Soviet] Jews to Palestine [Israel]? Who approved the crushing of Iraq after leaving Kuwait [in the recent Persian Gulf war]? Who gave the U.S. the chance to rampage world-wide, imposing its hegemony on us all? This is so because the Soviet Union has given over the reins and has surrendered without justification.

To Libyan military cadets
on 22nd anniversary of his revolution/
Los Angeles Times, 9-10:(A)15.

Qian Qichen
Foreign Minister of China

5

Some people say that human rights have no boundaries. This does not square with fact . . . If anyone thinks that human rights have international standards, then those standards must find expression in various international human-rights conventions. The sovereign states can either accede to those conventions . . . or they can just stay away. But it is impermissible to impose the standards worked out by one country, or a group of countries, on other countries.

News conference,
Beijing, March 27/
Los Angeles Times, 3-28:(A)6.

Dana T. Rohrabacher
United States Representative,
R-California

6

[Criticizing U.S. officials who do not want the independence movement among constituent republics in Yugoslavia, the Soviet Union and elsewhere to succeed]: I think it's time for our leaders to reread the Declaration of Independence. If the "new world order" means that we are going to stand beside tryants, I want nothing to do with it.

Los Angeles Times, 7-25:(A)10.

Jeswald Salacuse
Dean, Fletcher School of Law
and Diplomacy,
Medford, Mass.

1

Will this new world order be a *Pax America-na,* where the U.S. calls the shots, or will it be a *Pax United Nations,* where we really try to use the UN and to strengthen it for collective security in the future? . . . The history of the world shows that the international system abhors a single dominant power.

The Christian Science Monitor,
3-11:4.

Richard Schifter
Assistant Secretary
for Human Rights and
Humanitarian Affairs,
Department of State
of the United States

2

There is both good news and bad news [on human rights around the world]. The good news [is that] totalitarian and authoritarian dictator-ships are in a decline world-wide, and democracy and respect for the rights of the individual by governments are on the rise. [The bad news is] the problem of death and destruction associated with inter-ethnic and inter-communal conflict, [which] has moved to the foreground of human-rights concerns.

News conference,
Washington, Feb. 1/
The Washington Post, 2-2:(A)10.

Brent Scowcroft
Assistant to President
of the United States
George Bush for
National Security Affairs

3

[On U.S. policy in situations where, with the end of the Cold War, constituent republics of some countries try to secede and become independent states]: By and large we, and I think our NATO friends and allies, are opposed to the disintegration of states or the breakup of states.

We support the unity of Yugoslavia. We support the unity of Iraq. But there's a very practical reason—not that we think [Iraqi President] Saddam Hussein should repress the Kurds and the Shiites . . . But there is a political balance of power in the region among states that historically have been at least not friends, or they've been antagonistic . . . If you change the balance sig-nificantly, you could induce enormous instabili-ties. It is not possible to set down a hard and fast rule on self-determination. Why? Because you can get down to a single village, a tribe. It has to stop at some point . . . Small units like that are not very practical in a modern world.

Los Angeles Times, 7-25:(A)10.

Nevin S. Scrimshaw
Director, United Nations Food,
Nutrition and Human
Development Program

4

With modern communication, almost every-one in the Western world is aware of the ravages of famine. Civil war and government oppression create refugee populations that furnish the news media with graphic pictures and heart-rending descriptions of dying children and wasted adults. The developed world tries to respond to the crisis, but only after great suffering has occurred . . . Improved agricultural production can do very little for this kind of hunger, because it is rooted in government cruelty, disinterest, corruption and aggression. While drought may sometimes be an exacerbating factor, it is rarely famine's primary cause, as we have seen most recently in Ethiopia, Sudan, Somalia and Iraq . . . It is government actions that result in desperate refugees. Interna-tional assistance cannot eliminate hunger of this kind without changes in national government policy.

Washington, Oct. 14/
The Washington Post, 10-25:(A)26.

Eduard A. Shevardnadze
Former Foreign Minister
of the Soviet Union

5

Totalitarianism has revealed its total inade-quacy as a system for organizing the life of

185

(EDUARD A. SHEVARDNADZE)

society. I think that in the region of the Persian Gulf, the last military confrontation between democracy and totalitarianism has just occurred [with the U.S.-led war against Iraqi occupation of Kuwait].

Washington, May 6/
Los Angeles Times, 5-7:(A)12.

Eduard A. Shevardnadze
Co-chairman, Democratic
Reform Movement
(Soviet Union);
Former Foreign Minister
of the Soviet Union

1

[On the Soviet Union since the Cold War with the West has been ended]: New threats have emerged that are no less serious, and maybe even more serious and dangerous. These are our domestic problems and conflicts, which may become a source for serious and, I would say, major trouble. Even tragic events are a possibility. This is the principal and major threat to the world, not only to the Soviet Union. I think, in fact, that an unstable Soviet Union, our unstable country, is the main threat to the whole world today. This may be a bigger threat than the nuclear, the ecological, the economic dangers.

Broadcast interview/
Los Angeles Times, 11-20:(A)10.

John Shy
Military historian,
University of Michigan

2

[On the U.S.-led victory in the recent Persian Gulf war]: Put together with Grenada, with Libya, with Panama [where the U.S. used military force in recent years], it seems to be the triumphal culmination of a series of episodes in which military power was used as an instrument of foreign policy. I hope it does not induce an arrogance or bully-boy behavior in American foreign policy.

The New York Times,
3-4:(A)9.

Paul Simon
United States Senator,
D-Illinois

3

[On the UN economic sanctions that were applied to Iraq in the wake of that country's invasion and take-over of Kuwait last year]: If we had been able to show in Iraq that sanctions can work [instead of eventually turning to military force as was done to get Iraq out of Kuwait], we would have had a tool we could use in any kind of international situation where one country is an aggressor against another. As it is, it's not as proven a tool as we would have had if we'd stuck to sanctions.

The Christian Science Monitor,
4-10:9.

Stephen J. Solarz
United States Representative,
D-New York

4

[On U.S. policy in situations where, with the end of the Cold War, constituent republics of some countries try to secede and become independent states]: It's an issue of enormous importance that is going to loom larger. In the post-Cold War world, we're going to face a host of problems like this, and I don't think the [Bush] Administration has put in the effort to come up with any coherent, credible, consistent criteria for determining when we support self-determination.

Los Angeles Times, 7-25:(A)10.

Carl-Dieter Spranger
Minister of Economic Cooperation
of Germany

5

[Saying Germany will cut its foreign aid to countries that spend too much on weapons and that fail to meet other standards of behavior]: In our experience with the countries of the Third World, we have learned that development aid can only be effective under certain conditions. We are going to be looking closely at the level of

(CARL-DIETER SPRANGER)

spending for arms, and also at factors such as human rights and economic freedoms in the various countries. Our help will be directed to countries with efficient and honest administrations, countries that enjoy what is generally called good government.

Interview, Bonn, Aug. 2/
The New York Times, 8-3:3.

Margaret Thatcher
Former Prime Minister
of the United Kingdom

1

Is there a new world order? . . . I believe that [U.S.] President Bush is right to talk in these terms. A seismic change has occurred with the crumbling of Communism and the advance of democracy and free enterprise. It will be possible to achieve greater international cooperation in upholding peace. But we should also be cautious. Human nature itself does not change. This is not the first time that new [world] orders of a visionary kind have been conceived.

Before Los Angeles World Affairs
Council, Nov. 16/
Los Angeles Times, 11-22:(B)2.

Paul E. Tsongas
Candidate for the
1992 Democratic
U.S. Presidential nomination;
Former United States Senator,
D-Massachusetts

2

[The collapse of Communism and the end of the Cold War mean that] power will increasingly gravitate to those who cannot launch an army but can write a check, those who cannot push a nuclear button but can withhold credit to a debtor nation. Those with economic reserves will be the powers.

At George Washington University,
Sept. 4/
The Washington Post,
9-5:(A)2.

Stansfield Turner
Former Director
of Central Intelligence
of the United States

3

It's time to give the Director of Central Intelligence more authority over all these agencies that collect information. The head of the National Security Agency should be appointed by the Director of Central Intelligence, not by the Secretary of Defense. Same with the head of the reconnaissance office. The Director should be given additional authority to control the dissemination of the information collected by all these other agencies.

Interview/
USA Today, 9-16:(A)13.

I. T. "Tim" Valentine, Jr.
United States Representative,
D-North Carolina

4

[Arguing against Congressional approval of $650-million in foreign aid to Israel]: I do not believe the majority of Americans share the wish of this Congress to grant [the money] to the government of Israel . . . when we are struggling under the weight of a recession. We cannot afford to support the economies of other nations when our own economy is hurting . . . Foreign aid [in general] is completely out of control and an overwhelming majority of Americans are disgusted.

Washington, March 7/
The Washington Post,
3-8:(A)4.

Richard Viguerie
Chairman, United Conservatives
(United States)

5

I'm not one of those people who believe the cliche [that] we [the U.S.] can't be the world's policeman. Well, somebody has to be the world's policeman, or else a lot of people are going to be hurt.

The New York Times,
3-4:(A)9.

WHAT THEY SAID IN 1991

Sakuji Yoshimura
Professor, Waseda University
(Japan)

1

America today is a mighty country—and a frightening one . . . It is crucial to recognize that the [recent Persian Gulf] war began from America's own plan for a monolithic control of a post-war world. For better or worse, the Gulf war built a new world order, with America at the head . . . This will be fine as long as the rest of the world accepts its role as America's underlings.

The Washington Post,
3-13:(A)19,26.

Africa

Claude Ake
Fellow, Institute for
African Studies,
Columbia University
(United States)

1

[The end of the Cold War] has meant that factions and governments in Africa cannot count on the consistent support of anybody, no matter what. This has not only undermined people in authority, but it has given confidence to people fighting that authority . . . Africa is entering a period of fluidity that may last some time.

The Washington Post, 5-31:(A)22.

George Bush
President of the United States

2

[On his decision to lift U.S. economic sanctions against South Africa in response to the South African government's moves toward dismantling apartheid]: During the last two years, we've seen a profound transformation in the situation in South Africa. Since coming to office in 1989, President [Frederik] de Klerk has repealed the legislative pillars of apartheid and opened up the political arena to prepare the way for constitutional negotiations. And as I've said on several occasions, I really firmly believe that this progress is irreversible . . . I happen to think [lifting sanctions is] the right thing to do. I believe that this will result in more progress toward racial equity, instead of less, and certainly in more economic opportunity, rather than less. So the time has come to do it.

News conference, Washington,
July 10/The New York Times, 7-11:(A)6.

Mangosuthu Gatsha Buthelezi
President,
Inkatha Freedom Party
of South Africa;
Chief of the Zulu people

3

The whites in this country will not stand for [an ANC government]. They are armed, they are

mobile and, because of conscription, they are trained soldiers.

Interview, December/
The Christian Science Monitor,
12-19:2.

Frank Chikane
Secretary general,
South African
Council of Churches

4

[Criticizing the U.S.' lifting of economic sanctions against South Africa in response to the South African government's moves toward dismantling apartheid]: Unfortunately, the struggle is not over yet and we fear that the premature lifting of sanctions will mean that one of the major incentives motivating the South African government to change will be lost.

The New York Times, 7-11:(A)6.

Barber B. Conable
President, World Bank

5

There are a number of reasons to be positive about the future of Africa—and I say this without taking a romantic view of the very real life-and-death struggle that so many Africans face every day . . . The major reason that I am hopeful, and the major difference that I see in Africa today compared with five years ago, is the clear emergence of consensus—in Africa and between Africa and the international community—on Africa's development objectives and how they should be tackled . . . There is now widespread agreement on the priority of human-resource development and capacity building; the need for continued economic reform; the importance of agricultural productivity; the urgency of slowing the population growth rate and protecting the environment; promoting the role of women and the private sector generally; and on increasing economic cooperation within Africa.

Speech, Nigeria, June 4/
The Washington Post, 6-13:(A)20.

John Conyers, Jr.
United States Representative,
D-Michigan

1

By revoking the pillars of apartheid one by one, [South African President Frederik] de Klerk is only picking away at South Africa's walls of oppression. His actions . . . will not substitute for ripping down the walls once and for all.

Feb. 1/
The Washington Post, 2-2:(A)12.

Jeremy Cronin
Member, Central Committee,
Communist Party of South Africa

2

We've [the South African Communist Party] made horrific mistakes on international policy, and our nose keeps getting rubbed into those by the local press. But, for the factory worker in South Africa, what we said—and now regret saying—about the [Soviet] invasions of Afghanistan, Czechoslovakia and Poland is pretty insignificant. It's our domestic policy for which we are particularly proud . . . We think socialism is the way to go. But we are very realistic. We've got plenty of examples of heroic revolutions [in black Africa] that tried to pole-vault into Utopia far ahead of what the objective situation allowed . . . A lot of black South Africans, understandably but incorrectly, still see the Soviet Union as a kind of godfather figure. These are people who need to be told, "Why, yes, we believe in socialism, but there are profound lessons that have to be learned."

Interview/
Los Angeles Times, 9-20:(A)5.

Frederik W. de Klerk
President of South Africa

3

The elimination of racial discrimination [in South Africa] goes hand in hand with the constitutional process. The government has expressed its intention repeatedly to remove discriminatory laws and practices. Many of them have been abolished already. Those remaining could not be repealed out of hand, because their complex

nature required in-depth investigation . . . The South African statute book will be devoid, within months, of the remnants of racially discriminatory legislation which have become known as the cornerstones of apartheid.

Before South African Parliament,
Cape Town, Feb. 1/
The New York Times, 2-2:7;
Los Angeles Times, 2-2:(A)1.

4

Today [in South Africa] there is a psychosis of violence on both sides of the political spectrum. Also, in the reaction against violence, one sees growing signs of a justification of violence. This approach and culture of violence leads to polarization which may land us in a civil war.

Before South African Parliament,
Cape Town, April 29/
The New York Times, 4-30:(A)3.

5

We regard the ANC as nothing more or less than an important political negotiating party—as one of the many negotiators, albeit an important one, that will meet around the conference table to work out a new and just Constitution for our country.

Before South African Parliament,
Cape Town, May 2/
The New York Times, 5-3:(A)4.

6

[On the repeal of numerous racial laws in South Africa, including the Population Registration Act]: Now everybody is free of [apartheid]. Now it belongs to history.

Newsweek, 7-1:37.

7

[On his National Party's proposal for giving blacks the vote but requiring a shared, multi-tiered government]: [It is the only way to preclude that] a majority, however composed, could be able to misuse its power to suppress minorities, communities or individual rights . . . We are

(FREDERIK W. DE KLERK)

certainly not prepared to exchange one form of domination for another. Black domination is as unacceptable as white domination. Power domination spells catastrophe.

At National Party convention,
Bloemfontein, South Africa, Sept. 4/
The Washington Post, 9-5:(A)28.

Jose Eduardo dos Santos
President of Angola

1

[On the recent signing of peace accords ending Angola's 16-year civil war]: [This represents] a fundamental change in favor of peace and stability, the indispensable conditions for this country to govern itself. This is the first time the Angolan people are going to live in a state of peace in five centuries. That's 500 years. This is an event of extraordinary importance. We are going to re-begin, we are going to reorganize our lives from all points of view.

Interview/
The Washington Post, 7-12:(A)27.

Mervyn M. Dymally
United States Representative,
D-California

2

Under current South African law, black South Africans are prevented from voting and running for national office. The law also limits participation of blacks in the political process to the continuation of the racially divided bicameral parliament composed exclusively of whites, Indians and so-called "colored." Many other apartheid laws remain as a fixture of South African society. It is inconceivable . . . that the United States could in good conscience consider lifting sanctions [against South Africa] unless and until . . . all racial laws and repressive language that maintain sanctions [are repealed and] . . . there is agreement [on] . . . an interim government and elected constituent assembly and . . . there is clear and irreversible progress toward a nonracial, multi-party democracy where there is full participation . . . by South Africans of all races,

resulting in free and fair elections on the basis of "one person, one vote."

Before the House,
Washington, April 30/
The Washington Post, 5-2:(A)18.

Zwawi Ben Hamadi
Editor, "Algerie Actualite"
(Algeria)

3

[On the victory of an Islamic fundamentalist party in Algeria's first free Parliamentary election]: There is nothing surprising about what is happening here. We should have known it was coming. We are at the point where out of the entire population of this country, there are barely one million persons who are participating in a civilized cycle of life, in the sense that they have good jobs, collect a reasonable salary, deal with banks and sometimes can take vacations. The rest of the country lives at subsistence levels or below that. Yesterday [in the election] they got the right to express themselves.

Dec. 27/
The New York Times, 12-28:5.

Richard Joseph
Fellow, Carter Center,
Emory University
(United States)

4

[On political changes sweeping through many areas of Africa]: I see a number of factors [causing this], not least a growing demand for political pluralism and democratization. But there is also the geopolitical aspect . . . We are living in a unipolar world. The bipolariries of the past have ended and the U.S. has emerged as the lead player. Whether this is good or bad remains to be seen, but it is clear that it has become a critical factor in Africa.

The Washington Post, 5-31:(A)1.

Ambroise Kom
Professor of African literature,
University of Yaounde
(Cameroon)

5

The big problem is that the African mind is still very much a prisoner of the state. In the West,

(AMBROISE KOM)

the university and society are a cradle of free thought. We don't have such a cradle. Most of us can work only so long as we defer [to the state] and obey and don't cause trouble . . . A true intellectual leads a risky existence in Africa.

Interview, Yaounde, Cameroon/
The Washington Post,
7-4:(A)23.

Nelson Mandela
Deputy president,
African National Congress
(South Africa)

1

[On expectations of him as an anti-apartheid leader following his release from prison last year]: We are all men of flesh and blood and . . . if the people expected miracles, well, I was not worthy. If people regarded me as the Messiah who was overnight going to solve the problems of South Africa, then they were living in a fool's paradise. No human being could do that. Not even Christ succeeded in doing that—and I'm far from being a Christ.

Los Angeles Times, 4-2:(H)6.

2

Despite our own heroic efforts, we have not defeated the [white minority government of South Africa]. We see negotiations as a continuation of the struggle leading to our central objective: the transfer of power to the people. The point which must be clearly understood is that the struggle is not over, and negotiations themselves are a theatre of struggle, subject to advances and reverses as any other form of struggle.

At African National Congress
conference, Durban, South Africa,
July 2/The New York Times, 7-3:(A)3.

Nelson Mandela
President, African National Congress
(South Africa)

3

[On criticism of the ANC's ties to the South African Communist Party]: We have got an

agenda and we are carrying out that agenda. The SACP have not sought to undermine it . . . The SACP has declared that their cooperation with us is only up to the moment of the overthrow of the apartheid state. After that, they take their own line . . . which we will not follow. We won't follow socialism.

The Christian Science Monitor,
7-25:5.

4

[Calling for a transitional government as South Africa moves away from the apartheid system]: As we have often stated, such a government should be constituted so as to enjoy the support of the overwhelming majority of South Africans . . . The modalities of its installation and its actual composition can be a matter for discussion and negotiation among all the players in the political arena. We would want only two principles. The first is inclusivity, so that no body of political opinion feels excluded. The second is a definite and unambiguous time frame [for creation of the interim government] . . . The interim government would have to take charge of all armed and security forces in the country, adopt an interim bill of rights, supervise and conduct the elections to a constituent assembly, in addition to implementing other measures necessary to prepare the country for democracy.

Before Spear of the Nation,
Thohoyandou, South Africa, Aug. 9/
The New York Times, 8-10:2.

5

[On ending apartheid in South Africa]: . . . the minority of whites who have monopolized the resources of the country may resist every attempt to distribute the resources equitably among all groups. But it will be correct for us to go on with that process, whatever the resistance, because unless equitable distribution is effected, there can be no industrial peace in the country. Restructuring is absolutely necessary for the economic progress of the country . . . The framework of apartheid is being dismantled. But you must understand that this is a process, not just an event. It is going to take some time to dismantle

(NELSON MANDELA)

apartheid because, apart from the laws themselves, the practice has been there for decades and you'll find discrimination in education, housing, health care and in social services. It's not going to be a question of a decision overnight that balances up these inequities.

Interview/
USA Today, 12-10:(A)13.

Donald McHenry
Professor of diplomacy and
international affairs,
Georgetown University
(United States);
Former United States Ambassador/
Permanent Representative
to the United Nations

1

There are many [in the U.S.] who hate the ANC [of South Africa] because it has some Communists in it or because it took to arms [to fight apartheid]. There are many who love [Zulu leader] Chief [Mangosuthu] Buthelezi because he was opposed to sanctions or criticizes the ANC. This is a very simplistic approach. One ought to be cautious of all of the players and let them prove themselves. That's true of [South African President Frederik] de Klerk, Mr. Buthelezi, [ANC President Nelson] Mandela. It's their negotiation which has to be conducted. They have to live with their harvest, if you will, of apartheid.

Interview/
USA Today, 7-31:(A)9.

Meles Zenawi
Chairman, supreme council,
Ethiopian People's Revolutionary
Democratic Front

2

[On his rebel group's seizing control of Addis Ababa, Ethiopia's capital]: We expect that Ethiopia will be a really democratic and united country, a country not united by force of arms but by the expressed will of the various peoples concerned. It will be a country that is involved in the

process of building wealth for everybody, rather than making endless wars.

News conference, London, May 28/
The Washington Post, 5-29:(A)24.

Meles Zenawi
President of Ethiopia

3

Here 90 per cent of the population is peasants. For democracy to flourish in Africa you have to involve the population. Without rational economic policies you can't involve the population. Without democracy you cannot make rational economic policies work.

Interview/Time, 11-4:48.

Thandika Mkandawire
Director, Council for
Economic and Social Research
in Africa (Senegal)

4

[On South Africa's current moves toward ending apartheid]: For years, South Africa has been criticized for human-rights violations by states that are regular violators themselves. But I think we have entered an era now when such contradictions can no longer be overlooked. . . Many African regimes will have a tough case to put forward for their own authority. The hypocrisy is so glaring that [their continued rule] will essentially mean that true democracy is good and should be supported only in countries where there are whites; and that for blacks, one-party states and other restrictions on freedom are still best. That is a racial insult to ourselves.

The Washington Post, 7-11:(A)23,25.

Mobutu Sese Seko
President of Zaire

5

I am alleged to have a colossal fortune . . . As if my villa in Cap-Martin, my apartment in Paris, my castle in Brussels and my house in Portugal could save Zaire . . . Stop alleging that I have accounts everywhere . . . It is not true. I stake my honor on it.

Interview/
World Press Review, December:38.

193

Miguel Angel Moratinos
Director of North African Affairs,
Foreign Ministry of Spain

1

The situation in the Mahgreb [Arab nations of North Africa] is not explosive, but nor is it reassuring. The [Persian] Gulf crisis [Iraq's invasion and take-over of Kuwait and the U.S.-led coalition's use of force to oust the Iraqis] has accelerated the process of socio-political change [in the Mahgreb]. To create prosperity and stability in the Mahgreb is to assure peace and security in Spain. To permit instability and under-development in North Africa is to invest in crises and conflicts that, whether we like it or not, will be exported here.

The New York Times, 3-20:(A)7.

Makau Wa Mutua
Project director,
Human Rights Program,
Harvard University Law School
(United States);
Exiled Kenyan lawyer

2

Since independence in Africa, government has been seen as the personal fiefdom a leader uses to accumulate wealth for himself, his family, his clan. He cannot be subjected to criticism by anyone, and everything he says is final. The apex of this notion of owning government is the idea of a "life president" . . . Africans have just had it [with this system]. Whether these leaders like it or not, Africa is at the threshold of a new chapter in our history. They cannot separate Africa from ideals guiding the rest of the world. We want rule of law, we want accountable government and respect for human rights.

The Washington Post, 9-9:(A)20.

Nguza Karl-i-Bond
Prime Minister of Zaire

3

[Saying Zaire's economic problems are not conducive to democracy there]: My belief is that when people are starving, they are not free. You're free only when you eat, and not in need of vital necessities. And when people are starving,

you cannot bring them to understand or follow you when you're talking about democracy.

Interview, Kinshasa, Zaire/
The New York Times, 12-9:(A)3.

Rakiya Omaar
Director, Africa Watch
(Britain)

4

[On South Africa's current moves toward ending apartheid]: The changes in South Africa have left many [black African rulers] with nowhere to hide when it comes to their own rule. They seem so pathetic when they try . . . The fight against apartheid was an article of faith around the world. It was a hard fight and it was right. But it was also a way to avoid looking at ourselves. [Three or four years ago,] you could never mention the injustices of black Africa and those of South Africa in the same breath. It was just not correct to compare them . . . [Now] I think Africans in particular are taking the lead in pointing out this history of hypocrisy. I think they are willing to take the responsibility to be more self-critical. In the long run, this can only help.

The Washington Post, 7-11:(A)25.

Muammar el-Qaddafi
Chief of State of Libya

5

[Rejecting U.S. and British calls that he turn over two Libyans accused by those countries of carrying out the bombing of Pan Am flight 103 in 1988]: The evidence against Libya is less than a laughable piece of a fingernail. They affirm they have decisive evidence against Libya [which was also implicated in the bombing] . . . This is disinformation and deceit of public opinion. We are asking that these investigations not be closed, and we challenge them to produce evidence against Libya . . . Libyan law, like the law of any other country, does not permit the delivery to American, English and French authorities of Libyan citizens suspected of carrying out the Lockerbie [Scotland] bombing. There are no extradition treaties between us and the United States and Britain since our relations have been broken with these two states.

Italian broadcast interview,
Nov. 28/Los Angeles Times, 11-29:(A)40.

Harry Schwarz
South African Ambassador
to the United States

1

[Saying the U.S. should assist South Africa in its transition to a post-apartheid society]: Whether sanctions [imposed on South Africa in 1986 to protest the country's apartheid system] were right or wrong doesn't really matter any more. But my view is that the United States cannot now say, "We wash our hands of the post-apartheid South Africa." You've now got a moral obligation to ensure that the post-apartheid society conforms with your own ideas of democracy. You've got involved. Now stay involved and see to it that we get a proper democracy, a proper kind of market economy, and a proper exercise of human rights.

Interview/
Los Angeles Times, 2-12:(H)6.

2

[Saying apartheid is on its way out in South Africa]: Black South Africans have come to accept that the new age is about to come. It's not in 20 years' time or 10 years' time; it's around the corner. That's a very real change that's happened in South Africa . . . That's where irreversibility comes in . . . I think black South Africans accept that it's completely irreversible.

Interview/
The Washington Post, 3-1:(B)4.

3

Apartheid [in South Africa] is gone in many respects, but the reality is that it has not entirely disappeared, particularly economically. The drawing of the Constitution is probably not going to be the most difficult part. In relative terms to the problems of the economy, it's going to be easy because the one fundamental thing that has been argued about for years is no longer a matter of dispute . . . It is going to be agreed in any new Constitution that there will be one person, one vote. That's not even going to be debated. What is going to be debated will be whether it will be a federal-type Constitution similar to what you have in the United States or whether there will be

a unitary-type Constitution, such as in the United Kingdom, where there is no division of power and where you have a simple majority that decides everything.

Interview/USA Today, 10-3:(A)11.

Walter Sisulu
Deputy president,
African National Council
(South Africa)

4

It has now become patently obvious that the major obstacle in the path to negotiations [aimed toward ending apartheid] is the continuation in office of the present government. Given their track record, who can trust [South African President Frederik] de Klerk to govern our country during the transition? We all know he wants to be referee, player, linesman—and write the score.

Speech, Oct. 25/
The Washington Post, 10-26:(A)13.

Frederik van Zyl Slabbert
Director, Institute for
a Democratic Alternative
for South Africa

5

South Africa's transition [away from apartheid] is forcing a redefinition of relationships with nations and agencies, not only toward South Africa but amongst themselves. Increasingly, South Africa and other countries in Africa are beginning to experience the same international pressures: increasing marginalization, demands for good governance and sound management of the economy.

Before Africa Leadership Forum,
Windhoek, Namibia/
The Christian Science Monitor,
9-20:6.

Stephen J. Solarz
United States Representative,
D-New York

6

[On Zairian President Mobutu Sese Seko]: He has established a kleptocracy to end all klep-

(STEPHEN J. SOLARZ)

tocracies, and he has set a new standard by which all future international thieves will have to be measured. He makes [the late Philippine President Ferdinand] Marcos look like a piker by comparison.

The Washington Post, 10-3:(A)38.

Helen Suzman
Former member of
South African Parliament

1

[On her long-standing opposition to apartheid in South Africa]: What motivated me was not bleeding-heart liberalism. It was justice, simple justice. And acceptance that the black population didn't have equal opportunity and suffered many disabilities. You have to remove those disabilities. You have to give them equal opportunities. But after, I don't fall over backward agreeing with everything that every black leader says he wants. There are major principles that still have to be realized [by the government], such as universal franchise and removing the remaining discriminatory laws. But, on the [ANC] side, there's got to be an acceptance of checks and balances. I don't want to replace an authoritarian white minority government with an equally authoritarian—and maybe even worse—black majority government. That's never been my aim.

Interview, Johannesburg/
Los Angeles Times, 3-24:(M)2.

Lloyd Vogelman
Director, Project for
the Study of Violence,
Witwatersrand University
(South Africa)

2

[On violence between black groups in the townships of South Africa]: People are resorting increasingly to violence to settle political conflicts. In their view, violence is serving a positive social function. It is a quick and easy method of resolving conflicts. It increases their social standing and there is a growing sense of confidence that they can get away with it.

The Christian Science Monitor,
3-13:6.

Leon Wessels
Deputy Foreign Minister
of South Africa

3

Apartheid [in South Africa] was a terrible mistake that blighted our land. With the benefits of hindsight, we know that we have hurt our fellow countrymen . . . We had failed to listen to the laughing and the crying of our people . . . That must never happen again. I am sorry for having been so hard of hearing for so long, so indifferent.

Before South African Parliament,
Cape Town/
The Christian Science Monitor,
3-18:2.

Howard Wolpe
United States Representative,
D-Michigan

4

[On the civil war in Somalia aimed at ousting the U.S.-backed government]: It is a clear failure of American foreign policy, and we should bear some responsibility. We established a strong security assistance relationship [with Somalia] and transferred millions in weaponry, while we totally disregarded the internal policies of the regime, the human-rights violations that occurred over time . . . Now what you are seeing is a general indifference to a disaster that we played a role in creating.

Interview/
The Washington Post, 1-8:(A)8.

The Americas

Jean-Bertrand Aristide
President of Haiti

1

[On his being Haiti's first democratically elected President]: It took 200 years to arrive at our second independence. At our first independence we cried "Liberty or Death!" We must now shout with all our strength, "Democracy or Death!"

*Speech after being sworn in as
President, Port-au-Prince, Feb. 7/
The New York Times, 2-8:(A)3.*

2

Justice. First, Haitians need justice, okay? So I start by hearing the voice of *everybody*. This is the way to a government of democracy. And if you obey the Constitution, of course you will get justice. If you respect human rights, of course you will get justice. If you respect the rules of democracy, you will of course get justice. And I think what we are doing is exactly that. You cannot govern a country without law . . . and once you do that, *every*body will realize how their right is respected . . . You just have to obey the Constitution, to obey the law.

*Interview/
Los Angeles Times Magazine,
4-21:14.*

3

The "big powers" have never known the real face of our country. Since we had corrupt leaders who spent their time stealing and pillaging, today we have to struggle for credibility, honesty and openness. Time is needed for the international partners to come around. And if these international partners are not used to functioning with governments as credible and honest as ours, then probably more time will be needed for the rules of the game to be redefined, before we arrive at this new Haiti. For the moment, we see that, with certain countries, acceptance is moving along faster than with others. But over-all, I see a willingness

to harmonize relations. That's why I want to be patient.

*Interview, Port-au-Prince/
"Interview" magazine, October:128.*

Bernard W. Aronson
*Assistant Secretary for
Inter-American Affairs,
Department of State
of the United States*

4

[On the agreement between Brazil, Chile and Argentina to ban chemical weapons]: I think it's a good sign that Latin America is addressing the post-Cold War agenda. It shows that democratization yields important dividends in terms of security and peace and that these countries are not going to make the mistake of being trapped in a regional arms race and waste precious economic resources.

*Interview, Washington, Sept. 5/
The New York Times, 9-6:(A)3.*

George Bush
President of the United States

5

[On a possible U.S.-Canada-Mexico free-trade agreement]: . . . we intend to pursue a trilateral free-trade agreement that would link our three economies in bold and far-reaching ways. A successful conclusion of the free-trade agreement will expand market opportunities, increase prosperity and help our three countries meet the economic challenges of the future. A free-trade area encompassing all three countries would create a North American market of 360 million people with annual production of more than $6-trillion. This agreement would be a dramatic first step toward the realization of a hemispheric free-trade zone stretching from Point Barrow in Alaska to the Straits of Magellan.

*News conference,
Washington, Feb. 5/
The New York Times, 2-6:(A)8.*

(GEORGE BUSH)

1

Ninety-nine per cent of the people of this hemisphere live either in a democracy or a country that is on the road to democracy. One per cent live under the hemisphere's last dictator, [Cuba's] Fidel Castro . . . I ask Fidel Castro to free political prisoners in Cuba and allow the United Nations Commission on Human Rights to investigate possible human-rights violations in Cuba. I challenge Mr. Castro to let Cuba live in peace with its neighbors. Put democracy to a test. Permit political parties to organize and a free press to survive. Hold free and fair elections under international supervision. [If Castro did these things,] we can expect relations between our two countries to improve significantly.

Radio address to Cuba, May 20/
The New York Times, 5-21:(A)7.

2

Another obstacle [to better U.S.-Soviet relations] lies close to home for the United States—90 miles off the Florida coast, in Cuba. The United States poses no threat to Cuba. Therefore, there is no need for the Soviet Union to funnel millions of dollars in military aid to Cuba—especially since a defiant [Cuban President Fidel] Castro, isolated by his obsolete totalitarianism, denies his people any move toward democracy. Castro does not share your faith in *glasnost* [openness] and *perestroika* [reform].

Addressing Soviet President
Mikhail Gorbachev, in speech at
Moscow State Institute, July 30/
Los Angeles Times, 7-31:(A)9.

3

[The recent failed coup in the Soviet Union] clearly is the death knell for the Communist movement around the world. There's only a handful of people that stick out like a sore thumb. I think of one down there in Cuba [Fidel Castro] right now that must be sweating . . . The American people should take great pleasure.

News conference,
Kennebunkport, Maine,
Aug. 26/USA Today, 8-27:(A)5.

4

[On the recent coup in Haiti which ousted democratically elected President Jean-Bertrand Aristide]: I'm worried about Haiti. Here's a whole hemisphere . . . that's moving in a democratic way, and along comes Haiti now, overthrowing an elected government. We care very much about it. [But] I am disinclined to use American force. We've got a big history of American force in this hemisphere, and so we've got to be very careful about that.

To reporters, Washington, Oct. 2/
Los Angeles Times, 10-3:(A)9.

Ruben Carles
Comptroller General
of Panama

5

In a place like Panama, where you have absolute freedom to move capital in and out, where the dollar is the basis of the monetary system, and where there is almost no inflation, it is logical that people from many countries bring money. Drug dollars are, undoubtedly, one of those components. During the dictatorship [of Manuel Noriega], trafficking [in drugs] and laundering [of money] were protected by Noriega and his friends. I can't say that money-laundering has now disappeared. But if there is any, it is not protected by the government.

Interview, Panama City/
The New York Times, 6-6:(C)12.

Fidel Castro
President of Cuba

6

Capitalism has neither the capacity, nor the morality, nor the ethics to solve the problems of poverty. [Returning to pre-1959 Cuban capitalism would bring back] all the old vices of that society—illiteracy, prostitution, racial discrimination, children without schools . . . So why ever talk of such garbage?

Speech, Matanzas, Cuba, July 26/
Los Angeles Times, 7-27:(A)6.

7

It's good that we should talk about democracy, once and for all . . . So-called Western bourgeois

(FIDEL CASTRO)

democracy has nothing to do with democracy. It's complete garbage, truly.

At Cuban Communist Party Congress,
Santiago de Cuba, Oct. 12/
The New York Times, 10-14:(A)7.

1

[On whether he has considered retirement]: From the revolution? From my ideas? No. For me, power is like a form of slavery. I feel like a slave. It's my profession.

September/
The Wall Street Journal,
10-10:(A)14.

Violeta Barrios de Chamorro
President of Nicaragua

2

[On suggestions that she is not in control of the government]: I answer to nobody. I am taking the reins of the country . . . I only make pacts with God. [Minister of the Presidency] Antonio Lacayo has certain control, but the weight behind his decisions comes from me. I give my ideas, and they are executed. Definitively! And if we are not in agreement, he might say, "Look, I don't like this or that." But nobody governs me. I make the first decision and the last.

Los Angeles Times Magazine,
1-6:30.

3

[On her forthcoming visit to Washington)]: I imagine they are going to ask, "What have you done in this first year?" [of her Presidency], and I will say with great pride that I stopped a [guerrilla] war, reconciled everyone, gave an amnesty so Nicaraguans can return home, and a free press so everyone can say whatever he wants. I would love to have a wand of virtue and solve [the economic problem], but I don't. We have to advance little by little. I'll keep knocking on the doors of friendly countries to see if they can help.

Interview, Managua/
Los Angeles Times, 4-15:(A)12.

Fernando Collor (de Mello)
President of Brazil

4

[Saying he is more popular than the Brazilian Congress]: In public-opinion polls about credibility, politicians generally come in last. The President of the republic comes in third, after the church and radio. There is an enormous distance in popular perception between policies made by the President and policies made by Congress.

Interview/
The New York Times, 2-11:(A)9.

Alfredo Cristiani
President of El Salvador

5

The main objective here is to create a disarmed political party from the FMLN (rebels fighting his government) . . . They have to come in. They have to take the risks. It's not easy. They have killed and destroyed . . . There might be some lunatics out there who want to take things into their own hands. All we can do is to try and give them the same security that we give any other citizen here . . . Why should government take risks? . . . We didn't shoot our way in here . . . We are here because we expressed to the people what we would do, and they supported what we told them, and that is the legal and moral way of trying to promote your ideas . . . not by sort of shooting everybody down and trying to create a dictatorship . . . The only thing the FMLN [would give up] is stopping something that is totally illegal, which is trying to reach political power through violence.

Interview, San Salvador/
Los Angeles Times, 8-26:(A)4.

6

[Salvadorans have been] easy victims of that abusive and irrational polarity that divided the world into inevitable bands on the basis of an artificial ideological fanaticism. No one invented the Salvadoran [civil] war. Rather, it arose as a manifestation of grave shortcomings and errors in our society; but once set off it took on the colors of the world conflict.

At United Nations,
New York, Sept. 23/
The New York Times, 9-24:(A)8.

Alvaro de Soto
United Nations mediator
in peace talks between
the government of El Salvador
and Salvadoran rebels

1

[Saying the FMLN rebels are unlikely to agree to a cease-fire in their war with the government]: Unless you look at guarantees and conditions, for the FMLN the cease-fire will be like asking them to jump into an empty swimming pool. For this reason, the FMLN is asking for cease-fire terms that are tantamount to an armed peace. They want to be able to carry out maneuvers and continue to recruit in a large swatch of the country to be ready for the possibility of having to return to fighting. For the government, that would be unthinkable.

Interview, Connecticut/
Los Angeles Times, 8-26:(A)4.

Vilmar Faria
President, Cebrap,
the Brazilian Center
for Planning and Analysis

2

[In Brazil,] there are elections, political parties, a Congress. There's no threat on the horizon [to the system]. But if you understand democracy as a relationship among people, the country is far off.

The Christian Science Monitor, 3-12:4.

Mikhail S. Gorbachev
President of the Soviet Union

3

[Announcing plans to withdraw Soviet troops from Cuba and eliminate Soviet subsidies to that country]: . . . we plan to transfer our relations with Cuba to a plane of mutually beneficial trade and economic ties and we will remove the other elements of that relationship—elements that were born of a different time in a different era. In that context, we will soon begin discussions with the Cuban leadership about the withdrawal of a Soviet training brigade, which was stationed in Cuba some time ago and is still there.

News conference,
Moscow, Sept. 11/
The New York Times, 9-12:(A)6.

Jaime Gonzalez Graf
Director, Institute of Political
Studies (Mexico)

4

[Saying that if Mexico and the U.S. sign a free-trade pact, Mexico must retain its identity and individuality]: It's a question of diplomatic consistency and tradition. As much as [Mexican President Carlos] Salinas may want to alter this tradition, he can't. For example, the U.S. would like Mexico to help bring down [Cuban President Fidel] Castro. But I'm absolutely convinced Mexico would never do this. Not only because it would break a historic position, but because it would be an absolute submission to North American policy.

The Christian Science Monitor, 8-1:7.

Gillian Gunn
Specialist on Cuba,
Carnegie Endowment
for International
Peace (United States)

5

Diplomatically, the Latin American countries would just as soon have Cuba join the [international trade] club. But economically, I don't think [Cuban President Fidel] Castro can make much progress at the [current Latin American summit meeting]. His real problem isn't U.S. pressure on his neighbors or differing ideologies. His real problem is that Cuba is not paying the bills.

Los Angeles Times, 7-19:(A)6.

Jean-Jacques Honorat
Prime Minister of Haiti

6

[Criticizing foreign threats to institute a trade embargo against Haiti because of the recent coup there ousting President Jean-Bertrand Aristide]: Haiti cannot withstand an embargo for more than three days. It's a country that produces nothing. An embargo imposed on Haiti will mean civil war. Now, if the international community wants to declare civil war in Haiti . . . they have to take the responsibility.

Interview,
Port-au-Prince, Haiti, Oct. 23/
The Washington Post, 10-25:(A)19.

Jacques Jolicoeur
International-affairs specialist,
External Affairs Ministry
of Quebec, Canada

1

I think that there should be, and there will be, a referendum somewhere next fall about the way the people in Quebec wish to be in the future. It will be totally different [from the referendum in 1980 about the province's desire to become a sovereign state], because in 1980 there were still many Canadian federalists who gave the Quebecois some dreams, some possibilities, of making some [acceptable] new political organization in Canada. And this is no longer believable. The question [in the referendum] would be: How do you see your future—as a province of Canada, or as a sovereign state with an economic arrangement with Canada? I think at this point Quebecers feel strong enough, and feel that it would be good for themselves and probably good for the other Canadians, to make a definition of themselves which is different from the one at the moment.

Los Angeles Times, 1-1:(H)3.

D. Marvin Jones
Professor of law,
University of Miami

2

[On the current drug-trafficking trial of former Panamanian leader Manuel Noriega, who was captured and brought to the U.S. during the 1989 U.S. invasion of Panama]: Noriega comes to us as a political case. The reason he's here on trial is not because he's a drug dealer, but because we had certain interests in Panama which we could not achieve. What we really wanted was to depose a political figure who had become a thorn in the side of American foreign policy.

Los Angeles Times, 9-5:(A)4.

Enrique Krauze
Mexican historian

3

The Mexican Presidency has always resembled the enlightened despotism of late 18th-century Europe. The 18th-century despots made many changes in the right direction without the participation of the people. That is exactly the case [in Mexico] today... [But] in 1991, nobody can sell a hegemonic, one-party system in the world. You have to put makeup on it and say we are gearing toward democracy. But Mexico is not Mars and one-party systems do not work. The one way to modernize is to modernize in both the economy and politics.

Los Angeles Times, 10-22:(H)2.

Antonio Lacayo
Minister of the Presidency
of Nicaragua

4

We think we have to begin to move away from the Nicaraguan attitude that he who is in power is the one who orders and arranges, is the owner of life and wealth, and the other person has no right to express an opinion. The thinking has traditionally meant that if that person does express an opinion he should be taken prisoner, as [Anastasio] Somoza did and Daniel Ortgega did [both former Nicaraguan leaders]. That wasn't the discovery of Somoza or of Daniel. That comes from the last century. It's part of our culture.

The New York Times, 4-12:(A)4.

5

Here [in Nicaragua] we've always had liberals fighting conservatives to death, Somocistas [supporters of the former Somoza government] fighting Sandinistas to death, Sandinistas fighting contras to death. The only solution is to create a great force of the center... Nicaragua is a country that's born and then dies over and over again. We are determined that this system end and that democracy be installed.

Interview, Managua/
The Washington Post, 7-25:(A)28.

Barbara McDougall
Secretary of State
for External Affairs of Canada

6

[On the possibility of Quebec splitting off from Canada]: That's not going to happen. Or it will

(BARBARA McDOUGALL)

happen over my dead body and the dead body of the Prime Minister. [It is] not in anyone's interest that this country split apart. A lot of the messages that we [in the government] are delivering across Canada are much tougher . . . It would not be a friendly parting.

Interview, Nov. 21/
The Christian Science Monitor,
12-4:6.

Jim McKenzie
Professor of journalism,
University of Regina (Canada)

1

[On the Royal Canadian Mounted Police]: It's interesting to see how significant the Mounties are in Canadian society. This is a country that doesn't have a very high opinion of itself. There's a lot of sentiment about "Who are we?" We're not really Americans, and we're not really Brits. We don't make heroes out of our Prime Ministers. We really don't know who we are. But, by God, we've produced at least one good national institution that is worthy of admiration [the Mounties].

Los Angeles Times, 4-23:(H)4.

Carlos Saul Menem
President of Argentina

2

[On the Malvinas, or Falkland Islands, which were the object of an Argentine war with Britain in 1982]: Our position is that we still claim the Malvinas as Argentine territory, but we are going to go about regaining them through diplomatic channels, and not through war again.

To reporters/
The New York Times, 3-19:(A)3.

3

Argentina was a country that aligned with what was called the Third World. But, for me, there is no reason for that world to exist. We have resolved to align ourselves with the only world that does exist. And at this point, everyone

knows that within the context of the United Nations, there is one country that is the leader and that is the United States. There is no doubt of this. We are in a spirit of harmony, of excellent relations. It's the best level that Argentina and the United States have had.

The New York Times, 6-8:3.

4

Argentina and the United States were in opposite camps in recent years because of a false [Argentine] concept of what sovereignty is. We isolated ourselves from practically all the world, basically because of out-of-date neutralist attitudes . . . We are living in another Argentina now . . . We Peronists cannot continue thinking in 1991 as we did in 1945. Haven't there been changes in the thinking of the United States? Did you think a year or two ago that the Cold War would end, for example, and the Soviet Union would line up behind the United States or that there would be a new current of opinion based on a new international order? A country that doesn't live these realities . . . for all practical purposes disappears.

Interview/Newsweek, 7-15:28.

Carmelo Mesa-Lago
Specialist on Cuba,
University of Pittsburgh
(United States)

5

[On the anticipated cut in Soviet aid to Cuba in the wake of current political upheavals in the Soviet Union)]: The most important part of the equation all along has been the availability of Soviet supplies [for Cuba], and it is a fair assumption that they are going to decline even more dramatically. If there has been a marked deterioration in the internal situation between last July and this July, the next six months will be much worse. Popular discontent [in Cuba] is going to expand much faster. And if they [the Communist government] don't change—and tactical changes are not going to make the necessary difference—there is no way now that they can survive.

The New York Times, 9-3:(A)10.

Brian Mulroney
Prime Minister of Canada

1

Anyone who seeks to break up Canada will have this Prime Minister, this Cabinet, this caucus and the membership of this great Party to face right across Canada. And we will fight . . . with every ounce of our strength to achieve and preserve the unity of Canada.

> *To reporters at meeting of*
> *Progressive Conservative Party,*
> *Toronto, Aug. 9/*
> *The Washington Post, 8-10:(A)19.*

2

If you want a syrupy, sugar-coated, unrealistic Canada, you go ahead and talk to somebody else.

> *Los Angeles Times, 11-12:(H)2.*

Salvador Nava
1991 opposition candidate
for Governor of
San Luis Potosi, Mexico

3

[Charging fraud by the ruling PRI party in the recent gubernatorial election in San Luis Potosi]: I beg the people's pardon for having trusted the high officials whom I thought would respect the move toward democracy. I am convinced that we will not achieve democracy through elections.

> *At rally, Aug. 25/*
> *Los Angeles Times, 8-29:(A)11.*

Daniel Ortega (Saavedra)
Former President of Nicaragua

4

[Saying Sandinista leaders like himself gave away many government assets to their supporters after the party's defeat in last year's elections]: We gave away as many houses as we could—gave vehicles to the cooperatives, to the transport workers, to our bureaucrats, to the popular sectors. We gave trucks, cars, forgave outstanding debts, gave away all the construction materials we had warehoused, gave away all the money we could to the families of war casualties and veterans. We gave away everything we could, and in that way protected an important sector of Sandinista militancy.

> *Interview/*
> *The New York Times, 6-25:(A)5.*

Douglas W. Payne
Director of hemispheric studies,
Freedom House (United States)

5

It should be obvious by now that as long as major [illegal-drug] markets exist in the United States and other developed countries and as long as Latin America [from which much of the world's drugs eminates] remains in economic crisis, the drug trade will flourish. The prospects for reducing the world drug market and improving Latin economies are long-term propositions at best. In the meantime, by pressing for deeper involvement of Latin militaries in hopes of quick solutions [to the drug-trafficking problem], the United States risks undermining the authority of already weak civilian governments. Washington should therefore consider carefully the alternative proposals for assistance now being formulated by governments in the region. Finally, the United States must recognize that consolidating democracy requires a transformation of Latin political culture, a process of embracing new values that will require at least another generation. The United States can assist in the process by sharing the experience of democracy.

> *Before House Foreign Affairs Committee,*
> *Washington, February/*
> *The Washington Post,*
> *3-13:(A)16.*

Carlos Andres Perez
President of Venezuela

6

A new Latin American era is dawning. It will be a continent where the utopia of an authenic democracy of free and equal citizens reigns, the model for a prosperous new society that seeks to join the First World.

> *At Latin American summit meeting,*
> *Guadalajara, Mexico, July/*
> *Los Angeles Times, 8-6:(H)2.*

Thomas R. Pickering
United States Ambassador/
Permanent Representative
to the United Nations

1

[Addressing the new government of Haiti, which came to power in a coup that ousted the democratically elected President]: Your regime is illegitimate. It has no standing in the Western Hemisphere and the international community. Until democracy is restored, you will be treated in this hemisphere as a pariah—without assistance, without friends and without a future.

At United Nations,
New York, Oct. 11/
The Washington Post, 10-12:(A)18.

Charles B. Rangel
United States Representative,
D-New York

2

[Criticizing those in the U.S. Bush Administration and in Congress who do not want to allow Haitian refugees to enter the U.S.]: I've never seen a more clear-cut moral issue that people find so comfortable dismissing. Morally, nobody [in Congress] challenges me. But everybody tries to come up with an excuse not to let these people into the country.

Los Angeles Times, 12-3:(A)5.

Gil Remillard
Minister of Constitutional Affairs
of Quebec, Canada

3

Quebec within a profoundly renewed [Canadian] federalism is the option that the Quebec government prefers. But let's make this clear: not federalism at any price or on any condition.

The Christian Science Monitor,
6-26:4.

Federico Reyes (Heroles)
Mexican political scientist;
Editor, "Este Pais" magazine

4

If you think about political science in the United States, you think about polls, statistics,

that kind of thing. But, in Mexico, political science means philosophy. We don't have a tradition of fact in Mexico, even in economics.

The New York Times, 3-21:(A)4.

Carlos Salinas (de Gortari)
President of Mexico

5

Competitiveness calls upon us to forge new relations with the United States and also with other nations of the world. We must create and build up shared advantages through the complementarity of economies in order to compete with the new centers of financial and technological innovation. [As for the proposed U.S.-Mexico-Canada trade zone,] our economies are certainly different, but in their very differences lie sources of exchange and the possibility of creating the comparative advantages that will enable us to compete.

Before Texas Legislature,
Austin, April 12/
The Washington Post, 4-13:(A)8.

6

[Supporting a proposed free-trade agreement between the U.S. and Mexico]: There are already very strong economic interactions between Mexico and the United States, and we must introduce order into that very strong relationship. Second, geography put us together, but political will will now allow us to emphasize coincidences and respect the differences. And last . . . I want to avoid the very big migration of Mexicans to the United States looking for jobs. I want Mexicans to remain here and find in Mexico the opportunities for their well-being. That is why I emphasize that we want to export goods and not people.

Interview, Mexico City/
U.S. News & World Report,
7-8:41.

Jorge Serrano
President of Guatemala

7

[On Guatemala's long guerrilla war]: We are seeking total peace and not a simple truce or

(JORGE SERRANO)

cease-fire, conscious that the simple absence of conflict does not guarantee peace if the causes that motivated it remain.

Inaugural address,
Guatemala City, Jan. 14/
Los Angeles Times, 1-15:(A)20.

1

[Guatemala has] a culture of death. It is the history of this society, not just of the military . . . Everybody believes they can work outside the law.

Interview/
Los Angeles Times, 9-19:(A)1.

Robert G. Torricelli
United States Representative,
D-New Jersey

2

[Saying further U.S. military aid to the government of El Salvador should be deferred until late summer to give current peace negotiations between the government and anti-government rebel forces more of a chance to succeed]: A continuation of aid might convince the [Salvadoran armed forces] that a military solution would be possible. A decision to withhold aid [completely] might have convinced the [guerrillas] that the United States would withdraw from the conflict. The best way to send an appropriate message is to send no message at all.

June 6/
The Washington Post, 6-7:(A)15.

Roberto Troncoso
President, Panamanian Committee
for Human Rights

3

[On 1989's invasion of Panama by the U.S., which ousted Panamanian dictator Manuel Noriega]: No matter how good the invasion was for us, it was a trauma we can't shake. The United States overthrew the generals they tolerated for so many years, but this [new] government [of President Guillermo Endara]

hasn't been able to put the word "democracy" back into our dictionary.

The New York Times, 2-11:(A)1.

Margaret D. Tutwiler
Spokesman,
Department of State
of the United States

4

[On the recent coup in Haiti in which the elected President, Jean-Bertrand Aristide, was ousted from office]: Our view is that there is no constitutional vacancy [in Haiti] and we will not recognize a provisional government. President Aristide was forced from office illegally by force of arms. The Parliament acted yesterday at gunpoint. The legislators did not vote. They were forced to sign a petition. We do not accept the Parliament's forced action [swearing in a new provisional President] as a legitimate constitutional action.

Washington, Oct. 8/
The New York Times, 10-9:(A)3.

Joaquin Villalobos
Commander, Farabundo
Marti National Liberation
Front (rebels fighting the
government of El Salvador)

5

In El Salvador there is a need to isolate or cut off the extremes. In our case, that means the thinking of dogmatic Stalinism and traditional, classic Communism. At the other extreme, it is the orthodox right wing, which in El Salvador is something from the Stone Age.

Interview, Mexico City, March/
The New York Times, 3-7:(A)3.

6

I don't believe in Marxism as a religion but as a tool of analysis. After 100 years, any ideology is bound to be superseded. Traditionally, the left had to confront dictatorship. This meant our ideology was, in my view, almost religious and vertical in organization. In politics this is no good. Maybe [it was], 20-odd years ago, when

(JOAQUIN VILLALOBOS)

the FMLN was baptized as Marxist-Leninist. We are revolutionary but a pluralist group that came from social democratic and social Christian tendencies. In Nicaragua, the Sandinistas thought that traditional Marxism would work. They became rigid [and lost last year's elections] . . . Now they are correcting their errors. They are doing what they should have done in 1979, what they said they would do. The private sector and the left are cooperating. But [for this to work] international cooperation is needed, and a private sector that is modern. In El Salvador, we have dinosaurs.

Interview/
U.S. News & World Report,
5-6:49.

Peter D. Whitney
Director, Office of Regional
Economic Policy,
Bureau of Inter-American Affairs,
Department of State
of the United States

1

[Urging Latin American countries to reduce trade barriers among themselves]: We [the U.S.] benefit in practical terms, as well as in foreign-policy terms, from having more prosperous neighbors. The whole process of regional trade liberalization would be greatly enhanced if groups of Latin American and Caribbean countries organized to remove the many trade barriers that exist among themselves.

The Christian Science Monitor,
7-17:4.

Ralph Winter
Economist, Acadia University,
Nova Scotia (Canada)

2

[On the fate of Canada's Atlantic provinces if Quebec, which stands between those provinces and the rest of Canada, should become independent]: I'm not sure people have realized how serious the situation is. The rest of Canada is becoming less and less concerned about the economy of this region. I'm sure the day after Quebec separates, you'd have [Ontario] Premier [Bob] Rae saying, "Oh, we'll look after our friends and fellow Canadians." But within a year, the rot would set in.

Los Angeles Times, 7-23:(H)1.

Ruben Zamora
Leader, Democratic Convergence
(El Salvador)

3

[On the recent elections in El Salvador]: We campaigned on the theme of peace and were the only party that spectacularly increased its vote. That, I think, is a clear signal to the government . . . When I returned [from exile], I shared the [Salvadoran rebels'] view that elections had to be put off until we negotiated a share of power. For the government, elections were a substitute for negotiations. Neither of us were right. These elections have served the negotiating process . . . We have to dignify the [Salvadoran] Assembly. We have to make it a center for negotiations, not of confrontation.

Interview/
Los Angeles Times, 3-13:(A)9.

Lal Krishna Advani
Leader, Bharatiya Janata Party
of India

1

[On charges that he is a Fascist]: You judge me not by what my adversaries say about me. You judge me by my track record. I wish someone were to point out to me anything from my manifesto, constitution, utterances, statements, anything that can be pinned down as being indexes of Fascism . . . Where is the authoritarianism? Where is the Fascism? These are trite and stereotyped words of political abuse. And, because everyone uses them, therefore they do stick. What can I do? And then, people meet me, talk with me, discuss with me and find that this is not correct. So then, they think I'm clever.

Interview, New Delhi/
Los Angeles Times, 6-11:(H)4.

Akihito
Emperor of Japan

2

After [World War II], looking back upon the past, Japan has determined to live as a peaceful nation. I would like to make efforts to convey the fact that the Japanese people love peace and have wishes to deepen friendship with people of each country.

To reporters, Tokyo/
The Christian Science Monitor,
9-26:2.

Chester G. Atkins
United States Representative,
D-Massachusetts

3

One single clear and continuing theme in United States policy to Cambodia has been our insistence on the inclusion of the Khmer Rouge in the interim government. That is really quite astonishing. It sent an enormous signal to the Cambodian people that the killing fields could very easily happen again.

Interview, Washington, Dec. 20/
The New York Times, 12-21:3.

Gurmit Singh Aulakh
President, Council of Khalistan
(India)

4

I have made it my life's work to spread the truth about India's brutality against the Sikh nation . . . The only appropriate response of the international community should be one of outright condemnation of the Indian government, its laws and the brutality it so fervently works to sustain. Indeed, under the Indian Constitution, the presumption of innocence is [converted into] a presumption of guilt. Confessions obtained through police torture are repeatedly admitted in the courts as evidence. Trial can be held in jail cells. The legal remedy of habeas corpus goes unhonored. The identity of witnesses can be suppressed, cross-examination denied and the accused can be detained up to a year before even being charged with a crime.

At National Press Club,
Washington, May 28/
The Washington Post, 6-7:(A)22.

James A. Baker III
Secretary of State
of the United States

5

To those who doubted America's commitment and staying power, the [recent Persian] Gulf crisis demonstrated that American global engagement is here to stay. America's global engagement definitely includes Asia. Our destiny lies across the Pacific as much or more than anywhere else. We intend to operate with you bilaterally and collectively. We will stand by our commitments to you.

To foreign ministers of
Association of Southeast Asian Nations,
Kuala Lumpur, Malaysia, July 22/
The Washington Post, 7-24:(A)24.

6

Mongolia has placed itself at the crossroads of a new order for Asia and the world—an order based on democratic values and free markets. You were the first country in Asia to embrace Communism. Now you are the first Communist country in Asia to choose democracy . . . To some, the democratic process appears to be a presciption for anarchy and chaos. Yet it is not . . . However daunting the obstacles you face may seem, retreat to the ways of the past can only make the move more difficult.

At People's Great Hural (legislature),
Ulan Bator, Mongolia, July 26/
Los Angeles Times, 7-27:(A)4.

Jim Bolger
Prime Minister
of New Zealand

1

[Saying New Zealand must cut its social and welfare spending to save its economy]: We have tried devaluation, tried protectionism, tried massive borrowing, tried almost everything except living within our means . . . We have come to the end of debtor's row. The next step takes us into the Third World. We must all have the honesty to accept that New Zealand can't run a first-class social system on the strength of a third-rate economy.

Speech, July 30/
Los Angeles Times, 10-4:(A)1.

Ashish Bose
Indian professor
of population studies

2

[On India's recent national census]: Here, all generalizations are true. Every possible situation exists. India is a great zoo and a museum rolled into one. The human beings have such a diversity of languages, of dress, of manners, of customs, of beliefs, of superstitions, of human behavior. In short, the census is a snapshot of this nation at a single point in time. And even in spite of the problems it reveals to us, it unfolds into this beautiful and diverse mosaic for all to see in its wonder.

Los Angeles Times, 4-29:(A)9.

George Bush
President of the United States

3

I think it's important that we have reasonable relations with China. I think it's important we have trade relations with China. But, on the other hand, China sometimes doesn't see eye-to-eye with us on some of the fundamental human-rights questions that concern me as President and concern all Americans. That's a long way of saying I don't know exactly what we're going to do on MFN.

News conference,
Washington, April 29/
Los Angeles Times, 5-1:(A)11.

4

[On U.S.-China relations]: I look at the big picture. I look at the support we got from China back in Desert Storm [the U.S.-led war against Iraq's occupation of Kuwait], the importance of China as a country. And I don't want to see us isolate them. I do want to see them come forward more on some of the things that we've been asking [such as human rights] . . . I go back to the days when I was in China as the equivalent of [U.S.] Ambassador and, though there are major problems in China, things we don't like about their system, things are an awful lot better than they were back in 1975.

To reporters, Washington, May 15/
The New York Times, 5-16:(A)1,5.

5

This week, I will [propose] formally that MFN trade status continue for China. This policy has generated considerable controversy [in the U.S. because of China's poor record on human rights]. Some critics have said revoke MFN, or endanger it with sweeping conditions—to censure China, cut our ties and isolate them. We are told this is a principled policy, a moral thing to do. This advice is not new, it's not wise, it is not in the best interest of our country, the United States and, in the end, in spite of noble and best intentions, it is not moral. First, MFN is special. It's not a favor. It is the ordinary basis of trade world-wide. Second, MFN is a means to bring the influence of the

(GEORGE BUSH)

outside world to bear on China. Critics who attack MFN today act as if the point is to punish China, as if hurting China's economy will somehow help the cause of privatization and human rights. The real point is to pursue a policy that has the best chance of changing Chinese behavior.

At Yale University commencement,
May 27/
The New York Times, 5-28:(A)4.

1

China can easily affect the stability of the Asian-Pacific region, and therefore affect the entire world's peace and prosperity. The Chinese play a central role in working to resolve the conflict in Cambodia, to relax tensions on the Korean peninsula. China has a voice now in the multinational organizations, and its votes in the United Nations Security Council against Iraq's brutal aggression [against Kuwait] helped us forge the broad coalition that brought us victory in the [Persian] Gulf [war]. And so when we find opportunities to cooperate with China, we will explore them. When problems arise with China's behavior, we will take appropriate action.

At Yale University commencement,
May 27/
The New York Times,
5-28:(A)4.

2

Very candidly, there may be some elements [in Japan] of anti-American feeling, and I can't deny that some elements in [the U.S.] appear to want to bash Japan, to use a common expression. So, to those in either country that might harbor concerns about the other, let me simply say this relationship is big, it's broad, it's strong, it transcends any one issue or another. Where there are differences, they are outweighed by the common ground that we share and the common objectives that we share.

News conference,
Kennebunkport, Maine, July 11/
Los Angeles Times,
7-12:(A)8.

Jimmy Carter
Former President
of the United States

3

[On the reduction in high-level exchanges between the U.S. and China since China's violent crackdown on pro-democracy demonstrators in Beijing in 1989]: In order to restore the good relations forged by Chairman Deng Xiaoping and me and maintained until June, 1989, my hope is that the Chinese government will decide to grant amnesty to all non-violent dissidents . . . Our natioins must expect our policies to be scrutinized and analyzed by others. The exercise of these basic principles of inquiry involving such principles as freedom of expression and freedom of religion do not comprise "interference in the internal affairs" of another country.

At Beijing Foreign Affairs College,
April 14/
Los Angeles Times, 4-15:(A)4.

Dick Cheney
Secretary of Defense
of the United States

4

[On criticism that the U.S. is not doing enough to find out if there are any U.S. POWs remaining in Vietnam following the war there in the 1970s]: The suggestion that somehow we're not aggressively working these cases simply isn't a valid one. I can absolutely guarantee that if we had any evidence that there was an American POW still alive in Southeast Asia, and we knew where he was, I'd have thousands of volunteers lined up outside my office door to go get him.

Newsweek, 7-29:23.

Chu Chang Jun
North Korean Ambassador
to China

5

Because of the United States, we are still not able to reunify our country [North and South Korea]. Because of the United States, brothers and sisters are separated. The United States deployed nuclear weapons in South Korea that are hundreds or thousands of times stronger than

(CHU CHANG JUN)

the power of the nuclear weapons the United States dropped on Hiroshima and Nagasaki. We have very strong feelings about the United States. But we are not seeing only the past. We have to see the future, too. If the people of the United States can have good feelings toward the Democratic People's Republic of [North] Korea, if they take a good position and respect the sovereignty and independence of our country, then we have the intention to form ties with the people and with the United States.

News conference, Beijing, Nov. 27/
Los Angeles Times, 11-28:(A)13.

Edith Cresson
Prime Minister of France

1

I'm against the clear imbalance that exists between the European Community, which is not at all protectionist [in trade], and the Japanese system, which is hermetically sealed . . . The Japanese had several decades to acquire the strength that today is wiping out the American auto industry. I don't want Europe's auto industry to be wiped out. I don't want hundreds of thousands of jobs to disappear.

Broadcast interview/
The New York Times,
5-20:(C)2.

Dalai Lama
Exiled former ruler of Tibet

2

If the world truly hopes to see a reduction of tyranny in China, it must not appease China's leaders, [but must link] bilateral relations to respect for human rights.

Before members of Congress,
Washington, April 18/
Los Angeles Times, 4-19:(A)12.

Khairulah Dawalty
Professor of agriculture,
Kabul University (Afghanistan)

3

[On the current civil war in Afghanistan]: Afghanistan doesn't bother the world any more

[since the Soviets pulled out their forces in 1989]. It's just part of the culture of the world now, this war. Who is going to take care of the Afghan people from now on? This is a dark spot in the world, and there is no flashlight to see what's going on inside.

To journalists and educators,
Kabul, April 30/
Los Angeles Times, 5-3:(A)19.

Robert J. Dole
United States Senator,
R-Kansas

4

[On the probability that U.S. President Bush will veto the Senate's vote to eliminate most-favored-nation trade status for China]: I don't believe the Chinese leadership should take any great satisfaction because it appears now that the veto will be sustained. There might be a clear understanding in the People's Republic of China if a bipartisan group of United States Senators went to Beijing, met with the leadership, and spelled out some of the concerns we have [about human rights in China]. They're real; they're not going to disappear.

Washington, July 23/
The Christian Science Monitor,
7-25:7.

Juan Ponce Enrile
Philippine Senator;
Former Minister of Defense
of the Philippines

5

[Criticizing a proposed treaty that would extend the U.S. lease on military bases in the Philippines]: I cannot live with a treaty that assumed that without 8,000 servicemen and some passing warships, we shall fall flat on our faces. I cannot believe that the vitality of this country will be extinguished when the last bargirl in Olongapo turns off the light in the last cabaret [frequented by U.S. servicemen].

Before Philippine Senate,
Manila, Sept. 16/
The Washington Post, 9-17:(A)25.

Rajiv Gandhi
Former Prime Minister
of India

1

[India] needs a government that can function, a government that has a policy, a vision. Economically, if you look at the balance of what we did [when he was Prime Minister] from 1984 to 1989, I don't think the country ever progressed any faster than during those years. Our international prestige was never higher. Now India has disappeared from the map, economically and politically.

Interview, April/
The New York Times, 4-24:(A)4.

Richard A. Gephardt
United States Representative,
D-Missouri

2

Unless China stops selling arms around the world, stops stealing American products and starts respecting the human rights of its people, the [U.S. Bush] Administration should not extend most-favored-nation trading status to them. It would be unthinkable, and it shouldn't be approved by Congress.

Los Angeles Times, 4-27:(A)19.

3

[Saying the U.S. should toughen its trade laws to deal with Japan's difficult trade practices]: It's time to deal with the truth. Standard free-trade theory fails to recognize the deep differences between and fundamental incompatibility of our economic system and Japan's. Unless we change our ideas and our rules of engagement with Japan, these systems won't be reconciled... We persist in talking with the wrong people and we don't understand the dynamics of power in the Japanese political and economic system. There is no governmental conspiracy [by Japan] and no master plan. And because there isn't, there is no one to negotiate with when a foreign country tries to deal with Japan. The only real base of influence is the Japanese people.

Speech sponsored by Center for
National Policy,
Washington, Dec. 6/
Los Angeles Times, 12-7:(A)2.

Benjamin A. Gilman
United States Representative,
R-New York

4

[Arguing against renewing U.S. MFN trade status toward China]: If we deny [MFN] to the PRC, it's argued, China will happily withdraw into its cocoon, and we will hurt progressive elements in the ruling elite in addition to losing all our influence with that nation. The truth, however, is that we've already isolated China from the ethical and moral standards we expect from civilized nations. Years of moral and ethical isolation have emboldened China's Communist leaders. According to Amnesty International, pro-democracy forces in the PRC have been hunted down, rounded up and even executed. Asia Watch calls China's rule over Tibet "merciless repression"... The authorization of MFN since 1979 has apparently not put a stop to any of these violations. According to... authoritative sources, the Beijing Administration has re-centralized banking, credit, production planning, material allocation, foreign trade and other important elements in the economy. There are approximately 3 million private and semi-private Chinese enterprises that have been shut down and, in the majority of cases, only state-run enterprises are going to benefit from MFN... The problem with China is the harsh Communist system itself, and the world's industrialized nations continuing to do business with the People's Republic of China despite these violations.

Before House Foreign Affairs Committee,
The Washington Post, 5-30:(A)18.

Allan Goodman
Associate dean,
School of Foreign Service,
Georgetown University
(United States)

5

[U.S.-Japanese] relations are in a terrible state at all levels—economic, political and cultural. They probably haven't been as bad at any time in the post-World War II period... We completely misunderstand each other culturally. We are fierce economic competitors. After years of

211

(ALLAN GOODMAN)

effort and numerous negotiations, the Japanese still have enormous barriers to any outsider, and particularly the United States, doing business in their country.

Interview/
USA Today, 12-2:(A)13.

Mikhail S. Gorbachev
President of the Soviet Union;
General Secretary,
Communist Party
of the Soviet Union

1

Asia and the Pacific, whose inhabitants make up half of the world's total population, face a host of economic, ethnic, social, religious, environmental and other highly complex problems. No country can cope with them single-handedly. Therefore, we feel that the idea of a multilateral forum on security and cooperation remains as revelant as ever. Sooner or later, life will make us accept that idea.

Before Japanese Parliament,
Tokyo, April 17/
Los Angeles Times, 4-18:(A)9.

Joseph Gorman
Chairman, TRW, Inc.

2

Isn't it time for you [the Japanese] to step up to your obligations as a super-economic power—to provide world leadership on issues of trade? For there to be free and fair trade around the world, every regional and major national system must be fundamentally the same, or it won't work. If the Japanese don't materially alter their system to make it fundamentally the same as North America and Europe, then both North America and Europe will begin to erect trade protection barriers . . . and that will harm all regions of the world.

Interview, Cleveland/
The Christian Science Monitor,
8-8:8.

Donald Gregg
United States Ambassador
to South Korea

3

[On South Korea]: This is one of the most exciting, interesting economies in the world. I tell our businessmen, "This place is going to go crazy! Get in here!" This is an extraordinary country, but most Koreans don't realize it. They always think of themselves as a shrimp among whales.

Los Angeles Times, 5-21:(H)10.

Tito Guingona
Philippine Senator

4

[On the Philippine Senate vote to reject a new U.S. lease for the Subic Bay Naval Station]: This is a decision to break off the last shackles of the past. We want friendship with America. We want trade. But we do not want servitude. For 500 years this land has been occupied or dominated by foreigners in one form or another. It is time we came into our own, time to become truly self-reliant, time to end our dependence on the United States.

Before the Senate,
Manila, Sept. 16/
The New York Times,
9-17:(A)4.

Richard Halloran
Director of special projects,
East-West Center
(United States)

5

[On the new U.S. plan to bring much of its Pacific-based forces back to U.S. soil and use small military posts in several Asian countries rather than rely on large foreign bases as in the past]: It's probably the best of all possible worlds. You reassure your Asian friends that you can get there in a hurry and do the job. And you reassure them that you can go away.

Los Angeles Times,
10-15:(H)6.

Harry Harding
Specialist on China,
Brookings Institution
(United States)

1

[On calls in the U.S. for elimination of most-favored-nation trade status for China because of that nation's poor human-rights record]: Elimination of MFN would make the human-rights situation worse. It would provide a pretext for tightening of political controls and a cutback of exchanges with the U.S. The bottom line is that the U.S. does not have much leverage in [China].
The Christian Science Monitor,
7-25:7.

Takashi Hosomi
Director, Nissei Research Institute
(Japan)

2

Japanese are beginning to realize that just mimicking the United States, while hiding under the American umbrella, is not enough. We are coming to the realization that we must form our own opinions—that we must become one of the participants. That is a huge change.
Interview/
Los Angeles Times, 2-26:(A)5.

Yuichi Ichikawa
Secretary general,
Komeito Party of Japan

3

[On Japan's low profile in the recent Persian Gulf war]: The Gulf war had a strong impact. We watched the war in real-time on TV, with newscasters and scholars and pundits talking about what Japan's role in the world ought to be. And the new consensus that emerged is that our strong anti-war pacifism is still there. But beyond that, shouldn't Japan have some role in helping the UN preserve peace? . . . How can our country lock itself out of the world and sit here behind the closed door of anti-war pacifism?
Interview/
The Washington Post,
9-20:(A)20.

Jiang Zemin
General Secretary,
Communist Party of China

4

One thing I find difficult to understand is why some people in the West are so interested in the internal affairs of China. The concept of human rights, democracy and freedom are all relative. They have different meanings and natures under different social systems. If one tenth, or one one-hundredth, one one-thousandth or even one ten-thousandth of the Chinese population wanted to go to the West, and I, as the General Secretary of the Party and also our Premier, were to do nothing to stop them, then that would be 1 14,000 people who would like to go abroad and flood into the United States and the West. I joked to your [U.S.] Ambassador, James Lilley, that he wouldn't have time to issue all the visas. What's more, because the Chinese are so clever, they would probably fill all the fields in the United States, and you would be deprived of tranquility. So in terms of human rights, one of our major obligations is to try to provide this huge population with a good life in China.
Interview, Beijing/
U.S. News & World Report,
5-27:44.

5

[On the poor performance by China's state-run industries]: They are the state's main source of income and the backbone of the socialist economy. So whether we can revive them affects not only the stability of the national economy, but also the status of the public-ownership economy and the solidity of the entire socialist system.
The New York Times, 12-18:(A)6.

Toshiki Kaifu
Prime Minister of Japan

6

When it comes to Japan-U.S. relations, we believe that instead of bashing each other, we should be . . . basking together, looking ahead in the same direction.
News conference,
Kennebunkport, Maine, July 11/
Los Angeles Times, 7-12:(A)8.

Mikhail Kapitsa
Director, Institute of Oriental Studies
(Soviet Union)

1

Relations between the [Soviet Union and Japan] during the last 150 years have been relations of war, semi-war, pre-war or post-war . . . [To the Russian people,] Japan usually is regarded as a hostile country, and it is now as well . . . Whereas in Japan, the Japanese public considers the Soviet Union, Russia as a most unpleasant country.

The Christian Science Monitor,
4-10:3.

Paul Kreisberg
Asia specialist,
Carnegie Endowment
for International Peace
(United States)

2

[On Soviet President Mikhail Gorbachev's forthcoming visit to Japan]: The Gorbachev visit is no big deal in and of itself. But it's part of a larger process of change. And, if successful, it would be seen as the crossing of the Rubicon, in terms of the Soviets no longer being seen as a threat in Japan. An extended period of relaxed tensions between the Soviets and Japan would raise questions in Japan over the next five to seven years about security relations between the United States and Japan. People in Japan could ask, "Why do we need to have 50,000 Americans sitting on our turf now?"

Los Angeles Times, 4-9:(H)2.

Hiroomi Kurisu
Former Chairman,
Joint Chiefs of Staff,
Self-Defense Forces of Japan

3

Until now, Japan has run away from, or dodged, international [conflicts]. But after the UN resolutions [against Iraq's invasion and take-over of Kuwait] and the dispatch of troops to the Middle East by [28] countries, Japan realized that it would be forgotten, or isolated, in the international community if it did nothing . . .

[Even now,] neither the government nor the ruling party has the slightest desire to send troops overseas. But they fear that if Japan makes no contribution of personnel, it will become isolated in the world community.

Interview/
Los Angeles Times, 2-26:(A)5.

Nicholas Lardy
Professor of economics
and Chinese studies,
University of Washington

4

The decentralization [of the Chinese economy] has allowed the expression of all kinds of entrepreneurial activities in China in a way that we have not yet seen in the Soviet Union or in Eastern Europe. The best measure of that is the extent to which even manufacturing, traditionally the core of the socialist state-owned economy, has been decentralized. In China, about half of all industrial output is being generated by firms that are not under the direct control of the state government or provincial government. In other words, these are private firms—for example, collective township and village enterprises—that operate by and large in a much more market-like environment than state-owned enterprises. In contrast, almost two years after the collapse of the Communist regime in Poland, roughly about 90 per cent or more of all [Polish] manufacturing is still in the hands of state enterprises.

Interview/
Los Angeles Times, 7-15:(D)3.

Li Peng
Prime Minister of China

5

[Calling for strict enforcement of laws in China]: It must be emphasized that once a law is promulgated, any and all organizations and individuals must abide by it. We must . . . work toward the point where, when there is a law, it is obeyed, enforcement is strict and law-breakers are prosecuted. Those who take part in economic or other crimes, abuse power for their personal gain or practice favoritism in violation of the law,

(LI PENG)

no matter how high their position is, must be resolutely punished.

Before National People's Congress,
Beijing, March 25/
Los Angeles Times, 3-26:(A)10.

1

[Defending his government's violent crackdown on pro-democracy demonstrators in Beijing in 1989]: Any unbiased person who pays attention to the facts can agree with us that if the government and Communist Party had not at that critical moment taken those resolute measures—that is, had not been forced to take such resolute measures—then China today would not enjoy its present stability and prosperity. If we had not taken the measures that we were forced to take, China today might be bogged down in economic decline as well as political instability, no less severe than has happened to some countries that once practiced socialism. That is something that Chinese people would not like to see, so from a historical perspective I think that the resolute measures taken by the government will increasingly be proven correct.

News conference, Beijing, April 9/
The New York Times, 4-10:(A)3.

2

[Criticizing visiting British Prime Minister John Major for his bringing up the subject of human rights in China]: [I] received a letter from a Chinese historian. He reminded me not to forget that, for more than 100 years, China was bullied and humiliated. For 100 years, foreign powers totally disregarded the human rights of the Chinese people. China and Britain have different social systems, and their value systems, ideologies and historical traditions are different. So, regarding the problem of human rights, the two sides definitely will have differences here and there. This is natural. However, the two sides can exchange opinions on this and can enhance mutual understanding.

Beijing/
The New York Times, 9-4:(A)4.

3

We will never tolerate Taiwan independence under any pretext . . . and [we] are firmly opposed to any activities aimed at splitting the motherland.

At National Day reception,
Beijing, Sept. 30/
The Christian Science Monitor,
10-3:4.

Nguyen Van Linh
General Secretary,
Communist Party of Vietnam

4

In the present condition of our country, it is not objectively necessary to establish a political mechanism of pluralism and multi-party government. Socialism is the only right decision. For our country there is no other way to have freedom and happiness for the people.

At Vietnamese Communist Party
Congress, Hanoi, Jan. 24/
The New York Times, 1-25:(A)3.

Winston Lord
Former United States Ambassador
to China

5

China is important, but this doesn't mean we have to give them everything they want or send them high-level visitors or legitimize their regime. The Soviet Union is certainly important, too, but that hasn't prevented us from having a mixed policy toward them over the past 40 years. No one's talking about isolating China.

Los Angeles Times, 5-18:(A)6.

Alex Magno
Professor, University
of the Philippines

6

[Saying the political system in the Philippines is more and more being financed by the criminal world]: This is now a Mafioso democracy. The next election will be decided by who is most [financially] liquid: the smugglers, the gambling syndicates and the drug lords . . . We've pulled

215

(ALEX MAGNO)

away, mercifully, from the landed oligarchy that always ran the Philippines. We've moved, unfortunately, to the underground oligarchy. The people now pulling the strings are invisible.

Los Angeles Times, 12-6:(A)5.

John Major
Prime Minister
of the United Kingdom

1

[On his current trip to China, made despite criticism from human-rights groups in the West who cite 1989's violent government crackdown on pro-democracy demonstrators in Beijing]: China has had a period of isolation. It needs people going in and telling them face-to-face what the rest of the world thinks. An important part of the dialogue will be on human rights. I will raise the issue and I will carry it as far as I can without provoking a breakdown of communications.

Enroute to Beijing, Sept. 2/
Los Angeles Times, 9-3:(A)13.

Joseph A. Massey
Assistant United States
Trade Representative
for Japan and China

2

In the space of only 10 years, China emerged from self-imposed isolation to become a participant in the global trading community, aware of the community's rules and increasingly sensitive to its criticisms. Over the last two years, however, China's trade policies have skewed the bilateral trade relationship increasingly in China's favor. The United States now runs a substantial, and growing, trade deficit with China... The deficit reflects a decision [by China] to resort to protectionist measures.

Before Congressional Joint
Economic Committee,
Washington, June 28/
Los Angeles Times,
6-29:(A)4.

Farid Mazdak
Deputy Secretary,
Communist Party of Afghanistan

3

[On the future of Afghanistan's Communist government now that the Soviet Union appears to be ready to cut its military and financial support]: Let's assume that the government does have this potential for collapse. When the anarchy starts to spread, the government forces may even be able to stop it, but it will be very costly—it means war in every street, because a great portion of the forces on both sides [of the current Afghan civil war] are war-minded. And there is another alarm: If the Afghan problem is not settled urgently, then Islamic fundamentalism will grow, taking over not only in Afghanistan but throughout Soviet Central Asia, all the way to Kashmir. All this region of the world will become an Islamic continent, and this continent will be ruled by fundamentalists. Is this what Moscow wants? Is this what Washington wants? Do you want the Cold War to re-emerge against the Islamic world so soon after it ended in the East Bloc?

Interview/
Los Angeles Times, 9-13:(A)17.

George J. Mitchell
United States Senator,
D-Maine

4

[Criticizing the U.S. Bush Administration for not being tough enough on the Chinese government for its crackdown on pro-democracy demonstrators in Beijing two years ago]: It has been more than two years since the elderly Communist rulers of China sent tanks and soldiers to kill [the demonstrators]. It has been over two years since the President [Bush] sent the first of several high-level missions to talk with the Chinese leaders about human-rights violatioins and weapons-technology proliferation. Yet, there has been no progress... It is against our national interest to compound a mistake and continue a failed policy [such as preferential trade status for China].

Before the Senate, Washington,
July 23/Los Angeles Times, 7-24:(A)10.

Kiichi Miyazawa
*Former Minister of Finance
and former Deputy Prime Minister
of Japan*

1

[On criticism of continuing U.S. trade with China despite China's poor record on human rights]: Looking at the debate in America [on China], my opinion is closer to [U.S.] President Bush's. Americans who oppose [trade] are too puritan, too idealistic. For a people with a history of just 200 years to tell a people with a 3,000-year history what to do—the concept of time is different... Whenever you go to China, you feel this. They talk of 100 years or 200 years as if it were nothing, while America's entire history fits into that span ... So when people keep talking about human rights—well, in China there weren't any human rights until about 30 years ago. Little by little, they are trying to... change. To remove [China's] most-favored-nation [trade] status [by the U.S.] because they didn't [improve human rights] in two years, to penalize them [isn't right]. You have to think of the longer term.

*Interview, Tokyo/
Los Angeles Times, 10-13:(M)3.*

Mahathir Mohamad
Prime Minister of Malaysia

2

It would be condescending, to say the least, and suspect for the West to preach human rights to the East.

Los Angeles Times, 8-4:(M)3.

Akio Morita
*Chairman, Sony Corporation
(Japan)*

3

As a leading economic power, Japan should be more bold about modernizing our concepts and become a world citizen. But Japan has jumped ahead at high speed, and it is very difficult to match this speed in changing our social system. We need strong leadership. But leadership has many aspects. It means not only that we must have the right to say "no" sometimes. It also means that when we say "yes" we must have the

willingness to sacrifice our own interests for the greater good of the international order. The United States and Japan must learn how to share sovereignty. In Japanese we have a saying: *daido shoi*—it means "small differences are sublimated in a greater cause." That is part of what leaderhip implies for Japan.

*Conversation with former Chase
Manhattan Bank chairman
David Rockefeller/
Los Angeles Times, 12-4:(B)7.*

Yasuhiro Nakasone
*Former Prime Minister
of Japan*

4

[Saying it is time that Toshiki Kaifu, who became Prime Minister when Nakasone was forced from office under a cloud of a scandal in 1987, be removed from office]: When a person [Nakasone] with majority power within his own party becomes immobilized, it is sometimes necessary to use a rookie, usually without majority support within the party, as a relief pitcher. In this type of crunch, the pitcher usually takes time to read the facial expressions and signals of his coach and manager before winding up for a pitch. Regrettably, the [recent Persian] Gulf crisis occurred at such a time, resulting in the "too little, too late" response of the Japanese government.

*Before Japan-America Society,
Washington, Sept. 6/
The Washington Post, 9-7:(A)17.*

Robert Orr
*Director, Japan Center,
Stanford University
(United States)*

5

There is a difference in philosophy... between Japan and Western countries. In line with missionary beliefs, Western countries focus on basic human needs, whereas Japan stresses self-help of the recipients and expands the definition of aid to include assisting the country's infrastructure through economic cooperation.

The Christian Science Monitor, 10-23:7.

Ichiro Ozawa
A leader of the Liberal
Democratic Party of Japan
1

Japan has come to where it is today [a leading world economic power] due to the U.S. When America is in need of something, we should give it. I wouldn't call Japan a very fair country. The Japanese people have become big grown-ups, but we're still spoiled brats in a way. When we were young brats, the U.S. tolerated us. Now that we stand as tall as the Americans, they don't think it's cute any more.

The Christian Science Monitor,
12-24:2.

Nancy Pelosi
United States Representative,
D-California
2

[U.S. Secretary of State James Baker's announced plans to visit Beijing amounts to] an acceptance of [China's] repressive policy and a victory for the Chinese regime. It shows that the Chinese were right after the [1989] Tiananmen Square massacre [of pro-democracy demonstrators] when they said we are a paper tiger. China's repressive policy has continued in spite of everything that has been said about it . . . The [U.S. Bush] Administration has waffled every step of the way.

Nov. 4/
Los Angeles Times, 11-5:(A)12.

Douglas Pike
Director, Indochina Project,
Institute of East Asian Studies,
University of California,
Berkeley
3

There are five major impediments to economic development in Vietnam. One of these is infrastructure—in terms of education. There is a lack of training. They need people who know how to make a computer chip. The second problem is the top leadership itself. Power is concentrated in the Politburo [of the Communist Party]—they make all of the decisions themselves—and there isn't a

single one of them that has the equivalent of a high-school education. They don't understand the workings of a modern technically oriented system. They also have a problem getting a social consensus, which is a notion sociologists have that all people in a country have to have a general sense of what the country stands for and where it ought to go. Vietnam was two countries, and it still is two countries to a very large degree. Fourth, they need capital, vast amounts of capital. It costs about $7,000 per person to transfer a person from the farm to the factory, and their plans are to try to transfer 7 to 8 million people. The fifth thing they need is amicable relationships with their neighbors, which they don't have. They're surrounded by enemies.

Interview/
Los Angeles Times, 8-19:(D)3.

Aquilino Q. Pimentel
Philippine Senator
4

[Opposing a new U.S. lease on the Subic Bay Naval Station in his country]: Because of the American protection and tutelage, we have been reduced to an adolescent nation, growing old in age but not in our ability to guarantee our own survival . . . It is time for the Philippines to move into a new era.

Interview,
Manila, Sept. 11/
The New York Times, 9-12:(A)7.

Jonathan Pollack
Specialist on China,
Rand Corporation
5

There is an element in [the Chinese] leadership which is now very discomfited with the singularity of our [the U.S.] power position in global terms and with the power of our ideas in China. They're uncomfortable with a world in which there is only one superpower. It makes it much more difficult for them to parlay their international situation to strategic advantage.

Los Angeles Times, 10-1:(A)14.

Roh Tae Woo
President of South Korea

1

[On recent anti-government demonstrations in South Korea]: The country is faced with a critical situation, and the future of the country lies in whether the government can carry out its task with responsibility. I regret the excessive demonstrations. However, I admit that at the bottom of these protests there is discontent and friction, and I accept this discontent and friction as the voice of the people.

Broadcast address to the nation,
Seoul, May 28/
The Washington Post, 5-29:(A)26.

2

When I . . . ran for the Presidency [in 1987], many people—especially people in the armed forces—predicted that I would be defeated. But you know the results [a 37 per cent plurality], and the military upheld its integrity and accepted the result . . . It is no longer possible even to imagine military intervention in politics. In a democratic country, there can be no force that can negate the people's choice expressed through elections.

Interview, Seoul/
Los Angeles Times, 6-23:(M)3.

3

[On North and South Korea's recent admission to the United Nations]: Imperfect as it may be, the separate membership of the two Koreas in the United Nations is an important interim step on the road to national unification. It took the two Germanys 17 years to combine their UN seats. I sincerely hope that it will not take as long for the two Korean seats to become one.

At United Nations,
New York, Sept. 24/
The New York Times, 9-25:(A)6.

Patricia Schroeder
United States Representative,
D-Colorado

4

[Calling on Japan to get more involved in world affairs and giving foreign aid, such as

money, to help dismantle nuclear weapons in the former Soviet Union]: Japan has the money to do it. We [the U.S.] have a deficit; they have real money. We've been pressuring Japan to get into the world and do more. We tried to get them involved in [the Persian Gulf war]. I think we have the moral high ground to say the countries we rebuilt after World War II are now economically able to offer aid.

Interview, Denver/
The Christian Science Monitor,
12-27:9.

Chandra Shekhar
Prime Minister of India

5

It's not that [India] went for this parliamentary democracy without going into the merits of the Presidential form of government. A Presidential government gives a certain [amount] of permanency or stability. But in a parliamentary democracy there is always accountability. So in a country like India, where the disparities are so wide and people are suffering from so many inadequacies, the accountability of the people's representatives is more important than the stability of the Administration. Sometimes we go for personalities instead of policies, and that is the biggest problem of India today. Individuals matter, but I don't think that that should [be] the determining factor in political change.

Interview, Bhondsi, India, April 17/
The New York Times, 4-18:(A)4.

Manmohan Singh
Minister of Finance of India

6

India is now a new ball game. Our country is now prepared for big [economic] changes and I think we can launch a process of changing the mind-sets of our people . . . We have tremendous potential, a country of 850 million people, a vast internal market; we have a tremendous reservoir of managerial, entrepreneurial and technological skills; and our people, when they compete abroad, are second to none whether it's in terms of academic institutions or in terms of making money in the U.S. or U.K. Yet I found

(MANMOHAN SINGH)

India has become increasingly marginalized. There must be a deep examination of what has gone wrong. Why is it that South Korea is talked about? In 1960, South Korea had the same per capita income as India. Today, South Korea's income is 10 times India's . . . I get the feeling that now is the time to do big things because most people now, in their hearts, feel that the old habits of thinking have not yielded results.

Interview, New Delhi, July/
The New York Times, 7-8:(C)3.

Stephen J. Solarz
United States Representative,
D-New York

1

As someone who has been deeply moved and affected by the tragic fate which befell Cambodia during the years when the Khmer Rouge were in power, I believe that there is no greater moral imperative confronting the international community today than finding ways to prevent Pol Pot and his murderous minions from battling their way back to power in Phnom Penh.

News conference, Beijing, Sept. 5/
Los Angeles Times, 9-6:(A)17.

Sun Pinghua
President, China-Japan
Friendship Association

2

The present Japan-China ties are like the spring sun rising in the heavens. There exist no major obstacles in the Sino-Japanese relationship, and thus it should continue to develop on the present favorable basis.

Interview/
Los Angeles Times, 8-9:(A)5.

Robert G. Torricelli
United States Representative,
D-New Jersey

3

[Saying there should be human-rights conditions attached to any U.S. MFN trade policy toward China]: This is the fight that nobody wanted. We all believed that reason would prevail [in China], but there is today no evidence that that policy has yielded any success, or that it will in the future. MFN may be the norm among nations, but nothing is normal in China.

Washington, May 29/
The Washington Post, 5-30:(A)37.

B. N. Uniyal
Editor-in-chief, "Business &
Political Observer" (India)

4

[On India's new policy of opening up to foreign investment and cutting government interference in the economy]: In the Indian context, this is a very revolutionary step. It may not be as radical or revolutionary as you would expect for a foreign businessman or an overseas company. And, in the context of the global changes, it is possible it is not radical enough. But these steps have to be seen in the Indian context. It's basically a balancing act between the desperate need for economic change and the political realities of the day. The most important thing is to see this as a beginning step. This message is clear. India is moving toward an open economy, welcoming foreign investment with greater vigor and dismantling the roadblocks. It is a statement of intent. And there's just no going back now.

Los Angeles Times, 7-30:(H)2.

Wang Zhen
Vice President of China

5

Facing the present changeable international situation [in which Communist governments in the Soviet Union and Eastern Europe are falling], we should have firm confidence in socialism and Communism. The road is tortuous and the struggle intense, but the future is undoubtedly bright . . . Through the long struggles of one generation of revolutionaries after another, the socialist cause will go forward and true Communism will ultimately be achieved.

Xinjiang, China/
Los Angeles Times, 8-27:(A)7.

Yang Shang-kun
President of China

1

In my view, we are not yet quarreling with the United States. If we were really to quarrel, our quarrels would not be settled even after 10 or 20 years. Because the United States and China have different systems, different historical circumstances and a different understanding of some issues, it is natural that some points of dispute should appear. If there are some disagreements, they can certainly be negotiated, discussed and resolved through normal consultations. Groundless reports and accusations are not helpful to good relations. Frankly, we are worried about where the U.S. side intends to lead Sino-American relations. The voices which want to improve our relations are much quieter than the voices which are not beneficial to those relations.

Interview, Beijing, May/
U.S. News & World Report, 5-27:43.

2

[On U.S. most-favored-nation trade status for China]: We believe that if the most-favored-nation status is revoked, China would of course suffer losses. It would cause us to lose some hard currency and capital; our exports would be greatly reduced. But China's economy is in many ways a self-sufficient economy, and its ability to endure is very great. For 30 years, it was sealed off from the rest of the world, yet the heavens were not overturned. With our ability to adapt and to endure low living standards, China will not collapse under embargo. I don't think it is possible to seal off China now, because the world has changed and China has diplomatic and economic relations with more than 100 countries.

Interview,
Beijing, May/
U.S. News & World Report,
5-27:43.

Europe

Abel Aganbegyan
President, Soviet Academy
of National Economy

1

[Saying the Soviet transition to a market economy is irreversible]: All conservatives understand that going back is impossible because the command system has been destroyed. The old system was a bad system. Everyone knows that . . . Movement on the economic front depends on political stability. For our economy to move toward the market, we need effective political power.

At World Economic Forum,
Davos, Switzerland, February/
The New York Times, 2-18:21.

Askar Akayev
President of the Kirghiz Soviet
Socialist Republic

2

[On the push toward greater independence by many of the Soviet republics]: We have lived in a unitary state and today separatism and secessionism in republics, in varying degrees, is a natural freedom. Today there are three groups of republics. The first group is for federation, the second for confederation, and the third—the Baltics, Georgia—want to leave the union. So I believe we need a good architect who could build a house of union from federation and confederation bricks.

Interview, Frunze, U.S.S.R./
The Christian Science Monitor,
1-10:5.

Madeleine Albright
President, Center for National Policy
(United States)

3

Every time I go [to the Soviet Union], I'm stunned at what a Third World country it is. Many Americans think that because the Soviets have sophisticated weapons, the country must be a mirror image of the United States.

USA Today, 6-3:(A)10.

Alexi II
Patriarch of the
Russian Orthodox Church

4

[Addressing Boris Yeltsin at his inauguration as President of the Russian Republic]: You have taken responsibility for a country that is seriously ill. Three generations have been brought up under conditions which killed any wish and ability to work. First, the people were made to forget the labor of prayer. Then they were made to forget the labor of thought, the desire to search for truth.

The Christian Science Monitor,
7-11:4.

Viktor Alksnis
Member, Supreme Soviet
of the Soviet Union

5

For the last five years, it has been graphically demonstrated that [Soviet President Mikhail] Gorbachev has no program of *perestroika* [reform]. He has a program of destruction, but no program of construction. In 1985, Gorbachev was handed control of a country in a pre-crisis situation; now we are in a catastrophic situation . . . and Gorbachev is at fault. Civil war is already going on in Azerbaijan and Georgia, and there's a cold war in the Baltics and Moldavia.

Los Angeles Times, 2-26:(H)6.

Giulio Andreotti
Prime Minister of Italy

6

[Announcing an austerity program to deal with Italy's economic problems]: Soon, the European Community will examine our accounts. Europe can do without us, but it is we who cannot do without Europe. Italy is not autarkic. We are among the world's most industrialized countries, but there is a limit to how indebted we can become.

Broadcast address to the nation,
Rome, Oct. 1/
Los Angeles times, 10-3:(A)8.

Georgi A. Arbatov
*Director, Soviet Institute
of U.S.A. and Canadian Affairs*

1

[On the recent failed coup aimed at ousting Soviet President Mikhail Gorbachev]: He [Gorbachev] is tremendously guilty [in setting the stage for the coup]. He was the one who issued the decrees for joint military-police patrols, who gave tremendous power to the police and KGB. He grabbed more and more extra power. The package was there, waiting only to be used.

The New York Times, 8-27:(A)6.

James A. Baker III
*Secretary of State
of the United States*

2

[The Soviet Baltic states] should be free to pursue their own hopes and aspirations for self-determination . . . Since 1933, we [the U.S.] have recognized the territorial integrity of the Soviet Union, except for the Baltic states. There's a significant difference between the Baltic republics, on the one hand, and other [Soviet] republics, on the other. We will not permit—at least, we cannot go along with—the use of force to suppress peaceful dissent, peaceful political expression.

*Broadcast interview/
"This Week With David Brinkley,"
ABC-TV, 3-17.*

3

I am satisfied that the leadership of the Soviet Union has, as a fundamental goal, moving toward a market economy. But I think we should not lose sight of the fact . . . that you have here a situation where a country is trying to change 70 years of political and economic philosophy and change it in a way that moves it in exactly the opposite direction. Now, that is not easy.

*To reporters, Washington, May 29/
Los Angeles Times, 5-30:(A)16.*

4

The United States fully supports the concept of European integration. We stand ready to support the arrangements which our European allies decide are needed to express a new European security and defense identity. [But] it is clear to us that one of our key goals must be to insure that NATO remains the principal venue for our consultations and the forum for agreement on all policies bearing on the security and defense commitments of its members.

*To NATO foreign ministers,
Copenhagen, June 6/
The New York Times, 6-7:(A)6.*

5

[On U.S. financial aid to the Soviet Union]: The Soviets must start with self-help. If they do, we will support them. Indeed, we are developing a package of supportive measures, which we hope we can coordinate with you [NATO allies] and others. But I don't honestly think we can catalyze Soviet reform through a big-bang approach. Our effort is more likely to be a step-by-step process—certainly one with a grand goal—but ever a realistic and workable approach . . . We do not intend to stand idly by if the Soviets come to grips with these questions of political and economic legitimacy. *Perestroika* [Soviet reform] could be the most important revolution of this century. All of us have a profound stake in its outcome.

*To NATO foreign ministers,
Copenhagen, June 6/
The New York Times, 6-7:(A)6;
Los Angeles Times, 6-7:(A)13.*

6

[On the ethnic unrest threatening to break up Yugoslavia]: We came to Yugoslavia because of our concern about the crisis and about the dangers of a disintegration of this country. Instability and breakup of Yugoslavia, we think, could have some very tragic consequences, not only here but more broadly in Europe. We are obviously not alone in having these concerns. The concerns that we came to Yugoslavia with have not been allayed by the meetings we had today. We think that the situation is very serious. We worry, frankly, about history repeating itself. Frankly, we don't want to see that and I don't

(JAMES A. BAKER III)

think anyone in the international community wants to see that.

Belgrade, June 21/
The New York Times, 6-22:1.

1

[On the recent failed coup in the Soviet Union]: This crisis has demonstrated the importance of our NATO alliance; first, as a political instrument for supporting democracy and reform in Eastern Europe as well as the Soviet Union; second, as a forum to coordinate a Western response to common political as well as military challenges; and third, as a firm bulwark for our common security.

At meeting of NATO/
The Christian Science Monitor,
8-23:3.

2

[On the changes in the Soviet Union, including the recent failed coup and the move toward independence of many of the republics]: In the last two weeks, we've seen another revolution blowing with full force across the Soviet Union. Of course, it's obvious that we want to see this revolution remain democratic and we want to see it remain peaceful. Building democracy and free markets across the Soviet Union is not going to be an easy task after decades of totalitarianism and central planning. The work of freedom will be hard, and the transition will be painful. The Soviet peoples have to know that they have just embarked on what will be a very difficult road, but they must know, too, that there can be no turning away from democratic principles and tolerance if they truly hope to follow that road to its end and to join the democratic commonwealth of nations. We will help them move along that path of political and economic freedom.

Press briefing,
Washington, Sept. 4/
The New York Times, 9-5:(A)8.

3

[On the civil war in Yugoslavia]: Clearly, the Yugoslav federal military is not serving as an impartial guarantor of a cease-fire in [the Yugoslav republic of] Croatia. On the contrary, it has actively supported local Serbian forces in violating the cease-fire, causing deaths to the citizens it is constitutionally supposed to protect . . . It is equally clear that the Serbian leadership is actively supporting and encouraging the use of force in Croatia by Serb militants and the Yugoslav military. The apparent objective of the Serbian leadership and the Yugoslav military working in tandem is to create a "small Yugoslavia" or "greater Serbia."

At United Nations,
New York, Sept. 25/
The Christian Science Monitor, 9-27:4.

4

[On the current breakup of the Soviet Union into independent nations, and the poor state of their economies]: Politically, the dangers of protracted anarchy and chaos are obvious. Great empires rarely go quietly into extinction. No one can dismiss the possibility that darker political forces lurk in the wings, representing the remnants of Stalinism or the birth of nationalist extremism or even Fascism, ready to exploit the frustrations of a proud but exhausted people in their hour of [economic] despair. Strategically, both of these alternatives, anarchy or reaction, could become threats to the West's vital interests when they shake a land that is still home to nearly 30,000 nuclear weapons and the most powerful arsenal of conventional weaponry ever amassed in Europe . . . If during the Cold War we faced each other as two scorpions in a bottle, now the Western nations and the former Soviet republics stand as awkward climbers on a steep mountain. Held together by a single rope, a fall toward Fascism or anarchy in the former Soviet Union will pull the West down, too. Yet, a strong, a steady pull by the West now can help them to gain their footing.

At Princeton University, Dec. 12/
The New York Times, 12-13:(A)10,1.

Kurt Biedenkopf
Premier of Saxony, Germany

5

[Saying that while many citizens of what was formerly East Germany have gone to the former

(KURT BIEDENKOPF)

West Germany for better opportunities now that Germany is reunited, he believes the reverse will also be true because of the challenge of work that will be needed to build the economy of the former eastern states]: What do you do if you're a 30-year-old in West Germany? You live in a society of which your parents tell you that everything is perfect, and you should leave it just the way it is, and you should not disturb it, and it's going to be very difficult to find something new to do. Now, if you really are a man or a woman who wants something new to do, you'll come here [to eastern Germany]. And I'm quite sure they will.

Interview, Dresden, Germany/
The New York Times, 5-3:(A)4.

Nicholas F. Brady
Secretary of the Treasury
of the United States

1

[The Soviets] do believe the things they have been uttering [about changing their economy toward a more market-oriented one]. They say, "Look, we've made the commitment, we have no alternative." [But] is their economic understanding and vocabulary at a level that will let them do it rapidly? No. Will they eventually do it? Yes. The difficulty is, the reforms go against hundreds of years of Russian history and the lack of a commercial tradition in the land.

Newsweek, 7-29:18.

Zbigniew Brzezinski
Counsellor, Center for Strategic
and International Studies
(United States);
Former Assistant to the
President of the United States
(Jimmy Carter) for
National Security Affairs

2

[On U.S. policy toward the Soviet Union during that country's current upheaval]: This [U.S. President] Bush Administration is a tactically superb team without any evident sense of strategic direction. [In the Soviet Union,] the United States should be in the forefront, welcoming these developments [toward democracy and independence of the Soviet republics]. Instead, the President [Bush] is acting as if his greatest concern is preserving both [Soviet President Mikhail] Gorbachev and a reformed Soviet Union—at a time when no one in the Soviet Union calls himself "Soviet" any more.

Los Angeles Times, 9-5:(A)12.

Ylli Bufi
Prime Minister of Albania

3

[On reforms taking place in Albania]: The mistakes [of the past] are linked with the system [former Albanian leader] Enver Hoxha imposed. But rummaging in the past is the easiest thing to do. Our need is to look to the future. We must, as soon as possible, replace the totalitarianism with a democratic system and a market economy.

The Christian Science Monitor,
8-13:3.

Pavel Bunich
Soviet economist

4

[On reforms in the Soviet economy]: We are not talking about a better banking system or a plan to increase production, reduce inflation and eliminate the budget deficit or even a program of industrial development into the next century. We are talking about all that and more—matters of great complexity that nonetheless touch everyone's life. But there is even more, much more, to all this, for we are deciding the nature of the economic system, and consequently of the political system, that we will have. The very character of the nation, the way that we act toward one another, the position we occupy in the world . . .

Los Angeles times, 7-2:(H)2.

Daniel Burstein
Global business and
financial analyst

5

People don't realize how dominant an economic power the Germans are. They are a bigger

225

(DANIEL BURSTEIN)

trading nation than Japan, and they will become even more powerful because they will be the focal point of a European economic boom during the 1990s. That's because many German institutions—principally the Bundesbank, the country's central bank—will be the center of economic gravity.

Interview/
U.S. News & World Report,
4-1:50.

George Bush
President of the United States

1

When you look at the accomplishments of [Soviet President] Mikhail Gorbachev, they are enormous. And yes, the Soviet Union is fighting difficult economic times, but I am not about to forget history, and what he did in terms of [letting democracy develop in] Eastern Europe, what he's done in terms of *perestroika* [Soviet reform] and *glasnost* [openness], has my respect. And so we will deal with the facts as they come to us. But I don't want to see a breach in a relationship that is very strong, that has served us extraordinarily well in recent times, during the [Persian Gulf] war itself, where for the first time the Soviet Union and the United States worked in synch on those matters, and I give President Gorbachev great credit for that, because he was under some pressures at home.

News conference,
Washington, May 8/
The New York Times, 5-9:(A)12.

2

[On U.S. policy toward the Soviet Union and its republics]: We will support those in the center and the republics who pursue freedom, democracy and economic liberty. We will determine our support not on the basis of personalities but on the basis of principles. And we cannot tell you how to reform your society. We will not try to pick winners and losers in political competition between republics or between republics and the center. That is your business. That's not the business of the United States of America . . . Some people have urged the United States to choose between supporting [Soviet] President [Mikhail] Gorbachev and supporting independence-minded leaders throughout the U.S.S.R. I consider this a false choice . . . we will maintain the strongest possible relationship with the Soviet government of President Gorbachev, but we also appreciate the new realities of life in the U.S.S.R. and therefore, as a federation ourselves, we want good relations, improved relations with the republics.

Before Ukrainian Parliament, Kiev,
U.S.S.R., Aug. 1/
The New York Times, 8-2:(A)5.

3

[On the coup in the Soviet Union that just ousted President Mikhail Gorbachev]: We are deeply disturbed by the events of the last hours in the Soviet Union and condemn the unconstitutional resort to force . . . The apparently unconstitutional removal of President Gorbachev, the declaration of a state of emergency and the deployment of Soviet military forces . . . raise the most serious questions about the future course of the Soviet Union . . . Accordingly, we support [Russian Republic] President [Boris] Yeltsin's call for "restoration of the legally elected organs of power and the reaffirmation of the post of U.S.S.R. President M. S. Gorbachev."

News conference, Kennebunkport, Maine,
Aug. 19/USA Today, 8-20:(A)9.

4

The Baltic peoples of Estonia, Latvia and Lithuania, and their democratically elected governments, have declared their independence [from the Soviet Union] and are moving now to control their own national territories and their own destinies. The United States has always supported the independence of the Baltic states and is now prepared immediately to establish diplomatic relations with their governments. The United States is also prepared to do whatever it can to assist in the completion of the current process of making Baltic independence a factual reality.

News conference, Kennebunkport, Maine,
Sept. 2/USA Today, 9-3:(A)11.

(GEORGE BUSH)

1

[To NATO members]: Our premise is that the American role in the defense and the affairs of Europe will not be made superfluous by European union. If our premise is wrong—if, my friends, your ultimate aim is to provide independently for your own defense—the time to tell us is today.

At NATO summit meeting,
Rome, Nov. 7/
Los Angeles Times, 11-8:(A)1.

Ingvar Carlsson
Prime Minister of Sweden

2

[On his Social Democratic Party's loss in the recent election]: We've taken a number of difficult decisions during our term in office and lost support as a result. Now it's the Moderate's turn. [Once Swedes see] the consequences [of tax cuts in terms of lost benefits], the parties which stand for social responsibility will gain ground again.

Sept. 15/
The New York Times, 9-16:(A)3.

Lord Carrington
Chairman, peace conference
for Yugoslavia sponsored by
the European Community;
Former Foreign Secretary
of the United Kingdom

3

[On the civil war in Yugoslavia]: How can we go on having a peace conference if everyone is killing each other? I don't think the Serbs and the Croats have negotiation on their minds. If the cease-fire collapses totally, we shall probably see the bloodiest civil war in Europe for a very long time. It is a terrible prospect.

Interview, London/
The Christian Science Monitor,
9-20:6.

Dick Cheney
Secretary of Defense
of the United States

4

The Europeans clearly don't want us to eliminate our presence. Some of the staunchest advocates of NATO and a continued U.S. presence are the Czechs, the Poles and the Hungarians. If we're going to have a successful transition of those Eastern European governments to true democracies with functioning economies, they badly need the kind of security anchor that the U.S. presence in Western Europe provides.

Interview/USA Today, 6-27:(A)11.

5

[On the Soviet military situation if current moves toward independence by various Soviet republics and the lessening of power of the central government continue]: Five years from now, who will control the Soviet nuclear arsenal? Will there still be a central government in charge? Or will the Russian Republic have taken over that responsibility? Or will the four republics that currently have strategic nuclear weapons on their soil each have its own independently controlled arsenal of nuclear weapons in the future? ... If the center gives way and the Soviet Union as we've known it ceases to exist, what happens to existing treaties and arms-control agreements that have been negotiated with the Soviet Union? Interesting questions.

To political scientists,
Washington, Aug. 29/
The Washington Post, 8-30:(A)33.

6

Given the breakup of the Soviet Union, given the disintegration of their society, given the sad state of their economy, the only realistic thing for me to do as Secretary of Defense is to anticipate that one of the byproducts of the breakup of the Soviet Union will be a proliferation of nuclear capability [in many of the former Soviet republics]. If the Soviets do an excellent job at retaining control over their stockpile of nuclear weapons—let's assume they've got 25,000 to 30,000; that's a ballpark figure—and they are 99 per cent successful, that would mean you could still have as many as 250 that they were not able to control.

Broadcast interview/
"Meet the Press," NBC-TV,
12-15.

Stephen F. Cohen
*Professor of politics
and director of the Russian
studies program,
Princeton University
(United States)*

1

[On the current coup in the Soviet Union aimed at ousting President Mikhail Gorbachev]: For almost seven years, Gorbachev led a reformation which sought to reverse the Russian despotic tradition which existed long before the revolution. He sought to do this through political and economic democratization and opening the country to the West. At the same time, there have always been powerful forces that have opposed this for political, cultural and economic reasons. These forces are not just Communist—they go way back in Russian history. This has been an epic struggle. While this coup d'etat is a shock, it is not a surprise. These people and the institutions they represent—the military-industrial complex, the KGB, the Party apparatus, the Ministry of the Interior and the state collective farm structure—were the primary targets of Gorbachev's reforms.

The New York Times, 8-21:(A)10.

Jacques Delors
*President,
Executive Commission,
European Community*

2

We cannot limit the horizons of the new Europe. All around us, naked ambition, lust for power, national uprisings and under-development are combining to create potentially dangerous situations, containing the seeds of destabilization and conflict. The EC must face this challenge.

*London, March 7/
The Christian Science Monitor,
3-11:3.*

3

[On Europe's difficulty in bringing peace to strife-torn Yugoslavia]: The Community is like an adolescent facing the crisis of an adult. It now only has the weapons of recognition and economic aid. If it were 10 years older, it might be able to impose a military peace-keeping force.

The Washington Post, 9-5:(A)23.

4

[Supporting a federal European union, which Britain opposes]: There is a misunderstanding about what "federal" is in the first place, even if there is a special definition in the English dictionaries. We have to define who has the powers. There is not a single example of a group of nations which has survived purely on the basis of inter-governmental arrangements. That was not the vision of the EC's founding fathers.

*Before European Parliament,
Strasbourg, France, Nov. 20/
Los Angeles Times, 11-21:(A)7.*

Petur Dertliev
*Chairman, Social Democratic Party
of Bulgaria*

5

[On U.S.-Bulgarian relations]: Our friendship should not overheat so we are simply replacing the old Big Brother [the Soviet Union] with a new one. We don't need a Big Brother—we need a brother. It is impossible to have too many brothers.

The Washington Post, 11-11:(A)22.

Abdou Diouf
President of Senegal

6

You [in Europe] risk being invaded tomorrow by multitudes of Africans who, pushed by misery, will land in waves in the countries of the North. You can pass all the immigration legislation you want, you won't stop the tide.

*French newspaper interview/
The Christian Science Monitor,
8-7:12.*

Robert J. Dole
*United States Senator,
R-Kansas*

7

[Criticizing the use of force by the Soviet military against nationalists in the Baltic republics]: We want independence and freedom for the

(ROBERT J. DOLE)

Baltic states. We understand [Soviet President Mikhail] Gorbachev's dilemma, but you can't have it both ways. You can't win the Nobel Peace Prize [as did Gorbachev] and then start killing people in . . . Lithuania and Latvia.

USA Today, 1-23:(A)5.

Alexander Dzasokov
Ideology Secretary,
Communist Party
of the Soviet Union

1

We [Soviets] have moved so far from the monopoly of power, from the monopoly of one party, from the unitary nature of our state . . . that there is no way to reverse the process, let alone bring it back to where we started nearly six years ago. We can only go forward, developing the conditions we need to build humane socialism . . . If you asked me to distribute political opinion by sector—the left, the right, the center—frankly, I couldn't do it. Everything is shifting. There are very few clear standpoints, and none seems permanent.

Interview, Moscow, January/
Los Angeles Times, 1-28:(A)4.

Alexei Emelyanov
Soviet agricultural economist

2

Several generations of our people have lived under the collective-farm system in this country. They have got used to being responsible for nothing, just being obedient and getting a meager salary. To become a private farmer would mean a complete change in their life-style: working hard, not getting enough sleep at night, constant worry about where to find seeds and spare parts. Most people are not ready for this.

The Washington Post, 9-5:(A)33.

Amitai Etzioni
Sociologist,
George Washington University
(United States)

3

The Queen [of England] has her own pedestal. We [in the U.S.] used to see this in our Presi-

dency, but we've always been ambivalent about treating our Presidents with too much awe. They are, after all, politicians. But the Queen—she's above politics. She's not anti-abortion or anti-anything. She's a symbol rather than a person. We can all project on her our own values and views. There is no controversy with her.

The New York Times, 5-20:(A)10.

John R. Galvin
General, United States Army;
Supreme Allied Commander/
Europe

4

The first half of the 20th century was a pretty bad half when it came to fighting and dying. The second half hasn't been as bad . . . And the reason is that we have managed to keep a stable Europe. It might have been full of tension and confrontation, but it was stable. And a lot of the reason it was stable is that the U.S. had a shaping influence on security and the future in Europe.

Interview, Stuttgart, Germany/
The Washington Post, 10-15:(A)16.

Robert M. Gates
Assistant to President
of the United States George Bush
and Deputy for National
Security Affairs;
Nominee for Director
of Central Intelligence
of the United States

5

The forces of real reform are at last ascendant in the Soviet Union. Still, as ever, there are challenges, concerns and risks. The collapse of the Soviet and Russian empire offers the promise of democracy and economic transformation, but it also contains the seeds of grave instability, chaos and civil war, in a country possessing nearly 30,000 nuclear warheads, the most powerful of which are still aimed at us. We cannot yet divert our attention from the Soviet Union, but clearly our priorities and our concerns have changed.

At Senate Select Committee
on Intelligence hearing on his
nomination, Washington, Sept. 16/
The New York Times, 9-17:(A)14.

Charles Gati
Professor,
Columbia University
(United States);
Specialist on Europe

1

In the Soviet Union, the populace is uncertain about reform of the economy. [Soviet President Mikhail] Gorbachev's policies of the last two or three years, going back and forth, flirting with reform, then backtracking, were not simply the machinations of a politician. In point of fact, [they] reflected popular attitude . . . There is both a desire to get their economy on another beat [and] a tremendous fear of losing some of the previous benefits . . . When a toy store where 10 people work goes to a mom-and-pop operation, there are eight people who are not likely to celebrate market reform.

Los Angeles Times, 9-17:(H)2.

Vitaly I. Goldansky
Chairman, Soviet Pugwash
Committee; Member,
International Affairs
Committee of Supreme Soviet

2

[On the unrest in the Soviet Union resulting from economic problems and the country's withdrawal from Eastern Europe]: These are really feelings that touch on national humiliation. Many in the older generation, for example, believe we have lost our victory in World War II through the developments in Eastern Europe, that we have given up our laurels . . . Others realize that we have lost the Cold War. This is true, and although that may be a good thing for us and the world both, to admit it openly is again a national humiliation.

Interview/
Los Angeles Times, 1-15:(H)2.

Mikhail S. Gorbachev
President of the Soviet Union;
General Secretary,
Communist Party
of the Soviet Union

3

[On the use of Soviet military force against nationalists in Lithuania]: We did not want, and

do not want, this . . . [But by declaring the republic's independence from the Soviet Union on March 11, the Lithuanian Parliament] staged an overnight coup d'etat against the [Soviet] Constitution. All subsequent acts by the Soviet President, by the government, by all state institutions, including those of the army, could not be different from what they were . . . There could be no other actions, and no one could even hope for them.

Moscow, Jan. 14/
Los Angeles Times, 1-15:(A)1.

4

[On the democratic opposition to his leadership]: In fact, all these "democrats" are anti-Communist in nature. They do not want to cooperate with the Communists. They reject all propositions by the Communist Party. They want to call the Party a criminal organization and to put it on trial. It's ridiculous to try to put on trial more than 16 million people . . . What they are really up to is to take power. They failed to do this by means of the Congress [of People's Deputies], by means of the Supreme Soviet, but now they are using the tactics of the neo-Bolsheviks: struggles in the streets, demonstrations, strikes, hunger strikes. They wage constant psychological attacks on the existing structures.

Speech, Minsk, U.S.S.R., Feb. 26/
The Washington Post, 2-27:(A)14.

5

[Calling for a "yes" vote in a plebiscite on national unity, and criticizing the "no" stance of Russian President Boris Yeltsin]: If some madman should arise to provoke a breakup of our union, that would be a disaster for this country, for Europeans, for the entire world. What is in question is the fate of our people, the fate of our whole civilization. This is not a matter for someone's political ambitions.

Moscow, March 17/
Los Angeles Times, 3-18:(A)1.

6

[Saying if the West gives his country $100-billion in aid, the Soviet Union can proceed with

(MIKHAIL S. GORBACHEV)

massive economic reforms]: If we, together with you, find $100-billion to resolve the crisis and the question of cooperation with the Soviet Union in order to ensure that *perestroika* [Soviet reform] succeeds—that is, to enable the country through deep reforms to open up and reorient itself to the individual domestically and toward the world externally—than I think the game is worth the candle . . . I am convinced that the peoples of those [Western] countries need *perestroika* as much as we do, especially since the Soviet Union is one of the pillars of today's world. If that pillar falls, if it disappears, we all should calculate the consequences. It is not possible to remain indifferent or, worse, to fish in troubled waters. That would lead us to catastrophe. Whatever aspect you take—military, political, economic—these questions are all very serious.

News conference,
Moscow, May 22/
Los Angeles Times, 5-23:(A)1,13.

1

[On his forthcoming trip to the G-7 meeting in London where he will seek Western economic assistance]: Some of you may think Gorbachev is going to crawl on his knees and plead for help from the leaders of the leading industrial countries. This is just not serious. We realize there are no free financial resources in this world. Our main direction will be in investment projects . . . We know we cannot join the world economy without a steady transition to a free market. This doesn't mean, though, that we are departing from socialist ideals. On the contrary, through democracy we'll assert the principles of socialism.

News conference, Moscow, July 12/
The Washington Post, 7-13:(A)13.

2

It's of unique significance that we [the Soviet Communist Party] speak about ourselves as a party of democratic reforms. It is only the plurality of opinions and the democratic comparison of views within the framework of constitutional law that will make it possible to find the

truth . . . We will not find an answer to our questions within the framework of the old model. Our friends whom we had helped to "experiment" with this model have also failed to find the answers. This is indeed a crisis of socialism and the socialist idea. But the crisis can be overcome. It can be followed by recovery and a new, resolute step forward by the rejuvenated organism.

Before Soviet Communist Party
Central Committee, Moscow, July 26/
Los Angeles Times, 7-27:(A)12.

3

[On the recent failed coup by hard-line Communist Party members aimed at ousting him from office]: They wanted . . . to push people in a way which would lead the whole society to a catastrophe. [They] have not succeeded, and this is a great victory for *perestroika* [Soviet reform] . . . What did they do to the President and his family? For 72 hours, they surrounded him with troops, and they wanted to break his willpower, but they lost. And here is my respect to the Soviet people, and specifically to Boris Yeltsin, the President of Russia, and to all labor collectives, to all people who stood up in the way of reaction. This what we should be proud of.

Moscow, Aug. 21/
Los Angeles Times, 8-22:(A)22.

4

. . . I am one of those people who's never concealed his position. I am convinced that socialism is correct; I'm an adherent of socialism. I don't think it's anything abnormal, anomalous, and . . . many governments adhere to it . . . You cannot have socialism without democracy, without a more correct solution of social problems. When we, you and I . . . want to discuss this matter, we always get down to the Stalinist model, and what that led to, the Stalinist model of organizing society . . . And over these years I've always had the courage to say that unless we get rid of Stalinism we will never achieve the implementation of socialism.

News conference,
Moscow, Aug. 22/
The New York Times, 8-23:(A)10.

Mikhail S. Gorbachev
President of the Soviet Union

1

[On the recent failed coup aimed at ousting him as President]: . . . the coup was not entirely unexpected. It was not a bolt from the blue. It was prepared by the provocative statements of certain Generals and people in key positions and certain statements made in the Supreme Soviet . . . However, instead of decisive actions [that should have been taken to prevent the coup], there was a lack of determination, and I am also responsible for that lack of determination . . . [There was a] lack of decision in the implementation of democratic reforms, particularly in those structures that spearheaded the coup. And this is not only my responsibility but the responsibility of the Supreme Soviet, the [Communist] Party and the government. Our good intentions and plans were not implemented because the old mechanism and the old structure of power had not been changed. And I mean primarily the state apparatus, which was totally in agreement with the policy of the Party, and there were people in key positions who remained loyal to the Stalinist doctrine. We vacillated for a long time; and, even at this moment, we have not embarked on the road of decisive transformation.

Before Supreme Soviet,
Moscow, Aug. 26/
The New York Times, 8-27:(A)8.

2

[Criticizing the rapid move toward independence by many of the Soviet republics]: If the republics start categorically to secede from the union, and if, in an atmosphere of nationalism, we try to decide these extremely important issues related to the fate of this state which has existed for 1,000 years, and whose collapse would threaten the lives and properties of millions of people, and would relate to the defense potential of our country, which is a superpower. And those who think about such a thing should be aware of what their responsibility is, not only to their own people, but to humanity as a whole. We do not have the right to make a mistake of this nature.

Before Supreme Soviet,
Moscow, Aug. 27/
The New York Times, 8-28:(A)8.

3

[Calling on the West to provide his country with aid in the wake of the current economic and political upheaval in the Soviet Union]: If Europe does not want to face a torrent of refugees from armed conflicts, inter-ethnic hatred, killings and burned homes, then it must pay very close attention to the guarantees for human rights provided by all states on its territory. We need assistance, cooperation, solidarity. We are counting on it.

At Conference on Security and
Cooperation in Europe, Moscow,
Sept. 10/
Los Angeles Times, 9-11:(A)6.

4

Will we [in the Soviet Union] go forward together, or will every republic try to find its own way? Until we clear up this point, all programs will remain just wishful thinking. We'll remain stuck while the tension in society will continue to grow . . . Some are for maintaining the old super-centralized totalitarian state, others for an economic union without a political union. There is the opinion that the union no longer exists and we should go to the end in separating and disintegration. I'm convinced that if any one of these points of view prevails, the consequences will be catastrophic for all peoples and republics.

Before Supreme Soviet,
Moscow, Oct. 21/
The Christian Science Monitor,
10-22:3.

5

[On Russian President Boris Yeltsin]: A sincere man. I wish he could always be consistent without vacillating. I wish he wouldn't give in to pressure. And I would wish the same thing for myself. I wish he were more democratic. It wouldn't hurt him.

Broadcast interview/
"Face the Nation," CBS-TV, 12-22.

6

[On the creation of a commonwealth of former Soviet republics declared by Russia, Ukraine

(MIKHAIL S. GORBACHEV)

and Byelorussia]: Those three republics have no right to declare the Soviet Union non-existent. What do they mean—there's no such country as the U.S.S.R., not even as an object of international law? If there are no laws governing the union as a whole, then who controls the army? The borders of our state have also been established by union law. The same with our territorial waters and airspace, not to mention our relations with foreign countries. What kind of democrats are these? How can they even call themselves democrats? What about our shared commitment to develop a state governed by law? I said all this to them, and it sobered them up a bit. They tell me that back in '37, a troika [a three-person kangaroo court] could decide a person's fate. And now a troika is deciding the fate of entire nations!

Interview, Moscow/
Time, 12-23:25.

1

[On his efforts to reform the Soviet system, which has resulted in the breakup of the Soviet Union]: The main goal of my life has been accomplished. All the rest . . . well, maybe someone else will come and do it better. But you must understand, I wanted to succeed. What's special about me is that I can't accept defeat.

Meeting with reporters, Dec. 12/
The Christian Science Monitor,
12-26:3.

2

When I found myself at the helm of this state, it was already clear that something was wrong in this country. We were living much worse than people in the industrialized countries were living and we were increasingly lagging behind them. The reason was obvious even then. This country was suffocating in the shackles of the bureaucratic command system. Doomed to cater to ideology and suffer and carry the onerous burden of the arms race, it found itself at a breaking point . . . We had to change everything radically.

Broadcast address announcing his
resignation, Moscow, Dec. 25/
The Christian Science Monitor, 12-27:4.

Albert Gore, Jr.
United States Senator,
D-Tennessee

3

. . . I would like to draw attention to the Swiss, who have benefited enormously from the security we [the U.S.] have provided in Europe for the last 50 years. Switzerland has become a well-known haven for arms dealers and [weapons] proliferators. Its government values the security and tranquility of its own people, but in this area its contribution to the security of other people in the world is substantially negative. It is time for the Swiss to live up to their image of clean rectitude. Other countries may feel pinched by that same shoe. So be it.

Before the Senate,
Washington, Sept. 19/
The New York Times, 9-26:(A)19.

Bryan Gould
Spokesman, Labor Party
of Britain

4

[On the scrapping of Britain's unpopular poll tax by the Conservative Party, a tax that was instituted by the Conservatives Party under former Prime Minister Margaret Thatcher]: We have just heard the most complete capitulation, the most startling U-turn and the most shameless abandonment of consistency and principle in modern political history.

March 21/
Los Angeles Times, 3-22:(A)16.

Vissarion A. Gugushvili
Prime Minister
of the Georgian Soviet
Socialist Republic

5

[On the unrest in Soviet republics, such as Georgia, which have been exerting more independence from the central Soviet government]: The most well-ordered place in the world is a prison. We have gotten out of prison, but we now don't know how to act.

Interview/
Los Angeles Times, 10-7:(A)6.

233

Gus Hall
General secretary,
Communist Party
of the United States

1

[On the Soviet Parliament suspending the Communist Party's activities in that country]: We have to deal with something that never happened before, but this is not a memorial meeting. The setbacks are serious . . . but I am not downcast or pessimistic. As Engels said: "If current events are negative, focus on long-range events" . . . I would check the air-conditioning vents in the Soviet legislature to see if anything was put in it to produce this insanity, this hysteria. Maybe [suspending Party activity] was just an act of plain mass cowardice. The Soviet people will catch up with this hypocrisy.

News conference,
New York, Aug. 30/
Los Angeles Times, 8-31:(A)9.

Tom Harkin
United States Senator,
D-Iowa;
Candidate for the
1992 Democratic
Presidential nomination

2

I intend to ask the American people to make a choice. If they want to continue to spend $160-billion a year of their money to defend Europe from the Soviet Union . . . they can vote for [current U.S. President] Bush. But if they believe, like I do, that Europe is strong enough and rich enough and powerful enough to defend itself, and that we can take some of that $160-billion a year and start [spending it on U.S. domestic needs] . . . then they ought to [vote for] Harkin.

News conference, Manchester, N.H./
The Christian Science Monitor,
9-18:9.

Vaclav Havel
President of Czechoslovakia

3

From the time when I was young, I used to hear in my country from all the official authori-

ties, as well as from all media, one thing only about the North Atlantic alliance (NATO]: that it was a bulwark of imperialism, a devil incarnate that posed a threat to peace and wanted to destroy us . . . I am happy to be in a position to apologize to you today on behalf of the Czech and the Slovak peoples for all the lies which my predecessors, on behalf of the same peoples, were for years telling about you.

At meeting of North Atlantic Treaty
Organization, Brussels, March 21/
Los Angeles Times, 3-22:(A)14.

4

The West bears a tremendous responsibility [to help countries in Eastern Europe survive the difficult transition to freedom and market economies]. It cannot remain indifferent to what is happening in countries which, being constantly encouraged by the Western democracies, have finally shaken off the totalitarian regimes . . . The democracies established [in Eastern Europe] are very fragile and therefore can be easily hurt, as everything in them is undergoing a fundamental transformation.

At meeting of North Atlantic Treaty
Organization, Brussels, March 21/
The Washington Post, 3-22:(A)18.

5

You know, everyone is always facing some dilemmas. I used to have dilemmas in the opposition and I'm facing analogous dilemmas now. For example, I used to have the dilemma of whether to say everything I wanted to say openly and risk imprisonment [during the previous Communist regime], or whether to be more cautious and phrase things in a more careful way and reduce the risk. And nowadays I am faced with exactly the same dilemma. For example, should I be the first in the world to recognize officially the [independence of] the Baltic states [in the Soviet Union] and thus risk immediate interruption of Soviet oil supplies and the subsequent total collapse of our economy? Or should I take into account the circumstances and express my deeply felt opinion more cautiously? It is exactly the same dilemma in a slightly different form.

Interview, Prague/Vanity Fair,
August:157.

Francois Heisbourg
Director, International Institute
for Strategic Studies
(Britain)

1

[On the sentiment in Germany against the U.S.-led coalition's use of force in the Persian Gulf war]: I thought I understood German pacifism. But here Germany is not a target for attack, the war has been sanctioned by the United Nations, and it's far away. [German anti-war sentiment is] not going over well in Paris or London. How can there be a common European policy when the British and French take ground losses in Kuwait and the Germans keep themselves deliberately aloof?

The New York Times, 1-25:(A)7.

2

If you extend a de facto (NATO) security guarantee to the East Europeans, you dilute the alliance. The worst kind of security guarantees are ambiguous ones—the kind we had in Europe before 1914. NATO's advantage has come from the transatlantic link and from its commitment to collective defense. It will die if it ties its survival to obligations it cannot fulfill.

U.S. News & World Report,
11-11:50.

Volodymir Hriniev
Deputy Vice President
of the Ukrainian Soviet
Socialist Republic

3

The fate of any future union [of Soviet republics] depends on the participation of the Ukraine, and it's clear that the Ukraine wants real independence. We may participate in an economic union like the European Community, but Kiev is our capital and the Ukraine—not the union—will be our state. Have no illusions about that. That is fact, not euphoria . . . [But] if we make enemies of people, if we cause divisions along national or linguistic lines, then independence is dead before it ever lives. We have to begin realizing that building a sovereign state is not just a goal in and of itself, but also a vehicle to create a better life and opportunities for the people who live here.

The Washington Post, 9-23:(A)1,15.

Janis Jurkans
Foreign Minister of Latvia

4

During the last 75 years, two economic systems existed on the face of the Earth. One flourished, another collapsed. Unfortunately, Latvia was forced to be on the losing side. All that has made Japan powerful, the United States enormous, the European Community vibrant and full of opportunity—all of these things have passed us by.

At meeting of 24 industrial nations,
Brussels, Nov. 11/
Los Angeles Times, 11-12:(A)4.

Oleg Kalugin
Member, Supreme Soviet
of the Soviet Union;
Former Director of Foreign
Counterintelligence, KGB
(Soviet security police)

5

[The KGB should become] a regular police force concerned with the protection of the Constitution, with counterintelligence activities, intelligence—and that's all. No political functions, no troops, no secret laboratories where they manufacture poison and special weapons. Interception of communications will be taken from them, protection of the President will be taken from them. We shall make it a safe organization for a democratic society.

To reporters/
The Christian Science Monitor,
8-30:7.

Ruslan Khasbulatov
Chairman, Supreme Soviet
of the Russian Soviet
Federated Socialist Republic

6

If [the Russian Republic] is a progressive, democratic state, it will pull everyone around it along. But if it is consumed by, say, nationalism and torn by ethnic strife, then all in the new union [of Soviet republics] would suffer. These are decisive times for Russia and every republic, and the future of hundreds of millions of people,

235

(RUSLAN KHASBULATOV)

generations in fact, will depend on what we do and how well we do it . . . We know the theories, but really we are feeling our way.

To callers on Soviet radio program/
Los Angeles Times, 9-16:(A)9.

Neil Kinnock
Leader, Labor Party
of Britain

1

The leadership that most concerns the British people is the one that has brought a 700,000 rise in unemployment, a 50,000 rise in company bankruptcies, a 70,000 rise in household mortgage repossessions, a 20 per cent fall in investment, and put a million people on hospital waiting lists. That's the leadership of [Prime Minister] John Major and his government.

To reporters/
The Christian Science Monitor,
9-19:4.

Helmut Kohl
Chancellor of Germany

2

We in Germany know from our own experience that the transition from a centralized command economy to democracy, rule of law and social market economy is long and difficult. The huge challenge we are facing in the new federal states [after the unification of East and West Germany] foreshadows the problems that the nations of Central and Eastern Europe, including the Soviet Union, will have to cope with. Their transition to democracy and a market economy demands courage, patience and a strong predisposition for change—not the least on the part of the people.

To foreign ministers at meeting of
Conference on Security and Cooperation
in Europe, Berlin, June 19/
The New York Times, 6-20:(A)6.

3

It would be foolish for the Western countries to sit back and calmly watch what happens in the Soviet Union. I believe we, not the Germans alone but all Western countries, must help the [Soviet] reformers. The Soviet Union must provide the essential pre-conditions, but then we cannot sit on the sidelines. I told [Soviet President Mikhail] Gorbachev in Kiev that we want his [reform] policies to be successful. That would benefit not only the Soviet Union, and not only the reformed nations of central and Eastern Europe. It would strengthen peace and security in the whole world.

Interview/
The New York Times, 7-9:(A)7.

4

[On the dangers in the disparity of wealth between Eastern and Western Europe]: It is unthinkable that we in Western Europe, in the European Community, can maintain our prosperity over the long term, while next to us, directly on our border, things don't develop well. More than before, we've become one world.

German broadcast interview/
Los Angeles Times, 9-10:(H)5.

5

The way to European unity is irreversible . . . When this Europe in 1997 or 1999 has a common currency from Copenhagen to Madrid and from The Hague to Rome, when more than 350 million people live in a common space without border controls, then no bureaucrat in Europe is going to be able to stop the process of political unification. . . . The member states of the European Community are now bound in such a way that it is impossible for them to split apart and fall back into the concept of the nation-state, with all of its consequences.

Before German Parliament,
Bonn, Dec. 13/
The New York Times, 12-14:5.

Karin Konig
Director,
Committee to Support
Politically Persecuted Foreigners
(Austria)

6

Immigration from Third World countries [to Europe] will continue to increase for the simple

(KARIN KONIG)

reason that people have no other choice. But that is going to mean growing problems of the kind we see across Europe—the street battles, and crime, and ghettos, the xenophobia and far-right political movements—because the cultures involved are so different.

The Christian Science Monitor,
8-7:12.

Vitaly Korotich
Editor, "Ogonyok"
(Soviet Union)

1

We [Soviets] are all products and victims of the same system, from [Soviet President Mikhail] Gorbachev down to the last child. We are a nation of welfare bums. We expect the state to look after us, even if it does it badly. Seven out of 10 Soviets do not want to work.

The Washington Post,
9-5:(A)1.

2

[On the current breakup of the Soviet Union]: [Soviet President Mikhail] Gorbachev took this country like my wife takes cabbage. He thought that, to get rid of the dirt, he could just peel off the top layer of leaves. But he had to keep going until there was nothing left.

The Christian Science Monitor,
12-26:2.

Leonid Kozhendayev
General and member
of the General Staff,
Soviet Armed Forces

3

[Criticizing the breakup of the Soviet Union into independent states]: We need new leaders. I think they will be advanced by the people, who are sick and tired of standing in lines for bread and fearing the next day. And whether the ruling elite wants it or not, the armed forces are being politicized. The Army is losing patience. It will not tolerate for much longer this humiliation, this

living a hungry life in small rented flats and serving a country that is no more.

Interview/
Los Angeles Times, 12-6:(A)1,14.

Mathias Krafft
Director, Division for
International Law,
Department of Foreign Affairs
of Switzerland

4

Europe has entered a new phase of its post-war history in which the policies of the superpowers have changed. An internal European Community market is emerging, East-West relations further improve and disarmament has become a possibility and a necessity. Even a traditionally neutral country like Switzerland must continuously review its security policy and, at some point, even its neutrality.

Speech, London, May 17/
Los Angeles Times, 6-11:(H)5.

Leonid M. Kravchuk
President-elect of Ukraine

5

[On the Ukrainian people's recent vote to become independent of the Soviet Union]: As to the problem of [Soviet] nuclear weapons and strategic forces [now based in the Ukraine], we are going to pursue the principle of collective security. We will stand for the liquidation of nuclear weapons, tactical and strategic, and this should be done in a process of negotiations with all countries. The Ukraine only wants control over the weapons on its territory, but it doesn't want a button. We cannot allow several nuclear powers to form on the territory of the ex-Soviet Union.

Dec. 2/
Los Angeles Times, 12-3:(A)22.

Jan Krol
Member, Democratic Unity Party
of Poland

6

[Criticizing Polish President Lech Walesa, who he says is trying to assume too much power]:

(JAN KROL)

If the President is going to exercise power . . . through [street] rallies, if he is to try to subdue other Constitutional powers like the Parliament . . . then we will all pay the highest price, beginning with the "road to Europe," because Europe will turn its back on this sort of Poland.

Los Angeles Times, 6-29:(A)8.

Vladimir A. Kryuchkov
Chairman, Soviet State
Security Committee (KGB)

1

The KGB cannot work without firm regulation by the law as the basis for its activities. As we strive to establish a state run by laws, such legislation will be an important guarantee for the citizens exercising their Constitutional rights and freedoms, and I am sure that it will also enhance the KGB's efficiency and reliability in ensuring the country's security . . . We must reckon with the fact that the shadow of the mass repressions that the KGB bodies were involved in during the years of the [Stalin] personality cult falls, willingly or not, on our time as well . . . We always stress that the Soviet people must be sure that, neither today nor in the future, such lawlessness will not be repeated.

Before Supreme Soviet,
Moscow, March 5/
Los Angeles Times, 3-6:(A)16.

Catherine Lalumiere
Secretary General,
Council of Europe

2

I think, in a nutshell, what we are trying to do is turn the Council [of Europe] into a Pan-European organization. And we are bringing in those from Eastern Europe because they urgently need a structure capable of accommodating them and assisting them to democratic reform . . . They are first received as special guests to our meetings. Then as participants in ministerial conferences. And last, having adopted all the requirements for a democratic government that observes human rights, to full membership.

Interview, Paris/
Los Angeles Times, 3-19:(H)2.

Vytautas Landsbergis
President of the Lithuanian
Soviet Socialist Republic

3

[On the Soviet Union's reluctance to allow Lithuania to become independent]: Their position is that we are a constituent republic and, if we want to separate, we must go the way that involves Soviet loyalty. The Soviets feel that annexation obligates us in their Constitution. We adopted our own Constitution and declarations and believe that no other constitution is valid.

Interview/
Los Angeles Times, 5-26:(M)3.

4

We know that behind the crimes of any Soviet armed-forces units [in Lithuania] and the gangs supported by them stands the senior leadership of the Soviet Union, which cannot incessantly pretend that it knows nothing, does not control the situation and does not hear the demands, for example, of the Republic of Lithuania for the withdrawal of [Soviet special forces] from the territory of Lithuania . . . Attention must be drawn to repeated coincidences of circumstances. Whenever the United States has shown more favorable disposition toward the Soviet Union, the Baltic countries and especially Lithuania each time experienced the Soviets' armed blows. In fact, the United States makes concessions by not firmly demanding of the Soviet Union punishment of those guilty for the killings in Lithuania and Latvia in January, 1991, return of the buildings seized by Soviet forces and withdrawal of the [special-forces] terrorists from Baltic countries.

Vilnius, U.S.S.R., July 31/
The Washington Post, 8-1:(A)14.

5

Tens of millions murdered and hundreds of millions of spirits deliberately broken. Nations annihilated, poisoned lands. States seized by spastic hands so that they would never be released. Total war, so that the whole world would be conquered. Vengeance and hatred at the moment of retreat. That is Soviet Com-

(VYTAUTAS LANDSBERGIS)

munism named Bolshevism. Now the time has come for Bolshevism's Nuremberg. I will offer for Lithuania to initiate a juridical process, analogous to the liquidation of Nazi influence 45 years ago, and we would invite an international tribunal to come to Vilnius [Lithuania's capital]. If [the world] would support this as well, then perhaps our Lithuania will again be able to do something good for everyone.

Speech, Vilnius, Aug. 23/
Los Angeles Times, 8-25:(M)5.

Vytautas Landsbergis
President of Lithuania

1

[On his country's recently regained independence from the Soviet Union]: In what could we place our faith during these last decades, when brutal coercion and cynical pragmatism forced so many to believe in nothing at all in this world? We believed in simple, or should I say fundamental, things: truth and justice. When the people of Lithuania held on to the belief that independence would be regained and then had the brashness to declare it, many cynically smiled, thinking that unless backed by tanks and missiles, our right to independence was meaningless, that it was simply a piece of paper.

At United Nations,
New York, Sept. 17/
The Washington Post, 9-18:(A)25.

Yegor Ligachev
Member, Politburo,
Communist Party
of the Soviet Union

2

When we started this insane effort to create a market economy [in the Soviet Union] without establishing the proper economic and political logistics, it alienated everyone, and the crash began. The main thing behind the collapse is this over-emphasis on market economics. We succeeded brilliantly in destroying the central planning system, and there are no other methods to replace it. We must go back from where we started.

The Washington Post, 4-24:(A)27.

John D. Macomber
Chairman, Export-Import
Bank of the United States

3

[In the Soviet Union,] there's a lot of rhetoric about fundamental reform—politically, economically and socially. But among most of the leadership there is a healthy skepticism that they can get from here to there. A lot of them are walking through a little *Alice in Wonderland* and [are] rather naive about what it takes to participate in a free-market economy.

Interview/
The Washington Post, 10-5:(B)1.

Harry Maier
Professor,
University of Flensburg
(Germany)

4

[Saying the unification of East and West Germany has not resulted in an improved economy in what was East Germany]: The government had the naive notion that the free market would take care of everything. Instead, it has been a disaster. Given west German money, the east Germans only want to buy west German products. And western industry is interested, naturally enough, first in selling products there [in the east], not in building factories and making them. Right now, the government seems to have no over-all concept of how to proceed. In economic terms, Germany is more divided than before unity.

The New York Times, 2-13:(C)2.

John Major
Prime Minister
of the United Kingdom

5

I don't have a shred of regret about entering the [European] exchange-rate mechanism. I'm sure it was the right thing to do for the British economy. If you consider what has happened in the last four months: We have had a recession, we have had a war [in the Persian Gulf], we have lost a Prime Minister [Margaret Thatcher, who was forced out by her party] in very dramatic political

(JOHN MAJOR)

circumstances, we've seen a narrowing of two and one-half per cent in the differential between the Sterling and the Deutschmark rate, a critical rate for us in Europe, and Sterling has remained steady. Now, would that have happened if we hadn't been members of the exchange-rate mechanism? It would not. Sterling would have fallen. And what would have happened if Sterling had fallen? We would either have built-in inflation for next year, or we would have had to increase interest rates . . . I know some people think it [the exchange-rate mechanism] is a strait-jacket. In practice, it has been more a lifebelt than a strait-jacket.

Interview, London, Feb. 27/
The New York Times, 2-28:(A)3.

1

[On Britain's position in the European Community]: There are, I think, only three ways [for Britain] to go in the Community; to lead, which is unthinkable, to stand aside and let ourselves be dragged along by others, which is untenable, or to be at the very heart of the Community and to help frame the decisions—and that is our policy.

Before House of Commons,
London, March 12/
The Washington Post, 3-13:(A)19.

Ante Markovic
Prime Minister of Yugoslavia

2

[On the unrest in Yugoslavia resulting from moves for independence by several of its constituent republics]: Blind forces have the upper hand, and we are only a step from all-out war. In my opinion, the consequences would equal a natural calamity, that is, cataclysm. It would take decades to come out of that state, leaving a few thousand, or dare I say, perhaps millions of victims. We have to be very expeditious. We have no chance of reaching an agreement on the future of the country if we do not establish its functioning . . . No chance at all! We shall all kill ourselves and be done with!

To Federal Presidency, July 22/
The New York Times, 7-29:(A)3.

Jack F. Matlock, Jr.
United States Ambassador
to the Soviet Union

3

[On whether Soviet President Mikhail Gorbachev means what he says about reforms in his country]: Yes. The fact is, I think he is at heart a democrat with a little *d*, in the sense that he wants to lead the country to an open society and one where sovereignty resides in the people. Some would say, "Well, he really doesn't know where he is going." I don't agree. He's really sailing in uncharted seas in many ways . . . If there is a reef coming up, then you steer around it.

Interview, Moscow/
Los Angeles Times, 8-13:(E)1.

Jack F. Matlock, Jr.
Former United States Ambassador
to the Soviet Union

4

[On the recent failed coup aimed at ousting Soviet President Mikhail Gorbachev]: Basically, it failed because the spirit of democracy had begun to take root, sufficiently so that millions of people were willing to stand up [against the coup] and be counted and risk everything. This had not been true before. Second, although Gorbachev was increasingly unpopular . . . the last thing they wanted was reinstallation of Communist rule.

Interview, Boone, Tenn./
USA Today, 8-22:(A)4.

Hanns Maull
Deputy director, German Foreign Policy
Association

5

The Franco-German relationship has become both the concrete mechanism and the symbol that has made war in Western Europe unthinkable. The two countries have embraced each other so tightly that they have gone beyond the traditional ways of dealings between nations. This is the core of the [West] European experiment, the [West] European experience.

Los Angeles Times, 11-19:(H)1.

Martin McGuinness
Member, executive body,
Sinn Fein (political wing of
Irish Republican Army)

1

[On the IRA's campaign of violence to try to get Britain out of Northern Ireland]: There are a lot of people who would like to see an end to the suffering and death, and I am one of them. But we need an honest settlement—and that means a real commitment from Britain to withdraw from this island—before people like me can stand up and call for a truce.

The Washington Post, 6-1:(A) 15.

Robert S. McNamara
Former Secretary of Defense
of the United States

2

There were real threats in the Cold War, risks that some governments in Western Europe would be subverted or otherwise end up controlled by the Communists. Later we confronted very serious pressures against Berlin and other parts of the world. But I suspect we exaggerated, greatly exaggerated, the strength that lay behind those threats, and therefore I think we probably misused our resources and directed excessive resources toward responding to those threats at considerable cost to our domestic societies.

Interview,
Washington/Time, 2-11:70.

Roy A. Medvedev
Member, Supreme Soviet
of the Soviet Union

3

[Soviet President Mikhail] Gorbachev is having to face the fact that with the exception of some people in the [privately run] cooperative sector, *perestroika* reforms in six years have improved the material life of absolutely no one in the country. In most cases, life is worse.

The Washington Post, 4-10:(A)27.

4

There will be no split [in the Soviet Communist Party] for one simple reason. The Party

ceased some time ago to be a party in an ideological sense. It is a machine that distributes privileges and power. The membership understands that if the Party splits, they will lose this power.

U.S. News & World Report,
7-29:30.

5

[On the move toward independence by many Soviet republics]: The country was formed centuries ago under the czars as a centralized, united state. It is an illusion to imagine that a state like this can simply disintegrate. It only seems that way to people who live in Moscow or go on a short visit to Lithuania. We cannot change the system of railroads, which are all connected with Moscow. We cannot change the system of communications or the configuration of oil and gas pipelines. We have a united system of energy in this country—atomic power stations in the Ukraine are all managed from Moscow. It would cost billions of rubles to change all this.

The Washington Post, 9-5:(A)33.

Stipe Mesic
Former President of Yugoslavia

6

[On the current ethnic civil war among the Yugoslavian republics]: Now it's Yugoslavia's problem. Tomorrow it's Europe's problem. Then it will be the world's problem.

Interview, Zagreb, Yugoslavia,
Dec. 5/
Los Angeles Times, 12-6:(A)21.

Robert H. Michel
United States Representative,
R-Illinois

7

[Criticizing the Soviet government's use of the military to crack down on democratically elected governments in the Baltic republics]: The Communist government of the Soviet Union has reverted to form. The ghost of Lenin must be smiling as he sees his [Soviet President Mikhail] Gorbachev once again using the Party's ulti-

WHAT THEY SAID IN 1991

mate argument against people who want to be free. [Gorbachev] has chosen to ride a tank down the road to the past, waving his Nobel Peace Prize as he passes by.

Before the House,
Washington, Jan. 16/
The Washington Post, 1-17:(A)14.

Meinhard Miegel
Director, Institute for
Economy and Society
(Germany)

1

Somehow [German Chancellor Helmut] Kohl doesn't look any more like the figure who can supervise unification [of East and West Germany, which occurred last year] in all its enormous philosophical, mental and psychological dimensions. To truly unify two societies . . . requires more than a technocratic financial approach.

Newsweek, 4-1:28.

Slobodan Milosevic
President, Republic of Serbia,
Yugoslavia

2

[On the ethnic unrest threatening to break up Yugoslavia]: Our policy is to preserve the integrity of [Yugoslavia] in order to realize democratic changes within the country but not to liquidate the country as a state. Flexibility has some limits. I think we are very flexible but the limit to our flexibility is the integrity of our country. We think we have to have, on the level of Yugoslavia, some minimal function without which Yugoslavia cannot be a country. It means defense, foreign affairs, human-rights protection, national rights protection and one market with one central bank.

The New York Times, 6-22:4.

Constantine Mitsotakis
Prime Minister of Greece

3

[On Greece's part in the U.S.-led coalition that ousted Iraq from Kuwait in the recent Persian Gulf war]: These men of the Greek Navy . . . went to the Gulf in the belief that by opposing Iraq's aggression against Kuwait, they would help raise the consciousness of the world to the continued [Turkish] occupation of northern Cyprus . . . Greeks went to the Gulf not only because their country asked them to do it but also because they believed that the invasion of Kuwait was patently unjust. [Likewise, the occupation of northern Cyprus by Turkey] is patently unjust and in defiance of the international rules of conduct that the Gulf war was fought to defend.

To visiting U.S. President Bush,
Souda Bay, Crete, July 19/
Los Angeles Times, 7-20:(A)11.

4

While the United States is now the symbol of democracy in the world, Greece, where it was born, remains its soul. That creates a special bond between us that is crucial to the future of democracy, for all political systems need to return to the ideals that shaped them if they are to remain vital. Those ideals are Greek.

To visiting U.S. President Bush,
Souda Bay, Crete, July 19/
Los Angeles Times, 7-20:(A)11.

Francois Mitterrand
President of France

5

[On the current moves toward independence by many republics that are currently part of the Soviet Union and Yugoslavia]: The end of empires in Europe, particularly the Soviet, has liberated national aspirations constrained by force for too long . . . Thirty-three states [in Europe] yesterday, [but] how many tomorrow? This movement is healthy if it produces greater freedom. But let us be vigilant that it proceeds in a democratic way and conforms with treaties that ensure the security and peace of our continent.

News conference,
Paris, Sept. 11/
The Washington Post,
9-12:(A)30.

Jurgen Mollemann
Minister of Economics
of Germany

1

[Saying the West expects real positive change in the Soviet economic system in order to justify giving aid to the Soviet Union]: We want to make suggestions [to the Soviets], but we can't behave as if we were the World Bank going into Uganda, designing a plan for them and then saying they have to accept or else there is no money. It has to be a partnership of governments . . . The Americans are like us in that they don't want to waste their money over there . . . A lot depends on [Soviet President Mikhail] Gorbachev, whether he offers some real radical change or just window dressing.

Interview/
The New York Times, 6-25:(A)6.

2

[Saying Germany has Europe's strongest economy]: There are two especially important reasons. First, everything here is modern. Our country was totally destroyed in [World War II], and all of our factories had to be built new. The other reason is education. We connect the world of school to the world of work, and then we stress life-long learning to keep the quality level always improving. People with first-class educations have first-class ideas, and people with first-class ideas produce first-class products and services.

Interview/
The New York Times, 7-12:(A)2.

Akio Morita
Chairman, Sony Corporation
(Japan)

3

The unification of Europe after 1992 has caused great concern among many Japanese businessmen who fear they [Europeans] are building a "fortress." But my view is different. We must appreciate and admire the willingness of Europeans to sacrifice sovereignty to create a greater economic region. Despite their many different cultures, languages and traditions, and their deadly conflicts over the years, they know

now that to live together peacefully, every country has to sacrifice some of its own interests for the good of the greater whole.

Conversation with former Chase
Manhattan Bank chairman David Rockefeller/
Los Angeles Times, 12-4:(B)7.

Nursultan A. Nazarbayev
President of the
Kazakhstanian Soviet
Socialist Republic

4

It is clear to me that a renewed union [of Soviet republics] cannot be a federation. We have spent too long chasing after the past. The Ukraine's declaration of independence, and a similar decision by Byelorussia, witness a new historical reality that we cannot escape or ignore . . . In a future union what we have in mind is more economic relations with the center . . . Each republic should have its own army . . . We are used to the term U.S.S.R. We propose leaving it, and expanding it into the Free Union of Sovereign Republics. By this I mean all republics, including the autonomous republics that have declared or intend to declare their independence. We should give representatives of every nationality the right to speak in their own language at republic and union meetings, and each republic should have the right to hear their deputy in their mother tongue. Thus, we are in favor of a confederative treaty, and we are convinced that only in that way will we achieve equal rights among republics. Only in this way will we achieve a genuine federation.

Before Supreme Soviet,
Moscow, Aug. 26/
The New York Times, 8-27:(A)9.

5

[On the breakup of the Soviet Union into various independent states]: We should not scare the world. At least we have to agree upon a political and military union to keep the strategic [nuclear] weapons in one place . . . Even now I remain loyal to the idea that we should not break up our [union] in this most difficult time, although everyone wants to feel independent. After the

(NURSULTAN A. NAZARBAYEV)

many years of imperial totalitarianism, I understand this desire.

Interview,
Moscow, Dec. 8/
Los Angeles Times, 12-9:(A)10.

Richard M. Nixon
Former President
of the United States

1

[Comparing two political opponents, Soviet President Mikhail Gorbachev and Russian Republic President Boris Yeltsin]: I'd say this: Gorbachev is Wall Street and Yeltsin is Main Street; Gorbachev is Georgetown drawing rooms and Yeltsin is Newark factory gate. I can see where Yeltsin has enormous appeal as a political leader. He could become, if he had the desire to do so, the leader of a violent revolution. But the fact is, this has been a peaceful opposition in Russia, and that is a credit to Gorbachev, but also a credit to Yeltsin. Yeltsin is one who could be a revolutionary leader; he could charge people up. He has the animal magnetism. I also think he has the ruthlessness. But curiously enough, I doubt that Yeltsin wants Gorbachev's job.

Interview,
Moscow, April 3/
The Washington Post, 4-4:(A)31.

2

[The late Soviet leader Nikita Khrushchev, who predicted in 1959 that his country would catch up and overtake the U.S. within five years,] couldn't have believed that they would catch up that soon, but he believed that they would catch up. At that time and in the 1960s and even approaching the 1970s, the Russian people had faith that the system might work. Then it finally just ran out of gas, just collapsed. So what I see is a deep malaise that is affecting the Soviet people. The old beliefs have been discredited, and there is nothing to take its place.

Interview, Moscow/
The New York Times,
4-4:(A)8.

Robert C. Oaks
General, United States Air Force;
Commander, U.S. Air Forces/
Europe

3

I have had Germans tell me Germans are better people with Americans around. And if you talk to other countries, they would say NATO is a better place with Americans here . . . People have a hard time imagining the French and the Germans fighting today. But the history of mankind, as recorded, is a lot of fights in Western Europe. So I take a historical view and it's not unheard of.

Interview/
The Washington Post, 10-15:(A)16.

Turgut Ozal
President of Turkey

4

The Turkish role is very interesting. Turkey is the only Muslim country to sign the European security arrangement of 34 nations. The coming danger to the world is not Communism vs. capitalism but Christianity vs. Islam. I suggested that Turkey [enter] the European Community as a member. This way, you will build a bridge between the West and the Islamic countries. If the EC doesn't accept us, we will look to other solutions.

Interview, Ankara/
USA Today, 2-11:(A)11.

5

In Turkey, a politician should have a big heart. And a big stomach to take the punches.

Interview/
The New York Times, 3-9:2.

6

Turkey is on a cultural fault line, where two cultures mix. But in Ottoman times, Turkey was called "the sick man of Europe," so that means we were considered then a European country. Today, Turkey is basically of Western orientation. We have democracy, human rights and a free market. While 98 per cent of the population

(TURGUT OZAL)

is Muslim, we are also a secular state. It's a good example for the rest of the Islamic world. Turkey plays the role of a bridge between Western and Islamic societies, and this will become more important in the coming decades.

Interview, New York/
Time, 5-13:10.

Boris D. Pankin
Foreign Minister
of the Soviet Union

1

[On the move toward independence by many of the Soviet republics]: Our country will never be the same. Where an ossified empire once stood, a new union of free and truly sovereign nations bound together by common aspirations is being born. Democracy, human rights, openness toward each other and to the entire civilized world will be its main frame.

At United Nations,
New York, Sept. 24/
The New York Times, 9-25:(A)6.

Valentin Pavlov
Prime Minister
of the Soviet Union

2

[Criticizing proposals that the West provide financial aid to help the Soviet Union with its economic problems]: To give money to the Soviet Union, you have to go to Congress [in the U.S.] and convince the legislators and the taxpayers they represent that the Soviets must be given substantial aid, free of charge, just for the beauty of it. Let me tell you, this is not as simple as it sounds. What's more, should that happen, we will have to join the waiting line there after Israel, the Arabs and so forth. Those who are willing may stand there, but without me . . . I know some gentlemen from Harvard University, and they simply do not know our life or understand our views. They have their own criteria and values. They have their own ideas on how people should work and live. It is all but impossible to explain to them why we can't bring ourselves to

leave any potatoes or gravy on the plate . . . and I cannot let any of it be thrown away. They simply do not understand, and that's why there cannot be a joint program.

Before Supreme Soviet,
Moscow, June 17/
Los Angeles Times, 6-18:(A)1,7.

Rinaldo Petrignani
Italian Ambassador
to the United States

3

An American presence, diminished but still substantial, is essential to keeping the various European countries in balance with each other. And a more unified Europe will be able to play a larger role in the alliance than in the past, thus relieving the United States of some of its burdens.

Interview, Washington/
The New York Times, 5-27:7.

Mary Robinson
President of Ireland

4

I think Ireland has changed very significantly, but gradually, over about the last 10 years . . . by our membership in the European Community, now very much a part of the national psyche, by our young, well-educated population, by the vitality of our arts and culture. Irish people walk taller now.

Interview, Los Angeles/
Los Angeles Times, 10-21:(E)1.

Dana T. Rohrabacher
United States Representative,
R-California

5

[On the ethnic conflict in Yugoslavia]: The old centralized, Communist-controlled Yugoslavia is absolutely a thing of the past. We [the U.S.] should not be giving any encouragement to those people in Belgrade who still have that dream . . . The perception that Serbia is promoting a unified Yugoslavia is ridiculous. They are simply proposing the same old centralized, Serbian-

(DANA T. ROHRABACHER)

dominated Yugoslavia. That's not going to work in the Soviet Union, and it's not going to work here.

Interview, Zagreb, Yugoslavia,
Aug. 13/
Los Angeles Times, 8-14:(A)6.

Petre Roman
Prime Minister of Romania

1

Our democratization is a straight process. Every important aspect of this process is already functioning. There were some problems. There are still some interrogations. But these don't raise a question of whether we are deeply committed to the democratic process and the economic reform meant to re-orient our economy toward a market economy.

Interview, Washington/
USA Today, 4-16:(A)11.

Juergen Ruhfus
German Ambassador
to the United States

2

[On why the U.S. should keep troops in Europe now that the Soviet threat has disappeared]: The threat is not so much any more a combined force of the Warsaw Pact, but uncertainty. It has been pointed out that even if the Soviet Union changes, there are still 30,000 nuclear warheads in the Soviet Union. Your country [the U.S.] has stepped in twice, after World War I and after World War II, to be involved in the European scene. We would think it is in your interest to remain committed and involved.

Interview/USA Today, 5-15:(A)11.

Alexander V. Rutskoi
Vice President
of the Russian Soviet
Federated Socialist Republic

3

Some think democracy has already won [in the Soviet Union], but that's far from the truth.

Democracy will win only when the shelves of the stores are full and people don't have to wait in line.

To crowd honoring those killed in
the recent coup attempt,
Moscow, Sept. 29/
Los Angeles Times, 9-30:(A)14.

Patricia Schroeder
United States Representative,
D-Colorado

4

Here we are with all these [U.S. military] installations in West Germany protecting West Germany from East Germany, except [now] it's all one Germany, and all the East Germans are now in West Germany shopping at the mall.

The New York Times, 7-31:(A)12.

5

[On the breakup of the Soviet Union into independent states]: The Ukraine is [now] the third-largest nuclear power in the world, with 30,000 nuclear weapons [that used to belong to the united Soviet Union]. You don't want the Ukraine to turn into [strife-torn] Yugoslavia with nukes. We need to move very rapidly with this [nuclear] dismantling. I think everyone understands this. Clearly, we need those new republics on the nuclear non-proliferation treaty . . .

Interview, Denver/
The Christian Science Monitor,
12-27:9.

Francis Sejersted
Chairman, Norwegian Nobel
Committee

6

[On the selection of Soviet President Mikhail Gorbachev as winner of the 1990 Nobel Peace Prize]: During the late 1980s and the early 1990s, we have seen dramatic changes in relations between East and West. Old European nations have regained their freedom. The arms race is being reversed . . . The [Nobel] committee found that one man had made a decisive contribution to this process—the President of the

(FRANCIS SEJERSTED)

Soviet Union, Mikhail Sergeyevich Gorbachev, who has been described as the man responsible for starting the thaw.

*Introducing Gorbachev at Nobel
ceremony, Oslo, Norway,
June 5/
Los Angeles Times, 6-6:(A)9.*

Vladimir Seleznev
*Member, Supreme Soviet
of the Soviet Union;
Colonel, Soviet Army*

1

You [in the U.S.] were told that we were your mortal enemies. It was, to some extent, true for you and for us. The risk factor was there, and we had to be ready to defend our country. As for the Communist ideology, yes, it was the official set of slogans for the military. Nowadays, the situation is somewhat different [with the end of the Cold War and the retreat of Communism]. First of all, the Communist ideology is not as glorious, many people feel. We have a law [that says] the Communists should not play any role in the armed forces. Because of the new thinking, we feel much better about the U.S. armed forces . . . We don't have to be enemies to each other. We can collaborate.

*Interview,
Cambridge, Mass./
The Washington Post, 9-21:(A)3.*

Vasily Selyunin
Soviet economist

2

At this point, [Soviet President Mikhail] Gorbachev's own destiny may be interesting for its dramatic or tragic content, but that's about all. We are plunging into an economic depression that makes the American depression of 60 years ago look like a stroll in the park. Gorbachev has none of the tools—the legitimacy, the ideas, the will or even the power—to build a new order. His chapter is all but finished.

*The Washington Post,
4-24:(A)1.*

Vladimir I. Shcherbakov
*Chairman, Soviet
Confederation of Trade Unions*

3

The working people [in the Soviet Union] today demand that the breakup of the state be halted and the economy be brought to order so that people will have the opportunity to work and earn a decent salary. It's time that all who are vested with power be held to account . . . People do not understand what is happening. There is no war, no drought, no epidemic, no calamities, but we are talking about hunger. The half-measures taken by the government aggravate the crisis and hit the rank-and-file people the most.

*At May Day rally, Moscow, May 1/
Los Angeles Times, 5-2:(A)4.*

Vladimir I. Shcherbakov
*First Deputy Prime Minister
of the Soviet Union*

4

I told [U.S. President] Bush, "Maybe I'm wrong, but we have two very different psychologies. A certain type of person has been formed through your tradition with such a reserve of entrepreneurship, that your main government task is to restrain him from what is not allowed. But our system spent 73 years calculating those people who can act independently and catching them each time, so that a different type of passive person was formed. It's not enough now for us to tell this person that some action is no longer prohibited; we must convince him that the action is necessary. This will take more time than anything else."

*Interview/
The New York Times, 8-12:(A)4.*

Eduard A. Shevardnadze
*Former Foreign Minister
of the Soviet Union*

5

[Saying Soviet President Mikhail Gorbachev and Russian President Boris Yeltsin should stop their public quarrels with each other on the future of the nation]: I think this war, this war of parliaments, this war of laws and now a war of Presidents, must be ended. Everybody must think about the country, about the people, the fate of democracy in the Soviet Union. It seems to me the two Presidents, Gorbachev and Yeltsin, must meet and seriously discuss all problems which are now arising. They aren't simple, but the two leaders must find strength to overcome contradictions and difficulties.

To reporters, Moscow, Feb. 20/
The Washington Post, 2-21:(A)17.

Eduard A. Shevardnadze
President, Soviet Foreign
Policy Association;
Former Foreign Minister
of the Soviet Union

1

[On the possibility of dictatorship emerging in his country]: The threat has not diminished. I'd say the situation has become more tense, whether we're talking about the economy, society, politics or ethnic conflicts. But nobody can tell where the dictator might come from. History knows many examples when political unknowns have emerged. Take Hitler, for example. Who knew him? The situation in his country [Germany] was so bad that he managed to force his way into power and cause so much misery and tragedy. I don't mean to say this will happen here. But if we fail to stabilize events and the [Soviet Union] plunges into chaos, the people may demand a man with a strong hand and dictatorial inclinations who would bring about order.

Interview, Moscow/
Time, 5-13:36.

Eduard A. Shevardnadze
Co-chairman, Democratic
Reform Movement
(Soviet Union);
Former Foreign Minister
of the Soviet Union

2

The [Soviet Communist] Party is losing its cohesiveness. A lot of fractures are appearing. It is no longer able to act any more as a solid, unified party. After the elections in Moscow, Leningrad and Russia, it does not take a great deal of political skill to see which way the wind is blowing.

Interview, Moscow, July 26/
The Washington Post, 7-27:(A)18.

3

[Even] we [in the Soviet reform movement] have all sinned. We all bear the burden of our past. We all lived through [former Soviet leaders] Joseph Stalin, Nikita Khrushchev, Leonid Brezhnev, Yuri Andropov and Konstantin Chernenko. We all made speeches praising them. As a youth, I even wrote a poem in honor of Stalin. But we evolve—life forces us to. When we explain ourselves, people understand. I understand a certain reticence, but what should we do? Be afraid and do nothing? Certainly not! As long as our generation is still active, our task is to clear the way for the young, help them benefit from our experiences, good and bad. Their minds were molded by *perestroika* [reform], but they lack experience. Whether they are unemployed or the next generation's businessmen, they need a political umbrella. It is up to us to create the conditions that will protect them.

Interview/World Press Review,
September:24.

4

[On the recent failed coup in the Soviet Union aimed at ousting President Mikhail Gorbachev]: I was optimistic [that the coup would fail] because the people who illegally took power and illegally created the so-called committee were not able to get and cannot rely on the support of the people. Any government, or junta, or group that comes to power and does not have the people's support will inevitably go bankrupt.

Interview/
U.S. News & World Report,
9-2:31.

Krzysztof Skubiszewski
Foreign Minister of Poland

5

The fact that the Eastern bloc doesn't exist any more does not mean we intend to weaken our

(KRZYSZTOF SKUBISZEWSKI)

relations with the East and decrease our openness to the East. To the contrary. Belonging to
organized [Western] Europe and at the same
time maintaining relations with the East is the
role allocated to Poland by its geostrategic and
geopolitical position. This position has been
hurting us until now. Now we want to turn it to our
advantage and the advantage of Europe.

Before Polish Parliament,
Warsaw, Feb. 14/
The New York Times, 2-15:(A)4.

Hedrick Smith
Fellow,
Foreign Policy Institute,
Johns Hopkins School
of Advanced International
Studies (United States);
Pulitzer Prize-winning
journalist

1

[On Soviet President Mikhail Gorbachev]:
Our long-term interest is in the process of reform,
not in the fate of one man. As long as Gorbachev
is moving in a reformist direction, then we do
have an interest in his remaining in power. If
Gorbachev starts behaving like [the late Soviet
leader Leonid] Brezhnev and some of the others
before him, then it is less in our interest to back
him. Particularly when there are alternatives in
the Soviet Union as there are today. A lot of it
depends upon his policy. The answer is, which
Gorbachev?

Interview/USA Today, 3-21:(A)13.

Anatoly A. Sobchak
Mayor of Leningrad, U.S.S.R.

2

[Soviet President Mikhail Gorbachev's] main
mistake was that all the economic and political
changes in the country were presented as the
desire to reform a Communist society. So all
reforms were acceptable or not acceptable to the
degree they were acceptable to the Communist
Party. And so these six years of attempts to
reform the unreformable was our main mistake,

and this is something we should have recognized
a long time ago. We should have recognized that
this system could not be reformed, was not
capable of being reformed, and it should have
been dissolved from the beginning. This is something we just waited to do today. It took [the
recent failed] coup d'etat to do it.

Before Supreme Soviet,
Moscow, Aug. 26/
The New York Times, 8-27:(A)9.

Helmut Sonnenfeldt
Former senior member,
National Security Council
of the United States

3

The United States will continue in some ways
to be a preferred partner for the Soviets; when
they deal with us, it's evidence to them that they
are in the very big leagues. But the big issue for
the Soviets isn't arms control—it's how we and
other countries interact with them in this transformation they're attempting. They already have
a special relationship with Germany, based
partly on economics; they would like to have one
with Japan. They will be looking more and more
to the European Community, even Brazil and the
economic tigers of Southeast Asia.

Los Angeles Times, 7-18:(A)6.

Frederick Starr
President, Oberlin College
(United States);
Specialist on the Soviet Union

4

Despite [U.S.] President Bush's insistence on
calling [Soviet President Mikhail] Gorbachev
"the constitutionally chosen President of the
Soviet Union," the fact is that he has no political
legitimacy. He has not dared to test the popular
will and stand for President in a free election . . .
By contrast, [Russian Republic President Boris]
Yeltsin gambled on going to the voters, won big
and has the right to call himself a democratically
elected leader . . . The only way that Gorbachev
can regain any legitimacy and viability now is to
go before the voters and pass the test of a
democratic election.

The Washington Post, 8-22:(A)31.

Hans Stercken
Chairman,
Foreign Affairs Committee
of the German Parliament

1

We [Germans] cannot help but be concerned by what is happening around us. A terrible civil war is going on in Yugoslavia. There is great instability in the east. We cannot confront all of this by ourselves. Many of these unstable countries are going to need a great deal of help in the coming years. Otherwise, they are going to become security problems. Only the European Community as a whole, not Germany alone, can bear that burden. The German plan is to stabilize Europe by building a strong union, using the union to funnel aid into the poor republics to the east, and ultimately bringing those republics into the union so they can share the general prosperity.

The New York Times, 12-2:(A)3.

Robert S. Strauss
United States
Ambassador-designate
to the Soviet Union

2

[On his appointment as Ambassador]: It ain't an easy job and it's not comfortable surroundings, but the President [Bush] and [Secretary of State] Jim Baker talked me into it and I'm going to give it the best shot I got. If they want a Soviet expert, they made a mistake picking me. I'm as poor an example of a Soviet expert as they could find. But if they want a winner who's been successful at a lot of different things and understands relationships and how to help the Soviets with their terrible economic problems, then I was the right choice.

Washington, June 4/
The New York Times, 6-5:(A)1.

Lawrence H. Summers
Vice president and
chief economist,
World Bank

3

[On the economies of Eastern Europe]: The only thing that has collapsed faster than indus-

trial productivity is the consensus over quality of living standards. It will be closer to a lifetime than a generation before Eastern Europe's economies will be comparable to Western Europe's.

At conference sponsored by U.S. Agency
for International Development,
Prague, Czechoslovakia, March 24/
Los Angeles Times, 3-26:(D)1.

Roman Szporluk
Professor of Ukrainian history,
Harvard University
(United States)

4

[In the Soviet Union,] the Communist ego, internationalism and all the rest, has fallen apart, disintegrated. Now these various peoples [in the various Soviet republics] are trying to pick up the pieces and glue something together that works... The problem is the Soviet Union, the Communist Party, Marxism-Leninism. Nationalism [independence of the Soviet republics] is an answer... If someone told us that the peoples of Honduras, British Columbia, Maine and Cuba, for example, should be members of one state, we'd think they were crazy, [yet that same logic prevailed in the Soviet Union].

Los Angeles Times, 10-7:(A)7.

Levon Ter-Petrosyan
President of the Armenian
Soviet Socialist Republic

5

[Calling for power in the Soviet Union to be diffused through the independence of the republics]: For me, the center as a political factor doesn't exist any more. And now it's very dangerous not to use the chance to restructure our internal relations to get rid of the center and to transfer our way of life to structures similar to the European Community. If we again place the Army and KGB and Interior Ministry under central control, we'd be creating the same danger of a catastrophe that we have just lived through.

Interview, Moscow/
The Christian Science Monitor,
8-28:3.

Margaret Thatcher
Prime Minister
of the United Kingdom

1

I am often asked: Can we still do business with [Soviet President Mikhail] Gorbachev? We should not underestimate the future reforming zeal of a man who allowed Eastern Europe to grasp its freedom; who has begun the withdrawal of Soviet troops; accepted arms reduction for the first time; and cut support for Communist insurgencies across the world. We have to go on doing business with him. In the same way, he has to do business with the democratic reformers [in his country] if he is to succeed. The pessimists among you will perhaps reply that the Soviet leader embarked on reform so as not to be left behind by the military buildup and economic progress of the West in the 1980s. I am the last person—or maybe the second to the last person—to deny that these played a major role in Mr. Gorbachev's calculations. We had an economy driven by information technology; he had an economy fueled by vodka! And the very realism that prompted these reforms will persuade him to step up liberalization, if he can, when the present slowing of *perestroika* [reform] pushes the Soviet economy further into crisis, as it must. Perhaps it does not really matter whether the optimists or the pessimists are right. Because optimism and pessimism dictate the same policy. If Mr. Gorbachev remains a reformer at heart, as I believe, he will privately welcome Western pressure for reform and employ it against the hard-liners. If he himself has succumbed to the hard-liners, as others believe, the West's pressure will push him, too, in the direction of reform.
Speech, Washington, March 8/
The Washington Post, 3-19:(A)18.

2

[On her recent removal from office after being ousted as leader of the Conservative Party]: The pattern of my life was fractured. It's like throwing a pane of glass with a complicated map upon it on the floor, and all habits and thoughts and actions that went with it and the staff that went with it . . . You threw it on the floor and it shattered.
Interview, Washington/
Vanity Fair, June:122.

3

[Supporting the British poll tax, which was introduced during her Administration but was replaced after she left office]: If local government comes to rely entirely on subsidies from central government, in other words [to] rely on support from heavy taxes levied on the citizens as a whole, then, eventually, the entire country will go to ruin.
Interview/
Los Angeles Times, 6-14:(A)5.

4

[Saying she will devote her time to promoting democracy and free enterprise in Eastern Europe]: I intend to nurture democratic values in the former Communist states. My aim will be to perpetuate all the kinds of things I believe in. They know what they want to do. They don't know how to do it.
The journalists, June 29/
The Christian Science Monitor,
7-3:6.

Margaret D. Tutwiler
Spokesman for
the Department of State
of the United States

5

[On the ethnic civil war in Yugoslavia]: The continuing use of aggressive force and intimidation against Croatia and Bosnia by the Serbian leadership and its allies in Montenegro and by the Yugoslav military represents the greatest obstacle to a peaceful settlement. These continuing attacks against non-military targets and civilian urban centers are reprehensible.
Washington, Dec. 6/
Los Angeles Times, 12-7:(A)4.

Harry-Elmar Volmer
President, Land Bank,
Estonian Soviet
Socialist Republic

6

[On Estonia's economy as it moves toward independence from the Soviet Union]: We were

251

(HARRY-ELMAR VOLMER)

not prepared for it to happen so fast. We want a market economy, but we don't have the basic laws necessary—a law on bankruptcy or a law on monopolies. Our legislature also has not passed a law on land reform or on ownership. We don't have a free-market economy, we have a bazaar economy.

Los Angeles Times, 9-6:(A)8.

Edward Vorobiev
General, Soviet Armed Forces;
Commander of Soviet forces
in Czechoslovakia

1

[On the forthcoming completion of withdrawal of all Soviet troops from Czechoslovakia]: After signing the [withdrawal] agreement, I will drive my car to the airplane. Then I will drive my car *into* the airplane. I will take off in the airplane. You will never see me here again, unless as a tourist.

To reporters, Prague/
Los Angeles Times, 6-25:(A)4.

Franz Vranitzky
Chancellor of Austria

2

Many Austrians greeted the *Anschluss* [Nazi Germany's 1938 annexation of Austria], supported the [Nazi] regime and upheld many levels of the hierarchy. Many Austrians took part in the repressive measures and persecution [by] the Third Reich, some of them in prominent positions. Even today we cannot brush aside a moral responsibility for the deeds of our citizens. Austrian politicians have always put off making this confession. I would like to do this explicitly, also in the name of the Austrian government, as a measure of the relationship we today must have to our history, as a standard for the political culture of our country.

Before Austrian Parliament,
Vienna, July 8/
The Washington Post, 7-9:(A)12.

Lech Walesa
President of Poland

3

[Calling for wide-ranging immediate elections in Poland]: It is high time that all the elected authorities of the republic originate from the free choice of its citizens. I am convinced that Poland today needs instant elections. One has to put an end to growing disillusion and mistrust of political institutions, including Parliament . . . It's time to reject the outdated contract. It used to be useful, but today it ties up the nation's energy and demoralizes public life.

Letter to Polish Assembly,
March 7/
The New York Times, 3-8:(A)2.

4

[On his asking for U.S. economic aid]: Perhaps it's not good that we require so much from the U.S., but this is the only superpower now left in the battlefield. We are not coming to [the U.S.] to beg; in fact, we want to collaborate. But this revolution we pilot must be successful—in economic as well as political terms . . . So many people would like to squeeze something out of America. But all I want is [American] business. I want [Americans] to participate in a place where something is being created.

Interview, Warsaw, March 14/
The Washington Post,
3-15:(A)41.

5

[On whether being President is what he thought it would be like]: Oh no, it's worse. I knew it would be difficult and ungratifying, but it is worse and even more ungratifying . . . One is President as a punishment because it's too difficult and nothing is arranged. I must say, I don't like it. I'm really surprised to see people who want to fulfill such functions all their lives, but that could be ranked as a political deviation. There are various deviations; one of them is political, but I don't belong to such.

Interview,
Warsaw/
USA Today, 3-14:(A)13.

(LECH WALESA)

1

[On Poland's history of anti-Semitism]: Here in Israel, in the cradle of our culture and the land of your revival, I am asking your forgiveness. I ask for justice on behalf of the Polish people and that you remember the good things as well. We want to build a free Poland for all, regardless of religion or race . . . Let us learn from you.

Before Israeli Knesset (Parliament),
Jerusalem, May 20/
Los Angeles Times, 5-21:(A)1.

2

In almost all the issues as they stand today, we have non-classical times, and therefore the President is non-classic. I'm not fit to be a classic President, either in the first or second class. I do not fit, and I know it. The solutions I apply are not classical either.

Interview/
The New York Times, 5-31:(A)4.

3

[Saying the Polish Presidency should be a more powerful position]: There must be a strong executive, similar to the American or French system; the difficulties of Polish reform make this necessary . . . Democracy as regards elections and selection of people and programs, but then dictator-like decisiveness in carrying them out. There's no place for democracy when you are driving a bus. Imagine being in a bus where everyone wants to grab the steering wheel. The first tree will finish you off.

Interview, Warsaw, Oct. 31/
The Washington Post, 11-1:(A)33.

Vernon A. Walters
United States Ambassador
to Germany

4

[On German reluctance to become involved in foreign conflicts]: I think they understand that if they're going to play an important part in the Europe of tomorrow . . . it's going to be very hard for them to have a position whereby everybody else . . . can send troops in case of an emergency

and they don't . . . [The Germans] haven't been used to leading . . . The very word "Fuhrer" has become a bad word in the German language and it simply means "leader" or "guide." They're coming out of this psychosis.

Interview, Bonn/
The Christian Science Monitor,
3-6:3.

Shirley Williams
Director, Project Liberty,
Kennedy School of Government,
Harvard University
(United States);
Former Member
of British Parliament

5

[On Eastern Europe]: Trying to establish a free market if you have a society which has no sense of what contract is about, no sense of what relationships within a civic society is about, no sense of what law and free organizations are—is not to introduce a free market. You haven't got any of the internal sanctions, the relationships of trust, that we in the West—although they sometimes break down—at least operate under . . . In country after country, [there's] a perception that the great effort to get democracy is running into the ground. If we don't begin to create a civic society in the sense of what civic morality is about, with a sense about consensus creation, the spectrum of parties, different interests being represented through parties, I think this experiment could go badly awry. It's at the moment not doing well. Nobody should sit back and say, "It's likely that there will be flourishing democracies in Eastern Europe." The present bet is that the outcome is authoritarian governments on the right.

Interview, Boston/
The Christian Science Monitor,
4-3:14.

Susan Woodward
Visiting fellow
in foreign policy,
Brookings Institution
(United States)

6

The United States is in a difficult situation because it has been very vocal in calling for rights

(SUSAN WOODWARD)

of self-determination for such Soviet republics as Latvia, Lithuania and Estonia. But where Yugoslavia is concerned, the U.S. emphasis is on supporting the sovereignty and territorial integrity. That causes the various ethnic factions there either to accuse us of a double standard or to exploit what we say for their own purposes.

The Washington Post,
5-17:(A)21.

Alexander N. Yakovlev
Member, Politburo,
Communist Party
of the Soviet Union

1

The very idea of *perestroika* [Soviet reform] refutes and negates socialism of the Soviet type. I've grown disenchanted with Marxism as a framework for concrete action. Marxism had the right, and has a right, to exist as one of many theories of social development for the mid-19th century. But you cannot take this analysis and extrapolate from it a way of living in today's world . . . One should take things from life and adjust them every day. Our whole trouble is that we are inert, we think in dogmas. Even if reality tells us to change things, we always check first in a book. Even now.

Interview, Moscow/
The Washington Post, 8-16:(A)38.

Alexander N. Yakovlev
Adviser to Soviet President
Mikhail S. Gorbachev

2

Democracy [in the Soviet Union] has been installed only in Moscow and Leningrad. One should not believe the central squares of these cities represent the whole of the country. There is a danger of an explosion . . . Personally, I am afraid of a "revolution of empty plates." Any scoundrel capable of raping the nation could use such a situation.

Los Angeles Times, 11-12:(H)5.

3

[On the failed effort to reform Soviet Communism]: While the system completely rejected any attempt at sensible reform, Stalinist obstructions could be crushed only by a powerful ram. [The late Soviet leader Nikita] Khrushchev's direct and brave attack ended in defeat, although [the late Soviet leader Leonid] Brezhnev's refurbishing failed as well. A time of uncertainty settled in, but the outcome was already near and it came in the form of *perestroika* [the recent reform movement instituted by Soviet President Mikhail Gorbachev], elite revolution meant to develop in a peaceful way. Perhaps it couldn't have been otherwise. It was born within the politically active part of the CPSU and the society, and it was here that it encountered the most fierce resistance and rejection.

At conference of Soviet Movement
for Democratic Reforms, December/
The Christian Science Monitor,
12-26:2.

Gennadi I. Yanayev
Acting President
of the Soviet Union

4

[On why he took over the Soviet Presidency from Mikhail Gorbachev in a coup]: The Soviet Union has faced a deep crisis which can call into question further reform and bring major upheavals in the international scene. It is not a secret to anyone that a drastic drop in production, which is not being compensated by alternative economic structures, poses a real threat to further development and survival of the U.S.S.R. nations. The situation has gone out of control in the U.S.S.R. and we are facing a situation of multi-rule. This is a cause of popular discontent. We're also facing a threat of disintegration . . . And normal life under these circumstances is impossible . . . Under the circumstances, we have no other alternative but to take resolute action in order to stop the country from sliding down to a disaster . . . We stand for genuine democratic reforms . . . To do nothing at this crucial period means to take a grave responsibility for tragic, really unpredictable circumstances. Anyone who wants to live and work in

(GENNADI I. YANAYEV)

peace, who does not accept the bloodshed, who wants to see his homeland in prosperity, must take the only right choice.

News conference, Moscow, Aug. 19/
USA Today, 8-20:(A)9.

Boris N. Yeltsin
President, Russian Soviet
Federated Socialist Republic

1

I would say to [Soviet President Mikhail Gorbachev]: For three years, I have asked you, begged you, to lean to your left, rely on the leftist forces. Then the rightist front, which is crowding you right now, would be unable to develop any momentum. Today it is the rightists who would remove you, not the leftists. But then, you recently called the rightists leftists, and the leftists rightists, so now nobody can figure out what you think. I am not claiming your role; I will not be an alternative to you. But from one point I will not retreat: Allow Russia to breathe; give it autonomy. Russia has everything it needs to solve its problems, as long as a doomed system does not interfere.

Telephone call-in/
World Press Review, May:11.

2

Partial reforms [in the Soviet Union], gradual implemented reforms—this will destroy us. The people won't put up with this. When they [Soviet leaders] say that it's logical to stretch reforms over years, this is not for us. That's for a society where a tolerable level of life has been achieved and where people can wait. We have such a critical situation, plus such a massive bureaucratic system, that you have to finish with them not gradually, but radically.

Interview, May/
The New York Times, 6-19:(A)4.

3

[On Soviet President Mikhail Gorbachev]: If he is a reformer, then I am with him. If he holds up

reform, if he stops and goes backwards, if he takes half-hearted decisions, if he pressurizes the republics, including military pressure, I'm his opponent. [But] to a large extent I don't like him, I'm saying he's inconsistent . . . He has strength for a certain period of time and then, under pressure of other forces, he may lose his decision.

Broadcast interview, Washington/
"Nightline," ABC-TV, 6-18.

4

[On his being sworn in as the Russian Republic's first popularly elected President]: Great Russia is rising from its knees. We will turn it into a prosperous, democratic, peaceful, genuinely sovereign, law-abiding state . . . The President is not a god, not a monarch, not a miracle worker. He is a citizen . . . And in Russia, the individual will become the measure of all things . . . For centuries, the interests of the state were put above those of the individual. We were practically the last of the civilized peoples of the world to realize that the strength of the state lies in the well-being of its people.

Inaugural address,
Moscow, July 10/
The Washington Post, 7-11:(A)1,20.

5

[On the coup that just removed Soviet President Mikhail Gorbachev from office]: To the soldiers and officers of the army, the KGB and the Ministry of the Interior troops, countrymen: An attempt to stage a coup d'etat has been made. The President of the country, the Commander-in-Chief of the armed forces of the Soviet Union, has been removed from power. The Vice President, the Chairman of the KGB, the First Deputy of the Chairman of the Council of Defense have formed an unconstitutional body and have hereby committed a grave crime. The country is faced with the threat of terror. The "order," quote, unquote, promised by the self-appointed saviors of the country will create a situation where we will have concentration camps. These are all lies. Soldiers and officers, at this tragic hour I call on you: Don't let yourselves be misled; don't allow adventurists to use you as blind

(BORIS N. YELTSIN)

weapons. Soldiers, I call on you: Think about your loved ones, your friends and your people. At this difficult hour of decision, remember that you have taken an oath to your people . . . Clouds of terror and dictatorship are gathering over Russia, but this night will not be eternal, and our long-suffering people will find its freedom once again, for good.

Speech, Moscow, Aug. 20/
USA Today, 8-21:(A)9.

1

[On Communism in the Soviet Union]: I think this experiment which was conducted on our soil was a tragedy for our people, and it was too bad it happened on our territory. It would have been better if this experiment had been conducted in some small country, at least to make clear it was a stupid idea, although a beautiful one. I think gradually this will come to be understood by other countries.

American question-and-answer broadcast,
Moscow/ABC-TV, 9-5.

2

[On the new commonwealth proclaimed by and made up of the now-independent Russia, Byelorussia and Ukraine]: The main result is as follows: Three [former Soviet] republics that had acted as founders of the U.S.S.R. suspended the process of uncontrolled anarchic disintegration of that common space in which our nations live. The only possible formula was found for the life of the new circumstances: a Commonwealth of Independent States, rather than a state in which no one has independence. The agreement states the fact that the Soviet Union is ceasing to exist, but I reject the accusations against those who signed it alleging that they arbitrarily eliminated the U.S.S.R. The union is incapable of playing a positive role in the relations among its former members any longer. The world community has started to consider it bankrupt. The central bank has announced that it doesn't have anything to

cover its expenditures. Our states, as founders of the union, simply had no right to close their eyes to it. To delay this hard conclusion means to continue to live in a world of illusions, bring catastrophic consequences closer. It was not done to destroy something. Just the opposite: The task was to save everything that is healthy and can be saved, and to build a realistic model of the commonwealth on this basis.

Before Russian Parliament,
Moscow, Dec. 12/
The New York Times, 12-13:(A)8.

Boris N. Yeltsin
President of Russia

3

Russia is gravely ill. The economy is sick. But there are no incurable economic diseases, and today we have far greater possibilities to begin healing . . . I'm certain we will get through this difficult period. It will be hard, but the period will not be long. We are talking of six to eight months. We need patience. We cannot permit a breakdown or panic. Then reform would become impossible . . . It was not Russia that suffered a defeat, but the Communist idea, the experiment which was performed on Russia and which was inflicted on her people.

New Year's broadcast address to
the nation, Moscow, Dec. 29/
The New York Times, 12-30:(A)3.

Jean Ziegler
Professor of sociology,
Geneva University (Switzerland)

4

Switzerland is not a nation—it is a defense organization. As long as Europe [was] torn by war—400 years of the enemy at your doorstop—it all held together. But nowadays there are no enemies, no chaos on the borders, not even any Communists to rally against. Switzerland as a nation is finished.

Interview/
Los Angeles Times, 6-11:(H)5.

The Middle East

Haidar Abdel-Shafi
Leader, Palestinian delegation
to Middle East peace conference
in Madrid

1

[Addressing Israel]: We have seen some of you at your best and at your worst, for the occupier [of Arab lands] can hide no secrets from the occupied, and we are witness to the toll that occupation has exacted from you and yours. We have seen you anguish over the transformation of your sons and daughters into instruments of a blind and violent occupation, and we are sure that at no time did you envisage such a role for the children whom you thought would forge your future. We have seen you look back in deepest sorrow at the tragedy of your past and look on in horror at the disfigurement of the victim turned oppressor. Not for this have you nurtured your hopes, dreams and your offspring.

At Middle East peace conference,
Madrid, Oct. 31/
The Washington Post, 11-1:(A)36.

2

The issue [in the Arab-Israeli conflict] is land [occupied by Israel], and what is at stake here is the survival of the Palestinian people on what is left of our olive groves and orchards, our terraced hills and peaceful valleys, our ancestral homes, villages and cities. International legitimacy demands the restoration of the illegally occupied Arab and Palestinian lands to their rightful owners. Israel must recognize the concept of limits—political, legal, moral and territorial—and must decide to join the community of nations by accepting the terms of international law and the will of the international community. No amount of circumlocution or self-deception can alter that fact.

At Middle East peace conference,
Madrid, Nov. 1/
The New York Times,
11-2:5.

Yossi Ahimeir
Chief of Staff
to Israeli Prime Minister
Yitzhak Shamir

3

[Criticizing what he says is U.S. linkage of $10-billion in loan guarantees with Israeli cessation of new Jewish settlements in the occupied Arab territories]: Their bottom line was: "If you want the guarantees . . . you will stall all activities in the Golan Heights, Judea, Samaria and Gaza." We reject such a condition. It means handcuffs on Israeli hands on the whole Israeli approach to the territories.

The Christian Science Monitor,
9-20:7.

Bakhtiar Amin
Secretary general,
Kurdish Institute (France)

4

[Criticizing the U.S. Bush Administration for urging Iraqi Kurds to rise up against Iraqi President Saddam Hussein and then doing nothing to come to the aid of the Kurds when Hussein's forces began what some call genocide against them]: History is repeating itself. The [Bush] Administration encouraged the Iraqi people to rise up against the tyrannical regime and called Saddam Hussein the new Hitler. Now they [the U.S.] have turned their back on us and given a green light to the regime to massacre the people.

The New York Times, 4-5:(A)6.

Abdul Amir Anbari
Iraqi Ambassador/
Permanent Representative
to the United Nations

5

[On charges that Iraq has an on-going nuclear-weapons program and is hiding it from UN investigators]: We have cooperated with all United Nations agencies, commissions and missions, and we have done so particularly with the

WHAT THEY SAID IN 1991

commission entrusted with the task of destroying mass-destruction weapons . . . Iraq will continue to cooperate. We have made our commitment.

Before UN Security Council,
New York, June 26/
Los Angeles Times, 6-27:(A)12.

Yasir Arafat
Chairman, Palestine
Liberation Organization

1

We appreciated [U.S. President Bush's earlier] talk of [Israel] exchanging territories for peace [with the Arabs], withdrawal of Israel from the occupied territories. But during the meeting with [French] President [Francois] Mitterrand last month, he changed what he had said before [the U.S.] Congress. No, Bush told Mitterrand, on the self-determination of the Palestinian people; no, on the independent [Palestinian] state; no, on the role of the PLO; no, for the international conference . . . And now what is the U.S. proposing? They propose a two-track solution: Normalization of relations between Israel and the Arab states including, maybe, a new Camp David, to find not *the* but *a* solution [to the Palestinian question], some kind of autonomy or self-government, a Middle Eastern Bantustan, a "condominium" between Jordan, Israel and Palestine . . . It's not that I reject it; it can't work . . . No Arab state will be able to talk with Israel as long as the Palestinian issue is not resolved.

Interview, Tunis, Tunisia, April/
Los Angeles Times, 4-14:(M)5.

2

[Saying the U.S. efforts for peace in the Middle East following the recent Persian Gulf war should not ignore the Palestinians]: No one can hide the sun with his finger. No one can say no for the self-determination for 6.5-million Palestinians . . . You [the U.S.] have done all this big military operation to protect 300,000 Kuwaitis [from Iraqi occupation]. Why not do the same to protect the Palestinians from the

daily massacres, from the daily oppression, from the discrimination, from the aggressions they are facing from the Israeli army, from the Israeli armed settlers.

Interview, Tunis, Tunisia/
Los Angeles Times, 7-6:(A)16.

3

[Saying Israel must not have veto power over whom the Palestinians send to represent themselves at the possible forthcoming Arab-Israeli peace talks]: We have appreciated [U.S.] President Bush's initiative [for the talks] from the beginning, and I'm repeating my appreciation again for the same initiative and for the new initiative declared by President Bush and [Soviet President Mikhail] Gorbachev to hold very soon the peace conference. But I have the right to ask the whole international public opinion: With whom are you going to make peace if there is no place for Palestinians at the table of negotiations?

Interview, Tunis, Tunisia, Aug. 2/
Los Angeles Times, 8-3:(A)17.

4

[Criticizing Israel's refusal to have the PLO take part in proposed Arab-Israeli peace negotiations]: I want the same terms as being given to the other participants because the Palestinians are the main factor in the Middle East peach equation. It's a matter of principle. Why are only the Palestinians treated in this way? Would Israel accept if I only wanted to deal with the [Israeli] Peace Now movement, not the [Israeli] Likud government?

Interview, Tunis, Tunisia, Aug. 6/
The New York Times, 8-7:(A)4.

5

[On splits among members of the Palestine National Council]: Dear brothers, we are facing a catastrophe, and what weapons do we have? Do you want me to send bombs? I have no bombs. Do you want me to send missiles? I have no missiles. Do you want me to send chemical weapons? I have no chemical weapons. May God help us, the only missile I can give to my

(YASIR ARAFAT)

people, the only bomb I can give to my people, is your unity, your unity, your unity.

At Palestine National Council conference/
Los Angeles Times, 10-3:(A)15.

Moshe Arens
Minister of Defense of Israel

1

I think the source of greatest danger to the [Middle East] area has been the tremendous influx of arms. If countries like France, and I must add the United States, will continue to sell the most advanced type of weaponry to the Arab armies, then I think peace and stability are really very far away from us in the Middle East. If, on the other hand, the world understands that the first agreement that needs to be reached is an agreement among the arms-exporting countries that they will not export arms into the Middle East, then I think we will have taken a big step ahead.

February/
Los Angeles Times, 3-5:(H)1.

2

We have a new order in this part of the world, and it isn't a good order at all, because the Syrians are in the process of swallowing up Lebanon and, in effect, putting an end to Lebanese sovereignty. If this new order, in quotation marks, will bring about a worsening of the security situation, a danger to the civilian population in the northern part of Israel, then this is certainly something that we don't intend to live with.

May 22/
Los Angeles Times, 5-23:(A)16.

3

We have just seen how dangerous it is when a Middle East dictator [Iraqi President Saddam Hussein in the recent Persian Gulf war] gets his hands on a very large military machine. It took the United States and its allies—and a deployment of troops that took five months to put into place—to deal with that danger. So we in Israel

ask ourselves, what would have happened if Saddam Hussein had gone for Israel and not for Kuwait? He's not the only dictator in the area that has a large army. Today, I suppose the Syrians have the fourth-largest army in the world. I would say the most important step that should be taken is that weapons are not sold to dictators in this area. If you can't bring about a cessation, something I have suggested, you ought to bring about a reduction.

Interview, July/
Los Angeles Times, 7-16:(H)7.

Hanan Ashrawi
Palestinian representative at
Middle East peace conference
in Madrid

4

[On her return from the Middle East peace conference just concluded in Madrid]: There is spirit, enthusiasm, happiness and strength. After Madrid, we have to start a new phase. We have to start preparing for peace; we have to start to end the [Israeli] occupation [of Arab territory] and approach each other as equal human beings.

Jericho, Israeli-occupied
West Bank, Nov. 10/
The Washington Post, 11-11:(A)24.

Hafez al-Assad
President of Syria

5

[Criticizing the idea that Israel needs to hold on to some Arab territory for security reasons]: Will the map of the universe change according to the needs of each party in the world? If in order to guarantee its security Israel requires certain territory from Syria, and Syria sees that its security requires certain territory from Turkey, and Turkey needs for its own security some territory from the Soviet Union, and the Soviet Union from China, and the United States from Canada or Mexico, will the world approve, and be a stable world? Our territories do not exist so that Israel can take control of them for Israeli security. To call these territories "occupied" means the occupier should leave them. We have never grown accustomed nor shall we get used to

(HAFEZ AL-ASSAD)

the idea of giving our land to others. Without the return of territory, there is no peace. If the Arabs agreed to relinquish territory, it wouldn't mean peace but capitulation. We have not capitulated at any time in history. We were beaten, but we never capitulated. We never lost the will to preserve and regain our rights. If Israel is not going to quit the occupied land, when then should we want peace?

Interview, Damascus, July/
Newsweek, 8-5:20.

1

[On Arab terrorism]: The important thing is what is meant by terrorism. If it means committing a murder, for example, just for killing, for blackmail, for a fraud, then this is terrorism as we understand it. But if you mean the militants who fight for the liberty and independence of their country and for the liberation of their land, then it is a different thing. Those were not terrorists. They are patriots and militants. Palestinians, Lebanese and Syrians are people whose land is occupied. Will they give up their identity and land and homes without fighting for them? They do what was done by all people who were colonized. Acts such as kidnapping or hijacking or shooting down airplanes or murdering individuals in Europe and elsewhere have nothing to do with the struggle for peoples' rights. Such acts, indeed, serve the aims of the occupiers. We condemn terrorism.

Interview, Damascus, July/
Newsweek, 8-5:21.

Tarik Aziz
Foreign Minister of Iraq

2

[Saying his country, in the wake of its loss to U.S.-led forces in the Persian Gulf war, is committed to democracy]: We know we have made mistakes, which is bound to happen when you are in power that long [the Baath Party has ruled for 23 years]. But we think [Iraqi President] Saddam Hussein is popular enough to be elected and the people will give us the chance to carry on the

leadership in these difficult times. Besides, there is no concrete alternative.

Interview, Baghdad/
The Washington Post, 5-8:(A)1.

James A. Baker III
Secretary of State
of the United States

3

It is important that Palestinians . . . clearly and unequivocally demonstrate that they are committed to peace if they want to play a role in the search for peace . . . The PLO, in supporting [Iraqi President] Saddam Hussein [in the current Persian Gulf war], made the wrong choice. By doing that, the PLO signaled that it prefers confrontation to peace.

Before Senate Foreign Relations
Committee, Washington, Feb. 7/
Los Angeles Times, 2-8:(A)9.

4

We think it is reasonable, in the aftermath of [the Persian Gulf war, in which U.S.-led forces drove Iraq out of Kuwait], to approach the [Arab-Israeli] peace process from both sides of it. That is, from the Arab state-Israel side and from the Israel-Palestinian dialogue side. As you know, we have spent quite a bit of time early on trying to work to bring about an Israeli-Palestinian dialogue. That is still a very, very important component of the over-all process as we see it, but we don't think that either of these two tracks are mutually exclusive of the other, and that it would not be unreasonable, or unrealistic, to think that we could try and approach the peace process on this dual track . . . Let me give you a for-instance: It may be that both sides might have some interest in exploring confidence-building measures of some sort—an approach that was used in Europe with some degree of success. That doesn't take it all the way to recognition [of Israel by the Arabs] or to sitting down in formal negotiations, or anything like that; but all I am saying is that I think it is appropriate, given what's happened in the region, to look at both sides of the equation as far as the peace process is concerned.

To reporters, enroute to Middle East,
March 7/The New York Times, 3-8:(A)6.

(JAMES A. BAKER III)

1

[On his efforts to bring about a lessening of the Arab-Israeli conflict]: We do not intend to engage in what some have referred to as pressure [on Israel]. We intend to reason, to cajole, to plead and to offer our good offices to see if we can seize this opportunity and make progress for peace . . . The United States is willing to do the hard, nitty-gritty, repetitive work that will clearly be involved if we're going to make progress.

News conference,
Jerusalem, March 11/
Los Angeles Times, 3-12:(A)8.

2

[Saying signs from Israel and her Middle East enemies could indicate an Arab-Israeli peace agreement may be possible]: Now, maybe you don't think that's progress. And maybe it isn't, and maybe the wheels will come off, but let's give it a chance. I think all countries involved on all sides really want to try to seize this opportunity, if possible, to make progress. [But] nobody can impose peace . . . if the parties to the conflict don't want real, true reconciliation.

News conference, March 14/
The Washington Post, 3-15:(A)36.

3

[After visiting Kurdish refugees who are fleeing the Iraqi military's attacks on them following the uprising of Kurdish rebels against Iraqi President Saddam Hussein]: Today we have witnessed the suffering and despair of the Kurdish people. We have seen examples of cruelty and human anguish that really do defy description. Our relief efforts, including air drops of supplies, have begun, but they alone are not going to be enough. So the international community has to respond quickly and effectively . . . You will now have a major humanitarian relief effort undertaken by the international community, and it is hoped that the presence of humanitarian relief workers will act as a deterrent to future harassment and persecution of these people.

News conference,
Cukurca, Turkey, April 8/
The New York Times, 4-9:(A)4.

4

[On the proposed Arab-Israeli conference aimed at settling their conflicts, which the Arabs want called an "international conference" and the Israelis want called a "regional meeting"]: Do you know what's important here? Substance. Substance is important, not form. Names are not as important as whether or not there is truly a desire on the part of the parties to this conflict to seek true reconciliation. [But] in the Middle East, process and substance are the same thing.

News conference,
Damascus, Syria, April 12/
Los Angeles Times, 4:13:(A)6.

5

[Saying he still hopes that an Arab-Israeli peace conference can be arranged]: We are going to make another trip to the Middle East . . . I have reason to think that we should continue this effort, that it is worth continuing, and that there is some chance that we might be successful. We are still talking about a conference that would see direct face-to-face discussions and negotiations between Israel and each of its neighboring Arab states, as well as direct face-to-face discussions and negotiations between Israel and the Palestinians. And, in that sense, it would be a very, very broad conference of a nature and type that has never before taken place.

To reporters, Washington, May 5/
The New York Times, 5-7:(A)7.

6

Nothing has made my job of trying to find Arab and Palestinian partners for Israel more difficult than being greeted by a new [Jewish] settlement [in Israeli-occupied Arab territories] every time I arrive. I don't think that there is any bigger obstacle to peace than the settlement activity that continues not only unabated but at an enhanced pace . . . Every time I have gone to Israel in connection with the peace process, on each of my four trips, I have been met with the announcement of new settlement activity. This does violate United States policy. It's the first thing that Arab governments, the first thing the Palestinians in the territories—whose situation is

(JAMES A. BAKER III)

really quite desperate—raise with us when we talk to them. The Arabs and the Palestinians, of course, argue that this proves that the Israeli government is not interested in negotiating outcomes, but it's really interested in creating facts on the ground. And it substantially weakens our hand in trying to bring about a peace process and creates quite a predicament.

Before House Foreign Operations Subcommittee, Washington, May 22/ The New York Times, 5-23:(A)4.

1

[On the current Middle East peace conference in Madrid]: The United States is willing to be a catalytic force, an energizing force and a driving force in the negotiating process. The United States is and will be an honest broker. We have our own positions and views on the peace process, and we will not forego our right to state those views. But as an honest broker, with experience—successful experience—in Middle East negotiations, we also know that our critical contribution will often be to exert quiet, behind-the-scenes influence and persuasion. We will do our part. But we cannot do your [Arabs' and Israelis'] part as well. The United States and the Soviet Union will provide encouragement, advice, recommendations, proposals and views to help the peace process. None of this . . . will relieve you—the parties—of the obligation of making peace. Because if you don't do it, we certainly can't.

At Middle East peace conference, Madrid, Nov. 1/ Los Angeles Times, 11-2:(A)5.

Amatzia Baram
Authority on the Middle East, Haifa University (Israel)

2

[Saying that, despite Iraq's defeat in the recent Persian Gulf war, Israel doesn't want a democracy there]: If Iraq becomes a democracy, it will be an anti-Israeli democracy.

Newsweek, 4-15:29.

Tahseen Bashir
Former Egyptian Ambassador/ Permanent Representative to the United Nations

3

The volcano [of the recent Persian Gulf war] only lasted with a few days of war, and it ended in less than 100 hours. But now the whole landscape [of the Arab world] is changing. The stability of the Arab world today is being kept not from month to month but almost from day to day. What will happen to Jordan? What will happen to Kuwait? We ended a world system in the Middle East, but we have not yet established a new system, and what is being done is being done ad hoc, piece by piece. It is not now as dramatic or explosive as the war, but its impact on the human beings who live here will be graver. Each country in the Middle East is trying to save its own skin. The Arabs have not yet managed to recoup or regroup. We are living in a fractured Arab world, and in every fracture there are new problems.

Los Angeles Times, 7-30:(H)1.

Yosef Ben-Aharon
Director General, Office of the Prime Minister of Israel

4

[On the current move by some major Arab countries toward peace talks with Israel]: I don't believe they have given up their vendetta [against Israel]. They have shifted tactics and are making a bid for the heart, soul and mind of the United States—in order to drive a wedge between the U.S. and Israel. If the illusion is created that the U.S. has made a switch and is disengaging from Israel, it will create unreal expectations . . . We haven't yet succeeded in impressing on our Arab neighbors the logic of defeat on the battlefield. They cannot come to the table demanding the spoils [Israeli occupied Arab lands] of wars they started, as if they are the victims.

Interview, Jerusalem/ Los Angeles Times, 8-13:(H)3.

Joseph R. Biden, Jr.
United States Senator,
D-Delaware

1

[On his plan to halt or limit the sale of arms to the Middle East through formal cooperation among Western suppliers]: What we are proposing today is the creation of a cartel very different from OPEC. It would be a benign cartel, enabling the arms-producing nations to limit supplies, not for purposes of profit but indeed to forgo profit—in order to build peace and stability in a region that for decades has seen precious little of either.

May 14/
The Washington Post, 5-15:(A)24.

Hans Blix
Director General,
International Atomic
Energy Commission

2

[On Iraq's disclosures about its atomic-energy capabilities]: . . . we cannot be sure that the information they gave of having enriched about half a kilogram of uranium . . . is full disclosure. But I can say if a country has mastered the technique of enriching uranium, it's only a matter of time before they can make a bomb, and Iraq has mastered that technique.

American broadcast interview,
Vienna/"Today" show, NBC-TV, 7:26.

Hyman Bookbinder
Former Washington
representative,
American Jewish Committee

3

[On U.S. President Bush's desire to delay guarantees for $10-billion in loans to Israel pending a proposed Arab-Israeli peace conference, loans that would be used to finance Jewish settlements in occupied Arab lands]: We have to understand the limitation of our own power [as pro-Israel lobbyists in Washington]. The lobby has slowed up some arms sales to Arabs . . . But if the President of the United States goes to the American people and says "Enough, already," the Israeli lobby can't counteract that.

Los Angeles Times, 9-30:(A)16.

Richard A. Boucher
Deputy Spokesman for
the Department of State
of the United States

4

[On Iraq's reluctance to supply all information on its various military capabilities in response to UN demands following the recent Persian Gulf war]: The pattern throughout has been that Iraq has admitted to additional [military] facilities and capabilities only under the pressure of international inspections, and then only in a piecemeal fashion. In recent inspections, for example, Iraq admitted to having undeclared nuclear material, to having the "supergun" . . . to having a much larger number of chemical munitions and to having a biological-weapons research program for both offensive and defensive purposes. Based on the pattern of Iraqi behavior, there is every reason to believe that they have not yet disclosed all their capabilities.

Aug. 15/Los Angeles Times, 8-16:(A)16.

Faris Bouhafa
Director of public affairs,
Arab-American Institute
(United States)

5

What I think has happened is that over the weeks and months it took to put the [U.S.-led coalition fighting Iraq's invasion and take-over of Kuwait] together, there has been a gradual breakdown of one basic stereotype—that the Arab world is a monolithic region, basically anti-Western and hostile to American interests. Americans, I think, are beginning to understand that the Arab world is a diverse region with diverse interests and diverse leaders and diverse people, only some of which fit the stereotype. That is one of the positive spinoffs from this war. American interests are the same as Arab interests. Most Americans used to think of the Middle East only in terms of what's good or bad for Israel. They reacted to events as they affected Israel. Now they seem to be asking what's good or bad for the United States, Saudi Arabia, Kuwait? That's a big change, and it's as it should be. All countries, including Israel, should have equal status and equal importance.

Los Angeles Times, 2-12:(H)4.

Linda Brady
Professor of international affairs,
Georgia Institute
of Technology

1

The Middle East needs a security arrangement among countries. It could work much as NATO did in Europe during the Cold War. The U.S. should have no long-term military presence in the area. It would be destabilizing. A number of Persian Gulf states already belong to the Gulf Cooperation Council. But it's had serious problems with military cooperation. The GCC can work only if, in addition to the Gulf states, Egypt becomes a member. The U.S. role can only be encouragement and support.

USA Today, 2-28:(A)4.

George Bush
President of the United States

2

All of us know the depth of bitterness that has made the dispute between Israel and its neighbors so painful and intractable. Yet, in the conflict just concluded [the Persian Gulf war against Iraq], Israel and many of the Arab states have for the first time found themselves confronting the same aggressor [Iraqi President Saddam Hussein]. By now, it should be plain to all parties that peace-making in the Middle East requires compromise. At the same time, peace brings real benefits to everyone. We must do all that we can to close the gap between Israel and the Arab states—and between Israelis and Palestinians. The tactics of terror lead nowhere. There can be no substitute for diplomacy. A comprehensive peace must be grounded in United Nations Security Council Resolutions 242 and 338 and the principle of territory for peace. This principle must be elaborated to provide for Israel's security and recognition, and at the same time for legitimate Palestinian political rights. Anything else would fail the twin tests of fairness and security. The time has come to put an end to Arab-Israeli conflict.

Before joint session
of U.S. Congress,
Washington, March 6/
The Washington Post, 3-7:(A)32.

3

[Calling for better relations with Iran]: We have no animosity . . . Sometimes, when you have deep divisions, it takes a little more time. So we're not pressing Iran on bilateral relations. But Iran is a big country. I don't think they should be treated forever as enemies by all the countries in the region.

Interview, Washington, March 8/
The Washington Post, 3-14:(A)33.

4

I've said over and over again I'd like to see improved relations with Iran. They know what our bottom line is, and our bottom line is those [U.S.] hostages [long being held by Middle East terrorists]. I am not going to forget those Americans that are held hostage. And I'm not suggesting Iran holds them. But I am suggesting Iran could have a great deal of influence in getting them out of there.

News conference,
Washington, April 16/
The Washington Post, 4-17:(A)27.

5

[Saying Iraqi President Saddam Hussein is withholding information on his country's nuclear-weapons capabilities]: Saddam Hussein's continuation of lying and trying to go forward with some nuclear capability—that is a cause for alarm all over the world . . . There has been incontrovertible evidence presented to the United Nations Security Council that the man is lying and cheating. I can tell you I am still . . . very much concerned about his intentions—with reason. I'm not just thinking that way. I have evidence to back it up.

News conference,
Rambouillet, France, July 14/
Los Angeles Times, 7-15:(A)6.

6

[On the proposed Arab-Israeli peace conference]: We know that the Israelis are studying our proposal seriously. We hope that they will respond favorably to this historic opportunity for

(GEORGE BUSH)

peace and security. I know the Palestinians are closely examining their choices. Here, too, I would ask only that they do everything possible to take advantage of this unprecedented situation to attain their legitimate rights, and at the same time further the cause of peace. I will go the extra mile, walk the extra distance to try to bring . . . lasting peace, long-sought-for peace, to this troubled corner of the world. In the Middle East, as in Lebanon, our objective remains a peace that is fair to all parties, a peace that promotes the security of our friends and true stability in the region.

At Antiochian Orthodox Christian
convention, Arlington, Va., July 25/
The Washington Post, 7-26:(A)29.

1

A few days ago, I asked Congress to defer consideration for 120 days of Israel's request for $10-billion in additional U.S. loan guarantees meant to help Israel absorb its many new immigrants. I did so in the interests of peace . . . A good deal of confusion surrounds this request for deferral, confusion that I'd like to try to clear up. Let me begin by making clear what my request for delay is not about. It's not about the strength of my or this country's support for immigration to Israel. Both as Vice President and President, I've tried my hardest to do everything possible to liberate Jews living in Ethiopia and the Soviet Union, so that they could immigrate to Israel. Today, in no small part due to American efforts, hundreds of thousands of people are now living in Israel, able at last to live free of fear, free to practice their faith. Nor should our request for delay be viewed as an indication that there exists any question in my mind about the need for a strong and secure Israel. For more than 40 years the United States has been Israel's closest friend in the world. And this remains the case and will as long as I am President of the United States. This is a friendship backed up with real support . . . My request that Congress delay consideration of the Israeli request for $10-billion in new loan guarantees to support immigrant absorption is about peace. For the first time in

history, the vision of Israelis sitting with their Arab neighbors to talk peace is a real prospect. Nothing should be done that might interfere with this prospect . . . Quite simply, a 120-day delay [to allow Arab-Israeli peace talks to begin without interference] is not too much for a President to ask for with so much in the balance. We must give peace a chance; we must give peace every chance.

News conference,
Washington, Sept. 12/
The New York Times, 9-13:(A)4.

2

[Calling on the UN to repeal its 1975 resolution equating Zionism with racism]: To equate Zionism with the intolerable sin of racism is to twist history and forget the terrible plight of Jews in World War II and, indeed, throughout history. To equate Zionism with racism is to reject Israel itself, a member in good standing of the United Nations. This body cannot claim to seek peace and at the same time challenge Israel's right to exist. By repealing this resolution unconditionally, the United Nations will enhance its credibility and serve the cause of peace.

At United Nations,
New York, Sept. 23/
Los Angeles Times, 9-24:(A)1.

3

[After his defeat in the recent Persian Gulf war, Iraqi President] Saddam [Hussein] continues to rebuild his weapons of mass destruction and subject the Iraqi people to brutal repression. Saddam's contempt for UN resolutions was first demonstrated back in August of 1990 [when Iraq invaded Kuwait], and it continues even as I am speaking. His government refuses to permit unconditional helicopter inspections [of his weapons systems] and right now is refusing to allow UN inspectors to leave inspected premises with documents relating to an Iraqi nuclear-weapons program . . . We cannot compromise for a moment in seeing that Iraq destroys all of its weapons of mass destruction and the means to deliver them, and we will not compromise. This is not to say—and let me be clear on this one—

(GEORGE BUSH)

that we should punish the Iraqi people. Let me repeat: Our argument has never been with the people of Iraq. It was and is with a brutal dictator whose arrogance dishonors the Iraqi people.

At United Nations, New York,
Sept. 23/The New York Times, 9-24:(A)6.

1

[On the current Middle East peace conference in Madrid]: Our objective must be clear and straightforward. It is not simply to end the state of war [between the Arabs and Israel] and replace it with a state of belligerency. This is not enough. This would not last. Rather, we seek peace. Real peace. And by real peace I mean treaties, security, diplomatic relations, economic relations, trade, investment, cultural exchange, even tourism. What we seek is a Middle East where vast resources are no longer devoted to armaments; a Middle East where young people no longer have to dedicate and all too often give their lives to combat; a Middle East no longer victimized by fear and terror; a Middle East where normal men and women lead normal lives.

At Middle East peace conference,
Madrid, Oct. 30/
The Washington Post, 10-31:(A)35.

Dick Cheney
Secretary of Defense
of the United States

2

[Saying the U.S. should sell conventional arms to allies in the Middle East following the recent victory in getting Iraq out of Kuwait]: . . . I think our first concern ought to be to work with our friends and allies to see to it that they're secure. The policy we're pursuing now is one in which we want to minimize the U.S. military presence on the ground in the region. It's probably easier to do if we help out friends like the Saudis and the [Persian] Gulf states to have sufficient capability to be able to defend themselves long enough for us to be able to get back [if necessary].

Before House Foreign Affairs Committee,
Washington, March 19/
The New York Times, 3-20:(A)7.

Alfonse M. D'Amato
United States Senator,
R-New York

3

[Challenging U.S. secretary of State James Baker's comments that there was no greater obstacle to Arab-Israeli peace than Israel's permitting more Jewish settlements in the occupied territories]: Mr. Secretary, is the settlement activity more of a threat to peace than Syria's recent receipt of North Korean Scud missiles? More than the state of war that Arab nations have maintained against Israel since its inception? More than the continued refusal of Syria, Jordan, Saudi Arabia, Kuwait and all the other Arab states, except Egypt, to recognize and negotiate directly with Israel?

At Senate Foreign Operations
Subcommittee hearing,
Washington, May 23/
The New York Times, 5-24:(A)3.

Edward P. Djerejian
Assistant Secretary of State
of the United States

4

We've had a long-standing concern about Iran's nuclear intentions. The United States engages in no nuclear cooperation with Iran, and we have urged other nuclear suppliers, including China, to adopt a similar policy . . . We have been in touch with a number of potential nuclear suppliers [to warn] that engaging in any form of nuclear cooperation with Iran, whether under safeguards or not, is highly imprudent.

Before House Foreign Affairs subcommittee,
Washington, Nov. 20/
Los Angeles Times, 11-21:(A)4.

Stuart E. Eizenstat
Former Assistant
to the President
of the United States
(Jimmy Carter)
for Domestic Policy

5

[On the U.S. Bush Administration's desire to delay guarantees for $10-billion in loans to Israel pending a proposed Arab-Israeli peace con-

(STUART E. EIZENSTAT)

ference, loans that would be used to finance Jewish settlements in occupied Arab lands]: This is not just a typical flashpoint in U.S.-Israeli relations of the kind every [U.S.] President has. This one is over a basic policy disagreement that has been there since 1967—a fundamental difference over trading land for peace. The United States believes in that; the [Israeli Prime Minister Yitzhak] Shamir government does not . . . It is going to be a continuing and major source of problems.

Los Angeles Times, 9-30:(A)16.

Mohammed Hussein Fadlallah
Spiritual Leader of Hezbollah,
pro-Iranian Lebanese faction

1

[On recent indications that Lebanese terrorist groups may be ready to release Western hostages they hold]: If the drama of the captives ends and that problem is settled, America will feel liberated from its own constraints and can then move with new givens. America is still fighting Iran economically through hidden wars. Because of its binding political discourse, the United States cannot come forth with gestures of warmth [toward Iran]. I imagine that the ploys of hostage-dealing have been exhausted and everyone is looking for a way out, and the climate seems appropriate.

Interview, Beirut, Aug. 8/
The Washington Post, 8-9:(A)1,25.

Abraham H. Foxman
National director,
Anti-defamation League
of B'nai B'rith (United States)

2

[On U.S. President Bush's desire to delay guarantees for $10-billion in loans to Israel pending a proposed Arab-Israeli peace conference, loans that would be used to finance Jewish settlements in occupied Arab lands]: The reflexive reaction of many Americans to support Israel on the grounds of opposition to the Soviet Union no longer applies [since the Soviet Union has lost its

superpower status]. [And] in the light of the [recent Persian] Gulf war and progress toward a peace conference, there is a perception [by many Americans] that the Arabs are not necessarily the same bad guys as they have been . . . [President Bush] takes Israel's settlement policy personally . . . and to think that he won't exert his influence is to fool one's self. I think American policy is flawed . . . Up until now, America has been like Israel's brother. But when your brother starts undercutting your negotiating position, that hurts.

Los Angeles Times, 9-30:(A)16.

Graham Fuller
Middle East specialist,
Rand Corporation
(United States)

3

Ever since he came to power, [Syrian President Hafez] Assad's interests have not been fulfilled by going the peaceful route. What Syria got out of being the leader of the hell-no crowd—oil money, leadership of the Palestinian cause and Soviet arms—made him a dominant force for 15 years. Now, for the first time, Syria is benefiting more from peace than from controlled confrontation, and to me that is the real revolution in Syrian thinking.

The New York Times, 8-14:(A)6.

Gad Gilbar
Economist, Haifa University
(Israel)

4

[On the long-time Arab economic boycott of Israel]: In the beginning, the idea was, if you can't destroy Israel politically or militarily, let's try to strangle Israel economically. If this is the aim, it has not been achieved. On the contrary, Israel has over the years become—true, with enormous aid—one of the more developed countries of the world, with a very solid beginning of sophisticated industries, many of which the Arabs, with all their money, do not have. The boycott did not achieve anything near to destroying the Israeli economy. But who knows what would have happened if the Israeli economy would not have been faced with the boycott?

Los Angeles Times, 5-22:(A)14.

Edward W. Gnehm, Jr.
United States Ambassador
to Kuwait
1

[On possible changes in Kuwait's political system following the U.S.-led victory over Iraqi forces who were occupying Kuwait]: The U.S. is a country founded on democracy and principles of public participation, and it is going to stand strongly on those principles here and everywhere . . . We don't care if they call it a Parliament or a National Assembly, we don't care if they call the head of state an emir, as long as [the Kuwaiti] people indeed have a right to participate in the government.

The Washington Post, 3-5:(A)17.

2

[Kuwait is] the one country in the [Persian] Gulf with a constitution, that has had a parliament and several elections, and that has said it will have new parliamentary elections next year. There is more political debate going on today amongst Kuwaitis than in every other country in the region put together. That's where we want Kuwait to be and that's where we want Kuwait to go. It's worth helping a country trying to go in that direction . . . They were very disappointed with the support they got [during the recent Persian Gulf war] from some of their Arab brethren, like the Jordanians and the North Africans. So they are now more cautious than ever. Their close friends were in America, Britain and other coalition countries that were willing to send troops here and die for them. I don't think they'll ever forget that.

Interview, Kuwait City/
USA Today, 7-29:(A)9.

Mikhail S. Gorbachev
President of the Soviet Union
3

We have restored diplomatic relations with Israel. Now that deep-rooted democratic changes are taking place in our country and in the world and now that a real process toward settling the Middle East crisis is getting underway, the absence of relations with Israel was becoming

senseless. We hope and will try to make sure that this will be of benefit to the peoples of our two countries and the entire Arab world. Peace in the Middle and Near East would benefit all.

At Middle East peace conference,
Madrid, Oct. 30/
The Washington Post, 10-31:(A)35.

Mouloud Hamrouche
Prime Minister of Algeria
4

The Arab world has no answers to contemporary problems. It is at an impasse. There's no democracy, no freedom of expression. Regimes can maintain order, yes. But what is the societal base of these regimes? Today we want to build real power on the basis of the popular will.

U.S. News & World Report,
1-21:23.

David Hartman
Director, Shalom Hartman Institute
for Jewish Studies
(Israel)
5

[On new Arab overtures for peace talks with Israel]: For [Israeli Prime Minister Yitzhak] Shamir, this is the most difficult moment. On the one hand, he knows he can't say no to the peace process without demoralizing his own nation, alienating the Americans and inviting another [Arab-Israeli] war. On the other, he feels he can't trust the Arabs or the Americans. And finally, he's afraid that if he says yes, he'll be selling out the sacred trust he is supposed to defend. This is not a man who wants to make history, but he can't get away from this dilemma.

The Washington Post, 7-24:(A)24.

Hassan ibn Talal
Crown Prince of Jordan
6

[On the Middle East after the U.S.-led military victory in the recent war against Iraq's occupation of Kuwait]: I am very worried for the year ahead if we're going to go back to business as usual. By that, I mean massive purchases of

(HASSAN IBN TALAL)

weapons as the sole manifestation of dealing with the outside world. The issue has to be addressed; otherwise, any leader in this part of the world will consider it his right to put together an arsenal. We'll be back in another confrontation in a decade.

Interview, Amman/
USA Today, 3-4:(A)9.

political prisoners and common criminals. There has been systematic torture. There has been the arrest of non-violent political dissenters. There has been persecution of ethnic minorities, such as the Kurds, and of Syrians. We've seen use of chemical weapons against civilian populations in Kurdistan and elsewhere. It's a horrendous record.

Interview/
USA Today, 2-12:(A)11.

Khaled Hassan
Member, Palestine Liberation
Organization

1

[Criticizing the way the U.S. is handling Palestinian participation in the proposed Arab-Israeli peace talks]: We [Palestinians] have rights. The Americans are refusing to give us any of the rights they practice around the globe, including in the Soviet Union, when the Soviet Union was a country. All your ideas about human rights, when it comes to the Palestinian people, you keep silent. Why? God knows. Now America is the superpower. That means the leader of the world. A leader without ethics is not a leader, it's a jungle. Now we're living in a jungle . . . Give me one point to be optimistic. I am known as a moderate. I am known as a man of western thinking. Give me one point of justice . . . This [peace] conference is not for the Palestinian question. This is to naturalize Arab-Israeli relations, and you [the U.S.] need the Palestinians for icing the cake.

Los Angeles Times, 9-24:(A)8.

David Hinkley
Consultant, United States
Committee for Refugees;
Former chairman,
Amnesty International USA

2

Iraq, under [President] Saddam Hussein since 1968, has had one of the worst records of abuses of human rights in that region and in the world. It is guilty of large numbers of executions of both

Bruce Hoffman
Specialist on terrorism,
Rand Corporation

3

[On the recent release of all U.S. hostages being held in Lebanon by Arab terrorists]: Unfortunately, terrorism has its own momentum and it ticks to its own clock. The release of the last American hostage is something to exult over, but the terrorists also have a victory, as they got what they wanted out of it. Ten years ago, who knew about the [Shiites] in Lebanon? Today, there are very few people in the world who haven't heard of Islamic Jihad . . . State-sponsored terrorism is just another instrument of foreign policy in both [Syria and Iran] that will be used when it is in their interest, and won't be when it isn't in their interest.

Los Angeles Times,
12-5:(A)14.

Elias Hrawi
President of Lebanon

4

We are trying to boost the [Lebanese] military with men and material to the best of our abilities, not to declare war on anyone, but to keep the peace. A country with no army can have no sovereignty or independence, and we must hurry because the Syrians are pressing us to establish our own security so their soldiers can pull out of Lebanon. At least this is what Syrian President Hafez Assad keeps repeating to my ears.

Interview, Beirut/
The Washington Post,
9-28:(A)15.

269

Shirleen T. Hunter
Deputy director
of Middle East studies,
Center for Strategic and
International Studies
(United States)

1

The Iranians are quite eager for some sort of rapprochement [with the U.S.]. There is no complete agreement in the Iranian leadership, even among the moderate elements, on the extent to which it is necessary to have better relations with the United States. But without improving relations with the United States, there will always be limits on how far they can go with the Europeans. At least for the foreseeable future, the United States has the dominant position in the Middle East, especially in the Persian Gulf. The Iranians will have to come to terms with that.

Los Angeles Times, 11-23:(A)18.

Hussein ibn Talal
King of Jordan

2

Jordan has a very important part in any Arab-Israeli peace process. But I'm saying at the same time that Jordan should not be, cannot be, will not be a substitute for the Palestinians themselves as the major aggrieved party on the Arab side in a process that leads to peace. If it is the choice of the Palestinians at some time in the future to ask Jordan to join them, then they would certainly have the position of prominence in any process that seeks a comprehensive peace to deal with the Palestinian-Israeli problem.

Interview, Amman, March 12/
The New York Times, 3-13:(A)6.

3

We have a new national political charter here. It took nine months. We had people from the extreme right and the extreme left getting to know each other, discussing and debating. What they produced has put us on the threshold of having political parties. Experiences [like the recent Persian Gulf war] illustrate the need to create democratic institutions in this region. I hope our example might show the way—a country where

people share power, express their opinions, discuss and debate, where there is respect for human rights, where there is democracy. Because that is the only guarantee that things don't go haywire and that demi-gods are not created of leaders.

Interview, Amman/
Time, 7-22:42.

Saddam Hussein
President of Iraq

4

[On international criticism of his country's invasion and take-over of Kuwait last year]: Many have spoken of international legitimacy and law. But if we are reviewing international legitimacy and laws, let us start with Palestine. If the international community behaved in a balanced manner, all things would be open for application of international legitimacy. Whether they solve the problem according to international law or not, Palestine will return to the Palestinians.

At international Islamic conference,
Baghdad, Jan. 11/
The New York Times, 1-12:9.

Saad Eddin Ibrahim
Professor of sociology,
American University, Cairo

5

[Iraqi President] Saddam Hussein [whose move to take over Kuwait last year resulted in war with U.S.-led coalition forces] opened legitimate accounts. But he himself was not a legitimate accountant. So the accounts are still standing, they're overdue, they ought to be settled. One of the accounts is Palestine, but there is also the socio-economic account, the distribution among those [in the Middle East] who have and those who have not, and the civilizational conflict between the Arab-Muslin world and the West. Both the West and the [Persian] Gulf need to invest in less well-to-do countries, paying human-resource elements, putting money in education, health. Not handouts, not outright grants as much as real development that creates opportunities for a growing number of youngsters entering the labor force. If you resolve the ques-

(SAAD EDDIN IBRAHIM)

tion of equity and the question of disparity in the Arab world, then you would have taken the explosive elements out of the issues.

Los Angeles Times, 7-30:(H)5.

Martin Indyk
Executive director,
Washington Institute
for Near East Policy

1

There will always be an Arab-state component and a Palestinian component to any [Arab-Israeli] peace process. The last two years have focused on the Palestinians at the expense of the Arab-state dimension. After this [Persian Gulf] war, it could be both possible and necessary to engage the Arab states more. This, in turn, may make it easier to deal with the Palestinian dimension, because Israel's security concerns derive much more from Arab armies than Palestinian rock-throwers.

The New York Times, 1-21:(A)7.

2

[On Syria's current more friendly attitude toward the U.S.]: For [Syrian President Hafez] Assad . . . life is a struggle for power, it is not a struggle for peace . . . In his neck of the woods, his loss of a superpower patron [the Soviet Union] and his loss, through the destruction of Iraq's offensive capabilities [in the recent Persian Gulf war] . . . of a potential Eastern-front coalition partner for a prospective war against Israel, those two developments have meant that he needs some other way to balance Israel's power. And there is in this new world order only one other way: through serious relationship with the United States.

Washington, Aug. 6/
The Washington Post, 8-7:(A)14.

3

[On the current Middle East peace conference in Madrid]: At the end of the day, [U.S. Secre-

tary of State James] Baker got all the parties to accept things that they previously refused to consider. He did it by being the "Schoolmaster of State" and using the changed circumstances in the region to great effect. He admonished and coaxed the participants, alternating between teaching them how to behave and telling them that they need him more than he needs them. He will have to do the same, and more, to produce agreements. He now has a big stake in this. He can't walk away, but I don't think he wants to. It's the ultimate test of any Secretary of State's negotiating abilities.

Nov. 3/
The New York Times, 11-4:(A)1.

Kamel abu Jaber
Foreign Minister of Jordan

4

The core of the present Arab-Israeli conflict revolves around the [Israeli-] occupied [Arab] territories. To say that "the issue is not territory" is a gross reduction of the truth . . . Israel can have either land or peace, but it cannot have both. It can have the true security that comes from a negotiated political solution. Force alone will never provide security. It may be very well that Israel wants peace, but it wants the Arabs alone to pay the price.

At Middle East peace conference,
Madrid, Nov. 1/
Los Angeles Times, 11-2:(A)5.

Ahmed Jibril
Secretary general,
Popular Front for
the Liberation of Palestine-General
Command

5

We understand "peace" as the right of Palestinian return, self-determination and the establishment of a Palestinian state. Any Palestinian leader who would make a deal without those three conditions would be beheaded.

The Christian Science Monitor,
8-22:5.

271

Geoffrey Kemp
Senior associate,
Carnegie Endowment
for the Advancement of Peace
(United States)

1

More and more Arab countries are coming to recognize the need for a dialogue with Israel. Looked at in this context, the differences that separate the parties are still significant but not nearly as insurmountable as they were in the past. That doesn't mean that peace is at hand or there has been a breakthrough. But by plowing the same ground against a different background, you do make some progress.

Los Angeles Times, 5-28:(H)2.

2

There is no way out of a conclusion that there will be a U.S. [military] presence for the foreseeable future [in the Persian Gulf following the recent war against Iraq] . . . Everyone [in the area] will hedge their bets and want U.S. forces on the ground. The *quid pro quo* for a quick pullout may be increased U.S. arms sales [to the Gulf states]. That will run up against sentiment in [the U.S.] Congress for an embargo on arms sales.

Los Angeles Times, 5-31:(A)10.

Mohammed al-Khadiri
Leader, Democratic Forum
of Kuwait

3

We have no democracy in Kuwait [even after the recent Persian Gulf war]. It's very clear. We are asking for democracy, the implementation of the suspended Constitution, forming a real democratic government and to have human rights—individual rights to speak, to read, to write, to have a small conference, which is forbidden . . . We have the same problem as before. All we are asking for is a government that represents all political parties and respects the program of the people. This government does not represent the program of the people.

The New York Times,
4-23:(A)7.

Ali Khamenei
Spiritual leader of Iran

4

The Islamic Republic [of Iran] rejects relations with the U.S. regime, which is the symbol of bullying and unjust hegemonism and the manifestation of cruelty to the weak nations of the world. As long as it arrogantly does injustice to nations, interferes in governments and countries [and] supports such illegitimate regimes as the hated Zionist regime [Israel] . . . the vanguard Muslim nation of Iran and the risen Muslim nations will never establish relations with that regime.

Message to the nation, June 2/
The Washington Post, 6-8:(A)16.

Ahmad al-Khatib
Former member
of Kuwaiti Parliament

5

[Saying that, with the recent success by U.S.-led forces in getting Iraq out of Kuwait, the country should become more democratic]: This matter of constitutional democracy is no longer a question of negotiations or something to duck. We have arrived at a stage where we cannot have a constitutional legitimate government in Kuwait unless it is based on free elections, a free Parliament and Cabinet ministers who are approved by the Parliament.

Interview, London, April 3/
The New York Times, 4-4:(A)7.

Michael T. Klare
Associate professor of peace
and world security affairs,
Hampshire College
(United States)

6

In the Middle East, the Soviets and the United States have used arms [sales] to make alliances. This is the way we sought to spread our influence. It goes back to . . . 1954, when [then-Egyptian President Gamal] Nasser turned away from the West and toward the Soviets. Since then, both sides have played a game of trying to woo away the other guy's clients with arms.

Los Angeles Times, 3-18:(A)10.

Teddy Kollek
Mayor of Jerusalem

1

I personally think that eventually—after quite some time—the Palestinians will have their country. I don't know whether that country will be in Jordan or part of the West Bank, or what. Theirs is a growing nationalism that, in a sense, is a mirror reflection of our [Israeli] nationalism, and they'll have their land and their country, their state and their capital.

Interview,
Jerusalem/
Los Angeles Times, 2-17:(M)5.

Mohammed Javad Larijani
Member, National Security Council
of Iran

2

[Saying Iran is becoming more moderate in its policies]: I think there has been a great change in Iran in the last two years, in foreign affairs behavior and in economic behavior . . . There have been very many openings in Iran . . . The difficulty is this: We want to have freedom of thought, freedom of expression, but we don't want to annoy the general moral views and the Islamic sentiment of the people. It is a sign of the maturity of this system that, despite harsh criticism, it has not moved from one extreme to another.

Interview,
Teheran, Sept. 18/
The Washington Post, 9-19:(A)39.

3

The Arab countries in the southern flank of the Persian Gulf see a huge neighbor [Iran] sitting in the north. Even if we are not militarized, even if we are not going to nuclear weapons, still they see a huge neighbor to the north. So what to do with that neighbor? I think the best thing is to enter a kind of arrangement which has international guarantees, and even the United States could support and guarantee the Arab states.

Interview,
Teheran, Sept. 18/
The New York Times, 9-19:(A)7.

Patrick J. Leahy
United States Senator,
D-Vermont

4

[On U.S. President Bush's proposal to delay $10-billion in loan guarantees to Israel pending Arab-Israeli peace talks]: If the President of the United States asks for a delay in the guarantees to help the chances for peace in the Middle East, I believe I should support him. I think the American Jewish community will understand that Israel will be the greatest beneficiary of such talks, and that warrants a brief wait for the guarantee.

Interview, Vermont, Sept. 5/
The Washington Post, 9-6:(A)24.

Mel Levine
United States Representative,
D-California

5

There is an overriding need for a change in U.S. and Western policy on arming [the Middle East] region. A policy of unrestrained arms sales and high-technology assistance in the most volatile tinderbox on the globe does not yield stability. On the contrary, it creates instability.

Los Angeles Times, 3-18:(A)11.

David Levy
Foreign Minister of Israel

6

[On Syria's current moves toward negotiations with Israel]: If it becomes clear to us that there's a real change in the Syrian position, that finally it has begun to take the path of peace and is ridding itself of its stubbornness and isn't setting preconditions [for talks]—and that nothing has been said [between the U.S. and Syria] that's in conflict with what has been agreed with us—then we'll be able to welcome it.

July 19/
The New York Times, 7-20:4.

7

[Saying the U.S. may be siding with the Arabs and trying to force Israel to make concessions at

(DAVID LEVY)

the proposed forthcoming peace conference]: This is the real problem. It is the doubts of all Israelis about what will be at the conference and how the United States will act. We are going toward a situation where we are almost alone. What is our security? It is that every Israeli feels that the United States will treat Israel with special sensitivity. If this trust is broken, we go into the unknown without any security.

Interview, Sept. 19/
The Washington Post, 9-21:(A)18.

Moshe Maoz
Specialist on Syria,
Hebrew University (Israel)

1

[On Syrian President Hafez Assad's current moves toward peace talks with Israel]: Basically, Assad would like Israel to disappear. This is his ideology. And this hasn't changed. The change we've seen in recent days is tactical, procedural.

Israeli broadcast interview/
The Washington Post, 7-29:(A)16.

Tariq al-Moayid
Minister of Information
of Bahrain

2

Anything without a strong American [military] commitment [to the Persian Gulf states] is not worth the paper it is written on. We would support a very strong American commitment for long-term stability in the region and we understand this is done for the region and not for one country.

Interview/
The New York Times, 5-11:4.

Yitzhak Modai
Minister of Finance of Israel

3

[Criticizing the Israeli government for going ahead with new Jewish settlements in Israeli-occupied Arab territories even though it angers the U.S.]: There is no particular need to anger the

Americans [on the settlement issue] . . . Accelerated building in the territories as a deliberate provocation against [the U.S.] is an act of stupidity of the highest order.

Interview/
The Washington Post, 9-21:(A)1.

Ali Akbar Mohtashemi
Member of the Majlis
(Iranian Parliament);
Former Minister of the Interior
of Iran

4

[On U.S. President Bush and the others taking part in the current Arab-Israeli peace negotiations]: Let us be frank. From an Islamic legal point of view, these people are waging war against the true state of Palestine, against Islam and Muslims as they also did in the [recent Persian] Gulf war against Iraq. Bush and his aides are criminals. They are *moharebeen* people who in the eyes of Islam have no value and therefore can be struck down. Their blood is of no further value. They are the most hated and loathed of people. Therefore, it is up to every individual Muslim to carry out the execution of Islamic laws [including the execution of Bush and his aides].

Interview/Newsweek, 12-9:42.

Amir Moussa
Foreign Minister of Egypt

5

The starting point in [Persian] Gulf security [following the recent Persian Gulf war] is Arab. And there can be no discussion or implementation of any security order in the Middle East without a role for Egypt, since Egypt is the biggest of the region's states and the most influential internationally and regionally, militarily and politically.

To reporters/
Los Angeles Times, 7-9:(A)13.

6

[On the current Middle East peace conference in Madrid]: . . . whatever the positions of one

(AMIR MOUSSA)

party or the other, we cannot and we should not continue arguing, trading accusations and re-crimination. Old arguments and archaic strat-egies should be left at the wayside . . . Wild dreams of expansion must come to an end. Illegal acts, such as building [Israeli] settlements [in occupied Arab territory] should be frozen. More than anything else, and as never before, this con-ference places an awesome responsibility on the parties to demonstrate that peace has a chance and that coming here was not in vain.

> *At Middle East peace conference,*
> *Madrid, Nov. 1/*
> *Los Angeles Times, 11-2:(A)5.*

Hosni Mubarak
President of Egypt

1

[Saying Israel must give up occupied Arab lands in return for peace]: You cannot keep the land and peace together. [Israeli Prime Minister Yitzhak] Shamir will get very angry when I speak very frankly, and I'm still telling him, Mr. Shamir, I'm not against him. But I cannot sit like this, and he is saying no for land for peace, no for this, no for that. I can't understand Mr. Shamir, frankly, nor his intentions.

> *Interview/*
> *The New York Times, 6-15:5.*

Brian Mulroney
Prime Minister of Canada

2

[On Canadian arms sales to the Middle East]: We could be much more active in that area if we wanted. We have all the technology in the world. We have all the resources we need. We could be big arms merchants. We've chosen not to be, even though it's a very lucrative business. We've chosen not to because it's fundamentally incon-sistent with our policy to develop it, to peddle it, to finance it and then to deplore its use.

> *News conference,*
> *Ottawa, March 13/*
> *Los Angeles Times,*
> *3-14:(A)9.*

Suleiman Mutawa
Former Minister of Planning
of Kuwait

3

[Criticizing the now-returned Kuwaiti govern-ment for not acting fast enough in helping the country back on its feet following seven months of Iraqi occupation]: I think if one is to limit the responsibility of the government to fixing faucets, then the government has succeeded and done a wonderful job. But I don't think the government was sitting in exile for seven months trying to plan the fixing of faucets. The main task of the government is to have the country back in motion and in action, and this is not happening.

> *Los Angeles Times, 4-23:(A)8.*

Vitaly V. Naumkin
Deputy director,
Institute for Oriental Affairs
(Soviet Union)

4

As a former superpower, our [Soviet] position in the Middle East has changed fundamentally. Precisely because no superpower ambitions can be attributed to us, because we no longer have allies or clients there, we can give friendly advice to everyone.

> *Los Angeles Times, 11-5:(H)1.*

Benjamin Netanyahu
Deputy Foreign Minister
of Israel

5

Weakness in the face of tyranny and terror is not a virtue; in fact, it can result in horrible conse-quences. We have always sought peace with our enemies, and we would like to see them change and accept our life here with them in a path of coexistence and prosperity. But until the [Iraqi President Saddam Husseins] of this world dis-appear, we shall have to have the ability to defend the peace. I say that both as a Jew, as an Israeli and as a citizen of the free world. In the Middle East, the only kind of peace that will hold is the peace being defended. And I try to do my share in defending Israel in the trenches of public opinion.

> *Interview, Israel/*
> *USA Today, 1-29:(A)11.*

(BENJAMIN NETANYAHU)

1

You can make peace but only with an enemy that wants peace. [Iraqi President] Saddam [Hussein] and [PLO leader Yasir] Arafat seek our destruction. They share not only this goal but even the methods. The PLO was hurling missiles at our cities in the north well before the [Iraqi] invasion of Kuwait, way before Saddam's current firing of missiles at Tel Aviv. They are, in fact, brothers in blood and practitioners in the art of terror.

Interview, Israel/
USA Today, 1-29:(A)11.

Queen Noor
Wife of King Hussein
of Jordan

2

In Jordan, to date, the monarchy has served an essential and, I believe, desired role by the majority of people. We are servants of the people of Jordan and of the region in any way that we can serve the best interests. That is the role that the family will play as long as it is wanted and needed to play that role. I do not see the monarchy in Jordan as an end in itself, but as a means to ever-improving quality of life and opportunity for Jordan contributing peace to the region.

Interview, Los Angeles/
Los Angeles Times, 6-9:(M)3.

David R. Obey
United States Representative,
D-Wisconsin

3

[Calling for a limit to U.S. arms sales to the Middle East in the wake of the recent U.S.-led victory against Iraq in the Persian Gulf war]: What is the immediate threat? We have just blown the living hell out of the only threat in the region . . . If we give new arms to the Saudis, and the Saudis continue to supply aid to the Syrians, and the Syrians buy new arms, and then the Israelis ask us for more, then we're off to the races again.

Los Angeles Times, 3-18:(A)11.

Ehud Olmert
Minister of Health of Israel

4

[On the Arab-Israeli conflict]: Israel agrees there should be a two-track strategy for peace . . . We are ready to immediately embark on negotiations with all the Arab states—with Saudi Arabia, Kuwait, the [Persian] Gulf emirates, Syria and others—without any delays. Israel is prepared to sit at the table with each one and negotiate immediate peace. At the same time, we suggest an immediate process of negotiations with proper Palestinian representatives for interim arrangements leading to a permanent solution [for the Israeli-occupied West Bank and Gaza]. Both sets of negotiations should start simultaneously and right now. Let me be clear about what we mean by a "proper Palestinian delegation." I don't mean [PLO chairman Yasir] Arafat; I don't mean the PLO. The conduct of the PLO in supporting [Iraqi President] Saddam Hussein during the [recent] Persian Gulf war is proof they don't belong to the mainstream of history in our region.

Before American Israel Public
Affairs Committee,
Washington, March 17/
The Washington Post, 3-18:(A)17.

Amos Oz
Israeli author

5

It is in the nature of dreams that they cannot be fulfilled. This is the case in making love, in writing a novel, in building a country. Israel is a dream come true and thus inevitably flawed.

U.S. News & World Report,
4-15:62.

Shimon Peres
Leader, Labor Party of Israel;
Former Prime Minister
of Israel

6

[On the current Arab willingness for peace talks with Israel]: We support this process without a doubt. We are in favor of saying "yes" to an international peace conference. We are in

(SHIMON PERES)

favor of negotiating with the Syrians, the Palestinians and the Jordanians, beyond any doubt, and in favor of negotiating without any preconditions.

The New York Times, 8-1:(A)7.

William B. Quandt
Senior fellow,
Brookings Institution
(United States)

1

[On a possible Arab-Israeli peace conference]: If you can get the Palestinians, Jordan and Syria to sit across a table from Israel and negotiate directly, you will have crossed a divide. You'd have a kind of explicit Arab recognition of Israel—and Israeli recognition of the Palestinians—that you've never had before . . . The substantive issues are still extremely difficult. [Former U.S. Secretary of State] Henry Kissinger used the Geneva Conference in 1973 very cleverly, because he had already worked out the next steps. When he went to Geneva, he had the first Sinai disengagement agreement [between Israel and Egyptian forces] ready to go. I don't think [current U.S. Secretary of State James] Baker has the agreements lined up yet.

Los Angeles Times, 4-13:(A)6.

Hashemi Rafsanjani
President of Iran

2

Iran is not thinking about establishing [diplomatic] ties with the U.S. The U.S. is always trying to make the issue of establishing ties with Iran subject to conditions . . . The principle is to have relations [with other countries], but the United States has its own special case, and Israel is illegitimate in our view.

Seminar at Teheran University,
May 5/
Los Angeles Times, 5-6:(A)7.

3

[Criticizing the U.S. for trying to prevent Iran from acquiring nuclear technology from other countries]: With utter insolence, the United States declares that Iran does not have the right to utilize nuclear technology, even for non-military purposes. Iran desires peace, and will cooperate with all nations that seek and work for preserving peace in the world . . . We have learned that preserving our independence and survival in this unsuitable international climate is not possible without science, technology and the necessary tools.

To graduating class at Iranian air force
academy, Nov. 17/
The New York Times, 11-18:(A)4.

Othman al-Rawaf
Director (Persian) Gulf
Studies Center,
King Saud University
(Saudi Arabia)

4

[On a possible regional security force in the Persian Gulf area involving the six GCC countries, plus Egypt and Syria]: The six need the two as windows to the rest of the Arab world, while the two know that there is a limit to their influence. The Gulf countries may be weak and vulnerable, but they have links to the West. Both sides know their limits and their needs.

The Christian Science Monitor,
3-13:2.

Saeed Saadi
Leader, Rally for Culture and
Democracy Party of Algeria

5

What is the Arab world? Is it the feudal petrodollar culture of the [Persian] Gulf? Is it the bloody Baathist regimes of Iraq and Syria? We have had so many governments since 1962 that have repeatedly said we want to be Arab, but without defining what that means. There is also a need to recognize that the Arab world suffers from retardation. I am a Berberophone. I claim the wealth of three cultures: my own, the Muslim heritage we have, the French heritage we have, and in my view all that makes up Algeria. I reject one-dimensional culture. It puts us behind.

Interview, Algiers/
The New York Times, 7-26:(A)5.

Ali al-Salim al-Sabah
Minister of Defense of Kuwait

1

[In the aftermath of the recent Persian Gulf war], Kuwait has no intention of granting a permanent base to the United States or to allied troops, but friendly countries will definitely have a role in maintaining the security of the region and the defense of Kuwait . . . The presence of Arab troops—Egyptian, Syrian and Gulf—will be the basis of military presence in Kuwait.

To reporters, Cairo, May 27/
Los Angeles Times, 5-28:(A)4.

Saud al-Faisal
Foreign Minister
of Saudi Arabia

2

Saudi Arabia believes it is time to put an end to the Arab-Israeli conflict and to achieve a comprehensive and just solution to the Palestinian question. Therefore, Saudi Arabia supports the efforts of the United States for the convening of an early peace conference to achieve this objective.

To reporters, April 22/
Los Angeles Times, 4-23:(A)10.

Zeev Schiff
Military editor,
"Haaretz" (Israel)

3

[On the current U.S.-led air attacks against Iraq in the Persian Gulf war]: I don't think America's action in recent days can ever be a substitute for [Israel holding onto occupied Arab] territory. Yes, it shows the friendship of the United States [toward Israel] and that it can be relied on. But we remember quite well how we were pushed aside during the last five months of this operation [the U.S.-led effort to get Iraq out of Kuwait]. And we still believe that when it comes to political issues, Americans might be sometimes very naive about events in the Middle East. We remember [U.S. friendly] policy toward Iraq before August 2 [1990, when Iraq invaded and occupied Kuwait]. You [the U.S.] can make a big mistake and absorb it. We can't.

So it's good to know they can protect us sometimes, but don't look for any revolution in Israeli strategic thinking overnight.

The New York Times, 1-21:(A)7.

Charles E. Schumer
United States Representative,
D-New York

4

[Criticizing U.S. President Bush for proposing a 120-day delay in loan guarantees for Israel pending the forthcoming Arab-Israeli peace conference]: I think he believes he's substantively right and politically on the strong ground, and when that combination occurs, politicians tend not to yield. [But] I think he is wrong in both cases. I think he's substantively wrong, and I don't think the President wants to have the entire American Jewish community and other friends of Israel against him. The ephemeral points you pick up with certain Americans by bashing Israel in a subliminal way won't be worth the candle.

The New York Times, 9-14:5.

Yitzhak Shamir
Prime Minister of Israel

5

The end of the [Persian] Gulf war will be followed by the usual attempt to establish a new pattern of Middle East arrangements. There will be an effort to use political means to snatch from Israel what could not be snatched from us by force. We shall stand firm and not retreat. If negotiations do take place, we shall go into them with a number of advantages, and weather them successfully.

To Likud Party legislators,
Jerusalem, Feb. 26/
The Washington Post, 2-27:(A)18.

6

It is our earnest hope that the civilized world—led by the United States—will give up any notion that the PLO terrorist organization, which was [Iraqi President] Saddam Hussein's staunchest ally [in the recent Persian Gulf war], has any place in the future [Arab-Israeli] peace venture.

(YITZHAK SHAMIR)

Any attempt to involve them will set the clock of history back, rather than move us forward on the road to peace.

TV broadcast from Jerusalem
to meeting of American Israel
Public Affairs Committee
in Washington, March 17/
The Washington Post, 3-18:(A)17.

1

Syria has the right to ask us to withdraw from the Golan Heights. If Syria does ask, we shall say we do not agree to withdraw. [But] we can talk about peace, about the ways of peace, about economic cooperation. There are many things. We say we are ready to negotiate unconditionally with all the Arab states—nothing more than that . . . At the moment, we are in different states that range from preparations of infrastructure to actual construction of 1,200 housing units in the Golan Heights, and I intend to add the same number next year. There are 11,000 Jews on the Golan today, and we hope that next year the Jewish population there will be increased up to 20,000.

March 18/
The New York Times, 3-20:(A)7.

2

I will say it simply. With my whole history and the way I perceive the state, I will never abandon the [Israeli-occupied Arab] territories. I wouldn't want to enter national memory as someone who sold off part of Israel cheaply.

Interview, April/
The Washington Post, 7-24:(A)1.

3

[On the new Arab efforts for peace talks with Israel]: For us, it is not enough that they [Arab leaders] have realized that the United States is the paramount power today. We have to know that they have at the same time, finally, come to accept the reality of Israel's existence and they have moved peace—rather than territory—to the

top of their agenda. This is what we are, at present, trying to establish with the help and active involvement of the U.S. government.

At Hadassah conference,
Jerusalem, July 22/
The Washington Post, 7-23:(A)17.

4

[Criticizing suggestions that Israel give up the West Bank and Golan Heights in exchange for peace with the Arabs]: I do not believe in territorial compromise. Our country is very small. Where would you find among the nations of the world a people who would be ready to give up the territory of their homeland? I believe with all my heart and soul that we are eternally tied to this homeland. Peace and security go together. Security, and a territory, a homeland—it all goes together. That is our belief, that is the belief of the [Likud] Party I belong to and, in my opinion, that is the feeling of a large majority of the Jewish nation.

Israeli broadcast interview, July 24/
The New York Times, 7-25:(A)1.

5

[Saying Syrian President Hafez Assad must be more direct in his new approach for peace talks with Israel]: [The late Egyptian President Anwar] Sadat started his move with an appeal to Israel, not to the United States [as has Assad]. He came to Jerusalem, to the Knesset [Israeli Parliament], and said to the Jewish nation: "I want peace with you. I understand your security problems." Assad has not said that up to today. He turned first of all to the Americans, and only the Americans. Up to now, he has not spoken at all about peace. He talks about "resolving the dispute." It is not the same thing.

Israeli broadcast interview, July 24/
The New York Times, 7-25:(A)6.

6

[Saying Israel will agree to Arab-Israeli peace talks, with the proviso that Israel will reject certain Palestinians from taking part]: We have agreements with the representatives of the

(YITZHAK SHAMIR)

United States on the Palestinian composition of this delegation—that it will not include PLO members; that it will not include people from East Jerusalem; that it will not include people from outside Israel. Apparently, the Americans have not reached an agreement with the other side [the Palestinians].

Israeli broadcast interview, Aug. 1/
Los Angeles Times, 8-2:(A)12.

1

[Criticizing U.S. President Bush's decision to delay a $10-billion loan guarantee for Israel for 120 days pending the start of Arab-Israeli peace talks]: If the Arabs are handed such a gift without even asking for it, they will dance on the rooftops and make new and even bigger demands, and the peace process will become impossible . . . What really counts is that the population of Israel is expanding [with the influx of Soviet Jews], and it will expand in those areas [Israeli-occupied Arab territories] also, [which is why Israel is asking for the loan guarantee] . . . It is not true that [freezing those settlements] is the key to progress in the peace process as some people claim. Nobody has asked us for such a freeze. We do not accept any linkage, not with the problem of settlements and not with the other political problems.

Israeli radio interview, Sept. 8/
The Washington Post, 9-9:(A)17.

2

[On Israeli occupation of Arab territories it seized in the 1967 war]: Our first duty is to survive, and we cannot survive unless we have secure and defensible borders. Relinquishing this area is an invitation to war.

Oct. 22/
USA Today, 10-23:(A)1.

3

I appeal to the Arab leaders, those who are here and those who have not yet joined the process: Show us and the world that you accept Israel's existence. Demonstrate your readiness

to accept Israel as a permanent entity in the region. Let the people in our region hear you speak in the language of reconciliation, coexistence and peace with Israel. In Israel there is an almost total consensus for the need for peace. We only differ on the best ways to achieve it. In most Arab countries the opposite seems to be true: The only differences are the ways to push Israel into a defenseless position and, ultimately, to destruction . . . We appeal to you to renounce the Jihad [holy war] against Israel. We appeal to you to denounce the PLO covenant which calls for Israel's destruction. We appeal to you to condemn declarations that call for Israel's annihilation . . .

At Middle East peace conference,
Madrid, Oct. 31/
The Washington Post, 11-1:(A)36.

4

To the Lebanese people, our neighbors to the north, we send a message of sympathy and understanding. They are suffering under the yoke of Syrian occupation and oppression and are denied even the capacity to cry out in protest. We bear no ill-will to the courageous and suffering Lebanese, and we join them in the hope that they will soon regain their independence and freedom. We have no designs on Lebanese territory, and in the context of a peace treaty and the removal of the Syrian presence, we can restore stability and security on the borders between our two countries.

At Middle East peace conference,
Madrid, Nov. 1/
Los Angeles Times, 11-2:(A)5.

5

Syria's representative [to the current Middle East peace conference] wants us and the world to believe that his country is a model of freedom and protection of human rights, including those of the Jews. Such a statement stretches incredulity to infinite proportions. To this day, Syria is the home of a host of terrorist organizations that spread violence and death to all kinds of innocent targets, including civil aviation, and women and children of many nations. I could go on and recite a litany of facts that demonstrate the extent to

(YITZHAK SHAMIR)

which Syria merits the dubious honor of being one of the most oppressive, tyrannical regimes in the world.

At Middle East peace conference,
Madrid, Nov. 1/
Los Angeles Times, 11-2:(A)5.

1

Ever since the State of Israel was founded, we called for direct face-to-face negotiations between us and our neighbors. The first such meetings were [the recent ones] in Madrid. We didn't expect much. The gaps are still wide. The gulf is deep. But we shall meet again. And we hope the ice will begin to melt. We hope the Arab representatives will approach talks with a desire to make peace, not only to win concessions. If we are to bring down the wall, both sides must invest effort, energy and good-will . . . [But] peace without security spells disaster for our state. We live in an unstable, undemocratic, militaristic region, where force is king, terrorism is endemic and hatred of Israel universal.

Before Council of Jewish Federations,
Baltimore, Nov. 21/
Los Angeles Times, 11-22:(A)8.

Farouk al-Sharaa
Foreign Minister of Syria

2

[Saying conditions for peace talks between Israel and the Arabs include UN Resolutions 242 and 338 and a large UN role at such a conference]: They are prerequisites for peace. Without these, you cannot have peace. If the [Israeli-occupied Arab] land is not returned, there'll be no peace. If there's no mechanism, which is the international peace conference, there'll be no peace . . . I think the Palestinian people should be free to send their own representation to the peace conference because, after all, these people have been suffering for a long time under Israeli occupation and must decide for themselves who would represent them.

Interview, Damascus, April 14/
The New York Times, 4-18:(A)8.

3

I think the Israelis as a people desire peace. They are looking for peace. Israel is a special case, where the government is more hawkish than the people. In the Arab world, it is just the opposite. We are more flexible than the Arab people.

Madrid, Nov. 4/
The New York Times, 11-5:(A)1.

Bassam abu Sharif
Senior adviser to Palestine
Liberation Organization chairman
Yasir Arafat

4

[On the proposed Arab-Israeli peace conference]: [U.S. President Bush and Secretary of State James Baker] are serious about the effort to push the peace process forward, and I believe that President Bush wants to see the occupation by Israel of the Arab lands over, because this is the only way that will stabilize the Middle East. What we're looking for now is a reassurance by the American Administration that what President Bush declared in front of the [U.S.] Congress will be done—i.e., implementation of [UN Resolutions] 242 and 338, land for peace and the full legitimate political rights of the Palestinian people. For me, the only basic guarantee is the continuing involvement of the U.S. It will be an ongoing process that will have to end in the fulfillment of [these rights] . . . and other guarantees don't necessarily have to be spelled out.

Interview/
Los Angeles Times, 9-24:(A)6.

Ariel Sharon
Minister of Housing,
and former Minister of Defense,
of Israel

5

[Criticizing Israeli Prime Minister Yitzhak Shamir's statement that Syrian President Hafez Assad, who is currently trying to arrange peace talks with Israel, has become more like the late Egyptian President Anwar Sadat, who did make peace with Israel]: Until a day ago, Assad was

(ARIEL SHARON)

seen as the twin brother of [Iraqi President and enemy of Israel] Saddam Hussein. Suddenly, like with a magic wand, he became the younger and beloved brother of Sadat. Suddenly, they say Syria is a different country and is seeking peace. This phenomenon amazes me.

July 24/
The Washington Post, 7-25:(A)32.

Eduard A. Shevardnadze
Former Foreign Minister
of the Soviet Union

1

It seems to me that the potential participants of [a regional] conference [on the Arab-Israeli conflict] understand full well that it will give them a real possibility for getting out of the dead end ... But it will never be possible to achieve this if the sides are concentrating not on the substance of the issues but, let us say, on the question of what kind of clothes the participants in the negotiations are going to wear. And this has, in fact, been the case. What is important is to sit down at that table and start a dialogue on substance. And then it will become clear rather rapidly that the so-called issues of principle ... which have been the object of wearisome disputes, matter rather little for a solution to the conflict itself. World-wide experience has shown that procedures to which enormous significance was attached initially ultimately lose their meaning once a contact has been established and the dialogue has been engaged.

Before Center for Policy Analysis
on Palestine, May 7/
The Washington Post, 5-9:(A)20.

Dan Shomron
Lieutenant General
and Chief of Staff,
Israeli armed forces

2

[Saying Israel should consider giving up occupied Arab territory in exchange for peace]: On the question of territories or peace, territory bears some significance during wartime. [But] a

political settlement is worth much more than territory. The *intifada* [anti-Israeli violence by Palestinians in the occupied territories] cannot be quelled, just as the entire Middle East conflict hasn't been.

To reporters, March 18/
Los Angeles Times, 3-20:(A)9.

Zalman Shoval
Israeli Ambassador
to the United States

3

Although there are different currents and undercurrents, even American decision-makers who are less closely identified with Israel know the underlying reality. They know that whatever coalition there may be from time to time with America and [Arab] countries in the [Middle East] area, these coalitions are based on interests of a certain moment ... It is something that could change overnight because the regimes in these countries can change overnight ... Neither [Israel nor the United States] has a real alternative to each other in the long run.

Interview, Washington, Jan. 17/
The Washington Post, 1-18:(C)4.

4

The Arabs have been very successful over the last few years in creating the false image of a big Israeli superpower unfairly treating the poor little Palestinians. Whereas the reality, of course, is that we are still less than 4 million Jews facing 140 million Arabs—none of whom, except for Egypt, have made peace with us. All of whom still threaten us with extinction.

Interview, Washington, Jan. 17/
The Washington Post, 1-18:(C)4.

5

The very special [Israeli] relationship with America—both the relationship with the state and relations with the Jewish community—necessitate something that is more than routine diplomacy. The Jewish community expects a strong spokesman for Israel ... When I came here [as Ambassador] I set for myself certain

(ZALMAN SHOVAL)

objectives to achieve. One was to put an end to this perception of a standoff between [U.S.] President Bush and [Israeli] Prime Minister [Yitzhak] Shamir—the so-called lack of chemistry—to make a new start. Number 2, the Jewish community was not united enough. I had the feeling that they wanted to be unified, and I have devoted a good deal of time to that. Number 3, and this was a point that motivated my government in appointing me, the Ambassador should be able to communicate through the media.

Interview, Washington/
The New York Times, 5-10:(A)7.

1

[Criticizing U.S. President Bush's proposal to delay a $10-billion loan guarantee to Israel pending Arab-Israeli peace talks]: Politically, [delay] may be sending the wrong signals to the Arabs at a very crucial time. If there is any chance for the peace process, it is for the Arabs to feel they cannot gang up on Israel and cannot use pressure on the United States in order to blackmail Israel to make concessions, which Israel is not willing to make.

Interview/
USA Today, 9-9:(A)11.

Denis Sullivan
Senior Fulbright fellow,
Cairo University (Egypt)

2

The end of the [Persian Gulf] war could bring a new cold war to the Middle East. Already, many Saudis and Egyptians don't like the Jordanians or Palestinians for their support of [Iraqi President] Saddam [Hussein], so this could mean the end of Arab nationalism altogether.

The Washington Post, 3-1:(A)29.

William Sullivan
Former United States Ambassador
to Iran

3

We [the U.S.] have to stop trying to pick and choose between dictators. We made a fun-

damental mistake after Iran's revolution. The [Jimmy] Carter Administration encouraged Iraq to attack Iran. It helped Iraq acquire military equipment well beyond its defensive needs. The policy continued under [Ronald] Reagan and under Bush until last summer [when Iraq invaded and took over Kuwait]. We built a Frankenstein monster. The motive was vengeance against Iran rather than to promote a sensible geopolitical balance. When you have dictators, the less military equipment they have, the less of a threat they are. The flow of weapons has to be reduced.

USA Today, 2-28:(A)4.

James A. Traficant, Jr.
United States Representative,
D-Ohio

4

[Calling for a reduction in U.S. aid to Israel]: If we took as much time to look after the interests of America as we do to look after the interests of Israel, we'd be a hell of a lot stronger.

Washington, March 7/
USA Today, 3-8:(A)4.

Terry Waite
Former hostage held by
guerrilla groups in Lebanon

5

[On his being released after being held hostage for almost five years]: On this day, it would not be right for me to leave this podium without remembering all those, and all those in particular in the Middle East, who are held captive. It is wrong to hold people in such a way. It is self-defeating, and those who do it fall well below civilized standards of behavior, no matter who they are, no matter what nationality or what organization they belong to. We have lived in these last years through the appalling suffering of the people of Lebanon. We have been in the midst of shelling. We have seen people die and killed in most brutal ways. We know the people of Lebanon have suffered greatly, and those from whom I have just come can be assured that we in the church . . . will not rest until all are freed and there is justice and peace brought to people who deserve a better deal.

At Lyneham Air Base, England,
Nov. 19/Los Angeles Times, 11-20:(A)4.

Paul D. Wolfowitz
Under Secretary of Defense
of the United States

1

[Saying previous U.S. arms sales to friendly Arab countries made the recent U.S.-led victory over Iraq in the Persian Gulf war possible]: America's foreign military sales program has turned out to be everything we said it would. We haven't just been loading the Saudis and other Gulf states down, as some have said, with toys they could never use. Those sales made a big difference.

Before America-Arab Affairs Council,
March 1/
The Washington Post, 3-7:(A)33.

Yang Shang-kun
President of China

2

We [China] sold intermediate-range missiles to Saudi Arabia to help it defend its security. Apart from this, we have not sold any intermediate-range missiles. Not to Iran. Not to Syria. American opinion censures us for selling weapons. Yet the United States also sells weapons. Why does it not censure itself? Many of the weapons now in the Middle East are American. So there is a question of fairness here. It seems as if people are always beating us with this issue. Why is your America like this?

Interview, Beijing, May/
U.S. News & World Report, 5-27:43.

THE PERSIAN GULF WAR

The quotations in this sub-section pertain directly to the war in the Persian Gulf area (which began on January 16, 1991, and was dubbed Operation Desert Storm) conducted by a U.S.-led coalition against Iraq's occupation of Kuwait.

Bakar Amri
*Dean of economics
and administration,
King Abdulaziz University
(Saudi Arabia)*

1

We don't want war, but we also don't want [Iraqi] aggression. It is time now for America to change its image. It lost Vietnam because it yielded to public opinion. If it loses this, believe me, America will never have any effectiveness or influence in Third World countries.

Los Angeles Times, 1-15:(H)7.

Yasir Arafat
*Chairman, Palestine
Liberation Organization*

2

[On Iraqi missile attacks against Israel during the current Persian Gulf war]: It proves that Israel's security can't be protected by the Jordan River. The argument that Israel needs the West Bank and Gaza to protect its security has tumbled down. It's only a political solution that will bring security. What Israel has been feeling the last 14 days is something the Palestinians have been feeling for the last 40 years. Maybe this will awaken the Israelis that peace and not military dominance is the solution to the problem.

*Interview, Tunis, Tunisia/
The Christian Science Monitor,
2-5:2.*

3

[On his siding with Iraq in the recent Persian Gulf war]: My decision was built on my prin-

ciples. I am not with [Iraqi President] Saddam [Hussein] on Kuwait. I am with Saddam and the Iraqi people against any outside aggression. I will not change my position . . . As long as there is American soldiers in Iraqi territory [following the war], I am with [Saddam].

*Interview, Tunis, Tunisia/
USA Today, 4-19:(A)2.*

Les Aspin
*United States Representative,
D-Wisconsin*

4

You want an Iraq weak enough that it can't threaten the weakest of its neighbors, yet strong enough to deter the strongest of its neighbors.

Time, 1-28:39.

5

[Disagreeing with those who say U.S.-led forces should have gone all the way to Baghdad and pushed Iraqi President Saddam Hussein out in the recent Persian Gulf war]: We probably should have continued the war, closed the loop and prevented the several hundred [Iraqi] tanks from going back north of Basra. [But] we should not have gone on to Baghdad. That was not the plan. It's always risky to add to your objectives in the middle of the war. That was not part of the UN resolution; it was not part of the mandate to go on to Baghdad and, frankly, if we had gone into Baghdad and pushed Saddam Hussein off, we would have inherited an even bigger mess than the mess we inherited with the [Kurdish] refugee problem.

Interview/USA Today, 4-18:(A)11.

Tarik Aziz
Foreign Minister of Iraq

1

Iraq does not yield to pressure, but Iraq is open to genuine exchange of views. If there is a genuine, sincere, serious intention to make peace in the whole region of the Middle East, we are ready to reciprocate. If we are going to hear the same kind of talk that has been reiterated in the last few months [that Iraq must leave Kuwait unconditionally], then we are going to give the proper response.

Airport arrival statement,
Geneva, Jan. 8/
The New York Times, 1-9:(A)6.

2

[On his rejection of a letter given him by U.S. Secretary of State James Baker from U.S. President George Bush to Iraqi President Saddam Hussein about the possibility of imminent war]: I told him [Baker] I am sorry, I cannot receive such a letter. The language in this letter is not compatible with the language that should be used in correspondences between heads of state. When a head of state writes to another head of state a letter and he really intends to make peace, he should use polite language.

News conference, Geneva, Jan. 9/
The New York Times, 1-10:(A)4.

James A. Baker III
Secretary of State
of the United States

3

[On the UN-set deadline of January 15 for Iraq to pull out of Kuwait or face possible military action]: We have been dealing with this issue for five months. The Security Council gave Iraq and [Iraqi President] Saddam [Hussein] a 45-day pause for peace. We should not be talking about postponing deadlines that we have been saying for five months, or for 45 days certainly, are real deadlines. We have been making the point over and over and over that this deadline is real, and the only real chance we have for peace in my opinion is if Saddam Hussein begins to understand that the deadline is real and we are serious.

London, Jan. 7/The Washington Post, 1-8:(A)13.

4

[Addressing Iraqi Foreign Minister Tarik Aziz]: There will be harsh consequences if you use chemical or biological weapons. The United States will tolerate no terrorism against Americans nor will it tolerate the destruction of Kuwaiti oil installations. We are not trying to threaten but to inform. We want to leave as little room as possible for any further tragic miscalculations [by Iraq].

Geneva, January/
U.S. News & World Report,
1-21:21.

5

[On his just-concluded meeting with Iraqi Foreign Minister Tarik Aziz]: Regrettably, in over six hours of talks, I heard nothing today that suggested to me any Iraqi flexibility whatsoever on complying with the United Nations Security Council resolutions [demanding that Iraq leave Kuwait]. The choice is Iraq's. If it should choose to continue its brutal occupation of Kuwait, Iraq will be choosing a military confrontation which it cannot win and which will have devastating consequences for Iraq.

News conference, Geneva, Jan. 9/
The New York Times, 1-10:(A)1.

6

... there have been too many Iraqi miscalculations. And we fear yet another miscalculation, a truly tragic one. We believe that if Iraq is going to withdraw from Kuwait, [Iraqi President] Saddam Hussein will probably wait until he is on the very brink [when U.S.-led forces will launch an attack] before he moves. And our worry is that in his usual style, he will miscalculate where the brink exactly is. Just so there is no misunderstanding, let me be absolutely clear: We pass the brink at midnight, January 15.

To U.S. troops,
Saudi Arabia, Jan. 11/
The Washington Post, 1-12:(A)8.

7

[Criticizing a recent speech by Jordanian King Hussein in which he appeared to support Iraq in

(JAMES A. BAKER III)

the current Persian Gulf war]: We have a major disagreement with the King and what he said in that speech and the position that he has taken. To allege that our effort against Iraq is unjust and exceeds the UN resolution is something that is patently not true. We have repeatedly emphasized that our objective [in the war] is not the destruction of Iraq, it is the liberation of Kuwait and, quite frankly, we find it very sad that the King omitted in this rather long speech any reference whatsoever, not one single reference, to Iraq's invasion of Kuwait, and omitted any reference therefore to any call for withdrawal [by Iraq].

Before Senate Foreign Relations
Committee, Washington, Feb. 7/
The New York Times, 2-8:(A)7.

1

[On criticism that the U.S. is doing nothing to help Iraqi Kurdish and Shiite rebels fighting the government of Saddam Hussein following the end of the war]: We are not prepared to go down the slippery slope of being sucked into a civil war [in Iraq]. We cannot police what goes on inside Iraq, and we cannot be the arbiters of who shall govern Iraq. As [U.S.] President Bush has repeatedly made clear, our objective was the liberation of Kuwait. It never extended to the remaking of Iraq. We repeatedly said that that could only be done by the Iraqi people. However, we cannot be indifferent to atrocities and human suffering in Iraq, and we haven't been. We will make certain that humanitarian assistance, in both northern and southern Iraq, gets to those who most need it. We will not tolerate any [Iraqi government] interference with this humanitarian relief effort.

Ankara, Turkey,
April 7/
Los Angeles Times, 4-8:(A)8.

2

[On criticism in the U.S. that the Persian Gulf countries it defended in the recent war are not moving to democracy and human rights for their

people]: When we went in, we went in because it was the right thing to do, and we went in because we did not think that unprovoked aggression should be permitted to succeed, and we went in because we had some substantial national interests at stake. You can't say you're doing this to keep the world safe for democracy, because these aren't democracies that you're going in here to assist. But it was still the right thing to do.

Before Senate
Foreign Operations Subcommittee,
Washington, May 23/
The New York Times, 5-24:(A)3.

Bandar bin Sultan
Saudi Arabian Ambassador
to the United States

3

[Criticizing King Hussein of Jordan for supporting Iraq in its take-over of Kuwait]: He earned our disrespect and he earned [Iraqi President] Saddam Hussein's contempt. He was our friend for 40 years, and he sold us out, just like this. He cheered Saddam for five months. In fact, [King] Hussein was more eloquent than Saddam in expressing his cause. And when the chips were down, and we [the U.S.-led coalition] were hammering Saddam like hell, Hussein of Jordan said, "But I'm neutral."

Interview,
Washington/
Los Angeles Times, 2-22:(A)8.

Lloyd Bentsen
United States Senator,
D-Texas

4

[Arguing against the U.S. going to war at this time]: If we go to war, the estimate is we'll be spending an additional $1-billion to $2-billion a day. And that's with all of our deficit problems, with a recession in our country, with unemployment going up. Most experts believe that [current UN economic sanctions against Iraq] will work with time, and the estimates range all the way from 12 to 18 months.

The Christian Science Monitor,
1-15:6.

Howard L. Berman
United States Representative,
D-California

1

[On the possibility of war]: If we do not deal with [Iraqi President] Saddam Hussein now, the world and the United States will be facing a more heavily armed, a more powerful, more dangerous Saddam Hussein five or 10 years from now . . . This is a man who is hell-bent on establishing hegemony over the entire Middle East region . . . [He] is a very dangerous, potentially very powerful tyrant. And even though there is inadequate burden-sharing and even though it sickens me that some of our allies are not participating the way they shou!d . . . we have to deal with him now. If we don't, we'll pay a much greater price in the future.

Los Angeles Times, 1-12:(A)6.

Joseph R. Biden, Jr.
United States Senator,
D-Delaware

2

I think our willingness to shed American blood in the Persian Gulf to defend these oil-rich monarchies permits us to expect progress toward democracy and economic development [in those countries]. To those who say this might offend those Gulf monarchies, I say that promoting democracy should not be an offense to anyone. It seems like the least we can expect.

June 11/
The Washington Post, 6-13:(A)37.

Abdullah Bishara
Secretary General,
(Persian) Gulf
Cooperation Council

3

[Criticizing those Arab countries that do not support Kuwait in the war]: Farewell to the slogans of the past [about solidarity and brotherhood among Arab nations]. The GCC countries were shocked to discover that when the chips were down, those who had benefitted from their munificence [Jordan, Yemen, Algeria, Sudan, for example] turned against them, that economic contributions [made by the GCC in the past] went unrewarded. The new order will be based on a new approach. We used our economic clout in the past for charity. Now we are going to use it for mutuality of benefits. Economies in the Arab world have to be de-politicized, they must be free-market. If I invest in Damascus, I want to be sure I have a reward and that my interest will be protected.

Interview,
Riyadh, Saudi Arabia/
The Christian Science Monitor,
1-29:5.

4

[Criticizing PLO chairman Yasir Arafat for siding with Iraq in the war]: Mr. Arafat shot from the hip. He turned his back on legitimacy [of Kuwait] . . . And more than that, he called on Palestinians to fight the Kuwaitis. For us as Kuwaitis, we will never forgive. He's unpardonable [and has] lost any residue of credibility. I can say he is *persona non grata*; not only he, but his cohorts who rallied to his side.

To reporters,
Damascus, Syria, March 6/
Los Angeles Times, 3-7:(A)7.

Barbara Boxer
United States Representative,
D-California

5

Have you ever seen a body that is shot apart? Have you ever seen it up close? From a distance, from very far away, it may look still and peaceful. But up close you see the violence, the pain, the suffering, the horror . . . Make no mistake; we will win this war quickly. Maybe two weeks, maybe two months; that's quick. Maybe, at most, six months. That's quick, I guess. But, my colleagues, it won't come free. There's a huge price if we choose this route, even in the best of circumstances. The price is in body bags, in babies killed, in an uncertain, unstable Middle East, even after the crisis.

Before the House,
Washington, Jan. 11/
The Washington Post, 1-12:(A)12.

George Bush
President of the United States

1

[On the possibility of war between U.S.-led forces and Iraq]:. . . Iraq has accepted my initiative for a meeting between [U.S.] Secretary [of State James] Baker and [Iraqi] Foreign Minister [Tarik] Aziz. The meeting will take place on Wednesday, January 9, in Geneva. And this is a useful step. I hope that Iraq's acceptance of the meeting indicates a growing awareness of the seriousness of the situation and a willingness to heed the international community's will as expressed in 12 United Nations Security Council resolutions. There can be no compromise or negotiating on the objectives contained in those UN resolutions. And so it is now for [Iraqi President] Saddam Hussein to respond to the international community's plea for reason. I took this initiative yesterday with the view of going the extra mile to achieve a peaceful solution to the current crisis in the [Persian] Gulf. Secretary Baker's mission to Geneva is to convey to Iraq the gravity of the situation and the determination of the international community to overcome Iraq's aggression against Kuwait. Iraq knows what is necessary: the complete and unconditional and immediate withdrawal of all Iraqi forces from all of Kuwait and the restoration of the legitimate government of Kuwait.

News conference,
Washington, Jan. 4/
The New York Times, 1-5:4.

2

The current situation in the Persian Gulf, brought about by Iraq's unprovoked invasion and subsequent brutal occupation of Kuwait, threatens vital U.S. interests. The situation also threatens the peace. It would, however, greatly enhance the chances for peace if Congress were now to go on record supporting the position adopted by the UN Security Council on 12 separate occasions [that Iraq must get out of Kuwait]. Such an action [by the U.S. Congress] would underline that the United States stands with the international community and on the side of law and decency; it also would help dispel any belief that may exist in the minds of Iraq's leaders

that the United States lacks the necessary unity to act decisively in response to Iraq's continued aggression against Kuwait . . . I am determined to do whatever is necessary to protect America's security. I ask Congress to join with me in this task. I can think of no better way than for Congress to express its support for the President at this critical time. This truly is the last best chance for peace.

Letter to Congressional leaders
asking for authorization for the use
of force against Iraq,
Washington, Jan. 8*/
The New York Times, 1-9:(A)6.

3

[Announcing the start of air attacks by U.S.-led forces against Iraq]: Five months ago, [Iraqi President] Saddam Hussein started this cruel war against Kuwait; tonight the battle has been joined. This military action, taken in accord with United Nations resolutions and with the consent of the United States Congress, follows months of constant and virtually endless diplomatic activity on the part of the United Nations, the United States and many, many other countries. Arab leaders sought what became known as an "Arab solution," only to conclude that Saddam Hussein was unwilling to leave Kuwait. Others traveled to Baghdad in a variety of efforts to restore peace and justice. Our Secretary of State, James Baker, held an historic meeting in Geneva only to be totally rebuffed [by Iraq's Foreign Minister]. This past weekend, in a last-ditch effort, the Secretary General of the United Nations went to the Middle East with peace in his heart—his second such mission—and he came back from Baghdad with no progress at all in getting Saddam Hussein to withdraw from Kuwait. Now the 28 countries with forces in the [Persian] Gulf area have exhausted all reasonable efforts to reach a peaceful resolution, have no choice but to drive Saddam from Kuwait by force. We will not fail. As I report to you, air attacks are under way against military targets in Iraq. We are determined to knock out Saddam Hussein's nuclear-bomb potential. We will also destroy his chemical-weapons facilities. Much of Saddam's artillery and tanks will be destroyed . . . Our

(GEORGE BUSH)

3

objectives are clear. Saddam Hussein's forces will leave Kuwait. The legitimate government of Kuwait will be restored to its rightful place, and Kuwait will once again be free.

Broadcast address to the nation,
Washington, Jan. 16/
Los Angeles Times, 1-17:(A)24.

1

As we meet here tonight, we are exactly one week into Operation Desert Storm. But it is important to date this conflict not from January 16 [1991] but from its true beginning: the assault of August 2 [1990]—Iraq's unprovoked aggression against the tiny nation of Kuwait. We did not begin a war seven days ago. Rather, we began to end a war—to right a wrong that the world could not ignore. From the day [Iraqi President] Saddam's [Hussein] forces first crossed into Kuwait, it was clear that this aggression required a swift response from our nation and the world community. What was—and is—at stake is not simply our energy and economic security, and the stability of a vital region—but the prospects for peace in the post-Cold War era: the promise of a new world order, based upon the rule of law.

Before Reserve Officers' Association
of the United States, Jan. 21/
USA Today, 1-24:(A)9.

2

[I] pledge to you and to all Americans: This [war] will not be another Vietnam. Never again will our armed forces be sent out to do a job with one hand tied behind their back. They will continue to have the support they need to get the job done—get it done quickly and with as little loss of life as possible. And that support is not just military but moral . . . When the brave men and women of [Operation] Desert Storm return home, they will return to the love and respect of a grateful nation.

Before Reserve Officers' Association
of the United States,
Washington, Jan. 23/
The Washington Post, 1-24:(A)27.

[Iraqi President] Saddam [Hussein] tried to cast this conflict as a religious war, but it has nothing to do with religion *per se.* [But] it has everything to do with what religion embodies— good versus evil, right versus wrong, human dignity and freedom versus tyranny and oppression.

Before National Religious Broadcasters
Association, Washington, Jan. 28/
The Washington Post, 1-29:(A)1.

4

[The war] will require time and sacrifice, but we will prevail—make no mistake about that. And when we win, and we will, we will have taught a dangerous dictator [Iraqi President Saddam Hussein]—and any tyrant tempted to follow in his footsteps—that the U.S. has a new credibility and that what we say goes. There is no place for lawless aggression in the Persian Gulf and in this new world order that we seek to create. And we mean it, and he will understand that when the day is done.

Speech, Fort Stewart, Ga., Feb. 1/
Los Angeles Times, 2-2:(A)11.

5

Within the last 24 hours alone, we have heard a defiant, uncompromising address by [Iraqi President] Saddam Hussein, followed less than 10 hours later by a statement in Moscow that, on the face of it, appears more reasonable. I say "on the face of it," because the statement promised unconditional Iraqi withdrawal from Kuwait, only to set forth a number of conditions. And needless to say, any conditions would be unacceptable to the international coalition and would not be in compliance with the United Nations Security Council Resolution 660's demand for immediate and unconditional withdrawal. More importantly and more urgently, we learned this morning that Saddam has now launched a scorched-earth policy against Kuwait, anticipating perhaps that he will now be forced to leave. He is wantonly setting fires to and destroying the oil wells, the oil tanks, the export terminals and other installations of that small country. Indeed, they are destroying the entire oil-

(GEORGE BUSH)

production system of Kuwait. And at the same time that that Moscow press conference was going on and Iraq's Foreign Minister was talking peace, Saddam Hussein was launching Scud missiles . . . The coalition will give Saddam Hussein until noon [tomorrow] to do what he must do, begin his immediate and unconditional withdrawal from Kuwait. We must hear publicly and authoritatively his acceptance of these terms.

Washington, Feb. 22/
The Washington Post, 2-23:(A)14.

1

[On the success of U.S.-led forces in pushing Iraq out of Kuwait]: Kuwait is liberated. Iraq's army is defeated. Our military objectives are met. Kuwait is once more in the hands of Kuwaitis in control of their own destiny. We share in their joy, a joy tempered only by our compassion for their ordeal. Tonight, the Kuwaiti flag once again flies above the capital of a free and sovereign nation, and the American flag flies above our Embassy. Seven months ago [when Iraq invaded Kuwait], America and the world drew a line in the sand. We declared that the aggression against Kuwait would not stand. And tonight America and the world have kept their word. This is not a time of euphoria, certainly not a time to gloat, but it is a time of pride, pride in our troops, pride in the friends who stood with us in the crisis, pride in our nation and the people whose strength and resolve made victory quick, decisive and just.

Broadcast address to the nation,
Washington, Feb. 27/
The New York Times, 2-28:(A)12.

2

[On Jordan's siding with Iraq in the war]:. . . we have had differences with Jordan. And it's going to take some time. I think the Jordanians have to sort out their internal problems the way they look at this matter . . . We have no lasting pique with Jordan. Everybody knows we've had very pleasant relations with Jordan in the past.

But I have tried to be very frank with His Majesty the King and with the government of Jordan, pointing out a certain sense of disappointment that all Americans feel that they [Jordan] moved that close to [Iraqi President] Saddam Hussein. But I think it's just going to take time. And I can't say how much, but clearly we do not want to see [a] destabilized Jordan. I have no personal animosity toward His Majesty the King. So we'll just have to wait and see.

News conference,
Washington, March 1/
The New York Times, 3-2:5.

3

In terms of rebuilding Iraq [after the damage caused in the war], my view is this: Iraq, had they been led differently, is basically a wealthy country—they are a significant oil producer, they get enormous income . . . Iraq has a big reconstruction job to do, but, I'll be honest with you, at this point I don't want to see one single dime of the United States taxpayers' money to go into the reconstruction of Iraq. Now, you want to talk about helping a child? You want to talk about helping disease, something of that nature? Of course the United States will step up and do that which we've always done, lay aside the politics and help the health-care requirements, or help the children especially. But not reconstruction. They must work these things out without any help from the American taxpayer.

News conference,
Washington, March 1/
The New York Times, 3-2:5.

4

Tonight in Iraq, [President] Saddam [Hussein] walks amidst ruin. His war machine is crushed. His ability to threaten mass destruction is itself destroyed. His people have been lied to, denied the truth. And when his defeated legions come home, all Iraqis will see and feel the havoc he has wrought. And this I promise you: For all that Saddam has done to his own people, to the Kuwaitis and to the entire world, Saddam and those around him are accountable. All of us grieve for the victims of war, for the people of

(GEORGE BUSH)

Kuwait and the suffering that scars the soul of that proud nation. We grieve for all our fallen soldiers and their families, for all the innocents caught up in this conflict. And, yes, we grieve for the people of Iraq, a people who have never been our enemy. My hope is that one day we will once again welcome them as friends into the community of nations.

Before joint session of U.S. Congress,
Washington, March 6/
The Washington Post, 3-7:(A)32.

1

[On the Kurdish refugee problem in Iraq caused by Iraqi President Saddam Hussein's military crackdown on them after the Persian Gulf war]: Eleven days ago, on April 5, I announced that the United States would initiate what soon became the largest U.S. relief effort mounted in modern military history. Such an undertaking was made necessary by the terrible human tragedy unfolding in and around Iraq as a result of Saddam Hussein's brutal treatment of Iraqi citizens . . . Do I think the answer is now for Saddam Hussein to be kicked out? Absolutely. Because there will not be normalized relations with the United States . . . until Saddam Hussein is out of there . . . Do I think that the United States should bear guilt because of suggesting that the Iraqi people take matters into their own hands with the implication being given by some that the United States would be there to support them militarily? That was not true. We never implied that.

News conference,
Washington, April 16/
The New York Times, 4-17:(A)7.

2

[On criticism that he should have sent U.S.-led forces all the way to Baghdad and removed Iraqi President Saddam Hussein, rather than settling just for ending Iraqi occupation of Kuwait]: I don't think that even given hindsight, that I would say we should have done something different . . . because what I foresee would have been march-

ing into Baghdad, coalition forces getting sniped and maybe not finding Saddam Hussein and being bogged down in an urban guerrilla warfare. Now, how do I feel about Saddam Hussein today? Do I think he's a liar? Do I think he's broken his word over and over again? Yes. Will we ever have normal relations with this country as long as he's there? No.

Interview, Washington/
Los Angeles Times, 7-10:(A)4.

Dick Cheney
Secretary of Defense
of the United States

3

[On yesterday's U.S. bombing of what it calls an Iraqi command-and-control center in Baghdad but which contained hundreds of Iraqi civilians]: I think you all know that we sincerely regret any damage or any deaths caused to the civilian population. We've done everything we can to avoid that. Our forces, I think, have done an excellent job of targeting military targets and avoiding collateral damage to non-military targets. But the facility that was struck yesterday, we've gone back and checked very carefully on, and it was indeed a military facility, a hardened bunker, camouflage painted on top and plugged into [Iraqi President Saddam Hussein's] military communications system. We did in fact drop two bombs on it. They hit with great precision, and there's no question in my mind or in the mind of our key people that what we hit was a military target.

Before United States Chamber of
Commerce, Feb. 13/
USA Today, 2-14:(A)11.

4

[Arguing against U.S. military intervention to stop the Iraqi government's persecution of its Kurdish and Shiite citizens following the recent U.S.-led victory against Iraq]: It is just as important knowing when to use force as knowing when not to use force. When the [U.S.] President [Bush] made the decision to go to war, we had a very clear-cut military objective [to get Iraq out of Kuwait]. Once we cross over the line and start

(DICK CHENEY)

intervening in a civil war inside Iraq, it's a whole different proposition. I am as appalled and angry at seeing what [Iraqi President] Saddam Hussein's forces are doing to their own citizens as everybody else is . . . The only organized military force inside Iraq today, 20-some divisions, is the Iraqi Army. And there is no question that if we wanted to commit U.S. forces, we could go in and clean up the Iraqi Army or take Baghdad or intervene and defend the Kurds or the Shiites against the onslaught of the Iraqi Army. But that's not what we went over there to do. That would be a significant extension, a whole new set of military objectives for us to try to pursue. It would without doubt cost a lot of American lives, and it raises the very real specter of getting us involved in a quagmire trying to figure out who the hell is going to govern Iraq.

Interview, April/
U.S. News & World Report,
4-15:31.

Ramsey Clark
Former Attorney General
of the United States

1

Only one force on Earth can stop this war and only one force will start it—the President [of the U.S., Bush]. And the only power that will stop him is the people. If you and I take to the streets every day and tell everyone who will listen, "No war," it won't happen.

Los Angeles Times, 1-12:(A)8.

Anthony Cordesman
Military analyst; Specialist
on Persian Gulf conflicts

2

No matter how this [war] ends, we must take strong measures to control arms as the next step. We can't afford to let Iraq rearm. We can't afford to let Iran benefit. And we can't allow a situation where we push arms into Saudi Arabia to stop either Iraq or Iran. This odd business of trying to find a pillar on which to center policy is something that does not work. The idea that one northern Gulf state is better than another is an illusion that is only going to lead to conflict after conflict in the region.

Los Angeles Times,
1-18:(A)11.

Jerry F. Costello
United States Representative,
D-Illinois

3

[On whether to vote yes or no to giving U.S. President Bush authority to start hostilities against Iraq]:. . . if every member of Congress had a son or daughter in the Middle East, if the President had his son or his daughter in the Middle East in combat now, it might change their attitude to some extent when it comes to the issue of either war or pursuing options that take patience and time [UN economic sanctions against Iraq] . . . It's very difficult for me as a parent and as a member of Congress to risk either my son's life or the sons and daughters of other families in my district and around this country, when I know that in a matter of months that we can accomplish the same results [using the sanctions] without jeopardizing American lives.

Interview/
The Washington Post,
1-10:(A)23.

William J. Crowe, Jr.
Admiral, United States Navy
(Ret.);
Former Chairman,
Joint Chiefs of Staff

4

There's no guarantee that we'll be better off if we win [the war] . . . Either way it goes, it has a problem. If if goes badly, we'll be in the soup. It will probably pre-empt American intervention for a long time. If it goes well, it may not teach us the right lesson. It could encourage us to do something stupid in the future. If we dash into Iraq and cut off Kuwait and do it in a month, then some people will want to do something else [afterward].

Los Angeles Times,
1-18:(A)11.

Ronald V. Dellums
United States Representative,
D-California

1

[Criticizing the start of air attacks by U.S.-led forces against Iraq]: I am outraged by and oppose the commencement of the war in the Gulf. I continue to believe that if [international] sanctions [against Iraq] and other diplomatic efforts had been pressed, we could have resolved this crisis without the needless potential loss of life and unfathomable destruction that has occurred with the bombing tonight and which will occur in the fighting in the days and weeks ahead. I view this as an inestimable tragedy, one for which it will take us a lifetime to atone.

Jan. 16/USA Today, 1-17:(A)11.

Kenneth T. Derr
Chairman,
Chevron Corporation

2

[U.S.] President Bush has tried to downplay the oil part of the equation. I suspect that's because he's concerned that use of the word "oil" is not a very good idea, politically. But 30 per cent of the world's oil comes from the Persian Gulf. Sixty-five per cent of the reserves of oil are in that region. So I don't think I'm going to quite say it's a war over oil, but the existence of such a large piece of the world's oil supplies in the Persian Gulf clearly makes this situation one that is critical.

Interview/USA Today, 1-15:(A)11.

Byron L. Dorgan
United States Representative,
D-North Dakota

3

[On the U.S.-led coalition against Iraq]: It is a fig leaf to call this a "multinational force." It is an American force and would be an American war. And we will decide to spend money we don't have, borrowed from our allies, to send American kids to risk their lives to protect allied oil. When will we understand that it is time for America to ask our allies to bear their fair share of the burden? . . . I'm concerned about Iraq, concerned about war, concerned about our role in the world. But I'm concerned about something else. I'm concerned about America. Choking on debt and threatened with an economic crisis from within, I see a President and a Congress standing tall, exhibiting steely resolve in the Persian Gulf; willing to borrow money from abroad and risk our troops' lives to protect our allies' oil.

Before the House,
Washington, Jan. 11/
The New York Times, 1-12:6.

Fahd ibn Abdel Aziz al-Saud
King of Saudi Arabia

4

[Urging Iraqi President Saddam Hussein to withdraw his forces from Kuwait]: It will be in his favor if he withdraws [and] will make matters easy for him to [escape] any further punishment. And always, there is a way to negotiate and discuss and make agreements in the future so that what is happening now will not be repeated. [But] first [Iraq must] withdraw. Then, if there is any demand by Iraq to Kuwait, the two countries should sit together and discuss the matter between themselves, and whatever they agree on we will support.

During inspection tour of U.S.-led forces,
Hafr al-Batin, Saudi Arabia, Jan. 6/
The Washington Post, 1-7:(A)1.

Peter Galbraith
Staff member, U.S. Senate
Foreign Relations Committee

5

The first lesson of this crisis is that it was avoidable. We got into this situation because we abandoned our principles in favor of a politically expedient and economically greedy policy toward [Iraqi President] Saddam [Hussein]. There was an appalling period in the 1980s when, on the issue of chemical-weapons use, we condemned it without naming the country [Iraq]. And we were indifferent to Saddam's treatment of the Kurds and clear-cut human-rights abuses. All that sent a message that he could quite literally get away with murder. It would have been a lot cheaper if

(PETER GALBRAITH)

we'd sanctioned him earlier for use of chemical weapons on the Kurds and condemned him for attacking Iran. Instead, we saw dollar signs and a bulwark against [Islamic] fundamentalism whenever we looked at Iraq. It was nothing short of appeasement. And look at the price we had to pay to redress it when we were finally forced to face up to our own principles.

Los Angeles Times, 3-4:(A)11.

Geoffrey Garin
U.S. Democratic Party
consultant

1

[U.S. President Bush deserves praise for] being remarkably disciplined in focusing this on [Iraqi President] Saddam [Hussein] personally. Bush has used Saddam to claim the unquestionable moral high ground . . . [Former U.S. President Ronald] Reagan tried to do the same thing to [former Nicaraguan President Daniel] Ortega, [former Panamanian leader Manuel] Noriega and [Libyan leader Muammar] Qaddafi. But Reagan never established their capacity to do serious damage. Americans took Saddam Hussein very seriously. He was not just a bad guy; he came to be seen as a genuine threat.

The Washington Post, 2-23:(A)17.

Robert M. Gates
Assistant to President
of the United States
George Bush
and Deputy for National
Security Affairs

2

[Saying the U.S. favors keeping international sanctions against Iraq, which was recently defeated in the war, until Iraqi President Saddam Hussein leaves office]: Iraqis will pay the price while he is in power. All possible sanctions will be maintained until he is gone. Any easing of sanctions will be considered only where there is a new government. [Iraq] will be nothing but a pariah state [as long as Hussein rules]. Iraqis will not participate in post-crisis political, economic

and security arrangements until there is a change in regime.

Before American Newspaper Publishers
Association, Vancouver, Canada, May 7/
The New York Times, 5-21:(A)6.

John Glenn
United States Senator,
D-Ohio

3

[On the possibility of war]: Certainly Iraq is an ideal [economic] embargo target. And if the embargo ends in failure, we still have the military option. And I will fully support that course at that time. I believe the Persian Gulf is that important. But to again loose the terrors of war, and the thousands of lives that hang in the balance, should not be the first resort. And just saying that Kuwait was attacked or that hostages have been mistreated will not be of much solace if flag-draped coffins for both male and female soldiers and sailors and Marines and airmen line up in the hangars in Dover, Delaware.

Before the Senate,
Washington, Jan. 11/
The New York Times, 1-12:6.

Edward W. Gnehm, Jr.
United States Ambassador
to Kuwait

4

The rape of Kuwait [by Iraq] is not something abstract against sand and concrete. The rape is against men and women and children. The land is not murdered but the young men. [They] were picked up by Iraqi patrols in the night, shot on the front steps of their homes in full view of their families and their neighbors, who were forcibly collected to watch the execution . . . This crisis is about people and how people will live in the world in the years to come. That world cannot be a place for brutal aggressors, but it must be a place for those who wish to live in peace.

Swearing-in address,
Washington, Jan. 3/
Los Angeles Times, 1-4:(A)9.

Albert Gore, Jr.
United States Senator,
D-Tennessee

1

I support [U.S. President Bush's] moves to force [Iraqi President] Saddam Hussein to comply with the terms of the Gulf [war] cease-fire. But I disagree with [Bush's] policy at a more fundamental level—namely, his persistent view of Saddam Hussein as an acceptable part of the landscape, if and when we finally get him cut down to size . . . We can no more look forward to a constructive long-term relationship with Saddam Hussein than we could hope to house-break a cobra. But it is not just enough to say that there will not be normal U.S. relations with Iraq while he is in power. It is time to get down to cases. Sooner or later, he will go. Sooner is better. And with him, the entire Baathist [Party] rule by terror has to go as well, or we may simply exchange one brutal character for the next.

Before the Senate,
Washington, Sept. 19/
The New York Times, 9-26:(A)19.

Ghazi al-Gosaiby
Saudi Arabian Ambassador
to Bahrain

2

[Saying the forthcoming holy month of Ramadan will not cause his country to withdraw from fighting in the war]: We hope this battle will not last long, because nobody wants a war to last long, but not because of any particular date. I mean, we are defending our country. We will do that in Ramadan, we will do that during the pilgrimage season, if need be. We will do that at any time. A just war is just at any time. It is not a war that you fight in March, and in April you decide it is not a good time to fight a war. On the contrary, I think Ramadan will probably have the people even more willing to sacrifice themselves in order to liberate and defend their country.

Los Angeles Times, 2-13:(A)15.

3

I think it was a very stupid thing of [Iraqi President] Saddam Hussein when he declared this war. I think we should always remember *he* declared this war—not us, not America, not the [U.S.-led] coalition. He went and invaded a country that is a weak, peaceful, friendly neighbor . . . So if somebody comes now and says this is a war against Iraq, or that Iraq's infrastructure is being destroyed [by coalition forces], we would simply remind him of a very simple fact: Who started this? Who declared war? Who started the aggression? Who defied the international community? We have always known—anybody with any sense realized—that when he invaded Kuwait he was not going to be allowed to get away with it. Because if he did, no country, no small country would ever be safe . . . The blame should be put squarely, entirely and completely upon Saddam Hussein. He's the one who asked for it. He's the one who was determined to lead himself to this destiny.

Interview, Manama, Bahrain/
Los Angeles Times, 2-24:(M)3.

4

[Criticizing Palestinians who sided with Iraq in its invasion and take-over of Kuwait]: I think those people who are now, and in particular [PLO chairman] Mr. Yasir Arafat, those people who stood with [Iraqi President] Saddam Hussein, who are supporting him, have lost all their credibility with the man in the street in the GCC countries. I don't know about the government, but I can tell you nobody in the Gulf now trusts those who stood with Saddam Hussein or could deal with them in the future. So I think . . . if the Palestinian cause is to recover, then they should find some new leaders.

Interview, Manama, Bahrain/
Los Angeles Times, 2-24:(M)3.

Jeffrey Greenhut
Colonel, United States Army;
Arts, monument and archives
officer for U.S. Army
in Kuwait

5

[On the looting and destruction of the Kuwait National Museum by Iraqi forces who occupied Kuwait since last August until they were forced

(JEFFREY GREENHUT)

out in the war]: What [Iraqi President Saddam Hussein] did to the people of Kuwait was a crime against humanity. The torching of the [Kuwaiti] oil wells was a crime against the planet. But what he did here [to the Museum] was a crime against civilization. I have devoted my life to the acquisition and dissemination of knowledge, and this makes me angry. I want to shoot somebody.

Los Angeles Times, 3-11:(A)1.

Sadoun Hammadi
Deputy Prime Minister of Iraq

1

[On the war]: What is currently taking place is unrelated to Kuwait. The question now is a question of the American aggression, a violent and imperialist aggression, which is intended to destroy Iraq and subjugate the region . . . The issue of Kuwait has been used as a cover for aggression.

News conference,
Amman, Jordan, Feb. 10/
Los Angeles Times, 2-11:(A)1.

David Hannay
British Ambassador/
Permanent Representative
to the United Nations

2

[On the defeat of Iraq in the war]: There are many small countries in each region of the world that have cause to worry from their larger, better-armed neighbors. They should be able to sleep more securely in their beds after this episode. Just think on the contrary how they would have felt had [Iraqi President] Saddam Hussein been allowed by the United Nations to enjoy the fruits of his aggression.

Before UN Security Council,
New York, April 3/
Los Angeles Times, 4-4:(A)6.

Tom Harkin
United States Senator,
D-Iowa

3

[Arguing against U.S. Congressional approval for giving President Bush the authority to begin

hostilities against Iraq]: Just because the President, with his Lone Ranger type of policy, has put us in an untenable position doesn't mean we have to rubber-stamp it and send young men and women into war at this time.

The Washington Post, 1-10:(A)28.

4

When [Iraqi President Saddam Hussein] indicated he was going to invade Kuwait [last year], we didn't do a darn thing. When he started making moves, we should have been there with aircraft carriers and military support and said, "You take one step and that's it." I don't think he'd have ever done it. And I think [U.S. President] George Bush has got to be held accountable for all of the events that led up to that.

To reporters, Washington/
The Christian Science Monitor,
7-22:2.

Ernest F. Hollings
United States Senator,
D-South Carolina

5

[Addressing U.S. Secretary of State James Baker on the recent U.S.-led victory in forcing Iraq out of Kuwait]: What did we win? We've still got [Iraqi President] Saddam [Hussein]. We've had to adopt the Kurds [who suffered post-war persecution by the Iraqi government]. We have strengthened Iran. Down in Kuwait . . . the torture and rape of Saddam . . . continues under the [Kuwaiti] Emir.

At Senate Appropriations
Committee hearing,
Washington, June 12/
The Washington Post, 6-13:(A)37.

Robert E. Hunter
Director of European studies,
Center for Strategic and
International Studies
(United States)

6

What has happened in the past month [the start of military force against Iraq by the U.S.-led coalition] is clearly American leadership with a

297

(ROBERT E. HUNTER)

lot of "followership." There's been a facade of multilateralism . . . but in practice it's an American thing. If the "new world order" concept is going to have any validity, first there has to be an intelligent effort in the Middle East with a lot of sharing of ideas and responsibilities among countries. It won't work if the United States defines the new world order and the others are simply expected to salute.

Los Angeles Times, 2-18:(A)10.

Douglas Hurd
Foreign Secretary
of the United Kingdom

1

[Urging Israel not to retaliate against Iraq for that country's launching of Scud missiles against Israel following the start of the war, of which Israel is not a party]: We understand fully the anger of the Israeli government and people and their responsibility for the defense of their country. We have asked them to understand in turn the need to retain the greatest possible support for the military action being undertaken against Iraq, including among the Arab nations who have joined us in that action or who support it. Israel has the right of self-defense, and no one can take this decision from them. But we believe that restraint by Israel at this time would be interpreted as strength, not weakness, given the powerful operation now under way against Iraq in pursuit of the objectives laid down by the United Nations [getting Iraq out of Kuwait].

Before British House of Commons,
London, Jan. 18/
Los Angeles Times, 1-19:(A)10.

2

Those of us who have contributed a lot to the [war] effort now have a stake. We have to make sure in the post-war that [Iraqi President] Saddam Hussein was completely a bogus, puffed-up frog of a man insofar as he claimed to be spokesman for the Arab world.

Before House of Commons
Foreign Affairs Committee,
London, Feb. 25/
The New York Times, 2-26:(A)11.

Hussein ibn Talal
King of Jordan

3

[Criticizing the war against Iraq]: The talk [in the West] about a new world order whose early feature is the destruction of Iraq . . . leads us to wonder about the identity of this order and instills in us doubts about its nature. Fire rains down upon Iraq from airplanes, from battleships, from submarines and rockets, destroying mosques, churches, schools, museums, powdered-milk factories, residential areas, Bedouin tents, electricity-generating stations and water networks. This bombing started from the first hours and took the form of a war that aims to destroy all the achievements of Iraq and return it to primitive life.

Broadcast address to the nation,
Amman, Feb. 6/
The Washington Post, 2-7:(A)24.

4

[Asking Arab nations to forgive him for siding with Iraq in the war]: You know that after Iraq and Kuwait, Jordan suffered most from this crisis . . . Gloating and apportioning blame are not Arab traits, nor are they compatible with their spiritual values because they lead to enmity, hatred and alienation. On the other hand, forgiveness and burying the past lead to healing the wounds and closing the ranks of the [Arab] nation once again. Let us turn over a new page, thanking God that the Gulf war has ended, the bleeding has stopped and that the people of Kuwait enjoy their independence once again . . . On this day, we urge the world again to address the question of Palestine by the same criteria that has applied over the question of Kuwait. We should also like to renew our pledge to the world that we are committed to striving for the attainment of a just and durable peace that guarantees the national rights of the Palestinian people on their national soil. Foremost among these rights is their right to self-determination and to representation in a peace process aimed at resolving the Arab-Israeli conflict.

Broadcast address to the nation,
Amman, March 1/
The New York Times, 3-2:4.

(HUSSEIN IBN TALAL)

1

[On criticism by the U.S. and Persian Gulf countries of his seeming support for Iraq during the war]: We were never for the Iraq invasion [of Kuwait last year], never a party to it and never aware it was going to happen. But a majority of the world, including the U.S., adopted an attitude that "you are either with us or against us." Let me be very, very clear: We were against Iraq's action, and we were against Iraq's intransigence in not taking any of the opportunities to resolve this question peacefully. We never conspired against anybody. When people realize this, maybe they are going to feel what any decent people would: that they have wronged a country [Jordan] and wronged the people and wronged the leader of those people, a friend of theirs for many years.

Interview, Amman/
Time, 7-22:42.

Ahmed Hussein
Foreign Minister of Iraq

2

[Criticizing U.S. President Bush's handling of the war]: We would wonder what to call one who killed women, children and the elderly with his planes and missiles, who bombarded a shelter killing more women and children, who gave the orders to bury Iraqi soldiers alive, whose forces targeted baby-food factories, and who insists on depriving a population of 18 million [Iraqis] from food and medicine, and all other means of livelihood.

At United Nations,
New York, Sept. 27/
The Washington Post,
9-28:(A)14.

Saddam Hussein
President of Iraq

3

It is the role of the faithful to fight against tyranny, against injustice, against corruption and against the foolish and tyrannical U.S. Administration and its puppet, the Zionist entity [Israel], and against those bad people who have formed with them an alliance of tyranny and injustice.

For these reasons, the battle in which you are locked today is the mother of all battles.

Broadcast address to the nation,
Baghdad, Jan. 6/
Los Angeles Times, 1-7:(A)1.

4

We are not the type that bows to threats, and you will see the trap that America will fall into. If the Americans are involved in a Gulf conflict, you will see how we will make them swim in their own blood.

At meeting of Baath Party officials,
Baghdad, Jan. 9/
Los Angeles Times, 1-10:(A)12.

5

We have prepared all possible means to confront the aggressors. The Americans will come here to perform some acrobatics like in the Rambo movies, but wherever they land, they will find masses who will confront them. We are people who do not speak from military manuals but from eight years of combat experience [in the Iran-Iraq war]. All these sophisticated weapons [possessed by U.S. forces] will be under the test on the battlefield, and they will see how their weapons will be rendered useless . . . We fight for the sake of dignity. We fight for the sake of our Lord . . . To think that the infidel can fight with such commitment—this will never happen. The showdown today is not a showdown for land . . . but a showdown between the infidels and the true believers.

At international Islamic conference,
Baghdad, Jan. 11/
The Washington Post, 1-12:(A)9.

6

[When] it was decided that the [UN] Security Council would meet to look into the Soviet peace initiative, which we supported . . . the treacherous [U.S. President] Bush and his filthy agent [Saudi Arabian King] Fahd, and others who have consorted with them in committing crimes, shame and aggression, committed the treachery [and] waged their large-scale ground assault at our

(SADDAM HUSSEIN)

struggling forces this morning. If [our army is defeated], God forbid, there will only be the deep abyss to which the enemies are aspiring to push you [Iraqi forces], and a lengthy darkness will prevail over Iraq. Fight them and show no mercy toward them, for this is how God wishes the faithful to fight the infidel. Your sons, mothers, fathers and kin, and the entire population of Iraq and the world, are beholding your performance today.

Addressing Iraqi forces, Feb. 24/
USA Today, 2-25:(A)2.

1

[Announcing Iraq's withdrawal from Kuwait]: As of today our noble armed forces will complete their withdrawal from Kuwait. Today, our fight against aggression and atheism in a 30-country coalition that has officially waged a U.S.-led war on us, will have lasted from the night of January 16-17 until this moment—two months of legendary showdown. This showdown is a clear evidence of what God meant it to be: a lesson that would lead the believers to faith, immunity and capability, and the unfaithful, criminals, traitors, evil and depraved to abyss, weakness and humiliation . . . Today, special circumstances led the Iraqi army to withdraw because of different reasons, including the aggression and abominable embargo carried out by 30 allied countries led by the criminal machine and entity in America and its chief allies . . . The Iraqis will remember and will never forget that on 8-8-90 A.D. it [Kuwait] became a meaningful part of Iraq. Legally, constitutionally and actually it continued to be so until last night, when the withdrawal began . . .

Speech to the Iraqi nation, Feb. 26/
The Washington Post, 2-27:(A)32.

Saad Eddin Ibrahim
Professor of sociology,
American University, Cairo

2

[On Iraqi President Saddam Hussein, following Iraq's recent defeat in the war]: I don't think Saddam Hussein will survive for very long,

metaphorically or literally . . . He's not going to give up without a stiff fight, though. His legacy will disintegrate. But this will take some time, until the facts are revealed to the deceived masses who thought of him as a messiah of Arab nationalism. I think there will be intense disappointment, frustration, anger, sadness . . . among his supporters, among those who wanted to believe that there is an Arab leader who can stand up to the West. This, of course, does not change how people feel about the West. Even the most anti-Hussein forces in the Arab world will never forgive the West for a long list of grievances, the latest of which is that the West helped Hussein to become the Frankenstein he became. The biggest grievance is the double standard— the implicit racism in many of the Western policies toward this part of the world. When Hussein pinpointed that, he was right.

Interview/
Los Angeles Times, 3-3:(M)2.

3

The only winners [in the war were] the U.S. and Israel; there are no Arab winners at all. The war has destroyed two Arab countries and divided the Arab world without any redeeming outcome.

The Wall Street Journal,
8-1:(A)1.

Latif Jassim
Minister of Information
of Iraq

4

Deep dialogue is very important for the two countries [Iraq and the U.S.] because you have these huge forces on the two sides that are very dangerous. We are ready to understand the point of view of the United States, and the United States must understand our point of view about the crisis, about the situation in that Middle East. A dialogue for one year is better than war for one day.

Interview,
Baghdad, Jan. 8/
The New York Times, 1-9:(A)8.

(LATIF JASSIM)

1

[On Iraq's invasion and take-over of Kuwait]: Our troops are there to stay forever. Kuwait is the 19th province of Iraq and there is no way that this will change. The issue of Kuwait is finished.

Interview, Jan. 12/
The Christian Science Monitor, 1-15:4.

Thomas W. Kelly
Lieutenant General,
United States Army;
Director of Operations,
Joint Chiefs of Staff

2

[In this war,] you had a good combination of an evil enemy who was recognized, a very capable U.S. military that was able to respond, a national will [in the U.S.] that supported that, and a clear-cut objective. I think those four things are really very important as we analyze why we went to the Persian Gulf and why we did as well as we did while we were there.

Interview/USA Today, 3-20:(A)13.

Edward M. Kennedy
United States Senator,
D-Massachusetts

3

I urge the [U.S.] Senate to vote for peace, not war [by not authorizing President Bush to use force against Iraq] . . . At this historic moment, it may well be that only Congress can stop this senseless march toward war . . . The American people stand united in opposing [Iraqi President] Saddam Hussein . . . But America is deeply divided on whether war at this time, and on President Bush's timetable, is the only way to accomplish these goals. We have given peace a chance, but we have not given peace enough chance . . . We have arrayed an impressive international coalition against Iraq. But when the bullets start flying, 90 per cent of the casualties will be American. It is hardly a surprise that so many other nations are willing to fight to the last American to achieve the goals of the United Nations. It is not their sons and daughters who will do the dying.

Before the Senate,
Washington, Jan. 10/
Los Angeles Times, 1-11:(A)7.

Joseph P. Kennedy II
United States Representative,
D-Massachusetts

4

We're there to help our so-called Kuwaiti and Saudi friends. Need I remind the members of this chamber what the Kuwaitis and Saudis did to this country in 1973 [the oil embargo]? Did to us again in 1979? We're there to protect these so-called friends? Ladies and gentlemen, these fickle friends have never proven that they are worth the kind of price that [U.S.] President Bush is committing.

Before the House, Washington, Jan. 11/
The New York Times, 1-12:6.

Bob Kerrey
United States Senator,
D-Nebraska

5

[Criticizing the U.S. Bush Administration's handling of the crisis and the possibility of war]: [The Administration] came with this nonsense and said, "Gee, our way of life is threatened here [because of dependence on Persian Gulf oil]." Our way of life wasn't threatened. We're discovering that life goes on here in the United States without a great deal of disruption; 20 cents a gallon [increase in price] and maybe it's contributing a bit to the downturn in the economy. But if we're asking more than 400,000 guys potentially to die over there, it's a relatively small price for us to pay. There's been some economic disruption, but not a colossal disruption.

Interview, Los Angeles/
Los Angeles Times, 1-6:(M)3.

Ali Khamenei
Spiritual leader of Iran

6

[U.S. President] George Bush is a murderer who slaughters Iraq's innocent people. [But] those who support [Iraqi President] Saddam Hussein are wrong. What Saddam has done in Kuwait is unjustifiable. This is in no way a war between Islam and the blasphemy as Saddam Hussein tries to portray it. This is just a war between two evils.

Speech, Jan. 24/
The Christian Science Monitor, 2-5:3.

Helmut Kohl
Chancellor of Germany

1

[Criticizing those demonstrators in Germany who protest the U.S.-led war against Iraq]: I can well understand if people take to the street out of their desire for peace. But I do not understand at all when such actions turn against the United States, which is defending international law in the Gulf. Those who demonstrate must be asked where they were on August 2 [1990], the day Kuwait was taken over. I am dismayed by the moral indifference, the crass twisting of facts and the definite fomenting of emotions at some demonstrations.

Bonn, Germany, Jan. 23/
The Washington Post, 1-24:(A)17.

Charles Kupchan
Professor of politics,
Princeton University
(United States);
Specialist on the Persian Gulf

2

Victory now means two things: It means getting Iraq out of Kuwait, but it also means leaving the Iraqi military in such a degraded state that a permanent American presence is not necessary in the Gulf. We need to destroy Iraq's military infrastructure, but we need to preserve its political, economic and social infrastructure. If you turn the country into a parking lot, it could alter the alignment in the region for years to come in ways the United States may well not find advantageous.

The Washington Post, 1-24:(A)27.

Jim Leach
United States Representative,
R-Iowa

3

[Supporting U.S. President Bush's request for Congressional authorization to use military force against Iraq]: [The] liberal leadership in Congress [which is against giving war authority] appears on the verge of repudiating the philosophical heritage of Wilson and Roosevelt, as well as Truman and John Kennedy, in favor of

more flocculent "wait-and-see" nostrums that lack historical and philosophical perspective. What is the morality of the Congressional leadership's "wait-and-see" approach? [Iraqi President] Saddam Hussein has conducted two wars in the last 10 years which resulted in a million casualties; he has made rape a daily instrument of coercive state policy; executions are of epidemic proportions, frequently with family members asked to witness and pay for the bullets. In this context, is it moral to stand by? Can we allow Saddam's model of behavior to be rewarded or replicated elsewhere?

Before the House,
Washington/
The Washington Post, 1-12:(A)12.

John Major
Prime Minister
of the United Kingdom

4

[On Iraqi President Saddam Hussein]: It is perfectly clear that this man is amoral. He takes hostages. He attacks population centers. He threatens prisoners. He is a man without pity. And whatever his fate may be, I for one will not weep for him.

Before British House of Commons,
London, Jan. 22/
The New York Times, 1-23:(A)8.

Clovis Maksoud
Chief Arab League representative
to the United Nations

5

Iraq's fundamental mistake was not only confined to what it did to Kuwait. By its behavior, it made itself the vehicle for allowing the area to become an arena for outside nations to project power. There's a certain bitterness you find throughout the Third World and the Arab world about [Iraqi President] Saddam Hussein's actions. Iraq has brought back certain memories which we thought were overtaken by events.

The Christian Science Monitor,
8-2:6.

Michael Mandelbaum
Director of East-West studies,
Council on Foreign Relations
(United States)

1

There will only be a cease-fire if U.S. opinion turns completely against the war. Arab opinion and Soviet opinion don't count. We count. We should consider [world opinion]; but once we're on this course, there are drawbacks to stopping. If the British get antsy, that would make a difference. If [German Chancellor Helmut] Kohl gets antsy, that would make a difference. But the fact there are 200,000 people marching in Morocco [against U.S. war policy], that doesn't count. The Egyptians count, the Saudis count.

USA Today, 2-14:(A)4.

Mohamed al-Mashat
Iraqi Ambassador
to the United States

2

God knows we don't want this war; the Americans are starting the war, not us. It was Americans who made deadlines; Americans who were planning to attack Iraq in the first place. We consider it will be mass murder because there's nothing Iraq has done to the United States; Iraq has not touched U.S. interests . . . We want peace with justice, and we will never accept any humiliation or surrender. It's an Arab problem and you should let Arabs solve it . . . You should consider all the animosity that will be created by U.S. aggression among all the millions of Arabs and the billion Muslims in the world. The blood that will be shed, we put that responsibility on the Americans because they have blocked the Arab solution.

Interview, Washington, Jan. 15/
Los Angeles Times, 1-16:(A)9.

Barry McCaffrey
Major General,
United States Army;
Commander, 24th Infantry Division
(Mechanized)

3

[On U.S. involvement in the war]: . . . it seems to me that fighting for oil is okay. That is a vital American interest. The rights of 2 million people in Kuwait are absolutely worth fighting for. The United Nations came together and said [Iraq] cannot swallow [its] weaker neighbors. If you can't make it work here, if you can't demonstrate the rule of law, you will have endless warfare. I think that's what finally happened with the American people: They decided enough's enough. This [fighting Iraq] is a principle. And Americans are big on fighting for principles.

Interview/
U.S. News & World Report,
3-4:37.

John McCain
United States Senator,
R-Arizona

4

In this new world order, it is clear to me that if we fail to act [to get Iraq out of Kuwait] there will be inevitably a succession of dictators, of [Iraqi President] Saddam Husseins—of which around this globe there are an abundance, either in reality or would-be. And those dictators will see a green light, a green light for aggression, a green light for annexation of its weaker neighbors. And, indeed, over time a threat to the stability of this entire globe.

Before the Senate,
Washington, Jan. 11/
The New York Times, 1-12:6.

George S. McGovern
Former United States Senator,
D-South Dakota

5

I hope my foreboding about the war is wrong. But I don't have a good feeling about it at all. Not that I accept [Iraqi President] Saddam Hussein's invasion of Kuwait. That obviously makes it a different situation than we faced in Vietnam where there was no invasion—and where all the people we were fighting lived in Vietnam. I supported the sanctions [aimed at getting Iraq out of Kuwait], the condemnation, and even the defensive deployment to see that [Iraq] didn't get into the central oil fields in Saudi Arabia. But I think this war is extremely ill-advised. I seriously ques-

(GEORGE S. McGOVERN)

tion the military and political judgment of the President [Bush]. I think he made a costly mistake and there are all kinds of problems ahead.

Interview/
The Christian Science Monitor,
2-5:18.

Robert H. Michel
United States Representative,
R-Illinois

1

[Iraqi President] Saddam Hussein not only invaded Kuwait, he occupied, terrorized, murdered civilians, systematically looted and turned a peaceful nation into a wasteland of horror. He seeks control over one of the world's vital resources [oil], and he ultimately seeks to make himself the unchallenged anti-Western dictator of the Mideast. Either we stop him now, and stop him permanently, or we won't stop him at all . . . We're told by some that we must show patience. We must wait for [economic] sanctions to work. We must wait six months or a year before [military] forces are used. We must stay the course. My question is this—stay what course? A course that allows Saddam to know he is freed from surprise attack, free from sudden offensive movement for six months or a year or more?

Before the House,
Washington, Jan. 10/
The New York Times, 1-11:(A)4.

Hisham Milhelm
Lebanese journalist

2

[On the beginning of hostilities by U.S.-led forces against Iraq]: When I learned of the attack, the first thing that crossed my mind is how little control Arabs have over their own destiny. [Iraqi President] Saddam Hussein invaded Kuwait without consulting anyone. [Saudi Arabia's King] Fahd invited the U.S. in [to protect his country from Iraq] without consulting anyone. In the battle to reshape the Arab world, the Arabs are on the sidelines.

U.S. News & World Report,
1-28:26.

George J. Mitchell
United States Senator,
D-Maine

3

Most Americans and most members of Congress, myself included, supported the President's [Bush] initial decision to deploy American forces to Saudi Arabia to deter further Iraqi aggression . . . The change began on November 8, when President Bush announced that he was doubling the number of American troops in the Persian Gulf to 430,000 in order to attain a credible offensive option . . . In effect, the President, overnight, with no consultation and no public debate, changed American policy from being part of a collective effort to enforce economic and diplomatic sanctions into a predominantly American effort, relying upon the use of American military force. Despite the fact that his own policy of international economic sanctions was having a significant effect upon the Iraqi economy, the President, without explanation, abandoned that approach and instead adopted a policy based first and foremost upon the use of American military force. As a result, this country has been placed on a course toward war. This has upset the balance of the President's initial policy, the balance between resources and responsibility, between interest and risk, between patience and strength.

Before the Senate,
Washington, Jan. 10/
The New York Times, 1-11:(A)4.

4

In the event of war, why should it be an American war, made up largely of American troops, American casualties and American deaths? Just this morning I heard it said that there may be "only" a few thousand American casualties. But for the families of those few thousand—the word *only* will have no meaning. And the truly haunting question, which no one will ever be able to answer, will be: Did they die unnecessarily? For if we go to war now, no one will ever know if [international] sanctions [against Iraq] would have worked if given a full and fair chance.

Before the Senate,
Washington, Jan. 10/
Los Angeles Times, 1-11:(A)7.

Francois Mitterrand
President of France

1

[On French cooperation in the U.S.-led military offensive against Iraq]: France affirmed its difference [with the U.S. before the war broke out] and was right to do so. But during combat, while soldiers are fighting as comrades for the same cause, are we going to indulge in some kind of game of divergence? We are linked, we are allies, and we intend to do what we are committed to do.

Broadcast interview, Feb. 24/
The Washington Post, 2-26:(A)10.

Amir Moussa
Foreign Minister of Egypt

2

[Criticizing PLO leader Yasir Arafat's support of Iraq in the war]: We are all upset with what happened, with all those who supported the occupation of Kuwait. We think they did a very big injustice to the Arab system and the Arab image and morale. They have made a grave mistake . . . Nobody is called upon to forgive and to forget. But the world goes on. We will have to continue cooperating and working with each other. But not the previous terms, not on terms of just kissing and hugging and "Yes, okay" and "Mafaat mat" ["What's past is past; let's look to the future"]. I don't believe in that.

Interview/
The Christian Science Monitor,
8-22:5.

Daniel Patrick Moynihan
United States Senator,
D-New York

3

[Criticizing U.S. President Bush for his stance against Iraq that may lead to war]: What we find here is a kind of time warp in which we're acting in an old mode with response to a new condition. I find it, for example, extraordinary that the President should so personalize the encounter with this particular thug in Baghdad [Iraqi President Saddam Hussein]—the most recent thug in Baghdad, not the last by any means; there'll be

others, they'll succeed each other. We are not in an international crisis in the sense that events that took place on August 2, [1990, Iraq's invasion of Kuwait] necessitate the confrontation of the largest set of armed forces since World War II. Nothing large happened. A nasty little country [Iraq] invaded a littler, but just as nasty, country [Kuwait].

Before the Senate,
Washington, Jan. 10/
The New York Times, 1-11:(A)4.

Hosni Mubarak
President of Egypt

4

We still insist on the Iraqi troop withdrawal from Kuwait, for the occupation of one Arab country by another using force is a very serious matter, and nobody can accept this move at the turn of the 20th century.

To reporters, Cairo, Jan. 22/
The Washington Post, 1-23:(A)21.

5

[Criticizing Iraq's use of Scud missiles against population centers in Israel and Saudi Arabia during the war]: [Iraqi President] Saddam [Hussein] once told me they [Scuds] were nonsense, just something that makes a hole in the ground. Political missiles can trigger a misguided demonstration, but they never win a war.

Life, March:70.

Jim Muir
Correspondent, British
Broadcasting Corporation

6

[On Kurds fleeing Iraqi forces in the wake of Kurdish rebellions against the Iraqi government following Iraq's loss of the Persian Gulf war]: Hundreds of thousands of Kurds are now on the move, cramming their families and whatever they could carry into lorries, tractor-trailers, cars, taxis and any other vehicles they could find. Refugee families are now scattered through the snow-covered Kurdish mountains, ill-equipped to face the bitterly cold nights and with no idea

305

(JIM MUIR)

what future lies ahead for them. Again and again, refugees and many other Iraqi Kurds asked Western correspondents why the [U.S.-led] coalition powers that urged the Iraqi people to rise up against [Iraqi President] Saddam [Hussein] now seem to be standing by and leave them to face the consequences of having done so.

Radio dispatch, April 1/
The New York Times, 4-2:(A)4.

Vitaly V. Naumkin
Deputy director,
Institute for Oriental Affairs
(Soviet Union)

1

Enormous losses do not demoralize [Iraqi President] Saddam [Hussein]. If, like in the war with Iran, he loses today, he will merely say, "Fine, I will win tomorrow." In my view, the Americans have totally misunderstood this . . . Saddam is counting on ecological weapons [the release of oil], on land battles, on the Americans' loss of morale. He is betting that if enough Americans are killed in land operations, then the climate in America will change, and he will be able to save himself.

Interview/
Los Angeles Times, 2-2:(A)5.

Benjamin Netanyahu
Deputy Foreign Minister
of Israel

2

[On Iraq's launching Scud missiles against Israel in the current war, in which Israel is not a combatant]: I won't say what Israel's response will be, but it's important that Europe and the entire world not have a shadow of doubt about the principle of response and the certainty of an Israeli response. The period of Jews getting beaten and not hitting back, that period of history is gone.

Jan. 23/
The New York Times, 1-24:(A)9.

Don Nickles
United States Senator,
R-Oklahoma

3

[Criticizing Jordan's support for Iraq in the war, despite U.S. aid to Jordan in the past]: What did we get in return for our generosity? We got more than a slap in the face. After billions of dollars of aid from the United States, Jordan actively opposed the United States and the United Nations by giving political and moral support to [Iraqi President] Saddam Hussein . . . We ought to send a very strong signal that we don't send money to countries that turn around and blast the United States.

Before the Senate,
Washington, March 20/
The New York Times, 3-21:(A)6.

Richard M. Nixon
Former President
of the United States

4

[Saying that, if he were President, he would try to have Iraqi President Saddam Hussein killed]: If I could find a way to get him out of there, even putting out a contract on him, if the CIA still did that sort of thing, assuming it ever did, I would be for it.

Broadcast interview/
"60 Minutes," CBS-TV, 4-14.

Augustus Richard Norton
Senior research fellow,
International Peace Academy
(United States)

5

The great irony is that the United States spent the better part of the 1980s striving to prevent Iranian dominance in the Persian Gulf, but the outcome of this war is transparently likely to produce just that result. The Persian Gulf may, as a result of these events, indeed become the *Persian gulf* . . . Throughout the course of the war, Iran has benefitted on a number of levels. It has regained diplomatic respectability. It has enjoyed significant international financial support, with promises of more. And it has watched, no

(AUGUSTUS RICHARD NORTON)

doubt with some joy and satisfaction, while its enemy Iraq has been pummeled and bled by the international coalition.

Los Angeles Times, 2-5:(H)1,5.

Abdullah Nubari
Leader of Kuwaiti opposition
to the government of
the Emir of Kuwait

1

It's sad to see all the Arab intellectuals and political groups allow themselves to be deceived by [Iraqi President] Saddam Hussein, knowing his history and knowing that his is the most vicious Fascist regime in history. Just by raising the banner of fighting the U.S., they overlook the facts of life—that he brought these calamitous events on himself, on Kuwait, on the rest of the Arab world. We thought they should have the foresight to see that he wasn't serious about helping the Palestinian to get his rights; he was only using that slogan. Because for 20 years, he has done nothing for the Palestinians; he has done nothing for social justice in the Arab world; he has done nothing for sound development in Iraq. Iraq is poorer now than it was 20 years ago . . . Democracy in the Arab countries is a complementing process. We will not have democracy in one country, especially in small countries like Kuwait, unless we have democracy all over the place. That's why we look very, very anxiously to have democracy in Iraq, because in that case, that will give democracy a great push in the whole area.

Interview, Kuwait City/
Los Angeles Times, 4-14:(M)3.

Sam Nunn
United States Senator,
D-Georgia

2

A [UN economic] sanctions policy [against Iraq] is not perfect. No guarantees here. But it has to be weighed against the alternatives. The [U.S.] Bush Administration is correct when they point out that sanctions do not guarantee that

Iraq will leave Kuwait. But the story does not end there. What guarantees do we have that war will be brief? [That] American casualties will be light? No one can say whether war will last five days, five weeks or five months . . . Those who support prompt military action argue that delay will allow Iraq to strengthen its defensive positions in Kuwait, thereby adding to the eventual cost of forcing Iraq out of Kuwait . . . This would have been a better argument in September of last year, and October, than it is today. Iraq already has had five months to dig in and to fortify and they have done so in a major way . . . I believe that on balance there is a reasonable expectation that continued economic sanctions backed up by the threat of military force and international isolation can bring about Iraqi withdrawal from Kuwait.

Before the Senate,
Washington, Jan. 11/
The New York Times, 1-12:6.

Edward Peck
Former chief United States
diplomat in Iraq, 1977-1980

3

The whole problem can be summed up in one word: miscalculation. [Iraqi President] Saddam Hussein miscalculated Western reaction. We miscalculated what Saddam Hussein was going to do with his armed forces. I'm not sure there's much that can be done to stop it from happening again. We won't learn much because next time the circumstances will be different. It's like a diplomatic Murphy's Law: Events that happen permit you to recognize the same mistake when you make it again.

USA Today, 2-28:(A)4.

Javier Perez de Cuellar
Secretary General
of the United Nations

4

[On whether he has lost hope of averting war]: In some ways, yes. I have not been offered anything from the Iraqi authorities [during his just-

WHAT THEY SAID IN 1991

completed visit to Baghdad] which I can consider a step toward peace. You have an expression in English—"You need two to tango"—and I wanted very much to dance, but I didn't find a nice lady to dance with.

New York, Jan. 14/
Los Angeles Times, 1-15:(A)1.

1

As 15 January advances [the deadline set by the UN for Iraq to pull out of Kuwait], and the world stands poised between peace and war, I most sincerely appeal to [Iraqi] President Saddam Hussein to turn the course of events away from catastrophe and toward a new era of justice and harmony based on the principles of the United Nations Charter. All our efforts in this direction will fail unless Iraq can signify its readiness to comply with the relevant resolutions of the Security Council, beginning with Resolution 660. If this commitment is made, and clear and substantial steps taken to implement these resolutions, a just peace, with all its benefits, will follow. I therefore urge President Saddam Hussein to commence, without delay, the total withdrawal of Iraqi forces from Kuwait.

At United Nations,
New York, Jan. 15/
The New York Times, 1-16:(A)7.

Richard N. Perle
Former Assistant Secretary
for International Security Policy,
Department of Defense
of the United States

2

[On the start of the U.S.-led air war against Iraq]: There is a considerable risk, if you wait, that unforeseen political developments will make it more difficult to act. Psychologically, when you have a deadline as prominent as the 15th [of January] and nothing happens, you run the risk of a letdown—like letting the air out of a balloon.

Jan. 16/
Los Angeles Times, 1-17:(A)8.

Daniel Pipes
Director, Foreign Policy
Research Institute
(United States)

3

[On Iraqi President Saddam Hussein, whose forces were driven out of Kuwait during the war]: Hussein will have three legacies. Inside Iraq, he will be remembered as the man whose folly led to devastation, whose ambitions caused a rich country to become suddenly destitute and a proud country to be humiliated. In the Muslim world, Hussein will be fondly remembered as the standard-bearer who ran into a force much greater than his own; there'll be considerable affection and admiration for him, despite his poor showing. In the non-Muslim world, he will be a symbol, much like Hitler or Stalin, of an unbridled tyrant who indulged his ambitions, who let his own *machismo* determine the destiny of millions of people, and who eventually ended up destroying both them and himself.

Interview/
Los Angeles Times, 3-3:(M)8.

Colin L. Powell
General, United States Army;
Chairman, Joint Chiefs of Staff

4

Our strategy to go after this [Iraqi] Army is very, very simple. First we're going to cut it off, and then we're going to kill it.

Pentagon briefing/
Newsweek, 2-4:30.

Marwan Qasem
Foreign Minister of Jordan

5

[Warning the U.S. against using military force to get Iraq out of Kuwait]: An American victory at the end of the day will mean no oil, no credibility, no humanity, no morality. This is the irony of American gunboat diplomacy. Your victory is your total loss.

The Christian Science Monitor,
1-16:2.

William B. Quandt
Senior fellow, Brookings Institution
(United States)

1

If we achieve the strategic objective of crippling [Iraqi President Saddam Hussein's] military might and getting his forces out of Kuwait, why bother going after him personally? Do we really care which particular thug is in power in Baghdad?

2

[Criticizing the U.S. decision not to help Iraqi rebels who are fighting the government of President Saddam Hussein in the wake of the recent U.S.-led victory in pushing Iraq out of Kuwait]: We don't want to feed the illusions of the Iraqi people, but we simply cannot appear to be neutral toward a regime that has no respect for the human rights of its own people. The thing I find least appealing is that we have shifted from a rhetorical stance that Saddam is Hitler to one that says what happens inside Iraq doesn't really matter to us.

The New York Times,
4-4:(A)6.

Donald W. Riegle, Jr.
United States Senator,
D-Michigan

3

I'm convinced in my own mind that if the sons and daughters of all of us, of the President, the Vice President, the Cabinet, were all over there in the Persian Gulf right now, right up on the front line, and were going to be part of that first assault wave that would go on into Kuwait, I think we'd be taking more time [on deciding whether to go to war]. I think we'd be working harder on the [economic] sanctions policy. I think we'd be trying to squeeze [Iraqi President] Saddam Hussein in every other way that we could, short of a shooting war.

Before the Senate,
Washington, Jan. 11/
The New York Times,
1-12:6.

Michel Rocard
Prime Minister of France

4

[On the increasing possibility of war]: The fact—the only one that counts—is the painful recognition that Baghdad has resolutely refused all offers of dialogue compatible with UN resolutions [ordering its withdrawal from Kuwait] . . . In any international police operation, the fatal moment comes when one must act. Alas, after everything we have done to avoid it, that moment has now arrived.

Jan. 15/
The New York Times, 1-16:(A)7.

Eugene V. Rostow
Former Director,
Arms Control and
Disarmament Agency
of the United States

5

[On the start of air attacks by U.S.-led forces against Iraq]: I'm very pleased that the thing has gotten into motion. What the President [Bush] is doing, I think, is to do exactly what President Truman was doing in Korea and for the same reasons—that is, to try to accomplish a small military step that will prevent something very much worse later on. The President is standing in the tradition of Wilson, Truman and Franklin Roosevelt, and it's just where the U.S. has to be.

Jan. 16/USA Today, 1-17:(A)11.

William V. Roth
United States Senator,
R-Delaware

6

One can only imagine what devastating consequence would fall should [Iraqi President Saddam Hussein's] dominance be allowed in the oil-rich Middle East . . . I'm not talking about consequences to major oil companies. Quite simply, I'm talking about jobs; I'm talking about the raw material of human endeavor. Oil runs the economy of the world. It fuels our factories, heats our homes. Carries our products from manufacturer to market. It's as basic to the economy as water is to life. And the free trade and interna-

(WILLIAM V. ROTH)

tional supplies is critical, not only for the industrial democracies, but the fragile Third World nations that depend on this precious resource even more than we do. Any attempt to disrupt these supplies will send a devastating quake to these economies, lengthening unemployment lines, boosting inflation in the industrialized democracies and crushing the economies of developing countries where day-to-day existence depends on imported energy sources.

Before the Senate,
Washington, Jan. 10/
The New York Times, 1-11:(A)4.

Martin A. Russo
United States Representative,
D-Illinois

1

[Lamenting the possibility of war]: If diplomacy and international cooperation is not an alternative we embrace, then why do we have a State Department? Why do we have the United Nations? Why do we sign treaties? *Diplomacy does work.*

Before the House,
Washington, Jan. 11/
The New York Times, 1-12:6.

Nawaf al-Sabah
Exiled Minister of Defense
of Kuwait

2

What has really bothered me is the cowardly way [Iraqi President] Saddam Hussein invaded. He gave a lot of promises to high-ranking persons—presidents and kings—and then, he came in the night, cheating the international community. He put the knife in my back. Of course, as Minister of Defense, what really affected me was that I hadn't prepared my army on the border. I know we are a small force against this huge [Iraqi] army. But to die defending my country is better than to be attacked in my house without any preparation.

Interview, Taif, Saudi Arabia/
USA Today, 2-18:(A)9.

Michael J. Sandel
Professor of government,
Harvard University
(United States)

3

[On the U.S. decision not to help Iraqi Kurdish rebels fighting the government of President Saddam Hussein in the wake of the recent U.S.-led victory in the Persian Gulf war]: If, as it appears, we decide that the most important thing is to uphold Iraq's territorial integrity, even at the price of maintaining Saddam's dictatorship, then what we are really saying is that the [Persian] Gulf war was about maintaining the status quo and nothing more; but then its moral authority will be diminished. If we decide that we cannot simply stand by and watch while the Kurds are brutally suppressed, but must help them, then we are saying that the principle of self-determination is the value we hold most dear.

The New York Times, 4-4:(A)6.

Alexander M. Schindler
President, Union of American
Hebrew Congregations

4

[Supporting U.S.-led forces in the war against Iraq]: Had the Western nations responded to Hitler with resolve early on, when he entered the Rhineland, there would have been no World War II with its 50 million casualties, and one-third of the Jewish people would not have become wisps of smoke or blackened ashes. While war has a fearsome price, compromise also has a fearsome price.

Los Angeles Times, 1-19:(A)28.

Arthur M. Schlesinger, Jr.
American historian

5

[On the recent start of hostilities against Iraq by the U.S.-led coalition]: I am against the whole damn thing. I don't think anything there is worth the life of a single American soldier. But if we have to do something, I prefer to rely on air power and a blockade to starve them [Iraqis] out.

The New York Times,
1-23:(A)6.

Patricia Schroeder
United States Representative,
D-Colorado

1

[On Iraq's recent defeat in the war]: My guess is that the Arab community is going to be split. There will be those who think [Iraqi President Saddam] Hussein was the greatest, and there will be others who disagree. Incredible amounts of energy will be expended arguing that issue. There will be a raging debate about whether the Arab community left him high and dry: Could he have won if there had been solidarity? I would hope it wouldn't continue for a long time . . . [but] that region tends to rehash history over and over again. It's important that we [the U.S.] not be there as a colonizing force . . . It's the Arab neighborhood, and the Arabs ought to be policing their own neighborhood.

Interview/Los Angeles Times, 3-3:(M)8.

Charles E. Schumer
United States Representative,
D-New York

2

[On the forthcoming vote in Congress on whether to give U.S. President Bush authority to use military force to get Iraq out of Kuwait]: It's one of the most difficult decisions I've had to make in 16 years of government. Each side has some very good arguments—and some major weaknesses. The crux of the issue is whether [UN economic] sanctions [against Iraq] will work. If the sanctions don't work and we fail to act, we'll have made a major mistake that we'll pay for—significantly—later. If the sanctions would have worked and we act precipitously, we will have made a major mistake.

Washington, Jan. 10/
The Washington Post, 1-11:(A)23.

H. Norman Schwarzkopf
General, United States Army;
Commander, Operation
Desert Storm
(U.S.-led forces against Iraqi
occupation of Kuwait)

3

[Saying U.S. air strikes against Iraq are designed to limit civilian casualties]: I will state

once again, we are absolutely doing more than we ever have and any nation has in the history of warfare to use our technology [to avoid civilian casualties]. By requiring that the pilots fly in a certain direction or use a certain type of munition that requires them to go to altitudes that they normally wouldn't be required to go to, those pilots are at much more risk than they otherwise would be. But we have deliberately decided to do this in order to avoid unnecessary civilian casualties . . . and I think we should be pretty proud of the young men who are willing to do that to minimize damage.

Jan. 27/USA Today, 1-28:(A)3.

4

[On being Commander of Desert Storm]: I get enough sleep, but I don't get enough rest because I wake up 15, 20, 25 times in the middle of the night, and my brain is just in turmoil over some of these agonizingly difficult decisions that I have to make. Every waking and sleeping moment, my nightmare is the fact that I will give an order that will cause countless numbers of human beings to lose their lives. I don't want my troops to die. I don't want my troops to be maimed. It's an intensely personal, emotional thing for me. Any decision you have to make that involves the loss of human life is nothing you do lightly. I agonize over it.

Interview,
Riyadh, Saudi Arabia, Feb. 4/
Los Angeles Times, 2-5:(A)7.

5

It has been the pattern of [Iraqi President] Saddam Hussein since he became a leader of Iraq that he is totally indifferent to the suffering his decisions inflict on . . . the people of his country. I do think that a certain amount of fatalism is in every action he takes; I think he considers himself a man of destiny, that his destiny is already set out, predetermined in some way. I would also tell you that we have several reports that Saddam is a very distraught man, that he has three doctors treating him with tranquilizers, which may say something about his mental state.

Interview, Saudi Arabia/
U.S. News & World Report,
2-11:36.

(H. NORMAN SCHWARZKOPF)

1

[On Arab-U.S. relations following the war]: We don't want to win the war and lose the peace. We have designed our campaign to take this into account. I think when all the evidence comes out—that we did not target civilians, that our intentions were exactly what we stated all along, that we respected regional cultural sensitivities— I think this will stand us in good stead in the Arab world.

Los Angeles Times, 2-25:(A)17.

2

As far as [Iraqi President] Saddam Hussein being a great military strategist, he is neither a strategist, nor is he schooled in the operational art, nor is he a tactician, nor is he a general, nor is he a soldier. Other than that, he's a great military man—I want you to know that.

News conference,
Riyadh, Saudi Arabia, Feb. 27/
USA Today,
2-28:(A)11.

3

Frankly, my recommendation [to U.S. President Bush] had been, you know, continue the march [against Iraq after they left Kuwait]. I mean, we had them in a rout and we could have continued to reap great destruction on them. We could have completely closed the door and made it a battle of annihilation. And the President made the decision that we should stop at a given time, at a given place that did leave some escape routes open for them to get back out, and I think it was a very humane decision and a very courageous decision on his part.

Broadcast interview/
"Talking With David Frost,"
PBS-TV, 3-27.

4

[Thanking the American people for supporting U.S. forces in the war]: The prophets of doom, the naysayers, the protestors and the flag-burners all said that you would never stick by us. But we knew better. We knew you'd never let us down. By golly, you didn't.

Before joint session of U.S. Congress,
Washington, May 8/
The New York Times, 5-9:(A)9.

Brent Scowcroft
Assistant to President
of the United States
George Bush
for National Security Affairs

5

[Saying the U.S. is not getting involved in the conflict between Iraqi Kurdish and Shiite rebels and the Iraqi government in the wake of the recent U.S.-led victory in the Persian Gulf war]: It's a real tragedy [the conflict in Iraq]. There's no question about it. And it's horrible to see the pictures of innocent people being savaged or even killed. But the policy has to be clear, and for us to get involved in a civil war in Iraq means occupying it, means replacing the government, means setting up a new government which undoubtedly would be overthrown as soon as the coalition troops left. That's a horrible morass into which to get, and from a policy standpoint it's just unacceptable.

Broadcast interview/
"Meet the Press," NBC-TV, 4-7.

U. S. Grant Sharp
Admiral, United States Navy
(Ret.);
Former Commander-in-Chief,
Pacific Command

6

[Comparing the current Persian Gulf war with the Vietnam war]: In Vietnam . . . we'd bomb for 10 days and then back off. We're doing the opposite here [in the Persian Gulf]; we're hitting hard, right at [Iraq's] war-making capability. [U.S. President Bush] is running a war the way it ought to be run. We're using military power the way it should be used. In Vietnam, I ran the air campaign from headquarters in Honolulu. I was never allowed to hit the targets I wanted to hit with any consistency. Each week, I had to submit a list of targets to the White House where

(U. S. GRANT SHARP)

[Defense Secretary] Robert McNamara, [President] Lyndon Johnson and two or three other civilians decided what targets we'd hit next week. That's no way to run a war.

USA Today, 1-28:(A)4.

Paul Simon
United States Senator,
D-Illinois

1

[Saying UN economic sanctions against Iraq, rather than resorting to the recent war, might have worked to get Iraq out of Kuwait]: Historically, when the GNP of a nation has been affected adversely by 3 per cent, you have a modification of policy. The most we've ever affected a nation is 16 per cent. In the case of Iraq it was 50 per cent, and by spring it would have been 70 per cent. I think that there is every possibility that not only would we have had a withdrawal from Kuwait without massive loss of life, but you would have had enough economic pressure to overthrow [Iraqi President] Saddam [Hussein].

The Christian Science Monitor,
4-10:9.

Ike Skelton
United States Representative,
D-Missouri

2

... have we learned anything from the lessons of history? It's 1936; Adolf Hitler entered the Rhineland. Those great powers of the day, Great Britain and France, did nothing. Nineteen thirty-eight; Adolf Hitler demanded part of Czechoslovakia and got it, based upon a promise of no more territorial demands. It was Great Britain's [Neville] Chamberlain, the Prime Minister, who returned from the Munich meeting with Adolf Hitler, proclaiming "peace in our time." How wrong he was. The lesson in history of which I speak is found in the phrase, "We should have stopped him when we could." How many British, French and, yes, American families said that about Adolf Hitler after World War II? Applying

that sad lesson of history, we must stop [Iraqi President] Saddam Hussein now.

Before the House,
Washington, Jan. 11/
The New York Times, 1-12:6.

Stephen J. Solarz
United States Representative,
D-New York.

3

[Saying the UN should demand that Iraqi President Saddam Hussein resign because of his brutal treatment of Iraqi Kurds who revolted after Iraq's defeat in the Persian Gulf war, and that force to accomplish his removal should be authorized]: It is morally and politically unacceptable to stand by and do nothing while Saddam brutally crushes a revolt we helped inspire [by urging Iraqis to overthrow Hussein following the war]. We need to act in ways that will bring the killing to an end. There is no way to do this while Saddam is in power . . . The principle of non-intervention [in a country's internal affairs] should not be used as a rationale for paralysis. Having encouraged the Iraqi people to rebel, we incurred a moral obligation to help them succeed.

April 10/
The Washington Post, 4-11:(A)32.

Steven L. Spiegel
Specialist on
American-Israeli relations,
University of California,
Los Angeles

4

[On the use of Scud missiles against Israel in the current Persian Gulf war, of which Israel is not a party]: Through television, millions of Americans heard the sirens wail in Tel Aviv, they watched Israelis put on their gas masks [in case the missiles carried chemical warheads], they watched them go into sealed rooms and they experienced just about everything Israelis did, except the thud of missiles. I think many Americans will have a lot more sympathy for some of Israel's security problems after this. Put that together with the restraint the Israelis have

(STEVEN L. SPIEGEL)

shown in not retaliating and you have to say that Israel has not looked so good in American eyes since the late 1960s.

The New York Times, 1-21:(A)7.

Lily Sprangers
Director, Atlantic Commission
(Netherlands)

1

[On the European attitude about possible war in the Persian Gulf]: There is something schizophrenic at work here. The Europeans agree that Iraq is a problem for the whole Western world, but they would be quite satisfied with a partial solution, even a solution that will lead to new problems in six months. The Americans would really like to see [Iraqi President] Saddam Hussein go and are willing to pay the price. That view is too optimistic for Europeans, who feel that with the end of the Cold War a peaceful world is within reach.

The Washington Post, 1-4:(A)21.

Gerry E. Studds
United States Representative,
D-Massachusetts

2

If we go to war now, we will never know whether that war was necessary. Think about that. Think about the lives that'll be cut short, the families that will be shattered, the heartbreak that will be endured; and ask yourself how much greater the pain will be if we are not certain whether those sacrifices had to occur . . . Our choice today is whether to persevere on the path of patience and determination and peace or to stray from that path into the wilderness of war. Whether to walk together the extra mile or the extra two miles in pursuit of a bloodless resolution to this crisis or to declare war and fight war and count the bodies and bury the bodies and never know whether a single American soldier really had to die.

Before the House,
Washington, Jan. 11/
The New York Times, 1-12:6.

Mike Synar
United States Representative,
D-Oklahoma

3

[Arguing against war between U.S.-led forces and Iraq]: We are not under attack; Iraq has not claimed a single American life; it occupies not a single square foot of American soil; we do not need its oil and I have yet to meet a mother or father who would send their son and daughter into battle for a 20-cent differential in the price of regular unleaded [gasoline].

Before the House, Washington/
The Washington Post, 1-12:(A)12.

Israel Tal
Deputy Minister of Defense
of Israel

4

[On the U.S.-led victory in the war]: There was brilliance and genius at the level of grand strategy. The plan was exactly tailored to the circumstances and goals of America in this theatre, which involved expending an enormous amount of ammunition and ordnance to win the war without American casualties . . . When we [Israelis] fought our wars [against the Arabs], we were the few against the many. Those were basically wars among equals. The war in Iraq was decided by America's overwhelming technological advantage on the first day the air raids began.

Interview/
The Washington Post, 3-15:(A)23.

John N. Turner
Leader, Liberal Party
of Canada

5

[Supporting the use of force against Iraq]: The failure of the United Nations to act upon their resolutions [that Iraq get out of Kuwait] would lead eventually to instability, to non-credibility and perhaps to international anarchy. Aggressors would have hope of profiting from their aggression . . . If the alliance against Iraq were to fall into disarray from good intentions, from walking too many last miles, the impact upon the

(JOHN N. TURNER)

future of the United Nations would be devastating to the future efforts of collective security. The United Nations would be fatally exposed as the League of Nations was so ruthlessly, as being simply incapable of standing up to aggression, even to a brutal bully like [Iraqi President Saddam] Hussein.

Before Canadian Parliament,
Ottawa, Jan. 16/
The Wall Street Journal,
1-22:(A)8.

Caspar W. Weinberger
Former Secretary of Defense
of the United States

1

If Iraq were allowed to go unpunished, Saudi Arabia would have been captured, the [Gulf] emirates would have been captured, and 70 per cent of the world's oil supply would have been in the hands of a blackmailer of the most brutal kind [Iraqi President Saddam Hussein]. That would have been intolerable and we would have had to try to get him out of there later, at a greater cost. People who talk about [opposing Iraq as] being for oil or to try to help the oil companies, or a war over a few cents' difference at the gas pumps, are just totally wrong.

Interview/USA Today, 2-4:(A)9.

Paul D. Wellstone
United States Senator,
D-Minnesota

2

The policies that I am afraid the [U.S. Bush] Administration is pursuing, the rush to war that I am afraid is so much of what is now happening in our country and the world, will not create a new order. It will create a new world disorder. What kind of victory will it be? What kind of victory will it be if we unleash forces of fanaticism in the Middle East and a chronically unstable region becomes even more unstable, further jeopardizing Israel's security . . . Some causes are worth fighting for. This cause is not worth fighting for right now. We must stay the course with economic sanctions [against Iraq], continue the pressure, continue the squeeze, move forward on the diplomatic front, and we must not rush to war.

Before the Senate,
Washington, Jan. 10/
The New York Times, 1-11:(A)4.

War and Peace

Joseph R. Biden, Jr.
United States Senator,
D-Delaware

1

[On the possibility of war between U.S.-led forces and Iraq, which invaded and took over Kuwait last year]: The [U.S.] Constitution's language says that the war powers rest with the Congress. And, from James Madison to John Marshall, the Constitution's fathers all understood this to be a key principle of the republic . . . I'm raising [this point] because the President [Bush] continues to insist he does not need, does not need the will of the people spoken through the Congress as envisioned by the Constitution to decide whether or not to go to war. On Tuesday, President Bush asked this Congress to debate and decide whether to take the nation to war, yet unfortunately the President stopped short of abandoning his previous claim that he has the power acting alone to start a war. And just yesterday . . . the President himself said that he alone has the Constitutional authority to initiate war. No President before him has ever said anything like that. No President in our history has ever made such an assertion. To put it simply, these views are at odds with the Constitution.

Before the Senate,
Washington, Jan. 10/
The New York Times, 1-11:(A)4.

Walter E. Boomer
Lieutenant General,
United States Marine Corps;
Commanding General,
U.S. Marines in Saudi Arabia

2

There are things worth fighting for. A world in which brutality and lawlessness are allowed to go unchecked isn't the kind of world we're going to want to live in.

USA Today,
1-17:(A)2.

Ramsey Clark
Former Attorney General
of the United States

3

[Criticizing the build-up of U.S.-led forces in the Persian Gulf area in response to Iraq's invasion and take-over of Kuwait]: Look at the speed and determination with which we rush these huge planes and send huge ships bristling with the capacity to destroy. What about the human tragedy that surrounds us? . . . I think we have no greater challenge or duty but to prevent war. I don't consider myself as a pacifist. I consider myself as actively committed to preventing wars.

USA Today, 1-17:(A)2.

Mario M. Cuomo
Governor of New York (D)

4

Before you go to war, you should pursue every reasonable alternative. That is not called surrender. That is intelligence and civility in progress.

U.S. News & World Report,
3-25:28.

Ronald V. Dellums
United States Representative,
D-California

5

I have a profound respect for human life. I think that war is anachronistic. I think that war is archaic. I think war is not an appropriate vehicle for a civilized world trying to find a high level of maturity in terms of how we live and deal with each other. That's marching backward—that's killing and dying and suffering and broken bodies and broken homes.

Interview, Washington/
The Washington Post, 2-20:(C)8.

Elizabeth II
Queen of England

6

Some people believe that power grows from the barrel of a gun. So it can; but history shows

(ELIZABETH II)

that it never grows well nor for very long. Force, in the end, is sterile.

Before joint session of U.S. Congress,
Washington, May 16/
The New York Times, 5-17:(A)8.

Wes Fox
Colonel, United States
Marine Corps;
Winner, Congressional Medal
of Honor

1

[As a soldier in a war,] when it gets down to the zero hour, and it's you and almost certain death, it is the *team*, the immediate family members [your fellow soldiers], that send you over the ridgeline. In those kinds of situations—in the dark, moving into machine-gun fire—the guys to the right and left of you are more important than Mom, the flag and apple pie. You don't see the flag, Mom's not with you, and apple pie's the farthest thing from your mind.

Los Angeles Times, 2-26:(A)8.

Allan Goodman
Associate dean,
School of Foreign Service,
Georgetown University

2

Sneak attacks can happen again. There were sneak attacks by the Viet Cong on U.S. forces in the Vietnam War. The North Korean invasion of South Korea was similar in that we had indications we didn't read correctly. We didn't call it right when it came to the invasion by Iraq of Kuwait [in 1990]. The risk of such attacks remains fairly high, though the scale of war is probably much lower today in the post-Cold War era.

Interview/USA Today, 12-2:(A)13.

Mikhail S. Gorbachev
President of the Soviet Union;
General Secretary,
Communist Party of the Soviet Union

3

Today peace means an ascent from mere coexistence to cooperation and common en-

deavor among countries and nations. Peace is movement toward globality and universality of civilization. Never before has the idea that peace is indivisible been as true as it is now. Peace is not unity in similarity, but unity in diversity, in the juxtaposing and reconciling of differences. And, ideally, peace means the absence of violence, an ethical value.

Lecture as winner
of 1990 Nobel Peace Prize,
Oslo, Norway, June 5/
The New York Times, 6-6:(A)6.

Alexander M. Haig, Jr.
Former Secretary of State
of the United States;
Former Supreme Allied
Commander/Europe

4

[In war,] nobody can predict [casualties] and anybody that's been in war can tell you that any war is completely surprising and uncertain. But I think logical calculations and detailed homework generally minimizes these kinds of surprises. It doesn't eliminate them.

USA Today, 1-18:(A)6.

Richard A. Harrison
Associate professor of history,
Pomona College

5

[On the U.S.'s first obtaining UN approval before embarking on the Persian Gulf war]: By so deliberately seeking UN Security Council approval, the U.S. has set a very important precedent. I think it will be very difficult for the U.S. or any of the other permanent members to undertake unilateral action after this . . . It's quite possible, given good statesmanship, that there will be a new world order.

The Christian Science Monitor,
3-11:4.

Bruce Jentleson
Political scientist

6

[In wartime,] there's a difference between [the government] giving out limited information and

(BRUCE JENTLESON)

misinformation. The press doesn't like limited information, but the American public doesn't seem to be bothered very much by that. But if it starts to become misinformation or intentional deception, then you have a credibility-gap problem and the trust of the public could be broken really quickly.

The Washington Post, 2-14:(A)33.

John Paul II
Pope

1

It is the terrible logic of war that the conflict tends to involve other states and indiscriminately threaten even civilian populations. The deplorable bombardment we have seen [by U.S. air forces against Iraq in the current Persian Gulf war] is a painful confirmation of this . . . The tragic reality of these days has made it ever clearer that weapons don't solve problems; they simply create new and bigger tensions between peoples.

Vatican City, Jan. 20/
USA Today, 1-21:(A)3.

Robert H. Kupperman
Senior adviser,
Center for Strategic and
International Studies,
Georgetown University

2

Fighting terrorism is not a question of increasing the number of tanks or missiles. It is an irregular form of warfare, and its success depends upon inflicting terror. Warfare of the future is going to be of an irregular nature, and terrorism is very much a part of it.

Interview/USA Today, 1-16:(A)9.

Douglas Lackey
Professor of philosophy,
Baruch College,
City University of New York

3

The phrase "just war" is very ambiguous and causes a lot of confusion. In the weak sense, it

means that war is permissible, it is not contrary to morality to fight the war. But, in the stronger sense, it means the war is obligatory, it is your moral duty to fight it.

The Washington Post, 2-2:(G)1.

Joseph E. Lowery
President,
Southern Christian
Leadership Conference

4

Let us call upon the nations to spend our resources on medical supplies, not military supplies; to make tractors, not tanks; to beat missiles into morsels of bread to feed the hungry; to build housing, not foxholes.

At celebration of the late civil-rights
leader Martin Luther King, Jr.'s birthday,
Philadelphia, Jan. 21/
The New York Times, 1-22:(A)12.

Wesley McDonald
Admiral, United States Navy,
(Ret.);
Leader of U.S. invasion
of Grenada in 1983

5

There's a lesson [we have learned] in the application of force. In Vietnam, we used the gradual application of force. But over the last 10 years, the philosophy has been to use enough force to make an attack credible and victorious. To attack quickly and decisively can turn the battle quickly into a rout. We've learned in Grenada and Panama and presumably here [in the Persian Gulf war] that overwhelming force minimizes our own losses.

USA Today, 2-25:(A)4.

Merrill A. McPeak
General and Chief of Staff,
United States Air Force

6

Battles go through stages, and there's a stage in which the enemy force is defeated. After that comes the real victory, when you consolidate that defeat in the exploitation or chase phase. Our

(MERRILL A. McPEAK)

obligation is to our young men and to end the war [such as the recent Persian Gulf war] as rapidly as possible. That often requires that we be very brutal. War is a brutal thing.

Interview/USA Today, 3-20:(A)13.

Francis Meehan
Former board member,
Pax Christi,
international Catholic
peace organization

1

[On the use of the term "just war"]: I am left wondering whether the language of just-war teaching is being co-opted so that people simply are beginning to know the public-relations thing to say, and one has to worry about what's really happening in the real world of war . . . Now even the [U.S.] President [Bush] is cloaking himself in just-war language [in describing the current Persian Gulf war], and one has to wonder if he is using the power of that language to intimidate people from dissenting.

The Washington Post, 2-2:(G)1.

George J. Mitchell,
United States Senator,
D-Maine

2

[On whether the Congress should grant President Bush the authority to use military force against Iraq, which invaded and took over Kuwait last year]: If we now say in the United States that the President has the authority at some unspecified future time, any time of his choice in the future under some as yet undefined circumstance, to initiate war, then how is the United States different from a monarchy or a dictatorship . . . ?

Broadcast interview, Jan. 3/
The Washington Post, 1-4:(A)20.

Linus Pauling
Nobel Prize-winning chemist

3

I'm not surprised that scientists feel so strongly about the need to eliminate war from the world and to replace it by a system of world law, based upon the principles of morality and justice. The idea appeals to scientists partially because they think about problems in a very large way, and are not thinking about just the next four years, the way politicians are.

Interview, Palo Alto, Calif./
The Christian Science Monitor,
3-19:14.

Leo Ribuffo
Professor of history,
George Washington University

4

[On the celebrations in the U.S. following the recent Persian Gulf war in which U.S.-led forces ended Iraq's occupation of Kuwait]: This is the 1990s analogue to what Secretary of State John Hay called the "splendid little war" against Spain in 1898. Short, quick wars with few casualties against evil regimes are popular.

The Washington Post, 3-5:(A)16.

Ronald Rotunda
Professor of law,
University of Illinois

5

[Saying U.S. President Bush has the Constitutional authority to commit American troops to battle in the current Persian Gulf crisis without obtaining approval of Congress]: [He] has all the authority to do whatever he wants. The [Constitution's] framers debated and changed the phrase [requiring Congressional approval from] "make war" to "declare war" because they did not want to tie the President's hands.

USA Today, 1-7:(A)11.

H. Norman Schwarzkopf
General, United States Army;
Commander, Operation
Desert Storm
(U.S.-led forces
in the Persian Gulf war)

6

If anyone thinks [war] is an enjoyable experience, they're dead wrong, dead wrong. I've

WHAT THEY SAID IN 1991

(H. NORMAN SCHWARZKOPF)

known a lot of Generals who were war lovers. They scare the living hell out of me, and they're also not very good Generals, not by my measure. Custer loved war, and look at what he accomplished.

Interview,
Riyadh, Saudi Arabia, Feb. 4/
The New York Times, 2-5:(A)5.

Joseph Sisco
Former Assistant Secretary
for Near Eastern and
South Asian Affairs,
Department of State
of the United States

1

With the new world interdependency, with regional issues globalized, with modern technology and weapons of mass destruction now in the hands of a number of regional powers—all superimposed on old enmities and territorial issues—warfare is going to be more dangerous.

Los Angeles Times, 1-18:(A)11.

Elie Wiesel
Historian;
Winner, 1986 Nobel
Peace Prize

2

I believe that all wars are blasphemy. I do not believe that wars can be glorious, and surely not holy. War means death, and death is ugly. But some wars are less offensive than others. To help victims of war defend themselves is commendable. To wage war against wars with all the means at our disposal can be an act of solidarity with the victims, an act which I am ready to applaud, for I believe in justice as the victims see it, not the aggressors . . . Let history record our determination that whenever an aggressor will launch war against defenseless countries, history will inexorably lead him before an international court of justice. His sentence will almost be irrelevant. His personal future will matter little. What will matter is the exposure of his criminal deeds. What will matter is that he will remain in the annals of history as an example of what human beings, driven by fanaticism or ambition, can do to one another.

Before Senate Foreign Relations
Committee, Washington,
April 9/
The Washington Post, 4-11:(A)20.

Theodore Windt, Jr.
Associate professor
of communications,
University of Pittsburgh

3

War rhetoric is a moral rhetoric. People are not willing to die unless there's some kind of a moral goal or value that transcends private interest.

The Christian Science Monitor,
1-15:5.

PART THREE

General

The Arts

Walter H. Annenberg
Publishing entrepreneur

1

[On art collecting]: Only when you are moved by a painting should you buy it. Being *moved* is what collecting is all about.

Connoisseur, February:37.

Les AuCoin
United States Representative,
D-Oregon

2

[Saying there is censorship of the arts in the U.S.]: The greatest irony of our time is that just as the shackles and chains of oppression are being broken in Eastern Europe and the Soviet Union, and just when we [in the U.S.] mark the bicentennial of our own Bill of Rights, the censorship threat is clearly on the rise in America . . . I believe that censorship in the arts leads to censorship elsewhere. It is a sign of a much deeper problem, of a poisonous intolerance, an intolerance that fears what is different and what is not understood . . . We all too often misunderstand that the test of a democracy is not that the majority gets its way, but rather that the minority is protected in its access to the fullest choice of ideas and in its ability to express those ideas.

Panel discussion sponsored by
Freedom of Expression Network,
Los Angeles, Dec. 4/
Daily Variety, 12-6:6.

Barbara Boxer
United States Representative,
D-California

3

[Criticizing obscenity restrictions put on NEA grants]: In my opinion, this controversy is largely manufactured by right-wing members of the House and Senate and ultra-conservative direct-mail specialists who needed new ogres as the Cold War drew to an end. Historians, at some future date, will ponder the irony that the death of

Communism, and the ensuing rebirth of freedom in Eastern Europe, has produced a vicious attack on creative freedom here in the United States.

At briefing held by House
Government Activities and
Transportation Subcommittee,
Los Angeles, Sept. 30/
Daily Variety 10-1:2.

Richard L. Brodsky
New York State
Assemblyman (D)

4

I think it's fair at this time to characterize the art market as a sort of commodities market. Art-market practices are no longer merely of concern to a privileged few, but to the general public, and it's time for the art community to take a hard look at itself.

Interview/
The New York Times, 1-16:(B)6.

Chick Corea
Jazz pianist

5

[An artist] is one who lightens the load of his audience and kind of gets them out there floating into the participation of creation that's occurring, whether it's a movie, or a painting, or whatever. It's a measure of success to me.

Interview/
Down Beat, February:19.

Miguel Angel Corzo
Director, Getty Conservation
Institute

6

I think of cultural patrimony like photographs of your grandparents. You keep the photographs at home in a special place. They represent your relationship to the past and a springboard to the future. If those photographs are down on the ground being trampled on, if they are van-

(MIGUEL ANGEL CORZO)

dalized, flooded, burned or ignored . . . we lose symbols of the past and the hope of our children's future. Like the photographs, cultural patrimony deserves a place of dignity, love and respect.

Los Angeles Times, 6-2:(Calendar)5.

Pablo Antonio Cuadra
Nicaraguan poet

1

The government has no business with culture. The state hinders culture. It is better if freedom dominates.

Los Angeles Times, 6-11:(H)6.

John E. Frohnmayer
Chairman, National Endowment for the Arts of the United States

2

[On calls for restrictions on NEA funding of obscene art]: The intent of the Congress, after vigorous debates, was that it doesn't make any sense if you have an agency whose business it is to promote creativity, to then try and shackle it with all sorts of content restrictions. I think the more restrictions you have, the less able you are to fill a mission of promoting creativity. I don't see restrictions and creativity as being compatible . . . The statue of the Venus de Milo was put on trial for nudity and convicted in 1853. In the 1920s during the birth of jazz, pregnant women were told that if they listened to it, they would have deformed children. The passage of time has had little to do with creating tolerance. And, right now, the agency is at a fork in the road. We need to ask ourselves, "What happened? And now what?" Who owns the truth when it comes to contemporary art? We cannot judge what will and will not survive the test of time. And time is the ultimate judge.

Before Town Hall,
Los Angeles, Jan. 23/
Daily Variety, 1-24:3,38.

3

[On charges that some work funded by the NEA is pornographic]: We are not here to be censors; we are not here to create a blacklist; we are not here to tell what subject matter should be . . . What I think is really objectionable . . . is for people who have not confronted the art to make statements about it, because art must be confronted.

Washington, March 29/
The Washington Post, 3-30:(C)1.

4

Art does a lot of different things. It reflects a kind of piety and faith. But it also holds up a mirror to the dark side of human nature. It holds up a mirror to social problems and sometimes that art is unflinching so that you can't duck it. You confront the art, you confront the problem, and that makes people uncomfortable sometimes.

The New York Times, 5-3:(A)10.

5

There is, I guess, a fairly understandable degree of paranoia in the arts world, particularly in the very tenuous existence of the individual artist, where you are so susceptible to a bad review, or somebody who willingly or ignorantly misunderstands your art or mischaracterizes it. I really believe that for the good of the individual artist and the good of the country both, we need to try to make the climate for the individual artist more nurturing. It's a tough life. I think anything we can do to make that environment better for the individual artist is worth doing.

Interview, Washington/
Los Angeles Times, 12-22:(Calendar)88.

Carlos Fuentes
Author

6

There seems to be a mark of Cain on the human race. But at the same time I am a writer, so I have to believe in the power of words and the imagination of love and hope. Though death is inevitable, life is continuous. Between those two elements you have a contradiction, and of course out of contradiction you make art.

Interview, New York/
Publishers Weekly, 10-25:43.

Karl Glenn
President, Music Educators
National Conference

1

[Saying the arts should be an integral part of education]: It's important not to separate the arts from other parts of life. Art and life are one.

Interview/
The Christian Science Monitor,
4-1:12.

Jesse Helms
United States Senator,
R-North Carolina

2

[Calling for the banning of NEA funding of obscene or offensive works]: From burning the American flag to desecrating one another's bodies, the depravity of these artists knows no bounds. Shame, shame on the United States Senate [for permitting such funding]. These so-called artists are leading Senators around by their noses.

Before the Senate,
Washington, Sept. 19/
The Washington Post, 9-20:(B)1.

3

[On his measure to impose strict anti-obscenity restrictions on Federal grants to the arts]: These "artists" who have their minds in the gutter are free to do what they want to with their own time and their own money, but don't ask John Q. Public to pay for it.

USA Today, 9-20:(A)5.

Nancy Landon Kassebaum
United States Senator,
R-Kansas

4

Many Americans have legitimate concerns about the way in which their tax dollars are being used with respect to arts funding . . . With respect to the NEA, there seems to be an atmosphere that anything presented as art deserves public support.

Before the Senate,
Washington, Sept. 19/
The Washington Post, 9-20:(B)2.

Alex Katz
Painter

5

I'm a lot more skillful than the average painter. I put a lot more information in. But I don't really understand all of my paintings. Some, I don't even know if they're good. I know they're finished because people come in and say, "Gee, this is the best thing you've ever painted," or something like that. When you're working way out on the edge, you try to take yourself into an area where you're frightened of what you're doing.

Interview, New York/
Lear's, November:24.

David Levy
President and director,
Corcoran Gallery of Art,
Washington

6

I am very committed to the notion that museums are places in which people are educated . . . To teach the history of art in a way that would lead to its disconnection from its cultural context is almost useless . . . To teach the students about the Renaissance and never say a word about Dante, or to talk about Michelangelo or Giotto and never talk about what's going on intellectually, politically or culturally is a great mistake.

Interview, Washington/
The Christian Science Monitor,
9-27:12.

Witold Lutoslawski
Composer

7

I think the world in which we live doesn't need to be expressed in art—it is too much with us as it is! [But] the world in which we live while creating something is an ideal world, a dream world, the world of our wishes. Our duty is to give expression to this *ideal* world and make it accessible to everybody.

Interview/
Los Angeles Times, 1-7:(F)10.

325

WHAT THEY SAID IN 1991

Gian Carlo Menotti
Composer; Artistic director,
Spoleto Festival U.S.A.

1

Great art must have what I call *inevitability*. I am a neo-Platonist, I suppose. I believe there is a Platonic ideal of beauty, and artists are given a fleeting vision of that beauty. The rest is a process of remembering. You try to catch the beauty you've seen, and it is a torture, because you can never quite do it. Why should an artist spend three days working on a single measure when nobody will really notice, nobody will really care?

Interview, New York/
Los Angeles Times, 5-19:(Calendar)90.

2

An artist's real love is art. It always comes first. I've never met an artist's wife who didn't complain about being second. In a way, I think all artists suffer from a certain guilt over this, especially toward people close to them.

Interview/
Opera News, June:15.

Eric Oddleifson
President, Center for Arts
in the Basic Curriculum

3

[Saying the arts should be an integral part of education]: We think about the arts as somehow inspirational or entertainment, but the actual fact is, when you're engaged in arts production, you're using your mental capacities in a very intensive and broad way. [This] spills over into academic subjects as well.

The Christian Science Monitor,
4-1:12.

David A. Ross
Director, Whitney Museum
of American Art,
New York

4

I do see art in a social context, to some extent, but I find myself on the line between those who believe in the transcendent power of art and those who question it. I think art has both the power to delight and the responsibility to question.

Interview/
The New York Times, 1-12:15.

Kathleen Turner
Actress

5

[Criticizing proposed standards for NEA funding]: Standards of decency—a short phrase, but very disquieting to me. I looked up decency in the dictionary and found that its first meaning is fitting, followed by orderly and appropriate. How can these words ever be used to define art?

Before House Government Activities
and Transportation Subcommittee,
Washington, Oct. 28/
Daily Variety, 10-29:2.

Stan Wojewodski, Jr.
Dean, School of Drama,
Yale University;
Artistic director,
Yale Repertory Theatre

6

What I find so discouraging is that art becomes increasingly marginal in American society, that it's something we can do without, or that people should pay for. But then, is it all that surprising that there's no arts policy when there's no [Bush Administration] domestic policy?

Interview, San Diego/
Los Angeles Times, 8-11:(Calendar)54.

Journalism

Jonathan Adler
Journalist,
"Newsweek" magazine

1

[On journalistic plagiarism]: In its worst forms, plagiarism is a sickness. In its lesser forms, it's a kind of carelessness that I think every journalist sweats over at one time or another . . . Everybody in journalism borrows, so it's a question of how much you borrow and what kind of credit you provide. You have to reserve the label "plagiarism" for cases that are unambiguous.

USA Today, 7-25:(B)1.

Peter Arnett
Correspondent,
Cable News Network

2

[On his reporting for CNN from Baghdad during the recent Persian Gulf war between U.S.-led forces and Iraq]: The United Nations [and] the whole world decided to take measures against the Iraqi government and to get it out of Kuwait. And the whole world was interested in what was happening, and CNN was fortunate to be able to be here to talk about the consequences of what the world was doing. And the Pope was watching the broadcasts apparently, leaders all over the world, the average person in Jordan and in Tunisia and certainly in the United States and elsewhere, my own 89-year-old mother was following it. And there were criticisms about what we [at CNN] were doing. But I felt from the beginning, why can't we be an eyewitness to what our decisions lead to? Why can't I be here and talk about where the bombs are really falling? . . . But I felt very proud to be an eyewitness so the rest of the world would know how its policy was being implemented . . . And I like to think the record will show that we as journalists here . . . were able to reflect pretty much accurately on aspects that the world wanted to know.

Broadcast interview, Baghdad/
Cable News Network, 3-6.

Lee Baggett
Admiral, United States Navy
(Ret.);
Former Commander-in-Chief,
Atlantic Command

3

[On complaints by the press that the military isn't providing enough information to journalists about the current Persian Gulf war]: You've got to control the news you let out. If you put out too much, you give aid and comfort to the enemy. The military can't be expected to tell too much, especially in this day of satellite communication. When you start talking bomb damage assessments and targets hit, you give information to the opposition. That could cost us lives. The military should not be expected to provide play-by-play coverage, like a football game. But it is the press' roll to be skeptical and get all the information it can.

USA Today,
1-25:(A)4.

Louis D. Boccardi
President,
Associated Press

4

[On a meeting with U.S. Defense Secretary Dick Cheney in which the press criticized the way the Defense Department handled press coverage of the recent Persian Gulf war]: We didn't threaten him. We raised with him the danger that, if the Gulf was the model for the way they set up future rules [controlling war coverage], they risked very seriously any kind of cooperation with the press. And we made the point that, in our view, this wouldn't serve the public interest in the least. We told him [Cheney] we could go our way and he could go his, and that would be that, but we added that we felt that really wasn't the way to serve the public's interest at all.

Interview/
Los Angeles Times, 9-13:(A)22.

Roy Bode
Editor,
"Dallas Times Herald"

1

[On the closing of his newspaper]: Newspaper people are unique in a certain respect. They subordinate their personal lives to their work and make an enormous emotional investment in it. This is like the loss of a family member.

Interview, Dallas/
The Christian Science Monitor,
12-19:12.

Nora Boustany
Correspondent,
"The Washington Post"

2

[Defending the U.S. press in Iraq against criticism that it is being used for propaganda purposes by the Iraqi government during the current Persian Gulf war]: The main constraint on reporters in Iraq appears to be danger. I've seen a lot of footage. I don't think it's as staged or managed as people think. When you have a bomb shelter blow up and men cry and pull at their hearts, that's genuine and spontaneous. The reporter has to use his or her sensitivity to judge [the truthfulness of] what's being said. My editors want me to tell it like it is. That's what counts at the end of the day. No one wants to think of his leaders as killers. The natural inclination is to think you're on the right side. In the end, you have to look through both prisms to get a balanced picture.

USA Today, 2-15:(A)4.

L. Brent Bozell III
Executive director,
Media Research Center

3

The media is the only institution that wields as much power as the three branches of government but doesn't have any system of checks and balances like the other ones do. And it has gotten away with it . . . That's why there's a need for a private-based system of checks and balances . . . There's no such thing as an objective press. You can't fault a reporter for being biased, conserva-tive or liberal. You can, however, fault a reporter or a media institution for not being balanced—and that is the problem.

Interview/
The Christian Science Monitor,
6-27:12.

Benjamin C. Bradlee
Executive editor,
"The Washington Post"

4

Most people get their first bite of news out of television or radio; I think that's probably right. But the longest story on the *CBS Evening News* will be a hundred words and, you know, that's two paragraphs of a newspaper. For those people who want to know more, they still have to take a newspaper.

Interview/
The Christian Science Monitor, 7-11:11.

5

If you are a reporter and you cover a Mayor or a Governor, you are going to develop a relationship with that person, and it could be dislike, it could be hatred, it could be esteem, it could be a whole lot of different things. The important thing is that the editors know what that relationship is and be sure that it's not abused by either the source or by the reporter . . . I would love to have reporters who have the access to governmental officials that I had, and the editors will take care of the possible abuses. None of these people who say I was too close to [the late President John] Kennedy say that I ever abused that access. I didn't.

Interview/
The Christian Science Monitor, 7-11:11.

Hodding Carter III
Columnist,
"The Wall Street Journal";
Former spokesman for
the Department of State
of the United States

6

[On complaints by the press that the military isn't providing enough information to journalists

(HODDING CARTER III)

about the current Persian Gulf war]: What needs to be done right now, before the killing starts on the ground, is for the reporters to go and challenge the system. To directly test it. The government would be happy to see coverage contained to press pools, but that's no way to cover a fast-moving war on multiple fronts. We didn't do it that way in World War II or any other war. It's like a closed society.

USA Today, 1-25:(A)4.

Richard J. Cattani
Editor, "The Christian
Science Monitor"

1

News, as a first telling of what happens, has been devalued. It is, like oxygen, everywhere. It is content—the ideas, the integrity, the balance of treatment—that marks successful publication. News has energy. It affects, attracts. Newspapers should center on the news. They should report the creative process of our times—in politics, economics, the arts. They should report the news that makes history—which implies context, analysis and conceptual framework.

Upon receiving Distinguished
Service Award from International
Communication Division of
Association of Educators
in Journalism and Mass Communication,
Boston, Aug. 8/
The Christian Science Monitor,
8-14:19.

Dick Cheney
Secretary of Defense
of the United States

2

[Addressing the press on its criticism that they are not being given enough information about the current Persian Gulf war]: I want to caution you that a military operation of this intensity and complexity cannot be scored every evening like a college track meet or a basketball tournament. I know how hard it is for you to cover this kind of operation when you cannot see what's going on

inside Iraq or occupied Kuwait. Some of you've been critical of us for not putting information out more quickly. I understand your point, but we want to be certain that we don't rush down here with premature words of success.

News briefing,
Washington, Jan. 23/
The New York Times, 1-24:(A)5.

Tony Clifton
Correspondent,
"Newsweek" magazine

3

[Criticizing U.S. government restrictions on journalists covering the current Persian Gulf war]: I have never had movement so controlled, reporting so restricted. In Vietnam, you went anywhere nerve or foolishness would take you. [Today,] in Saudi Arabia, men who have never heard a shot fired in anger dog your footsteps, and unless you break their petty regulations you see nothing.

Newsweek, 2-11:4.

Shelby Coffey III
Editor, "Los Angeles Times"

4

[On his plans for the future of the *Los Angeles Times*]: I don't think there will come a day when a voice like rolling thunder comes out of the sky and says, "This is the best newspaper." Because the day that happens is the day somebody starts gaining on you.

Time, 4-15:47.

Walter Cronkite
Former anchorman,
CBS News

5

[Saying there are too many restrictions put on reporters by the military in the current Persian Gulf war]: [The press] should be free to go where it wants when it wants . . . [But] I don't see what this rush to print, or this rush to transmit, is all about. It doesn't really matter in a wartime situa-

(WALTER CRONKITE)

tion if we learn something this minute . . . or the next day.

Before Senate Governmental
Affairs Committee,
Washington, Feb. 20/
The Washington Post, 2-21:(A)28.

Faith Daniels
Broadcast journalist,
NBC News

1

Women broadcasters still face much more criticism than men for things that have nothing to do with their jobs—their appearance, for one thing, and how they dress. More often than not, when people stop me on the street they don't say, "I really liked the way you reported the news out of the Middle East." It's usually, "Boy, you had on a great outfit today" . . . I think people make assumptions about a man sitting in the anchor or reporter's chair, about his track record, his years in the field, the work he did to get there. I think the assumptions people most often make about how a woman got to sit in that same chair are different: They assume she got the job because of the way she looks or because somebody fancies her. These are the negative kinds of assumptions female broadcasters have to fight.

Interview/
McCall's, April:26.

John B. Evans
Executive vice president,
News Corporation

2

[On the possibility that technology may provide for future newspapers to consist of electronic or computerized editions viewed on a TV screen]: I cannot imagine a time in the future when there will not be newspapers in the home. A newspaper is a data base. It happens to be on crushed trees right now. I don't think a newspaper proprietor . . . should care how it is delivered as long as it's his information.

Los Angeles Times,
6-3:(A)18.

Marlin Fitzwater
Press Secretary to
President of the United States
George Bush

3

[On criticism of U.S. news reports emanating from Baghdad during the current Persian Gulf war between U.S.-led forces and Iraq]: Journalists operating in the capital of the enemy country, operating under complete control of the enemy government, sending instant pictures here [is unique and a problem]. The power of the image on television is so much stronger than the power of the word. It doesn't matter how much caveats you put in there [about enemy government control of the press], the picture tells a story that establishes itself in the mind's eye no matter what it said.

Press briefing,
Washington, Feb. 13/
The Washington Post, 2-14:(A)29.

Steve Friedman
Executive producer,
"Evening News," NBC-TV

4

Going live and doing an edited piece [in TV news] are two separate things. With live, you don't know what the results are, it's not a calm presentation, it's not well balanced with both sides; but who cares [as long as viewers] understand this is one kind [of news] and the other is the other kind.

The Christian Science Monitor,
2-7:13.

Vladislav A. Fronin
Editor-in-chief,
"Komsomolskaya Pravda"
(Soviet Union)

5

[On the increased freedom for Soviet newspapers]: We [his paper] were born as an official organ of the central committee of a Communist organization, the Communist Youth League, but we have changed a great deal in the last couple of years. We are fully in the marketplace and determined to compete—journalistically, politically,

(VLADISLAV A. FRONIN)

ideologically, commercially. We don't want to put out a "nice" paper that nobody reads nor a paper that millions might read but that really says nothing. We want readers to buy us because we have something to tell them, something to say . . . A journalist must have the freedom to state his opinions, and we have that oxygen now. It's quite heady, this oxygen; but once you begin to breathe it you [get] hooked on it. That's how we are now, journalists and readers alike, absolutely hooked on this new freedom of the press. And if they turn it off, we'll all suffocate.

Interview/
Los Angeles Times, 2-5:(H)2.

David Frost
Broadcast interviewer

1

. . . the most important thing in an interview is seizing the moment, is listening, is getting the underlying motives as well as the words on the surface. And that involves all sorts of techniques. Sometimes it's a chess game in which you know somebody is prepared to go so far and you want them to go further . . . Although this may sound simplistic, I believe in getting people to come over as they really are. Very often they have been doing themselves a disservice, and, reluctant though they are to reveal it, the real person is more interesting than the image they are trying to project.

Interview/
"Interview" magazine,
February:60.

Michael G. Gartner
President, NBC News

2

[On NBC's decision to reveal the name of a woman who is charging rape against a member of the Kennedy political family]: I'm in the business of disseminating information, not withholding it. Names add credibility; they round out a story.

Newsweek, 4-29:29.

Katharine Graham
Chairman,
Washington Post Company

3

Because of new technologies, the number of media alternatives available to advertisers and to readers and viewers has multiplied exponentially. Instead of competing with a few newspapers, magazines and radio, we [in the newspaper business] have all of those to deal with, plus network television, independents, cable in all its forms, VCRs, and anything ever known by man available over the computer . . . The advertising environment has been altered, probably permanently, by the [leveraged buyouts], takeovers and bankruptcies of the '80s. There are fewer retail advertisers today. And many of them have diminished financial resources to devote to advertising because of heavy debt . . . There are threats from the efforts of the phone companies to compete with newspapers in the information business. Postal rates are grossly unfair to newspapers and magazines—and a totally unjustified boon to bulk advertising mailers. In my view, this may be the biggest immediate challenge our industry faces.

At Washington Post Co.
annual meeting, Washington, May 9/
The Washington Post, 5-10:(D)3.

Lawrence Grossman
Senior fellow,
Gannett Foundation
Media Center;
Former president, NBC News

4

I don't think there's any question that, in the next several years, there will not be three evening [network] newscasts. With CNN becoming the place where viewers turn for breaking news in a crisis, and local news also assuming a stronger role, the traditional dinner-hour network news is becoming an anachronism . . . ABC News has positioned itself as the dominant network news force. But NBC and CBS are bound to be coming under pressure from their managements, asking, "Why do we need this huge factory with staff and news-gathering facilities around the world?"

Los Angeles Times, 2-16:(F)1,6.

Brit Hume
White House correspondent,
ABC News

1

Compared to the adversarial posturing reporters do when they're covering the President, the atmosphere on Capitol Hill is incredibly chummy and cozy. When members of Congress come in to talk to the press, all you're usually trying to do is get them to make some sharp critical statement about the Administration, or whoever—something you can build a story around. The idea that you would seriously challenge any member of Congress to defend his or her position on any issue, and then follow up on the questions, is almost unheard of. I mean, members of Congress love to beat their breasts about being a coequal branch of government. Generally, Congress is an institution that reporters sort of laugh at—like a bunch of guys hitting each other with rubber chickens. With one exception: Congressional investigating committees are the most hallowed institutions in Washington. Reporters don't take Congress seriously unless it's conducting an investigation, at which point the press immediately gets in bed with it.

The Wall Street Journal,
7-29:(A)10.

Peter Jennings
Anchorman, ABC News

2

I don't believe newsmen should be celebrities. The one thing a good journalist wants is to blend into the background. We should never be the story.

Good Housekeeping, April:50.

3

There are Americans who believed during this [recent Persian Gulf] war that the American press should have quietly abided by all military restrictions in the name of "national security" . . . You know as well as I do that in this war, unlike any other in the nation's history, the U.S. military mounted a major effort to suffocate impartial reporting. The military establishment was apparently so fearful that the press would have an objective view of its behavior that thousands of man-hours, at taxpayers' expense, were spent trying to keep the American press corps in quarantine . . . Do we really want a military establishment in the United States which hides from the cameras? . . . I think it's rather sad there was no opportunity for millions of us to see anything of the bravery or dedication of U.S. soldiers on the battlefield.

At Gallaudet University commencement,
May 10/USA Today, 5-20:(A)11.

Rheta Grimsley Johnson
Columnist

4

The biggest mistake I see myself and other columnists making is resorting to writing merely a feature on a bad day. There should be a point to every column. However minor, however subtle, however obscure. We are paid to make a point. The feature writers can find the praying pigs and the 103-year-old birthday boys. We [columnists] have to make the oddities *mean* something. If you cannot mine the meaning, you're not a columnist. You're a feature writer with a mug shot above your story.

Interview/
Writer's Digest, January:38.

Marvin Kalb
Director, Barone Center
on the Press,
Politics and Public Policy,
Harvard University

5

The press very rarely sets the national agenda. The President sets the national agenda. The press is most happy when it is marching more or less in lock-step with majority sentiment in the country. It doesn't want to be out front and it doesn't want to be behind . . . The press wants to be with the majority of Americans because if you're with the majority of the Americans, the likelihood is that as a newspaper, you're going to be purchased, as a network you're going to be watched, as a magazine you're going to be read. If you're out of the mainstream, you may also be out of the economic mainstream, and that is really not what any news organization thinks is a very good idea.

Interview/ USA Today, 2-21:(A)11.

Thomas W. Kelly
Lieutenant General,
United States Army;
Director of Operations,
Joint Chiefs of Staff

1

[On criticism by journalists that the government is not releasing enough information to the press on the current Persian Gulf war]: We're releasing as much information as we can that is reasonable. You've got to remember that we're in a war. You have to remember there's another side in this war. You have to remember that there has to be a balance between the amount of information that's released and the amount of information that we possess.

USA Today, 1-22:(A)7.

2

[On the daily Pentagon news briefings for reporters during the recent Persian Gulf war]: I've just got to say that, believe it or not, I've enjoyed this little interlude . . . At no time were you [the press] ever impolite to me and at no time did I ever become offended. And as you know, I hold a lot of you in great respect. The last thing I'd like to say is that having a free press has served the United States well for 215 years. It is a crucial element in our democracy. And if anybody needs a contrast, all they have to do is look at the country that didn't have a free press [Iraq during the war] and see what happened.

To reporters,
Washington, March 4/
The Washington Post, 3-5:(A)14.

Joan Konner
Dean, School of Journalism,
Columbia University

3

I was struck by the United Nations Security Council vote to keep the press out [of its meeting on the crisis in the Persian Gulf] but release a transcript later. I'm an absolutist on freedom of the press, but I could see their point. A lot of manipulation is going on. I think about the old example: If the press had been present during the debate of the [U.S.] Constitution, we probably wouldn't have a Constitution and freedom-of-speech protections.

USA Today, 2-15:(A)4.

Robert Lichter
Co-director,
Center for Media
and Public Affairs

4

Through the mid-'80s it was a common scholarly complaint that there was no interest [in the U.S.] in foreign news, but three out of the top five stories [on the TV networks] in the past two years have been foreign because the technology was there [to broadcast it]. Technology is changing the whole public discourse and internationalizing it.

The Christian Science Monitor,
12-19:13.

Robert MacNeil
Co-host, "MacNeil/Lehrer
NewsHour," PBS-TV

5

[TV] network news employs a great many very capable journalists. Its fatal flaw is that they operate as part of a system which is forced to maximize its audience. The networks have created a show which gets into the tent at the same time all the uninterested, uninformed and incurious people, as well as the well-informed and sophisticated. It is an almost impossible communications proposition.

Interview/
The Christian Science Monitor,
9-19:12.

Newton N. Minow
Former Chairman,
Federal Communications
Commission

6

The fault I would give to the [three U.S. TV] networks is a failure to foresee what was happening in television. For example, when CBS started a cable network years ago, they made it a cultural network. Suppose they'd made it a news network—would CNN [the very successful cable news network started by Ted Turner] have succeeded? I have a theory that the reason that Ted Turner did what he did with CNN was that he came from outside broadcasting and didn't know all the rules.

Interview/
Los Angeles Times, 5-9:(F)10.

Michael Moore
Former editor,
"Quill" (journal of the Society
of Professional Journalists)

1

Our [the news media's] job is not to be another branch of government. Our job is to confront issues squarely and not to buy into slogans. If you're going to portray yourself as a watchdog, you've got to bark once in a while. We're too often lap dogs.

TV broadcast/
"Project Uncensored,"
PBS-TV, 2-25.

Bryce Poe
General,
United States Air Force (Ret.)

2

[Criticizing the U.S. news media's coverage of Persian Gulf-war events in Iraq, where press reports are controlled by the government]: The media is taking on faith what's said under controlled conditions in Iraq. Then, they dig and dig with questions that essentially call *our* representatives liars. I have a hard time with [U.S.] reporters being in Iraq. The American public can sort the information out. Americans are used to nonsense on TV. The problem is how it plays to standing-room crowds in coffee houses throughout the Arab world. You have large numbers of unsophisticated people not used to examining critically what they see. How would I run CNN? I don't think I could do it. My first duty is to my country. For most reporters, their first duty seems to be to the story.

USA Today, 2-15:(A)4.

Vladimir Pozner
Soviet news commentator

3

[Saying he is quitting Soviet broadcasting because it is again becoming tightly controlled by the government]: A journalist has a duty to comment on what he believes is happening and report what he sees as truth. But when you are told in advance that you cannot talk critically about this or that . . . then you compromise or quit . . . Freedom of the press is a lot like that genie who is released from the bottle, and there is no way he's going to be stuffed back in. As journalists, we might be criticized for not living up to our professed ideals in the past, and that is all the more reason why we must try to do so now.

Los Angeles Times, 4-27:(A)3.

Howell Raines
Washington editor,
"The New York Times"

4

[Criticizing the U.S. Defense Department's restrictions on press coverage of the Persian Gulf war]: The [Bush] Administration wants to use the legitimate theme of "security," in some cases, to install a kind of blanket news management that we've never had in this century. No one argues with legitimate security needs. There's a kernel of truth in [Defense] Secretary [Dick] Cheney's argument. But we are over a month into this conflict and we've never seen a photograph of a wounded American soldier.

The New York Times,
2-25:(A)17.

Dan Rather
Anchorman, CBS News

5

There is a side of this business that says when you anchor, your job is not to ask the tough questions, not to be a tough reporter, not to be even independent—your job is just to be popular and get along. I do not subscribe to that school of thought. I never have and I won't.

Interview,
Beverly Hills, Calif./
Los Angeles Times, 11-2:(F)1.

James Reston
Journalist

1

Mine was the Depression generation of journalists; we grew up on the wrong side of the tracks. Many of the very best people were not educated. Hell, when I went to London as a sportswriter I didn't know the difference between the Baltic States and the Balkins. But I learned the advantage of the dumb-boy technique. I found that people love to talk about themselves. You get more news by trust than by tricks—and I've tried both. But that is not a very popular idea in this generation. Because they went to college, they think that they know so many things—and to some extent they do. But they think that they know more than the guys who run the joint, and that's a pretense that doesn't work. Also, they like big shots. I always felt that the way to gather news in Washington is at the periphery and not at the center. You get it from the people who tell the big shots what to say.

Interview/
U.S. News & World Report,
10-28:81.

Cokie Roberts
Broadcast journalist,
National Public Radio
and ABC-TV

2

. . . we in the press censor ourselves all the time when we're in difficult situations. I was in Greece during the period when the junta was in power, and you're very careful about your sources because people can get in a tremendous amount of trouble for talking to you. There's a huge amount of self-censorship that goes on in difficult situations.

USA Today, 2-14:(A)10.

Jay Rosen
Associate professor of journalism,
New York University

3

[On the large audience that tuned in TV coverage of the Judge Clarence Thomas-Anita Hill sexual-harassment hearings and the rape trial

involving a relative of U.S. Senator Edward Kennedy]: It's polarizing and creates the illusion that the clash of utterly biased accounts produces the truth. But arriving at consensus is more difficult. These combative rituals make people small-minded, one-sided. [However,] it would be a mistake to assume the intensity of interest as a degradation of democracy or culture, to see the appetite for these as wholly debased. Ultimately, it's a desire to be part of the public world.

The Christian Science Monitor,
12-19:13.

Roger Rosenblatt
News commentator, PBS-TV

4

[On TV coverage of the Persian Gulf war]: The war does not come to us live. We do not see the presence, but a report on the presence. The presence exists either off-camera or is censored or is suppressed. What reports exist are frequently misleading . . . One thing TV is very good at, it brings us the people of the war, and the people are impressive, particularly the military, the Admirals and Generals who face the cameras . . . however reluctantly, [and] show themselves on the whole to be thoughtful, resolute and above all humane. We did not know about them before.

USA Today, 2-14:(A)10.

H. Norman Schwarzkopf
General, United States Army;
Commander-in-Chief,
Operation Desert Storm
(U.S.-led forces in the recent
Persian Gulf war

5

[Criticizing CNN's broadcasting of Iraqi television's showing of captured U.S. and British pilots during the recent Persian Gulf war]: I did resent CNN aiding and abetting an enemy who was violating the Geneva convention. [There may be a "public's right to know," but] I just think that in the future when people choose to justify their actions based on the American public's right to know, they'd better check with the American public first because the American public has made it very clear to me, in all the literally

(H. NORMAN SCHWARZKOPF)

hundreds of thousands of letters I have gotten, how they felt about the term "the American people's right to know" as it was being used by the people who were doing that sort of thing.

Broadcast interview/
"Talking With David Frost,"
PBS-TV, 3-27.

Bernard Shaw
Anchorman,
Cable News Network

1

I'm a celebrity and I don't like it . . . I tolerate it. Also, it's my way of keeping myself honest, because if you really dote on praise—incidentally, I learn more from criticism than I do praise—and dote on attention, eventually you start believing it. It distorts your perception. It affects your honesty. It affects the way you hear things, feel things, sense things and see things. And those are basic to good reporting. I don't ever want to lose that. I remember the problems that [former news anchorman] Walter Cronkite used to have. He'd try to get on the campaign trail and get on the bus with all of the other reporters and go cover a story. He'd get off the bus and more attention was given to him than to the candidate. That's repulsive. That's embarrassing. To me, the only way you can avoid that is to fight it every step of the way.

Interview, March 4/
Daily Variety, 3-22:25.

2

[On criticism of news reporters]: Messengers have always been targets. We'll continue to be targets. Unfortunately, a reporter's curse is that of not being liked many times. But the moment a reporter starts weighing his or her decisions based on whether or not what is reported will be liked or disliked, that is the time that a person should think about getting out of this profession.

Interview, March 4/
Daily Variety, 3-22:25.

3

[Saying journalists should take a harder line on political advertising that distorts and on politicians who do not address issues]: [Journalists should show their] sensitivity to the harm this garbage is doing to American politics by reporting on the attack ads, pointing to their distortions and exposing candidates who work harder at ducking issues than discussing issues . . . There is nothing wrong with leading your newscast that night by saying "Democratic [Presidential] candidate Tom Harkin thought enough of San Jose voters to spend 22 minutes at the airport today before going on to Los Angeles for a Hollywood fundraiser. The Senator said nothing he hasn't said before, but he did note ours was the best weather he's seen in days." [Viewers are] keen for those kinds of reporting distinctions. They want them, they expect them [and] they need them for perspective on the sleights-of-hand they are subjected to by politicians lusting for votes but lacking in so many ways.

Before Radio-Television
News Directors Association,
Denver, Sept. 25/
Daily Variety, 9-27:3.

Richard Stott
Editor, "The Daily Mirror"
(Britain)

4

The whole secret of tabloid newspapers is a balance between the heavy, the light, the funny and the sad. [*The Daily Mirror* gives its readers] some entertainment, some escapism [as well as normal news, heavy sports and photos]. That's what tabloid papers are about, and that's what we cater to, unashamedly and delightedly.

Interview, London/
The New York Times, 4-23:(C)17.

Mark Thompson
Defense correspondent,
Knight-Ridder Newspapers

5

[On the letdown for news reporters following the recent Persian Gulf war]: There's nothing

(MARK THOMPSON)

better for a journalist than to know what the story of the day is. The worst thing for reporters is to mope around, sifting through ashes looking for a story, and that's what everyone is doing now. [Covering the war] was tough, but, boy, it was fun. The surge of adrenalin masked some of the problems. You had beer in the newsroom for a change, pizza every night.

The Washington Post,
3-25:(C)6.

Jeff Wald
News director, KCOP-TV,
Los Angeles

1

[On television stations' buying amateur video-tapes of newsworthy happenings, such as the recent beating of a suspect by Los Angeles Police]: Our policy is if it's good video, we'll buy it. These kinds of tapes can provide a real check and balance on police agencies and other public officials. I think it's very healthy.

Los Angeles Times, 3-9:(F)1.

Mike Wallace
Co-host and reporter,
"60 Minutes," CBS-TV

2

[On interviewing]: I have always been fascinated by the weak spots in other people because I am well aware of the weak spots in myself—the insecurities, the sense of inadequacy. I know what my own Achilles' heels are and, when I go on television, all I have to do is frame them in questions to others . . . You role-play to a certain degree. If you succeed in persuading your object of scrutiny that you know a great deal more about him than you do, he opens up all the more easily. You try to establish a chemistry of confidentiality. You want to give him a psychological excuse to reveal himself.

Interview,
Martha's Vineyard, Mass., July/
Vanity Fair, November:197.

Av Westin
Senior vice president
of reality-based programming,
King World Productions;
Former executive producer,
ABC News

3

[Comparing TV news with newspapers]: There is a permanence to the printed word. Television is a ribbon of time; if you get distracted while that ribbon is going by, you've lost forever what was said. A newspaper gives you an opportunity to put it down if the phone rings, go back and pick it up afterward, and you haven't lost anything. I would sound the death knell for the [TV] network news at dinner hour before I would the death knell for newspapers.

Interview/
USA Today, 5-6:(A)9.

Bill Wheatley
Director of political coverage,
NBC News

4

[On press coverage of elections]: If you decide what is important in a campaign is recording what the candidates say, then you will get a certain kind of coverage. If you decide determining who is going to be elected is the principal question, then you will get another kind of coverage. And if you decide to focus your reporting on what challenges face the country and how the candidates might deal with them, you will get still a different type of reporting.

Los Angeles Times, 7-11:(A)5.

Pete Williams
Assistant Secretary
for Public Affairs,
Department of Defense
of the United States

5

[On Pentagon restrictions on press reporting during the current Persian Gulf war]: Our goal is the same as those of our predecessors—to get as much information as possible to the American people about their military without jeopardizing the lives of the troops or the success of the opera-

337

tion . . . The plan for combat coverage was not drawn up in a vacuum. We worked closely with the military and with the news media to develop a plan that would meet the needs of both . . . Unlike World War II, this will not be an operation in which reporters can ride around in jeeps going from one part of the front to another, or like Vietnam where reporters could hop a helicopter to specific points of action. If a ground war begins on the Arabian Peninsula, the battlefield will be chaotic and the action violent. This will be modern, intense warfare.

Before Senate Government
Operations Committee,
Washington, Feb. 20/
USA Today, 2-21:(A)11.

Shirley Williams
Director, Project Liberty,
Kennedy School of Government,
Harvard University
(United States);
Former Member
of British Parliament

1

The Eastern European press is undergoing a colossal upheaval. For example, there's only one east German paper that is still alive. All the others were bought out by the great west German chains. Which means that, for the moment, east German indigenous culture has been effectively destroyed. I think it will come back, because of things like desktop publishing and so on. But it'll come back as small, regional papers.

Interview, Boston/
The Christian Science Monitor,
4-3:14.

Robert C. Wright
President,
National Broadcasting Company

2

Network television [news] still has the advantage [over cable-TV news] of having 100 per cent coverage of the country. CNN doesn't have that. That still makes the difference between ourselves and cable really meaningful. We just haven't yet figured out how to arrange the economics. It used to be that at the beginning of the year you would budget five, six, ten million dollars for crisis coverage. Everybody in the company would hope the year would go by and nothing would happen so we wouldn't have to spend that money. Now, all of a sudden, we look for those moments to happen.

Interview/
The New York Times, 12-30:(C)6.

Barry Zorthian
Former Director,
Joint U.S. Public Affairs Office
during Vietnam war

3

[On military information supplied to the press during wartime]: The military information-gathering system isn't designed to meet the requirements of the media. It's a compilation from the front, up the line. On the ground, the platoon leader reports at the end of the day in bare-bones form, [and the] company passes it up the line. By the time it gets to headquarters, it's pretty distilled and dry. It serves military purposes; it is not designed to contain the eyewitness observation, the flavor and smell of battle. Therefore, it's almost always unsatisfactory to the media.

The Washington Post, 2-21:(A)19.

Literature

Shirley Abbott
Author

1

Anyone who thinks a memoir is the truth, the way something happened, is of course fooling herself, because memory is a knave. You forget what you don't want to remember, and you remember things the way you wished they had happened. You're constantly questioning and probing. Writing a memoir is not the same as writing fiction, but it's close.

Interview/
Publishers Weekly, 7-5:48.

Clive Barker
Author

2

Solid research gives you [the writer] a great place to move off from. It allows you a springboard, if you like, out into the fantastical. And also sometimes it throws up extraordinary things that you could never have guessed. Going to a prison for a couple of days gave me more insight than I could have imagined. The danger of not doing research is that what you end up doing is using other people's work as the basis for the reality which you're creating . . . It's wonderful to have inspiration from other artists and from the tradition in which you feel you're working. But it can really be dangerous if that's what's shaping your creativity, because what should be shaping it is the life which is being lived on the street outside. You've got to get drunk and be in danger once in a while. You've got to fall in love, you've got to be hurt—this is an old story but it's exactly true. It's not just about prisons and it's not just about autopsies. It's about experiencing stuff. It's about writing out of your pain, writing out of your own doubt, writing out of your own anger.

Interview/Writer's Digest, March:24.

Ray Bradbury
Author

3

If you stuff yourself full of poems, essays, plays, stories, novels, films, comic strips, magazines, music, you automatically explode every morning like Old Faithful. I have never had a dry spell in my life, mainly because I feed myself well, to the point of bursting. I wake early and hear my morning voices leaping around in my head like jumping beans. I get out of bed quickly, to trap them before they escape.

Writer's Digest, February:28.

Barbara Taylor Bradford
Author

4

[On writing novels]: Creating believable characters is the hardest part. That was what I had to get to grips with and, if you're serious about novel-writing, so will you. You will be a close people-watcher, observant of mannerisms, susceptible to inner reactions, a bit of a psychologist and emotionally able to get under their skin. I always start my novels with the character . . . [Also,] sound research gives a novel reality. A lot of people can string words together, but you are not a novelist unless you are able to tell monumental lies around invented people and make them seem believable. That's what I failed to do in my earliest attempts in the '60s. I set tales in exotic places I hardly knew—and my fibs failed to convince even me. Result: I scrapped them.

Interview/
The Writer, September:10,11.

Pete Dexter
Author

5

It always gets me when you see an interview with somebody who writes a book, who will step out there and presume to say anything about what authors are like or what the creative process is. That stuff, really—what a bunch of bullshit! 'Cause if you're honest at all, you know that it changes from day to day. The whole process of categorizing it or explaining it—even if it exists and even if you could say things about it that are true for you—why talk about how you do it instead of doing it?

Interview/Publishers Weekly, 10-4:71.

WHAT THEY SAID IN 1991

Thomas M. Disch
Author

1

[On his versatility in writing in many genres]: I've never been reviewed in *The New York Review of Books*. My poetry is not reviewed in *The New York Times*. Usually, anytime a book of mine is assigned, it's given to another science-fiction writer or to somebody who has that as part of their bailiwick. And then when I do books that live outside of those areas, they're dealt with as novelties. It would have been very easy for me to perform according to the publishers' expectations and turn out a succession of books that could be marketed as, "Here's another one just like the last one!" It's easy to market product that way. As it is, I present difficulties to the sales force.

Interview/
Publishers Weekly, 4-19:49.

Stephen Dobyns
Author

2

Writing poems is like waiting for lightning to strike. But it's hard to order your life around that. When I begin a novel, I'm beginning a long process that requires me to order my life in a conservative way over a period of months. I have to go to bed early and get up early and work, and this gives a structure to my life that poetry doesn't. If you're going to be a lightning rod, you're spending a lot of time running around looking for lightning. I don't think I could have a wife and family if I didn't write fiction.

Interview, New York/
Publishers Weekly, 6-21:44.

Leslie Fiedler
Author, Critic

3

I want to change people's minds with the revolution of the word. Yet one of my deep beliefs is that literature never really changes anything— it only makes you feel for a moment as though the world has changed. Maybe that's the best we can do. There's no flood prevention in literature. You can't even change the direction of the stream.

Interview, Buffalo, N.Y./
Publishers Weekly, 6-28:85.

Carlos Fuentes
Author

4

We're living in an age when I don't think "national literature" has any sense. Something that seemed absurdly utopian in the early 19th century when Goethe spoke about it, *"veiter Literatur"*—or world literature—is today a fact. It is national literatures that have become obsolete, anachronistic. You see, the geography of the novel of the world today is made up of many, many men and women of very different nationalities. You could not understand the novel today without Gunther Grass, Nadine Gordimer, Salman Rushdie, Garcia Marquez, Joan Didion or Julian Barnes. It is varied, but it makes up one great corpus of narrative writing that goes well beyond nationality, and which distinguishes itself by the stress on the quality of the imagination, the communicability of the imagination, which matters more than nationality or even languages.

Interview,
New York/
Publishers Weekly, 10-25:43.

Alice Fulton
Poet

5

[On the difference between poetry and prose]: Poetry is written in lines, prose isn't. Everyone thinks they know that, but often people don't think about what the line is doing and what it *can* do in poetry. I love the sense of all that white space around a little unit of language that becomes framed by the whiteness. What you do with the language itself is also much more important in poetry. Often, poems are about familiar subjects, but the language and the way words are put together make it poetry. I use rhythm, sound, music, the line, assonance, consonance, all the devices that make poetry different. Not that prose writers don't give any attention to these things. But poetry brings them to the fore. It's a more compressed form. People forget that. They think it's prose with wide margins.

Interview/
Writer's Digest,
September:38.

Henry Lewis Gates, Jr.
Professor of English,
Duke University

1

When I was in grad school, in the 1960s, everything [racially] black that could be found [in literature] was reproduced. But some of it was terrible. We've got to make discriminations within the corpus of black literature, and keep that which is worth keeping. We have to allow ourselves to be co-opted, and to co-opt. Sure, this means joining the establishment, but what's wrong with that? We are needed to keep those guys honest. I'm much more conservative than my colleagues. I do believe that some works are better than others. Some texts, black or white, use language that is more complex, more compelling, richer. I'm not in favor of Chinese-lantern literature—you know, paper-thin and full of hot air. I believe we can find works by blacks that are complex and reflect layers of experience otherwise scarce, otherwise ignored. My friends on the left think I'm hopeless . . . [But] you can't criticize black people too much or you'll be called a racist.

Interview/
The Atlantic Monthly, March:71.

Dana Gioia
Poet

2

Poetry is the art of using words charged to the greatest intensity. Poetry tends to be written in a language which is rhythmically organized. It tends to be written in lines. For thousands of years, poetry was almost exclusively written in meter, language which is rhythmically regular. That's no longer the case . . . The so-called free-verse revolution brought a great deal of vitality into modern poetry. It also, however, confused the general audience. In general, the average person prefers poetry written in rhyme and meter. It also prefers poetry which tells a story. Modernist poetry was not, for the most part, written in rhyme or meter, and modernist poetry declared that telling stories in verse was dead. That modernist revolution, while producing a great deal of magnificent poetry, also alienated poetry from the common reader.

Interview/USA Today, 8-29:(A)9.

Nadine Gordimer
Author;
Winner, 1991 Nobel Prize
in Literature

3

I never thought about the [Nobel] Prize when I wrote. The Prize is not important to the writing. Writing is not a horse race. It's very nice for a writer to have recognition, just as it is nice to have a truly understanding, favorable review and to know that the reviewer got from your work what you had hoped for. But it has no effect at all on what's going on in the writing. The best way to be read is posthumously. That way it doesn't matter if you offend a friend or a relative or a lover. It's absolutely fatal to your writing to think about how your work will be received. It's a betrayal of whatever talent you have.

Interview/
The New York Times, 10-10:(B)2.

Sue Grafton
Author

4

There is no finer form of fiction than the mystery. It has structure, a story line and a sense of place and pace. It is the one genre where the reader and the writer are pitted against each other. Readers don't want to guess the ending, but they don't want to be so baffled that it annoys them. Reading mysteries is a way for people to deal with the crime they see in their newspapers, on television or in their daily lives, in a safe, impersonal way.

Interview/
Writer's Digest, January:45.

Jim Harrison
Author

5

[As a writer, you] don't create something so that people can draw conclusions, but to enlarge them, just as you have been enlarged by the experience of making it up. Art should be a process of discovery, or it's boring.

Interview/
The Writer, January:3.

John Irving
Author

1

[A story] may be as comic as you can make it in tone or vein, but if something serious doesn't happen in it, it isn't really about anything that's worth our attention.

The Writer, December:3.

Susan Isaacs
Author

2

. . . although I love writing screenplays, I get more satisfaction out of my novels. In writing a novel, you're God, even though what you're creating might be a third-rate universe. In writing a screenplay, you're collaborating.

People, 4-15:98.

John Jakes
Author

3

For too many years, I tried to write like Ray Bradbury, then John Dickson Carr, then John D. MacDonald—always with negligible, not to say wretched, results. Find your own voice, listen to it, write it. Only by doing this will you be recognized in your own right. Over and over again, to writing groups, I offer a quote I ran across years ago, whose origin and author are lost to my memory. "Originality does not consist of saying what has never been said before; it consists of saying what you have to say."

Writer's Digest, February:33.

Erica Jong
Author; President,
Author's Guild

4

[On author-publisher relations]: In the last 10 years, we have seen contract boilerplates get tougher and tougher, relationships between authors and editors get weaker and weaker; a few celebrity business tycoons, television actresses and celebrity authors get millions of dollars for their work, while the majority of authors get lower royalties, lower advances, and in many cases cannot be published at all.

Accepting the presidency,
New York/
The New York Times, 3-6:(B)3.

Ryszard Kapuscinski
Polish author

5

I don't need the speed of writing [that a computer can give]. I need, rather, quiet, small, slow. My writing is a very slow process. If I include a computer, it's just this other being which asks me, Quick, quick, quick, give me something. This makes me nervous, this makes me de-concentrate. And if I just sit with a plain piece of paper, it's silent, it's quiet.

Interview/
Publishers Weekly, 4-5:125.

Stephen King
Author

6

Writers are secret agents. We are observers and should not be the observed. I like to live with one foot in the twilight zone.

The New York Times, 6-3:(B)3.

Louis H. Lapham
Editor, "Harper's Magazine"

7

I myself believe that the real world, at least as I understand it, is better approached through fiction than non-fiction. If one were to describe the sexual, psychological, political, social reality of the United States at the moment, I think you would be better with a fiction writer than a non-fiction writer.

The New York Times, 4-23:(B)1.

Norman Mailer
Author

8

A lot of us just aren't certain how long the novel has to live. The serious novelist 20 years from now may be absolutely the spiritual and

(NORMAN MAILER)

economic equal of a poet . . . which is, he's doing something because he or she is absolutely determined to do it, but that's the only reason to do it.

Interview, New York/
Los Angeles Times, 10-3:(E)9.

1

We live in crazy times. And the role of fiction now is to make non-fiction believable. That's what the novel has become . . . the only way to *explain* behavior and show that the bizarre world around us is real.

Interview, New York/
Los Angeles Times, 10-3:(E)9.

Robert Massey
Author

2

The "satisfactory manuscript" clause [in an author's contract with a publisher] is what bugs me the most. When that goes wrong and a publisher rejects a manuscript and then comes back after the advance, which of course the writer has spent—there's no first proceeds, you haven't sold it anywhere else, but they want [the advance] back anyway. The "satisfactory manuscript" clause ought to be deader than a doornail; publishers should be ashamed of themselves.

Interview, New York/
Publishers Weekly, 11-8:47.

Daniel Menaker
Fiction editor,
"The New Yorker" magazine

3

If there is any cultural significance in what the literary community is doing, it resides in the short story. I think it's an important part of American culture right now in a way that I truly believe novels are not.

The New York Times, 4-23:(B)1.

Mary McGarry Morris
Author

4

I am not part of any literary world. I have no writer friends or connections. And I have no

desire to move into a literary world. I am wary of letting an aura take the place of the effort of writing.

Interview, Andover, Mass./
The New York Times, 1-28:(B)3.

5

I start with a sense of the story first. I feel such a need for a story, which is something that often seems to be missing from contemporary fiction in this country, where a mood seems enough for many writers.

The Writer, June:3.

John Mortimer
Author

6

Nothing is more depressingly snobbish than the idea that good writing can't be popular; but high sales are not necessarily a proof of literary excellence.

The Writer, February:5.

V. S. Naipaul
Author

7

Flaubert began to write *Madame Bovary* 140 years ago, and it is accessible to all of us. But we cannot write the Flaubertian novel [today]. It's done. We have to do our own work. It would be nonsensical for me to write the same kind of novel I wrote 34 years ago. My theory is that Dickens was driven to an early grave by the Dickensian novel. I think he carried it like a burden. When you think he began *Oliver Twist* at the time Balzac was doing *Pere Goriot* and *Eugenie Grandet,* those lovely books. Then the French novel developed and de Maupassant came along, all the excitement. And there was Dickens still writing this Dickensian thing. No wonder he died at the age of 58; it was too much for him.

Interview,
New York/
The New York Times, 1-30:(B)3.

WHAT THEY SAID IN 1991

1

An autobiography can distort, facts can be realigned. But fiction never lies. It reveals the writer totally.

The Writer, June:3.

Tim O'Brien
Author

2

I guess if there's one thing I really care about beyond anything else in the writing world, the main obsession is the story. I don't mean to sound so simple because it's so complex, but still, the story's *it* for me. Story means more than just narrative or plot. It means *aboutness*. In *Huckleberry Finn,* the story's more than Huck's being on a raft on the river; it's the aboutness—the things that surround the boy along the way—that makes the story.

Interview/
Writers Digest, April:34.

Anna Quindlen
Columnist,
"The New York Times";
Author

3

I find fiction oddly liberating, precisely because it isn't fact. Reporting on a story, there's always the anecdote you didn't get or the quote that you know would have been there if you had more time to dig for it. In fiction, you don't have to give up, and you don't have to worry about spelling names right. But if you're liberated by the form, you're imprisoned by the characters. You find that out the first time you try to make them say or do something they wouldn't really say or do.

Interview, New York/
Publishers Weekly, 3-15:41.

Shannon Ravenel
Former editor,
"The Best American
Short Stories"

4

The short story is kind of hot these days, even though there is not a lot of support in the slick end of the magazine world. There is a very real community of American short-story writers. Everybody knows who everybody is, although there is no real way to make much of a splash.

The New York Times, 4-23:(B)1.

Anita Shreve
Author

5

... my politics and my feminism do not really enter into my fiction. I write stories out of my subconscious. I try in my fiction to tell human truths, not necessarily political ones. Political writing has an agenda, a message—but literature doesn't fit quite as neatly into political categories.

Interview, Rockland County, N.Y./
Publishers Weekly, 4-12:40.

Charles Simic
Poet

6

Poetry is an orphan of silence. The words never quite equal the experience behind them. We are always at the beginning, eternal apprentices, thrown back again and again into that condition.

The Writer, February:5.

William Stafford
Poet

7

I have this feeling of wending my way or blundering through a mysterious jungle of possibilities when I am writing. This jungle has not been explored by previous writers. It never will be explored. It's endlessly varying as we progress through the experience of time. The words that occur to me come out of my relation to the language which is developing even as I am using it . . . I am not learning definitions as established in even the latest dictionary. I'm not a dictionary-maker. I'm a person a dictionary-maker has to contend with . . . I'm a living element in the development of language.

Interview, Oregon/
The Christian Science Monitor,
8-21:17.

Danielle Steel
Author

1

I know my characters. I know where they came from, who their grandmothers were, how their parents treated them when they were little. It's the characters' history that makes them who they are.

The Writer, June:3.

Mark Strand
Poet Laureate
of the United States

2

[Poets] tend to be cheerleaders for the universe. That's why it's dangerous for them to align themselves with political causes. People will say they've [poets] been taken in. They should stick to the broad issues, and the broadest issues of our experience are life and death. That's the stuff of all great poems.

Interview/
Los Angeles Times Magazine, 1-13:30.

3

You don't choose to become something like a poet. You write and you write, and the years go by, and you are a poet.

People, 2-4:100.

Alice Walker
Poet

4

I have learned that I can't force poems. But if I spend a long time in silence, which is really love, that's very good for my writing. The main thing is just to live intensely and to feel. If there's the slightest little bubble from the spring coming up, I try to go with the bubble until it gets to the top of the water and then try to be there for it, so that I can begin to understand what is happening down in the depths.

Interview/
U.S. News and World Report,
6-3:51.

Yevgeny Yevtushenko
Soviet poet

5

[Poetry became important in the Soviet Union because] it was only possible for the conscience of the people to be expressed in a metaphorical way. That's why poetry was a kind of spiritual newspaper of the people. Sometimes we published our unpublished poetry in the pages of the open air, with our own voices. Published poetry was a great spiritual power. Being oppressed, being sometimes not published, a poet in Russia is a little bit like a holy man—they are always martyrs in the understanding of people.

Interview, Washington/
The Christian Science Monitor,
3-8:11.

6

[On censorship as it existed until recently in the Soviet Union]: I just finished writing a long article: "Censorship as the Best Reader." It's a bitter irony. I am talking how I am longing for censorship—because nobody better than censors understood all the subtle nuances of poetry. Nobody appreciated us so highly.

Interview, Washington/
The Christian Science Monitor,
3-8:11.

Medicine and Health

Henry J. Aaron
Director of economic studies,
Brookings Institution

1

National health insurance is the hands-down winner for universal coverage [in the U.S.]. It does so directly and in the simplest way—one insurer for all. It also changes the spending incentives, though whether it really controls costs depends on government's political will. But the price [of such coverage] is very high. My own view is that whatever the virtues of national health insurance in the long haul, and I think they are considerable, the chances of moving directly to such a system from where we are now are pretty slight because of the enormous redistribution of income and the huge increase in the size of government [required under such a system].

Interview/
USA Today, 6-26:(A)13.

Brock Adams
United States Senator,
D-Washington

2

Women will continue to be at unnecessary risk until the study of the health concerns of midlife and older women become a top priority in the United States. Many of the health problems women face . . . begin in midlife, but little attention or resources have been directed to menopause where it is believed women's susceptibility to many of these diseases begins. Women pay the price for this inattention. As a result of the lack of research, particularly on gender differences in aging and the development of disease, women receive second-class health care.

Los Angeles Times, 4-20:(A)23.

Drew Altman
President,
Henry J. Kaiser
Family Foundation

3

You can't operate in today's health-care world effectively without quickly seeing the main ball-game is government. Government policy and financing drives our health-care system. And it's not doing it well enough.

Los Angeles Times, 4-13:(A)1.

Marion S. Barry, Jr.
Former Mayor of Washington

4

[On his past drug abuse]: Mind-altering chemicals are destroying America. Lives are destroyed. Families are broken up. I got caught up in this drug culture but, let me say, it's not the way. I stand here clear, bright . . . Thanks to God, with a strong commitment on my part, I kicked it. So many don't make it. We must develop a revolutionary attitude about drugs. We can't say, "It ain't my thing; it's their thing." If it's a wrong thing, it's our thing [to fight]. There's no such thing as a little line [of cocaine]. [If] you take a little line, you take a big line. I ought to know that.

At University of the District of
Columbia, Sept. 5/
The Washington Post, 9-6:(A)22.

Margaret P. Battin
Professor of philosophy,
University of Utah

5

In a society that can't agree when human life begins, it's no surprise that we have trouble deciding when it should end. If you think the abortion issue was emotional, just wait until we get fully into euthanasia and death.

Los Angeles Times, 11-2:(A)1.

William J. Bennett
Former Director,
Federal Office of
National Drug Control Policy

6

I believe with Harvard psychiatrist Robert Coles that drugs are fundamentally a spiritual

(WILLIAM J. BENNETT)

problem for many people. Drug use is a misguided attempt to find meaning in life. When people take drugs, they get a feeling of transcendence, of power, of control. That's a great deception. I said in one of the first speeches I gave in the job that if drugs aren't a sin and if this isn't a form of idolatry, I don't know what is.

Interview/
Christianity Today, 2-11:46.

Lloyd Bentsen
United States Senator,
D-Texas

1

[Criticizing Bush Administration proposals to cut Medicare spending]: Medicare cuts of the size we're hearing about would put severe strains on the ability of hospitals to cover rising medical costs. I don't see how they can propose another $20-billion cut when half our hospitals already lose money each time they treat a Medicare patient. It's obvious to me—and to most of you— that a growing number of hospitals are simply not in a position to take another hit.

Before American Hospital Association,
Washington, Jan. 28/
Los Angeles Times, 1-29:(A)4.

Robert C. Bonner
Administrator, Drug
Enforcement Administration
of the United States

2

[Saying his office will go after those who traffic in or abuse the use of anabolic steroids]: I want to send a loud and clear signal to doctors and pharmacists that it will not be business as usual with steroids. Doctors who prescribe anabolic steroids for other than legitimate purposes will be prosecuted. Profits made from such sales will be forfeited, and I will revoke their license to prescribe drugs.

Washington, Feb. 21/
The Washington Post, 2-22:(A)3.

Michael Bromberg
Executive director,
American Federation
of Health Systems

3

If you have national health insurance [in the U.S.] run by the Federal government, you destroy the insurance industry. If you mandate that all employers provide health insurance—or if they fail to do so, be forced to pay a tax to finance a government program for them—small business will get hurt . . . If you subsidize purchase of policies through Federal tax credits, you'd have to raise taxes and President Bush would scream. If you have strong cost controls, the providers would scream.

The Washington Post,
4-29:(A)5.

George Bush
President of the United States

4

[On AIDS]: I'm not in favor of Federally funded needle programs [to provide clean needles to drug-users]. I am in favor of the most efficient and effective research possible. I'm in favor of compassion. I'm in favor of behavioral change. Here's a disease where you can control its spread by your own personal behavior. So if the message is compassion, I got it loud and clear.

News conference,
Kennebunkport, Maine, Sept. 2/
The New York Times, 9-3:(A)14.

Daniel Callahan
Director, Hastings Center,
Briarcliff Manor, N.Y.

5

The new interest in euthanasia is very much a response to the failure of medicine to adequately reassure people about their dying. As fast as we have been trying to figure out how to allow people to die more peacefully, we keep improving the [life-prolonging] technology that makes it all the harder to do . . . Medicine has really not managed to control people's dying very well.

Los Angeles Times, 4-19:(A)1.

Arthur L. Caplan
Director,
Center for Biomedical Ethics,
University of Minnesota

1

[On suggestions that medical providers such as doctors, dentists and nurses be tested for the HIV virus to guard against transmission of this AIDS virus to patients]: The future of HIV testing has almost nothing to do with actuarial facts or risk assessments. Our health-care system is driven by liability concerns. It will only take a few more million-dollar awards to infected patients before insurance companies and those who write malpractice insurance insist on testing as a precondition for coverage [of medical providers].

At conference sponsored by
Centers for Disease Control,
Atlanta, Feb. 21/
The Washington Post, 2-22:(A)6.

2

[Saying drug companies could reduce high prices for many drugs by cutting their expenses for other activities]: We should be asking some tough questions about what is going on with respect to these prices. We have a special moral obligation to take this seriously, because lives really hang in the balance . . . Drug companies spend a lot of money on advertising, promotional activities, junkets and assorted other activities. They subsidize every prize given to every medical student. They give away stethoscopes, note pads—you name it. They find out who their markets are early—in medical school—and they stay with them until they retire.

Los Angeles Times, 4-11:(A)26.

Eric J. Cassell
Clinical professor
of public health,
Cornell University
Medical College

3

[On euthanasia]: I don't think doctors should be killers. The decision to assist someone in their death should be agonized and private. Doctors administering injections is bad for doctors and bad for medicine, not because it is too hard but because it is too easy.

The New York Times, 10-28:(A)15.

John H. Chafee
United States Senator,
R-Rhode Island

4

[Criticizing a proposed health-insurance bill that would require employers to either provide health coverage for their employees or pay a tax into a fund for the uninsured]: You care for the middle class by demonstrating you don't want to put small businesses out of commission, and clearly that's what the "play or pay" provision does. The good news [about this bill] is individuals have health-care coverage; the bad news is they are out of a job.

USA Today, 12-2:(A)4.

Robert Chilcote
Pediatric oncologist,
School of Medicine,
University of California,
Irvine

5

[Calling for better communications skills for doctors when they deal with patients]: We have our powerful scientific tools, our MRIs, our DNA-based testing, our methods of studying the heart and brain no one dreamed of 10 years ago. But we can't order those expensive tests in lieu of talking to the patient.

Los Angeles Times, 10-1:(A)20.

Larry R. Churchill
Professor and chairman
of social medicine,
University of North Carolina,
Chapel Hill

6

I think [national health care in the U.S.] is inevitable. The question is how soon and what form it's going to take because health-care costs are out of control. If people think 12.5 per cent [of GNP] is too much to spend on health care, wait until the turn of the century when we're spending

(LARRY R. CHURCHILL)

17 per cent to 20 per cent. We're paying a price for having the system we do . . . [If the U.S. goes to national health care, we'll] have to give up our aspiration that the health-care system can do anything and everything for us—this idea that there's no amount of money that's too great to spend to prolong somebody's life for a few months. But what we will gain is an idea of health care as a common right of every citizen.

Interview/
USA Today, 12-30:(A)11.

Mario M. Cuomo
Governor of New York (D)

1

Health care is a metaphor now. It is a metaphor for taking care of people's real problems, taking care of the middle class. Health care is a middle-class issue . . . The poor people are on Medicaid . . . The problem is the middle-class people, the people who go into nursing homes with a little money in their pockets and a house and a car; the people who don't have health insurance.

Interview, Nov. 6/
Los Angeles Times, 11-7:(A)27.

James Curran
Director, AIDS program,
Centers for Disease Control
(United States)

2

[Encouraging the testing of hospital patients for the AIDS virus]: In a lot of these studies, as many as two-thirds of infected people who enter and exit a hospital do so without their infection being recognized. In many cases, knowing that condition may be very important for treatment. It also represents a lost opportunity to diagnose, refer and counsel HIV-infected people.

The Washington Post, 9-20:(A)3.

Howard B. Dean
Governor of Vermont (D);
Physician

3

Health care is going to be the Number 1 problem over the next five years, and doctors are doing their profession and the public a terrible disservice by not getting into politics. If doctors don't get in there trying to lead the movement toward cost containment, the public and doctors will lose from the mistakes.

Interview/The New York Times, 9-3:(B)6.

Nancy Dickey
Physician;
Member, board of trustees,
American Medical Association

4

[On proposals that doctors should be tested for the AIDS virus and that patients should be notified of the results]: If doctors are at risk, due either to their practice or life-style, they have an obligation to know their HIV status. If they are doing invasive procedures, they have an obligation to stop voluntarily, or tell their patient, and let the patient decide whether to go further . . . Until we know the numbers and know the science, we must take a patient-protective, conservative public-health stance.

Chicago, June 26/
The New York Times, 6-27:(A)9.

Lee Dogoloff
Executive director,
American Council
for Drug Education

5

[On a survey showing young people are using less cocaine and crack than in the past]: . . . for any drug to enjoy widespread use, there must be a public perception of safety—and that perception has been shattered for crack and cocaine. But what is most disconcerting is that we have not made any significant dent in either alcohol or tobacco. And that is what is likely to take our children from us before they reach maturity.

Jan. 24/Los Angeles Times, 1-25:(A)4.

Fran DuMelle
Deputy managing director,
American Lung Association;
Chairman, Coalition
on Smoking OR Health

6

There's bad stuff in side stream [passive or second-hand tobacco] smoke and nobody need

349

(FRAN DuMELLE)

be exposed to it. Environmental tobacco smoke is the easiest indoor pollutant to deal with. You just don't have smoking anymore. It's not like the glue that holds down your carpeting or the particleboard in your furniture. It's easy to remove [tobacco smoke].

April 18/Los Angeles Times, 4-19:(A)4.

Robert DuPont
Former director,
National Institute
on Drug Abuse

1

[On teen-age alcohol consumption]: Society looks the other way. Nobody does anything about it. When parents or anybody else— teachers, counselors—try to deal with the teen-age drinking problem, they're treated as if they're [temperance crusader] Carry Nation. We ought to have a genuine prohibition of under-age drinking—that is, enforce it across the board. It's not just law enforcement, it's social enforcement.

Los Angeles Times, 6-7:(A)29.

Anthony Fauci
Director, National Institute
for Allergy and Infectious Diseases
of the United States

2

The NIH is still the best place in the world to do basic research. The atmosphere is electric. Certainly there are gripes, but to say that morale is reaching a new low here is completely incorrect. Do I think I should be making more money? Yes. Is my morale low? No. Morale is how you feel about the place and about your work and your colleagues. Most of us believe that the benefits of working here are worth the differential in salary [between the NIH and the private sector].

Los Angeles Times, 3-19:(A)5.

Joel Feinberg
Professor of philosophy and law,
University of Arizona

3

[On whether there is a moral difference between a doctor stopping life-sustaining medical

treatment and a doctor assisting a patient who wants to die]: A doctor discontinuing a treatment often thinks he isn't morally responsible but thinks that he is when he gives a lethal injection. That is superstitious—he's responsible either way.

The New York Times, 10-28:(A)15.

Harvey Field
President,
Board of Rabbis
of Southern California

4

The basic [Jewish] tradition is that you allow life to take its course; you neither foreshorten nor prolong it . . . But I believe that where there is clearly a terminal situation, and the quality of life has deteriorated and will continue to deteriorate, the person really ought to have the choice in determining how he or she wishes to die.

Los Angeles Times, 11-2:(A)25.

Betty Ford
Founder, Betty Ford Center at
Eisenhower Medical Center,
Rancho Mirage, Calif.;
Wife of former President
of the United States
Gerald R. Ford

5

[Saying government support for substance-abuse treatment, such as her Betty Ford Center, is not keeping up with the need]: From a society that was beginning to understand and become part of the solution so desperately needed, we've moved back to punishing people by keeping them from accessing the health-care benefits to which they should be clearly entitled. We're seeing a rebirth of the stigma that encourages them not to seek treatment for fear of consequences . . . As someone who knows the joy of recovery, this kind of thinking leads me to believe that our public policy has gone badly awry. Questionable reasoning, ignorance and our failure to face the facts are not a good basis for decision-making . . . If we do not continue to educate, if we do not attempt to change the current trend of public policy, if we continue to focus on enforcement

(BETTY FORD)

and interdiction [of illegal drugs] to the virtual exclusion of prevention and treatment, we will have succeeded in dismantling our treatment system to the point of no return. If we do that, we will never make a dent in alcoholism and drug dependency in this country.

Before House Subcommittee on
Health and Long-Term Care,
Washington, March 25/
The Washington Post, 4-2:(A)20.

Jacob Fox
Neurologist

1

A diagnosis of Alzheimer's [disease] used to be reserved for younger people who became prematurely senile. Senility in older people was believed to be due to something else, like hardening of the arteries. But now we know that the difference between senile old people and normal old people is that one group generally has Alzheimer's and the other doesn't. We also know that Alzheimer's becomes more common as people grow older and, since the population of this country is aging, we are seeing more patients with Alzheimer's. A colleague of mine estimates that 10 per cent of people over 65 have Alzheimer's, and past the age of 85 the number may approach 50 per cent. So sometime in the next century, when we have 80 million people in the country above the age of 65, we might have 8 million Alzheimer's patients.

Interview, Chicago/
Time, 4-15:12.

William A. Galston
Professor of public affairs,
University of Maryland;
Democratic Party analyst

2

. . . cost increases for health care outpace family incomes by a factor of two or three. The anxiety is increased because more and more employers are requiring more and more employees to pay a higher share of health-care costs. What's worse, many people find them-

selves locked into jobs they don't like simply because they're afraid of losing their existing health plans if they change employment. As the inadequacy of health care is no longer simply an underclass problem, it becomes a more important issue politically.

Time, 11-11:51.

Albert Gore, Jr.
United States Senator,
D-Tennessee

3

Can we afford a prescription drug-pricing policy whose bottom line is whatever the market will bear? What is saving a life worth?

Los Angeles Times, 4-11:(A)26.

Norton J. Greenberger
President, American College
of Physicians

4

The last decade has seen increasing regulation of physicians with resultant loss of clinical autonomy and the imposition of numerous hassle factors that are leading to ever increasing frustration with the practice of medicine. Primary-care physicians, and especially general internists, are bearing the brunt of this.

Los Angeles Times, 1-1:(A)3.

Jack Hadley
Co-director, Center for
Health Policy Studies,
Georgetown University

5

[Saying Americans without health insurance receive cheaper medical care]: Where it is clear-cut that a procedure or test needs to be done to save a person's life, I have no doubt that the test or procedure is done. But unfortunately for people without insurance, there are a lot of situations where this is not so clear-cut . . . There are borderline situations where medical coverage is likely to be an important consideration [in deciding whether or not a test or procedure is done].

The Washington Post, 1-16:(A)1.

Peter B. Hutt
Drug-industry consultant;
Authority on the U.S. Food
and Drug Administration
1

We have found, especially with AIDS and other life-threatening diseases, that if [the FDA holds new] drugs off the market until the last i is dotted, you are subjecting patients to another risk, the risk of not getting a drug to them that might help. Of course, if new drugs reach the market faster, the American public will be accepting a greater risk. It may well happen that a drug will get on the market that shouldn't. But the purpose of [a current proposal to get new drugs to market faster] is to consider both risks.

The New York Times,
11-9:7.

Linda Jenckes
Vice president
for Federal affairs,
Health Insurance Association
of America
2

[On the health-care industry]: I don't think there's any other industry or any other social problem that has quite as many dynamics or intractabilities. The problem is that, politically, it's a no-win constituency. There are no natural allies.

The Washington Post,
7-1:(A)12.

James C. Johnson
President,
American College
of Emergency Physicians
3

[On reports of emergency-room patients having to wait sometimes days for in-patient beds]: Our nation's emergency health-care system is in crisis, jeopardizing access to life-saving medical care for all Americans regardless of who they are, where they live, or whether they are covered by medical insurance.

News conference, Aug. 26/
The Washington Post, 8-27:(A)3.

Albert R. Jonsen
Professor of ethics in medicine,
University of Washington
4

If medicine ever embarks on [euthanasia], it should probably surround the physician decision with some sort of review and consultation. I just don't like the idea of a kind of privatization of killing. That is the big danger.

Los Angeles Times, 4-19:(A)25.

Larry Joyce
Chief spokesman,
American Medical Association
5

[On the AMA's new media campaign to improve the image of the medical profession]: There's a common perception amongst physicians that the public does not fully understand or appreciate the work that they do. That's what this campaign is designed to address, but we're not naive enough to think that this, in and of itself, is going to solve the problem . . . The whole purpose of this is to personalize physicians so that people will see that physicians across the country are much like their own individual doctors.

Los Angeles Times, 8-14:(A)5.

Sanford Kadish
Criminal-law specialist,
Boalt Hall Law School,
University of California,
Berkeley
6

[Laws to legalize euthanasia by physicians would] constitute a radical affront to accepted life-and-death mores [of much of the population]. It is a threatening business to give the power to kill someone to a private person without much guidance except that in their judgment someone is terminally ill.

Los Angeles Times, 4-19:(A)24.

Edward M. Kennedy
United States Senator,
D-Massachusetts
7

We have a competitive health-care system today, in which the best of health care and the

(EDWARD M. KENNEDY)

worst of health care are competing side by side—and the worst is winning.

At Senate Labor and Human Resources
Committee hearing, Washington/
Los Angeles Times, 2-10:(D)2.

David A. Kessler
Commissioner,
Food and Drug Administration
of the United States

1

[On advertising of prescription drugs]: The Food and Drug Administration is kind of grappling with its policy on direct-to-consumer advertising. It's very hard, in my opinion, to achieve fair balance . . . For example, I'm not overly impressed with the information conveyed in any pharmaceutical drug advertisements . . . While I'm personally supportive of efforts to educate patients about drugs, once one crosses the line into promotional aspects, I become skeptical about the benefits . . . Once you're into the realm of promotion, it's very hard to control the messages.

The Washington Post, 5-24:(F)3.

Louis J. Kettel
Vice president
for academic affairs,
Association of
American Medical Colleges

2

In the 1940s and 1950s, medicine was too much an art and not enough of a science. Now we have more science than we know what to do with.

U.S. News & World Report,
4-29:84.

John Kitzhaber
President of the
Oregon State Senate (D)

3

[On Oregon's new program that provides health insurance for everyone through a plan of care rationing]: Most Americans believe that everyone should have access to health care and Congress has toyed for nearly half a century with the idea. Yet today, the number of Americans without coverage continues to grow. In Oregon, we've created an approach that provides coverage for everyone and we've reached the political consensus necessary to make it happen.

Los Angeles Times, 7-1:(A)1.

4

[Oregon's] current Medicaid program will give a kid five liver transplants and let his mom die from preventable breast cancer. Most of the things that get people in trouble are not strange cancers or rare bone diseases. They are the routine problems of fundamental health care. We don't have an endless supply of money. It's time we were fair about how we use what we have.

The Washington Post, 7-1:(A)12.

C. Everett Koop
Former Surgeon General
of the United States

5

One of the things that frightens me now more than anything else is the public belief that we have turned the corner on AIDS. The disease still is moving along relentlessly. Because of this attitude, we're unable to reach the people we need to reach. One group that worries me is 14-to-17-year-olds, who are sexually promiscuous. It gives teen-agers a sense there's no problem at all.

U.S. News & World Report,
6-17:26.

6

I care about animals, but I care about people more. Any legislation that bans animal-based research that ensures product safety is, quite literally, hazardous to human health.

Washington/
Los Angeles Times, 9-10:(A)3.

John Lewin
Director of Health of Hawaii

7

[On Hawaii's system of health insurance that provides coverage for 98 per cent of the popula-

(JOHN LEWIN)

tion either through employer-paid plans or state subsidies]: One criticism I hear is that we [in Hawaii] are different, as if we're all sipping mai tais on the beach and dancing in coconut-shell bras. We have a lot of poor people in Hawaii. We have all the health problems of the rest of the states. But what makes us different is that we decided to do something about it . . . The secret of our success, the secret that many in the American medical establishment do not want to hear, is prevention. We have twice as many outpatient visits, that is, people see their doctors several times a year, and half as many hospital stays, as the national average.

The New York Times, 7-23:(A)1,7.

David Lewis
Director,
substance-abuse program,
National Basketball Association

1

If you compare the professional athlete to the general population [on drinking alcoholic beverages], you will find use and abuse and addiction is almost identical. Alcoholism is a genetic illness exacerbated by environment and stress. People who have the illness use alcohol to treat their feelings. If you look at when we tend to pick up people [to the NBA's abuse program], it's usually in the second half of the season. The road schedule is a bear.

USA Today, 4-23:(A)11.

George D. Lundberg
Editor,
"Journal of the American
Medical Association"

2

[On euthanasia]: It is a real tough area. I think in the next century death without pain and with dignity and perhaps even at a pre-arranged time will be the norm. But I hope that we do not get there quickly because there is a tremendous gulf of philosophical and historical experience that runs counter to that.

Los Angeles Times, 4-19:(A)25.

Marc O. Mayer
Analyst,
Sanford C. Bernstein & Company

3

[Saying drug companies have little incentive to limit price increases for prescription drugs]: In our system, one person prescribes a drug, another person dispenses it, somebody else takes it and somebody else pays for it.

The New York Times, 5-11:27.

Ruth McCorkle
Professor of nursing,
University of Pennsylvania

4

Nursing has the best bag of tricks for helping people live day to day with chronic problems, and it is far ahead of physicians in its ability to monitor patients' quality of life.

The New York Times, 8-13:(B)6.

Jim McDermott
United States Representative,
D-Washington

5

Every other industrialized country in the world has been able to develop a system that meets their health-care needs, but not in this country [the U.S.] . . . [In Canada,] you can choose your own doctor, you can choose your own hospital, but all the bills are paid through the government, through a single payer. They set the rates with respect to doctors and hospitals . . . Everybody gets the health care, they live two years longer, their infant-mortality rate is lower than ours. In every respect, it's at least as good if not better than our system.

Interview/"Morning News,"
Cable News Network, 10-10.

Gerald Mossinghoff
President, Pharmaceutical
Manufacturers Association

6

[On criticism of the high cost of drugs]: Last year, our companies invested $8.1-billion in research-and-development; this year, they will

(GERALD MOSSINGHOFF)

invest $9.2-billion. What pays for that $9.2-billion is sales revenues. The percentage of sales that our companies put into research and development will be about 17 per cent this year—about five times higher than the average industrial investment for research and development for other industries . . . If you look at the over-all health-care dollar, as much as our critics would like to deny it, drugs amount to less than a nickel. It's the most cost-effective form of therapy there is. You're really lucky as a patient if there *is* a pharmaceutical that goes right to your problem and cures it. Otherwise, you'd be spending a lot more money in hospitals.

Los Angeles Times, 4-11:(A)26.

Jack Needleman
Health-policy specialist,
Harvard University

1

[Saying health insurance and other financial considerations affect the way health care is provided to an individual]: One of the myths we keep repeating is that we can't start rationing care in the United States. But . . . we already are. The other myth is that U.S. health care is the best in the world . . . At its best, U.S. health care is unmatched. But the health-care system we have, with the millions of uninsured, is not the best.

The Washington Post, 1-16:(A)20.

Herbert Nickens
Vice president
for minority health,
American Association
of Medical Colleges

2

[On the increasing incidence of AIDS in minority-group populations]: When the image of AIDS was as a white, gay disease, it had the advantages of the activism and social power that the gay community brought to it. But as it gets perceived as a minority disease, this will change. Minority diseases, particularly those of IV drug users and their sexual partners and children, do not have great power in society . . . The real

danger is that this could be labeled as a disease of people who are expendable.

The Washington Post, 6-5:(A)3.

John D. (Jay) Rockefeller IV
United States Senator,
D-West Virginia

3

[Saying arriving at a compromise on the health-care financing issue requires all sides to accept it, grumpily]: None of this works unless everyone is unhappy. It's like orchestrating a symphony of unhappiness.

The Washington Post, 7-1:(A)12.

4

. . . health-care [legislation] is very difficult. It is not approached lightly. It is a world of acronyms, of conflicts, of incredibly palpable interests. It's a hard subject . . . In health-care legislation, your only attitude can be full speed ahead. Assault on all fronts.

Interview/USA Today, 7-25:(A)9.

Dan Rostenkowski
United States Representative,
D-Illinois

5

There is no more important problem confronting our country today than health care. It is time to abandon the catchy slogans and gear up for the legislative long march. [But] absent Presidential leadership, we will not be able to achieve a major reform of the health-care system. [Health care could be] the cornerstone issue of the next Presidential election. [President] George Bush is wrong to duck this issue.

Washington, Aug. 2/
The New York Times, 8-3:6.

6

As long as health spending consumes 12 per cent or more of our gross national product, doomsday is just around the corner.

Washington, Aug. 2/
The Washington Post, 8-24:(A)2.

(DAN ROSTENKOWSKI)

1

A recent survey found that the American people believe we should spend more on health, but that they were unwilling to pay more individually. Nice work if you can get it. So I conclude that people want a system where someone else will pay the bills and they don't have to make any changes themselves. On a personal level, I can certainly understand that view. On a political level, I can tell you that it is unrealistic. There are going to be some changes made. And we are going to be the victims as well as the beneficiaries of them. The public doesn't realize that yet. In some cases, people will have to pay more money. In others, they'll have to compromise on convenience. But the bottom line is that virtually no one—except those who are denied adequate care now and thus have absolutely nothing to lose—will be exempt from the burden-sharing required . . . Basically what people want is unlimited access to the physicians and hospitals of their choice with the bills paid by someone else. I sympathize with that. But the sad fact is that there's no health fairy and that there's no way we can achieve that unrealistic goal without one.

At meeting sponsored by
National Consumers League,
Washington, Oct. 9/
The Washington Post, 10-10:(A)21.

Thomas B. Stoddard
Adjunct professor of law,
New York University;
Executive director,
Lambda Legal Defense
and Education Fund

2

[Criticizing expected Federal recommendations that physicians and health workers who engage in invasive medical procedures be tested for the AIDS virus and not practice if they test positive]: These recommendations will be interpreted by every liability lawyer in the United States to require health professionals to disclose their HIV status. The idea that these guidelines are voluntary is totally illusory. What is voluntary at this moment will, within six months,

become mandatory. And, in another year, we will see testing for patients as well.

Los Angeles Times, 7-15:(A)17.

Louis W. Sullivan
Secretary of Health
and Human Services
of the United States

3

[Criticizing tobacco companies for sponsoring sporting events]: The tobacco companies are trading on the prestige and image of the athletes to barter their deadly products. They are using the vigor and energy of these athletes as a subtle—but incorrect and dishonest—message that tobacco use is compatible with good health . . . It is immoral for civilized societies to condone the promotion and advertising of products which, when used as intended, cause disability and death . . . We must seriously question values which allow activities that ostensibly represent the essence of fun, fitness and health to be exploited to such a large degree by the merchants of suffering, disease and death.

At First International Conference
on Smokeless Tobacco,
Columbus, Ohio, April 10/
The Washington Post, 4-11:(A)1,4.

4

There is clear, demonstrable, undeniable evidence of discrimination and racism in our health-care system. Each year since 1984, while the health status of the general population has increased, black health status has actually declined. This decline is not in one or two health categories; it is across the board.

At health-care conference,
Minneapolis/
The New York Times, 6-3:(A)8.

5

As physicians, we must recognize that health care is not the only public good. As Americans, as well as physicians, we must be concerned that consuming ever larger portions of GNP on health care necessarily diverts resources from other

(LOUIS W. SULLIVAN)

good uses—for example, increased wages, savings, capital investment, research and development and human services such as drug rehabilitation, foster care and family support.

Before American Medical Association,
Chicago, June 23/
The Washington Post, 6-24:(A)4.

Jean Thorne
Oregon State Medical Director

1

[On Oregon's new Basic Health Services plan that rations coverage to include only certain basic health-care needs]: To those who say the current Medicaid program can be restructured to help all the poor who need health care, I say, "Dream on." To those who say [the new plan] is not the perfect plan, I say we are not in the business of philosophy. We are trying to increase access to health care for the poor. And to those who say that this legitimates a two-tiered health-care system in the United States, I can only ask why do they think there should be one tier of health care? Is there one tier of housing in America or education or of food?

The Washington Post, 7-1:(A)12.

James S. Todd
Executive vice president,
American Medical Association

2

Medicare as an entitlement is going to absolutely destroy the health-care system. Just think what would happen in this country if somebody suddenly decided that everyone was entitled to air travel. On its current course, Medicare will soon exceed our expenditures for defense, our expenditures for Social Security. There are a lot of people on Medicare who could very easily support themselves . . . The way to help the poor is to get Medicare patients to support themselves and take that money that is now being poured into Part A [hospital costs] and give it to the poor. We've got a terrible disconnect.

Interview/
The Washington Post, 10-8:(Health)11.

Nat Walker
Director of public relations
for sports marketing,
RJR Nabisco Corporation

3

[On HHS Secretary Louis Sullivan's criticism of tobacco companies' sponsorship of sporting events, which, Sullivan says, gives an image of health to an unhealthy product]: We think we have a right to sell and market our [tobacco] products, including the use of sports sponsorships. It's an insult to the American people to say they are unable to make their own personal choices and that government somehow must make those decisions for them.

April 10/
The Washington Post, 4-11:(A)1.

Henry A. Waxman
United States Representative,
D-California

4

[Arguing against a Federal ban that prohibits research involving transplants of fetal tissue]: By banning such research, the [Bush] Administration has implicitly told those Americans afflicted with such disabilities and diseases that the cure for their disease is too controversial to study, too political to pursue. The Administration is suppressing the truth from people whose very lives depend on it.

Before House Subcommittee
on Health and the Environment,
Washington, April 15/
The Washington Post, 4-16:(A)5.

5

[On the AMA's new willingness to consider major changes in health financing]: It is remarkable to me that the organization that is most famous for opposing Medicare is now leading the call for reform, and they're calling on the Federal government as the only agency that can bring that about. The old AMA—they were against everything that might have the government involved in health care. Now they see the private system has not worked.

The Washington Post, 10-8:(Health)10.

Gail R. Wilensky
Administrator, Health Care
Financing Administration,
Department of Health
and Human Services
of the United States

1

[Saying drug companies should limit their price increases for prescription drugs if they don't want government cost controls]: Pharmaceuticals is a successful, internationally competitive industry and we want to make sure it stays that way. There are some individuals who would just as soon see the industry as a regulated public utility. I would hate to see the companies doing anything that would give those groups any encouragement.

The New York Times, 5-11:27.

Harris Wofford
United States Senator,
D-Pennsylvania

2

The Constitution says that if you are charged with a crime, you have a right to a lawyer. But it's even more fundamental that if you're sick, you should have the right to a doctor.

Time, 11-11:51.

Sidney Wolfe
Director, Public Citizen
Health Research Group

3

[On the AMA's new media campaign to improve the image of the medical profession]: The response [by the AMA] should be to do something about the reality that is causing people to have this [negative] view rather than treating the public like an idiot and trying to solve the fundamental problem with an image campaign . . . There's a real problem in the house of medicine, and AMA wants to solve it by just taking out ads saying "everything's okay, let's go back to the good old days when ignorance is bliss."

Los Angeles Times, 8-14:(A)5.

4

[On proposals to speed the approval process for new drugs]: We [in the U.S.] have the highest safety and effectiveness standards in the world, and this proposal can hardly avoid lowering that to allow privatization of the review process and moving toward other countries' standards. It could be a major step backwards. Lowering standards will ultimately make American products less credible and thus less competitive.

The New York Times, 11-9:7.

The Performing Arts

BROADCASTING

Pat Aufderheide
Professor of communications,
American University,
Washington

1

[On MTV, the successful rock-music cable-TV channel]: They're not just selling the record. They're selling a life-style. MTV has transformed commercials into programs, and well expressed the fact that popular culture's defining feature is commercial. What bothers me about MTV is it represents consumption as identity. The way that you define yourself is as a consumer. The way that you become real to yourself is by purchasing the right song, assuming the right attitude.

The Christian Science Monitor,
8-6:10.

Robert Batscha
President, Museum of
Television and Radio,
New York

2

Five hundred years ago, Columbus discovered the New World. Wouldn't it have been wonderful if television had been there. Wouldn't it be wonderful if we had on tape Columbus saying to his sailors, "We've found India"? Well, 500 years from now, people will see man landing on the moon because television did go there.

The Washington Post, 9-11:(B)12.

Levar Burton
Host, "Reading Rainbow,"
PBS-TV

3

I'm very critical when it comes to children's [TV] programming because it's so important to the growth and development of children. I believe

that too many people want to attribute more harm and the potential for too much good to TV than it possesses. It is really our *use* of television that has any real meaning . . . Make sure you know what it is your kids are watching and be willing to search out the kind of television that is being produced by people who exercise a sense of responsibility where this medium is concerned.

Interview/USA Today, 3-20:(A)7.

Peggy Charren
President, Action for
Children's Television

4

When it's good, TV can be an adjunct for learning. TV could be kind of a children's video library. Instead, it's mostly manufacturers' catalogs and comic books.

USA Today, 3-20:(A)7.

Bill Cosby
Actor

5

[Saying the major TV networks will not dominate in the future]: Because syndication is the future. [The] Fox [network] is more in line with what the future is going to bring than CBS, NBC or ABC, and that's because Fox is almost a syndicator. Five years from now it won't make any difference whether it's the [NBC] peacock or the local syndication station. Syndication is about the local station, about the local commercials and the local news, and that's what people are going to respond to.

Interview, New York/
USA Today, 9-19:(D)2.

Brian Dennehy
Actor

6

[As an actor,] coming off a TV series is a tough deal, and you go in limbo-land for a while, if not

359

(BRIAN DENNEHY)

forever. Most actors go immediately to the "Island of Lost Actors" and stay there. Troy Donahue is the mayor.

Interview, Marina del Rey, Calif./
Los Angeles Times, 5-8:(F)1.

William Dietz
Associate professor
of pediatrics,
Tufts University
Medical School

1

Not only do we believe that food ads [aimed at children on TV] should be eliminated but also parents' control of the television set should be increased . . . Television viewing promotes inactivity and food consumption . . . What we have is a tightly woven net of commercialism that now surrounds children's television in which it often begins with toys like the Teenage Mutant Ninja Turtles [and ends with a cereal for the toy].

Chicago, July 23/
The Washington Post, 7-24:(A)13.

Keith Geiger
President, National
Education Association

2

If America's children are to become more literate, more numerate, more civic-minded, more prepared for formal schooling, and more prepared for lifelong learning, we need more children's TV programming—and better programming.

The Christian Science Monitor,
6-25:15.

Bob Keeshan
Television's
"Captain Kangaroo"

3

One of the worst things a parent can do is to use the television as a babysitter. Using it to fill a vacuum is not appropriate. It can have a wide range of effects and deprive a growing child of

important experiences. Parents are busy today, but it's not excusable.

Interview/USA Today, 3-20:(A)7.

Larry King
Television and Radio
talk-show host

4

[Comparing TV with radio]: The most powerful medium is television by far. Everything else is a distant, distant . . . More people saw [TV's] *Murphy Brown* tonight than will listen to radio this week. Our [radio's] impact is there, but it ain't *there* there! Nobody loves this business more than me, but [in radio] you are not being heard by 80 million people. Nobody has the impact any more. There ain't no Walter Winchell.

Radio broadcast/
The Washington Post, 8-27:(C)7.

Angela Lansbury
Actress

5

[On mature actresses]: We don't have to be a "bankable" proposition to make it on TV. In movies, we have to be big box-office, otherwise they can't raise the money. So, luckily, we've been afforded many, many more opportunities in television. It didn't used to be that way in the '40s. The world changed tremendously after World War II, and with it women kind of lost their mystique. [But on TV,] the home audience is made up of a huge volume of older people, and they appreciate and thoroughly enjoy seeing a woman of their years who's out there doing it. Living it, and being a vital, healthy, liberated, opinionated, fair, honest, just person. *That* is the truth behind the success of [her series] *Murder She Wrote.*

Los Angeles Times, 4-14:(Calendar)82.

Margaret Loesch
President, Fox
Children's Network

6

We [in TV] have inherited the responsibilities of being a baby sitter for millions of kids. We

(MARGARET LOESCH)

better come up with a good mix between entertainment and education, with a really diverse schedule. We can do a lot better than we do now.

The Christian Science Monitor,
6-25:15.

Penny Marshall
Actress, Director

1

I think television is an invaluable experience because you're under the gun every single week. You never have time. You're running for your life. After TV, as a performer, you can do anything. That's why I like working with television actors. They're fast. They walk and talk at the same time.

People, 4-15:98.

Newton N. Minow
Former Chairman, Federal
Communications Commission

2

Television is one of our most important enterprises in this country [the U.S.], and yet, as a nation, we have never paid very much attention to what we expect of television. As technology changes, the TV business will change. Technology must be accompanied by some thought about public policy. That's the trick in our free society.

Interview/
Los Angeles Times, 5-9:(F)10.

3

I think the most troubling change over the past 30 years is the rise in the quantity and quality of violence on television. In 1961, I worried that my children would not benefit much from television. But in 1991, I worry that my grandchildren will actually be harmed by it . . . If television is to change, the men and women in television will have to make it a leading institution in American life rather than merely a reactive mirror of the lowest common denominator. Today, [my] 1961 speech is remembered for two words [his calling

TV a "vast wasteland"], but not the two I intended to be remembered. The words we tried to advance were "public interest." To me, the public interest meant, and still means, that we should constantly ask: What can television do for our country?

At celebration of 30th anniversary
of station WETA,
National Press Club, Washington,
Oct. 2/
The Washington Post, 10-3:(C)9.

Bill Moyers
Broadcast journalist,
PBS-TV

4

I think PBS has to find a different mission from what it's had the last 10 or 15 years. I hope it goes for education in the broadest sense of that word and doesn't try to compete with high-brow entertainment. I don't think we can be the Disney Channel or A&E or HBO. I think our concerns should be the people who take seriously the life of this republic. That means public-affairs and educational programs—not instructional programs, although we have a role there, too, in the daytime—but educational programs in prime time that are well done.

Interview, New York/
Los Angeles Times, 10-1:(F)8.

Ralph Nader
Lawyer; Consumer advocate

5

The trivialization of the broadcast industry has reached grotesque proportions. [TV has become] 90 per cent entertainment, 10 per cent redundant news and zero per cent civic values.

Before House Telecommunications
Subcommittee, Washington, May 13/
Daily Variety, 5-14:9.

Ron Reagan
Television talk-show host

6

Television is relentlessly stupid because it's not an entertainment or information medium, but

361

(RON REAGAN)

a marketing outlet. As we all know, it's the commercials that count, not the shows. More money, more thought, more emphasis is placed upon the commercials. Even the volume on your set goes up when they [commercials] come on. Motive is everything. If what you are trying to do is sell largely useless products to the public, that's what you are going to do best, and the shows will fall by the wayside.

Interview, Los Angeles/
The Washington Post, 8-12:(B)8.

Fred Rogers
Host, "Mr. Rogers'
Neighborhood," PBS-TV

1

Used indiscriminately, television can impoverish [children's] lives. Television offers messages and dramas that are just the opposite of what's helpful: stereotypes and put-downs, fear and distrust, quick pace and fragmented images. Furthermore, too much television viewing robs children of the vital time they need to play and to be alone in quiet, for time to think and make sense of the world around them. But, used carefully, television can enrich them beyond measure.

Interview/
USA Today, 3-20:(A)7.

Allen Sabinson
Executive vice president,
motion pictures for television
and miniseries, ABC-TV

2

With the exception of the Barbra Streisands and the Meryl Streeps and the Chers, [actresses] are finding the only roles available for them [in movies are] as the third and fourth leads, sometimes in good films, more often than not in just sort of mass entertainment material. And what TV can represent [for the mature actress] is serious drama with terrific roles, and frequently with some degree of social conscience.

Los Angeles Times, 4-14:
(Calendar)82.

Brandon Stoddard
President, ABC Productions

3

My own feeling is that "reality programming" doesn't necessarily have to mean exploitation of human misery or bad taste. I just don't believe that. There are many areas of the human condition that haven't been touched yet—programming about families, for instance. My instinct says that is true. There are basic audiences that like those kinds of shows. They are not necessarily as huge as those that watch *Roseanne.* But the networks' share of the audience has lowered, and some executives will be happy with a 16 per cent share in certain time periods nowadays.

Interview,
Los Angeles/
Los Angeles Times, 5-12:(Calendar)81.

4

I think there's going to be a shift in the next couple of years away from hard-core, in-your-face, cancer-ridden drama on television. I think that people would like to come home and watch a television show that lifts their spirits but also underlines their capacity to control their lives and destinies—programs that show the possibilities of human beings.

Los Angeles Times, 6-16:
(Calendar)4.

Brian Stonehill
Professor of English,
Pomona (Calif.) College

5

There's absolutely no social or informational benefit built into TV. You can't expect a commercial medium to necessarily inform us well, or to ennoble us, or enrich our lives visually or culturally. What happens on TV between commercials is just to get people to watch the commercials.

Interview,
Boston/
The Christian Science Monitor,
12-19:13.

Brandon Tartikoff
Chairman,
NBC Entertainment Group;
Chairman-designate,
Paramount Pictures Corporation

1

I'm worried about network television . . . The end of network television will come if all it is is an endless sea of sitcoms and reality shows . . . [Network TV must] do something that's totally different, that's not on cable, not on your competitors. You get a nucleus of viewers that you can build. Really take chances. Take a 40-1 shot.

Interview, May3/Los Angeles Times, 5-6:(F)1,8.

Scott Thomson
Former executive director,
National Association of
Secondary School Principals

2

If we don't find a way to control TV and make it educational, we're going to have a generation of kids who are literate only in entertainment and who won't have any of the creative working skills they'll need to compete in the world market.

USA Today, 3-20:(A)7.

Grant Tinker
Producer

3

I think this thing, network television, in which I've spent most of my adult life, could have been, should have been, a lot better. I think too much of it has been witless and forgettable, really a precious resource wasted. I don't want to sound too pompous, but I think it's worth saying.

Interview/Emmy, May-June:75.

Lynn Walters
Associate professor
of communications,
Texas A&M University

4

[On the trend toward more half-hour situation comedies on TV]: Hour-long programs are expensive, requiring multiple changes of scenery, car chases, etc. Most half-hour sitcoms, on the other hand, are in one or two locations. Your primary expense is with the stars . . . Americans just want to be entertained. They're looking for humor. It's hard to sustain the drama in most hour-long programs . . .

The Christian Science Monitor,
7-2:11.

Donald E. Wildmon
Media critic

5

[On his movement against what he sees as objectionable programming on TV]: When I started this in 1977, I thought I was dealing with sex and violence on TV. I've discovered we are dealing with a war between the Christian view of man and a secular, or humanistic or materialistic, view of man . . . You may think that [evangelist] Billy Graham is the leading evangelist in America, but he's not. The leading evangelists in America are those people who make the TV programs.

Interview/
Christianity Today,
8-19:16.

MOTION PICTURES

Robert Aldrich
Director

1

The Academy Awards are strictly a money thing. It's about "the industry" and its image. Awards should not be given by the group getting them. They say, "Oh, we're getting this from our *peers!*" That's bull. You get hate from your peers; jealousy, competition . . . and *sometimes* a friendship kind of thing, because you're working together.

Interview, Santa Monica, Calif./
Los Angeles Times, 9-29:(Calendar)32.

Julie Andrews
Actress

2

I just think that the [movie] industry to a great degree is about beauty and youth. Generally, people would prefer to see youth. Youth would prefer to see youth, and that seems to be where the money is.

Interview/
Los Angeles Times, 4-14:(Calendar)7.

James Bacon
Entertainment columnist

3

It was much easier to [write on the movie business] back in the '50s, the end of the Golden Era. Stars loved the press and the press loved stars. You'd go out to the studio and sit down with Gable and Tracy and people like that; you'd have a column in a minute. You didn't have to deal that much with press agents. It was a lot more fun in those days because every studio was a big family. You'd go over to Warner Bros., and they had Bogie and Errol Flynn and Jimmy Cagney, Ronald Reagan and the second team. Nowadays, a lot of the stars are pretty much inaccessible.

Back in those days they were very accessible. The studios wanted their stars to be publicized. If I wanted to talk to Ava Gardner, I just called up and talked to Ava Gardner; that was it. Of course, in those days, they didn't have television, didn't have [TV's] *Entertainment Tonight* or anything else. The print medium was the big thing.

Interview/
Los Angeles Times, 3-24:(Calendar)8.

Warren Beatty
Actor, Director

4

As a director, you want to be in control, but if you're any good, you want to be a little bit out of control of being in control. Whereas if you're an actor, you're trying as hard as you can to be out of control all the while that you also have to be in control of being out of control.

Interview/
Vanity Fair, November:226.

Elmer Bernstein
Soundtrack composer

5

Music generally gives a film emotional exhilaration, but not in a way that you have to necessarily be aware of. All you have to do is see any film without any music and you know what music does.

Interview, Santa Monica, Calif./
Los Angeles Times, 2-10:(Calendar)84.

Dirk Bogarde
Actor

6

[On acting]: When I say the camera photographs thought, it does, but it's a total concentra-

(DIRK BOGARDE)

tion on identifying with your character. If you don't do that, if the thought is not there, the camera will just photograph an empty cranium. It's no good saying you can do the laundry list at the same time. You can't. You should be drained for a little while afterward, so the body can recharge—because you're someone else.

Interview, Paris/
"Interview" magazine, January: 78.

Mark Canton
Chairman, Columbia Pictures

1

The dilemma of the [film] business today is that movies are so expensive that you don't have many chances. In baseball, you lead the league if you bat .300. In football, winning 12 out of 16 is a great year. No one wins all the time. In the old Hollywood, they judged Alfred Hitchcock on the breadth of his career. He certainly had a clinker or two. Today, like in the rest of society, everything in the movie business is very "immediate." And that's not good.

Interview,
Culver City, Calif./
Los Angeles Times, 11-10:(Calendar)27.

Glenn Close
Actress

2

Theatre really helps feed your soul [as an actress] in a way that movies might not, because in a movie you're under a microscope, and you don't have the audience to give you back what you give to them. To put it very simply, theatre is in control and movies are out of control. I used to think there was one way to do something. I don't think that way any more, especially in movies, because you don't know what nuances a scene might have when it's cut together. You have to trust your director, because you're totally in his hands, and trust that at the moment you'll have inspiration. That's what is frightening and thrilling about film acting.

Interview, Los Angeles/
Connoisseur, August: 42.

Joan Collins
Actress

3

I realize that any actress over 40 has a hard time finding roles. As you get older, it doesn't matter how you look—people think of you as your age. And you know the way the business is—it's still sexist to the extent that you can have [actors] Michael Caine, Jack Nicholson or Robert Redford, all of whom are in their 50s, playing romantic leading men. But I don't see too many women in their 50s—not even Jane Fonda any more.

Interview, San Francisco/
Los Angeles Times, 12-15:(Calendar)83.

Kevin Costner
Actor

4

My goal [as an actor] was not driving down Sunset [Boulevard] in a big old limo. I'm not immune to the perks in this business, but my goal was to brush shoulders with the best minds in the business . . . I've always been able to live with disappointment, but I like to get it from the source. What you should never get caught doing is not trying to make a good movie.

Interview/
Los Angeles Times, 3-19:(F)5.

5

I believe in the magic of the movies, in the opportunity that something great will happen. I remember when I was four years old, in those PJs that have the feet in them, going with my mother to drop my brother off at the movies, and looking out the back window of the car at the big marquees with the red letters in the rain, and my mother telling me they spelled Ben Hur. And I never forgot that. But I never realistically thought I'd be in the movies. I thought those people were somehow mysteriously born on the screen.

Interview/
Ladies' Home Journal, April: 227.

Tony Curtis
Actor

6

There is no such thing as learning the craft of acting. Everybody thinks that's so. Bullshit.

(TONY CURTIS)

Acting is of the moment. Acting is living. It's not more complicated than that. That's why I don't believe in any *method* to acting . . . Cary Grant once told me that the way you judge a bottle of white wine is that, when it's chilled, it tastes like a glass of cool water. It is so artful it comes out artless. Nice, isn't it? Well, I feel acting is that.

Interview/
"Interview" magazine, June:86.

Jonathan Demme
Director

1

You've got to have a gifted writer in order to get a good script, because no director, no matter how many ideas he has in his head, is going to help make a good script out of the work of a bad writer. It's important to sit down, and you tell the writer what you like and what you don't like. And you tell him if you feel there's something missing, and you discuss it a little bit, and then you let him go write it. And then you come back and read it again.

Interview/
Film Comment, Jan.-Feb.:37.

Lem Dobbs
Screenwriter

2

Being a [screen-] writer is a great life, lousy career. It is incredibly lucrative . . . The trouble is, there's a quality of giving up in Hollywood. It's very mysterious. Maybe people just lose their talent. But in so many cases you can't sit through films that were made by people who once made great films . . . I get the Writers Guild newsletter, and it's pitiful. They have these glowing memorial tributes to these guys who made terrific films, guys who wound up writing episodes of [TV's] *Gilligan's Island.* It's a pathetic existence. At some point, people just stay here [in Hollywood] too long. It's like being at the roulette table. One more roll of the dice, and you say you'll walk away . . . One of the ridiculous myths of Hollywood is that it's a collaborative medium. It's not. And it shouldn't be. Movies are made by directors. Paying too much attention to screenwriters is silly because, after all, they really don't count very much in Hollywood.

Interview, Los Angeles/
The New York Times, 12-30:(B)1,3.

Kirk Douglas
Actor

3

When I play a weak character, I always try to look for the elements where he's strong. If I play a strong character, I try to look for the elements within him that are weak. It's *chiaroscuro;* light and shade.

Interview/
American Film, March:35.

Clint Eastwood
Actor, Director

4

I think the directing personality is just being able to lead the platoon up the hill, and the acting personality is "Okay . . . What are we going to shoot at on the way to protect ourselves?" It's a life of escapism. Maybe that's why so many actors get screwed up along the way. They tend to rely on the escapist part rather than the reality part . . . I think I've always been a realist. Your brain can go fast. After a while you forget that you once bagged groceries or worked in a gas station or dug ditches.

Interview, Burbank, Calif./
"W" magazine, 4-29:31.

Jodie Foster
Acress, Director

5

[On directing]: Film-making is 85 per cent the social dynamics of sitting on a set. If you don't know what a *set* is, then you're *really* in trouble. It's the proving ground. It doesn't matter how you can sell your idea at the Polo Lounge—you get here at 5 o'clock in the morning and you have to come up with something. It's the sort of instinct that says, "That doesn't feel right to me. This does, that doesn't, so this is the way we're doing it."

Interview, Newport, Ky./
Film Comment, Jan.-Feb.:38.

(JODIE FOSTER)

1

Acting is all about being in the hands of someone else. You embrace it, because you have to embrace a director's vision. But you're always fighting the fact that he could do something horrible; it's just not in your control. And that is a tremendous strain. It is tiring to have your whole job be about pleasing someone else—pleasing the lighting guy, pleasing the audience. And then also maintaining the character of the character. It's just exhausting. Much more exhausting than directing.

Interview/
"Interview" magazine, October:84.

David Geffen
Producer

2

[On the current economic problems of the film industry]: It's a continual slide. The audiences have become trained to accept less and less because of television. The material available is not very good and the quality of the writing has declined. And everything is over-priced—the actors, the directors, the writers, the movies. There's the stupidity of the studios who don't say, "Enough is enough." They're afraid. That's the prevailing emotion now—fear.

Interview/
The New York Times, 10-15:(B)1.

Larry Gelbart
Screenwriter

3

A [screenwriter] can never get rich enough or old enough or famous enough to be safe. You're paid for the pain now. With iron-pumpers getting eight-figure salaries, some of the insanity spills over on us, and it's better to get a million-dollar insult than a $300,000 insult. You can buy more expensive salve for your wounds.

Esquire, July:80.

Judd Hirsch
Actor

4

All I ever wanted to do was be believable as an actor. That's how you touch people—by being real. It's almost mathematical: Reality equals Believability equals Emotion.

Interview, Los Angeles/
Redbook, July:25.

Nicholas Kazan
Screenwriter

5

Everyone else in the film business is an alchemist. They change one thing into another. We [screenwriters] are like gods, creating out of a void.

Esquire, July:80.

George Lucas
Director

6

. . . unless we [in the creative end of U.S. film-making] are able to obtain protection of moral rights under the Berne Convention, the agony of [American] film-makers who have suffered as their work has been chopped, tinted, and compressed [by a film's copyright owner] is nothing to what is going to be happening in the future . . . I see a future of indifferent copyright-owning corporations with unlimited power to tamper continually with filmed dramatic works as if they were revising an acceptance speech—not by Orwell's Big Brother, but by a legion of Little Brothers, all with no regard for the original contributors, and changing what they like to refer to as "product" . . . Unless the United States achieves uniformity with the rest of the world in the protection of her motion-picture creations, we may live to see them [electronically] re-cast with stars we never directed, utter dialogue we never wrote—all in support of goals and masters we never imagined we would serve.

At dedication of Artists Rights
Foundation, Los Angeles, Dec. 4/
Daily Variety, 12-6:6.

Karl Malden
Actor; President,
Academy of Motion Picture
Arts and Sciences

7

[On Japanese corporations buying U.S. film companies]: . . . I was here when Jack Warner

(KARL MALDEN)

was head of a studio, Louis B. Mayer, Zanuck, Cohn . . . and I never felt I'd see the day when I say I wished they were back. The studios today are even different than they were then. And if the Japanese buy what they're buying, so it'll change [some more]. How they'll change, who knows? Another 10 years somebody will buy from Sony. It's just changing, and I don't worry about those things. And I honestly don't think the Academy should worry about those things. [Film] is an art-form. We just hope, I just hope that they hold on to a kind of integrity about film-making—keep it at a level where people will be proud to be a part of this industry.

Interview, Beverly Hills, Calif./
Los Angeles Times, 1-20:(Calendar)33.

Joseph L. Mankiewicz
Director, Screenwriter

1

Directing, whether it be a play or a film, is the second half of a writer's work. And I'm talking now about my type of film. I'm not talking about a primer on how to kill people, a primer on how to terrorize schools, a primer on intergalactic war-fare. The films I'm talking about are films about the conflicts and arrangements and relation-ships and situations between human beings, and their effect upon each other in varying aspects of life; falling in love, out of love, the non-visible aspects of existence. I don't think that's a major film concern today . . . Today's films don't seem to exist without the destruction of property, the destruction of human beings, the actual stripping of any kind of mystery or individuality, really, from sex, by putting as much as possible on the screen. Sex . . . hell, we used to fight for the right to have lips touch.

Interview, Bedford, N.Y./
Los Angeles Times, 5-6:(F)7.

2

I feel deep sorrow at the condition of film today. It's on its way out. There are no values. Some of the films pretend to be moral. Bull. Maybe the good guys win in the end . . . get to go

home to the wives in the last reel . . . have destroyed the villain . . . but there have been 10 reels in which the bad guys have had a ball. They've killed people, they've humped people, they get all the money . . . they get all of every-thing. That's what the young person watching the film is going to remember . . . not the final fade . . . the "morally" happy ending. They're going to remember what the bad guys did for the majority of the film. I wish someone would take the time and spend the money to do a survey on how some of the scenes they film today affect kids . . . Whatever [happened] to love stories? I can't remember the last time I saw a love story. Even that *Pretty Woman*. I like that film, but it was about a guy falling in love with a prostitute! It may have been picking up crumbs, but there was a human relationship there. How few films even bother about human relationships. I wouldn't know how to make a film today. I really wouldn't.

Interview, Bedford, N.Y./
Films in Review, August:244.

Steve Martin
Actor

3

[In film-making,] your only guidepost is your own instinct—and judicious editing. In my [stand-up comic] act, I learned that, in the first 10 minutes, I could say anything and it would get a laugh. Then I'd better deliver. In [a] movie, it's the same thing. You get a lot of laughs when people first sit down and then the story better kick in. My 20 years in front of an audience, I would hope, gives me a sense of what works.

Interview, Los Angeles/
Los Angeles Times, 2-3:(Calendar)25.

Robert R. McCammon
Author

4

In books and movies, horror has moved away from classic psychological suspense, losing the Hitchcockian touch. Horror stories have grace and character for dumbness influenced by the garbage that Hollywood throws out as entertain-ment. It's also a matter of losing, or discarding, aesthetic distance. Now writers and movie-

(ROBERT R. McCAMMON)

makers shove the horror in your face. I don't like that. I think you can do a lot more with a lot less.

Interview, New York/
Publishers Weekly, 8-2:54.

Michael Medved
Film critic; Co-host,
"Sneak Previews," PBS-TV

1

In years past, in the heyday of Gary Cooper, Jimmy Stewart and Katherine Hepburn, Hollywood was accused of creating characters who were larger than life, more deeply lovable and admirable than people in the real world. Today, the movie business regularly offers us characters who are smaller than life, who are less decent, less intelligent, less noble than our own friends and neighbors. Four years ago, George Roche wrote an eloquent and important book that highlighted the threat within our culture to those values of civility and faith that many of us hold most dear. The name of that book was "A World Without Heroes." And that is precisely the sort of world that Hollywood portrays again and again on screen.

At Hillsdale (Mich.) College/
The Wall Street Journal,
3-15:(A)10.

Arthur Miller
Playwright

2

. . . we have the movies. Which is the signal art—no way around it. Having written one, I think that its potential is enormous, but I have a prejudice against them which is that it deals with our most infantile side. A baby of a month old can lie in a bed looking up and follow images. And I think that that's the way we approach movies. It makes you more and more passive, and more and more helpless, and I think that the brain closes down to that degree. I don't get affected by movies as much as I do even by moderately good theatre works.

Interview, Connecticut/
Vanity Fair, November:244.

Ennio Morricone
Soundtrack composer

3

Music in a film must not add emphasis but must give more body and depth to the story, to the characters, to the language that the director has chosen. It must, therefore, say all that the dialogue, images, effects, etc., cannot say.

Interview/
American Film, February:41.

Mike Nichols
Director

4

The director creates the events. That is to say, the director has to create the things that happen, that aren't talk, that aren't words. And he has to choose the mood and the rhythm, the speed with which things happen, the speed with which actors talk—movies are all mood, really. A movie scene is a mood. You have to pick the style. I figured out very early in my life what I think style is. I thought of it watching a play when I was in college. It seemed to me then, as it does now, that style is beginning something in the manner which will make it necessary for the things that happen later to happen. So there are certain subliminal jobs you have to do in a play or in a movie. You have to say to the audience, first of all, "Don't worry, you're in good hands, we all know what we're doing." Second of all, "This is what we're doing, and it starts like this." And just like a child—really, we are all children when we're in an audience—the audience first says, "Why are you telling me this?" You have to have a very good answer for that.

Interview/
Film Comment, May-June:28.

Joyce Carol Oates
Author

5

A number of us [writers] have written prose fiction for many years and won awards which are perceived as external signs of success. But to think that we can sit down and write a play or a movie is a complete mistake. The tools are more limited. [In films,] all exposition, except flash-

(JOYCE CAROL OATES)

backs and voiceovers, must be done in the present. Everything must be obvious, or the audience won't "get it" . . . They need to be cued. It's like the difference between jogging and swimming. You have to use a whole different set of muscles, beginning again—virtually at zero! What a great lesson in humility.

Interview, Santa Monica, Calif./
Los Angeles Times, 5-9:(F)10.

Leon E. Panetta
United States Representative,
D-California

1

[Supporting legislation that would place a maximum of 50 per cent on foreign ownership of American cultural institutions, such as the movie industry]: It is increasingly apparent that our cultural industries, particularly the entertainment and motion-picture industries, are in danger of being dominated by foreign powers. It seems to me that this is not healthy for America, nor would it be accepted by any other nation . . . We ought not to allow our motion-picture industry and related firms to be run from abroad. The United States . . . stands to lose both its artistic license and its integrity as a truly American institution through the intangible but sure process of foreign owners' discreet direction, implicit censorship or pervasive corporate philosophy . . . Most foreign owners of the entertainment industry are responsible global citizens. But I would like to leave in place a suitable fail-safe mechanism to ensure that America continues to receive the full range of independent artistic expression on a mass scale.

Before the House, Washington/
Daily Variety, 10-11:1,4.

Mandy Patinkin
Actor

2

The minute, the second, the millisecond [a performance is] over, it's over. It has little or no value to me. I have friends who can live off what they did 10 years ago, but I'm not like that. I'm only interested in what I can do. For me, it's always the next concert or the next performance or shooting the next scene. That's where the fun is. My favorite thing would be just to rehearse for the rest of my life, with nothing planned whatsoever.

Interview,
New York/
The Washington Post, 9-5:(C)3.

Sean Penn
Actor

3

At some point, every actor's got to face his own limitations, and the only thing limitations are to me are differences, because everybody's got that power—it's the power of being an individual. You've got something to offer that no one else on earth has. And it's getting in touch with that, and working to be concentrated and relaxed enough, whether on a stage or on camera or in someone else's words or someone else's clothes, so that you continue to be an individual.

Interview/
Film Comment, Sept.-Oct.:66.

Julia Phillips
Producer

4

[On film executives]: . . . they don't like visionaries. They distrust visionaries. And there don't seem to be a lot of people like me, whose job it is to be between the money and the vision— people who understand both . . . [There is] the money factor and the meanness of the way business is concluded. The ruthlessness. "I'm bored this afternoon. Who can I run around the room?" All these instant billionaires in the '80s—what did they create and put back in the system that they made their money from? A lot of paper. Or meaningless celluloid. Or cars that blow up. Do you think in the dead of night these guys are really proud of the product?

Interview/
"Interview" magazine,
February:32.

Tom Pollock
Chairman,
motion-picture group,
MCA, Inc. (Universal Pictures)

1

There's a finite pool of talent [in the film industry]. More movies are being made than there are talented people to make them. That results in a dilution of quality.

Interview, Universal City, Calif./
The New York Times, 10-15:(B)1.

Julia Roberts
Actress

2

I wouldn't be in this business if I wasn't [ambitious]. But "ambition" has a bad connotation. People don't understand all the hues. It's not just money, greed, fame. My ambitions are to seek out challenges, to discover new things about myself—maybe some things I haven't wanted to deal with. I also want to be part of a group I respect, from whom I can get an influx of ideas and creativity.

Interview/
Los Angeles Times, 6-9:(Calendar)9.

Joe Roth
President, 20th Century Fox
Film Corporation

3

[On the current economic problems of the film industry]: So many movies, so many *bad* movies. Ticket prices are up. Attendance is down. The economy is bad. Disposable income is leveling off. The numbers just don't add up.

Interview, Los Angeles/
The New York Times, 10-15:(B)1.

Susan Sarandon
Actress

4

It is not only sexism that threatens to strangle and pervert this [film] business; it is greed. The greed that dictates that movies must turn astronomical profits in order to be considered successful. The greed that links violence and sex to turn a profit. The greed that turns a well-intentioned script into pabulum . . . We are communicators of stories, ideas and images. And our bottom line, our strongest tool, is language. We should be vigilant in our knowledge of words and fierce in our protection of their purity. We must not allow our words and our images to be distorted in order to pacify us. *Kinder* and *gentler*. What a shame to lose those words.

Before New York Women in Film/
Lear's, May:61,94.

John Schlesinger
Director

5

You make a film, but your concern for it doesn't end with the first print. I'm interested in how they sell the film afterwards. You have to be. Your future can depend on the success or failure of each project. You've got to nurse a project diligently from the very first moment. Passion and personal involvement are essential. Sometimes the passion grows. You may go into something and feel, I'm not sure, maybe we'll give the script a whirl, and then, once you see it starting to work, you've got to tenaciously hold onto it and fight for its life right through. When it's done, make trouble if necessary, phone up the front office, complain to the head of publicity or distribution . . . It's a constant, constant fight. Your head is on the line, and it's your film.

Interview/
American Film, January:21.

Maurice Sendak
Author of children's books

6

[Criticizing some of today's movies because of their effect on young audiences]: *Home Alone* is a nightmare to me because it's violent. And yet I've been yelled at, "Oh, relax, Maurice. You take everything so seriously. It's just a funny movie and it's not meant to be serious." But it really bothers me a lot because it's full of the most incredible violence and because it's not *true* that a child could protect himself in the face of this dementedness, or that his parents—it's not *funny* that they forgot him. I don't get it . . . [And in the

371

(MAURICE SENDAK)

Rambo movies where Rambo was] blowing up villages and annihilating hundreds of people, and you see them on fire. Kids [in the audience] were laughing. I'm lost on this planet! I no longer know how to respond to these things.

Interview/
The Christian Science Monitor,
12-23:13.

James Stewart
Actor

1

In the days of the big studios, as a contract player you went to work every day. You got there at 8 o'clock and you left at 6:30. Whether you were working on a picture or not, you had something to do . . . You had big parts in little pictures and little parts in big pictures. You were working all the time. You were learning your craft by working at it. Someone would come to you and say, "Here's a script. You will play the role of George. Go down to wardrobe and get fitted for what you're going to wear. Shooting starts Tuesday . . . " [Today,] so many of the actors sit at home and either their agents tell them, "I'll let you know when something comes," or they keep getting scripts and reading them and saying, "No, this isn't right for me."

Interview/
Los Angeles Times, 11-21:(F)4.

Tom Stoppard
Playwright

2

[On the idea that writing for film precludes the use of long speeches and verbiage when compared with writing for the stage]: I don't think there ought to be any rules like that. In fact, I think it's absolute bilge. I don't believe there is something called "film" and something called "theatre," and that words belong in the theatre. Some rather bad films have few words in them; some good films have a lot of words in them.

Interview/
"Interview" magazine, March:48.

Jessica Tandy
Actress

3

[On the success of *Driving Miss Daisy,* in which she starred]: Maybe it's just that everyone's happy not to see one more spitty kiss or a movie where people actually bite one another. Those films are dreadful. Quite unnecessary. They show parts of a man close up that a woman who's married 50 years has never even seen in the dark. Our picture was an on-again-off-again project because it was difficult for the producers to raise the money. The "wise" people were saying it would never make a nickel . . . too soft . . . has no action . . . and whatever the hell else they were saying in those high places. Therefore, I thought it's such a small picture that not only wouldn't I be nominated [for an Academy Award, which she was], but I wouldn't even be noticed.

Interview, New York/
Ladies' Home Journal, April:63.

Kathleen Turner
Actress

4

I think as you get older you do more theatre [as opposed to film]. Honest to god, the more interesting roles for women are in plays and you look forward to the time you are not the love interest, which means you have a man protagonist and you are the second banana. The roles for women like that are much stronger in theatre and I think that should translate into film. I mean, there is such a strong body of women actresses working today, and we make them [film studios] so much money, that they [should] have to write for us.

Interview, East Hampton, N.Y./
Los Angeles Times, 7-21:(Calendar)30.

Jack Valenti
President, Motion Picture Association
of America

5

[On the MPAA's rating system]: I've said over and over again that the whole rating system is based on parental responsibility. If parents abandon that responsibility, the rating system has no

(JACK VALENTI)

meaning . . . I think there has to be an educational approach to the public re-emphasizing what the purpose of the rating system is . . . It is information for parents, and the parent is the one that has to be in control of their children, whatever their age. They can't just assume an exhibitor [theatre owner] is going to have to do the parent's work for them. We try—and probably are the only industry in the world—that will turn away business. We don't want those kids to get in [to restricted films], but accidents happen. Errors occur. The bottom line is the parents' responsibility for what their kids do or do not do.

Interview/
Daily Variety, 2-5:23.

Gore Vidal
Author, Screenwriter

1

[On today's screenwriters]: They are cleverer or luckier than my generation. Many of them make their own movies. They marry money or have a rich aunt who comes up with the money to make their first movie. I was president of the jury at the Venice Film Festival [last year] and we had to watch 32 movies. That rich aunt is living in Bulgaria, Yugoslavia, Turkey and India, [because] nobody else in their right mind would have financed the movies I saw. During one screening, a judge was crying. When it was over, I said, "Why were you crying? That was a piece of junk." And he said, "I was crying because I want to know where they get their money. I've got five movies and can't get the money to put on one."

Interview/
Emmy, May-June:84.

Irwin Winkler
Producer, Director

2

As a producer, the most important call you can get is on Saturday morning, when the Friday-night [theatre] grosses come in. As a director, you want your film to be successful; but your outlook is a bit different. You become very conscious of the reviews . . . The stakes are higher: If the film succeeds, you take the bow. If it fails, there is no one else to blame.

Interview, Los Angeles/
Los Angeles Times, 3-10:(Calendar)23.

Yevgeny Yevtushenko
Soviet poet

3

[On his directing films]: My "passion" for movies comes from the fact that I have always sought contact with as large an audience as possible—both domestically and internationally. More people will see a film than will read a poem.

World Press Review, April:45.

Richard Zanuck
Producer

4

[On whether winning an Oscar automatically increases the clout of a producer]: Obviously, your standing is elevated in the eyes of those people in positions of power, those who can either say yea or nay to your project. But, in the final analysis, I've found that for a producer it pretty much boils down to what you have in your trunk. You're going to be judged on your material.

Interview, Houston/
The New York Times, 3-26:(B)1.

MUSIC

Jay Berman
President, Recording Industry Association
of America

1

[Arguing against censorship of objectionable lyrics in popular music]: Last year we beat back the forces of censorship everywhere they raised their ugly head. But anyone who thinks the pop-music obscenity battle is over ought to think again . . . Under the test that the Supreme Court laid down in 1973, for something to be called obscene it has to meet certain criteria. It has to be without artistic merit. Now, whether you enjoy a certain kind of song or not, music is a creative art-form. And our basic position from the beginning has been that it would be virtually impossible to find any legitimate music per se . . . obscene.

Los Angeles Times, 4-21:
(Calendar)68.

Ray Charles
Jazz musician

2

I haven't heard anybody in the modern [music] field that I would say has blown my head off. Partly, that might be my own fault, because I don't get around to hear maybe as much stuff as I could, and you ain't gonna discover nobody that's going to blow your head off listening to the radio. The radio is dead. Most of what you hear on the radio is very, very simple. It seems like the record companies want everybody to sound the same. And that's another thing: When I was coming up, you could hear artists sing two notes and you knew who they were. You don't see that now. Maybe I saw an awful lot in my life, but what bothers me is that I don't see anything coming through to replace it.

Interview/
"Interview" magazine, November:92.

Jonathan Eaton
Opera director;
Associate professor of opera,
University of Cincinnati

3

Tradition [in opera] is a very odd word, and when I've crossed swords on it, usually with academics, I've found it very difficult to elicit what people mean by it. Does it mean that there are musical and theatrical ideas that help make sense of the music, and help project it to a contemporary audience—for instance, in Mozart or Rossini works, where period costumes and movement help articulate the social context of the pieces? If that's tradition, then it's very useful and it should be taught. But where tradition means acting badly and evolving awkward stage blocking, so that the primary focus of the opera is always vocal, then it's a bad idea and we should chuck it out the window. Wherever tradition means cheating, I have no respect for it. Where it means communicating the operas to an audience, I'm a great supporter.

Interview/
The New York Times, 8-13:(B)3.

Al Edwards
Texas State Representative (D)

4

[Criticizing obscenity in popular music]: These vulgar lyrics are a disgrace before humanity and God. The owners of these record companies need to be punished for preying on tender minds. They don't care what this stuff does to the youth of America. They're just out to make a buck. What these guys need is to be hung up by their toes . . . The obscenity codes in our country just do not go far enough. Music is as dangerous as drugs nowadays. To be quite frank with you, I wish we could make it illegal for anyone to perform or record this dirt at all. Sure, I

(AL EDWARDS)

realize that the entertainment industry is going to send their little lobbyists down here trying to stop me, but it's only going to make me work harder to get it [legislation against objectionable lyrics] passed.

Los Angeles Times, 4-21:(Calendar)8,68.

Henry Fogel
Executive director,
Chicago Symphony Orchestra

1

[Saying the Chicago Symphony has a commitment]: That commitment manifests itself in a lot of ways. In most orchestras, if you walk into a concert hall 60 minutes before a concert, you would find two or three players, at most, getting used to the hall and warming up. But you'd find 30 or 40 Chicago Symphony members sitting on that stage an hour before the concert when they are on tour. In their own hall, 30 minutes before the performance—when other orchestras would be just beginning to fill the stage—almost all our musicians are out there.

Interview, Chicago/
The Christian Science Monitor,
3-13:14.

David Gockley
General director,
Houston Grand Opera

2

I think there's a big, big challenge in keeping opera and opera institutions alive and vital [in Houston] in a time of so many other civic priorities. Those civic priorities are going to shift even more as the slender white majority becomes a white minority, and all of the political and social and philanthropic [agendas] are going to shift away from the direction of Euro-oriented work. Something that has appeal to 3 or 4 per cent of the population, I think, isn't deserving of any media coverage, isn't deserving of any real corporate or foundation or government support . . . I think that probably we need to follow on the heels of theatre companies in being able to offer a lot more new work, find new composers, librettists,

and stake them and develop audiences for them. It's not going to be the same old game.

Interview, Houston/
The Christian Science Monitor,
12-2:11.

Gwyneth Jones
Opera singer

3

The number of singers that have come up like shooting stars and then disappeared again during my career is horrific. The problem is to allow this talent to grow and develop so that they have a healthy career. There are many more opera houses today than there used to be and most of these houses want to play all the big pieces, which they didn't used to do. And so of course, there just are not enough singers to go around for them all. The result is that quite a lot of the small houses are persuading young people into doing these roles too soon, and this is very dangerous.

Interview, Costa Mesa, Calif./
Los Angeles Times, 6-5:(F)4.

James King
Opera singer;
Professor of voice,
Indiana University,
Bloomington

4

I don't think there is anything more difficult than learning to use your voice properly. You've got to discover what your timbre is on each of those 25 to 30 tones in your voice range, and at the same time be able sometimes to sing darker or lighter, depending on the expression you want to put into what you are singing. It took me nearly 20 years to get all my problems worked out to the point where I could step out with the big-timers.

Interview/
Opera News, 3-2:17.

Alfredo Kraus
Opera singer

5

. . . the present situation in the opera world is bad. Productions are so expensive, and adminis-

(ALFREDO KRAUS)

tration costs are bigger and bigger every year. They make new offices every year; they take new employees. The prices of things are really crazy. Practically all the money they can get goes for administration, and no money for the important things—music, opera and singers. Then the conductors don't have time for rehearsal. In many theatres, even great ones, you go directly to rehearsal with the orchestra, without seeing each other before to agree how to manage the whole musical situation. You arrive, you do one rehearsal, maybe not even one. You go directly to the stage, you do your performance, and you fly to another place. This is really terrible, because you don't have the possibility of communicating with each other. Every conductor is different, every singer is different. We have different voices. Everybody sings in a different way, and the conductor has to realize from the very beginning what kind of company he has in his hands. A conductor can't have just one way of accompanying a particular opera—he has to have many different ways. It depends on the cast, the characteristics of every voice. Also for that reason, a rehearsal period of at least one week between conductor and singers is really necessary. Of course, everything looks and seems okay, because we sometimes do operas superficially, but the audience doesn't realize.

Interview/
Opera News, November:12.

Witold Lutoslawski
Composer

1

I've always been very involved with large-scale closed forms, taking as a base my experience as a listener. I compose my big pieces basically in two movements. First, an introduction to engage and intrigue the listener, but never satisfy him. It creates a pressure, an expectation of something more substantial, which the main movement then delivers.

Interview/
Los Angeles Times,
1-7:(F)10.

Gian Carlo Menotti
Composer; Artistic director,
Spoleto Festival U.S.A.

2

I must say that I am very disappointed in many young composers. It is all very well and good to talk about the return of "emotion" to music. But music is more than just emotion. It is craft. It is style. It is a personal voice.

Interview, New York/
Los Angeles Times, 5-19:(Calendar)6.

Yehudi Menuhin
Violinist

3

My contribution is not only musicianship, it's a sense of style. Young musicians often play the notes clearly and cleanly, but classical music needs interpretation. That's where I feel I can be useful.

Interview, London, March/
The New York Times, 3-26:(B)1.

Ennio Morricone
Composer

4

I have never needed collaborators to write for me. On the contrary, this revolts me. The great classic musicians in the history of musical composition have never had such need. This habit of not writing one's own music is a negative practice of composers who are lazy, or incapable, or who take on too much work. In my opinion, it is an immoral system because it takes advantage of creative qualities of others for one's own exclusive purposes.

Interview/
American Film, February:41.

Riccardo Muti
Music director,
Philadelphia Orchestra

5

The conductor looks like he is on a pedestal, but he is not. Even if he is surrounded by the orchestra in front and the audience behind, he is lonely. He must find the source of inspiration in

(RICCARDO MUTI)

himself. His instrument is outside; he must bring it to his ideas. The public is the other entity, to whom he must convey his vision. Loneliness is the first sacrifice of the conductor.

Interview/
Connoisseur, January:104.

Oscar Peterson
Jazz pianist

1

My audience has nothing to do with anything I do when I'm on stage. And it never has. I don't think it's a matter of being insensitive to the audience, either. I'm sensitive only to my group when I go on. What happens on stage is my concern. What happens in the audience is theirs.

Interview, Toronto/
Down Beat, January:26.

Paul Plishka
Opera singer

2

[On opera critics]: The only thing I really get upset with is when a writer reviews your performance *the way he would like to see it*. Because I do believe there are so many ways to create characters. If every Leporello were identical, you could see one show and never have to see another. A reviewer should try to make sense of what the performer is trying to do with the character, and the way he's trying to plumb it, and review his effort in creating that impression. He can say, "Well, this is not my idea of the way this should be done, but . . . he achieves 'x' and 'y' and not 'z'."

Interview/Opera News, 3-30:16.

Andre Previn
Conductor

3

. . . I have a very antiquated feeling that the music director should be there for musical reasons. And whatever else he's expected to do should be done if he's so inclined, or if he has the time, or if it is absolutely necessary. But it is true

in a lot of American orchestras that they want a kind of social creature who also conducts. I always used to resent that, and it got me into fights everywhere.

Interview,
Bedford Hills, N.Y./
Connoisseur, October:118.

Shulamit Ran
Composer-in-residence,
Chicago Symphony Orchestra;
Winner, 1991 Pulitzer Prize
for music

4

I'm not interested in music that is one-dimensional, where what you hear the first time is what you get. I think music must reflect life, or, at least, life as the composer sees it . . . What I can say about my work, really, has very little to do with pinning it down in strict technical terms. I like to say that I want my music to challenge both the mind and the heart, and to do so in equal fashion.

Interview,
Chicago, April 10/
The New York Times, 4-11:(B)4.

Max Rudolf
Conductor;
Former music director,
Cincinnati Symphony Orchestra

5

I always try to be fair in my estimation of music critics. However, no journalist, regardless of his talent, has the training or technical experience of a conductor. And a journalist's schedule makes it impossible to do what a conductor does by virtue of his profession—namely, to study a score for weeks until you know from bar to bar what every musician is doing. It would be unfair to expect this from a critic. But the public does expect to be informed of what is happening in the world of music. And *this* is the critic's function . . . Certainly you have an opinion. But having an opinion doesn't necessarily mean you have founded it on deep knowledge.

Interview/
Opera News, 12-7:18.

Carlos Santana
Guitarist

1

I play music because I know it can elevate the spirit, because it has the power to build the bridge of love between people. It speaks more clearly than passports or nationalities or religions or caste systems. Music can break down borders and divisions. I believe Western music helped to break down the Berlin Wall. Musicians can be healers more so than politicians, senators, presidents or generals. That's why Louis Armstrong and Duke Ellington were called peace ambassadors.

Interview/Down Beat, August:29.

Nello Santi
Conductor

2

[On "interpretation" of the composer's work]: You have to study the music and have a true understanding of the style and intention of the composer. For example, you must put Verdi in the framework of his life. His career began nine years after Rossini stopped composing, and he worked almost to the beginning of the 20th century. Verdi was a different man throughout his career, molded by different experiences. Only by studying the historical context and the man, and knowing the musical style in which he composed, can you understand his source of inspiration, so that you can respect his wishes. The works themselves are complete. And it is useless to "interpret" them, since it's all there in the composition.

Interview/Opera News, 3-2:20.

Jascha Silberstein
Principal cellist,
Metropolitan Opera Orchestra,
New York

3

[On conductors who aren't around enough]: A music director has to be there, day in and day out. Otherwise, orchestra musicians tend to get to be like Dead End Kids, desperados. They get a guest conductor and walk all over him. And anyone who comes in as a guest conductor wants to be on his best behavior. When an orchestra plays with so many different conductors, it becomes ragged—there is no goal, no togetherness.

Interview/Opera News, 3-30:23.

Leonard Slatkin
Conductor

4

We cannot sit back and assume that what was acceptable [in opera] 50 years ago remains acceptable now. We've got to allow new technologies from outside the opera world to affect how things within the opera world are going to be done. For instance, what about involving holography in a production of *L'Enfante et les Sortileges,* so that those animated teapots and chairs really come out of the wall? Or why not use closed-circuit technology to project people in other rooms or other sets onto the stage? True, it's expensive, but done the right way, it could enhance the music drama *and* bring in the crowds.

Interview/Opera News, October: 10.

Isaac Stern
Violinist; President,
Carnegie Hall, New York

5

[On Carnegie Hall's 100th anniversary]: All the things you fight for and dream about, in the final analysis it's what actually happens on the stage that counts. I'm trying to keep from being too emotional, not to bubble over. But this is a consecrated house. It's not consecrated because *we* say so, but because of the musicians who play there. The name "Carnegie Hall" is synonymous with the United States for musicians and performers from around the world.

New York, May 5/
The New York Times, 5-6:(A)1.

Kiri Te Kanawa
Opera singer

6

I started with Mozart when I started my career, and it's been the saving grace of my career, singing Mozart almost exclusively. My

(KIRI TE KANAWA)

teacher says, "Mozart is a lubricant for your voice. If you can sing Mozart, you can sing anything." Mozart's charm is his brilliance. It's breathtaking to think you're singing a particular song which he composed when he was 12; it was just tumbling out of him.

Interview/
The Christian Science Monitor,
3-5:11.

Blanche Thebom
Former opera singer

1

It has become the accepted norm that the way to prepare for an opera career in America is to take a degree at a university or conservatory and then perhaps even a master's degree, so you have six years of higher education before you begin to become a professional. And the curriculum is not specialized. Voice majors do not specialize in *performance*. Instead, singers are required to take music courses and lots and lots of chorus. The worst thing you can do to a person who has solo capabilities and a big personality is to require them to participate in a chorus, where they are constantly held back, where they can never express themselves, where someone else takes control of their musicality. It's like hitching a Kentucky Derby winner to a plough.

Interview/
Opera News, November:19.

Michael Tilson Thomas
Principal conductor,
London Symphony Orchestra

2

In the United States there has been so much divisiveness in the world of music, the musicians on one side, the management on another side, the board of directors and the trustees on still some other, social side, the press very often taking potshots from some other side—well, nothing will ever be good enough or right enough or anything like that. It can't be that way. The music and the traditions that it represents are too special and too fragile to survive that.

Interview/
The New York Times, 8-9:(B)3.

Dawn Upshaw
Opera singer

3

I think we're going through the "director phase" in opera. A few years ago, we went through the "conductor is God" phase, and then, a long time ago, the singers were gods and goddesses. Now the incredible egos that used to belong to singers and conductors have been passed on to directors. I really look forward to the day when we can all work together a bit more. I won't point a finger at anyone, but some people in the opera business have decided that huge productions are the important thing right now.

Interview/Opera News, 2-2:14.

Carol Vaness
Opera singer

4

[On conductors and artistic directors who have believed in her]: Their confidence *inspires* confidence. That's the great passion of our profession! To work with people who make you want to go out there! With great colleagues you learn to do things you didn't know you could do— musically, artistically, vocally, dramatically. And what you send out, a great audience sends back. That gives you energy, heart. Then all the loneliness and the hard work and the scares are really worth it.

Interview/Connoisseur, April:141.

Joseph Volpe
General director,
Metropolitan Opera,
New York

5

I remember when it was first proposed to bring our productions to television. There was concern that we would lose audience for our own performances if people could stay home and watch. Instead, having opera on television has increased our audience and given us more members of our opera guild. The radio and TV performances of the Met are what makes the Met a national company.

Los Angeles Times,
9-23:(F)10.

379

THE STAGE

Alan Alda
Actor

1

[Comparing acting on the stage with acting in movies and TV]: I love the chance to start a play and not come out of it for two hours. The hardest thing about going into movies and TV was to leave that and learn to chop a performance up into little fragments, never getting the pleasure of tying them together. In movies, the director "acts" for you, but in theatre the actor has final cut every night.

Interview, London/
Los Angeles Times, 9-29:(Calendar)4.

Jay Presson Allen
Playwright

2

[On getting a "household name" to star in a Broadway play]: It can't guarantee success. It *can* guarantee big advance ticket sales and initial excitement. *The Merchant of Venice* was a limited run, and it sold out every seat, which it certainly would not have done without a big name like Dustin's [Hoffman] . . . If you want to put a play on Broadway without a star, you're in very deep trouble. You're going to have to start Off-Broadway someplace unless you've got backers with very deep pockets, who don't give a damn what they lose.

Interview/
Cosmopolitan, January:78.

Reid Anderson
Artistic director,
National Ballet of Canada

3

Dance is like a coloring book. When you give the dancers choreography, it's like giving them crayons. What they do with the crayons will determine the final picture. I've been in dance my whole life, and I always know when a dancer uses those crayons brilliantly. That's what makes a great artist.

Dance Magazine, March:60.

Alan Ayckbourn
British playwright

4

A lot of people in America thought I was another Neil Simon and tried to play my [productions] as such, and you can't play them like Neil Simon's; they are different beasts . . . [In Britain,] we have a whole code of half-things we say, which mean something else. And if you're not attuned to that, you don't really know what people are communicating. It's a terrible generalization, but Americans, to my mind, tend to speak much more plainly and directly. Whereas, my plays use the coded language of the English. It's like the difference between the American game of pool and our snooker; Most of the snooker [points] come off the cushions; you rarely make a direct shot.

Interview, London/
The Christian Science Monitor,
12-4:14.

Mikhail Baryshnikov
Ballet dancer

5

[Comparing ballet with modern dance]: There is just good dancing and bad dancing, good choreography and bad choreography. You can't *separate* dance. During the 10 to 15 years when I discovered contemporary dance—and a lot of possibilities and horizons which I had never dreamed existed—it took quite a few years first just to really understand the beauty of that choreography—and to go out and to *see* . . . I

(MIKHAIL BARYSHNIKOV)

don't ever go for an evening of dance and say, "Okay, I'm seeing Balanchine ballets and I have to prepare myself *differently.*" The curtain is opened and it excites me or not. It takes me with it or not.

Interview/
Dance Magazine, January:41.

Masazumi Chaya
Associate artistic director,
Alvin Ailey American
Dance Theatre

1

I watch [dancers] and I think about the dynamics of the performance, and what the difference is between this superstar and that good dancer. When I go out into the theatre with a notebook, I don't go as police. Sometimes the choices made onstage tickle me. Some choices stink so bad. People dance differently. They even sweat differently.

Interview, New York/
The New York Times, 12-23:(B)2.

Robert Desrosiers
Choreographer, Desrosiers
Dance Theatre, Toronto

2

My inspiration comes from my heart and my demons. From the heart comes the humor in my work, the simple ways of dealing with the colorful side of life. The nightmarish qualities are the demons—the fears that man has because of ignorance. When we die our life becomes a memory, and the soul remembers these lives as we remember dreams. This universal drama fascinates and amazes me, and this is what I express in dance.

Interview/
Dance Magazine, January:60.

Molissa Fenley
Dancer, Choreographer

3

I hated the fact that very little [in dance school] was about training and a lot of it was about ego

and peoples' problems and therapy sessions. I didn't want to have anything to do with that. Also, I wanted my dances to deal with universals. It was something about my perceptions, and how dancing didn't necessarily have to be about the person dancing but about these very strong feelings of universal knowledge or of sensations that belonged to all people. I didn't want my dances to be secularized, which a lot of dance tends to be. I mean, it tends to get locked into an idea of being just about *itself.* Well, I wanted to get outside of that.

Interview/
Dance Magazine, May:40.

Judith Fugate
Principal dancer,
New York City Ballet

4

I've always been interested in full-length ballets—I mean for a ballerina to carry a character through a full evening. I love the idea of telling a story with a ballet, and if it's done properly so that the audience can understand, then that's all the better. They should be able to tell from the action onstage what the story is, and that involves clear acting—and clear pantomime whenever necessary . . . It's very different when you have to act in a ballet. It's not something that people feel comfortable with from the beginning. Dancers don't feel comfortable unless they're dancing. The only thing worse than acting or doing a pantomime is standing still—that's the worst thing in the world.

Interview/
Dance Magazine, April:42.

5

I'm not interested in technical feats, in dancers kicking their legs up to here [their ears]. The most important thing is to see an artist make a ballet come alive. That's the difference between being an artist and a dancer, or an artist and a gymnast . . . It's not very American or very today to appreciate the artistry of a dancer. It's much more American and '90s to appreciate how many turns someone can do, or how high they can lift their leg. It's often a sport instead of an art.

Interview/
Dance Magazine, December:60.

WHAT THEY SAID IN 1991

Cynthia Gregory
Ballerina,
American Ballet Theatre

1

[Ballet dancers] don't have specialties any more. Maybe that's old-fashioned. Sometimes I feel like I'm a little old-fashioned. But there aren't the real strong personalities. And we've lost some of the die-hard fans for that kind of thing. I can't say anything against the dancers today, because they're beautiful. But there's nothing—special . . . I see special things in some of our ballerinas that aren't being developed. They all have their own particular personality, but they don't know it. They're out there trying to hit a beautiful pose, and they're skimming the surface of the roles. But they're not finding the real essence of the role for themselves and making it their own. I like to see risks. I like to see someone pushing to the limit, even if it means faltering a bit. It adds to the excitement.

Interview/
Dance Magazine, June:49.

Yuri Grigorovich
Artistic director,
Bolshoi Ballet (Soviet Union)

2

. . . you cannot separate the life of the Bolshoi from the life of the [Soviet Union] as a whole. The theatre is like a drop of water that reflects the general situation in the country. So there's a struggle and a fight on. The republics all want to secede and there's confusion and fighting all over the place. There's nothing to eat in the country. Everything is falling apart; the shop windows are empty . . . There's nothing really amazing happening at the Bolshoi. In fact, the situation at the Bolshoi is probably much better than in the country in general, because we dance—and we don't dance so badly! And we go abroad, and people buy tickets to come and see us, so we are actually still well off. In fact, the Bolshoi is leading a very good life. The dancers work regularly and not a single performance has been canceled so far. Every day, work goes on as usual. But, of course, where is there a theatre without intrigues?—without infighting? The theatre is the theatre.

Interview/
Dance Magazine, February:71.

Lincoln Kirstein
Co-founder and
president-emeritus,
School of American Ballet,
New York

3

The whole thing about ballet—it's so clear to me and so unclear to so many other people—is that it is a language. The words are steps. It has its own grammar. It is not a personal style. And it's the grammar we teach.

Interview/
The New York Times, 1-9:(B)2.

Jiri Kylian
Artistic director,
Netherlands Dance Theatre

4

[Saying choreography to him is the freedom in the mind to find something that already exists]: It's like the famous statement of Michelangelo as he stood beside a block of marble. You see part of the face, an elbow, and a knee coming out of the stone. The people around Michelangelo were saying, "You make all those marvelous things," and he answered, "But it's already inside. I just have to scrape out the unnecessary bits." Choreography is the same; all the movement is out there. You only have to make a choice when you have enough freedom in you to creatively deal with it. All you have to do is to leave out the unnecessary.

Interview/
Dance Magazine, June:60.

Paul Lazarus
Artistic director,
Pasadena (Calif.) Playhouse

5

Theatre is about great ideas, great humor, great music expressed in human terms to human beings sitting there. Or it's a simple act of story-telling.

Interview/
Los Angeles Times,
2-10:(Calendar)47.

382

Paul Libin
Producing director,
Jujamcyn Theatres, New York

1

[On foreign investment in Broadway productions]: Foreign investors have been buying [U.S.] real estate and service corporations and investing in theatre and motion pictures, and we love them. Some clearly are allocating their money for Broadway productions. There's English money and European money, but none of the magnitude of Japanese investments.

Los Angeles Times, 2-17:(Calendar)5.

Kenneth MacMillan
Choreographer

2

I think critics [especially in the U.S.] have too many preconceived ideas of what ballet can be about. What they're really saying is that ballet should only be light entertainment. I think ballet would die if it were just the old pas de deux and *Swan Lake* and *Giselle* endlessly. We have to go on renewing and looking at it afresh. Of course, there are certain stories that are unsuitable for dance. You just don't do ballets about mothers-in-law. But there are all sorts of other things you can say.

Interview/Dance Magazine, September:52.

Peter Martins
Ballet master-in-chief,
New York City Ballet

3

One of the biggest problems with the ballet, to my mind, is its pace. Frankly, I've always found it deadly, so I wanted to find a way that wouldn't let people out of the theatre at 11:30 p.m. I wanted them to have an evening that didn't involve three intermissions and six drinks! My approach [to his version of *The Sleeping Beauty*] was [George] Balanchines's approach to *A Midsummer Night's Dream*. These ballets are really structured like a Broadway show. Look, today people are used to sitting for an hour and ten minutes for the first act, taking a break for intermission, coming back and sitting for another forty-five minutes, and then going home. And that's what I've done with *Sleeping Beauty.*

Interview/Dance Magazine, April:40.

Arthur Miller
Playwright

4

I believe the theatre as one knew it is gone. It's a social arrangement—theatre always is—which was simply washed out by various events. Something else is there, which is in some formative stage, perhaps. But we don't have any longer what I can detect as being a theatre culture.

Interview, Connecticut/
Vanity Fair, November:246.

Al Pacino
Actor

5

Sometimes . . . we get into habits, and we don't even know why any more, but we're in a habit. That is what you try to do in acting, too. When you're acting in a scene, in the theatre, say, you do something and you know it's right. You're lucky enough to get a moment. And then the next night you try to repeat it. Then pretty soon all you're doing after many, many nights is repeating the moment, and it's gone bad. You've forgotten about the source, how you got there, what made that moment possible.

Interview/
"Interview" magazine, February:92.

Maurice Sendak
Author of children's books;
Artistic director,
The Night Kitchen children's
repertory theatre

6

[On his Night Kitchen theatre]: I will use my experience as a writer and illustrator and stage designer, fuse all of that, and really try to create something . . . I'm not a pioneer; I'm just trying to put my oar in a situation where children's entertainment might be improved on some level . . . [You should] feed them stuff that's rich and thick and intellectually stimulating and emotionally stimulating. That's the whole point, to be there and show your respect for that . . . Why shouldn't children be empowered by art? That's what I'd like to see happen.

Interview/
The Christian Science Monitor, 12-23:13.

Oliver Smith
Co-director,
American Ballet Theatre

1

There is never a multiplicity of great dancers and choreographers. And interestingly, the younger ones, like my favorite of all, Paul Taylor, are very involved with having their own companies. It is a whole different world [from the early days of the American Ballet Theatre]. When Ballet Theatre began, the only other major company was the Ballet Russe de Monte Carlo. We were building an audience then. There was always this devoted cult of people who admired ballet, but it wasn't a popular art-form. I think Ballet Theatre was very important in developing that population. Being a touring company, we went to every state in the union, every size auditorium—and there were some terrible theatres—spreading a gospel. Now there are innumerable ballet companies all over the United States, and some are very good.

Interview,
New York/
The New York Times,
4-22:(B)3.

Danny Thomas
Actor, Comedian

2

[On today's comics compared with those of his era]: Most of the new comics have about six or seven great minutes. After that, they have to garbage it up to be out there for maybe 20 minutes. In our day, you did an hour . . . The new comics' subject matter is not deep enough. They don't get to the core of the people. There's really no substance, no universality to what they're doing. There's no artistry there. They have one big problem. They have to start at the top. They go on the talk shows or to the big comedy clubs and the first time out they must be scared to death. They have no place to stink. We did. Oh, did we stink!

Interview, New York/
The New York Times, 1-10:(B)4.

Helgi Tomasson
Artistic director,
San Francisco Ballet

3

Too often today the term "classical" is used as a bad word. Classical doesn't mean boring. To me, classical ballet means the use of classical technique, and it would be a terrible tragedy to see that disappear. Classical can be exciting, but very few people attempt to make it so.

Dance Magazine, September:40.

Tommy Tune
Dancer, Choreographer

4

Once you're a dancer, you're a dancer. There's something about that feeling that I can't describe. It's a divine feeling. There's a quote, I think it's from the Bible, that goes: "He who danceth not, knoweth not what we are knowing." Yes, it's a special feeling. It's why people go out dancing! Martha Graham called it the landscape of a man's soul; Agnes de Mille called it "non-utilitarian movement set to music." I don't know what I call it. It's a *feeling.*

Interview, Philadelphia/
Dance Magazine, November:39,40.

Stan Wojewodski, Jr.
Dean, School of Drama,
Yale University;
Artistic director,
Yale Repertory Theatre

5

When [the newer] theatres were made, they were under-capitalized artistically and financially most of the time. I don't think people understood—because it's such a new thing—just what resources it's really going to take to make a difference as far as the artistic climate. People were initially optimistic that theatres could prove that they could make theatre, people would come see it and funding would follow. It never followed. Now to come to understand that it's going to happen even less is pretty hard.

Interview, San Diego/
Los Angeles Times, 8-11:(Calendar)53.

Philosophy

Jean-Bertrand Aristide
President of Haiti

1

Love is the air that I breathe, like oxygen. When I lack it, I feel atrophied, asphyxiated. When I have it, I feel I am growing. And so this growth is linked to others, or to a collective other. If I realize that I do not love you, my faith diminishes, and I breathe less and less of the oxygen of life. When I feel linked to you, in communion with you, there is a current of love that passes between us, and the intensity can multiply. And the more this love grows, the more the faith becomes luminous, the more I feel linked to the collective other. I am speaking of God.

Interview, Port-au-Prince, Haiti/
"Interview" magazine, October:90.

Russell Baker
Columnist,
"The New York Times"

2

There is a hunger in us for something more than the money standard, for some assurance that our lives have been not merely successful, but valuable—that we have accomplished something grander than just another well-heeled loudly publicized journey from the diaper to the shroud. In short, that our lives have been consequential.

At celebration of 75th anniversary
of Pulitzer Prizes, New York, Sept. 22/
The New York Times, 9-23:(A)8.

Daniel Bell
Sociologist,
Harvard University;
Scholar in residence,
American Academy of Arts
and Sciences

3

Wisdom is the tears of experience, the bridge of experience and imagination over time. It is the listening heart, the melancholy sigh, the distilla-

tion of despair to provide a realistic, if often despondent, view of the world.

At Brandeis University commencement,
May 26/The New York Times, 5-27:8.

Steven Berglas
Psychologist, Harvard University
Medical School

4

[On successful people]: Individuals who suffer from success have what I call the four A's—arrogance, a sense of aloneness, the need to seek adventure, and adultery. These are the core attributes of people who achieve stellar successes without the psychological bedrock to prevent disorder. All my patients and the individuals I've studied suffer from at least three out of four of these patterns.

Interview/Time, 11-4:14.

Jacqueline Bisset
Actress

5

We get to think of life as an inexhaustible well. Yet everything happens only a certain number of times, and a very small number, really . . . How many more times will you watch the full moon rise? Perhaps twenty. And yet it all seems limitless.

Interview, Los Angeles/
Lear's, February:118.

Erma Bombeck
Columnist

6

Most of you, if you're lucky, will lead two lives. You'll walk a tightrope between a personal life and a career . . . I'm a card-carrying feminist who has worked to bring about equality for women . . . But if I blow raising my kids, nothing else I do will have any importance . . . Several of you will have the courage to conquer an illness or a handicap you never thought was possible . . . These are

(ERMA BOMBECK)

successes . . . Don't confuse fame with success. One is Madonna; the other is Helen Keller.

At Meredith College commencement,
May 12/USA Today, 5-20:(A)11.

Leo Braudy
Professor of English,
University of Southern California

1

The status of film criticism and books about popular culture are an indication of . . . how the perception [of fame] has changed. People like Fred Astaire, who were once thought to be just entertainers, have become icons. Since World War II, the salient vocation in America has been performance. No matter what you do, you measure the standards of your success by those of a performer. Go to a real-estate awards ceremony, and you realize it's modeled on the Oscars.

Los Angeles Times, 3-24:(Calendar)9.

Albert Brooks
Actor, Director

2

. . . I've been fascinated with how the media invades our lives. With the advent of cameras and microphones we can preserve everything. And that makes us different, I think, from the people who came before us. If somebody in vaudeville 100 years ago did a bad performance, it would fade away. But now, your stuff is there forever. And the idea that your *life* is there forever is very intriguing.

Interview, New York/
The Christian Science Monitor,
4-5:14.

George Bush
President of the United States

3

History gives our lives meaning and continuity. Any nation that tries to repudiate history—tries to ignore the actors and events that shaped it—only repudiates itself.

At Babi Yar monument near Kiev,
Soviet Union, Aug. 1/
Los Angeles Times, 8-2:(A)15.

Robert Coles
Child psychiatrist,
Harvard University

4

[On religion being used negatively]: So is everything else. So is intellectual life. Look at the sectarianism in the name of psychoanalysis, the way we've learned to hate one another. Look at the Ivy League colleges; the meanness you find there rivals Belfast. Religion becomes a scapegoat. We see clearly the hatred in the name of religion, but we don't see so clearly the hatred generated in the different departments within these fancy universities or different political worlds. There's no sphere of human activity that lacks smugness, arrogance, self-importance, divisiveness and all the other sins we're capable of. And I say *sins.* If you look at what the religious tradition tells us, it warns about this sin of pride. No amount of secular progress, social or economic or educational, has so far enabled us to get beyond that darker side of ourselves.

Interview/Time, 1-21:17.

Hume Cronyn
Actor

5

Some of the people who I have had the greatest affection for have been people who had many faults, and because of those flaws they were very vulnerable. It's very touching. Take someone who has had enormous success and who's been a huge power. And you suddenly discover they've got the most appalling Achilles' heel. That they drink a hell of a lot. Or that they're capable of real meanness. Or that they are betrayers. Or that they are greedy beyond belief. To watch someone who is so loaded with talent and yet who completely messes up his or her gift is so sad. And yet I think you very often want to put your arms around people like that. I mean, I'm loaded with my own faults. And I'd like when I'm at my worst to have somebody put an arm around me.

Interview,
New York/
The New York Times,
9-23:(B)2.

Elizabeth Hanford Dole
President, American Red Cross;
Former Secretary of Labor
of the United States

1

What you believe matters less than your capacity for belief—and your willingness to translate belief into constructive action . . . It is your moral compass that counts far more than any bank balance, any resume and, yes, any diploma. Whether on the floor of Congress or in the boardrooms of corporate America or in the corridors of a big city hospital, there is no body of professional expertise and no anthology of case studies which can supplant the force of character which provides both a sense of direction and a means of fulfillment. It asks, not what you want to be, but who you want to be.

At Dartmouth College
commencement, June 9/
The New York Times, 6-10:(A)12.

Clint Eastwood
Actor

2

Rigidity is death and flexibility is birth. God gave you a brain to think and, if you don't use it, it's going to get rigid, and it's going to get smaller, until it's just a tiny pea inside your skull.

Interview, Burbank, Calif./
"W" magazine, 4-29:31.

David Geffen
Motion-picture and
record producer

3

On the day you die, you will be the only one who knows what lies you told. And how well, or badly, you behaved at any given moment. How brave you were. That's why you have to forgive people. Because each of us has to live with what we've done.

Interview/Vanity Fair, March:228.

Kenneth J. Gergen
Professor of psychology,
Swarthmore (Pa.) College

4

We are now immersed in an array of relationships in a way that has not existed at any other time in history. We take in views and values from all over the world; we know as much about [Soviet President Mikhail] Gorbachev as we do about our Mayor. In a sense, we become a local representation of an enormous array of others. The self is located outside us; as we move from one locale and relationship to another, we change. We also take many of our cues from the media. We have seen on television what it is like to have a love affair and what it is to mourn. Hence, we know how things are done as rituals and act them out in our lives. As a result of all this, it becomes increasingly difficult to believe in the inner-core essences of romanticism or the cerebral essences of modernism. We begin to feel that we have no real center. It is our relationships that more and more define us and create our sense of who we are. Our identity is continuously reformed and redirected as we move through a sea of changing relationships. We realize that who and what we are is not so much the result of personal essence but of how we are constructed in social groups.

Interview/
U.S. News & World Report,
7-1:59.

Philip Glass
Composer

5

One of the most valuable properties often exhibited by young people is their idealism. However, after some years, too often this quality begins to lose its shine and a little bit later is often gone altogether. It's easy to be an idealist at 20, but much harder at 50, as is easy to observe. However, this quality of idealism, a natural for young people, is one of the most valuable assets we carry with us for the rest of our life. Recognize it for what it is and hold on to it!

Interview/Connoisseur, February:41.

Albert Gore, Jr.
United States Senator,
D-Tennessee

6

Genetically, people today are less than one-one-thousandth of one per cent different from the people of the Stone Age. But civilization is com-

(ALBERT GORE, JR.)

pletely different from any organized manifestation of the human species that's ever existed on this planet; because we're so numerous now, we're so powerful with our new technologies, and we have a weird way of thinking that the Earth is disposable, that we're not a part of the Earth, that we are a disembodied intellectual species capable of thinking our way through any problem, not burdened with the connections to the Earth that the lower animal species still carry from their evolutionary past.

At symposium sponsored by
Environmental Defense Fund,
May 17/The Washington Post, 5-22:(A)20.

Roderic Gorney
Professor of psychiatry,
University of California, Los Angeles;
Futurist

1

There is in the world today a degree of dread that we may have outlived our string on this planet through our own foolishness, which we don't seem to be able to control. And the result of it may be the extermination of our species. Everywhere people turn, there is this harbinger of decay—pollution, the airwaves, the propaganda we're fed. Everybody realizes that whether you believe the Desert Storm [Persian Gulf] war was a true protection against aggression or an effort to assure the United States of uninterrupted oil supplies, corruption lies at the bottom. I do think that the result of the sense that the world is corrupt and teetering is that everybody harks back to times when things were hopeful, like defeating Hitler and coming home. If you mean by nostalgia to include such things as regularity and hope—that if you do what's right in the world, you will be rewarded—then I think that nostalgia is the right word.

Los Angeles Times, 6-16:(Calendar)85.

Gary Hart
Former United States Senator,
D-Colorado

2

It is often much more difficult to learn from victory than from defeat. In defeat, questions are

asked about what went wrong, so that those mistakes will not be made in the future. But victory seldom creates the need to inquire as to its sources.

Before House Armed Services Committee,
Washington, April 30/
The Washington Post, 5-1:(A)17.

Vaclav Havel
President of Czechoslovakia

3

Communism isn't the only disaster in today's world, and if we dismantle Communism, this won't mean that this planet will start an era of paradise. The global problems are very deep. In the West, there are many disturbing omens, like frustration and the loss of purpose in life. In today's Czechoslovakia, it is quite sensible to repeat this from time to time because many people have excessive illusions.

Interview, Prague/
Newsweek, 7-22:31.

4

The power [of being President] naturally is accompanied by certain advantages. Nowadays, it is impossible that there would not be a table for me in a restaurant, or a ticket to the theatre or cinema. And I've discovered that despite my high salary I usually don't have to pay the bill in a pub. There are lots of people who can arrange things for me, so that I don't have to worry about ordinary tasks, and from this point of view my life is, of course, much more comfortable. On the other hand, I can now imagine how easy it is to be corrupted by power. I understand why so many people love power so much.

Interview, Prague/
Vanity Fair, August:157.

Timothy S. Healy
President, New York
Public Library

5

The more one is drawn into the maelstrom of human doing, the more one's days and nights are preoccupied by the sheer busyness of living, the

(TIMOTHY S. HEALY)

more distant becomes the "still small voice": that is all a discreet and self-effacing God permits himself in dealing with his creatures.

At Boston College
commencement, May 20/
The New York Times, 5-21:(C)18.

Jeremy Irons
Actor

1

. . . success is not to do with talent. You have to have the talent, yes. But you can learn an awful lot. It's to do with many other things: how open you are, how you get on with people, how you interview, how you look, and how you make choices. And I think if there's anything that I've been blessed with it's my ability to make the right choices . . . So careers are not just about talent. They're about other things. And then there's luck. But I think luck has to do with balance. Luck is the result of a mixture of many things. I think we all get chances in life, but probably a lot of us don't notice them—don't notice they've happened, don't notice we've missed them.

Interview, New York/
Los Angeles Times, 12-1:(Calendar)30.

Christopher Lasch
Chairman and professor,
department of history,
University of Rochester (N.Y.)

2

The rise of consumerism in this century—in which the individual's self-interest is the *only* good—created a society in which you don't need any public consensus as long as the economy can satisfy people's needs and expand them into ever increasing levels of desire and expectation. Beguiled by the prospect of limitless abundance, Americans came to believe that it was no longer necessary to grapple with underlying issues of justice and equality as long as the goods kept coming.

Panel discussion/
Harper's Magazine, February:45.

Sugar Ray Leonard
Boxer

3

Fame makes you realize your dreams. But, more importantly, it makes you understand your failures.

Interview/USA Today, 2-5:(C)2.

Bob McEwen
United States Representative,
R-Ohio

4

The reason people are standing in line for bread in North Korea, and in Moscow, and in Havana, and in Albania, is because of a lack of freedom. When there is a free economy and this [Albania] is a free country, there will be abundance.

Albania, March/
Los Angeles Times, 4-17:(A)10.

Willie Nelson
Singer

5

There are more serious problems in life than financial ones, and I've had a lot of those. I've been broke before and will be again. Heartbroke? That's serious. Lose a few bucks? That's not.

Interview/
The New York Times, 9-2:13.

Mike Nichols
Motion-picture director

6

I started out, because of my personal experiences in early life, not liking or trusting people much. And I'll never like or trust strangers very much—that's just the way I am. But I now do like people, and by and large trust them in certain controlled circumstances. And as you come to like them, it seems a very important aspect of both life and art not to come to conclusions about people. One of my favorite lines in any move is in *The Philadelphia Story:* "The time to make up your mind about people is never."

Interview/
Film Comment, May-June:29.

Oliver L. North
Lieutenant Colonel,
United States Marine Corps
(Ret.)

1

[Referring to his role in the Iran-contra scandal]: It's easy to make judgment calls between right and wrong . . . The tougher calls are the ones where you have to decide between good and better. And the worst of all are the ones where you have to decide between bad and worse.

Interview/
Christianity Today, 11-25:44.

Robert Payton
Professor of philanthropic
studies, and director of the
Center on Philanthropy,
Indiana University

2

[Philanthropy is] where we get involved with the needs of the community on a voluntary, non-political, non-economic basis. And it's the thing that makes our democracy work. It's the right of people to come together to do the public's business with no public mandate, not for private gain but for the public good or the common good, for the sake of the community . . . When you were in college, you didn't ever take a course that had anything to do with this. And some of the courses you took—like your economics course, maybe your psychology course—say that people don't behave that way, they just behave in terms of their self-interest in some sense, or they are required to do so. So if you want good works to be done, [you are taught that] the government has to do it, or you have to pay people for it.

Interview, Indiana University/
The Christian Science Monitor,
12-3:14.

Martin Scorsese
Motion-picture director

3

I really believe that suffering is a thing people have to go through to be redeemed in life. Some may never. Some will, some won't . . . One needs a sense of a spiritual in life. I really believe that.

And from our culture in the early '80s on to now I think the emphasis has become the worst possible kind of materialism. You make a lot of money. You spend it. And then what? You still feel funny when you go to sleep. You still wake up. You still have a chill when you think about dying and the void.

Interview, New York/
Los Angeles Times, 11-10:(Calendar)30.

Maurice Sendak
Author of children's books

4

I think I like as few children as I like people in general, because often they are as tedious as their parents, even at an early age. There's nothing magical about children. Well, there is, but they all don't have it.

Interview, Los Angeles/
Los Angeles Times, 12-4:(E)1.

Clarence Thomas
Judge, United States
Court of Appeals
for the District of Columbia;
Nominee for Associate Justice,
Supreme Court
of the United States

5

When I spoke earlier about changing the world, I think I would distinguish between the way that as a youth you feel that you can go out and take on everything tomorrow morning and get it all accomplished tomorrow morning. At some point I think you realize that you have to take a step back and begin to approach it more—not so much in a rush or impatiently, but persistently. And if there is one lesson that I learned during that period, it was the difference between impatience and persistence, the difference between being upset and being committed to something.

At Senate Judiciary Committee
hearing on his nomination,
Washington, Sept. 13/
The New York Times, 9-14:6.

Tommy Tune
Dancer, Choreographer

1

Here's what I've found thus far in my life: There's love and there's work. Everything else is fear, and God knows we try to divest ourselves of that. Because fear is what stops us in life.

Interview, Philadelphia/
Dance Magazine, November:36.

Ted Turner
Chairman,
Turner Broadcasting System

2

In the last couple of years, we've seen a lot of people go to jail for cheating in the business world. There are a lot of temptations to take a shortcut. They've always been with us. But when you cheat in any form, all you're doing is cheating yourself. You don't feel good about the rewards that you get from cheating. They are meaningless. The only thing that means anything are the things you really earn. So keep your ethics at a very, very high level. That's very important if you're going to have a happy life.

At Tufts University commencement,
May 14/USA Today, 5-20:(A)11.

Peter V. Ueberroth
Former Commissioner
of Baseball

3

Start volunteering immediately. There's no job that you can possibly take that's not going to allow you six hours or four hours a week to go do something that's fun and vibrant, gives you a broadening experience, and gets you into another game.

At Rensselaer Polytechnic Institute
commencement, May 17/
USA Today, 5-20:(A)11.

Lech Walesa
President of Poland

4

. . . I'm lazy. But it's the lazy people who invented the wheel and the bicycle because they didn't like walking or carrying things.

Interview, Warsaw/
USA Today, 3-14:(A)13.

Cornel West
Professor of religion
and director of Afro-American
studies program,
Princeton University

5

The most important indication of cultural decay is when a social breakdown takes place in the system of nurturing children. [This results in] spiritual impoverishment and the inability to transmit non-market values . . . I mean love, justice, solidarity, care, sacrifice. [Instead, the market ethic of] "get over any way you can" [prevails].

At New York Historical
Society forum/
The Christian Science Monitor,
3-11:14.

L. Douglas Wilder
Governor of Virginia (D)

6

Our societal values across the board have just disintegrated. Take the movie *Wall Street,* where the leading character says that greed is good. It is money, bucks. No one is saying the good life comes as a result of years of planning, saving for a college education for your kids, a sacrifice for your generation so the next generation will be better. All that's gone.

Interview/
USA Today, 4-11:(A)13.

Pete Wilson
Governor of California (R)

7

It does seem that as we acquired state-of-the-art comfort, we may have gone a little soft, have lost some discipline and direction. And yes, I do worry that in recent years we have stressed the rights of the individual while ignoring his or her duties . . . [But] if the young people, who are soon to be our next generation of leaders, are held fast by the moorings of ethical values, the winds of change needn't blow them in a headlong rush into mindless hedonism.

At Stanford University, Oct. 1/
Los Angeles Times, 10-2:(A)15.

Alexander N. Yakovlev
Member, Politburo,
Communist Party
of the Soviet Union

1

[Criticizing Marxism]: I have read a lot about Marx's and Engels' derisive attitude to the peasants. They wrote so much about class struggle and violence. Imagine—total harmony can only be achieved through a class struggle. First, one class eliminates another and then there is total harmony. Revolutionary maximalism— the dictatorship of the proletariat based on violence—these are horrible things.

Interview/
Los Angeles Times, 8-17:(A)11.

Yevgeny Yevtushenko
Soviet poet

2

This generation [in the Soviet Union] is more audio than we were. They imitate the superficial features of Western mass culture, and they think that is culture. They wear black-leather jackets and metal chains, and they feel themselves citizens of the world. They idolize America as a country with mountains made from blue jeans and rivers of Coca-Cola. If you chew American chewing gum, probably ignorance is chewing you at the same time.

Interview, Washington/
The Christian Science Monitor,
3-8:11.

3

Do not be afraid when you suffer . . . Forget the vulgar, insultingly patronizing fairy tale that has been hammered into your heads since childhood that the main meaning of life is to be happy. The only true happiness is to share in the sufferings of the unhappy . . . It is much better to have the screaming sensitivity of the soul uncovered by any protective skin than to have tear-proof rhinoceros skin in combination with the cold fish blood.

At Juniata College commencement/
U.S. News & World Report,
5-27:18.

Religion

William J. Bennett
Former Director,
Federal Office of National
Drug Control Policy;
Former Secretary of Education
of the United States

1

[On recent anti-Catholic sentiment in the U.S.]: We will attempt to speak in a level, even-tempered voice—nevertheless, a strong one—to say that as Catholics we don't like to be bashed, ridiculed, made fun of. Sooner or later, Catholics were bound to say: "Look, we're tired of being the easy target."

News conference,
Washington, Sept. 5/
Los Angeles Times, 9-9:(E)1.

George Carey
Archbishop of Canterbury;
Primate of all England

2

As someone who has an undisguised affection for football, I love the words of Bill Shankly of Liverpool, who once said to his players: "Football is not a matter of life and death—it's far more important than that." So is our Christian faith; far more important than life and even death.

Los Angeles Times, 5-28:(H)2.

Robert Coles
Child psychiatrist,
Harvard University

3

The spiritual interests of children have a lot to teach us . . . I have listened to children of eight or nine or 10 getting to the heart of the Bible. I have found in elementary schools a good deal of spiritual curiosity that does not reflect mere indoctrination. This is an interesting capacity children have, and I think we ought to pay attention to it.

Interview/Time, 1-21:17.

Dalai Lama
Exiled former ruler of Tibet

4

In the past, Buddhist institutions carried an important role in our society. However, that society is now completely changed. In the future, I'm quite sure the Buddhist role in our country will be important and positive. However, because of new circumstances, we should change deeply and properly. First, the standard of knowledge about Buddhism should be increased. In the past, the general public was contented to claim themselves as Buddhist. Actually, they had very little knowledge. As general education improves, education involving Buddhism also should improve. The second thing, I personally think, the number of monks and nuns may be better with lesser numbers and good quality. And there should be more participation of monks and nuns in social services, education and health. Then, the monastic institutions, I have no doubt, need some change. Now, already, in India, the monks and nuns in the monasteries already are something like self-sufficient. In the future, this practice must continue in our own land.

Interview, Mongolia/
Los Angeles Times, 10-8:(H)6.

Wendy Doniger
Professor of history of religions,
University of Chicago
Divinity School

5

There is no common agreement today about who we are [in the U.S.], what our culture is and where we are going. People are asking questions that traditional churches can no longer answer for them. Some are seeking answers in new cults. There are a lot of self-help, pseudo-therapy groups whose basic tenet is that Christian mythology has failed and consequently other mythologies are needed to reinvent ways of being religious. Unfortunately, what these groups often do under the name of neopaganism, neo-Hinduism and so forth, is take a very tiny part of mythology

(WENDY DONIGER)

and turn it into a fifth-rate form of psycho-therapy.

Interview/
U.S. News & World Report,
7-15:49.

Edward N. Gaffney
Dean, Valparaiso University
Law School

1

We are now at a point in our history where the courts can rewrite the meaning of the First Amendment and sharply curb the freedoms that are avilable. And what truly distresses me is that they don't think there is anything wrong with treating religious freedom as though it were any other part of the democratic process.

Christianity Today, 10-7:40.

George Gallup, Jr.
Public-opinion analyst

2

There's no question about it. The sex-related issues are going to be the most important issues facing all churches in the foreseeable future. Abortion, AIDS, premarital sex, homosexuality, all those are going to be at the vortex.

Los Angeles Times, 6-6:(A)1.

Jozef Cardinal Glemp
Roman Catholic Primate
of Poland

3

The church and state stand on different levels, should be independent from each other, but somehow bound to cooperate for the benefit of man. If such autonomy is called separation, that is acceptable.

Broadcast sermon, May 12/
The New York Times, 5-15:(A)7.

Andrew M. Greeley
Theologian

4

[On a survey that showed that only 1 per cent of Americans never pray]: How can one explain such frequent prayer, not only among those who believe in God and life after death but especially among those who do not believe in God or survival? Do they address their prayers "To whom it may concern"?

At conference, Dublin, Ireland/
The New York Times, 6-29:9.

Michael Green
Professor of evangelism
and New Testament,
Regent College,
Vancouver, Canada

5

. . . I get fed up with our churchly ghettos. Christianity in Canada—as in America—is receding among almost all the denominations. What happens when you and your friends start to recede? You go into a ghetto. You keep warm. Then, every now and then, you look around and say, "There are lots of pine benches where there used to be people. Send for an evangelist!" A lot of [church] people think they just need to shout louder in the KJV. All the while keeping away from where real people are.

Interview/
Christianity Today, 12-16:39.

Gregg Ivers
Assistant professor of government,
American University,
Washington

6

Respect for religion and the inability of government to interfere with private religious beliefs is what has enabled religion to flourish in the U.S . . . The record is replete with examples and concern of the framers [of the Constitution] of taxpayer funds supporting religious institutions. They were also concerned with the criminalization of religious belief. They firmly believed that persons had the right to freely exercise their religious beliefs, not merely hold them. When we put the pieces of the puzzle together, we come out with a robust formula for religious liberty, that government cannot intervene nor regulate, not have control over the religious opinions of people, and religion cannot and should not be

(GREGG IVERS)

dependent on government for its livelihood or existence.

Interview/USA Today, 9-25:(A)11.

Ann Lane
Professor of history and
director of women's studies,
University of Virginia

1

There are serious movements in all the major institutions of religion to expand religious views to incorporate a new view of women. But then, there are people, like me, who think that the major religious institutions are so compromised that they don't have anything to offer. I think religion has emerged as one of the major ways of keeping women in their place by teaching them obedience, self-sacrifice and that this is what God wanted. I do think that patriarchal notion is racist and sexist and has worked through history, at least in the West through Christianity and Judaism, to oppress women.

Interview/USA Today, 4-1:(A)9.

Robert F. Leavitt
President-rector,
St. Mary's Seminary & University,
Baltimore

2

The church can survive with fewer priests, but it cannot survive with bad priests . . . A pastor is running a business. He must pay the bills, fix the leaking roof; but he must also provide spiritual help to members of the parish. We're always tinkering with how to . . . strike that balance.

Interview, Baltimore/
The Washington Post, 9-28:(B)8.

C. Eric Lincoln
Professor of religion and culture,
Duke University

3

The expectation that with integration blacks would rush to join white [church] denominations never materialized. The fact is the black church has remained the institution that consistently reflects the aspirations and hopes and lives of African-Americans. That has given it a certain stability that white denominations can only hope to emulate.

Ebony, August:73.

Michael Novacek
Vice president
and dean of science,
American Museum
of Natural History

4

Evolution is not just the history of a species, but the whole evolution of life. To understand that, you have to find the road maps—the way in which species are related in evolutionary terms. [Systematics, the identifying and naming of species,] is our window backwards into evolution.

The New York Times, 12-10:(B)7.

Sandra Day O'Connor
Associate Justice,
Supreme Court
of the United States

5

[On church-state issues that may come up before the Supreme Court]: Conflict in this area seems unavoidable. Given the division among members of the Court over the proper interpretation of the religion clauses [of the Constitution], I would say existing doctrine in this area may be said to be quite fragile.

Speech to Constitutional scholars/
Christianity Today, 10-7:39.

Turgut Ozal
President of Turkey

6

If a state is religious, with a name like Islamic Republic, and so forth, then there will be people there who want to appear religious, but they are just pretending to be so. But if your state is a secular one, then nobody can claim to be religious unless he really is so.

Interview, New York/
Time, 5-13:10.

Metropolitan Spyridon Papagheorghiou
Representative of Bartholomeus,
Patriarch of Constantinople,
at assembly of European bishops
in Vatican City

1

[Saying Eastern Orthodox churches in newly free Eastern Europe are criticizing the Roman Catholic Church for trying to spread Catholicism in their area]: The whole of the Orthodox Church is understandably perplexed [and has] the impression that we are drifting further and further away from Vatican Council II. Territories and countries, for centuries traditionally Orthodox and now liberated from Communist regimes, are considered by our Roman Catholic brothers as missionary ground. The difficult work of reconciliation between the two churches is now seriously compromised.

At synod of European bishops,
Vatican City, December/
Los Angeles Times, 12-7:(A)22.

Girolamo Prigione
Special envoy to Mexico
of Pope John Paul II

2

[On the reconciliation between the Catholic Church in Mexico and the Mexican government]: After so many years of incomprehension, of struggles, of suffering and frustration between the state and the churches, we have reached an opening . . . In Mexico we have lived a paradox: that of a profoundly Catholic nation that has had to coexist with the most anti-clerical Constitution on the planet. By comparison, the Constitution of the Soviet Union sounded like a Christmas song.

Interview, Mexico City, Dec. 19/
The New York Times, 12-20:(A)1,6.

Juergen Ruhfus
German Ambassador
to the United States

3

The revolution that happened [in Eastern Europe] at the end of '89 in most cases started from churches—people leaving services and taking to the road, and then other demonstrators joining. The church has remained a moral force during the years even under very adverse situations and political repression.

Interview/USA Today, 5-15:(A)11.

Allan R. Sandage
Cosmologist,
Carnegie Institution,
Pasadena, Calif.

4

Science cannot answer the deepest questions. As soon as you ask why is there something instead of nothing, you have gone beyond science. I find it quite improbable that such order came out of chaos. There has to be some organizing principle. God to me is a mystery, but is the explanation for the miracle of existence— why there is something instead of nothing.

Interview, Pasadena, Calif./
The New York Times, 3-12:(B)9.

Robert Skolrood
Director,
National Legal Foundation

5

[Criticizing a Federal court ruling banning Christian displays in a public park in Ottawa, Ill., at Christmastime]: Where Christ is depicted as a drug addict or his crucifix is immersed in urine [as in the recent art-works given Federal monetary grants], the work magically becomes "art" and is paid for . . . with taxpayers' money. On the other hand, sincere religious expression is labeled un-Constitutional and banished from the public square.

Christianity Today, 8-19:44.

Arthur Teitelbaum
Southern area director,
Anti-Defamation League
of B'nai B'rith

6

[On recent anti-Catholic sentiment in the U.S.]: It is part of the mosaic of bigotry that exists in America. When anti-Catholicism raises its ugly head, it is the responsibility of every

(ARTHUR TEITELBAUM)

Catholic and non-Catholic alike to repudiate it and attempt to quarantine it.

Los Angeles Times, 9-9:(E)1.

Oliver Thomas
General counsel,
Baptist Joint Committee

1

[Criticizing the U.S. Supreme Court for deferring cases involving religious liberty back to the Federal and state legislatures]: The Court, like Pontius Pilate of old, is washing its hands of the great moral and legal issues of the day and throwing them back to the shouting mobs in the streets.

Christianity Today, 10-7:39.

James Wall
Editor, "The Christian Century"

2

The problem with liberal Christians is that in their embrace of pluralism, they went too far by saying "it really doesn't matter what my faith is; I can absorb all faiths." That is a serious error, because you can't be pluralistic unless you know the basis on which you stand. Pluralism means acknowledging and respecting the faith of others without assuming theirs is superior to your own or even equal to it.

Interview, Denver/
The Christian Science Monitor, 3-18:14.

Cornel West
Professor of religion
and director of Afro-American
studies program,
Princeton University

3

... so many religions themselves have been so commercialized and commodified that religious messages tend to be at times just gospels of health and wealth or the "American Way of Life."

Interview,
Princeton, N.J./
The Christian Science Monitor,
3-11:14.

Joseph Williamson
Dean of the chapel,
Princeton University

4

The basic problems for young people have to do with the irrelevancy of the church. Young people are not anti-religious and they're not anti-moral, but they find the ethical rigidity of the church does not satisfy their own sense of what is right and what is wrong. They want to have some way of understanding what the moral character of their faith is all about. And I think that this is what the church is trying to do.

Interview/
USA Today,
6-4:(A)11.

Science and Technology

Edward P. Bass
Entrepreneur

1

[On his sponsorship of Biosphere 2, a project involving eight people who will live in a specially built earth-like closed environment for two years]: There was a NASA cult that got us to the Moon in the '60s. If what's at work is mindless conformity, manipulation and so forth, that would be frightening, that would be shocking. But as far as dedication to a project discipline, hard work and so forth, I would say NASA's effort that got us to the Moon and Biosphere 2 have a lot in common . . . Leonardo da Vinci talked about flying machines. Centuries later, the Wright brothers built one. Biosphere 2 may prove to be the Kitty Hawk of biospheric life-support systems. Then again, it may prove to be one of those airplanes everybody sees in the movies and laughs at that had 16 wings flapping at the same time.

Interview, New York/
The New York Times, 9-24:(B)7.

D. Allan Bromley
Assistant to President
of the United States
George Bush for Science
and Technology Policy

2

We [the U.S.] have tremendous resources in our national laboratories and universities, but we haven't been very good at transferring technology [to industry]. It's very important to bring in the private sector in setting the direction [of government-financed research]. That's something the Japanese have done very well.

Los Angeles Times, 10-25:(A)19.

George E. Brown, Jr.
United States Representative,
D-California

3

[On his support for funding a U.S. space station]: If I have to make a choice between space science and the space station, then I'll come down for space science every time. We do a great disservice by trying to present something [the space station] for what it isn't. The space station is not the world's greatest science project. But it happens to be part of NASA's budget. And you don't go into an argument for that looking half-hearted.

Interview/
The Washington Post, 10-15:(A)21.

Edward E. David
Chairman, National Academy
of Sciences panel
charged with drafting
recommendations on
self-policing of ethics
in science

4

It is terribly important for the country that the science community keep its ability to self-govern. That is what is being called into question now—the ability of universities and laboratories to govern themselves. And if we don't perform well to maintain that, we are in trouble.

Interview, March 27/
The New York Times, 3-28:(A)12.

Anatoli Denisov
Member, Supreme Soviet
of the Soviet Union

5

[Sarcastically commenting on the questionable state of Soviet science and a liberalized emigration policy that could result in a brain drain]: Given the current state of Soviet science, if the entire Academy of Sciences moved to the United States, it would be tantamount to destroying American science from within.

Before Supreme Soviet,
Moscow, May 20/
The Washington Post, 5-21:(A)18.

Thomas S. Foley
United States Representative,
D-Washington;
Speaker of the House

1

I wish I could get just a little bit of the excitement the [Bush] Administration has of going to Mars with a manned space program, or with building a space station. [But we must rebuild] the basic sinews of our national economic life, which are deteriorating; they're crumbling in front of our eyes. Here's an Administration that wants to spend hundreds of billions of dollars in space and doesn't want to spend five cents a gallon [for a gas tax for] building the country's highways and bridges and physical infrastructure. I think it's madness. I have to assume it's political, because it doesn't make any rational sense.
To reporters, Washington, July 19/
The Washington Post, 7-20:(A)5.

John Kendrew
Nobel Prize-winning biologist,
Cambridge University (Britain)

2

Traditionally, science has been an open subject. But now there is a change, even within national communities of scientists, and in particular of biologists. Nowadays, they don't talk to one another so freely, because each feels that his research may be important industrially—in other words, that there may be money in it, and, specifically, money in it for him or her.
The New York Times,
3-22:(C)2.

John F. Kerridge
Geophysicist,
University of California,
Los Angeles

3

[Criticizing the proposed U.S. space station Freedom]: It was conceived as a result of an unholy alliance between the aerospace industry, who wanted a welfare program, and empire-builders within NASA, who wanted to strengthen those empires.
Los Angeles Times, 7-9:(A)14.

Daniel Kleppner
Professor of physics,
Massachusetts Institute
of Technology

4

If America's senior scientists cannot, in good conscience, persuade the next generation to follow in their own footsteps [and become scientists], the nation is finished scientifically.
Time, 8-26:49.

James S. Langer
Professor of physics,
University of California,
Santa Barbara

5

It is not just lack of vision or pig-headedness that causes American manufacturing industries to resist introducing new materials or advanced processes. The cost of introducing new technologies in this country is enormous; capital is expensive; licensing can be risky and time-consuming; and if the product is really novel, the materials manufacturer is exposed to a variety of legal hazards.
The New York Times, 3-22:(C)2.

Christopher Lasch
Chairman and professor,
department of history,
University of Rochester (N.Y.)

6

A social order founded on science, with its unnerving but exhilarating expansion of our intellectual horizons, seems to have achieved a kind of immortality undreamed of by earlier civilizations. In science, every revision is an improvement on what preceded it, and the process can go on forever.
U.S. News & World Report,
2-18:58.

Spencer Leyton
Senior vice president
of development,
Borland International

7

[Saying the boom years for new high-tech firms are over]: There's always the potential for

399

(SPENCER LEYTON)

bright developers to come up with some technology that's very valuable. But 99 per cent of the time, they are not going to have what it takes to create a company. The barrier to entry has gone like that [upward].

Interview/
The Christian Science Monitor,
3-13:11.

Walter E. Massey
Director, National Science
Foundation

1

[On scientific ethics]: Scrupulous attention is especially important now. Growing competition for funds, tenure and acclaim; increasing chances of financial conflicts of interest among researchers; even the scope of intellectual ferment—with disciplinary boundaries breaking down and new ideas and techniques challenging traditional paradigms—all these conditions make science and engineering more vulnerable to falsehoods.

At Massachusetts Institute of Technology
commencement, June 3/
The New York Times, 1-4:(A)11.

Linus Pauling
Nobel Prize-winning chemist

2

So many branches of science have developed to such a great extent that to master just one of these rather small branches takes up the years. When I began, there was not nearly so much knowledge about the nature of the world . . . It may be that life isn't quite so [easy] for young scientists.

Interview, Palo Alto, Calif./
The Christian Science Monitor,
3-19:14.

Mark Ptashne
Researcher,
Harvard University
Medical School

3

Scientists have a right to be wrong, and a right not to feel guilty for publishing things that are wrong. But they also have an obligation to find out if they are wrong and say so.

The New York Times, 3-22:(A)13.

Dan Quayle
Vice President
of the United States

4

Less than a decade ago, our space policy envisioned total reliance on the [space] shuttle. But circumstances have changed dramatically since then. Today, we rely on expendable rockets for nearly all of our unmanned launch requirements, and that's a sound policy. The space shuttle, with its precious human lives, is just too valuable to use on missions that don't need its unique capabilities. It makes no sense to use shuttle astronauts unless we absolutely have to.

At Vandenberg Air Force Base,
Calif., July 24/
The Washington Post, 7-25:(A)19.

Nicholas Samios
Director, Brookhaven
National Laboratory

5

When funding gets tight, [scientists] get more conservative and bureaucratic. You don't want to make mistakes. You want to make certain you do the right thing. But to have science flourish, you want people who take chances.

Time, 8-26:49.

Allan R. Sandage
Cosmologist,
Carnegie Institution,
Pasadena, Calif.

6

Astronomy is a science in which you are not able to touch anything you study. Suppose you were given a watch, a tube to sight with and a string, and then asked to determine the distance to the nearest star. Or you were asked the chemical composition, pressure or temperature of the Sun. A hundred or more years ago, these questions seemed impossible. Now astronomers are answering them all the time, and they believe

(ALLAN R. SANDAGE)

their answers. Why? Because there are many parallel ways and tests; and they all give the same answers.

Interview, Pasadena, Calif./
The New York Times, 3-12:(B)9.

Henry G. Small
Director of research,
Institute of Scientific
Information

1

[On the counting of footnote citations in articles to judge a country's or an institution's scientific influence]: The citation phenomenon is just one of continuing fascination. It embodies the judgments of so many individual scientists who choose what to put in their footnotes. And other than peer review, it's the only evaluation we have that's internal to science. This is the view from the inside. It's the scientists looking at each other and saying, "Hey, this is interesting," or "This is a neat discovery," or "This is a useful method."

The New York Times, 2-12:(B)8.

Richard H. Truly
Administrator,
National Aeronautics and
Space Administration
of the United States

2

. . . essentially, we need to build space station Freedom with our foreign partners to keep the leadership position the U.S. holds in space. Look at how foreign countries now hold the dominant economic positions in so many parts of American life. That's not true of space. In this area we are still the world's leader . . . Space station Freedom is an inevitable step in the march to space exploration. It is the linchpin of planning for the entire manned space program. It is the

only way to put humans in space, to learn about their physiology so that generations in the next century can explore the cosmos more safely and confidently. Keep in mind the fight we won in the House of Representatives to keep the station alive was about more than the space station. It was a fight for the entire space program. It's unthinkable that this nation, based on our history, science and technology for the past 30 years, would turn its back on manned space efforts.

Interview, Washington/
Time, 7-1:11.

Yuri Tsvetkov
Chief scientific secretary,
Siberian branch,
Soviet Academy of Sciences

3

The future of Soviet science is under threat. A young scientist can receive much higher pay in a private company. People are just quitting science . . . Scientists don't see any real future for themselves. Everybody is worried about how they can maintain a basic level of life.

Los Angeles Times, 10-25:(A)5.

James D. Watkins
Secretary of Energy
of the United States

4

. . . for eight years under [former] President [Ronald] Reagan, the official White House policy was to shut down the Department of Energy and the Department of Education. Can you think of anything more ridiculous than to shut down these departments when energy and education are two of the leading issues in the nation? We have a nation of scientific illiterates, a nation of kids who are not being educated to be competitive in modern society.

Interview, Washington/
Los Angeles Times, 8-11:(M)3.

Sports

Henry Aaron
Former baseball player,
Atlanta "Braves"

1

[Saying today's high player salaries may mean long-standing baseball performance records may never be broken]: Players today are making so damn much money, they don't need to play 23 years, like I did. Hell, when you talk about players like Jose Canseco and Darryl Strawberry, when they get finished with their contracts they ain't going to need to play any more. And they won't keep playing for the love of the game, because that's not what they're playing for now. I'm just thankful big money wasn't around when I was playing, because I don't know if I would have continued [and set the all-time home-run record he holds], and there are just some things that money can't buy.

People, 4-29:130.

2

No one talks about it any more, but it's still the same situation: Two black [baseball] managers, no black general managers, hardly any [black] doctors and lawyers affiliated with baseball on the major- and minor-league levels, and very few attempts to use black-owned companies for various services. You have teams changing managers all the time . . . and you don't see any blacks. Baseball was and continues to be a good-old-boy network. I'm not saying the Commissioner can force anyone to hire minorities, any more than the President of the United States can force IBM to. But the Commissioner and the President can be outspoken and forceful in what should be done.

New York, May 14/
The New York Times, 5-15:(B)11.

Sparky Anderson
Baseball manager,
Detroit "Tigers"

3

[Criticizing the decision to make Pete Rose ineligible for induction into the Baseball Hall of Fame because of his ouster from baseball for gambling]: If he's not in the Hall of Fame, do we really have one?

USA Today, 2-6:(C)9.

4

I myself love to watch a National League game. There are a lot more moves and strategy. The best thing that could happen to a young manager is for him to start out in the National League. If he never manages in the National League, he doesn't truly understand all the things that he needs to know. From the seventh inning on, you're wide awake in the National League. But I don't see anything tough about being over here [in the American League]. There's nothing to be alive about. At my age, you have to really watch it so you don't go to sleep.

USA Today, 7-9:(E)2.

5

I never make [critical] comments about an umpire [off the field]. I don't like to settle my problems with an umpire in the paper. If he missed a call, I know it, he knows it, the world knows it. Television shows the replays for everyone to see.

The New York Times, 8-13:(B)10.

Arthur Ashe
Former tennis player

6

The results of black athletes in some sports have been so good that young white athletes are actively discouraged from trying to make the professional level at certain positions. You now have a second generation of young whites, 10 to 15 years old, who have been told, either explicitly or implicitly, "If you want to be a sprinter on the Olympic team, forget it; that's a black position." The same is true when it comes to being a guard in the NBA or a wide receiver in the NFL. They are speed positions that call for a lot of creativity. So, in many cases, whites don't even try out for those positions any more.

Ebony, August:68.

Deane Beman
Commissioner,
Professional Golfer's Association
Tour

1

It's harder for a [golfer] to stay on top today than in other eras because there are so many financial opportunities. It's harder for him to discipline himself to stay focused on what he must do to maintain that high level. I think we are going through a period of time where players are taking advantage of opportunities, and many times it's to the detriment of their own performance. It's been happening for the last 10 years.

The New York Times, 4-8:(B)10.

Bill Bergman
Executive director,
North American Association
of State and Provincial Lotteries

2

[Supporting legalized, state-run gambling on team sporting events]: People want it. It's taking their office pools and formalizing them. And it's a new source of revenue for states . . . The indisputable fact is millions of Americans wager billions of dollars annually on sports events. This hasn't resulted in the demise of professional sports. Indeed, attendance and TV revenues are at an all-time high.

USA Today, 6-25:(C)1,2.

Gary Bettman
Vice president
and general counsel,
National Basketball
Association

3

[Arguing against state-sanctioned gambling on team sports]: Betting doesn't enhance our game. Betting changes the rooting interest. If there was widespread legal gambling we'd be less popular, because the environment of the game will change. Players will come under suspicion.

USA Today, 6-25:(C)2.

Matt Biondi
American Olympic
swimming champion

4

[Criticizing the U.S. Swimming Federation for restricting the financial rewards of American swimmers]: The current administration is pushing the sport back into the 1960s and '70s. They treat us like high-school and college kids. It's very disappointing . . . The administration tells us that we should swim for our country. They say it is okay for us to receive only a plane ticket and a bottle of shampoo . . . It's time that U.S. swimming administrators brought the sport up to the rest of the world.

The Washington Post, 1-2:(F)2.

Johnny Blanchard
Former baseball player,
New York "Yankees"

5

[A baseball manager] hopes, he prays that in the starting lineup, if he has three guys who have good years, then he'll be the happiest guy in the world. Out of three big heavy hitters, two will have good years, one mediocre. Or the other way around . . . The game has been the same for 100 years. It's the turkeys that play it who have changed.

Interview/
Los Angeles Times, 10-15:(C)6.

Jim Boeheim
Basketball coach,
Syracuse (N.Y.) University

6

[Saying players in the NCAA tournament should be allowed six fouls instead of five before fouling out]: I seem to state my case every year; I might as well do it again here. [Six fouls] allows guys to play more aggressively. It takes pressure off the officials. The game's gotten more physical in the last five years. The six-foul rule helps the referees keep control, but lets the players play a better game.

March 13/
The Washington Post, 3-15:(F)4.

Barry Bonds
Baseball player,
Pittsburgh "Pirates"

1

Your time in the game is limited. My strategy is to do it fast, do it often, and try and make sure the entire package is complete before my [baseball] days are over.

The New York Times, 9-24:(B)10.

Bill Bradley
United States Senator,
D-New Jersey;
Former basketball player,
New York "Knicks"

2

[Arguing against state-sanctioned gambling on team sports]: I don't want to see athletes turned into roulette chips. I experienced a conflict when I played. Was it my game? Or the gamblers' game? When states sanction gambling, states have nodded in the direction of the gamblers' game.

Before Senate Patents, Copyrights
and Trademarks Subcommittee,
Washington, June 26/
USA Today, 6-27:(C)3.

George Brett
Baseball player,
Kansas City "Royals";
Part-owner of a
minor-league hockey team

3

[On a possible NHL players strike]: There's going to come a time where I think the greed of athletes is going to destroy all sports.

USA Today, 9-9:(C)11.

Jim Brock
Executive director,
Cotton Bowl football game

4

[Arguing against a proposed college-football playoff system]: I just don't know why anybody would want to mess with a [bowl] system that's been good for college football for so many years.

I don't want to do anything to diminish our game. We're against it and we'll fight until hell freezes over.

The Washington Post, 1-5:(D)10.

Bobby Brown
President,
American (baseball) League

5

[On whether Pete Rose, who has been barred from baseball because of a gambling scandal, should be allowed to be inducted into the Hall of Fame]: I felt from the very outset the main issue has always been, if you have somebody on [baseball's] ineligible list and you're considering bestowing baseball's highest honor on him . . . that didn't seem to be very sensible to me. I never felt that was a reasonable way to proceed . . . What got him on the ineligible list or gets him off the ineligible list is sort of immaterial to me. It boils down to the fact the Commissioner says this person is not to participate in baseball activities of any kind. That makes it very difficult for me to feel he's eligible for the Hall of Fame or any other honorable pursuit.

Interview/USA Today, 2-5:(C)8.

6

[Baseball] keeps you coming back for more. You sit in comfort, you munch peanuts, you talk to friends. With the progression of time, you observe the excitement increase until that is what consumes you.

The New York Times, 4-8:(B)9.

Maurice Cheeks
Basketball player,
New York "Knicks"

7

[On his team's internal problems]: I've seen a lot of things, but I've never really seen a professional team totally break apart. Everyone at this level should respect one another's abilities, because we all reached this level for one reason or another. We all know how to play the game. But when you're losing, guys get frustrated. That's when you're tested. We don't have to love

(MAURICE CHEEKS)

each other. But we have to work together and respect each other.

The New York Times, 1-12:31.

Ben Crenshaw
Golfer

1

[On why Europeans have been winning more and more high-level golf tournaments, which used to be dominated by Americans]: Actually, it's a number of things. First of all, they have some outstanding individual players. They are extremely motivated, they work very hard at their games, and they have all the shots you need to win under any conditions. The courses they play on the European tour are rustic, natural and unkempt. And they're confronted with more natural elements—rain and wind especially—that makes them better players. And agronomy has a lot to do with it. It's gotten so good in this country [the U.S.], and this may sound wild, but it's almost gotten too good. On tour, we [Americans] almost never get a bad lie. Our courses are soft, we hit it and it stops, so we make the same kind of shots all the time. Everything is so predictable, and some of our players today are not enamored with less than perfect conditions. They [Europeans] play bump-and-run over there; we never see it.

Interview, July/
The Washington Post, 7-15:(C)1.

Harry Dalton
General manager,
Milwaukee "Brewers"
baseball team

2

Basketball and football have made great strides at all levels [in developing and recruiting new players], at least partly at our [baseball's] expense. They're the major sports in the colleges, so kids who hope to turn their talents into scholarships concentrate on them. In some areas, you now have summer high-school basketball leagues or year-around football conditioning programs, and in the cities you have equipment and space

problems. So a lot of the better athletes hardly play baseball at all . . . we've been doing a good job of marketing lately, as shown by our attendance figures, but we've got to start paying more attention to player development at the grass roots. We've got to put baseball within the reach of more kids, and convince them that it's worth their while to play. We can start by telling them it's fun, and there's a chance it can make them millionaires. It shouldn't be a hard sale.

Interview, Milwaukee/
The Wall Street Journal,
6-28:(A)9.

Ben Davidson
Former football player,
Oakland "Raiders"

3

[Criticizing those who are against state-sanctioned gambling on team sports]: There are a lot of hypocrites running around here. Let's 'fess up, admit sports gambling is out there and get some good out of it for the states.

Before Senate Patents, Copyrights
and Trademarks Subcommittee,
Washington, June 26/
USA Today, 6-27:(C)3.

Richard deFlon
Architect

4

[On his design for the new Comiskey Park baseball stadium in Chicago, which recently opened]: What's happening in baseball architecture is what you see here today. This is the first of the new single-purpose stadiums. Baltimore's next, then Cleveland. There is a return to the intimacy and the character of the old ball parks.

Time, 4-29:80.

Len DeLuca
Vice president of
programming, CBS Sports

5

[Saying his network would support a college-football playoff system]: Our experience with the NCAA basketball tournament shows that

(LEN DeLUCA)

American viewers are drawn to a single-elimination, natural national championship process. The interest curve in football is totally askew. It heightens in late November, then the viewer has to wait three weeks until the major bowls. There are issues that have to be surmounted, like class-time and exams. They seem to be surmountable. If these issues are confronted and satisfied, then you have a hot property.

The Washington Post,
1-5:(D)10.

Rob Dibble
Baseball pitcher,
Cincinnati "Reds"

1

[On his new contract which more than doubles his income]: People come out to see Rob Dibble throw the ball 100 miles per hour. They pay to see me strike out Darryl Strawberry or Bobby Bonilla or Barry Bonds. We're entertainers, and we should be paid accordingly.

Interview/
The New York Times, 3-5:(B)11.

Joe DiMaggio
Former baseball player,
New York "Yankees"

2

. . . I could never have been a manager because I would have worried too much. I was like that. When you manage, too much of what happens depends on other people, and I didn't want that.

Interview/
Los Angeles Times, 7-22:(C)2.

Mike Ditka
Football coach,
Chicago "Bears"

3

This game is a 60-minute game and it will always be a 60-minute game and you must play it for 60 minutes. You must play it right. You must listen to what the coaches tell you and play the defenses that are called accordingly, and call the

plays that are called accordingly, and know what to do with them. [In a recent game,] we had—I can't tell you how much—miscommunication and errors. The penalties . . . were enough to make you sick.

The Washington Post, 10-1:(C)5.

Dwight Evans
Baseball player,
Baltimore "Orioles"

4

The older you get in this game, I guess, the more set you become in your ways. You kind of gain an understanding over the years of what preparation really means, what goes into being able to truthfully say that you were as ready as you possibly could be to go out onto the field and play that particular game . . . I guess you do become more inflexible as you go along. I think it's because you know what you have to accomplish with your time, and you know what's detrimental to the preparation that you need to do.

The Washington Post, 7-18:(B)3.

Chris Evert
Tennis player

5

When you're young, you have no fear; when you get older, you get nervous. I remember feeling real uptight whenever I had to play [younger players Andrea] Jaeger and [Tracy] Austin when they had nothing to lose. [Being young] is a real equalizer.

USA Today, 8-26:(E)2.

Donald Fehr
Executive director,
Major League (baseball) Players
Association

6

Of the athletes that make the really big money—and there are only a few of them—almost none ever make the big money forever. So the athletes try to get as much as they can before it all ends. Sometimes [because of injuries] it ends before they want it to.

The Washington Post, 6-19:(D)6.

Jim Finks
General manager,
New Orleans "Saints"
football team

1

[Arguing against free-agency for NFL players]: The [current] system has been very, very beneficial to everyone—players, owners, fans, the media. If they feel that free agency is a panacea, remember, management has its rights, too. Management has the right to dictate the number of coaches, the number of players. There's a lot of fat in this league today.

Interview, New Orleans/
USA Today, 7-11:(C)7.

Dick Floyd
California State
Assemblyman (D)

2

[On proposals for state-sanctioned gambling on team sports]: Gambling *per se* isn't so evil any more. Look at all the grannies piling into buses and heading to Las Vegas. Hey, if grannies can do it, it's not so evil . . . It's time we woke up to what's happening all around us. Legalized sports gambling is on the way nation-wide in one form or the other . . .

USA Today, 6-25:(C)8.

George Foreman
Former heavyweight boxing champion
of the world

3

I thought Muhammad Ali would be the easiest fight of my career. I trained hard, but the mental state wasn't there. Once somebody tells you that you got a pushover, you're not ready for a tough fight. It's like [his upcoming fight with] Evander Holyfield: They told him this would be an easy fight. Now it's too late for him to get serious. It's the initial seed that's planted. Like when I fought Gerry Cooney, everybody told me he was nothing. When he hit me with that left hook, I said, "Somebody told me a big lie."

Interview, Atlantic City, N.J./
The New York Times, 4-19:(B)13.

Jim Frey
Professor of sociology,
University of Nevada,
Las Vegas

4

[Saying the relationship between fans and players in professional sports is becoming hostile]: At one time, fans loved ballplayers because they were the way fans wanted to be. Now [athletes] are more vulnerable targets because they make so much money . . . and flaunt values like greed, lack of humility and late-night activity.

The Washington Post, 6-17:(B)3.

William Friday
Co-chairman, Knight
Foundation Commission on
Intercollegiate Athletics;
Former president,
University of North Carolina

5

[On whether television has taken over college sports]: The president of CBS Sports once said that, when schools take network money [for televising their games], they should play when the networks want them to—and that's about the way it has washed out. Several years ago, the University of North Carolina, where I was then president, played basketball on Sunday. We stopped because there is still a religious tradition in the South and the game interfered with church-going. Then, just the other Sunday during the NCAA tournament, there was my team playing on CBS at noon. You yield here and yield there and pretty soon TV has gotten a grip on things.

Interview/
U.S. News & World Report,
4-1:13.

Jean-Claude Ganga
President, National Olympic Committees
of Africa

6

[On the IOC's decision to readmit South Africa to Olympic competition after 21 years, as a result of that country's recent repeal of key apartheid statutes]: [Readmission is] a political decision to help point them [South Africans] in

(JEAN-CLAUDE GANGA)

the right direction. We will know we have succeeded when we see a black South African win a race and watch the whites cry when they see their flag raised and their anthem played.

July 9/
Los Angeles Times, 7-10:(A)8.

Joe Gibbs
Football coach,
Washington "Redskins"

1

Ten years ago, we went for players with character and ability. Character is still first, of course, but now our goal is character, intelligence and ability . . . You realize after a while that your offense is better if every player has a thorough understanding of your whole concept. The same goes for defense, and the smarter a player is, the easier to grab the concept. Another thing: The smarter they are, the less likely [they are] to get into trouble—I mean off-the-field trouble as well as on.

Interview, Washington/
Los Angeles Times, 10-16:(C)3.

Wayne Gretzky
Hockey player,
Los Angeles "Kings"

2

A lot of people in Canada feel hockey should just be a Canadian game, since that was where it was invented. But we need U.S. exposure to grow, and in order to get that, we need to eliminate fighting [among players]. But getting rid of fighting will probably never happen in my career, because too many owners think we've grown as far as we can grow—even though there's no consistent TV revenue.

The Washington Post, 9-30:(B)11.

John Hannah
Former football player,
New England "Patriots"

3

[Football is] the greatest game that's ever been and ever will be, as long as people who are trying

to sell it as a business don't destroy it. It's getting close.

USA Today, 7-25:(C)9.

Bud Harrelson
Baseball manager,
New York "Mets"

4

[On being manager]: Of course, I'm going to make all the final decisions, but I have people to remind me of things. I doubt that I'm getting too much advice. All managers lean on their people. Otherwise, what are they there for? To be figureheads? . . . I've been around the game long enough to understand that the game is mostly made up of standard situations, some creative additions and pure guts. And I think your guts get better the more you manage. And the public acceptance of those guts gets better.

Interview, Port St. Lucie, Fla./
The New York Times, 3-11:(B)12.

Doug Harvey
Baseball umpire

5

[For umpires,] one-nothing games [in the playoffs or World Series] can be the best games, the most exciting games, the ones you remember most. You walk off the field with a sigh of relief. You feel the tension. You've got 10 million people at home watching and TV and newspapers tearing up every judgment call [by an umpire]. You've got the bases loaded, the guy pops up—that's one thing. [But if] you've got a guy taking a [called] third strike with a runner on third for the last out, people say [about the umpire], "How could he? How could he?" But a player can recover from that and do something special. He can make himself a hero some other time. An umpire can't be a hero.

Interview/
The New York Times, 10-18:(B)13.

Robert H. Helmick
President,
United States
Olympic Committee

6

A lot of people say, "Why are we [the U.S.] participating in the Pan American Games?" If

(ROBERT H. HELMICK)

we bring our very best athletes, we get criticized that we're beating up our Latin colleagues. If we don't bring a top team in every sport, then we get criticized by our Latin friends that we're not taking them seriously.

Havana, Cuba, Aug. 11/
The Washington Post, 8-12:(C)1.

1

I have stated, and I still believe, that the USOC should consider at some time in the future compensating the president [of the USOC] and requiring the president to take a leave of absence from his or her ordinary profession. We should not set ourselves up so that the president can only be someone who's retired or has wealth sufficient to do this job. We must make sure that people who come from sport and who have devoted their life, probably too much of their life, to sport—and not to their business—can be president.

Interview/USA Today, 9-6:(C)8.

Tom House
Pitching coach,
Texas "Rangers"
baseball team

2

On my ballclub, there are probably 10 guys who don't know how to balance a checkbook. Some probably have problems writing a check. They're supposed to go out and deal with mortgage agreements and car payments. When they should have been learning about trusting people and how to judge character and make decisions, they were swinging at a little white ball and learning about running and sliding . . . There is a total lack of understanding with athletes that their career is a terminal thing, that it's going to die. One's status as an athlete—a performer who happens to gain recognition from doing something better than anybody else—gets in the way of developing the proper fit for one's role as a human being.

The Washington Post,
6-20:(C)3.

Hale Irwin
Golfer

3

[On the recent Ryder Cup golf match in which the U.S. played poorly but eventually won]: The pressure you feel in the Ryder Cup goes beyond what you've ever felt before. When the people started chanting "U.S.A., U.S.A.," I couldn't breathe, I couldn't swallow. I couldn't do anything. I could barely hit the ball. On that course, in that wind, under that pressure, the shots played were ugly and we were made to look ugly.

The Washington Post,
9-30:(B)9.

Phil Jackson
Basketball coach,
Chicago "Bulls"

4

When you're a basketball coach, you're a little like a minister in that you do a lot of preaching. A coach has to be a combination of teacher, a boss and a friend. At times you have to be a person concerned with the welfare of the individuals under your care. Other times you need to be ready to give advice, not only in basketball but things with regard to one's personal life.

The New York Times,
6-12:(B)12.

Eli Jacobs
Owner, Baltimore "Orioles"
baseball team

5

No one has established that there's a correlation between players' salaries and baseball performance. Perhaps the best illustration is the Cincinnati *Reds,* who had a payroll of approximately $15-million last year. They beat the Oakland *A's,* who had a payroll in the 30 millions of dollars, in the World Series. And they beat them in four games. If you look at the empirical data, and you look at the clubs that spend large amounts of money—Kansas City and the *Yankees* being illustrations—it doesn't necessarily correlate with success.

Interview/
The Washington Post, 6-6:(A)16.

Mike Jarvis
Basketball coach,
George Washington University

1

[On his team's playing Boston University, where he once coached and where his son plays on the team]: I have never gone to a game involving my son where I did not want him to win. This will be the first time. He and my wife are my best friends, but when he walks onto that court, he will not be my son. When the game is over, he will be my son again.

The Washington Post, 1-5:(D)3.

Bob Knight
Basketball coach,
Indiana University

2

[On his being inducted into the Naismith Memorial Basketball Hall of Fame]: A player coming into the Hall of Fame, or the baseball Hall of Fame, is a totally different proposition than a manager or a coach. Totally different. [A coach is] representative of. He's symbolic of. It's not his accomplishments. It's the fact that a lot of people have come together and put a team on the floor, or on the field, in such a way that the coach may have some thoughts reflected through the way the team plays.

Springfield, Mass./
The New York Times, 5-13:(B)8.

Chuck Knox
Football coach,
Seattle "Seahawks"

3

There's two things in coaching. One, is winning and two, is misery.

Los Angeles Times, 1-14:(C)2.

Alan LeForce
Basketball coach,
East Tennessee
State University

4

[On his becoming head coach at 55 years of age]: The thing that was disturbing to me was that

you could become President of the United States at 70, but you couldn't become a head coach. You were either too old or you couldn't relate to the players. That made me almost hate the profession. People don't understand that when you're 55, you're in the prime of your life. You can't buy wisdom.

Los Angeles Times, 1-5:(C)5.

Sugar Ray Leonard
Boxer

5

When do you quit [boxing]? When you get cut? When you get knocked down a couple of times? When the other guy hits you more than you hit him? When is it time to quit? When *you* feel it is. I always want more. Always. So there can never be enough. Never.

USA Today, 2-5:(C)2.

Jim Leyland
Baseball manager,
Pittsburgh "Pirates"

6

No, I don't resent the money the players are making. And the people who complain about them would be taking the money, too, if they had the chance. And I have nothing against the players. I love them. If it weren't for them, I wouldn't have a job.

The New York Times, 3-16:30.

7

I'll never forget the first time I had to tell a kid [player] he was released. I couldn't even look him in the eye. I was looking down, saying to myself, "Please, please, help me say the right words." Then I looked up, and the kid was bawling. Once you see that, you don't ever forget what it means to be a part of this game.

Interview, Pittsburgh/
Los Angeles Times, 10-16:(C)5.

James E. Loehr
Sports psychologist,
Nick Bollettieri Tennis Academy,
Bradenton, Fla.

8

[On today's tennis stars who win big when they are young]: That's a real problem. Imagine

(JAMES E. LOEHR)

waking up [at age 25 or younger] and saying, "I've done it all and I have $20-million in the bank." If that happens, that person had better find some new goals and vistas if life, fast. That's why careers are not going to last very long in the future. Tennis is a great opportunity to experience fulfillment, but it's also very hard to sustain. It's going to become increasingly difficult for fans to grow old with their stars.

USA Today, 8-26:(E)6.

Roy Love
Athletic director,
Portland (Ore.)
State University

1

[On the Oregon state sports lottery, which allows the public to bet on sports events and which uses the funds to help college sports]: The lottery money is vital to us. If we can't receive state help out of the general fund, this is the appropriate way to do it. The sports lottery is doing no harm to anyone, and it allows people to support athletics and have fun, too.

USA Today, 6-25:(C)8.

Ron Luciano
Former major-league
baseball umpire

2

When I started, baseball was played by nine tough competitors on grass in graceful ball parks. By the time I was finished, there were 10 men on each side, the game was played indoors, on plastic, and I had to spend half of my time watching out for a man dressed in a chicken suit who kept trying to kiss me.

Los Angeles Times, 7-25:(E)1.

Willie Mays
Former baseball player,
San Francisco "Giants"

3

The most money I ever made [as a player] was $180,000. I think I made that in 1972 and 1973.

Back then you could buy a nice car for $6,000 and a big house for $75,000 or $80,000. These days, [players] want to buy $3-million homes and cars that cost $100,000. So you see, I don't think these guys have it that much better. I could do a lot more with my money than they can with theirs. People like to criticize players for the money they make. I say, get all you can. If the owners are going to give it to you, you've got to take it.

Los Angeles Times, 4-8:(C)2.

Tom Meeker
President, Churchill Downs
race track,
Louisville, Ky.;
President, Thoroughbred
Racing Associations
of North America

4

[Lamenting the proliferation of off-track betting, TV coverage of horse races and other away-from-the-track electronic aspects in racing]: We may yet rue the day when racing is conducted before empty stands . . . The goal should be to bring people to the track to watch horses. We've got to get people to the race track: feeling it, seeing it, smelling it . . . When I came into racing, we were trying to see the entertainment value of racing, the color, the horses coming down the stretch, all that collage of excitement. Then along comes off-track betting, and TV gets a new use. Off-track betting in New York was first. Then came all the other forms of betting away from the track: satellite, inter-track, everything. I'm concerned when a horseman says we ought to have more inter-track wagering because the purses will go up. But I say, "Where will you get new owners to invest in our track?" The way you get new owners interested is to bring them to the paddock all gussied up and let them feel the horse is Secretariat. And then let them watch their horse run. Let them run up to the winner's circle and have that moment in the sunshine. You don't get any of that by sitting in a cold OTB parlor.

Interview,
Hallandale, Fla./
The New York Times, 2-23:33.

John Miller
Baseball sportscaster,
Baltimore "Orioles"

1

Doing baseball on radio is like writing a novel. Doing baseball on television is like doing the television version of a novel. The "action" at a ball game takes place only partly between the foul lines, but that's where the TV camera is almost always pointed, and TV's first rule is to follow the camera. But when a fan goes to a game, he also notices what goes on in the dugouts, the stands and the sky, and a good radio guy will weave those elements into his description. Get the mix right, and engage the listener's imagination, and you can make the game as vivid for him as being there; maybe more so.

Interview/
The Wall Street Journal,
3-15:(A)9.

Joe Morgan
Former baseball player,
Cincinnati "Reds"

2

[On the controversy over whether Pete Rose, who has been barred from baseball because of a gambling scandal, should be allowed to be inducted into the Hall of Fame]: I'm prejudiced in this situation, because Pete and I are close . . . As a friend, I've said they should let him go on the [Hall of Fame] ballot . . . Pete didn't kill somebody or sell drugs. He hurt himself and his family more than anyone else . . . If you make a mistake and pay for it, how long do you have to pay for it? He paid a bigger price than anybody knows.

Feb. 4/USA Today, 2-5:(C)8.

Jay Moyer
Vice president
and legal counsel,
National Football League

3

[Arguing against state-sanctioned gambling on team sports]: It's like a cancer. If states say citizens can legally bet on sports, you risk turning fans into gamblers. And if that happens, we'll diminish the significance of sports.

USA Today, 6-25:(C)2.

Robert Nederlander
Managing partner,
New York "Yankees"
baseball team

4

[On the *Yankees*]: Although I am a sports fan, I have to remember that it is a business. It's a franchise which is probably the most famous of all franchises, so you want to see if you can bring it back, for fans, for the city. But you also have to look at the tools that you have. You look at the free-agent market, where the prices are sky-rocketing. You look at your budget. You look at your talent, your young people. You look at your in-house personnel. And you say to yourself, "How can you combine this mix to provide the best team possible?"

Interview, New York/
The New York Times, 1-21:(B)12.

Peter O'Malley
President,
Los Angeles "Dodgers"
baseball team

5

The running of a major-league franchise today requires more attention and effort than ever before. The issues are too complex and too varied to look on it as a hobby. It's not fair to the fans, the players and the franchise to work at it on a part-time basis. Look at the franchises that are doing the best, generally speaking, and they are the ones that have the full-time support of an owner, president, CEO—a definite stability at the top.

Santa Monica, Calif., June 11/
Los Angeles Times, 6-12:(C)3.

Bill Parcells
Football coach,
New York "Giants"

6

[Saying give and take between coach and players is important]: If you're sensitive, you're not going to last too long around here. That's a two-way street. Players can say what they think. If you're a teacher, and that's what a coach is,

(BILL PARCELLS)

you've got to get some response from your pupils or you don't know where you are.

News conference,
Tampa, Fla., Jan. 24/
The New York Times, 1-25:(B)15.

Richard Petty
Auto-racing driver

1

[Saying next season will be his last as an auto-racing driver after a 34-year career]: Age has got something to do with it, not winning races has got something to do with it, just the idea that every once in a while you say, "I really love to drive this race car, but do I really need to do this?" Maybe the burning desire's not there the way it was 10 years ago.

News conference,
Level Cross, N.C., Oct. 1/
Los Angeles Times, 10-2:(C)10.

Richie Phillips
Head, Major League (baseball)
Umpires' Association

2

Owners realize that umpires have heightened [pay] expectations, given the rise in players' salaries and the rise in television revenues. Obviously, the money is there. Each team is making $15-million more a year as the result of the national television contracts. There is enormous wealth. Umpires feel there should be fairer distribution.

Interview, Philadelphia, Feb. 13/
The New York Times, 2-15:(B)14.

Cal Ripken, Jr.
Baseball player,
Baltimore "Orioles"

3

[Baseball] has become a whole lot more specialized. Everyone's role seems to be scientifically defined. Before, you just put nine people out there, and a starter was expected to pitch most of the game. I don't think it's taken any-

thing away from the game; it's just been modified to get the best performance out of everyone.

USA Today, 7-18:(C)4.

Dan Rooney
President,
Pittsburgh "Steelers"
football team

4

[On the high salaries being demanded by football players]: In baseball, it's eight players and the pitchers. We [in football] have 55 players on a team. It's going to take diplomacy and intelligence on both sides [of the negotiating table] to see that the game isn't destroyed. For us, competitive balance means so much. What I'm saying to you is that if it [a contract] becomes a problem, a lot of teams are going to be in financial difficulty. There's plenty of money out there, and the players should definitely share in the fruits of the game. But we should try to get this thing worked out on both sides.

Interview/USA Today, 8-5:(C)7.

Pete Rose
Former baseball player and
manager, Cincinnati "Reds"

5

[On his ineligibility for induction into the Hall of Fame because of being banned from baseball due to alleged sports gambling]: When you talk about the Hall of Fame, what you're talking about is really getting something you think you earned. I did a lot of things on the baseball field, and I'd hate like hell to think I was never going to the Hall of Fame because I gambled on other sports other than baseball—that's really what it amounts to.

News conference, July 23/
Los Angeles Times, 7-24:(C)4.

Juan Antonio Samaranch
President, International
Olympic Committee

6

[On the IOC's decision to readmit South Africa to Olympic competition after 21 years, as

(JUAN ANTONIO SAMARANCH)

a result of that country's recent repeal of key apartheid statutes]: It is a very important day, not only for the Olympic movement but for all sports around the world. I would like to see very soon athletes and players from South Africa taking part in major sports competition around the world.

Lausanne, Switzerland, July 9/
Los Angeles Times, 7-10:(A)1.

Pete Sampras
Tennis player

1

[On his fame as U.S. Open champion]: I've found out what Michael Chang meant when he said being the youngest champion of a slam is like carrying a backpack full of bricks around for the next year. If I lose in the early rounds [of the next U.S. Open], well, I know that bagful of bricks is going to come right down on me . . . The only time I'm really happy around tennis is when I'm playing tennis, and that's it; win or lose, as soon as the last point is hit, I wish I could disappear.

The New York Times, 8-26:(B)7.

Ray Schoenke
Former football player,
Washington "Redskins"

2

Athletes in our society are catered to and pampered. It's a tremendous high. Then there is that abrupt ending [at the end of one's career]. Dealing with that period is when the shock sets in.

The Washington Post, 6-20:(C)3.

Tex Schramm
Former general manager,
Dallas "Cowboys"
football team

3

[On how NFL free agency, which he does not favor, would affect the way he ran a team]: If I were still going to be running a football team and I knew I was only going to have a player four or five

years, I think I'd go about assembling the team in a different manner. So I might go ahead and take the backs coming out of college. I don't give a damn what I pay them because they're going to be gone, but I'm going to get the best five years of their lives. Maybe with the linemen, I'd wait until they played out their [other] contracts.

Los Angeles Times, 8-29:(C)11.

Richard D. Schultz
Executive director,
National Collegiate
Athletic Association

4

In 1960, when I started coaching at the University of Iowa, virtually all our coaches taught some class in the physical-education department, whether a skills class or a theories class. Over the years, you saw less and less of that happening, especially in football and basketball. And now, unfortunately, we are starting to see the same thing happen in Divisions II and III in those two sports. A lot of football and basketball coaches have been given a release to just coach. If coaches taught just one course, it would be beneficial to the coach and I think it would be beneficial to the institution.

Interview, Worcester, Mass./
The Christian Science Monitor,
10-11:14.

Leigh Steinberg
Sports agent

5

[Favoring a free-agent system in the NFL]: I think we'll see [fewer] holdouts and contract hassles and those difficulties. I think with or without a salary cap, it'll be much more difficult for a player who has been the beneficiary of free agency to have any team's sympathy for being out of training camp or renegotiating his contract. If there's an agreement between labor and management, [then] the internecine warfare of labor vs. management, the cannibalization of the League, would stop. And the whole thrust would be different. We have to remember that free-agency restrictions were not handed down by Moses on Mount Sinai. These things change and

(LEIGH STEINBERG)

people accept them and, 10 years from now, very few people will remember the days when there wasn't free agency in football.

Los Angeles Times, 8-29:(C)11.

Darryl Stingley
Former football player,
New England "Patriots"

1

[On the playing injury that made him a quadriplegic]: Fans and other people think players are asking for too much money. I don't think they are being greedy at all. Every time you step out there, you stand a chance to never walk off. The money I'm receiving now could never be enough for what I lost. One of the reasons a lot of football players are asking for so much now is because of people like myself.

The Washington Post, 6-19:(D)6.

Darryl Strawberry
Baseball player,
Los Angeles "Dodgers"

2

I've never doubted myself and my ability to play the game of baseball. It's what I've been blessed to do . . . I've been around long enough to know that the game is a game of inches. There will be mistakes. Separate the good from the bad, and it works out.

Interview, San Diego/
The New York Times, 9-27:(B)13.

Paul Tagliabue
Commissioner,
National Football League

3

After four years of litigation [between players and the NFL] in which neither side has a definitive success, the thing to do is to sit down and work out a "win-win" agreement. If we don't have an agreement for this season, it'd be the fifth year without one. With no increase in benefits, pensions, severance, health insurance and other benefits for players, we'll have an entire genera-

tion of players who have come into the League and out under outmoded benefits packages.

Interview/USA Today, 6-13:(A)13.

4

[Arguing against state-sanctioned gambling on team sports]: Sports gambling should not be used as a cure for sagging fortunes of Atlantic City casinos or to boost public interest in state lotteries. The question is, are we teaching youth to head to the goal line or the betting line?

Before Senate Patents, Copyrights
and Trademarks Subcommittee,
Washington, June 26/
USA Today, 6-27:(C)3.

Jerry Tarkanian
Basketball coach,
University of Nevada,
Las Vegas

5

I've never said we're unbeatable. There are so many things that can beat you . . . What if five shots roll around the rim and out instead of around and in? There are probably 10 [referees'] calls in a ballgame that can go either way, and if you get five of them you're okay. But what if you only get three? What about foul trouble or guys getting sick or guys having off nights? No one is unbeatable.

The Washington Post, 3-15:(F)6.

Joe Theismann
Former football player,
Washington "Redskins"

6

When a [player] would get hurt really bad, all guys would do is look at the guy and say: "Gee, that's a shame." And that's as much time as you think about it. You can't think too much about it. If you do, if you begin to see yourself lying on the ground some day, you're through as a pro football player. You might as well start looking into another career. None of us ever thinks that it's going to end, or going to end in an instant. It's a reality that is going to happen but it's never going to happen to you. It's always going to happen to

415

(JOE THEISMANN)

the other guy. You have to understand that once you get hurt or leave the game, you're no longer a part of the family. That hurts. Nobody wants to think about that.

The Washington Post, 6-19:(D)6.

Lee Trevino
Golfer

1

You can talk about baseball, apple pie and fried chicken, but man, don't leave out golf. This is America's sport, in my opinion. Baseball players retire, football players retire, hockey players retire, basketball players retire, [then] they play golf, don't they? I've never seen a golf pro retire to take up hockey, baseball or football. This is it. This is the game.

Los Angeles Times, 6-13:(C)2.

2

I wish they'd burn [golf carts] up. That way we could get the kids back out to caddying, and we'd have more minority players, more blacks, more Mexicans, more poor Anglos. The only reason the poor kids made it in golf before, like myself and Lee Elder and all these old pros, is because they didn't have golf carts when we came up. We were caddies. Every golf course had caddies. We got exposed to the game. They got a chance to play the course. Today, they're exposed to drugs on the streets.

Los Angeles Times, 8-22:(C)2.

Bubba Tyer
Trainer,
Washington "Redskins"
football team

3

[On player injuries]: It seems to me that the more severe the injury, the more strength that person has to cope with it. There is especially a certain calmness immediately after they get hurt. The more severe the injury, the more calm and rational they are. It seems your body kind of goes into shock a little bit. They get this look that says, "I guess my time has come."

The Washington Post, 6-19:(D)6.

Jim Valvano
Sportscaster, ABC-TV;
Former basketball coach,
North Carolina State University

4

The fact that we [the U.S.] were beaten [in basketball] in the '88 Olympics is a testament to the improvement of countries around the world. Basketball's the second most popular sport in the world. Everybody's getting better. Losing the Olympics should have been a sign to us to revamp amateur basketball to find ways to improve ourselves.

Interview/
The New York Times, 8-2:(B)7.

Fay Vincent
Commissioner of Baseball

5

[Criticizing the high salaries paid to baseball players]: Baseball is poised for a catastrophe. And it might not be far off. The major markets will continue to attract players, and they'll win. What will happen to the smaller markets, like Seattle? Last season, eight to 10 teams lost money.

Feb. 21/
The Washington Post, 2-23:(G)3.

6

[Arguing against state-sanctioned gambling on team sports]: Bear in mind that when gambling is permitted on team sports, winning the bet may become more important than winning the game. Fans may, in turn, become suspicious of every strikeout or error, and the game's integrity would be open to question, play by play, day after day.

Before Senate Patents, Copyrights
and Trademarks Subcommittee,
Washington, June 26/
The New York Times, 6-27:(B)11.

7

[Saying he frowns upon franchise moves by baseball teams to other cities]: Some people would like to see it be the way it is in football. But one of the major differences in our game, and others, is that the Commissioner has the authority to prevent transfers. [Los Angeles *Raiders* football team owner] Al Davis and [Indianapolis

(FAY VINCENT)

Colts football team owner Robert] Irsay couldn't do what they did [move their franchises] if they were in baseball. I believe it would be chaotic to have it that way. I would never say never, but any request for a transfer would have to be looked at very closely. It would be considered only if the city had demonstrated it just could not support baseball.

Milwaukee, July 1/
USA Today, 7-2:(C)4.

Rudy Washington
Basketball coach,
Drake University

1

Blacks dominate [college] basketball and play a significant part in football. That's the reason the percentage [of blacks] is so high with assistant coaches. You need blacks. At least, the feeling is, you need blacks to recruit blacks. That's a lot of jobs, but I'd like to see more go toward head coaching jobs, managerial positions. But I think for the most part America looks at blacks as laborers.

Interview/USA Today, 3-19:(A)11.

Rob Whiteley
Director of horse-racing
operations for entrepreneur
Carl Icahn

2

Horses, like people, are mortal. Flesh and blood. Some horses have more ability than others, some have more competitive quality than others. But the ability to compete continuously is limited by the toll that training and racing imposes on them.

Oct. 7/The New York Times, 10-8:(B)12.

Ted Williams
Former baseball player,
Boston "Red Sox"

3

Pitchers are the dumbest part of a ball club. They don't play as often. They're pitchers because they can't do anything else.

Broadcast interview, July 9/
Los Angeles Times, 7-10:(C)2.

Ralph Wilson
Owner,
Buffalo "Bills" football team

4

Sometimes when you leave the stadium [the fans] ask for your autograph; the next time they throw the program at you. If you don't understand that, you should get out of professional sports. You don't win every day.

USA Today, 1-25:(E)19.

Jerry Yeagley
Soccer coach,
University of Indiana

5

Having been with [U.S. soccer] for more than 20 years at the college and youth level, I've seen great change. Once, you could only find players in Chicago or St. Louis, but now there are quality players everywhere. The game's grass roots have spread. Youth soccer is solid, the national team is improved, but the pros are missing part of the puzzle. Soccer is like softball, a participant sport. It hasn't translated from player to spectator yet. We're seeing better facilities and more fan support, but as long as it's played in the fall, it will always be second to football.

Los Angeles Times, 8-29:(C)2.

Gary Yeatts
Baseball coach,
Fairfield (Ohio) High School;
"USA Today"'s 1991 national
high school baseball
coach of the year

6

We really believe it is important to win, but also to lose with dignity and class. I like to feel you can enjoy the kids on both sides. It's still a game we're playing—the real role is handling kids. I give them [his players] credit when we win. I think coaching probably is one of the more overrated professions around . . . Coaching is like being a sculptor. You take what you have and turn it into something beautiful.

Interview/
USA Today, 6-24:(C)12.

The Indexes

Index to Speakers

A

C

Index to Subjects

A

Abortion—*see* Women

Acquired immune deficiency syndrome (AIDS)—
see Medicine

Acting/actors:
  ambition, 371:2
  believability, 367:4
  characters:
    identifying with, 364:6
    weak/strong, 366:3
  contract players, 372:1
  control, out of/not in, 364:4, 367:1
  directors aspect, 365:2, 367:1, 380:1
  end of performance, 370:2
  escapism, life of, 366:4
  inaccessibility of, 364:3
  individuality, 370:3
  learning to act, 365:6
  limitations, 370:3
  the method, 365:6
  older/mature actresses, 360:5, 362:2, 365:3,
    372:4
  perks, 365:4
  stage/theatre, 365:2, 372:4, 380:1, 380:2,
    383:5
  stars, 364:3, 380:2
  television, 359:6, 360:5, 361:1,, 362:2, 380:1
  women—*see* older actresses, *this section*

Advertising—*see* Broadcasting; Commerce; Medicine: drugs, prescription; Politics

Afghanistan, 171:5, 210:3, 216:3

Africa, pp. 189-196
  changes sweeping continent, 191:4
  consensus in, 189:5
  fluidity, period of, 189:1
  future, positive, 189:5
  intellectuals, 191:5
  North Africa/Mahgreb, 194:1
  rulers/Presidents for life/one-party states,
    193:4, 194:2, 194:4
  state, deference to, 191:5
  foreign relations/policy with:
    Europe, 228:6
    Soviet Union, 190:2
    U.S., 191:4
  See also specific African countries

Agriculture/farming, 12:6, 75:4, 229:2

Air transportation—*see* Transportation

Alaska, 102:1, 102:2, 104:2, 108:1

Albania, 225:3

Alcohol—*see* Medicine: drug abuse

Algeria, 191:3, 288:3

Ali, Muhammad, 407:3

Ambition, 371:2

America/U.S.:
  best it can be, 9:4
  confidence, 11:3
  criticism, self-, 11:1
  decline of, 13:2
  demographic problems, 10:2
  doing things well, 11:1
  dream, American, 13:3, 68:7
  foreign vs. domestic issues, 9:1, 9:3, 9:4, 10:1,
    10:3, 12:3, 12:4
  freedom, danger to, 13:1
  future, 9:2
  great country, 11:3
  infrastructure, 399:1
  irresponsibility, glorification of, 9:5
  Main Street, 12:6
  melting pot/multi-racial/diversity, 10:5, 11:2,
    11:4
  optimism, 27:3
  preeminence, 13:2
  pride, 12:4
  renewal, self-, 11:5
  rights vs. responsibilities, 10:4, 391:7
  risk-taking, 11:5
  safety, personal, 9:1
  thinking like an American, 12:5
  traditions torn away, 10:2
  unity, 10:5, 12:1
  universal nation, 12:2
  weakness, 11:4
  where we are going, 393:5

American Broadcasting Companies (ABC)—*see*
  Broadcasting

American Civil Liberties Union (ACLU)—*see*
  Civil rights

American scene, the, pp. 9-13

Americas/Latin America, pp. 197-206
  defense/military/chemical weapons, 197:4
  democracy, 198:1, 198:4, 203:5, 203:6
  drugs, 203:5
  economy, 203:5

F

J

M

T